Lecture Notes in Compute

Edited by G. Goos, J. Hartmanis and J.

Springer
Berlin
Heidelberg
New York
Barcelona
Budapest
Hong Kong
London
Milan
Paris
Santa Clara
Singapore
Tokyo

Hans Kleine Büning (Ed.)

Computer Science Logic

9th International Workshop, CSL '95
Annual Conference of the EACSL
Paderborn, Germany, September 22-29, 1995
Selected Papers

Springer

Series Editors

Gerhard Goos, Karlsruhe University, Germany

Juris Hartmanis, Cornell University, NY, USA

Jan van Leeuwen, Utrecht University, The Netherlands

Volume Editor

Hans Kleine Büning
Universität Gesamthochschule Paderborn
Fachbereich 17, Mathematik-Informatik
Warburger Straße 100, D-33098 Paderborn, Germany

Cataloging-in-Publication data applied for

Die Deutsche Bibliothek - CIP-Einheitsaufnahme

Computer science logic : 9th international workshop ; annual conference of the EACSL ; selected papers / CSL '95, Paderborn, Germany, September 22 - 29, 1995. Hans Kleine Büning (ed.). - Berlin ; Heidelberg ; New York ; Barcelona ; Budapest ; Hong Kong ; London ; Milan ; Paris ; Santa Clara ; Singapore ; Tokyo : Springer, 1996
(Lecture notes in computer science ; Vol. 1092)
ISBN 3-540-61377-3
NE: Kleine Büning, Hans [Hrsg.]; CSL <9, 1995, Paderborn>; GT

CR Subject Classification (1991): F.4, I.2.3-4, F.3

ISSN 0302-9743
ISBN 3-540-61377-3 Springer-Verlag Berlin Heidelberg New York

Typesetting: Camera-ready by author
SPIN 10513160 06/3142 - 5 4 3 2 1 0 Printed on acid-free paper

Preface

The 1995 *Annual Conference of the European Association for Computer Science Logic, CSL'95,* was held at the University of Paderborn (Germany) from September 22 to September 29, 1995.

CSL'95 was the ninth in a series of workshops and the fourth to be held as the Annual Conference of the EACSL.

The scientific program included a tutorial on Finite Model Theory (September 22–24), invited lectures, and contributed papers (September 25–29). The tutorial was organized by H.-D. Ebbinghaus with lectures by J. Flum and E. Grädel, and was attended by 42 participants.

The conference was attended by 100 participants from 16 countries. Invited talks were given by C. Compton, A. Dawar, A. Goerdt, Y. Gurevich, G. Huet, J.-W. Klop, and E.-R. Olderog.

Thirty-three contributed papers selected from 74 submissions were presented. The selection was done by the Program Committee consisting of S. Artemov, J. Bergstra, J. Bowen, H.-D. Ebbinghaus, G. Gottlob, E. Grandjean, J.-P. Jouannaud, H. Kleine Büning, S. Martini, W. Thomas, and J. Tiuryn.

We gratefully acknowledge the generous sponsorship by the following institutions:

- European Union (HCM Euroconferences Program)
- University of Paderborn
- Universitätsgesellschaft Paderborn.

The EU sponsorship enabled us to offer grants to young scientists from all over Europe.

Following the usual procedure for CSL volumes, papers were collected after the presentation at the conference. Through the regular reviewing procedure 27 papers were selected for publication. We thank the numerous referees who made the preparation of this volume possible.

Finally, we would like to thank Ulf Dunker, Theo Lettmann, and Tanja Prior for their decisive help in the organization of the conference.

April 1996 Hans Kleine Büning

Table of Contents

Incompleteness of a First-Order Gödel Logic and Some Temporal Logics of Programs

Matthias Baaz[a,*], Alexander Leitsch[b], Richard Zach[b]

[a] *Institut für Algebra und Diskrete Mathematik E118.2, Technische Universität Wien, A–1040 Vienna, Austria*
[b] *Institut für Computersprachen E185.2, Technische Universität Wien, A–1040 Vienna, Austria*

Abstract. It is shown that the infinite-valued first-order Gödel logic $\mathbf{G}^0$ based on the set of truth values $\{1/k : k \in \omega \setminus \{0\}\} \cup \{0\}$ is not r.e. The logic $\mathbf{G}^0$ is the same as that obtained from the Kripke semantics for first-order intuitionistic logic with constant domains and where the order structure of the model is linear. From this, the unaxiomatizability of Kröger's temporal logic of programs (even of the fragment without the nexttime operator $\bigcirc$) and of the authors' temporal logic of linear discrete time with gaps follows.

Keywords: temporal logic, intermediate logic, many-valued logic
MR Classification: 03B45, 03B50, 03B55

1 Introduction

In [4], Kurt Gödel introduced a sequence of finite-valued logics $\mathbf{G}_n$ in order to show that there are infinitely many propositional systems intermediate in strength between classical and intuitionistic propositional logic. In [3], Dummett considers the natural infinite-valued analogue **LC** of Gödel's systems and shows that it is axiomatized using the intuitionistic propositional calculus plus the axiom schema $(A \supset B) \vee (B \supset A)$. Little is known about first-order versions of Dummett's **LC** and related systems and about infinite-valued first-order logics in general. The most famous result (Scarpellini [8]) in this area is that the infinite-valued first-order Lukasiewicz logic is not recursively axiomatizable.

We arrive at a first-order Gödel logic by taking the truth functions for the propositional connectives and defining truth functions for universal and existential quantifiers as infimum and supremum over the truth values, respectively. It is worth pointing out right away that which logic we get depends crucially on the order type of the set of truth values. In Section 2 we define these logics and describe their differences. The main result of this paper is that a particular Gödel logic $\mathbf{G}^0$, namely that based on the set of truth values $V^0 = \{1/k : k \in \omega \setminus \{0\}\} \cup \{0\}$, is not recursively axiomatizable. Indeed, already the $\exists$-free fragment is not r.e. We give the proof in Section 3.

* Corresponding author. Email addresses: {baaz, leitsch, zach}@logic.tuwien.ac.at.
This work is supported by FWF grant P–10282 MAT.

The main interest of Dummett's **LC** is that it axiomatizes *linear* intuitionistic Kripke semantics: **LC** is the set of all propositional formulas valid in all Kripke trees consisting of just one branch. We see that there is a strong connection between infinite-valued Gödel logic and logics based on linearly ordered models. In the first-order case it turns out that the logic defined by linearly ordered Kripke structures and constant domains **ILC** is exactly the same as $\mathbf{G}^0$. The logic we get by dropping the requirement that the domains are constant, **IL**, is arguably the more natural analogue to **LC** in the first-order case. We obtain the result that the set of validities of **IL** is not r.e. as a corollary to the result for $\mathbf{G}^0$ (which is equal to **ILC**).

Other logics based on linearly ordered Kripke structures are, e.g., variants of Kröger's [5] *Temporal logic of programs* **TL**. **TL** is based on the temporal operators $\Box$ (henceforth) and $\bigcirc$ (nexttime) and is characterized by temporal structures order isomorphic to ω. It is known [9, 6, 7] that first-order **TL** is not axiomatizable. The logic arising from temporal structures that have the form of trees of segments each of which is order-isomorphic to ω is axiomatizable [2]. It has been an open question whether the logic based on chains of segments order-isomorphic to ω is axiomatizable or not. In Section 4 we use the incompleteness result to give a negative answer to this question. We also strengthen the result of [6]: Already first-order **TL** *without* $\bigcirc$ is not axiomatizable.

2 First-order Temporal, Intuitionistic and Gödel Logics

We shall work in a usual language L of predicate logic containing countably many variables (x, y, z, ...), function symbols (s, h, ...), predicate symbols (P, Q, R, ...), connectives ($\land$, $\lor$, $\supset$, $\neg$) and the universal ($\forall$) and existential ($\exists$) quantifiers. The language L extended by the temporal operators $\Box$ (henceforth always) and $\bigcirc$ (next time) is denoted L_t. The set of (closed) formulas of L resp. L_t is denoted $\mathrm{Frm}(L)$ resp. $\mathrm{Frm}(L_t)$. For a given interpretation $\mathfrak{K}$ we will also consider *extended languages* $L^{\mathfrak{K}}$ where the elements of a given domain are added as constant symbols the interpretation of which is fixed.

We proceed to define Kripke semantics for first-order temporal logics. These logics are all based on discrete time; this reflects their use in theoretical computer science where "time" is taken to be the discrete states of program executions (see [5]).

Definition 2.1. Let T be a denumerable partially ordered set. T belongs to the class $\mathcal{L}$ of *linear discrete orders* iff it is order isomorphic to ω; it belongs to the class $\mathcal{T}$ of *trees* if it is order isomorphic to a rooted tree; it belongs to the class $\mathcal{G}$ of *linear discrete orders with gaps* if it is order isomorphic to an ω-chain of ω-segments (i.e., to $\omega \cdot \omega$); it belongs to the class $\mathcal{B}$ of *linear discrete orders with branching gaps* iff it is order isomorphic to a rooted tree of ω-segments.

Definition 2.2. Let $\mathcal{W}$ be $\mathcal{L}$, $\mathcal{G}$, or $\mathcal{B}$, and let $\mathrm{Frm}(L_t)$ be the set of formulas over some first-order temporal language. A *temporal structure* $\mathfrak{K}$ *for* L_t is a tuple $\langle T, \{D_i\}_{i\in T}, \{\mathbf{s}_i\}_{i\in T}, \mathbf{s}\rangle$, where $T \in \mathcal{W}$, D_i is a set called the *domain* at state i,

$D_i \subseteq D_j$ if $i \leq j$, s_i is a function mapping n-ary predicate symbols to functions from D_i^n to $\{\top, \bot\}$, and s is a function mapping n-ary function symbols to functions from $\bigcup D_i \to \bigcup D_i$ s.t. $\mathsf{s}(f)(d_1, \ldots, d_n) \in D_i$ for $d_i \in D_i$, in particular for $d \in D_i$, $\mathsf{s}(d) = d$. The valuation function s can be extended in the obvious way to a function on all terms.

We define the *valuation functions* $\mathfrak{K}_i$ from $\mathrm{Frm}(L^{\mathfrak{K}})$ to $\{\top, \bot\}$ as follows. Suppose $A \in \mathrm{Frm}(L^{\mathfrak{K}})$.

(1) $A \equiv P(t_1, \ldots, t_n)$: $\mathfrak{K}_i(A) = \mathsf{s}_i(P)(\mathsf{s}(t_1), \ldots, \mathsf{s}(t_n))$
(2) $A \equiv \neg B$: $\mathfrak{K}_i(A) = \top$ if $\mathfrak{K}_i(B) = \bot$, and $= \bot$ otherwise.
(3) $A \equiv B \wedge C$: $\mathfrak{K}_i(A) = \top$ if $\mathfrak{K}_i(B) = \mathfrak{K}_i(C) = \top$, and $= \bot$ otherwise.
(4) $A \equiv B \vee C$: $\mathfrak{K}_i(A) = \top$ if $\mathfrak{K}_i(B) = \top$ or $\mathfrak{K}_i(C) = \top$, and $= \bot$ otherwise.
(5) $A \equiv B \supset C$: $\mathfrak{K}_i(A) = \top$ if $\mathfrak{K}_i(B) = \bot$ or $\mathfrak{K}_i(C) = \top$, and $= \bot$ otherwise.
(6) $A \equiv (\forall x)B(x)$: $\mathfrak{K}_i(A) = \top$ if $\mathfrak{K}_i[d/x](A(d)) = \top$ for every $d \in D_i$, and $= \bot$ otherwise
(7) $A \equiv (\exists x)B(x)$: $\mathfrak{K}_i(A) = \top$ if $\mathfrak{K}_i[d/x](A(d)) = \top$ for some $d \in D_i$ and $= \bot$ otherwise
(8) $A \equiv \Box B$: $\mathfrak{K}_i(A) = \top$ if $\mathfrak{K}_j(B) = \top$ for every $j \geq i$, and $= \bot$ otherwise.
(9) $A \equiv \bigcirc B$: $\mathfrak{K}_i(A) = \top$ if $\mathfrak{K}_{i+1}(B) = \top$, and $= \bot$ otherwise

A is *satisfied* in a temporal structure $\mathfrak{K}$, $\mathfrak{K} \models_t A$, iff $\mathfrak{K}_0(A) = \top$.

Definition 2.3. We define the following logics:

Linear discrete temporal logic **TL** is the set of all $A \in \mathrm{Frm}(L_t)$ s.t. $\mathfrak{K} = \langle T, \{D_i\}_{i \in T}, \{\mathsf{s}_i\}_{i \in T}, \mathsf{s}\rangle$ with $T \in \mathcal{L}$ satisfies A.

Linear discrete temporal logic with constant domains **TLC** is the set of all $A \in \mathrm{Frm}(L_t)$every $\mathfrak{K} = \langle T, \{D_i\}_{i \in T}, \{\mathsf{s}_i\}_{i \in T}, \mathsf{s}\rangle$ with $T \in \mathcal{L}$ and $D_i = D_j$ for all $i, j \in T$ satisfies A.

Linear discrete temporal logic with gaps **TG** is the set of all $A \in \mathrm{Frm}(L_t)$ s.t. $\mathfrak{K} = \langle T, \{D_i\}_{i \in T}, \{\mathsf{s}_i\}_{i \in T}, \mathsf{s}\rangle$ with $T \in \mathcal{G}$ satisfies A.

Linear discrete temporal logic with gaps and constant domains **TGC** is the set of all $A \in \mathrm{Frm}(L_t)$every $\mathfrak{K} = \langle T, \{D_i\}_{i \in T}, \{\mathsf{s}_i\}_{i \in T}, \mathsf{s}\rangle$ with $T \in \mathcal{G}$ and $D_i = D_j$ for all $i, j \in T$ satisfies A.

Linear discrete temporal logic with branching gaps **TB** is the set of all $A \in \mathrm{Frm}(L_t)$ s.t. $\mathfrak{K} = \langle T, \{D_i\}_{i \in T}, \{\mathsf{s}_i\}_{i \in T}, \mathsf{s}\rangle$ with $T \in \mathcal{B}$ satisfies A.

As indicated in the introduction, the logic **TL** is not axiomatizable. This was shown for the original formulation of Kröger by Szalas [9] and Kröger [6] (two binary function symbols have to be present for the results to hold). If the operator **until** is also present, or if local variables (i.e., variables whose interpretation may me different for each state) are allowed, then the empty signature suffices, as was shown by Szalas and Holenderski [10] and Kröger [6], respectively. These results were strengthened and extended in various ways by Merz [7]. In fact, to be precise, Kröger's original formulation **TLV** differs from **TL** as defined here in several respects: it has (1) constant domains, (2) rigid predicate symbols (i.e., the interpretation of the predicate symbols is the same for each state) and (3) local variables. Merz [7, Lemma 1] shows that the validity problem for **TLC** can be reduced to to the validity problem for **TLV**. Hence, our results extend also to Kröger's original formulation. On the other hand, **TB** is axiomatizable by a sequent calculus presented in [2].

Next we give Kripke semantics for various fragments of first-order intuitionistic logic. We use the term "intuitionistic logic" par abus de langage: "Real" intuitionistic logic is defined not via Kripke- or any other semantics but by Heyting's calculi which he extracted from the writings of Brouwer. It is a more recent discovery that one can give Kripke semantics for these logics which are complete for the calculi. This completeness result, however, is of doubtful value from the intuitionistic point of view.

Definition 2.4. Let Frm(L) be the set of formulas over some first-order language, and let T bei in $\mathcal{T}$ or $\mathcal{L}$. An *intuitionistic Kripke-structure* $\mathfrak{K}$ *for* L is a tuple $\langle T, \{D_i\}_{i\in T}, \{\mathsf{s}_i\}_{i\in T}, \mathsf{s}\rangle$, where D_i is a set called the *domain* at state i, $D_i \subseteq D_j$ if $i \leq j$, s_i is a function mapping n-ary predicate symbols to functions from D_i^n to $\{\top, \bot\}$, and s is a function mapping n-ary function symbols to functions from $\bigcup D_i \to \bigcup D_i$ s.t. $\mathsf{s}(f)(d_1, \ldots, d_n) \in D_i$ for $d_i \in D_i$, in particular for $d \in D_i$, $\mathsf{s}(d) = d$. The valuation s_i has to satisfy a *monotonicity requirement:* if $\mathsf{s}_i(P(\bar{d})) = \top$ then $\mathsf{s}_j(P(\bar{d})) = \top$ for all $j \geq i$. The valuation function s can be extended in the obvious way to a function on all terms.

We define the *valuation functions* $\mathfrak{K}_i$ from Frm($L^{\mathfrak{K}}$) to $\{\top, \bot\}$ as follows. Suppose $A \in$ Frm($L^{\mathfrak{K}}$).

(1) $A \equiv P(t_1, \ldots, t_n)$: $\mathfrak{K}_i(A) = \mathsf{s}_i(P)(\mathsf{s}(t_1), \ldots, \mathsf{s}(t_n))$.
(2) $A \equiv \neg B$: $\mathfrak{K}_i(A) = \top$ iff $\mathfrak{K}_j(B) = \bot$ for all $j \geq i$, and $= \bot$ otherwise.
(3) $A \equiv B \wedge C$: $\mathfrak{K}_i(A) = \top$ iff $\mathfrak{K}_i(B) = \mathfrak{K}_i(C) = \top$, and $= \bot$ otherwise.
(4) $A \equiv B \vee C$: $\mathfrak{K}_i(A) = \top$ iff $\mathfrak{K}_i(B) = \top$ or $\mathfrak{K}_i(C) = \top$, and $= \bot$ otherwise.
(5) $A \equiv B \supset C$: $\mathfrak{K}_i(A) = \top$ iff for all $j \geq i$, $\mathfrak{K}_j(B) = \bot$ or $\mathfrak{K}_j(C) = \top$, and $= \bot$ otherwise.
(6) $A \equiv (\forall x)B(x)$: $\mathfrak{K}_i(A) = \top$ if $\mathfrak{K}_j[d/x](A(d)) = \top$ for every $j \geq i$ and every $d \in D_j$, and $= \bot$ otherwise.
(7) $A \equiv (\exists x)B(x)$: $\mathfrak{K}_i(A) = \top$ if $\mathfrak{K}_i[d/x](A(d)) = \top$ for some $d \in D_i$ and $= \bot$ otherwise.

A is *satisfied* in an intuitionistic Kripke structure $\mathfrak{K}$, $\mathfrak{K} \models_i A$, iff $\mathfrak{K}_0(A) = \top$.

Definition 2.5. We define the following logics:

Intuitionistic logic **I** is the set of all $A \in$ Frm(L) s.t. every $\mathfrak{K} = \langle T, \{D_i\}_{i\in T}, \{\mathsf{s}_i\}_{i\in T}, \mathsf{s}\rangle$ with $T \in \mathcal{T}$ satisifies A.

Linear intuitionistic logic **IL** is the set of all $A \in$ Frm(L) s.t. every $\mathfrak{K} = \langle T, \{D_i\}_{i\in T}, \{\mathsf{s}_i\}_{i\in T}, \mathsf{s}\rangle$ with $T \in \mathcal{L}$ satisfies A.

Linear intuitionistic logic with constant domains **ILC** is the set of all $A \in$ Frm(A) s.t. every $\mathfrak{K} = \langle T, \{D_i\}_{i\in T}, \{\mathsf{s}_i\}_{i\in T}, \mathsf{s}\rangle$ with $T \in \mathcal{L}$ and $D_i = D_j$ for all $i, j \in T$ satisfies A.

As usual, if $\mathbf{L}$ is some logic, we write $\mathbf{L} \models A$ for $A \in \mathbf{L}$.

First-order Gödel logics are given by a first-order language, truth functions for the connectives and quantifiers, and a set of truth values. The sets of truth values for the systems we consider are subsets of $[0,1]$; the designated truth value is 1. The propositional versions of these logics were originally introduced by Gödel [4], and have spawned a sizeable area of logical research subsumed under the title "intermediate logics" (intermediate between classical and intuitionistic logic).

Interpretations are defined as usual:

Definition 2.6. Let $V \subseteq [0,1]$ be some set of truth values which contains 0 and 1 and is closed under supremum and infimum. A *many-valued interpretation* $\mathfrak{I} = \langle D, \mathbf{s} \rangle$ *based on* V is given by the *domain* D and the *valuation function* $\mathbf{s}$ where $\mathbf{s}$ maps atomic formulas in $\mathrm{Frm}(L^{\mathfrak{I}})$ into V and n-ary function symbols to functions from D^n to D.

$\mathbf{s}$ can be extended in the obvious way to a function on all terms. The valuation for formulas is defined as follows:

(1) $A \equiv P(t_1, \ldots, t_n)$ is atomic: $\mathfrak{I}(A) = \mathbf{s}(P)(\mathbf{s}(t_1), \ldots, \mathbf{s}(t_n))$.
(2) $A \equiv \neg B$:

$$\mathfrak{I}(A) = \begin{cases} 0 & \text{if } \mathfrak{I}(B) \neq 0 \\ 1 & \text{otherwise.} \end{cases}$$

(3) $A \equiv B \wedge C$: $\mathfrak{I}(A) = \min(\mathfrak{I}(B), \mathfrak{I}(C))$.
(4) $A \equiv B \vee C$: $\mathfrak{I}(A) = \max(\mathfrak{I}(A), \mathfrak{I}(B))$.
(5) $A \equiv B \supset C$:

$$\mathfrak{I}(A) = \begin{cases} \mathfrak{I}(C) & \text{if } \mathfrak{I}(B) > \mathfrak{I}(C) \\ 1 & \text{if } \mathfrak{I}(B) \leq \mathfrak{I}(C). \end{cases}$$

The set $\{\mathfrak{I}(A(d)) : d \in D\}$ is called the *distribution* of $A(x)$, we denote it by $\mathrm{Distr}_{\mathfrak{I}}(A(x))$. The quantifiers are, as usual, defined by infimum and supremum of their distributions.

(6) $A \equiv (\forall x)B(x)$: $\mathfrak{I}(A) = \inf \mathrm{Distr}_{\mathfrak{I}}(B(x))$.
(7) $A \equiv (\exists x)B(x)$: $\mathfrak{I}(A) = \sup \mathrm{Distr}_{\mathfrak{I}}(B(x))$.

$\mathfrak{I}$ *satisfies* a formula A, $\mathfrak{I} \models_m A$, if $\mathfrak{I}(A) = 1$.

In considering first-order infinite valued logics, care must be taken in choosing the set of truth values. In order to define the semantics of the quantifier we must restrict the set of truth values to those which are closed under infima and suprema. Note that in propositional infinite valued logics this restriction is not required. For instance, the *rational* interval $[0,1] \cap \mathbb{Q}$ will not give a satisfactory set of truth values. The following, however, do:

$$V_R = [0,1]$$
$$V^0 = \{1/k : k \in \omega \setminus \{0\}\} \cup \{0\}$$
$$V^1 = \{1 - 1/k : k \in \omega \setminus \{0\}\} \cup \{1\}$$

The corresponding infinite-valued Gödel logics are $\mathbf{G}_R$, $\mathbf{G}^0$, and $\mathbf{G}^1$.

Definition 2.7. $\mathbf{G}_R$ is the set of all $A \in \mathrm{Frm}(L)$ s.t. for every $\mathfrak{I}$ based on V_R, $\mathfrak{I} \models_m A$.
$\mathbf{G}^0$ is the set of all $A \in \mathrm{Frm}(L)$ s.t. for every $\mathfrak{I}$ based on V^0, $\mathfrak{I} \models_m A$.
$\mathbf{G}^1$ is the set of all $A \in \mathrm{Frm}(L)$ s.t. for every $\mathfrak{I}$ based on V^1, $\mathfrak{I} \models_m A$.

Note that V^0 is order isomorphic to the set of truth values for **LC** ($\omega + 1$, with 0 designated and reverse order); hence $\mathbf{G}^0$ is the natural generalization of **LC** to first-order. The corresponding propositional systems all have the same sets of tautologies, as can easily be seen. In other words, propositional infinite-valued logic is independent of the cardinality or order type of the set of truth values. The finite-valued versions are all distinct, however, and in fact **LC** is the intersection of all finite-valued Gödel logics.

The first-order infinite-valued systems are *not* equivalent, however.

Proposition 2.8. *Let*

$$C = (\exists x)(A(x) \supset (\forall y)A(y)) \text{ and}$$
$$C' = (\exists x)((\exists y)A(y) \supset A(x))$$

Then

(1) $\mathfrak{I}(C) = 1$ *if* $\mathrm{Distr}_{\mathfrak{I}}(A(x))$ *has a minimum (w.r.t.* $\mathfrak{I}$*) and* $= \mathfrak{I}((\forall y)A(y))$ *otherwise.*
(2) $\mathfrak{I}(C') = 1$ *if* $\mathrm{Distr}_{\mathfrak{I}}(A(x))$ *has a maximum and* $= \mathfrak{I}((\exists y)A(y))$ *otherwise.*

Proof. (1) Let us assume that $\mathrm{Distr}_{\mathfrak{I}}(A(x))$ has the minimum d. $\mathfrak{I}(A(d)) = \mathfrak{I}((\forall y)A(y))$ and therefore $\mathfrak{I}(A(d) \supset (\forall y)A(y)) = 1$ and $\mathfrak{I}(C) = 1$. If $\mathrm{Distr}_{\mathfrak{I}}(A(x))$ does not have a minimum then $\mathfrak{I}(A(d)) > \mathfrak{I}((\forall y)A(y))$ for all $d \in D(\mathfrak{I})$ and, by definition of the semantics of $\supset$, $\mathfrak{I}(A(d) \supset (\forall y)A(y)) = \mathfrak{I}((\forall y)A(y))$ for all $d \in D(\mathfrak{I})$; thus also the supremum $\mathfrak{I}(C)$ gets this value.

(2) If $\mathrm{Distr}_{\mathfrak{I}}(A(x))$ has the maximum d then, similarly, $\mathfrak{I}(A(d)) = \mathfrak{I}((\exists y)A(y))$ and $\mathfrak{I}(C') = 1$. If $\mathrm{Distr}_{\mathfrak{I}}(A(x))$ does not have a maximum then we always have $\mathfrak{I}((\exists y)A(y)) > \mathfrak{I}(A(d))$ and $\mathfrak{I}((\exists y)A(y) \supset A(d)) = \mathfrak{I}(A(d))$, whence $\mathfrak{I}(C') = \sup \mathrm{Distr}_{\mathfrak{I}}(A(x)) = \mathfrak{I}((\exists y)A(y))$. $\square$

Corollary 2.9. *Let C and C' be defined as in Proposition 2.8. Then C' is valid in both $\mathbf{G}^0$ and $\mathbf{G}^1$. C is valid in $\mathbf{G}^1$ but not in $\mathbf{G}^0$. Neither C nor C' are valid in $\mathbf{G}_R$.*

Proof. C' is valid in $\mathbf{G}^0$ because every supremum is a maximum; it is also valid in $\mathbf{G}^1$ because the only supremum which is not a maximum is 1.

C is not valid in $\mathbf{G}^0$ because there exists a sequence of truth values converging to 0, having no minimum and $\mathfrak{I}((\forall y)A(y)) = 0$. In $\mathbf{G}^1$ every infimum is also a minimum and thus C is valid in $\mathbf{G}^1$.

C and C' are both nonvalid in $\mathbf{G}_R$ because – at arbitrary places in the open interval $(0, 1)$ there are infinite (increasing and decreasing) sequences without maximum and minimum. $\square$

Note that both C and C' are valid in classical logic and not valid in intuitionistic logic. Dummett's formula $(A \supset B) \vee (B \supset A)$ is also not valid intuitionistically, but—of course—it is true in all three infinite-valued Gödel logics: Whatever A and B evaluate to, one of them is certainly less than or equal to the other.

Proposition 2.10. *For any first-order formula A, $\mathbf{G}^0 \models A$ iff $\mathbf{ILC} \models A$.*

Proof. Only if: Let $\mathfrak{K} = \langle \omega, D, \{\mathbf{s}_i\}_{i\in\omega}, \mathbf{s}\rangle$ be an **ILC** interpretation. Define the maps $\hat{\varphi}_{\mathfrak{K}}\colon \mathrm{Frm}(L^{\mathfrak{K}}) \to \{\top, \bot\}^\omega$ and $\varphi_{\mathfrak{K}}\colon \mathrm{Frm}(L^{\mathfrak{K}}) \to V^0$ as follows:

$$\hat{\varphi}_{\mathfrak{K}}(A) = \langle \mathfrak{K}_i(A)\rangle_{i\in\omega}$$
$$\varphi_{\mathfrak{K}}(A) = \begin{cases} 1/(\min\{i : \mathfrak{K}_i(A) = \top\} + 1) & \text{if } \mathfrak{K}_i(A) = \top \text{ for some } i \\ 0 & \text{otherwise} \end{cases}$$

Note that the monotonicity proviso in the definition of **ILC**-interpretations implies that $\hat{\varphi}(A)$ is of the form $\{\bot\}^n{}^\frown\{\top\}^\omega$ for some $n \in \omega$, or equals $\{\bot\}^\omega$.

We can now associate to each **ILC**-interpretation $\mathfrak{K}$ a many-valued interpretation $\mathfrak{I}_{\mathfrak{K}} = \langle D, \mathbf{s}_{\mathfrak{K}}\rangle$ by setting $\mathbf{s}_{\mathfrak{K}}(A) = \varphi_{\mathfrak{K}}(A)$ for A atomic in $L^{\mathfrak{K}}$. It is then easily proved, by induction on the complexity of a formula A, that $\mathfrak{I}_{\mathfrak{K}}(A) = \varphi_{\mathfrak{K}}(A)$.

The only nontrivial induction step is that concerning implication. Suppose

$$\mathfrak{I}_{\mathfrak{K}}(A) = \varphi_{\mathfrak{K}}(A), \qquad \mathfrak{I}_{\mathfrak{K}}(B) = \varphi_{\mathfrak{K}}(B). \tag{IH}$$

(1) $\mathfrak{K}_0(A \supset B) = \top$: By definition of the **ILC**-semantics we get $\mathfrak{K}_i(A) = \bot$ or $\mathfrak{K}_i(B) = \top$ for all $i \in \omega$. Moreover, by definition of $\varphi_{\mathfrak{K}}$, we have $\varphi_{\mathfrak{K}}(A \supset B) = 1$.
   (a) $\mathfrak{K}_0(A) = \top$: By definition of the **ILC**-semantics, $\mathfrak{K}_i(A) = \top$ for all $i \in \omega$. From $\mathfrak{K}_0(A \supset B) = \top$ we thus get $\mathfrak{K}_i(B) = \top$ for all $i \in \omega$. By definition of $\varphi_{\mathfrak{K}}$, $\varphi_{\mathfrak{K}}(A) = \varphi_{\mathfrak{K}}(B) = 1$ and, by (IH), $\mathfrak{I}_{\mathfrak{K}}(A) = \mathfrak{I}_{\mathfrak{K}}(B) = 1$. So the $\mathbf{G}^0$-semantics yields $\mathfrak{I}_{\mathfrak{K}}(A \supset B) = 1$.
   (b) $\mathfrak{K}_0(A) = \bot$: Let $m_A = \min\{j : \mathfrak{K}_j(A) = \top\}$, $m_B = \min\{j : \mathfrak{K}_j(B) = \top\}$. m_A and m_B may be undefined. But by $\mathfrak{K}_0(A \supset B) = \top$ and the **ILC**-semantics m_B can only be undefined if m_A is too. If both are defined then $m_B \leq m_A$. By definition of $\varphi_{\mathfrak{K}}$ this gives us $\varphi_{\mathfrak{K}}(A) \leq \varphi_{\mathfrak{K}}(B)$. (IH) yields $\mathfrak{I}_{\mathfrak{K}}(A) \leq \mathfrak{I}_{\mathfrak{K}}(B)$ and the semantics of $\mathbf{G}^0$ that $\mathfrak{I}_{\mathfrak{K}}(A \supset B) = 1$.

(2) $\mathfrak{K}_0(A \supset B) = \bot$: By definition of the **ILC**-semantics there exists a $j \in \omega$ s.t. $\mathfrak{K}_j(A) = \top$ and $\mathfrak{K}_j(B) = \bot$. Let m be the least such. By the **ILC**-semantics $\mathfrak{K}_j(A) = \top$ for all $j \geq m$ and $m < \min\{j : \mathfrak{K}_j(B) = \top\}$ giving $\varphi_{\mathfrak{K}}(B) < \varphi_{\mathfrak{K}}(A)$. From (IH) we thus derive $\mathfrak{I}_{\mathfrak{K}}(B) < \mathfrak{I}_{\mathfrak{K}}(A)$ and, by the semantics of $\mathbf{G}^0$, $\mathfrak{I}_{\mathfrak{K}}(A \supset B) = \mathfrak{I}_{\mathfrak{K}}(B)$.

If $\mathfrak{K}_j(B) = \bot$ for all $j \in \omega$ then, by definition of $\varphi_{\mathfrak{K}}$, $\varphi_{\mathfrak{K}}(A \supset B) = \varphi_{\mathfrak{K}}(B) = 0$. From $\mathfrak{I}_{\mathfrak{K}}(B) = \varphi_{\mathfrak{K}}(B) = 0$ we get $\varphi_{\mathfrak{K}}(A \supset B) = \mathfrak{I}_{\mathfrak{K}}(A \supset B)$.

If, on the other hand, $\mathfrak{K}_j(B) = \top$ for some $j \in \omega$ then $\varphi_{\mathfrak{K}}(B) = \varphi_{\mathfrak{K}}(A \supset B)$. By (IH) we get $\varphi_{\mathfrak{K}}(B) = \mathfrak{I}_{\mathfrak{K}}(B)$ and finally $\varphi_{\mathfrak{K}}(A \supset B) = \mathfrak{I}_{\mathfrak{K}}(A \supset B)$. This concludes the induction step.

It immediately follows that if $\mathbf{ILC} \not\models A$ then $\mathbf{G}^0 \not\models A$.

If: Conversely, let $\mathfrak{I} = \langle D, \mathbf{s}\rangle$ be a $\mathbf{G}^0$-interpretation. Let $\mathfrak{K}_{\mathfrak{I}} = \langle \omega, D, \{\mathbf{s}_i\}_{i\in\omega}, \mathbf{s}'\rangle$ be given by:

$$\mathbf{s}_i(A) = \begin{cases} \top & \text{if } \mathfrak{I}(A) \geq \frac{1}{i+1} \\ \bot & \text{otherwise.} \end{cases}$$

for atomic A, and $\mathbf{s}'$ according to the interpretation of the function symbols in $\mathbf{s}$. Again by induction on the complexity of formulas we have $\mathfrak{I}(A) = \varphi_{\mathfrak{K}_{\mathfrak{I}}}(A)$, in particular, $\mathfrak{K}_{\mathfrak{I}} \not\models_i A$ if $\mathfrak{I} \not\models_m A$. □

3 Incompleteness of $\mathbf{G}^0$, ILC and IL

We proceed to prove that the valid formulas of $\mathbf{G}^0$are not recursively enumerable. In contrast to this result, all finite-valued Gödel logics are r.e. [1] as well as $\mathbf{G}_R$ [11] ($\mathbf{G}_R$ there appears as *intuitionistic fuzzy logic*).

Proposition 3.1. *Let $\mathfrak{I}$ be a $\mathbf{G}^0$- interpretation, A a formula and*

$$v = \mathfrak{I}((\forall x)\neg[A(x) \supset (\forall y)A(y)])$$

Then $v = 0$ if $\mathrm{Distr}_{\mathfrak{I}}(A(x))$ has a minimum and $v = 1$ otherwise.

Proof. Just as in Proposition 2.8: Suppose $\mathrm{Distr}_{\mathfrak{I}}(A(x))$ has a minimum v, let $d \in D$ be s.t. $\mathfrak{I}(A(d)) = v$. Then $\mathfrak{I}(A(d)) = \mathfrak{I}((\forall y)A(y))$, so $\mathfrak{I}(\neg[A(d) \supset (\forall y)A(y)]) = 0$. Conversely, if $\mathrm{Distr}_{\mathfrak{I}}(A(x))$ has no minimum, then $\mathfrak{I}((\forall y)A(y)) = 0$ and $\mathfrak{I}(A(d)) > 0$ for all $d \in D$. Hence $\mathfrak{I}(A(d) \supset (\forall y)A(y)) = 0$, and $\mathfrak{I}(\neg[A(d) \supset (\forall y)A(y)]) = 1$ for all $d \in D$. □

In order to prove the main theorem of this chapter we need some tools from recursion theory.

Definition 3.2. Let ψ be an effective recursive enumeration of the set PR^1_1 of all primitive recursive functions from ω to ω. We define a two place function φ (which enumerates a subclass of PR^1_1):

$$\varphi_k(x) = \begin{cases} 0 & \text{if } x = 0 \\ 0 & \text{if } \psi_k(y) = 0 \text{ for } 1 \leq y \leq x \\ 1 & \text{otherwise} \end{cases}$$

The index set O_φ is defined as $\{k : (\forall y)\varphi_k(y) = 0\}$.

Proposition 3.3. *The index set O_φ is not recursively enumerable.*

Proof. By definition of φ, $\{k : (\forall y)\varphi_k(y) = 0\} = \{k : (\forall y)\psi_k(y) = 0\}$. But for every $g \in \mathrm{PR}^1_1$ the index set $\{k : (\forall y)\psi_k = g\}$ is Π_1-complete. Therefore O_φ is Π_1-complete and thus not recursively enumerable. □

The essence of the incompleteness proof is represented by a sequence of formulas $(A_k)_{k\in\omega}$ constructed via φ s.t.

$$\mathbf{G}^0 \models A_k \Longleftrightarrow k \in O_\varphi$$

i.e. O_φ is m-reducible to the validity problem of $\mathbf{G}^0$.

Definition 3.4. Let P be a one-place predicate symbol, s be the function symbol for the successor function and $\bar{0}$ be the constant symbol representing 0 (in particular, we choose a signature containing this symbol and all symbols from Robinson's arithmetic Q).

Let A_1 be a conjunction of axioms strong enough to represent every recursive function (e.g. the axioms of Q) and a defining axiom for the function φ s.t. every atomic formula is negated or doubly negated. We define the formulas A_2, A_3^k, A_4^k, A_5^k for $k \in \omega$; for formulas representing the equality $\varphi_k(x) = 0$ we write $[\varphi_k(x) = 0]$.

$$\begin{aligned}
A_2 &\equiv (\forall x)\neg\neg P(x) \\
A_3^k &\equiv (\forall x, y)(\neg[\varphi_k(x) = 0] \wedge \neg\neg x \leq y \supset \neg[\varphi_k(y) = 0]) \\
A_4^k &\equiv (\forall x)(\neg[\varphi_k(x) = 0] \supset (P(\bar{0}) \supset P(x)) \\
A_5^k &\equiv (\forall x)\{\neg\neg[\varphi_k(s(x)) = 0] \supset \\
&\qquad \supset [(P(x) \supset P(s(x))) \supset P(s(x))] \wedge [P(s(x)) \supset P(\bar{0})]\}
\end{aligned}$$

Finally we set

$$B_k \equiv A_1 \wedge A_2 \wedge A_3^k \wedge A_4^k \wedge A_5^k$$

and

$$A_k \equiv B_k \supset ((\forall x)\neg[P(x) \supset (\forall y)P(y)] \vee P(0)).$$

The double negations in Definition 3.4 serves the purpose of giving classical truth values to the formulas; note that, for a $\mathbf{G}^0$-interpretation $\mathfrak{I}$, $\mathfrak{I}(B) > 0$ implies $\mathfrak{I}(\neg\neg B) = 1$ (clearly $\mathfrak{I}(B) = 0$ implies $\mathfrak{I}(\neg\neg B) = 0$). Therefore the formulas in A_1, A_2 and A_3^k may only the receive the truth values 0 and 1 and thus have a classical meaning. Intuitively A_2 expresses that P is always true, A_k^3 states that $\varphi_k(x) = 0$ implies that $\varphi_k(y) = 0$ for all y greater than x. A_4^k and A_5^k are not classical in the sense that they may assume truth values between 0 and 1. $\mathfrak{I}(A_4^k) = 1$ means (according to the $\supset$-semantics of $\mathbf{G}^0$) that for all x with $\varphi_k(x) \neq 0$, $\mathfrak{I}(P(0))$ is less or equal to $\mathfrak{I}(P(x))$.

Lemma 3.5. *If $\mathfrak{I}$ is a $\mathbf{G}^0$-interpretation s.t. $\mathfrak{I}(B_k) < 1$, then $\mathfrak{I}(A_k) = 1$.*

Proof.

(1) $\mathfrak{I}(A_1 \wedge A_2 \wedge A_3^k \wedge A_4^k) < 1$: If $\mathfrak{I}(A_1 \wedge A_2 \wedge A_3^k) < 1$ then the value is actually 0 and thus $\mathfrak{I}(B_k) = 0$; $\mathfrak{I}(A_k) = 1$ is a trivial consequence. If $\mathfrak{I}(A_1 \wedge A_2 \wedge A_3^k) = 1$ and $\mathfrak{I}(A_4^k) < 1$ then there must be some d s.t. $\mathfrak{I}(\neg[\varphi_k(d) = 0]) = 1$ and $\mathfrak{I}(P(\bar{0}) \supset P(d)) < 1$. But then, by the semantics of $\mathbf{G}^0$, $\mathfrak{I}(P(d)) \leq (P(\bar{0}))$. Therefore $\mathfrak{I}(A_4^k) \leq \mathfrak{I}(P(\bar{0}))$ and also $\mathfrak{I}(B_k) \leq \mathfrak{I}(P(\bar{0}))$. But $P(\bar{0})$ occurs disjunctively in A_k and so $\mathfrak{I}(A_k) = 1$.

(2) $\mathfrak{I}(A_1 \wedge A_2 \wedge A_3^k \wedge A_4^k) = 1$: If $\mathfrak{I}(P(\bar{0})) = 1$ then clearly $\mathfrak{I}(A_k) = 1$. Thus let us assume that $\mathfrak{I}(P(\bar{0})) < 1$. As $\mathfrak{I}(B_k) < 1$ we must have $\mathfrak{I}(A_5^k) < 1$. That means there exists some d s.t. $\mathfrak{I}(\neg\neg[\varphi_k(s(d)) = 0]) = 1$ and

$$\mathfrak{I}(((P(d) \supset P(s(d))) \supset P(s(d))) \wedge (P(s(d)) \supset P(\bar{0}))) < 1. \qquad (*)$$

For such a d we either have ($\mathfrak{I}(P(d)) \leq \mathfrak{I}(P(s(d)))$ and $\mathfrak{I}(P(s(d))) < 1$) or $\mathfrak{I}(P(\bar{0})) < \mathfrak{I}(P(s(d)))$. In the latter case we get $\mathfrak{I}(P(s(d)) \supset P(\bar{0})) = \mathfrak{I}(P(\bar{0}))$. Thus in any case $(*)$ gets a value $\leq \mathfrak{I}(P(\bar{0}))$ and $\mathfrak{I}(B_k) \leq \mathfrak{I}(P(\bar{0}))$. Again we obtain $\mathfrak{I}(A_k) = 1$. □

Theorem 3.6. *The $\exists$-free fragment of $\mathbf{G}^0$is not recursively enumerable.*

Proof. We show that $\mathbf{G}^0 \models A_k$ iff $k \in O_\varphi$ (i.e. iff for all x, $\varphi_k(x) = 0$). The sequence $(A_k)_{k \in \omega}$ is $\exists$-free and (trivially) r.e. Thus a recursive enumeration of all A_k with $\mathbf{G}^0 \models A_k$ would give a recursive enumeration of the set O_φ which, by Proposition 3.3, does not exist.

Now let us assume that $\mathbf{G}^0 \models A_k$. We define a specific $\mathbf{G}^0$-interpretation $\mathfrak{N}_k$: The domain of $\mathfrak{N}_k$ is the set of natural numbers ω and the evaluation function s for the atoms is defined by:

$$\mathrm{s}(P(s^n(\bar{0}))) = \begin{cases} \frac{1}{n+2} & \text{if } \varphi_k(n) = 0 \\ 1 & \text{if } \varphi_k(n) > 0 \end{cases}$$

For all other atoms A we set $\mathrm{s}(A) = 1$ if $\mathbb{N} \models A$ and $\mathrm{s}(A) = 0$ otherwise ($\mathbb{N} \models A$ means that A is true in the standard model $\mathbb{N}$). Note that $P(\bar{0})$ receives the value $\frac{1}{2}$.

By definition of $\mathfrak{N}_k$ all conjuncts of B_k are verified and so $\mathfrak{N}_k(B_k) = 1$. By $\mathbf{G}^0 \models A_k$ we must have $\mathfrak{N}_k \models_m A_k$ and therefore

$$\mathfrak{N}_k \models_m (\forall x)\neg[P(x) \supset (\forall y)P(y)] \vee P(\bar{0}).$$

From $\mathfrak{N}_k(P(\bar{0})) = \frac{1}{2}$ we infer

$$\mathfrak{N}_k \models_m (\forall x)\neg[P(x) \supset (\forall y)P(y)].$$

By Proposition 3.1 the last property only holds if $\mathrm{Distr}_{\mathfrak{N}_k}(P(x))$ does not have a minimum.

We show now that φ_k must be the constant function 0. We assume that there exists a number r s.t. $\varphi_k(r) \neq 0$ and derive a contradiction: By definition of s we obtain $\mathrm{s}(P(s^r(\bar{0}))) = 1$. But $\mathfrak{N}_k \models_m A_3^k$ what implies that for all number terms (i.e. successor terms) $s^p(\bar{0})$ with $p \geq r$ the formula $\neg[\varphi_k(s^p(\bar{0})) = 0]$ evaluates to 1. As A_1 represents φ we obtain $\varphi_k(p) \neq 0$ for all $p \geq r$ and, by definition of φ_k, $\varphi_k(p) = 1$ for all $p \geq r$. By definition of s we thus obtain

$$\mathrm{s}(P(s^p(\bar{0}))) = 1 \text{ for all p } \geq r$$

But $\mathfrak{N}_k(P(\bar{0})) = \frac{1}{2}$ and, consequently, for almost all p $\mathfrak{N}_k(P(s^p(\bar{0}))) > \frac{1}{2}$. Therefore $\mathrm{Distr}_{\mathfrak{N}_k}(P(x))$ has a minimum; a contradiction. Note that by the choice of the standard model $\mathbb{N}$ we only have standard elements in our domain (i.e. elements which are represented by successor terms). So there cannot be another sequence in the set $\mathrm{Distr}_{\mathfrak{N}_k}(P(x))$ which converges to 0. We infer that φ_k must be identical to 0, and so $k \in O_\varphi$.

For the other direction let us assume that $k \in O_\varphi$, i.e. $\varphi_k(n) = 0$ for all n. As A_1 represents φ the formula $[\varphi_k(s^\ell(0)) = 0]$ is provable for all $\ell \in \omega$. Now let $\mathfrak{I}$ be an arbitrary $\mathbf{G}^0$-interpretation of A_k. If $\mathfrak{I}(B_k) < 1$ then, by Lemma 3.5, $\mathfrak{I}(A_k) = 1$. Thus it remains to investigate the case $\mathfrak{I}(B_k) = 1$. By definition of B_k, $\mathfrak{I}(B_k) = 1$ implies $I(A_5^k) = 1$. We substitute all ground terms $s^n(\bar{0})$ into the matrix of A_5^k. These instances are true in $\mathfrak{I}$ either if all $P(s^n(\bar{0}))$ evaluate to 1 (in which case A_k is true because also $P(\bar{0})$ is true) or the sequence $\mathfrak{I}(P(s^n(\bar{0}))_{n\in\omega}$ is strictly decreasing. In the last case the sequence must converge to 0. By the axiom A_2 no element of this sequence is actually $= 0$; this property also holds for all (potential) nonstandard elements, which may be present as the domain is arbitrary. As a consequence $\mathrm{Distr}_{\mathfrak{I}}(P(x))$ does not have a minimum. Proposition 3.1 then implies that

$$\mathfrak{I} \models_m (\forall x)\neg[P(x) \supset (\forall y)P(y)].$$

But the last formula occurs disjunctively in the consequent of A_k and thus $\mathfrak{I} \models_m A_k$. Putting things together we see that A_k evaluates to 1 under all $\mathbf{G}^0$-interpretations, i.e., $\mathbf{G}^0 \models A_k$. □

Corollary 3.7. *(1)* **ILC** *is not recursively enumerable.*
(2) **IL** *is not recursively enumerable.*

Proof. (1) Immediate by Proposition 2.10.

(2) We show: **IL** $\models A_k$ iff $\varphi_k(n) = 0$ for all n. If $\varphi_k(n) \neq 0$ for some n, then $\mathbf{G}^0 \not\models A_k$ by Theorem 3.6. Since $\mathbf{G}^0 = $ **ILC**, there is some **ILC**-interpretation $\mathfrak{K}$ s.t. $\mathfrak{K} \not\models_i A_k$; but $\mathfrak{K}$ is also an **IL**-interpretation, so **IL** $\not\models A_k$.

So suppose that $\varphi_k(n) = 0$ for all $n \in \omega$. Let $\mathfrak{K} = \langle \omega, (D_i)_{i\in\omega}, \{s_i\}_{i\in\omega}, \mathrm{s}\rangle$ be an **IL**–interpretation. Then, by definition of the formulas A_k and B_k, $\mathfrak{K}_0(B_k) = \bot$ implies $\mathfrak{K}_0(A_k) = \top$. It remains to investigate the case $\mathfrak{K}_0(B_k) = \top$.

All domains D_i of $\mathfrak{K}$ must contain the interpretation of the number terms $s^n(\bar{0})$. Therefore either $\mathfrak{K}_0(P(\bar{0})) = \top$, in which case $\mathfrak{K}_0(A_k) = 1$ by definition of A_k, or (by the proof of Theorem 3.6) the sequence $\varphi_{\mathfrak{K}}(P(s^n(\bar{0})))_{n\in\omega}$ is strictly decreasing. Note that we may define $\varphi_{\mathfrak{K}}$ and $\hat{\varphi}_{\mathfrak{K}}$ exactly like in Proposition 2.10 (although $\mathfrak{K}$ need not be an **ILC**–interpretation).

So let us assume that $\varphi_{\mathfrak{K}}(P(s^n(\bar{0})))_{n\in\omega}$ is strictly decreasing. We will show that $\hat{\varphi}_{\mathfrak{K}}((\forall x)P(x)) = \{\bot\}^\omega$. Suppose, by way of contradiction, that $\hat{\varphi}_{\mathfrak{K}}((\forall x)P(x)) \neq \{\bot\}^\omega$, i.e. there exists an $i \in \omega$ s.t. $\mathfrak{K}_i((\forall x)P(x)) \neq \bot$. As $(\forall x)P(x)$ does not contain function symbols, $\mathfrak{K}_i((\forall x)P(x))$ cannot be undefined and so $\mathfrak{K}_i((\forall x)P(x)) = \top$. By definition of the **IL**-semantics this implies that for all $j \geq i$ and $d \in D_j$, $\mathfrak{K}_j(P(d/x)) = \top$. In particular, we get

$$\text{for all } d \in D_i : \mathfrak{K}_i(P(d/x)) = \top.$$

As D_i contains the interpretation of all number terms we also obtain $\mathfrak{K}_i(P(s^n(\bar{0}))) = \top$ for all $n \in \omega$. Consequently $\min\{j : K_j(P(s^n(\bar{0}))) = \top\} \leq i$ for all $n \in \omega$. By definition of $\varphi_{\mathfrak{K}}$ we thus obtain

$$\varphi_{\mathfrak{K}}(P(s^n(\bar{0}))) \geq \frac{1}{i+1} \quad \text{for all } n \in \omega$$

and

$$\varphi_{\mathfrak{K}}(P(s^n(\bar{0}))) = \frac{1}{k_n + 1} \quad \text{for } k_n \in \omega,\ k_n \le i,\ n \in \omega.$$

This however contradicts our assumption that the sequence $\varphi_{\mathfrak{K}}(P(s^n(\bar{0})))_{n \in \omega}$ is strictly decreasing. So we obtain $\hat{\varphi}_{\mathfrak{K}}((\forall x)P(x)) = \{\bot\}^\omega$. However, there are no i and $d \in D_i$ s.t. $\mathfrak{K}_i(P(d/x)) = \bot$, since $\mathfrak{K}_0((\forall x)\neg\neg P(x)) = \top$ by A_2 in B_k. Therefore $\mathfrak{K}_i(P(d/x) \supset (\forall y)P(y)) = \bot$ for all $i \in \omega$ and $d \in D_i$. By the semantics of **IL** this implies

$$\mathfrak{K}_0((\forall x)\neg[P(x) \supset (\forall y)P(y)]) = \top.$$

But then $\mathfrak{K}_0(A_k) = \top$ and the reduction of O_φ to **IL** is completed. □

4 Incompleteness of temporal logics

We now proceed to show that (a) ○-free **TL** and **TLC** and (b) **TG** and **TGC** are also not recursively axiomatizable. This strengthens the incompleteness result for **TL** of Szalas and Kröger [6] and answers a question left open in [2]. In contrast to **TG**, however, **TB** *is* r.e. [2]. An axiomatization is given by adding to first-order **S4** the axioms:

$$\begin{gathered} \bigcirc(A \supset B) \supset (\bigcirc A \supset \bigcirc B) \\ \neg\bigcirc A \leftrightarrow \bigcirc\neg A \\ \bigcirc\Box A \wedge A \leftrightarrow \Box A \end{gathered}$$

and the rule $A/\bigcirc A$.

Definition 4.1. We define the operator Ψ as follows:

$$\begin{aligned} \Psi(A) &= \Box A \qquad A \text{ atomic} \\ \Psi(A \vee B) &= \Psi(A) \vee \Psi(B) \\ \Psi(A \wedge B) &= \Psi(A) \wedge \Psi(B) \\ \Psi(A \supset B) &= \Box[\Psi(A) \supset \Psi(B)] \\ \Psi(\neg A) &= \Box(\neg\Psi(A)) \\ \Psi((\forall x)A(x)) &= \Box(\forall x)\Psi(A(x)) \end{aligned}$$

Proposition 4.2. *Let A be an $\exists$-free first-order formula. Then*

(1) **TL** $\models \Psi(A)$ *iff* **IL** $\models A$ *and*
(2) **TLC** $\models \Psi(A)$ *iff* **ILC** $\models A$.

Proof. Suppose **IL** $\not\models A$, let $\mathfrak{K} = \langle \omega, D_i, \{s_i\}, s\rangle$ be a countermodel. We can interpret $\mathfrak{K}$ as a **TL**-interpretation $\mathfrak{K}^t$. By induction on the complexity of a formula A and using the monotonicity property of $\mathfrak{K}$ we have $\mathfrak{K}^t_i(\Psi(A)) = \mathfrak{K}_i(A)$. Hence, $\mathfrak{K}^t \not\models_t \Psi(A)$.

Conversely, let $\mathfrak{K}^t = \langle \omega, D_i, \{\mathbf{s}_i^t\}, \mathbf{s} \rangle$ be a **TL**-interpretation s.t. $\mathfrak{K}^t \not\models_t \Psi(A)$. Then define $\mathfrak{K} = \langle \omega, D_i, \{\mathbf{s}_i\}, \mathbf{s} \rangle$ by $\mathbf{s}_i(A) = \mathfrak{K}_i^t(\Box(A))$. Again, by an easy induction on the complexity of A we have $\mathfrak{K}_i^t(\Psi(A)) = \mathfrak{K}_i(A)$. Thus, $\mathfrak{K} \not\models_i A$.

Similarly, for **TLC** and **ILC**. □

Corollary 4.3. *The* $\exists$- *and* $\bigcirc$-*free fragments of* **TL** *are not r.e.*

Proof. By Corollary 3.7 and Proposition 4.2. □

The reader will note the similarity between the above embedding of **IL** in **TL** with Gödel's, and McKinsey and Tarski's embeddings of intuitionistic predicate logic into **S4**.

In contrast to first order **TL**, propositional **TL** is axiomatizable (even with $\bigcirc$). In [5] it is shown that we get $\mathbf{TL}_{\mathrm{prop}}$ by adding to $\mathbf{TB}_{\mathrm{prop}}$ the rule

$$\frac{A \supset B \quad A \supset \bigcirc B}{A \supset \Box B}$$

Definition 4.4. The set $S^*(A)$ of *strict subformulas* of a formula A is defined as follows:

$$S^*(A) = \{A\} \cup \begin{cases} S^*(B) & \text{if } A \equiv \neg B \\ S^*(B) \cup S^*(C) & \text{if } A \equiv B \wedge C,\ B \vee C, \text{ or } B \supset C \\ S^*(B(x)) & \text{if } A \equiv (\forall x)B(x) \text{ or } (\exists x)B(x) \end{cases}$$

Let $P_1, \ldots, P_m$ be the predicate symbols with occurring in A with arities $r_1, \ldots, r_m$ and $\bar{x}_{r_1}, \ldots, \bar{x}_{r_m}$ corresponding variable vectors. Then we define

$$S(A) = S^*(A) \cup \{P_i(\bar{x}_{r_i}) : i = 1, \ldots, m\}$$

Definition 4.5. Let A be a first-order formula without $\exists$. Define

$$C_A \equiv \Box \bigwedge_{B(\bar{x}) \in S(A)} (\forall \bar{x})(B(\bar{x}) \leftrightarrow \bigcirc B(\bar{x}))$$

Let $\mathbf{TG}^*$ be the logic based on **TG**-interpretations where the domains within an ω-sequence are equal, i.e., for all i, j we have $D_{i\cdot\omega+j} = D_{i\cdot\omega}$.

Proposition 4.6. *Suppose* A *is* $\bigcirc$- *and* $\exists$-*free. Then* $\mathbf{TG} \models C_A \supset A$ *iff* $\mathbf{TG}^* \models C_A \supset A$.

Proof. Only if: Immediate. If: Let $\mathfrak{K}$ be a **TG**-interpretation s.t. $\mathfrak{K} \not\models_t C_A \supset A$. Let $\mathfrak{K}^* = \langle D_i^*, \mathbf{s}_i^* \rangle$ be defined by $D_{i\cdot\omega+j}^* = D_{i\cdot\omega}$ and $\mathbf{s}_i^* = \mathbf{s}_i \restriction D_i^*$. We prove by induction on the complexity of $A(\bar{c})$ (for $\bar{c} \in D_{i\cdot\omega}^*$) that $\mathfrak{K}_{i\cdot\omega+j}(A) = \mathfrak{K}_{i\cdot\omega+j}^*(A)$. This is immediately seen for A atomic or with outermost logical symbol a propositional connective. If $A \equiv (\forall x)B(x)$ we argue as follows: Let (i, j) denote $i \cdot \omega + j$. If $\mathfrak{K}_{i,j}(A) = \top$ then $\mathfrak{K}_{i,j}(B(d)) = \top$ for all $d \in D_{i,j} \supseteq D_{i,0}$. By induction hypothesis, $\mathfrak{K}_{i,j}^*(B(d)) = \top$ for all $d \in D_{i,j}^*$, so $\mathfrak{K}_{i,j}^*(A) = \top$.

If $\mathfrak{K}_{i,j}(A) = \bot$ then for some $d \in D_{i,j}$, $\mathfrak{K}_{i,j}(B(d)) = \bot$. Suppose for all $d \in D_{i,0}$, $\mathfrak{K}_{i,j}(B(d)) = \top$. Then we have $\mathfrak{K}_{i,0}((\forall x)\bigcirc^j B(x) \wedge \neg\bigcirc^j (\forall x)B(x)) = \top$. Since we have $\mathfrak{K}_{i,0} \models (\forall x)(B(x) \leftrightarrow \bigcirc B(x))$ and $\mathfrak{K}_{i,0} \models (\forall x)B(x) \leftrightarrow \bigcirc(\forall x)B(x))$ this gives $\mathfrak{K}_{i,0} \models (\forall x)B(x) \wedge \neg(\forall x)B(x)$, a contradiction. Hence actually there is $d \in D_{i,0}$ s.t. $\mathfrak{K}_{i,j}(B(d)) = \bot$. By induction hypothesis, $\mathfrak{K}^*_{i,j}(B(d)) = \bot = \mathfrak{K}^*_{i,j}(A)$. □

Let $\mathbf{TG}^{**}$ ($\mathbf{TGC}^{**}$) be the logic based on $\mathbf{TG}$($\mathbf{TGC}$)-interpretations where the worlds within an ω-sequence are equal, i.e., for all i, j we have $D_{i,j} = D_{i,0}$ and $\mathsf{s}_{i,j} = \mathsf{s}_{i,0}$.

Proposition 4.7. *Let A be a $\bigcirc$ and $\exists$-free formula.*

(1) $\mathbf{TGC}^* \models C_A \supset A$ *iff* $\mathbf{TGC}^{**} \models C_A \supset A$.
(2) $\mathbf{TG}^* \models C_A \supset A$ *iff* $\mathbf{TG}^{**} \models C_A \supset A$.

Proof. Obvious, since A does not contain $\bigcirc$. □

Proposition 4.8. *Let A be an $\bigcirc$- and $\exists$-free formula.*

(1) $\mathbf{TGC}^{**} \models C_A \supset A$ *iff* $\mathbf{TLC} \models A$.
(2) $\mathbf{TG}^{**} \models C_A \supset A$ *iff* $\mathbf{TL} \models A$.

Proof. (1) Only if: Suppose $\mathbf{TLC} \not\models A$, let $\mathfrak{K} = \langle \omega, D, \{\mathsf{s}_i\}, \mathsf{s}\rangle$ be a countermodel. Define $\mathfrak{K}^g = \langle \omega \cdot \omega, D, \{\mathsf{s}^g_i\}_{i \in \omega\cdot\omega}, \mathsf{s}\rangle$ by $\mathsf{s}^g_{j,k} = \mathsf{s}_j$ where $i, j, k \in \omega$. Clearly, $\mathfrak{K}^g \not\models_t C_A \supset A$.

If: Suppose $\mathbf{TGC}^{**} \not\models C_A \supset A$, let $\mathfrak{K} = \langle \omega \cdot \omega, D, \{\mathsf{s}_i\}, \mathsf{s}\rangle$ be a countermodel. Since $\mathfrak{K} \models C_A$ and the domains are constant, $\mathfrak{K}_{j,k}(A) = \mathfrak{K}_{j,\ell}(A)$ for A, and in particular $\mathsf{s}_{j,k} = \mathsf{s}_{j,\ell}$. Define $\mathfrak{K}^\ell = \langle \omega, D, \{\mathsf{s}^\ell_i\}, \mathsf{s}\rangle$ by $\mathsf{s}^\ell_j = \mathsf{s}_{j\omega}$ for $j \in \omega$. Again by induction on the complexity of A it is easily shown that $\mathfrak{K}^\ell_j(A) = \mathfrak{K}^\ell_{j,k}(A)$. So $\mathfrak{K}^\ell \not\models_t A$.

(2) Similarly. □

Corollary 4.9. *The $\exists$-free fragments of* $\mathbf{TG}$ *and* $\mathbf{TGC}$ *are not r.e.*

Proof. By Corollary 4.3 and Propositions 4.6, 4.7 and 4.8. □

For an axiomatization of the propositional logic $\mathbf{TG}_{\mathrm{prop}}$ it is convenient to introduce a new connective $\triangle$ defined by $\mathfrak{K}_{i,j}(\triangle A) = 1$ iff $\mathfrak{K}_{i+1,0}(A) = 1$. Then $\mathbf{TG}_{\mathrm{prop}}$ is axiomatized by **S4** plus

$$\bigcirc(A \supset B) \supset (\bigcirc A \supset \bigcirc B) \qquad \triangle(A \supset B) \supset (\triangle A \supset \triangle B)$$
$$\bigcirc\neg A \leftrightarrow \neg\bigcirc A \qquad \triangle\neg A \leftrightarrow \neg\triangle A$$
$$\bigcirc\triangle A \leftrightarrow \triangle A \qquad \bigcirc\Box A \wedge \triangle\Box A \wedge A \leftrightarrow \Box A$$

and the rules

$$\frac{A}{\bigcirc A} \qquad \frac{A}{\triangle A} \qquad \frac{A \supset B \quad A \supset \bigcirc A \quad A \supset \triangle A}{A \supset \Box B}$$

5 Conclusion

We used the main result of this paper, the incompleteness of the infinitely valued first-order Gödel logic based on the domain of truth values $V_0 : \{1/k : k \geq 1\} \cup \{0\}$, to demonstrate the incompleteness of first-order discrete linear temporal logics with/without time gaps and with/without constant domains. The first-order discrete branching time logic with time gaps, however, is complete, but it is an open question whether the same applies for the same logic with constant domains. The infinitely valued first-order Gödel logics define another field of future research; we conjecture that the logic based on $V_1 = \{1-1/k : k \geq 1\} \cup \{1\}$ and the $\exists$-fragment of the Gödel logic based on V_0 are recursively axiomatizable.

References

1. M. Baaz, C. G. Fermüller, and R. Zach. Elimination of cuts in first-order finite-valued logics. *J. Inform. Process. Cybernet.* **EIK**, **29**(6), 333–355, 1994.
2. M. Baaz, A. Leitsch, and R. Zach. Completeness of a first-order temporal logic with time-gaps. *Theoret. Comput. Sci.*, 1996 to appear.
3. M. Dummett. A propositional calculus with denumerable matrix. *J. Symbolic Logic*, **24**, 97–106, 1959.
4. K. Gödel. Zum intuitionistischen Aussagenkalkül. *Anz. Akad. Wiss. Wien*, **69**, 65–66, 1932.
5. F. Kröger. *Temporal Logic of Programs.* EATCS Monographs in Computer Science 8. (Springer, Berlin, 1987).
6. F. Kröger. On the interpretability of arithmetic in temporal logic. *Theoret. Comput. Sci.*, **73**, 47–60, 1990.
7. S. Merz. Decidability and incompleteness results for first-order temporal logics of linear time. *J. Applied Non-Classical Logics*, **2**(2), 139–156, 1992.
8. B. Scarpellini. Die Nichtaxiomatisierbarkeit des unendlichwertigen Prädikatenkalküls von Łukasiewicz. *J. Symbolic Logic*, **27**, 159–170, 1962.
9. A. Szalas. Concerning the semantic consequence relation in first-order temporal logic. *Theoret. Comput. Sci.*, **47**, 329–334, 1986.
10. A. Szalas and L. Holenderski. Incompleteness of first-order temporal logic with until. *Theoret. Comput. Sci.*, **57**, 317–325, 1988.
11. G. Takeuti and T. Titani. Intuitionistic fuzzy logic and instuitionistic fuzzy set theory. *J. Symbolic Logic*, **49**, 851–866, 1984.

Semantics of Non-terminating Rewrite Systems Using Minimal Coverings

José Barros *
Departamento de Informática
Universidade do Minho,
Braga, Portugal
Internet: jbb@di.uminho.pt

Joseph Goguen **
Programming Research Group
Oxford University
Oxford, U.K.
Internet: goguen@comlab.ox.ac.uk

Abstract. We propose a new semantics for rewrite systems based on interpreting rewrite rules as inequations between terms in an ordered algebra. In particular, we show that the algebra of normal forms in a terminating system is a uniquely minimal covering of the term algebra. In the non-terminating case, the existence of this minimal covering is established in the completion of an ordered algebra formed by rewriting sequences. We thus generalize the properties of normal forms for non-terminating systems to this minimal covering. These include the existence of normal forms for arbitrary rewrite systems, and their uniqueness for confluent systems, in which case the algebra of normal forms is isomorphic to the canonical quotient algebra associated with the rules when seen as equations. This extends the benefits of algebraic semantics to systems with non-deterministic and non-terminating computations. We first study properties of abstract orders, and then instantiate these to term rewriting systems.

1 Introduction

Term rewriting is the the basic computational aspect of equational logic and is fundamental to prototyping algebraic specifications. The vast majority of the literature in this area focuses on terminating rewrite systems, i.e., systems where no infinite rewriting sequence occurs. But there is now increasing research on the semantics of non-terminating systems. Non-strict functional languages such

* Supported in part by JNICT under contracts BD-1102-90/IA and PRAXIS XXI / BD / 4069 / 94.

** The research reported in this paper has been supported in part by the Science and Engineering Research Council, the CEC under ESPRIT-2 BRA Working Groups 6071, IS-CORE (Information Systems COrrectness and REusability) and 6112, COMPASS (COMPrehensive Algebraic Approach to System Specification and development), Fujitsu Laboratories Limited, and under the management of the Information Technology Promotion Agency (IPA), Japan, as part of the Industrial Science and Technology Frontier Program "New Models for Software Architectures," sponsored by NEDO (New Energy and Industrial Technology Development Organization).

as MIRANDA [23] provide a practical reason to study such systems, since one can write non-terminating functions that "compute" infinite structures, such as the list of all prime numbers. Moreover, it is often desirable to write terminating functions using other functions whose termination cannot be established. Such use of intermediate non-terminating functions may seem less peculiar if we note an analogous technique in imperative languages: it is not unusual to see in a terminating C program a loop of the form

```
while (1) { ... }
```

Another application is in specifying reactive or stream-based programs: for example, an operating system should not terminate. Also, studying non-terminating rewrite systems deepens our knowledge of rewrite systems in general. More specifically, it shows us which properties of a terminating rewrite system arise just because it terminates, and which are independent from termination.

The usual semantics for rewrite system is based in interpreting rewrite rules as equations and rewriting as a particular case of equational reasoning. Our proposal is different. Rules have a computational meaning – rewriting a term is computing it, i.e., finding its **value**, which is just a non-reducible term (a normal form). The connection with equations is seen in another way – in certain cases, we can replace equational reasoning by another type of reasoning: two terms are equal if they have the same value, i.e., if the result of computing them is equal. This can only be done if we guarantee that every term has a unique value and every term is equal to its value. The termination of a rewrite system ensures that every term has a value (normal form). But, in general we cannot guarantee this.

The research that has been done on non-terminating rewrite systems [21, 4, 6, 17, 20, 22, 7, 5, 16] is centered on seeking semantics for these systems where the usual properties of confluent systems (like uniqueness of normal forms) still hold. Most research that has been done on the semantics of non-terminating rewrite systems follows ideas of the ADJ Group on continuous algebras [12], where the authors give an elegant algebraic definition of finite and infinite terms as a way of completing the term algebra: they show not only that the algebra of finite and infinite terms is continuous but also that every infinite term is the least upper bound of a set of finite terms. These approaches extend the original set of terms (with infinite terms) in such a way that every term has a value. The problem with these approaches is that the connection referred above between rewriting and equational reasoning is not preserved: terms that are not equal can have the same value! Kennaway *et al.* [16] show that even in confluent systems, the ω-normal forms defined in [7] are not unique. Also the existence of these ω-normal forms, as well as infinite normal forms [16] is not only dependent on the confluence of a rewrite system, but on other properties like left-linearity and top-termination.

Our answer to this problem is to interpret rewrite rules as **inequations**. We then have a variant of equational logic (the logic of replacing equals for equals)

called **inequational logic** – the logic of replacing terms by larger terms[3]. The models in this logic are **preordered algebras** – algebras whose carrier is a preordered set. The term algebra is now a preorder – a term t is above a term t' iff all values of t are values of t' – and the set of values is nothing more than the maximal elements in this preorder. This view of rewriting is somehow similar to the algebraic definition of refinement (e.g. [14]). This view is also consistent with the work of Meseguer [19, 18], where it is argued that rules express change in a computational system. The main difference from inequational logic and Meseguer's **rewriting logic** is that, apart from limiting ourselves to the unconditional case, we do not record in any way how a reduction was performed. In rewriting logic, each reduction $t \rightarrow^*_{\mathcal{R}} t'$ is associated with the sequence of (parallel) rule applications. Since we omit this information, we cannot distinguish between two different reductions with the same start and end points. However, the simplicity of our approach makes it quite elegant where it applies, as demonstrated by the proofs of completeness and soundness of inequational logic given in Section 4.

In the case of terminating and confluent rewrite systems, normal forms constitute an initial algebra. We show that this algebra has a very special property: it is a **uniquely minimal covering** of the term algebra. It is this property that makes it the obvious choice for implementing the abstract data type described by the rules, and moreover, its initiality is provable from just that property. We also show that for globally finite rewrite systems, the results proved by Goguen [8] follow from the existence of a uniquely minimal covering of the term algebra.

To deal with arbitrary non-terminating systems, instead of extending the preorder of terms, we use another preorder – of the rewriting sequences – together with an injective embedding from the original preorder into this other one. This preorder has the important property mentioned above about the preorder of terms in the terminating case: all elements have a value, that we call a *normalizing sequence*. In other words, this preorder has a minimal covering. In the case of confluent systems these values are unique, allowing us to generalize the properties of the algebra of normal forms to this one. Among the differences between the results obtained here and in the cited approaches, we would emphasize the existence of normal forms for arbitrary systems, the uniqueness of these normal forms in confluent systems, and in this last case, the isomorphism between these normal forms and the canonical quotient algebra. We feel that the success of the approach presented here paves the way to applications of rewrite systems to concurrency, e.g., results along the lines of Hennessy [13] and Meseguer [19, 18].

Section 2 introduces the notation that we will use. In Section 3 we present some abstract properties of complete preorders and minimal coverings. Finally, we apply these properties to the particular case of term rewriting systems in Section 4. For simplicity of exposition we present here only the unsorted case, but everything extends smoothly to the many-sorted case.

---

[3] In standard rewriting texts (e.g., [15]) rewriting is often associated with simplification; thus we should have said *replacing terms by smaller terms*. The reason for using our terminology comes from the fact that in a great part of the examples of non-terminating rewrite systems, rewriting increases the size of terms.

2 Preliminaries

A **preorder** $(X, \sqsubseteq_X)$ consists of a set X and a reflexive and transitive binary relation $\sqsubseteq_X$ over X. A preorder is a **partial order** iff $\sqsubseteq_X$ is anti-symmetric; it is an **equivalence** iff $\sqsubseteq_X$ is symmetric. Let $(A, \equiv)$ be an equivalence; for each $a \in A$, let $[a]_\equiv$ denote the set $\{b \in A \mid a \equiv b\}$ and let $A/_\equiv$ denote the set $\{[a]_\equiv \mid a \in A\}$. Given preorders $(X, \sqsubseteq_X)$ and $(Y, \sqsubseteq_Y)$, a mapping $f : X \to Y$ is **monotonic** iff $f(x) \sqsubseteq_Y f(y)$ whenever $x \sqsubseteq_X y$. It is an **order embedding** iff for every $x, y \in X$, $x \sqsubseteq_X y$ iff $f(x) \sqsubseteq_Y f(y)$. Given a subset X of A, an upper bound of X is an element $a \in A$ such that $\forall x \in X\ x \sqsubseteq a$. An upper bound a of X is a **least upper bound (lub)** iff for any upper bound a' of X, $a \sqsubseteq a'$.

Given a preorder A, a non-empty subset C of A is a **chain** iff it is totally ordered (i.e., for every $x_1, x_2 \in C$ either $x_1 \sqsubseteq x_2$ or $x_2 \sqsubseteq x_1$). A chain is an **ω-chain** iff it is denumerable. A non-empty subset Δ of A is **directed** iff for every pair of elements d_1 and d_2 of Δ there exists an element d in Δ such that both $d_1 \sqsubseteq_A d$ and $d_2 \sqsubseteq_A d$. A preorder A is **ω-complete** iff every ω-chain has a lub in A, and is **complete** iff every directed subset of A has a lub in A. If $\sqsubseteq$ is a partial order then the lub of any set Δ, if it exists, is unique and is denoted by $\bigsqcup \Delta$. A monotonic mapping $f : A \to B$ between ω-complete preorders is **ω-continuous** iff it preserves least upper bounds of ω-chains, i.e., for every ω-chain X, if x is a lub of X then $f(x)$ is a lub of $f(X)$. Similarly, if A and B are complete preorders, f is **continuous** iff for every directed subset X of A, if x is a lub of X then $f(x)$ is a lub of $f(X)$.

Given a preorder A we define its kernel, denoted $\simeq$, as the largest equivalence contained in it, i.e., for all x in A,

$$x \simeq y \text{ iff } x \sqsubseteq y \text{ and } y \sqsubseteq x$$

We also define the partial order $A/_\simeq = (A/_\simeq, \sqsubseteq_\simeq)$ by

$$[x]_\simeq \sqsubseteq_\simeq [y]_\simeq \text{ iff } x \sqsubseteq y$$

For each monotonic mapping $f : A \to B$, we define the monotonic mapping $f_\simeq : A/_\simeq \to B/_\simeq$ to send each $[a]_\simeq$ to $[f(a)]_\simeq$.

Given a preorder $A = (A, \sqsubseteq)$, we define $(A_\omega, \ll)$ to be the preorder where A_ω is the set of ω-chains of elements of A, and

$$a \ll b \text{ iff } \forall i\ \exists j\ a_i \sqsubseteq b_j$$

For each monotonic mapping $f : A \to B$, we define the mapping $f_\omega : A_\omega \to B_\omega$ by

$$f_\omega(\langle a_0, a_1, \ldots \rangle) = \langle f(a_0), f(a_1), \ldots \rangle$$

It is well known [3] that A_ω is an ω-complete preorder, and that f_ω is ω-continuous. Moreover,

Proposition 1 [1]. *If A is denumerable then A_ω is complete and f_ω is continuous.*

Given a preorder $(A, \sqsubseteq_A)$, let $\equiv_A$ be defined as $a \equiv_A b$ if there exists a sequence $\langle a_0, \ldots, a_n \rangle$ of elements of A such that $a = a_0$, $b = a_n$, and for each $0 \leqslant i < n$ $a_i \sqsubseteq_A a_{i+1}$ or $a_{i+1} \sqsubseteq_A a_i$. In other words, $\equiv_A$ is the symmetric and transitive closure of $\sqsubseteq_A$. We denote by $A_\equiv$ the set $\{[a]_{\equiv_A} \mid a \in A\}$. Given a monotonic mapping $f : A \to B$, $f_\equiv : A_\equiv \to B_\equiv$ sends each $[a]_{\equiv_A}$ to $[f(a)]_{\equiv_B}$.

2.1 Algebras and Equations

A **signature** Σ is a family $\Sigma = \{\Sigma_n\}_{n \in \omega}$. An element $\sigma \in \Sigma_n$ is called a **function symbol of arity** n, and in particular, an element of Σ_0 is called a **constant symbol**. A signature Σ where $\Sigma_n = \emptyset$ for all $n > 0$ is called a **ground signature**, and is basically just a set of symbols. Given signatures Σ and Ω their union $\Sigma \cup \Omega$ is defined as $(\Sigma \cup \Omega)_n = \Sigma_n \cup \Omega_n$; Σ and Ω are said to be **disjoint** if $\bigcup_n \Sigma_n$ and $\bigcup_n \Omega_n$ are disjoint.

The set T_Σ of all Σ-terms is the smallest set of *strings* over $(\bigcup_n \Sigma_n) \cup \{\underline{(}, \underline{)}, \underline{,}\}$ (where $\underline{(}$, $\underline{)}$, and $\underline{,}$ are special symbols disjoint from Σ) that contains Σ_0 and such that $\sigma\underline{(}t_1\underline{,}\ldots\underline{,}t_n\underline{)} \in T_\Sigma$ whenever each $t_i \in T_\Sigma$. We will often omit the underlying of these symbols. For a ground signature X, we denote by $T_\Sigma(X)$ the Σ-algebra $T_{\Sigma \cup X}$.

A **Σ-algebra** is a set A together with a function $A_\sigma : A^n \to A$ for each $\sigma \in \Sigma_n$. In particular, if $n = 0$, A_σ is just an element of A. A **Σ-homomorphism** between Σ-algebras A and B is a mapping $h : A \to B$ such that $h(A_\sigma(a_1, \ldots, a_n)) = B_\sigma(h(a_1), \ldots, h(a_n))$ for every $\sigma \in \Sigma_n$.

T_Σ and $T_\Sigma(X)$ can be seen as Σ-algebras in the obvious way. A key property of this Σ-algebra is **initiality**:

Theorem 2. *For any Σ-algebra A, there exists a* **unique** *Σ-homomorphism from T_Σ to A.*

Corollary 3. *For any ground signature X disjoint from Σ, Σ-algebra A, and mapping $\theta : X \to A$ (such a mapping is often called an* **assignment***), there exists a unique Σ-homomorphism $\overline{\theta} : T_\Sigma(X) \to A$ that extends θ in the sense that $\overline{\theta}(x) = \theta(x)$.*

In the particular case where A is $T_\Sigma(Y)$ then an assignment θ is often referred as a **substitution** and $\overline{\theta}$ is the mapping that applies the substitution θ to terms.

Given a signature Σ, a **Σ-equation** (or equation if the signature is understood from the context) is a triple (X, l, r) where X is a set of variables (i.e., a ground signature) disjoint from Σ, and l and r are Σ-terms. We often write an equation in the form $(\forall X)\ l = r$. A Σ-algebra A **satisfies** the equation $(\forall X)\ l = r$ if for all assignments $\theta : X \to A$, $\overline{\theta}(l) = \overline{\theta}(r)$. A Σ-algebra A satisfies a set E of equations if it satisfies each of the equations in that set.

Given a set E of Σ-equations, $(T_\Sigma, \equiv_E)$ is the least equivalence that such that

- for all equations $(\forall X)\ l = r$ in E and assignments $\theta : X \to T_\Sigma, \overline{\theta}(l) \equiv_E \overline{\theta}(r)$,
- for each $\sigma \in \Sigma_n$, $\sigma(t_1, \ldots, t_n) \equiv \sigma(t'_1, \ldots, t'_n)$ whenever for all $1 \leqslant i \leqslant n$, $t_i \equiv_E t'_i$.

We can make $T_\Sigma/_{\equiv_E}$ into a Σ-algebra:

- for each $\sigma \in \Sigma_0$, $(T_\Sigma/_{\equiv_E})_\sigma = [\sigma]_{\equiv_E}$,
- for each $\sigma \in \Sigma_n$, $(T_\Sigma/_{\equiv_E})_\sigma([t_1]_{\equiv_E}, \ldots, [t_n]_{\equiv_E}) = [\sigma(t_1, \ldots, t_n)]_{\equiv_E}$

Again this algebra has an important property:

Theorem 4. *For any Σ-algebra A that satisfies the equations in E, there exists a* **unique** *Σ-homomorphism from $T_\Sigma/_{\equiv_E}$ to A.*

2.2 Preordered Algebras and Inequations

A **preordered** (resp. **partially ordered**) **Σ-algebra** is a preorder (resp. partial order) $(A, \sqsubseteq_A)$ called the carrier of the algebra, together with a monotonic mapping $A_\sigma : A^n \to A$ for each $\sigma \in \Sigma_n$. A preordered Σ-algebra is **continuous** (resp. **ω-continuous**) if its carrier is complete (resp. ω-complete) and each of the functions is continuous (resp. ω-continuous).

Given a preordered algebra A we define:

- the partially ordered Σ-algebra $A/_\simeq$ as having carrier $(A/_\simeq, \sqsubseteq_\simeq)$, and for each $\sigma \in \Sigma$, $(A/_\simeq)_\sigma = (A_\sigma)_\simeq$;
- the ω-continuous preordered Σ-algebra A_ω as having carrier $(A_\omega, \ll)$, and for each $\sigma \in \Sigma$, $(A_\omega)_\sigma = (A_\sigma)_\omega$;
- the Σ-algebra $A_\equiv$ as having carrier $A_\equiv$ and for each $\sigma \in \Sigma$, $(A_\equiv)_\sigma = (A_\sigma)_\equiv$.

Given a signature Σ, a **Σ-inequation** (or just inequation if the signature is understood from the context) is a triple (X, l, r) where X is a set of variables disjoint from Σ and l and r are Σ-terms. We often write an inequation in the form $(\forall X)\ l \sqsubseteq r$. A preordered Σ-algebra A **satisfies** the inequation $(\forall X)\ l \sqsubseteq r$ if for all assignments $\theta : X \to A$, $\overline{\theta}(l) \sqsubseteq_A \overline{\theta}(r)$; A satisfies a set $\mathcal{R}$ of inequations if it satisfies each of the inequations in that set.

Theorem 5. *If A is a preordered Σ-algebra that satisfies a set $\mathcal{R}$ of inequations then so do $A/_\simeq$ and A_ω (and thus $A_\omega/_\simeq$).*

The relation between equations and inequations is expressed by the following:

Theorem 6. *If A is a preordered Σ-algebra that satisfies the inequation $(\forall X)\ l \sqsubseteq r$ then $A_\equiv$ satisfies the equation $(\forall X)\ l = r$.*

The implication is proper and truly characterizes the relationship between equations and inequations.

3 Complete Orders and Minimal Coverings

A preorder $(A, \sqsubseteq)$ is **terminating** if there exists no infinite chain

$$a_0 \sqsubset a_1 \sqsubset \cdots \sqsubset a_n \sqsubset \cdots$$

where $a \sqsubset a'$ iff $a \sqsubseteq a'$ and $a \neq a'$.

The first and more obvious order theoretical property that termination establishes is that any terminating preorder is a partial order. Moreover, if $(A, \sqsubseteq)$ is terminating then for any (possibly infinite) sequence

$$a_0 \sqsubseteq a_1 \sqsubseteq \cdots \sqsubseteq a_n \sqsubseteq \cdots$$

there exists an $N \geqslant 0$ such that, for all i, $a_i \sqsubseteq a_N$. If $i < N$ then $a_i \sqsubseteq a_{i+1} \sqsubseteq \cdots \sqsubseteq a_N$ and so $a_i \sqsubseteq a_N$; if $i \geqslant N$, then $a_i = a_N$ and so $a_i \sqsubseteq a_N$. In other words, for any chain C there exists a finite sub-sequence C' of C that dominates it. This can be used to show that any terminating preorder is a a complete partial order. And thus we may establish that any preordered Σ-algebra whose carrier is terminating is in fact a complete partially ordered Σ-algebra.

A **covering** of a preorder $(A, \sqsubseteq)$ is a subset $X \subseteq A$ such that for every $a \in A$ there exists a $x \in X$ such that $a \sqsubseteq x$. A covering X is **minimal** if no proper subset of it is a covering of $(A, \sqsubseteq)$ (or equivalently, of $(X, \sqsubseteq)$). The relation of terminating relations with the existence of minimal coverings is expressed by:

Proposition 7. *If $(A, \sqsubseteq)$ is terminating then $\mathcal{N}_A = \{a \in A \mid a$ is maximal$\}$ is a minimal covering of $(A, \sqsubseteq)$.*

The following examples show that this implication is proper:

Example 1. Consider the preorder

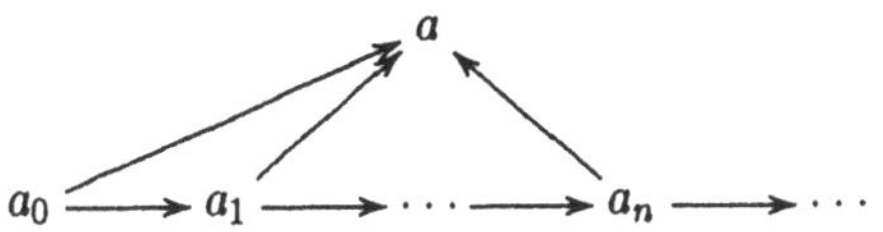

There exists a minimal covering of $\{a_i\}_{i \geqslant 0} \cup \{a\}$, namely the set $\{a\}$. However the preorder is non-terminating.

Example 2. Other examples of non-terminating preorders where there exists a minimal covering are:

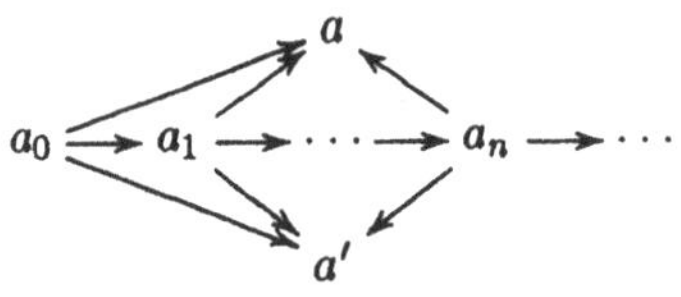

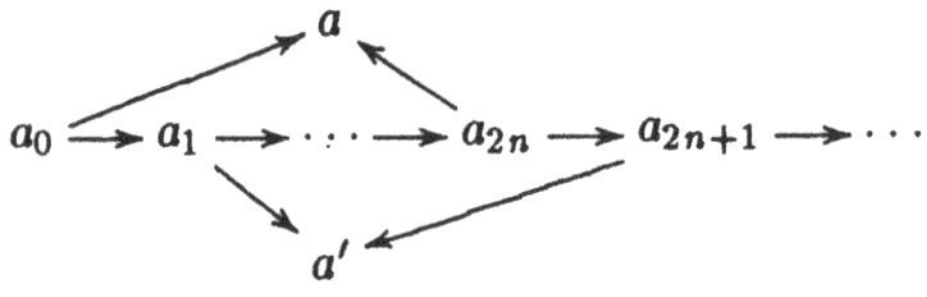

In both cases the set $\{a, a'\}$ is a minimal covering of the depicted preorders and these are non-terminating.

The main difference between these and Example 1 is that in the first one the minimal covering has an extra property: for each $a \in A$ there exists a unique element in $\mathcal{N}$ above a. This motivates the following definition:

Definition 8. Given a preorder $(A, \sqsubseteq)$, a minimal covering X of A is a **uniquely minimal covering** if for any element a of A there exists a unique element x in X such that $a \sqsubseteq x$.

These definitions of coverings, minimal coverings, and uniquely minimal coverings, correspond to the definitions of floorings in [9]. The only difference is that we are defining these concepts with respect to an arbitrary preorder rather than for the particular case of the underlying preorder of a given category. The importance of uniquely minimal coverings is that:

Lemma 9. *Given an preordered Σ-algebra $(A, \sqsubseteq)$ and a uniquely minimal covering $\mathcal{N}$ of A then the unique mapping $\mathrm{nf}_A : A \to \mathcal{N}$ satisfying $a \sqsubseteq \mathrm{nf}_A(a)$ for any element a in A, also satisfies: (1) if $a \sqsubseteq a'$ then $\mathrm{nf}_A(a) = \mathrm{nf}_A(a')$; (2) for any element $a \in A$, $\mathrm{nf}_A(\mathrm{nf}_A(a)) = \mathrm{nf}_A(a)$; (3) for any element $a \in \mathcal{N} \subseteq A$, $\mathrm{nf}_A(a) = a$.*

Proof. Note that nf_A sends each element a of A to the unique element a' of $\mathcal{N}$ such that $a \sqsubseteq a'$. Then, as $a \sqsubseteq a' \sqsubseteq \mathrm{nf}_A(a')$, and $\mathrm{nf}_A(a)$ is the unique element of $\mathcal{N}$ above a, then $\mathrm{nf}_A(a) = \mathrm{nf}_A(a')$, proving (1). Using the above and the fact that $a \sqsubseteq \mathrm{nf}_A(a)$ we have that $\mathrm{nf}_A(\mathrm{nf}_A(a)) = \mathrm{nf}_A(a)$, proving (2). Finally (3) follows because $a \in \mathcal{N}$ and $a \sqsubseteq a$.

Using this Lemma we can show that

Proposition 10. *Given a preordered Σ-algebra A and a uniquely minimal covering $\mathcal{N}$ of its carrier then we can make $\mathcal{N}$ into a Σ-algebra: for each $\sigma \in \Sigma_n$ we define $\mathcal{N}_\sigma$ as*

$$\mathcal{N}_\sigma(\overline{a}_1, \ldots, \overline{a}_n) = \mathrm{nf}_A(A_\sigma(\overline{a}_1, \ldots, \overline{a}_n)$$

for all elements $\overline{a}_i \in \mathcal{N}$. Moreover the mapping nf_A as defined above is a Σ-homomorphism from A (when seen as a Σ-algebra) to $\mathcal{N}$.

A preorder $(A, \sqsubseteq)$ is **confluent** if, whenever $a \sqsubseteq a_1$ and $a \sqsubseteq a_2$ there exists a' such that $a_1 \sqsubseteq a'$ and $a_2 \sqsubseteq a'$.

Remark. If $(A, \sqsubseteq)$ is confluent then, for every $a \in A$, the set $\{a' \mid a \sqsubseteq a'\}$ is directed.

Hence, if $(A, \sqsubseteq)$ is also complete, the least upper bounds of these sets exist. The following Proposition shows how uniquely minimal coverings are related to confluent preorders.

Proposition 11. *Given a preorder $(A, \sqsubseteq)$, a minimal covering $\mathcal{N}$ of A is uniquely minimal iff $\sqsubseteq$ is confluent.*

Proof. We prove the 'if' part by contradiction. Assume that $\mathcal{N}$ is a minimal covering of A and that there exists $a \in A$ for which there exist $a_1, a_2 \in \mathcal{N}$ such that $a \sqsubseteq a_1$ and $a \sqsubseteq a_2$ and $a_1 \neq a_2$. Then there exists $a' \in A$ such that $a_1 \sqsubseteq a'$ and $a_2 \sqsubseteq a'$. Let a'' be an element of $\mathcal{N}$ such that $a' \sqsubseteq a''$; this element exists because $\mathcal{N}$ is a covering of A. Then the set $(\mathcal{N} - \{a_1, a_2\}) \cup \{a''\}$ is a covering of A and is a proper subset of $\mathcal{N}$ because $a_1 \neq a_2$. Thus $\mathcal{N}$ is not a minimal covering contradicting the assumption. Hence $a_1 = a_2$. For the 'only-if' part assume that for some $a, a_1, a_2 \in A$ we have that $a \sqsubseteq a_1$ and $a \sqsubseteq a_2$. Let $a'_1, a'_2 \in \mathcal{N}$ be such that $a_1 \sqsubseteq a'_1$ and $a_2 \sqsubseteq a'_2$; these elements exist because $\mathcal{N}$ is a covering of A. But then $a \sqsubseteq a'_2$ and $a \sqsubseteq a'_1$. As there exists a unique element of $\mathcal{N}$ above a, $a'_1 = a'_2$ and so $a_1 \sqsubseteq a'_1$ and $a_2 \sqsubseteq = a'_1$.

Uniquely minimal coverings need not be unique. Consider the preorder

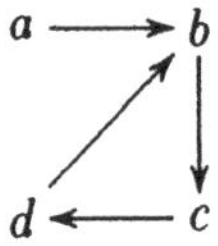

Any of the sets $\{b\}$, $\{c\}$, or $\{d\}$ is a uniquely minimal covering of $\{a, b, c, d\}$. However,

Proposition 12. *Given a preordered Σ-algebra A and two uniquely minimal coverings $\mathcal{N}$ and $\mathcal{N}'$ of its carrier, the associated Σ-algebras $\mathcal{N}$ and $\mathcal{N}'$ are isomorphic.*

But in the case where A is a partial order, uniquely minimal coverings are indeed unique. We can now relate the completeness of a partial order with the existence of a uniquely minimal covering.

Proposition 13. *If A is a complete and confluent partial order then there exists a uniquely minimal covering of A.*

Proof. for any a in A let $\overline{a}$ be defined as $\overline{a} = \bigsqcup\{a' \mid a \sqsubseteq a'\}$. That A is confluent ensures that this set is directed and as A is complete that lub exists. Define $\mathcal{N}$ as $\mathcal{N} = \{\overline{a} \mid a \in A\}$. We show that $\mathcal{N}$ is a uniquely minimal covering of A by showing that (1) it is a covering, (2) it is minimal, and (3) it is uniquely minimal. To prove (1), let a in A. Then $\overline{a}$ in $\mathcal{N}$ and $a \sqsubseteq \overline{a}$. Now, let $\mathcal{N}' \subseteq \mathcal{N}$ be another covering of A. We show that $\mathcal{N} \subseteq \mathcal{N}'$ and thus $\mathcal{N} = \mathcal{N}'$, proving (2). Let $n \in \mathcal{N}$; then, for some $a \in A$, $n = \bigsqcup\{a' \mid a \sqsubseteq a'\}$. Let $n' \in \mathcal{N}'$ be such that $n \sqsubseteq n'$ (n' exists because by assumption $\mathcal{N}'$ is a covering of A and $n \in \mathcal{N} \subseteq A$); then $a \sqsubseteq n \sqsubseteq n'$ and so n' belongs to the set $\{a' \mid a \sqsubseteq a'\}$. As n is the maximum of this set, $n' \sqsubseteq n$. The anti-symmetry of $\sqsubseteq$ establishes that $n = n'$ and thus $n \in \mathcal{N}'$. (3) follows directly from Proposition 11

Lemma 14. *If A is a complete partial order and $\mathcal{N}$ is a uniquely minimal covering of A, then the mapping $\mathrm{nf}_A : A \to \mathcal{N}$ is a continuous mapping from A to the complete partial order $(\mathcal{N}, =)$.*

Proof. Let Δ be a directed subset of A whose lub is d. Note that as $\mathcal{N}$ is a uniquely minimal covering, there exists $n \in \mathcal{N}$ such that $d \sqsubseteq n = \mathrm{nf}_A(d)$ for all $d \in \Delta$. Moreover $d \sqsubseteq n = \mathrm{nf}_A(d)$. Then,

$$\bigsqcup\{\mathrm{nf}_A(\delta) \mid \delta \in \Delta\} = \bigsqcup\{n\} = n = \mathrm{nf}_A(d)$$
$$= \mathrm{nf}_A(\bigsqcup \Delta)$$

The results we have presented so far can be extended to some kind of non-termination, namely for globally finite preorders. A binary relation $\sqsubseteq$ over A is **globally finite** if for any $a \in A$ the set $\{a' \mid a \sqsubseteq a'\}$ is finite.

If $\sqsubseteq$ is a globally finite binary relation, then for any sequence

$$a_0 \sqsubseteq a_1 \sqsubseteq \cdots \sqsubseteq a_n \sqsubseteq \cdots$$

there exists an $N \geqslant 0$ such that $a_i \sqsubseteq a_N$ for all $i \geqslant 0$. This allows us to show that any globally finite preorder is in fact a complete preordered set. And so, we can show that a preordered Σ-algebra whose carrier is globally finite is a complete preordered Σ-algebra. The main difference from the terminating case is that here we cannot ensure that $\sqsubseteq$ is a partial order.

If $(A, \sqsubseteq)$ is a globally finite and confluent preorder we define $(\!|\_|\!)$ as the mapping from A to $A/_{\simeq}$ that sends each $a \in A$ to the class

$$(\!|a|\!) = \bigsqcup\{[a']_{\simeq} \mid a \sqsubseteq a'\}$$

The well-definedness of $(\!|\_|\!)$ follows from the fact that if $\sqsubseteq$ is confluent the set $\{a' \mid a \sqsubseteq a'\}$ is directed and so is $\{[a']_{\simeq} \mid a \sqsubseteq a'\}$; if $\sqsubseteq$ is globally finite, $A/_{\simeq}$ is complete and so that lub exists.

Proposition 15. *Let A be a preordered Σ-algebra and C be a minimal covering of A. Then the set*

$$C/_{\simeq} = \{[c]_{\simeq} \in A/_{\simeq} \mid c \in C\}$$

is a minimal covering of $A/_{\simeq}$. Moreover, if C is uniquely minimal $C/_{\simeq}$ is **the** *(unique) uniquely minimal covering of $A/_{\simeq}$.*

The proof of this Proposition, shows that we could also prove that if A is a preorder such that there exists a (uniquely) minimal covering of $A/_{\simeq}$, then there exists a (uniquely) minimal covering of A. This proof uses the Axiom of Choice. It can also be shown that in fact it is equivalent to this Axiom. Another use of the Axiom of Choice, or more precisely of Zorn's Lemma, is in the proof of the following generalization of Proposition 7:

Proposition 16. *If $(A, \sqsubseteq)$ is a complete preorder then there exists a minimal covering of it.*

From which we can immediately establish that:

Corollary 17. *If $(A, \sqsubseteq)$ is a globally finite preorder then there exists a minimal covering of it.*

We can strengthen this result for the case of confluent preorders:

Proposition 18. *If $(A, \sqsubseteq)$ is a globally finite and confluent preorder then there exists a uniquely minimal covering of it, and a unique uniquely minimal covering of the partial order $A/_{\simeq}$.*

These results can again be lifted to algebras.

We have seen in the previous sections how termination ensures the existence of a minimal covering (which is uniquely minimal in the case where $\sqsubseteq$ is confluent). We have also seen that in some cases of non-termination (global finiteness) these properties still hold. But in general they don't: just consider the natural numbers ordered in the usual way; then the chain

$$\langle 0, 1, 2, \ldots, n, \ldots \rangle$$

doesn't have any upper bound; moreover there is no minimal covering of ω.

4 Applications to Term Rewrite Systems

Given a signature Σ, a **Σ-rewrite rule** (or simply rewrite rule) is a triple (X, l, r) where X is a set of variables disjoint from Σ and l and r are $(\Sigma \cup X)$-terms. It is often required that the variables that occur in r also occur in l and that l is not a single variable. In the present work we **do not** impose either of these restrictions. We often write a rewrite rule in the form $(\forall X)\ l \rightarrow r$. A **term rewrite system** (TRS) is just a set rewrite rules.

Given a TRS $\mathcal{R}$ and a ground signature X, the **one-step rewrite** relation is denoted by $\rightarrow_{\mathcal{R}}$ and defined as the least relation over $T_\Sigma(X)$ such that

- for all rewrite rules $(\forall A)\ l \rightarrow r$ in $\mathcal{R}$ and assignments $\theta : A \rightarrow T_\Sigma(X)$, $\overline{\theta}(l) \rightarrow_{\mathcal{R}} \overline{\theta}(r)$,
- for each operation symbol $\sigma \in \Sigma_n$, and terms $t_1, \ldots, t_n, t'_k$, such that $t_k \rightarrow_{\mathcal{R}} t'_k$, then $\sigma(t_1, \ldots, t_{k-1}, t_k, t_{k+1}, \ldots, t_n) \rightarrow_{\mathcal{R}} \sigma(t_1, \ldots, t_{k-1}, t'_k, t_{k+1}, \ldots, t_n)$.

We define the rewrite relation $\rightarrow^*_{\mathcal{R}}$ as the reflexive and transitive closure of $\rightarrow_{\mathcal{R}}$, and say that a rewrite system $\mathcal{R}$ is **confluent** if for all X, $\rightarrow_{\mathcal{R}}$ is confluent.

The similarities between the definition of a rewrite rule and an inequation are very important. In fact, when we see each rule $(\forall X)\ l \rightarrow r$ of a TRS $\mathcal{R}$ as the Σ-inequation $(\forall X)\ l \sqsubseteq r$, the definition of the rewrite relation establishes that $(T_\Sigma(X), \rightarrow^*_{\mathcal{R}})$ is a preorder. Moreover, this enables us to define the preordered Σ-algebra $OT_{\Sigma,\mathcal{R}}(X)$ as having carrier $(T_\Sigma(X), \rightarrow^*_{\mathcal{R}})$ and, for each operation symbol σ, the corresponding function $(OT_{\Sigma,\mathcal{R}}(X))_\sigma$ defined as

$$(OT_{\Sigma,\mathcal{R}}(X))_\sigma(t_1, \ldots, t_n) = (T_\Sigma(X))_\sigma(t_1, \ldots, t_n) = \sigma(t_1, \ldots, t_n)$$

That these functions are monotonic follows because $\sigma(t_1, \ldots, t_n) \rightarrow^*_{\mathcal{R}} \sigma(t'_1, \ldots, t'_n)$, whenever $t_i \rightarrow^*_{\mathcal{R}} t'_i$ for all i. The above definition of the rewrite relation shows that $OT_{\Sigma,\mathcal{R}}(X)$ satisfies the inequations in $\mathcal{R}$, allowing us to establish the following completeness result:

Theorem 19. *If, for some set of inequations $\mathcal{R}$, an inequation $(\forall X)t_1 \sqsubseteq t_2$ is satisfied by all preordered Σ-algebras that satisfy $\mathcal{R}$, then $t_1 \rightarrow^*_{\mathcal{R}} t_2$.*

Moreover,

Proposition 20. *Let A be a preordered Σ-algebra satisfying $\mathcal{R}$ and $\theta : X \rightarrow A$; then the unique Σ-homomorphism $\overline{\theta} : T_{\Sigma}(X) \rightarrow A$ that extends θ is a monotonic mapping from $OT_{\Sigma,\mathcal{R}}(X)$ to A.*

This allows us to establish:

Theorem 21. *Given a ground signature X, a preordered Σ-algebra A satisfying $\mathcal{R}$, and an assignment $\theta : X \rightarrow A$, there exists a unique ordered Σ-homomorphism $\overline{\theta} : OT_{\Sigma,\mathcal{R}}(X) \rightarrow A$ that extends θ.*

And thus, for any preordered Σ-algebra A satisfying $\mathcal{R}$, there exists a unique monotonic Σ-homomorphism from $OT_{\Sigma,\mathcal{R}}$ to A. In other words, $OT_{\Sigma,\mathcal{R}}$ is **initial** in the class of preordered Σ-algebras that satisfy the inequations of $\mathcal{R}$.

These results point out the benefit of treating rules as inequations. They do not depend on confluence, termination, or any other property of $\mathcal{R}$, thus representing the answer to the problem of providing an algebraic semantics for rewrite rules with a much wider field of application than the traditional (equational) solution (e.g., Huet and Oppen [15], Goguen [8]). A typical example appears in [19]: the specification of a non-deterministic operation CHOICE described by the two rules

$$(\forall x, y)\ \mathrm{CHOICE}(x, y) \rightarrow x$$
$$(\forall x, y)\ \mathrm{CHOICE}(x, y) \rightarrow y$$

It does not make sense to interpret these rules as equations: only the trivial model satisfies them! But taking this new approach, models of this rewrite system are preordered algebras where all the values of the expressions E and E' are possible values of the expression $\mathrm{CHOICE}(E, E')$. The initiality of $OT_{\Sigma,\mathcal{R}}$ states that for any such model there exists a **unique** way of interpreting a term, and that this interpretation is in fact monotonic. Furthermore, Theorem 4 can be obtained as a corollary of this last one. Notice that the preorder $(T_{\Sigma}(X), \rightarrow^*_{\mathcal{R}})$ is nothing more then the underlying preorder of the category $\mathcal{T}_{\mathcal{R}}(X)$ defined by Meseguer [19]. Hence, the differences with Meseguer's approach are that we do not distinguish different rewritings between two terms (for a careful comparison of these two formalisms see Section 3.6 of [19]). The simplicity of our definitions is reflected in the proof of the Completeness Theorem above and of the following soundness result:

Theorem 22. *Let $\mathcal{R}$ be a TRS, X a ground signature and $t_1, t_2 \in T_\Sigma(X)$. Then, for any preordered Σ-algebra A that satisfies the inequations in $\mathcal{R}$, if $t_1 \rightarrow^*_\mathcal{R} t_2$ then A satisfies the inequation $(\forall X)\ t_1 \sqsubseteq t_2$.*

Proof. Let $\theta : X \rightarrow A$ be any assignment. As $\overline{\theta}$ is monotonic then $\overline{\theta}(t_1) \sqsubseteq_A \overline{\theta}(t_2)$.

4.1 Terminating Rewrite Systems

A TRS is **terminating** if the one step rewrite relation is a terminating relation. This, in conjunction with the results of the previous section, allows us to conclude that, given a terminating TRS $\mathcal{R}$ and an arbitrary ground signature X disjoint from Σ, the preorder $(T_\Sigma(X), \rightarrow^*_\mathcal{R})$ is complete, and $OT_{\Sigma,\mathcal{R}}(X)$ is a continuous Σ-algebra satisfying the inequations in $\mathcal{R}$. Furthermore, if A is a continuous preordered Σ-algebra satisfying the inequations of $\mathcal{R}$, and $\theta : X \rightarrow A$ is an assignment, then the unique monotonic Σ-homomorphism that extends θ is continuous. This enables us to prove the following freeness result:

Theorem 23. *Let $\mathcal{R}$ be a terminating TRS. Then, given a ground signature X, a continuous Σ-algebra A satisfying $\mathcal{R}$, and an assignment $\theta : X \rightarrow A$, there exists a unique continuous Σ-homomorphism $\overline{\theta} : OT_{\Sigma,\mathcal{R}}(X) \rightarrow A$ that extends θ.*

Thus, if $\mathcal{R}$ is a terminating TRS, $OT_{\Sigma,\mathcal{R}}$ is initial in the class of continuous Σ-algebras that satisfy the inequations of $\mathcal{R}$. We can now use the results of the previous section to show:

Proposition 24. *If $\mathcal{R}$ is confluent and $(T_\Sigma(X), \rightarrow^*_\mathcal{R})$ is a continuous Σ-algebra, then for each term t, the normal form $[\![t]\!]_\mathcal{R}$, if it exists, is defined as $[\![t]\!]_\mathcal{R} = \bigsqcup\{t' \mid t \rightarrow^*_\mathcal{R} t'\}$*

Proposition 25. *If $\mathcal{R}$ is a terminating and confluent TRS there exists a (unique) uniquely minimal covering of the set of terms.*

This minimal covering is exactly the set of normal forms – $\mathcal{N}_{\Sigma,\mathcal{R}}(X)$. We can now use Proposition 11 to justify the following:

Definition 26. If $\mathcal{R}$ is confluent and $(T_\Sigma(X), \rightarrow^*_\mathcal{R})$ is a continuous Σ-algebra, we define the Σ-algebra $\mathcal{N}_{\Sigma,\mathcal{R}}(X)$ as having as carrier the set $\mathcal{N}_{\Sigma,\mathcal{R}}(X)$ and for each $\sigma \in \Sigma_n$, the corresponding operation in $\mathcal{N}_{\Sigma,\mathcal{R}}(X)$ is defined as

$$(\mathcal{N}_{\Sigma,\mathcal{R}}(X))_\sigma(\overline{t}_1, \ldots, \overline{t}_n) = [\![\sigma(\overline{t}_1, \ldots, \overline{t}_n)]\!]_\mathcal{R}$$

for all $\overline{t}_i \in \mathcal{N}_{\Sigma,\mathcal{R}}(X)$

Using Proposition 11 again, we can show that

Lemma 27. *The mapping $[\![\_]\!]_\mathcal{R} : T_\Sigma(X) \rightarrow \mathcal{N}_{\Sigma,\mathcal{R}}(X)$ as defined above is a Σ-homomorphism.*

This result, which was proved using only the order theoretical properties of confluent and terminating systems, allows us to show a basic property of normal forms – that, for any $\sigma \in \Sigma_n$ and terms $t_i \in T_\Sigma(X)$,

$$\begin{aligned}\llbracket\sigma(t_1,\ldots,t_n)\rrbracket_{\mathcal{R}} &= (\mathcal{N}_{\Sigma,\mathcal{R}}(X))_\sigma(\llbracket t_1\rrbracket_{\mathcal{R}},\ldots,\llbracket t_n\rrbracket_{\mathcal{R}})\\ &= \llbracket\sigma(\llbracket t_1\rrbracket_{\mathcal{R}},\ldots,\llbracket t_n\rrbracket_{\mathcal{R}})\rrbracket_{\mathcal{R}}\end{aligned}$$

Another property that follows from these order theoretical results is well known [8]:

Theorem 28. *If $\mathcal{R}$ is a terminating and confluent TRS, the algebra $\mathcal{N}_{\Sigma,\mathcal{R}}(X)$ is initial in the class of Σ-algebras that satisfy the equations of $\mathcal{R}$.*

The previous section pointed out how rewriting is naturally linked with preordered algebras. We showed here which order theoretical properties are associated with terminating systems. These include the existence of a minimal covering of the preorder $(T_\Sigma(X), \to_{\mathcal{R}}^*)$ and the fact that this preorder is a complete partial order.

The rewrite relation partitions the set of terms into *connected components.* Each of these components corresponds to an equivalence class when we forget the orientation of the rules, that is, when we consider the reflexive-transitive-symmetric closure of $\to_{\mathcal{R}}$, i.e., when we see rules as equations. Termination ensures that we can find a minimal covering of the set of terms. This minimal covering corresponds exactly to the set of values mentioned in the Introduction; the fact that it is a covering means that every term has at least one value, i.e., that every term is computable. This minimal covering is composed of the maximal elements of each connected component: for a given term a maximal element of the component where it lies is a value of it. Additionally, if the system is confluent then this covering is uniquely minimal, meaning that maximal elements in each component are unique. This implies that each term has a unique value.

When we see each rewrite step as a step in the computation of a term, and each rewriting sequence as a computation of its first element, the completeness of $OT_{\Sigma,\mathcal{R}}(X)$ means that we will always find the result of a computation. In this perspective, the confluence of a system means that any computation of a particular term t, represented by the set $\Delta^*(t) = \{t' \mid t \to_{\mathcal{R}}^* t'\}$ will always give the same result – the least upper bound of $\Delta^*(t)$.

The minimal covering referred above is what Bergstra and Tucker [2] call a **traversal** of the quotient induced by the rules when seen as equations. Our starting point is the ordered set of terms, rather than that quotient. As a consequence, our minimal covering is unique whereas their traversals aren't. Still according to these authors, the choice of a particular traversal fixes an operational view of the abstract data type defined by the rules (when seen as equations). But this is exactly the point of the present paper – the meaning of rewrite rules is primarily linked with computation. This view is consistent with the ideas put forward by Meseguer in [19, 18] where it is argued that we should see rewrite rules as expressing change in a computational system rather than expressing static properties as equations do. Another related formalism is the concept of

canonical term algebra [11]. As proved by Goguen [8], the algebra of normal forms is a canonical term algebra. However this property does not follow from the fact that it is a uniquely minimal covering.

4.2 Globally Finite Systems

A TRS $\mathcal{R}$ is **locally finite** if, for any term t, the set $\{t' \mid t \rightarrow_{\mathcal{R}} t'\}$ is finite, and is **globally finite** if $\rightarrow^*_{\mathcal{R}}$ is globally finite. The systems that we are interested in are locally finite: we only consider finite stes of rules and each rule is composed only by finite terms. In these conditions it is straightforward to show that global finitness is a proper generalization of termination. The practical motivation for the study of globally finite rewrite systems was pointed out by Goguen [8] and comes for instance from the difficulty of dealing with a commutative rule: in fact if we add a commutative rule to a terminating systems we end up with a globally finite but not terminating TRS. We show in this section that, with the help of the kernel operation of preorders we can extend the results presented above to this particular kind of non-termination. As we will see, this process will not be enough to extend these results to arbitrary systems.

From an order theoretical point of view, the main difference between globally finite and terminating systems is that in the former, the rewrite relation is no longer a partial order. We can however use the results about the kernel of a preorder to establish that:

Theorem 29. *Let $\mathcal{R}$ be a globally finite TRS. Then, given a ground signature X, a continuous partially ordered Σ-algebra A satisfying $\mathcal{R}$, and an assignment $\theta : X \rightarrow A$, there exists a unique continuous Σ-homomorphism $\theta^{\#}$: $(OT_{\Sigma,\mathcal{R}}(X))/_{\simeq} \rightarrow A$ that extends θ, i.e., such that $\theta(x) = \theta^{\#}([x]_{\simeq})$.*

From this Theorem we can immediately establish that $OT_{\Sigma,\mathcal{R}}/_{\simeq}$ is initial in the class of continuous Σ-algebras that satisfy the inequations of $\mathcal{R}$.

We can again use Proposition 13 to justify the following:

Definition 30. If $\mathcal{R}$ is a globally finite and confluent TRS, for a given ground signature X disjoint from Σ, we define the Σ-algebra $\mathcal{N}^{\simeq}_{\Sigma,\mathcal{R}}(X)$ as having carrier the set

$$\mathcal{N}^{\simeq}_{\Sigma,\mathcal{R}}(X) = \{(\!|t|\!)_{\mathcal{R}} \mid t \in T_{\Sigma}(X)\}$$

and, for each $\sigma \in \Sigma_n$,

$$(\mathcal{N}^{\simeq}_{\Sigma,\mathcal{R}}(X))_{\sigma}((\!|t_1|\!)_{\mathcal{R}}, \ldots, (\!|t_n|\!)_{\mathcal{R}}) = (\!|\sigma(t_1, \ldots, t_n)|\!)_{\mathcal{R}}$$

The above observations allow us to prove that

Theorem 31. *If $\mathcal{R}$ is a globally finite and confluent TRS, the algebra $\mathcal{N}^{\simeq}_{\Sigma,\mathcal{R}}(X)$ is isomorphic to $T_{\Sigma,\mathcal{R}}(X)$. The isomorphism $h : \mathcal{N}^{\simeq}_{\Sigma,\mathcal{R}}(X) \rightarrow (T_{\Sigma}(X))/_{\equiv_{\mathcal{R}}}$ sends each $(\!|t|\!)_{\mathcal{R}}$ to $[t]_{\equiv}$.*

From this it follows immediately that if $\mathcal{R}$ is a globally finite and confluent TRS, then the algebra $\mathcal{N}^{\widetilde{=}}_{\Sigma,\mathcal{R}}$ (i.e., $\mathcal{N}^{\widetilde{=}}_{\Sigma,\mathcal{R}}(\emptyset)$) is initial in the class of Σ-algebras that satisfy the equations of $\mathcal{R}$. This extends Theorem 28 for the case of globally finite systems. We could use the results of the previous section to show that for globally finite systems, there exists also a uniquely minimal covering of $OT_{\Sigma,\mathcal{R}}(X)$. This implies that this covering is also isomorphic to $(T_\Sigma(X))/_{\equiv_\mathcal{R}}$. But in this case we cannot guarantee that this minimal covering is a canonical term algebra. We can prove (with a proof along the same lines of the one presented in [11]) that in the case of global finiteness, there exists one such minimal covering.

The ease which this extension was done is due to the fact that we are using very abstract properties of rewriting. As we will see, with another smooth step we can extend to arbitrary confluent systems.

4.3 Non-terminating Rewrite Systems

Other approaches to non-terminating TRS's extend the set of terms with infinite terms, in order that this extended set satisfies these properties. In this paper we use a different method: instead of extending the set of terms we use a different set, the set $\mathcal{R}_\omega(X)$ of term rewriting sequences, i.e., $\mathcal{R}_\omega(X) = (T_\Sigma(X), \rightarrow^*_\mathcal{R})_\omega$, to which there exists an injection[4] from the set of terms $(T_\Sigma(X))$: the mapping that sends each term t to the rewriting sequence $\langle t, t, \ldots\rangle$. As we will see, this set fulfills all the desired properties, i.e., the properties of the set of terms in the terminating case.

The major constraint that we will assume is the finiteness of the signatures involved (Σ and X). This has as major consequence the denumerability of the set of terms $T_\Sigma(X)$.

The first observation that we can make about $\mathcal{R}_\omega(X)$ is that it is a ω-complete preordered algebra satisfying the inequations of $\mathcal{R}$. Furthermore, for every ω-continuous Σ-algebra A in these conditions and mapping $\theta : X \rightarrow A$, there exists a unique ω-continuous Σ-homomorphism $\theta^\#_\omega : \mathcal{R}_\omega(X)/_{\simeq} \rightarrow A$ that extends θ, i.e., that, for each $x \in X$, $\theta(x) = \theta^\#_\omega([\langle x, x, \ldots\rangle]_\simeq)$. This implies that $\mathcal{R}_\omega/_\simeq$ is initial in the class of ω-continuous Σ-algebras that satisfy the inequations of $\mathcal{R}$. Moreover, if both Σ and X are finite then the preorder $(\mathcal{R}_\omega(X), \ll)$ is complete and the operations of $\mathcal{R}_\omega(X)$ are continuous, allowing us to prove:

Theorem 32. *If both Σ and X are finite then for every continuous partially ordered Σ-algebra A satisfying the inequations in $\mathcal{R}$ and mapping $\theta : X \rightarrow A$, there exists a unique continuous Σ-homomorphism $\theta^\#_\omega : \mathcal{R}_\omega(X)/_\simeq \rightarrow A$ that extends θ, i.e., satisfying $\theta(x) = \theta^*_\omega([\langle x, x, \ldots\rangle]_\simeq)$ for all x in X.*

Again this implies that if Σ is finite, then $\mathcal{R}_\omega/_\simeq$ is initial in the class of continuous Σ-algebras that satisfy the inequations of $\mathcal{R}$. Another implication of the completeness of $\mathcal{R}_\omega$ is that we can use Proposition 16 to establish:

[4] Recall that the existence of an injection $i : A \rightarrow B$ is an abstraction of the fact that A is contained in B.

Proposition 33. *The set*

$$\mathcal{N}^{\omega}_{\Sigma,\mathcal{R}}(X) = \{[t]_{\simeq} \mid t \in \mathcal{R}_{\omega}(X) \wedge t \text{ is maximal wrt } \ll\}$$

is a minimal covering of $(\mathcal{R}_{\omega}(X))/_{\simeq}$.

Each rewriting sequence can be seen as a computation of its first element. The ordering $\ll$ between these sequences is then a measure of relative accuracy between these computations. For $[s]_{\simeq}$ in $\mathcal{N}^{\omega}_{\Sigma,\mathcal{R}}(X)$ we call each $t \in [s]_{\simeq}$ a **normalizing rewrite sequence**. Each normalizing sequence $\langle t_0, t_1, \ldots\rangle$ being a maximal element wrt $\ll$, represents a very particular computation: none is more accurate than it. It is therefore a good substitute for the concept of normal form. Note that, unlike the other approaches to this problem, we impose no requirements to the rewrite system in order that these sequences exist.

If $\mathcal{R}$ is a confluent TRS then, for any term rewriting sequence t, the set $\Delta^{*}_{\omega}(t) = \{[t']_{\simeq} \mid t \ll t'\}$ is directed. A direct consequence of this is that the preorder $\mathcal{R}_{\omega}(X)$ is confluent. Hence, the limit $\bigsqcup \Delta^{*}_{\omega}(t)$ exists. This allows us to define, for any confluent TRS $\mathcal{R}$, the mapping $\langle\!|\_|\!\rangle_{\mathcal{R}} : \mathcal{R}_{\omega}(X)/_{\simeq} \rightarrow \mathcal{R}_{\omega}(X)/_{\simeq}$ that sends each class $[t]_{\simeq}$ to $\bigsqcup \Delta^{*}_{\omega}(t)$.

Given a confluent TRS $\mathcal{R}$ we define the S-sorted set $\mathcal{N}^{\omega}_{\Sigma,\mathcal{R}}(X)$ as

$$\mathcal{N}^{\omega}_{\Sigma,\mathcal{R}}(X) \;=\; \{\langle\!| t |\!\rangle_{\mathcal{R}} \mid t \in \mathcal{R}_{\omega}(X)\}$$

This set has an important property: it is a uniquely minimal covering of $(\mathcal{R}_{\omega}(X))/_{\simeq}$. This allows us to use the results of the previous section and define the algebra $\mathcal{N}^{\omega}_{\Sigma,\mathcal{R}}(X)$ has having $\mathcal{N}^{\omega}_{\Sigma,\mathcal{R}}(X)$ as its carrier, and for each $\sigma \in \Sigma_n$,

$$(\mathcal{N}^{\omega}_{\Sigma,\mathcal{R}}(X))_{\sigma}(\langle\!| t^1 |\!\rangle_{\mathcal{R}}, \ldots, \langle\!| t^n |\!\rangle_{\mathcal{R}}) = \langle\!| (\mathcal{R}_{\omega})_{\sigma}(t^1, \ldots, t^n) |\!\rangle_{\mathcal{R}}$$

Moreover $\langle\!|\_|\!\rangle_{\mathcal{R}}$ is a Σ-homomorphism from $\mathcal{R}_{\omega}(X)$ (when seen as a Σ-algebra) to $\mathcal{N}^{\omega}_{\Sigma,\mathcal{R}}(X)$. If we compose this Σ-homomorphism to the one that sends each term t to the class $[t]_{\simeq}$ we get a Σ-homomorphism from $T_{\Sigma}(X)$ to $\mathcal{N}^{\omega}_{\Sigma,\mathcal{R}}(X)$ that sends each term t to $\langle\!| \langle t, t \ldots\rangle |\!\rangle_{\mathcal{R}}$.

Lemma 34. *Let $\mathcal{R}$ be a confluent TRS, t a term, and t^1 and t^2 term rewriting sequences such that $t^1_0 \rightarrow^{*}_{\mathcal{R}} t \;{}_{\mathcal{R}}\!\!{}^{*}\!\!\leftarrow t^2_0$. then, if $[a^1]_{\simeq}$ and $[a^2]_{\simeq}$ are arbitrary elements of $\Delta^{*}_{\omega}(t^1)$ and $\Delta^{*}_{\omega}(t^2)$ respectively, there exists a class $[b]_{\simeq} \in \Delta^{*}_{\omega}(t^1) \cup \Delta^{*}_{\omega}(t^2)$ such that both $a^1 \ll b$ and $a^2 \ll b$.*

This shows that in these conditions $\langle\!| t^1 |\!\rangle_{\mathcal{R}} = \langle\!| t^2 |\!\rangle_{\mathcal{R}}$. Hence

Theorem 35. *If $\mathcal{R}$ is a confluent TRS, the algebra $\mathcal{N}^{\omega}_{\Sigma,\mathcal{R}}(X)$ is isomorphic to $(T_{\Sigma}(X))/_{\equiv_{\mathcal{R}}}$.*

From which it follows immediately that $\mathcal{N}^{\omega}_{\Sigma,\mathcal{R}}$ (i.e., $\mathcal{N}^{\omega}_{\Sigma,\mathcal{R}}(\emptyset)$) is initial in the class of Σ-algebras that satisfy the equations of $\mathcal{R}$.

Each normalizing sequence $\langle t_0, t_1, \ldots\rangle \in \langle\!| t, t, \ldots |\!\rangle_{\mathcal{R}}$, being the least upper bound of the set of computations of t represents a very particular computation: it is at least as accurate as any other! Note that, unlike the other approaches to this problem, confluence is the only requirement that we impose to the rewrite system to guarantee the uniqueness of this set of sequences.

We end our exposition by presenting an example that has an intriguing solution in the other approaches to this problem. Let Σ be defined as $\Sigma_0 = \{0, 1\}$, $\Sigma_1 = \{q\}$, and $\Sigma_n = \emptyset$ for $n > 2$. Consider the TRS's:

$$\mathcal{R}_1 = \{(\forall\emptyset)1 \to q(1), (\forall\emptyset)0 \to q(0)\}$$

$$\mathcal{R}_2 = \{(\forall\emptyset)q(1) \to 1, (\forall\emptyset)q(0) \to 0\}$$

In the equational interpretation of rewriting, these two systems are indistinguishable – the orientation of the rules is irrelevant when we see them as equations. This means that all models of one system are models of the other. The initial model has a two point set as carrier and interprets q as the identity mapping.

In the other approaches to the semantics of non-terminating rewriting these systems have very different interpretations: only the trivial model satisfies $\mathcal{R}_1$ (cf. [7]) whereas the initial model that satisfies $\mathcal{R}_2$ has a two point set as carrier and interprets q as the identity mapping.

Our approach allows us to view these systems in two different perspectives:

- when we see the rules as inequations, the models of $\mathcal{R}_1$ are models of $\mathcal{R}_2$ with the reverse ordering.
- applying the construction described in this section we have that $\mathcal{N}^{\omega}_{\Sigma,\mathcal{R}_1}(X)$ and $\mathcal{N}^{\omega}_{\Sigma,\mathcal{R}_2}(X)$ are isomorphic: $\mathcal{N}^{\omega}_{\Sigma,\mathcal{R}_2}$ has carrier the set $\{0, 1\}$ and $\mathcal{N}^{\omega}_{\Sigma,\mathcal{R}_1}$ has carrier the set $\{[\langle 0, q(0), \ldots, q^n(0), \ldots\rangle]_{\simeq}, [\langle 1, q(1), \ldots, q^n(1), \ldots\rangle]_{\simeq}\}$. In both cases q is interpreted as the identity.

5 Conclusions

We have presented an algebraic semantics for rewrite systems that does not depend on any special assumptions about these systems. Our approach views rewrite rules not as equations, but as inequations. This allows us to use (non-confluent) rewrite systems to specify non-determinism. For confluent systems, we have shown how rewriting, even in the non-terminating case, can be seen as an alternative to equational reasoning.

Other approaches to this problem have extended to the non-terminating case by using infinite terms as normal forms of non-terminating computations. The difficulties of these approaches are shown by the counter examples of Kennaway *et al.* [16]. These difficulties have made it hard to apply these formalisms to applications like reactive systems. We feel that the solution presented in this paper paves the way for such applications, along the lines of Hennessy [13] and Meseguer [19, 18]. It was for this reason that we avoided the usual restrictions to the form of the rewrite rules.

One particular difference between our approach and the others referred is the rôle played by the "converging" sequences. Consider the signature Σ with $\Sigma_0 = \{a, b, c\}$, $\Sigma_1 = \{f\}$, and $\Sigma_n = \emptyset$ for all $n > 1$, and the TRS

$$\mathcal{R} = \{(\forall\emptyset)\ a \to b, (\forall\emptyset)\ b \to a, (\forall\emptyset)\ c \to f(c)\}$$

Then both of the sequences $\langle a, b, a, b, \ldots\rangle$ and $\langle c, f(c), f(f(c)), \ldots, f^n(c), \ldots\rangle$ are normalizing sequences, and so are equally important for us. But in the previous approaches, only the second sequence has an important property – it converges. This ensures that c can be assigned a *normal form*, whereas a does not have one. As a result most of the important results of these approaches cannot be applied to systems like the one above. One might think that this restriction is reasonable and desirable; but it rules out some interesting examples of non-terminating processes: just think of a scheduler in an operating system – its behaviour does not converge to any particular state (apart from deadlock in some cases); nevertheless the scheduler is a "respectable" and important part of the operating system, it would be good to study. Finally notice that establishing a convergence criteria is not incompatible with our approach; the difference (or more accurately, the novelty) is that we do not need such a restriction.

One extension of the results presented here is rewriting modulo a set of equations. One approach is to consider the rewrite relation modulo the equations, i.e., to use the quotient induced by those equations as the set of the preorder. This solution follows the lines of Goguen [10] and Meseguer [19]. Another solution is to add for each equation $(\forall X)\ t_1 = t_2$, the rules $(\forall X)\ t_1 \rightarrow t_2$ and $(\forall X)\ t_2 \rightarrow t_1$. Note that if the system is confluent modulo that set of equations then this new rewrite rewrite system is confluent, so these two approaches give the same results. The ease with which we can treat this extension is a direct consequence of the abstract approach that we have taken.

References

1. José Barros. Semantics of non-terminating systems through term rewriting. Technical Report PRG-TR-21-95, Programming Research Group, Oxford University, June 1995. D.Phil. Thesis. Available through FTP at `ftp.comlab.ox.ac.uk/pub/Documents/techreports/TR-21-95.ps.gz`.
2. Jan Bergstra and John Tucker. Characterization of computable data types by means of a finite equational specification method. In *Automata, Languages and Programming, Seventh Colloquium*, pages 76–90. Springer-Verlag, July 1980. Lecture Notes in Computer Science, Volume 85; also, Preprint IW 124, Mathematisch Centrum, Department of Computer Science, Amsterdam, November, 1979.
3. Steven Bloom. Varieties of ordered algebras. *Journal of Computer and System Sciences*, 13:200–212, 1976.
4. G. Boudol. Computational semantics of term rewriting systems. In *Algebraic Methods in Semantics*, pages 167–236. Cambridge University Press, 1985.
5. Y. Chen and M. O'Donnell. Infinite terms and infinite rewritings. In *2nd International Workshop on Conditional and Typed Rewriting Systems*, pages 45–52, 1990.
6. Bruno Courcelle. Infinite trees in normal form and recursive equations having a unique solution. *Mathematical Systems Theory*, 13:131–180, 1979.
7. Nachum Dershowitz, Stephane Kaplan, and David Plaisted. Rewrite,rewrite, rewrite, ... *Theoretical Computer Science*, 83(1):71–96, 1991. Preliminary versions appear in *Proceedings of the 16th ACM Symposium on Principles of Programming Languages*, 1989 and in *Proceedings of the 16th EATCS International Colloquium*

on Automata, Languages and Programming, Volume 372 of the Lecture Notes in Computer Science, 1989.

8. Joseph Goguen. How to prove algebraic inductive hypotheses without induction: with applications to the correctness of data type representations. In *Proceedings, Fifth Conference on Automated Deduction,* pages 356–373. Springer-Verlag, 1980. Lecture Notes in Computer Science, Volume 87.
9. Joseph Goguen. What is unification? – A categorical view of substitution, equation and solution. In *Resolution of Equations in Algebraic Systems,* volume 1. Academic Press, 1989. Preliminary version in *Proceedings, Colloquium on the Resolution of Equations in Algebraic Structures,* held in Lakeway, Texas, USA, May 1987.
10. Joseph Goguen. *Theorem Proving and Algebra.* MIT Press, To appear 1994.
11. Joseph Goguen, James Thatcher, and Eric Wagner. An initial algebra approach to the specification, correctness and implementation of abstract data types. Technical Report RC 6487, IBM Watson Research Center, October 1976. Appears in *Current Trends in Programming Methodology, IV,* Raymond Yeh, Ed., Prentice-Hall, 1978, pages 80–149.
12. Joseph Goguen, James Thatcher, Eric Wagner, and Jesse Wright. Initial algebra semantics and continuous algebras. *Journal of the Association for Computing Machinery,* 24(1):68–95, January 1977.
13. Matthew Hennessy. *Algebraic Theory of Processes.* MIT Press, 1988.
14. C. A. R. Hoare. *Communicating Sequential Processes.* Prentice-Hall, 1985.
15. Gerard Huet and Derek Oppen. Equations and rewrite rules: A survey. In Ronald Book, editor, *Formal Language Theory: Perspectives and Open Problems,* pages 349–405. Academic Press, 1980. Also Technical Report No. STAN-CS-80-785, Computer Science Department, Stanford University.
16. J. Kennaway, J. W. Klop, M. Sleep, and F. de Vries. Transfinite reductions in orthogonal term rewriting systems. *Lecture Notes in Computer Science,* 488:1–12, 1991. Extended abstract.
17. Michael Levy and T. S. E. Maibaum. Continuous data types. *SIAM Journal on Computing,* 11(2):201–216, 1982.
18. N. Martí-Oliet and José Meseguer. Rewriting logic as a logical and semantical framework. Technical report, SRI International, 1994.
19. José Meseguer. Conditional rewriting logic as a unified model of concurrency. *Theoretical Computer Science,* 96:73–155, 1992. Preliminary version appears as SRI International technical report n. SRI-CSL-90-02R.
20. T. Naoi and Y. Inagaki. Free continuous algebras and semantics of term rewriting systems. Technical report, Department of Information Science, Nagoya University, 1986.
21. Maurice Nivat. On the interpretation of polyadic recursive schemes. In *Symposia Mathematica,* volume 15. Academic Press, 1975.
22. J.-C. Raoult and Jean Vuillemin. Operational and semantic equivalence between recursive programs. *Journal of the Association for Computing Machinery,* 27(4):772–796, 1980.
23. David Turner. Miranda: A non-strict functional language with polymorphic types. In Jean-Pierre Jouannaud, editor, *Functional Programming Languages and Computer Architectures,* pages 1–16. Springer-Verlag, 1985. Lecture Notes in Computer Science, Volume 201.

Congruence Types*

Gilles Barthe[1,3] and Herman Geuvers[2,3]

[1] Centrum voor Wiskunde en Informatica (CWI),
Amsterdam, The Netherlands, gilles@cwi.nl

[2] Faculty of Mathematics and Informatics,
Technical University of Eindhoven, The Netherlands, herman@win.tue.nl

[3] Faculty of Mathematics and Informatics, University of Nijmegen, The Netherlands

Abstract. *We introduce a type-theoretical framework in which canonical term rewriting systems can be represented faithfully both from the logical and the computational points of view. The framework is based on congruence types, a new syntax which combines inductive, algebraic and quotient types. Congruence types improve on existing work to combine type theories with algebraic rewriting by making explicit the fact that the term-rewriting systems under consideration are initial models of an equational theory. As a result, the interaction gustavo:thesisween the type theory and the algebraic types (rewriting systems) is much more powerful than in previous work. Congruence types can be used (i) to introduce initial models of canonical term-rewriting systems (ii) to obtain a suitable computational behavior of a definable operation (iii) to provide an elegant solution to the problem of equational reasoning in type theory.*

1 Introduction

The combination of type systems with algebraic rewriting systems has given rise to algebraic-functional languages, a class of very powerful programming languages (see for example [4, 9, 12, 22]). Yet these frameworks only allow for a limited interaction between the algebraic rewriting systems and the type theory. For example, if $\mathbb{Z}$ is defined as an algebraic type, one cannot define the absolute value or prove that every integer is either positive or negative. This serious objection to algebraic-functional languages is in fact due to the absence of induction principles for algebraic types and so one might be tempted to formulate such principles. However, the task is not so easy if we want to have:

- *dependent elimination principles:* the naive approach which consists in adding the elimination principle directly to the algebraic type, as done in Clean ([27]), is limited to non-dependent elimination principles. For example, one could not prove from such an induction principle on $\mathbb{Z}$ that every integer is either positive or negative.

* This work was partially supported by the Esprit project 'Types: types for programs and proofs'.

- *confluence of the reduction relations on legal terms:* the computations attached to induction principles and those attached to algebraic types do not interact satisfactorily. What is usually required in programming languages is that the induction principle can only be applied to canonical values (i.e. closed algebraic terms in normal form). Without this restriction the reduction relation fails to be locally confluent.

To solve these problems, we opt for a two-level approach, in which every algebraic type is accompanied by the inductive type of its signature and related to it by suitable axioms for quotients[4]. For the case of $\mathbb{Z}$, this amounts to having an inductive type $\underline{Z}$ with constructors $\underline{0}, \underline{s}$ and $\underline{p}$ (the type of terms of the signature of $\mathbb{Z}$) and an algebraic type Z with constants $0 : Z$, $s : Z \rightarrow Z$ and $p : Z \rightarrow Z$ and rewrite rules $p(sx) \rightarrow x$ and $s(px) \rightarrow x$. The interaction between the types $\underline{Z}$ and Z is axiomatised by two maps: a 'class' map $[-] : \underline{Z} \rightarrow Z$ and a 'representant' map $\mathsf{rep} : Z \rightarrow \underline{Z}$, some reduction rules which specify the computational behavior of these maps (in particular, rep is forced to be the unique map which assigns to every 'class' a representant in normal form and $[.]$ is forced to be the unique morphism of algebras from $\underline{Z}$ to Z) and a logical axiom (which states that there is no confusion, i.e. that the $[.]$ map does identify exactly those terms which are provably equal for the theory of integers). In this way, one can transfer both the non-dependent and dependent induction principles (of $\underline{Z}$) to the algebraic type (Z) without affecting the confluence of the system. We claim that such a formalism, which we call *congruence types*, is suited for representing canonical term-rewriting systems in a faithful way (both from the logical and the computational points of view).

We see three important uses of congruence types.

- Represent initial models of term-rewriting systems, such as $\mathbb{Z}$. (They cannot be defined as inductive types, because they arise as a quotient of an inductive type). In this case we are mainly interested in the quotient type (Z) and we use the inductive type ($\underline{Z}$) to reason over the quotient type.
- Obtain a better computational behavior of a definable operation on an inductive type. This is achieved by defining an inductive type with 'extra' constructors and adding rewrite rules to specify the behavior of the extra constructor so that it represents the function we have in mind. How this works is best illustrated by an example. Consider the inductive type of natural numbers and the addition function $+$ on it. Then one has $+\ (sx)\ y \longrightarrow s(+\ x\ y)$ but (in general) not $+\ x\ (sy) \longrightarrow s(+\ x\ y)$. Hence $+$ has an unsatisfactory computational behavior. Now, consider the rewriting system (N, R), where N is the signature with constant 0, unary function s and binary symbol $+$ and the set of rewrite rules R consists of $+\ x\ 0 \rightarrow x$, $+\ 0\ x \rightarrow x$, $+\ (+\ x\ y)\ z \rightarrow +\ x\ (+\ y\ z)$, $+\ sx\ y \rightarrow s(+\ x\ y)$ and $+\ x\ sy \rightarrow s(+\ x\ y)$. The congruence type defined from this set of rewrite rules gives rise to an inductive type $\underline{N}$ with constructors $\underline{0}$, $\underline{s}$ and $\underline{+}$ and an algebraic type with the reduction rules R. In this framework, $+$ has a suitable computational

[4] The reader is refered to [6, 13, 20, 21] for a type-theoretic account of quotients.

behavior and N gives indeed a suitable representation of $\mathbb{N}$. Note that in this case we are again interested in the quotient type N.

- Use the quotient structure to prove properties of the algebra of terms (the inductive type). In this case the quotient structure acts as an *oracle* to derive a statement about the algebra of terms. Consider the congruence type associated to the theory of groups: the inductive type corresponds to the set of terms of the theory of groups and the quotient type corresponds to the free group over infinitely many elements. To know whether an equation (s, t) is a theorem of the theory of groups, it is enough to know whether $[s] = [t]$. The gain here is that if $[s]$ and $[t]$ have a common reduct, then the conclusion is immediate. This use of congruence types is very important in proof-checking and is the basis of lean proof-checking, a two-level approach to formal mathematics for efficient equational reasoning introduced in [7] and further developed in [10].

In this paper we want to emphasize especially the usefulness of congruence types and therefore we discuss three examples in quite some detail. Furthermore, we give a definition of the general syntax and an overview of the meta-theory of the system. The paper is organised as follows. In section 2, we discuss related work. In section 3, the more technical motivations of congruence types are discussed and we treat the integers as a motivating example of the syntax. In section 4, the syntax is given in detail (for the calculus of constructions) and we give some of the meta-theory (without proof). In section 5 we give two further examples of congruence types and their possible applications to programming and proof-checking. In the final section we suggest some extensions of the framework.

Related work

Congruence types are at the junction of several fundamental concepts and programming paradigms. They combine features of inductive ([25, 26, 24]), algebraic ([12, 4, 22]) and quotient types ([6, 13, 21]). Congruence types arise as a special form of quotient type where the underlying type is inductively defined and where the equivalence relation is given by a canonical term-rewriting system.

Congruence types and inductive types Congruence types are more expressive than inductive types because they allow to introduce initial models of canonical term-rewriting systems instead of initial models of signatures. They can be seen as a variant of the congruence types of Backhouse *et al.* which allow the introduction of initial models of arbitrary specifications ([2, 3]). Their work differs from ours in two respects; first, they focus on specifications and not on canonical term-rewriting systems, so there is no question of giving a computationally faithful representation of the rewrite rules. Second, their formalism requires a very strong form of equality as it is present for example in ITT.

Congruence types and pattern-matching It is possible to use congruence types to give a computationally faithful representation of definable operators on inductive types. In effect, congruence types share some of the power of pattern-matching as introduced by Coquand in [14]. See section 4.1.

Congruence types and algebraic rewriting Congruence types are also more expressive than algebraic rewriting because of the presence of elimination principles. They are closely related to Jouannaud and Okada's algebraic functional paradigm ([4, 22]). In algebraic functional languages, (higher-order) constants are defined by rewrite rules, whereas they are defined inductively in the framework of congruence types. An advantage of congruence types is that the elimination principles can be used to reason over the data structures, a possibility which is ruled out in algebraic-functional languages. See section 2.

Applications of congruence types to proof-checking Congruence types provide a suitable framework to ease the problem of equational reasoning in proof-checking. As argued in [10], they also lay the foundations for a theoretical study of the interaction between computer algebra systems and proof-checkers. See section 4.2.

Prerequisites and terminology

The paper assumes some familiarity with pure type systems ([5, 17]), inductive types (see for example [26]) and first-order term-rewriting ([15, 23]). A signature is a pair $\Sigma = (F_\Sigma, \mathsf{Ar})$ where F_Σ is a set (the set of function symbols) and $\mathsf{Ar} : F_\Sigma \to \mathbb{N}$ is the arity map. Term-rewriting systems are defined as usual. By canonical term-rewriting system, we mean confluent and terminating term-rewriting system. An algebraic type is a type corresponding to a term-rewriting system.

2 Motivation

For every term-rewriting system $\mathcal{S} = (\Sigma, \mathcal{R})$, one can reason on the initial model $T_\mathcal{S}$ of $\mathcal{S}$ by induction on the structure of the terms. This form of reasoning implicitly uses the universality of $T_\mathcal{S}$ as a quotient of T_Σ and the initiality of T_Σ. In type theory (or any formal system), such a reasoning is only possible if the relationship between T_Σ and $T_\mathcal{S}$ is made explicit. Congruence types provide an axiomatic framework in which the relationship between the initial Σ-algebra and the initial $\mathcal{S}$-model is described axiomatically. The idea is to introduce two types Σ and $\mathcal{S}$ simultaneously; these types should respectively correspond to T_Σ and $T_\mathcal{S}$ (so we will confuse Σ with T_Σ and $\mathcal{S}$ with $T_\mathcal{S}$). Every function symbol f of arity n induces two maps, $\underline{f}$ and f such that:

- if $q_1{:}\Sigma, \ldots, q_n{:}\Sigma$, then $\underline{f} q_1 \cdots q_n : \Sigma$,
- if $a_1{:}\mathcal{S}, \ldots, a_n{:}\mathcal{S}$, then $f a_1 \cdots a_n : \mathcal{S}$.

Hence every Σ-term t induces two terms $\underline{t}$ and t of respective type Σ and $\mathcal{S}$. Equality in $\mathcal{S}$ is forced by the rewriting rules of $\mathcal{R}$. Now the crucial step is to relate $\mathcal{S}$ and Σ by suitable axioms. As $T_{\mathcal{S}}$ is a quotient of T_{Σ}, we can inspire ourselves from the standard rules for quotients ([6]). First, there must be a canonical 'class' map $[-]$ from Σ to $\mathcal{S}$; it is the unique morphism of Σ-algebras and satisfies for every function symbol f of arity n and $t_1, \ldots, t_n$ elements of Σ,

$$[\underline{f}(t_1, \ldots, t_n)] = f([t_1], \ldots, [t_n])$$

Type theory is a computational framework, so it is natural to see this equality as a computation rule (from the left to the right). In a second instance, we must ensure that the two standard criterions for quotients hold:

- *no junk:* the map $[-]$ from Σ to $\mathcal{S}$ is surjective;
- *no confusion:* for every two terms s and t, $\mathcal{S} \vdash s \doteq t \quad \Leftrightarrow \quad [s] = [t]$, where the first equality $\mathcal{S} \vdash - \doteq -$ is the deductive closure of the rewrite rules.

In the syntax for quotient types, there are two alternatives to ensure the no junk condition: by the introduction of a map rep from $\mathcal{S}$ to Σ which picks a representative for each equivalence class or by adding a logical axiom that enforces the surjectivity of $[-]$. We prefer the first alternative over the more traditional second approach, because it can be given a computational meaning; the idea is that rep should assign to every equivalence class c the unique term t in 'normal form'[5] such that $[t] = c$. Note that the behavior of rep is completely specified on closed terms by the above requirement, hence rep is *not* a choice operator and does *not* alter the constructive character of type theory. The behavior of rep is forced by several rewrite rules. First, one must have the computation rule $[\mathsf{rep}\ x] = x$ for every x in $\mathcal{S}$. Second, we must impose the further computation rule

$$\mathsf{rep}(f(t_1, \ldots, t_n)) = \underline{f}(\mathsf{rep}\ t_1, \ldots, \mathsf{rep}\ t_n))$$

provided $f(t_1, \ldots, t_n)$ is a closed term in normal form (this corresponds exactly to our intuition of rep). The restriction to closed terms is necessary to preserve confluence.

As for the no confusion rule, it is ensured axiomatically. The rule expresses the fact that, if two elements of Σ are in the same class, then they are in the least equivalence relation that contains the rewrite relation (seen as a relation on Σ). This is achieved by adding a constant noconf that takes a proof p of $[a] =_{\mathcal{S}} [b]$ and returns a proof noconf p of $R_{\mathcal{S}}\ a\ b$, where $R_{\mathcal{S}}$ is the (impredicatively defined) least equivalence relation containing the rewrite relation.

A worked out example: the integers One of the starting points of our investigation was the representation of the set $\mathbb{Z}$ of integers in type theory. Despite being a fairly simple data type, it has no direct representation in type theory; it can either be defined as a "quotient" of $\mathbb{N} \times \mathbb{N}$, where $\mathbb{N}$ is the inductively defined type of natural numbers, or as an inductive type using some encoding ([11]), or as an algebraic type, i.e. a term-rewriting system (without induction principle).

[5] The rewriting relation is defined on $\mathcal{S}$ so the notion of a term (in Σ) in 'normal form' is an informal one.

However, none of these solutions captures adequately the structure of $\mathbb{Z}$. If we see $\mathbb{Z}$ as a canonical term-rewriting system, then the first two definitions are not computationally faithful. On the other hand, if $\mathbb{Z}$ is represented as an algebraic type, the representation of $\mathbb{Z}$ is unsatisfactory from a logical point of view; for example, one cannot prove that every integer is either positive or negative nor define the absolute value of an integer.

On the other hand, congruence types provide a suitable representation of $\mathbb{Z}$. $\mathbb{Z}$ can be defined with congruence types by introducing simultaneously an algebraic type Z corresponding to $\mathbb{Z}$ and an inductive type $\underline{Z}$ corresponding to the signature of $\mathbb{Z}$ and by relating them by suitable rules for quotient types. In this formalism, the representation of $\mathbb{Z}$ is computationally faithful and it is possible to derive from the induction principle on $\underline{Z}$ several standard induction principles on Z. The rules are as follows.

The inductive type $\underline{Z}$ of ground terms of the theory of integers with constructors $\underline{0}$, $\underline{s}$ and $\underline{p}$. $\underline{Z}$ is given by the standard rules for an inductive type

$$\frac{}{\vdash \underline{Z} : \Box} \qquad \frac{}{\vdash \underline{0} : \underline{Z}} \qquad \frac{\Gamma \vdash t : \underline{Z}}{\Gamma \vdash \underline{s}t : \underline{Z}} \frac{\Gamma \vdash t : \underline{Z}}{\Gamma \vdash \underline{p}t : \underline{Z}}$$

with the elimination rules

$$\frac{\begin{array}{ccc}\Gamma \vdash C : \underline{Z} \rightarrow * & \Gamma \vdash a : \underline{Z} & \Gamma \vdash f_0 : C\underline{0} \\ \Gamma \vdash f_s : \Pi x : \underline{Z}.Cx \rightarrow C(\underline{s}x) & & \Gamma \vdash f_p : \Pi x : \underline{Z}.Cx \rightarrow C(\underline{p}x)\end{array}}{\Gamma \vdash \epsilon\,[f_0, f_s, f_p]\; a : C\; a}$$

$$\frac{\begin{array}{ccc}\Gamma \vdash C : \Box & \Gamma \vdash a : \underline{Z} & \Gamma \vdash f_0 : C \\ \Gamma \vdash f_s : \underline{Z} \rightarrow C \rightarrow C & & \Gamma \vdash f_p : \underline{Z} \rightarrow C \rightarrow C\end{array}}{\Gamma \vdash \epsilon\,[f_0, f_s, f_p]\; a : C}$$

The term-rewriting system Z is introduced via the rules

$$\frac{}{\vdash Z : \Box} \qquad \frac{}{\vdash 0 : Z} \qquad \frac{\Gamma \vdash t : Z}{\Gamma \vdash st : Z} \frac{\Gamma \vdash t : Z}{\Gamma \vdash pt : Z}$$

The axioms for quotients, that relate Z and $\underline{Z}$, are represented by the rules

$$\frac{\Gamma \vdash a : \underline{Z}}{\Gamma \vdash [a] : Z} \frac{\Gamma \vdash a : Z}{\Gamma \vdash \mathsf{rep}\; a : \underline{Z}} \frac{\Gamma \vdash p : [a] =_Z [b]}{\Gamma \vdash \mathsf{noconf}\, p : R_Z\; a\; b.}$$

Here, R_Z is the least equivalence relation on $\underline{Z}$ that is closed under the rewrite rules. More precisely: for $a, b{:}\underline{Z}$,

$$R_Z a\; b := \Pi S{:}\underline{Z}{\rightarrow}\underline{Z}{\rightarrow}*.\mathrm{eqrel}\,(S){\rightarrow}(\Pi x{:}\underline{Z}.S\; (\underline{p}(\underline{s}x))\; x){\rightarrow}(\Pi x{:}\underline{Z}.S\; (\underline{s}(\underline{p}x))\; x){\rightarrow}S\; a\; b$$

where eqrel (S) denotes that S is an equivalence relation. There is a new conversion rule, which extends the reduction-expansion rule to take into account the new reduction relations[6].

[6] Note that in pure type systems, this rule is equivalent to the standard conversion rule; the equivalence follows from the subject reduction lemma and the Church-Rosser property of β-reduction on pseudo-terms ([5]). One consequence of the equivalence

$$\frac{\Gamma \vdash a : A \quad \Gamma \vdash A' : */\Box \quad A \twoheadrightarrow_{\beta\chi\iota\rho} A' \text{ or } A' \twoheadrightarrow_{\beta\chi\iota\rho} A}{\Gamma \vdash a : A'}$$

The computational behavior of the system is specified by β-reduction and three other reduction relations:

- ι-reduction (The computational meaning of the elimination principles over the inductive type $\underline{Z}$.)

$$\epsilon\ [f_0, f_s, f_p]\ \underline{0} \rightarrow_\iota f_0$$
$$\epsilon\ [f_0, f_s, f_p]\ (\underline{s}x) \rightarrow_\iota f_s\ x\ (\epsilon\ [f_0, f_s, f_p]\ x)$$
$$\epsilon\ [f_0, f_s, f_p]\ (\underline{p}x) \rightarrow_\iota f_p\ x\ (\epsilon\ [f_0, f_s, f_p]\ x)$$

These reduction rules are the standard ones for inductive types.

- ρ-reduction (Given by the term-rewriting system defining $\mathbb{Z}$.)

$$s(px) \rightarrow_\rho x \quad p(sx) \rightarrow_\rho x$$

- χ-reduction (The computational meaning of quotients.)

$$[\mathsf{rep}\ x] \rightarrow_\chi x$$
$$[\underline{0}] \rightarrow_\chi 0 \qquad [\underline{s}x] \rightarrow_\chi s[x] \qquad [\underline{p}x] \rightarrow_\chi p[x]$$
$$\mathsf{rep}\ 0 \rightarrow_\chi \underline{0} \quad \mathsf{rep}\ (st) \rightarrow_\chi \underline{s}\ (\mathsf{rep}\ t) \quad \mathsf{rep}\ (pt) \rightarrow_\chi \underline{p}\ (\mathsf{rep}\ t)$$

where in the last two rules it is respectively assumed that st and pt are closed algebraic terms (i.e built from 0, s and p) in normal form.

One of the main advantages of our definition is that it suppresses the burden of providing equality proofs when reasoning about integers. Indeed, the equality between integers is computational and handled by the reduction relations. It makes them very attractive to use in proof-checking. Furthermore, our definition also captures the logical content of $\mathbb{Z}$ as one can prove that all the standard induction principles for $\mathbb{Z}$ hold for Z. The first induction principle is proof by induction, which stipulates that for every predicate P on Z,

if $P0$ and $\forall x \in Z.\mathsf{pos}\ x, Px \rightarrow P(sx)$ and $\forall x \in Z.\mathsf{neg}\ x, Px \rightarrow P(px)$ then $\forall x \in Z.Px$

where being positive (pos) and being negative (neg) are suitably defined predicates. A similar non-dependent elimination principle over $\Box$ can be defined. For $P : \Box$, one can build from

$f_0 : P$, $f_s : \Pi x : Z.(\mathsf{pos}\ x) \rightarrow P \rightarrow P$ and $f_p : \Pi x : Z.(\mathsf{neg}\ x) \rightarrow P \rightarrow P$ a term $F(f_0, f_s, f_p)$ of type $Z \rightarrow P$.

---

is that for every two convertible legal types A and B, there exists a conversion path through legal types; this property is called soundness in [19]. Soundness is a very desirable property of the system because it ensures that non-typable terms do not play any role in derivations.

In presence of ρ-reduction, one cannot rely on subject reduction or confluence of the combined reduction relation on the set of pseudo-terms to prove soundness. The solution is to replace the conversion rule by the reduction-expansion rule (see [4]).

The construction of these terms is rather intricate and involves the definition of a normal form map $\mathsf{nf} : \underline{Z} \to \underline{Z}$ with suitable properties. The construction will be reported elsewhere.

The term F behaves as a kind of 'primitive recursor for the integers'. Indeed, one can check that the following equalities hold:

$$\begin{aligned} F\ f_0\ f_s\ f_p\ 0 &=_{\beta\iota\chi\rho} f_0 \\ F\ f_0\ f_s\ f_p\ (s\ t) &=_{\beta\iota\chi\rho} f_s\ t\ q\ (F\ f_0\ f_s\ f_p\ t) \\ F\ f_0\ f_s\ f_p\ (p\ t) &=_{\beta\iota\chi\rho} f_p\ t\ q\ (F\ f_0\ f_s\ f_p\ t) \end{aligned}$$

where in the second rule, st is a closed term in normal form and q a proof of pos t and in the last rule, pt is a closed term in normal form and q a proof that neg t. In contrast, the dependent elimination principle over $*$ does not have such a clear computational meaning. It seems to emphasize the necessity to separate between propositions and objects, as it is done in the present system by putting the sets on the *kind*-level. Our view is that only inhabitation is central to propositions, so that the computational meaning of the elimination principle over propositions is not crucial. On the contrary, both inhabitation and computational behavior of the inhabitants are important in the case of objects, so the computational meaning of the elimination principle over objects must be clear. Still, one can get an elimination principle for $*$ which is computationally meaningful by strengthening mildly the induction hypotheses. (So, this elimination principle is logically weaker). Indeed, one can easily construct a term G of type

$$\forall P : Z \to *.P0 \to (\forall x : Z.Px \to P(sx)) \to (\forall x : Z.Px \to P(px)) \to \forall x : Z.Px$$

that satisfies reductions that are similar to the ones for F above.

3 The calculus of constructions with congruence types

3.1 Syntax

We start from a (finite) collection $\mathcal{S}_1 = (\Sigma_1, \mathcal{R}_1)$, ..., $\mathcal{S}_1 = (\Sigma_n, \mathcal{R}_n)$ of canonical term-rewriting systems. We let $F = \bigcup_{i=1,\ldots,n} F_{\Sigma_i}$ and $\underline{F} = \{\underline{f} | f \in F\}$. The set of pseudo-terms is defined by the abstract syntax:

$$T = V | * | \Box | TT | \Pi V : T.T | \lambda V : T.T | \mathcal{S}_i | \Sigma_i | F\mathbf{T} | \underline{F}\mathbf{T} | [T] | \mathsf{rep}\ T | \mathsf{noconf}\ T | \epsilon_i[\mathbf{T}]\ T$$

The rules for derivation are those of the Calculus of Constructions (see Appendix) extended by the rules for congruence types. The rules are divided in four categories.

- *formation and introduction rules:* these rules introduce the congruence types and all the constructors. As motivated earlier, congruence types are introduced as kinds.

$$\frac{}{\vdash \mathcal{S}_i : \Box} \qquad \frac{}{\vdash \Sigma_i : \Box} \qquad \frac{\Gamma \vdash a : \Sigma_i}{\Gamma \vdash [a] : \mathcal{S}_i} \qquad \frac{\Gamma \vdash a : \Sigma_i}{\Gamma \vdash \mathsf{rep}\ a : \mathcal{S}_i}$$

$$\frac{\Gamma \vdash a_1 : \mathcal{S}_i \quad \ldots \quad \Gamma \vdash a_m : \mathcal{S}_i}{\Gamma \vdash f\ a_1\ \ldots\ a_m : \mathcal{S}_i} \qquad \frac{\Gamma \vdash a_1 : \Sigma_i \quad \ldots \quad \Gamma \vdash a_m : \Sigma_i}{\Gamma \vdash \underline{f}\ a_1\ \ldots\ a_m : \Sigma_i}$$

where it is assumed that $f \in \mathcal{F}_i$ has arity m;

- *elimination rules:* these are the standard elimination rules for inductive types; let Σ_i have constructors $f_1, \ldots, f_{n_i}$ of respective arity $m_1, \ldots, m_{n_i}$.

$$\frac{\Gamma \vdash a : \Sigma_i \qquad \Gamma \vdash P : \Sigma_i \to * \qquad \Gamma \vdash E_j : \Pi x_1 \ldots x_{m_j}{:}\Sigma_i . P x_1 \to \cdots \to P x_{m_j} \to P(\underline{f_j}\ x_1 \cdots x_{m_j})\ [1 \leq j \leq n_i]}{\epsilon_i[E_1, \ \ldots \ , E_{n_i}]a : Pa}$$

$$\frac{\Gamma \vdash a : \Sigma_i \qquad \Gamma \vdash P : \Box \qquad \Gamma \vdash E_j : \Pi x_1 \ldots x_{m_j}{:}\Sigma_i . P \to \cdots \to P \to P\ [1 \leq j \leq n_i]}{\epsilon_i[E_1, \ \ldots \ , E_{n_i}]\ a : P}$$

- *logical rule:* the no confusion rule is formalised by defining the closure of $\mathcal{R}_i$ as a relation on Σ_i. The relation is defined impredicatively and denoted by *abus de language* by $\mathcal{R}_i$.

$$\frac{\Gamma \vdash p : [a] =_{\mathcal{S}_i} [b]}{\Gamma \vdash \mathsf{noconf}\ p : \mathcal{R}_i\ a\ b}$$

- *reduction rule:* the reduction rule has to be extended so as to take into account the new reduction relations associated to congruence types.

$$\frac{\Gamma \vdash a : A \qquad \Gamma \vdash A' : */\Box \qquad A \twoheadrightarrow_{\beta\chi\iota\rho} A' \text{ or } A' \twoheadrightarrow_{\beta\chi\iota\rho} A}{\Gamma \vdash a : A'}$$

The new reduction relations are ι-reduction (which specifies the computational behavior of the elimination principles), χ-reduction (which specifies the computational behavior of quotient types) and ρ-reduction (which embeds the reduction relation of the term-rewriting systems into the type theory). The rules are:

- *ι-reduction:* if $f_j \in \mathcal{F}_i$ is of arity m_j, $\epsilon_i[\mathbf{E}](\underline{f_j} a_1 \cdots a_{m_j}) \to_\iota E_j a_1 \cdots a_{m_j} (\epsilon_i[\mathbf{E}]a_1) \cdots (\epsilon_i[\mathbf{E}]a_{m_j})$,
- *ρ-reduction:* for every rewriting rule $l \to r$, there is a rule $l \to_\rho r$,
- *χ-reduction:* the rules are

$$[\mathsf{rep}\ x] \to_\chi x$$

$$[\underline{f}\ t_1\ \ldots\ t_m] \to_\chi f\ [t_1]\ \ldots\ [t_m]$$

$$\mathsf{rep}\ (f\ t_1\ \ldots\ t_m) \to_\chi \underline{f}\ (\mathsf{rep}\ t_1)\ \ldots\ (\mathsf{rep}\ t_m)$$

In the last rule, it is assumed that $f\ t_1\ \ldots\ t_m$ is a closed algebraic term in (ρ-)normal form or that f is a *fundamental constructor*, i.e. for all Σ-terms $t_1, \ldots, t_m$, the normal form of $f(t_1, \ldots, t_m)$ is $f(t'_1, \ldots, t'_m)$ where the t'_i's are the normal forms of the t_i's. In section 4.1, we will justify this slight weakening of the proviso.

3.2 Meta-Theory

There are some important properties to be established before we can safely use the extension of CC with Congruence Types. These are the *Church-Rosser property* for the well-typed terms, *subject-reduction* (which ensures that reduction preserves typing), *consistency* (as a logical system, saying that not all types are inhabited by a closed term) and *decidability of typing* (it is decidable if in a given context Γ, a pseudo-term M has type A). These properties will of course depend on the specific algebraic rewrite rules that we have added, but remember that we only consider canonical (i.e. Church-Rosser and strongly normalizing) term-rewriting systems.

It turns out that all the standard results for the Calculus of Constructions hold for its extension with congruence types. Note however that proofs are complicated by the fact that $\beta\chi\iota\rho$-reduction is not confluent on pseudo-terms (see [12] for a counterexample). A relatively easy fact, but nevertheless a key observation is the following.

Lemma 1 *The $\beta\chi\iota\rho$-reduction is Weak Church-Rosser (WCR) on the set of pseudoterms. (That is, if $M \longrightarrow_{\beta\chi\iota\rho} M_1$ and $M \longrightarrow_{\beta\chi\iota\rho} M_2$, then there is a term Q such that $M_1 \twoheadrightarrow_{\beta\chi\iota\rho} Q$ $M_2 \twoheadrightarrow_{\beta\chi\iota\rho} Q$.)*

The subject reduction property (SR) can also be proved. Because $\beta\chi\iota\rho$-reduction is *not* Church-Rosser on the pseudo-terms, this involves some extra technicalities that were developped in [4] for the addition of algebraic rewriting to CC.

Proposition 2 (Subject Reduction) *If $\Gamma \vdash a : A$ and $a \rightarrow_{\beta\chi\iota\rho} a'$, then $\Gamma \vdash a' : A$.*

Termination is a modular property of CC with congruence types, under the mild restriction that the term-rewriting systems are non-duplicating[7]. We do not know whether strong normalisation pertains if the restriction to non-duplicating term-rewriting systems is dropped.

Theorem 3 (Strong Normalization) *Let $S_1, \ldots, S_n$ be canonical, non-duplicating term-rewriting systems. Then* CC *extended with the congruence types associated to $S_1, \ldots, S_n$ is strongly normalising.*

The proof is an adaptation of the semantical proof of strong normalisation for CC with (first-order) inductive types given in [18].

Corollary 4 *1. CC with Congruence Types satisfies the Church-Rosser property. (If M is well-typed and $M \twoheadrightarrow_{\beta\chi\iota\rho} M_1$ and $M \twoheadrightarrow_{\beta\chi\iota\rho} M_2$, then there is a term Q such that $M_1 \twoheadrightarrow_{\beta\chi\iota\rho} Q$ $M_2 \twoheadrightarrow_{\beta\chi\iota\rho} Q$.)*

[7] A term-rewriting system is non-duplicating if for every rule $l \rightarrow r$ and variable x, $\mathrm{occ}(x,l) \leq \mathrm{occ}(x,r)$ where for every term t, $\mathrm{occ}(x,t)$ denotes the number of occurences of x in t.

2. *CC with Congruence Types is consistent. (There is no closed term M with $\vdash M : \bot$.)*
3. *CC with Congruence Types has decidable typing.*

The first is due to Newman's Lemma (SN & WCR imply CR). The second follows by showing that a closed term of type $\bot$ ($:= \Pi\alpha{:}\, * \,.\alpha$) can never be in normal form in our system. This involves some more technical facts about the possible structure of inhabitants of types of a specific form. (Note that in presence of congruence types, this reasoning is slightly more complicated then for the Calculus of Constructions, because of the no confusion rules.) The consistency can also be proved in a more direct way by extending the proof-irrelevance model or the realisability model for CC to the case for congruence types. The third follows because for two well-typed terms it is decidable whether they have a common reduct.

4 Examples

4.1 The natural numbers with addition

Traditionally, the natural numbers are defined as an inductive type N with two constructors, zero and successor. Then addition, multiplication and other primitive recursive functions can all be defined inductively. One of the problems of this approach is that the computational behavior of these operations can be quite unsatisfactory. For example, if we define addition inductively on the first component, we have the reduction rule $sx + y \rightarrow s(x + y)$ but in general not $x + sy \rightarrow s(x + y)$ (if x and y are variables, then the reduction does not hold). Hence $+$ has not the expected computational behavior. This fact was already pointed out in [14] as a motivating example to introduce pattern-matching in type theory. Congruence types offer an alternative approach to define a type of natural numbers with well-behaved arithmetical operations. Consider the term-rewriting system $N = (\underline{N}, \mathcal{R}_N)$ where $\underline{N}$ is the signature consisting of one constant 0, one unary function symbol s and one binary function symbol $+$ and $\mathcal{R}_N$ is the term-rewriting system given by the reduction rules

$$
\begin{aligned}
+\; x\; 0 &\rightarrow x \\
+\; 0\; x &\rightarrow x \\
+\; (+\; x\; y)\; z &\rightarrow +\; x\; (+\; y\; z) \\
+\; sx\; y &\rightarrow s(+\; x\; y) \\
+\; x\; sy &\rightarrow s(+\; x\; y)
\end{aligned}
$$

We claim that N gives a suitable representation of $\mathbb{N}$. In particular, one can prove the standard induction principles for natural numbers. However, the weakening of the proviso in the rules for χ-reduction ($\mathsf{rep}\,(ft) \longrightarrow \underline{f}(\mathsf{rep}\,\mathsf{t})$ if f is a fundamental constructor) is essential to derive the standard elimination principles for N. The key fact is that in the present example s and 0 are fundamental constructors, hence $\mathsf{rep}\,(st) \longrightarrow \underline{s}(\mathsf{rep}\ t)$ for an arbitrary term t. Note that, as N is inductively definable, every closed algebraic term reduces to a *fundamental algebraic term*, i.e. one built from the fundamental constructors.

Congruence types and pattern-matching It is particularly interesting to compare our syntax with pattern-matching as introduced in [14]. Both offer a means to give a computationally adequate representation of definable operations on inductive types. Technically, this is achieved by different means. The most important differences between pattern-matching and congruence types are summarised below.

- Pattern-matching is schematic and can be used repeatedly to define new operators in the same way as the elimination principle. In contrast, congruence types are specific: they only provide a faithful representation of those operators introduced as constructors. For example, substraction will not have the expected computational behavior in the above definition of N. Moreover, pattern-matching can be used to define (for example) predicates, which is not possible with congruence types.
- The structure of rewrite rules allowed is more liberal in the syntax of congruence types than in the syntax of pattern-matching. For example, the rule $+\ (+\ x\ y)\ z \rightarrow +\ x\ (+\ y\ z)$ does not satisfy the criterion given in [14].

4.2 The free group over a set of atoms

Oracle types is another syntax for introducing term-rewriting systems in type theory, obtained from congruence types by forgetting the rep constructor and its associated reduction rules. In [10, 8], Barthe *et al.* have proposed oracle types as a theoretical framework to study the combination of proof-checkers and computer algebra systems. Indeed, oracle types can be viewed as an interface between a logical system (type theory with inductive types) and a calculational system (the computer algebra system, modelled by ρ-reduction). The two systems are correlated by the no confusion rule, which can be seen as some kind of soundness result. In this context, the no confusion rule can be read as follows.

> Let $(\Sigma, \mathcal{R})$ be a canonical term-rewriting system and let s, t be two Σ-terms. Every computation on $[s]$ and $[t]$ (the computer algebra representations of s and t) which yields a common reduct can be lifted to a proof that s and t are in the deductive closure of $\mathcal{R}$ (viewed as an equational theory).

In the remaining of this section, we illustrate how Barthe *et al.* have used congruence/oracle types to give a partial solution to the problem of equational reasoning in proof-checking.Consider the term-rewriting system $G = (\underline{G}, \mathcal{R}_G)$ where $\underline{G}$ is the signature of groups extended with infinitely many constants and $\mathcal{R}_G$ is the Knuth-Bendix completion of the axioms of the theory of groups. That is, $\mathcal{R}_G$ consists of the rules

$$
\begin{array}{rlrl}
o\ e\ x & \rightarrow_\rho x & i\ e & \rightarrow_\rho e \\
o\ x\ e & \rightarrow_\rho x & o\ (o\ x\ (i\ z))\ z & \rightarrow_\rho x \\
o\ x\ (o\ y\ z) & \rightarrow_\rho o\ (o\ x\ y)\ z & o\ (o\ x\ z)\ (i\ z) & \rightarrow_\rho x \\
o\ (i\ x)\ x & \rightarrow_\rho e & i\ (i\ x) & \rightarrow_\rho x \\
o\ x\ (i\ x) & \rightarrow_\rho e & i\ (o\ x\ y) & \rightarrow_\rho o\ (i\ y)\ (i\ x)
\end{array}
$$

The congruence type generated by G consists of two parts: the free group G over infinitely many elements and the inductive set of terms of the theory of groups (the infinite collection of constants serves as the set of variables). The interaction between the two types allows a simple solution to equational problems of the theory of groups. Assume we can derive

$$
\Gamma \vdash H : \Box \qquad \Gamma \vdash o_H : H \rightarrow H \rightarrow H \qquad \Gamma \vdash e_H : H \qquad \Gamma \vdash i_H : H \rightarrow H \rightarrow H
$$

and we have a proof of the fact that (H, o_H, e_H, i_H) satisfies the axioms of groups (we work with Leibniz equality). Assume that we want to decide whether $a =_H b$. One possible way to solve the problem is to find two inhabitants s, t of $\underline{G}$ and an assignment[8] α such that $[\![s]\!]_\alpha \twoheadrightarrow a$ and $[\![t]\!]_\alpha \twoheadrightarrow b$ (in fact, there are optimal such s and t). By the conversion rule, the problem can be reduced to $[\![s]\!]_\alpha =_H [\![t]\!]_\alpha$. But, by definition of $\mathcal{R}_G$, this is an immediate consequence of $\mathcal{R}_G\ s\ t$. (Note that we are implicitely using the soundness theorem for equational logic, which is an easy consequence of the impredicative definition of $\mathcal{R}_G$.) Now congruence types offer a decision procedure for solving $\mathcal{R}_G\ s\ t$, simply by checking whether $[s] = [t]$ (because of the no confusion rule).

5 Final remarks

We have presented a new syntax of congruence types and shown how the syntax can be used to give a faithful representation of canonical term-rewriting systems in type theory. In this paper, we have restricted our attention to unsorted term-rewriting systems. In the future, it seems natural to extend the framework to cover other case of term-rewriting systems such as:

- *many-sorted term-rewriting systems:* the extension would allow to introduce strongly normalising type theories (with explicit substitutions) as congruence types;
- *higher-order term-rewriting systems:* the extension of our framework to higher-order specifications would allow to consider congruence types generated by first-order languages (quantification has to be introduced as a higher-order constructor).
- *non-standard term-rewriting systems:* many theories, such as commutative theories, fall out of the scope of this paper because they do not yield canonical

[8] Assignments and their extension to interpretations of terms are defined as usual.

term-rewriting systems. It would be interesting to investigate the theory of congruence types when the term-rewriting systems under consideration are conditional or priority rewriting systems or are defined modulo a set of equations.

Another important direction for research is the application of congruence and oracle types in proof-checking. Extending the framework of oracle types to cover many forms of rewriting would enable the two-level approach of [8, 10] to be extended to a significant class of problems, including for example a decision procedure to detect logical equivalence of formulae of propositional logic.

References

1. S. Abramsky, D. Gabbay, and T. Maibaum, editors. *Handbook of Logic in Computer Science*. Oxford Science Publications, 1992.
2. R. Backhouse, P. Chisholm, and G. Malcolm. Do-it-yourself type theory (part I). *BEATCS: Bulletin of the European Association for Theoretical Computer Science*, 34:68–110, 1988.
3. R. Backhouse, P. Chisholm, and G. Malcolm. Do-it-yourself type theory (part II). *BEATCS: Bulletin of the European Association for Theoretical Computer Science*, 35:205–244, 1988.
4. F. Barbanera, M. Fernandez, and H. Geuvers. Modularity of strong normalisation and confluence in the algebraic λ-cube. In *Proceedings of LICS'94*, pages 406–415. IEEE Computer Society Press, 1994.
5. H.P. Barendregt. Lambda calculi with types. In Abramsky et al. [1], pages 117–309. Volume 2.
6. G. Barthe. Extensions of pure type systems. In Dezani-Ciancaglini and Plotkin [16], pages 16–31.
7. G. Barthe. Formalising algebra in type theory: fundamentals and applications to group theory. Manuscript. An earlier version appeared as technical report CSI-R9508, University of Nijmegen, under the title 'Formalising mathematics in type theory: fundamentals and case studies', 1995.
8. G. Barthe and H. Elbers. Towards lean proof checking. Manuscript, 1996.
9. G. Barthe and H. Geuvers. Modular properties of algebraic pure type systems. In G. Dowek, J. Heering, K. Meinke, and B. Möller, editors, *Proceedings of HOA'95*, Lecture Notes in Computer Science. Springer-Verlag, 1996. To appear.
10. G. Barthe, M. Ruys, and H. Barendregt. A two-level approach towards lean proof-checking. In S. Berardi and M. Coppo, editors, *Proceedings of TYPES'95*, Lecture Notes in Computer Science. Springer-Verlag, 1996. To appear.
11. G. Betarte. A machine-assisted proof that the integers form an integral domain. Master's thesis, Department of Computer Science, Chalmers University, 1993.
12. V. Breazu-Tannen. Combining algebra and higher-order types. In *Proceedings of LICS'88*, pages 82–90. IEEE Computer Society Press, 1988.
13. R.L. Constable, S.F. Allen, H.M. Bromley, W.R. Cleaveland, J.F. Cremer, R.W. Harper, D.J. Howe, T.B. Knoblock, N.P. Mendler, P. Panangaden, J.T. Sasaki, and S.F. Smith. *Implementing Mathematics with the NuPrl Development System*. Prentice-Hall, inc., Englewood Cliffs, New Jersey, first edition, 1986.

14. T. Coquand. Pattern matching in type theory. In B. Nordström, editor, *Informal proceedings of LF'92*, pages 66–79, 1992. Available from http://www.dcs.ed.ac.uk/lfcsinfo/research/types-bra/proc/index.html.
15. N. Dershowitz and J-P. Jouannaud. Rewrite systems. In J. van Leeuwen, editor, *Formal models and semantics. Handbook of Theoretical Computer Science*, volume B, pages 243–320. Elsevier, 1990.
16. M. Dezani-Ciancaglini and G. Plotkin, editors. *Proceedings of TLCA'95*, volume 902 of *Lecture Notes in Computer Science*. Springer-Verlag, 1995.
17. H. Geuvers. *Logics and type systems*. PhD thesis, University of Nijmegen, 1993.
18. H. Geuvers. A short and flexible proof of strong normalisation for the calculus of constructions. In P. Dybjer, B. Nordström, and J. Smith, editors, *Proceedings of TYPES'94*, volume 996 of *Lecture Notes in Computer Science*, pages 14–38. Springer-Verlag, 1995.
19. H. Geuvers and B. Werner. On the Church-Rosser property for expressive type systems and its consequence for their metatheoretic study. In *Proceedings of LICS'94*, pages 320–329. IEEE Computer Society Press, 1994.
20. M. Hofmann. A simple model for quotient types. In Dezani-Ciancaglini and Plotkin [16], pages 216–234.
21. B. Jacobs. *Categorical logic and type theory*. 199-. Book. In preparation.
22. J-P. Jouannaud and M. Okada. Executable higher-order algebraic specification languages. In *Proceedings of LICS'91*, pages 350–361. IEEE Computer Society Press, 1991.
23. J-W. Klop. Term-rewriting systems. In Abramsky et al. [1], pages 1–116. Volume 2.
24. Z. Luo. *Computation and Reasoning: A Type Theory for Computer Science*. Number 11 in International Series of Monographs on Computer Science. Oxford University Press, 1994.
25. B. Nordström, K. Petersson, and J. Smith. *Programming in Martin-Löf's Type Theory. An Introduction.* Number 7 in International Series of Monographs on Computer Science. Oxford University Press, 1990.
26. C. Paulin-Mohring. Inductive definitions in the system Coq. Rules and properties. In M. Bezem and J-F. Groote, editors, *Proceedings of TLCA'93*, volume 664 of *Lecture Notes in Computer Science*, pages 328–345. Springer-Verlag, 1993.
27. M.J. Plasmeijer and M.C.J.D. van Eekelen. Clean 1.0 reference manual. Technical report, Department of Computer Science, University of Nijmegen, 1996. In preparation.

The Calculus of Constructions

We now give a precise definition of the Calculus of Constructions and at the same time we fix some terminology. See for example [5, 17] for more information.

In CC there are two specific constants, $*$ and $\square$. The first represents the universe of *types* (so we shall say that σ *is a type* if $\sigma : *$) and the second represents the universe of *kinds* (so we shall say that A *is a kind* if $A : \square$). The universe $*$ is a specific example of a kind, so it will be the case that $* : \square$. To present the derivation rules for CC we first fix the set of *pseudoterms* from which the derivation rules select the (typable) terms.

Definition 5 *The set T of pseudoterms is defined by the following abstract syntax*

$$T = V \mid * \mid \Box \mid TT \mid \Pi V : T.T \mid \lambda V : T.T$$

where V is a countable set of variables. Both Π and λ bind variables and we have the usual notions of free variable *and* bound variable. *The substitution of N for v in M is denoted by $M[N/v]$. On T we have the usual notion of β-reduction, denoted by $\longrightarrow_\beta$. We also adopt from the untyped λ calculus the conventions of denoting the transitive reflexive closure of $\longrightarrow_\beta$ by $\twoheadrightarrow_\beta$ and the transitive symmetric closure of $\twoheadrightarrow_\beta$ by $=_\beta$.*

The typing of terms is done under the assumption of specific types for the free variables that occur in the term. These are listed in a *context*, which is a sequence of declarations $v_1{:}T_1, \ldots, v_n{:}T_n$, where the v_i are distinct variables and the T_i are pseudoterms. Contexts are denoted by the symbol Γ. For Γ a context and v a variable, v is said to be *Γ-fresh* if it is not among the variables that are declared in Γ.

Definition 6 *The Calculus of Constructions (CC) is the typed λ-calculus with the following deduction rules.*

Axiom	$\vdash * : \Box$	
Start	$\dfrac{\Gamma \vdash A : */\Box}{\Gamma, x : A \vdash x : A}$	*if* $x \notin \Gamma$
Weakening	$\dfrac{\Gamma \vdash t : A \quad \Gamma \vdash B : */\Box}{\Gamma, x : B \vdash t : A}$	*if* $x \notin \Gamma$
Product	$\dfrac{\Gamma \vdash A : s_1 \quad \Gamma, x : A \vdash B : s_2}{\Gamma \vdash \Pi x : A.B : s_2}$	$s_1, s_2 \in \{*, \Box\}$
Application	$\dfrac{\Gamma \vdash t : \Pi x : A.B \quad \Gamma \vdash u : A}{\Gamma \vdash tu : B[u/x]}$	
Abstraction	$\dfrac{\Gamma, x : A \vdash t : B \quad \Gamma \vdash \Pi x : A.B : */\Box}{\Gamma \vdash \lambda x : A.t : \Pi x : A.B}$	
Conversion	$\dfrac{\Gamma \vdash u : A \quad \Gamma \vdash B : */\Box}{\Gamma \vdash u : B}$	*if* $A \to_\beta B$ *or* $B \to_\beta A$

The set of terms of CC *is defined by* $\mathsf{Term} = \{A \mid \exists \Gamma, B[\Gamma \vdash A : B \vee \Gamma \vdash B : A]\}$.

Deduction by Combining Semantic Tableaux and Integer Programming*

Bernhard Beckert & Reiner Hähnle

University of Karlsruhe
Institute for Logic, Complexity and Deduction Systems
Am Fasanengarten 5, 76128 Karlsruhe, Germany
{beckert,haehnle}@ira.uka.de, http://i12www.ira.uka.de/

Abstract. In this paper we propose to extend the current capabilities of automated reasoning systems by making use of techniques from integer programming. We describe the architecture of an automated reasoning system based on a Herbrand procedure (enumeration of formula instances) on clauses. The input are arbitrary sentences of first-order logic. The translation into clauses is done incrementally and is controlled by a semantic tableau procedure using unification. This amounts to an incremental polynomial CNF transformation which at the same time encodes part of the tableau structure and, therefore, tableau-specific refinements that reduce the search space. Checking propositional unsatisfiability of the resulting sequence of clauses can either be done with a symbolic inference system such as the Davis-Putnam procedure or it can be done using integer programming. If the latter is used a number of advantages become apparent.

Introduction

In this paper we propose to extend the current capabilities of automated reasoning (AR) systems by combining the inference procedure *semantic tableaux* with integer program (IP) solvers. We show that the resulting system has properties which are interesting for such applications as formal program verification. In Section 1 we summarize some facts on semantic tableaux in order to make the paper reasonably self-contained. In Section 2 we give a tableau-based polynomial time translation from propositional logic into IPs. This translation will be lifted to full first-order logic in Section 3. With an extended example we illustrate how the system is supposed to work (Section 4) and in Section 5 we summarize the possible synergy effects from marrying AR and operations research (OR) in the way suggested. Finally we mention related and ongoing work. We had to omit all proofs due to limited space.

* This research was supported by Deutsche Forschungsgemeinschaft within the Schwerpunktprogramm *Deduktion*.

1 Semantic Tableaux

First we state some standard notions of computational logic that will be used in the following; consult (Fitting, 1996) for details. Let us fix a first-order language whose terms and formulae are built up from countable sets of predicate symbols, function symbols, constant symbols and object variables in the usual manner (for each arity there are countably many function and predicate symbols). We use the logical connectives $\land$ (conjunction), $\lor$ (disjunction), $\supset$ (implication) and $\neg$ (negation), and the quantifier symbols $\forall$ and $\exists$. An *atom* is a formula of the form $p(t_1, \ldots, t_n)$, where p is a predicate symbol and $t_1, \ldots, t_n$ are terms. Atoms and their negations are called *literals*. A *clause* is a disjunction of literals. A formula is in *conjunctive normal form* (CNF) if it is a conjunction of clauses. A variable is *free* if it is not bound by a quantifier ($\forall$ or $\exists$). A *sentence* is a formula not containing any free variables. We use the standard notions of *satisfiability* and *model*. A sentence is called a *tautology* if it is true in all models, i.e., if its negation is unsatisfiable. *Substitutions* are mappings from variables to terms and are extended to formulae as usual. We denote a substitution by $\{x_1 \leftarrow t_1, \ldots, x_n \leftarrow t_n\}$, where $\{x_1, \ldots, x_n\}$ are the variables that occur in the term it is applied to. The application of σ to a term t is denoted by $t\sigma$.

Semantic (or analytic) tableaux are a sound and complete calculus for doing logical inferences in full first-order logic. They were developed in the 1950s from Gentzen systems. For an introduction which covers the material needed here, see (Fitting, 1996). Following Fitting we divide the set of formulae into four classes: α for formulae of conjunctive type, β for formulae of disjunctive type, γ for quantified formulae of universal type, and finally δ for quantified formulae of existential type. This is called *uniform notation*; it simplifies presentation and proofs considerably. The classification is motivated by the *tableau expansion rules* which are associated with each formula. The rules characterize the assertion of a truth value to a formula by means of asserting truth values to its direct subformulae. For example, $\phi \land \psi$ holds if and only if ϕ and ψ hold. In the upper part of Table 1 the rule schemata for the various formula types are given. Premises and conclusions are separated by a horizontal bar, while vertical bars in the conclusion denote different *extensions* which are to be thought as disjunctions. In the lower part of Table 1 the correspondence between formulae and formula types is shown.

We use *free variable* quantifier rules (Fitting, 1996). Instead of "guessing" ground terms that are instantiated for universally quantified variables, a new *free* variable is introduced, that is instantiated later "on demand" with a term that is useful.

For our purposes it is sufficient to visualize a *tableau* as a finite binary tree, whose nodes are first-order formulae, constructed as follows:

1. A finite linear tree whose nodes are formulae taken from a set Φ of formulae is a tableau for Φ.
2. If T is a tableau for Φ and ϕ is a node from T then a new tableau T' for Φ is constructed by extending a branch of T that contains ϕ by as many new

α	β	γ	δ
α_1 α_2	$\beta_1 \mid \beta_2$	$\gamma_1(y)$ where y is a new free variable.	$\delta_1(f(x_1,\ldots,x_n))$ where f is a new (Skolem) function symbol, and $x_1,\ldots,x_n$ are the free variables occurring in δ.

α	α_1	α_2
$\phi \wedge \psi$	ϕ	ψ
$\neg(\phi \vee \psi)$	$\neg\phi$	$\neg\psi$
$\neg(\phi \supset \psi)$	ϕ	$\neg\psi$
$\neg\neg\phi$	ϕ	ϕ

β	β_1	β_2
$(\phi \vee \psi)$	ϕ	ψ
$\neg(\phi \wedge \psi)$	$\neg\phi$	$\neg\psi$
$(\phi \supset \psi)$	$\neg\phi$	ψ

γ	$\gamma_1(y)$
$(\forall x)\phi(x)$	$\phi(y)$
$\neg(\exists x)\phi(x)$	$\neg\phi(y)$

δ	$\delta_1(f(x_1,\ldots,x_n))$
$\neg(\forall x)\phi(x)$	$\neg\phi(f(x_1,\ldots,x_n))$
$(\exists x)\phi(x)$	$\phi(f(x_1,\ldots,x_n))$

Table 1. Formula types and tableau rule schemata.

linear subtrees as the rule[1] corresponding to ϕ has extensions, the nodes of the new subtrees being labeled with the formulae in the extensions.[2]

A *branch* B of T is a maximal path in T. It is often identified with the set of formulae it contains. A tableau *branch* is *closed* iff it contains a pair of complementary formulae, i.e., formulae of the form ϕ and $\neg\phi$.[3] A *tableau* is *closed* (under σ) iff there is a substitution σ such that all branches $B\sigma$ of $T\sigma$ are closed.

To prove tautologyhood of a formula ϕ we begin with a tree whose single node is labeled by $\neg\phi$, that is we assume that ϕ is false in some model. A tableau proof represents a systematic search for such a model. Every tableau branch corresponds to a partial possible model in which the formulae on the branch are valid. Therefore, a complementary pair of formulae, and thus a closed branch, denotes an explicit contradiction, since in no model both a formula and its negation can be true.

A proof of the following theorem, that states soundness and completeness of semantic tableaux, can be found in (Fitting, 1996).

Theorem 1. *Let ϕ be any first-order sentence. Then there is a closed tableau for $\{\neg\phi\}$ iff ϕ is a first-order tautology.*

[1] It is obtained by looking up the subformulae corresponding to ϕ and instantiating the matching rule schema (Table 1).

[2] From the two formulae in the conclusion of a double negation only one copy needs to be kept. Moreover, it is is sufficient for completeness to apply α-, β- and δ-rules only once to every formula in each branch. Consequently, formulae of these types may be deleted locally to the current branch after rule application. Note, however, that γ-formulae must be used repeatedly sometimes and hence may not be removed.

[3] It is sufficient merely to consider complementary pairs of *atomic* formulae.

Using the deduction theorem for first order logic[4], an immediate corollary of Theorem 1 is that for all sentences $\phi_1, \ldots, \phi_n, \phi$: $\{\phi_1, \ldots, \phi_n\} \models \phi$ iff there is a closed tableau for $\{\phi_1, \ldots, \phi_n, \neg\phi\}$.

Tableau construction for a set of formulae Φ is a highly non-deterministic procedure. We did not specify, for example, in which order the tableau rules should be applied to the formulae on a branch, or how a closing substitution should be searched for.

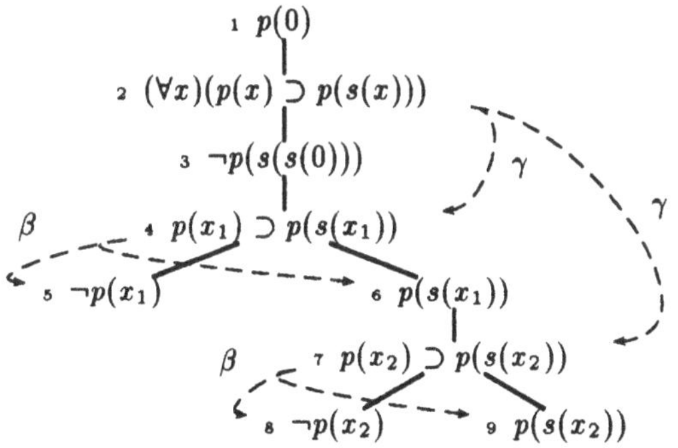

Fig. 1. The tableau proof described in Example 1.

Example 1. The tableau shown in Figure 1 proves that $p(s(s(0)))$ is a logical consequence of $\{p(0),\ (\forall x)(p(x) \supset p(s(x)))\}$. Formulae (1)–(3) are put on the tableau initially. Formula (4) is derived from (2) by applying the γ-rule, and then (5) and (6) are added by applying the β-rule to (4). Now, the left branch is closed under the substitution $\{x_1 \leftarrow 0\}$ by (1) and (5). The right branch of the tableau is not closed under $\{x_1 \leftarrow 0\}$; thus, the γ-rule has to be applied a second time to (2) to derive (7), and then (8) and (9) from (7). At that point the whole tableau is closed under the substitution $\{x_1 \leftarrow 0,\ x_2 \leftarrow s(0)\}$, the middle branch by (6) and (8), and the right branch by (3) and (9). The middle branch could have been closed under the substitution $\{x_2 \leftarrow 0\}$ as well (using (1) and (8)); this, however, would have been useless and does not close the branch on the right. There is a refinement of semantic tableaux called regularity (Letz *et al.*, 1992) that can avoid such closures: it is not allowed to put two identical formulae on a branch. This condition would be violated under the substitution $\{x_2 \leftarrow 0\}$, because (6) and (9) would then become identical.

2 Translating Semantic Tableaux into Integer Programs

In this section we describe a method using semantic tableaux for translating a *propositional*[5] formula ϕ (which *needs not* to be in any normal form) into a

[4] For all sentences $\phi_1, \ldots, \phi_n, \phi$: $\{\phi_1, \ldots, \phi_n\} \models \phi$ iff $(\phi_1 \wedge \ldots \wedge \phi_n) \supset \phi$ is a tautology (where $\models$ denotes the logical consequence relation).

[5] Lifting of this method to full first-order logic is described in Section 3.

0-1-IP C such that ϕ is satisfiable iff C is feasible. Tableau rules are used to split and transform ϕ, whereas IP methods are used to check whether the resulting tableau is closed.

For propositional CNF formulae there is a well-known standard translation into 0-1-IPs: Each clause of the form

$$p_1 \vee \ldots \vee p_k \vee \neg p_{k+1} \vee \ldots \vee \neg p_m \qquad (1 \leq k \leq m)$$

corresponds to the constraint

$$p_1 + \cdots + p_k + (1 - p_{k+1}) + \cdots + (1 - p_m) \geq 1 \ .$$

The question whether a single tableau branch B is closed can as well be easily transformed into a 0-1-IP: B is closed iff the set of constraints

$$\{p \geq 1 \ : \ p \in B, \, p \text{ is an atom}\} \cup \{p \leq 0 \ : \ \neg p \in B, \, p \text{ is an atom}\}$$

is infeasible. Using this translation, the question whether a whole tableau T is closed results in a disjunctive programming problem: T is closed iff there is a solution to one of the IPs constructed for each of its branches; that way, nothing is gained by using IPs, because the transformation does not make use of their expressiveness.

Instead, we use techniques similar to that of disjunctive programming to encode a whole tableau, including its structure, into a single 0-1-IP. This translation makes use of *signed* formulae[6]. A signed formula is a string of the form $\boxed{\geq i}\,\phi$, where ϕ is a (propositional or first-order) formula and i is a linear expression (for example $1 - j_1 + j_2$). The sign associates a logical truth value with the formula. For example, $\boxed{\geq 1}\,\phi$ means that ϕ is true. One could add signs of the form $\boxed{\leq i}\,\phi$ to express "ϕ is false" by $\boxed{\leq 0}\,\phi$; this, however, is not necessary as we may use $\boxed{\geq 1}\,\neg\phi$ instead. By employing signed formulae, tableau rules that are linear for β-formulae (in contrast to the rules in Table 1) can be defined, see the second rule in Table 2. To generate a 0-1-IP, two additional rules are needed that translate literals into constraints, see the two rules on the right of Table 2.

$\dfrac{\boxed{\geq i}\,\alpha}{\begin{array}{l}\boxed{\geq i}\,\alpha_1 \\ \boxed{\geq i}\,\alpha_2\end{array}}$	$\dfrac{\boxed{\geq i}\,\beta}{\begin{array}{l}\boxed{\geq i-j}\,\beta_1 \\ \boxed{\geq i+j-1}\,\beta_2\end{array}}$ where j is a new IP variable.	$\dfrac{\boxed{\geq i}\,p}{p \geq i}$	$\dfrac{\boxed{\geq i}\,\neg p}{1 - p \geq i}$

Table 2. Propositional rules for signed α-formulae, β-formulae, and literals (p is an atomic formula).

[6] Signed formulae (with different types of signs) are frequently used in semantic tableaux for non-classical logics, e.g. multiple-valued logics (Hähnle, 1994a).

There is, of course, a price to be paid for the linearity of the disjunctive β-rules. New variables are introduced by their application, that we call *branching variables*. Each assignment of 0/1-values to the branching variables in the resulting IP corresponds to one of the tableau branches and, thus, to a partial model. If, for example, by assigning values to $j_1, \ldots, j_k$, a linear expression $i = i(j_1, \ldots, j_k)$ evaluates to 1, then $\boxed{\geq i}\,\phi$ means that ϕ is part of the branch B corresponding to that assignment and is valid in the partial model associated with B.

The rules from Table 2 can be used to step by step transform a set of signed formulae into an IP:

Definition 2. Let $\Phi = \{\phi_1, \ldots, \phi_k\}$ be a set of propositional formulae, and let the sequence $C_0, \ldots, C_n$ be formed according to the following rules:

1. $C_0 = \{\boxed{\geq 1}\,\phi_1, \ldots, \boxed{\geq 1}\,\phi_k\}$,
2. C_m is derived from C_{m-1} by applying one of the tableau rules from Table 2 to $\psi \in C_{m-1}$ and replacing ψ by the result of the transformation $(1 \leq m \leq n)$.
3. C_n consists only of constraints (i.e., there are no a signed formulae left).

Then C_n is a *0-1-IP associated with* Φ.

The following soundness and completeness theorem holds:

Theorem 3. *If C is a 0-1-IP associated with a set Φ of propositional formulae (Def. 2), then:*

C is infeasible iff Φ is unsatisfiable.

Theorem 3 implies that a propositional formula ϕ is a tautology iff the IP(s) associated with $\{\neg\phi\}$ are infeasible.

Example 2. Let $\Phi = \{p \vee \neg p\}$; then $C_0 = \{\boxed{\geq 1}\,(p \vee \neg p)\}$. By applying the β-rule we obtain $C_1 = \{\boxed{\geq 1-j}\,p, \boxed{\geq 1+j-1}\,\neg p\}$; the literal rules are applied to derive the 0-1-IP

$$C_3 = \{ \quad p \geq 1 - j\,, \quad 1 - p \geq 1 + j - 1\}$$

that is associated with Φ. Since C_3 is feasible, $p \vee \neg p$ has to be satisfiable (which is, of course, true).

The two possible assignments of values (0 or 1) to the branching variable j correspond to the two branches of the semantic tableau for $p \vee \neg p$, and thus to the two possible models, in which p is either true or false.

In case β_1 or β_2 is a literal, the β rule can be optimized inasmuch as the introduction of an additional variable can be avoided; the variable is simply replaced by the literal itself, which then becomes part of the constraint (Table 3).

Using this optimization, the formula from Example 2 is transformed into the single constraint $1 - p \geq 1 - p$ whose feasibility (for all values of p) can be seen immediately. Taking this optimization into account our translation collapses into the standard translation mentioned at the beginning of this section in the case of CNF input.

$$\frac{\boxed{\geq i}\,(p \vee \beta_2)}{\boxed{\geq i-p}\,\beta_2} \qquad \frac{\boxed{\geq i}\,(\beta_1 \vee p)}{\boxed{\geq i-p}\,\beta_1} \qquad \frac{\boxed{\geq i}\,(\neg p \vee \beta_2)}{\boxed{\geq i-(1-p)}\,\beta_2} \qquad \frac{\boxed{\geq i}\,(\beta_1 \vee \neg p)}{\boxed{\geq i-(1-p)}\,\beta_1}$$

Table 3. Optimized β-rules in the case when β_1 or β_2 is a literal (p is an atom).

3 Lifting to First-order Logic

Our lifting of the method described in the previous section to first-order logic is based on Herbrand's Theorem[7]. A set Φ of first-order sentences is first transformed into an IP containing free variables[8]. Then, new instances of the parts of the IP that correspond to universally quantified (sub-)formulae are added to the problem until it becomes infeasible (if Φ is satisfiable this process does, in general, not terminate, because satisfiability of first-order sentences is undecidable).

The transformation rules for quantified formulae (γ- and δ-rules) from Table 1 can be adapted to signed formulae straightforwardly. The α-rules and the rules for literals (Table 2) remain unchanged for first-order logic. The β-formulae, however, become slightly more complicated. It is necessary to parameterize the branching variables with some of the free variables. The first-order rules are shown in Table 4.

$\dfrac{\boxed{\geq i}\,\beta}{\boxed{\geq i-j(x_1,\ldots,x_n)}\,\beta_1 \quad \boxed{\geq i+j(x_1,\ldots,x_n)-1}\,\beta_2}$	$\dfrac{\boxed{\geq i}\,\gamma}{\boxed{\geq i}\,\gamma_1(y)}$	$\dfrac{\boxed{\geq i}\,\delta}{\boxed{\geq i}\,\delta_1(f(x_1,\ldots,x_n))}$
where j is a new n-ary predicate symbol, and $x_1,\ldots,x_n$ are the free variables occurring both in β_1 and β_2.	where y is a new free variable.	where f is a new (Skolem) function symbol, and $x_1,\ldots,x_n$ are the free variables occurring in δ.

Table 4. First-order constraint rules for β-, γ-, and δ-formulae.

The definition of IPs associated with a set of formulae has to be adapted. Since more than one instance of universally quantified (sub-)formulae may be needed, a mechanism has to be added that allows to duplicate and instantiate parts of the IP (Rule 2(b) in the definition):

---

[7] A set Φ of clauses is unsatisfiable iff there is an unsatisfiable *finite* set of *ground* (i.e. variable-free) instances of clauses from Φ.

[8] These free variables should not be confused with IP variables in constraints (e.g. branching variables). IP variables correspond to atomic formulae and, thus, might *contain* free variables.

Definition 4. Let $\Phi = \{\phi_1, \ldots, \phi_k\}$ be a set of first-order sentences and let the sequence $\mathcal{C}_0, \ldots, \mathcal{C}_n$ be formed according to the following rules:

1. $\mathcal{C}_0 = \{\boxed{\geq 1}\,\phi_1, \ldots, \boxed{\geq 1}\,\phi_k\}$,
2. (a) $\mathcal{C}_m$ is derived from $\mathcal{C}_{m-1}$ by applying the α- or the literal rules from Table 2, or the β, γ-, or δ-rules from Table 4 to $\psi \in \mathcal{C}_{m-1}$ and replacing ψ by the result of the transformation $(1 \leq m \leq n)$;[9] or
   (b) there is a substitution σ such that $\mathcal{C}_m = \mathcal{C}_{m-1} \cup (\mathcal{C}_{m-1}\sigma)$.
3. $\mathcal{C}_n$ consists only of constraints (that is, no signed formulae are left).

Then $\mathcal{C}_n$ is a *(first-order) 0-1-IP associated with* Φ.

Optimized versions of the β-rule in case when β_1 or β_2 is a literal (similar to those in Table 3) can still be used.

The following soundness and completeness theorem for first-order logic holds; note, that in general not every IP associated with an unsatisfiable set of formulae is infeasible (in contrast to the propositional case, Theorem 3).

Theorem 5. *A finite set* Φ *of first-order sentences is unsatisfiable iff at least one of the first-order 0-1-IPs associated with* Φ *is infeasible.*

This theorem implies soundness and completeness of the following procedure that can be used to prove a first-order formula ϕ to be a tautology:

1. Apply α-, β-, γ-, δ-, and literal rules as long as possible to derive from $\mathcal{C}_0 = \{\boxed{\geq 1}\,\neg\phi\}$ the 0-1-IP $\mathcal{C}$
2. **if** the 0-1-IP $\mathcal{C}$ is *infeasible*
   then STOP ($\neg\phi$ is unsatisfiable; ϕ is a tautology)
3. Choose a solution L of $\mathcal{C}$, $L :$ Atoms$(\mathcal{C}) \rightarrow \{0, 1\}$
4. **if** there are σ, p, q, such that $\sigma(p) = \sigma(q)$ but $L(p) \neq L(q)$
   then $\mathcal{C} := \mathcal{C} \cup \sigma(\mathcal{C})$; GOTO 2
   else STOP ($\neg\phi$ satisfiable; ϕ is not a tautology)

Note, that the choice of the solution L is non-deterministic; for completeness backtracking has to be used or fairness strategies have to be employed. Since the substitutions σ, that are applied to generate new instances, are computed by analyzing the solutions of the IPs, and since this analysis is global (and is not restricted to single tableau branches), the search space is much smaller than that for semantic tableaux.

The pairs of atoms p, q that can be used to remove a solution are called *links*. It is a good heuristic to prefer links that involve an atom (p or q) that is part of as few links as possible. This heuristic can be encoded into a minimization problem and integrated into the IP.

[9] Note, that γ-rules, too, are removed and replaced by γ_1.

4 Example

As an example we use the procedure described above to prove (again) the formula from Example 1 to be a tautology, i.e., that $\Phi = \{p(0),\ (\forall x)(p(x) \supset p(s(x))),\ \neg p(s(s(x)))\}$ is unsatisfiable. We initialize

$$\mathcal{C}_0 = \{\boxed{\geq 1}\,p(0),\ \boxed{\geq 1}\,(\forall x)(p(x) \supset p(s(x))),\ \boxed{\geq 1}\,\neg p(s(s(x)))\}\ .$$

By applying the literal rules (Table 2) to $\boxed{\geq 1}\,p(0)$ and $\boxed{\geq 1}\,\neg p(s(s(x)))$ we derive the constraints

$$p(0) \geq 1 \tag{1}$$

$$1 - p(s(s(0))) \geq 1 \tag{2}$$

From $\boxed{\geq 1}\,(\forall x)(p(x) \supset p(s(x)))$ we derive $\boxed{\geq 1}\,(p(x) \supset p(s(x)))$ using the γ-rule (Table 4), then $\boxed{\geq 1-(1-p(x))}\,p(s(x))$ by applying the optimized β-rule[10], and finally using the literal rule $p(s(x)) \geq 1 - (1 - p(x))$, i.e.,

$$(1 - p(x)) + p(s(x)) \geq 1 \tag{3}$$

The 0-1-IP $\mathcal{C}$ consisting of (1)–(3) is feasible. We (arbitrarily) chose the solution L_1, where $L_1(p(0)) = L_1(p(s(x))) = 1$ and $L_1(p(s(s(0)))) = L_1(p(x)) = 0$. This solution can be removed using the link $p(0), p(x)$, since $L_1(p(0)) \neq L_1(p(x))$, but $\sigma_1(p(0)) = \sigma_1(p(x))$, where $\sigma_1 = \{x \leftarrow 0\}$. Thus, we carry on with the IP $\mathcal{C} \cup \mathcal{C}\sigma_1$, i.e., we add the constraint

$$(1 - p(0)) + p(s(0)) \geq 1 \tag{4}$$

The new problem (1)–(4) is still feasible. One solution is L_2, where $L_2(p(0)) = L_2(p(s(0))) = L_2(p(s(x))) = 1$ and $L_2(p(s(s(0)))) = L_2(p(x)) = 0$. We remove the solution using the link $p(s(0)), p(x)$ and apply $\sigma_2 = \{x \leftarrow s(0)\}$ to add

$$(1 - p(s(0))) + p(s(s(0))) \geq 1 \tag{5}$$

The resulting 0-1-IP (1)–(5) is infeasible, which proves Φ to be unsatisfiable.

It is obviously useless to use the link $p(0), p(x)$ to remove the solution L_2, because (4) would be added a second time. In general it is not as easy to recognize useless links; fortunately, it is possible to adapt regularity (described in Example 1) and other strategies known from semantic tableaux to avoid using such links.

---

[10] Applying the non-optimized β-rule from Table 2 results in the two formulae $\boxed{\geq 1-j(x)}\,\neg p(x)$ and $\boxed{\geq 1+j(x)-1}\,p(s(x))$ containing a branching variable, and finally in the constraints $j(x) + (1 - p(x)) \geq 1$ and $(1 - j(x)) + p(s(x)) \geq 1$.

5 Synergy Effects

The fact that logical formulae and the linear fragment of arithmetic are mapped into the same domain allows an efficient representation of the search space associated with formulae as they typically occur in verification conditions during formal program verification. Arithmetic properties are awkward to define by purely logical means. On the other hand, if a special machinery for dealing with purely arithmetical subproblems is used, tough problems with redundancy and fairness tend to emerge. It is possible to view first-order formulae over linear arithmetic as an *extension* of IP and the presented mechanism as a solver that makes use of AR techniques to gain efficiency.

As a tableau procedure is used to produce instances of formulae, the input is not restricted to any normal form; for the same reason an adaptation of the technique to certain non-classical logics is possible, see (Hähnle, 1994b; Hähnle & Ibens, 1994). Both properties are important for many applications.

Reductions of the search space (such as the regularity restriction defined above) as they are commonly found in tableau-oriented procedures can be built into the translation. The same holds for polynomial CNF transformation, cf. (Plaisted & Greenbaum, 1986), and for an optimized version of skolemization (Hähnle & Schmitt, 1994).

The amount of backtracking which normally occurs in tableaux is greatly reduced due to the efficient representation of a whole tableau which still can be checked rapidly for closure (unsatisfiability). This kind of representation makes it also possible to define subsumption within the IPs. Moreover, the cost function of integer programs can be employed to suggest substitutions that lead to a favorable structure of the search space. In addition, a meaningful cost function often improves the behavior of IP solvers.

Many IP solvers allow incremental solutions. Moreover, IP solvers tend to find solutions of satisfiable problems quickly. Hence, they promise to be efficient for large, combinatorially not too hard, and mostly satisfiable problems such as they result from large formal specifications. Specific techniques for managing sparse matrices will be of advantage for such problems as well.

Problem dependent heuristics can often be encoded as arithmetical properties in which case they can be represented at the same level as the problems themselves.

Some IP techniques such as detection of simple (polynomially solvable) cases, generation of certain strong cuts or various pre-processing aids have no direct logical counterparts. Therefore, it can be hoped that such techniques can solve some problems quickly, where symbolic inference is in trouble.

Conclusion

Related Work The inference procedure as sketched in this paper is reminiscent of the *Primal Partial Instantiation Method* developed by Hooker (1993) and

Rago (1994). The latter derives its name from the analogy between the generation of new inequalities in the primal simplex method of Dantzig (1963) for solving linear programs and the generation of new clauses/inequations in the procedure outlined above. Our proposal differs from Hooker and Rago's mainly in the following points: (i) we work with full first-order logic, not only with function-free universal clauses; (ii) our procedure encodes part of the structure of a semantic tableau into the generated inequations; (iii) we take advantage of the optimizing part of IP solvers for computing links (*blocks* in the terminology of Hooker and Rago) with a minimal number of alternatives, whereas Rago (1994) does not consider the use of IPs, but generates sequences of ground (variable-free) clauses.

Further related work is (Kagan *et al.*, 1994) which provides a translation (working as well by partial instantiation) from definite logic programs into linear programs. It is restricted to the area of logic programming and, as the authors concede, linear programming is not specifically exploited and could be substituted by a symbolic inference procedure.

Ongoing and Future Work A prototypical implementation of the suggested procedure has been completed (it is written in Prolog and is based on a commercial IP solver); using this implementation we are now evaluating various heuristics.

Summary On the meta-level the potential synergy effects of putting together AR and OR can be summarized as follows:

1. A mixed approach can switch implementation paradigms whenever it is of advantage.
2. Some techniques of AR have no OR counterpart and vice versa. A mixed procedure can employ all of them.
3. Finally, an occasional change of the point of view often results in new ideas such as the usage of cost functions to compute substitutions.

References

DANTZIG, GEORGE B. 1963. *Linear Programming and Extensions.* Princeton University Press.

FITTING, MELVIN C. 1996. *First-Order Logic and Automated Theorem Proving.* 2nd edn. Springer.

HÄHNLE, REINER. 1994a. *Automated Deduction in Multiple-valued Logics.* International Series of Monographs on Computer Science, vol. 10. Oxford University Press.

HÄHNLE, REINER. 1994b. Many-Valued Logic and Mixed Integer Programming. *Annals of Mathematics and Artificial Intelligence*, **12**(3,4), 231–264.

HÄHNLE, REINER, & IBENS, ORTRUN. 1994. Improving Temporal Logic Tableaux Using Integer Constraints. *Pages 535–539 of: Proceedings, International Conference on Temporal Logic, Bonn, Germany.* Springer LNCS 827.

HÄHNLE, REINER, & SCHMITT, PETER H. 1994. The liberalized δ-rule in free variable semantic tableaux. *Journal of Automated Reasoning,*, **13**(2), 211–222.

HOOKER, JOHN N. 1993. New Methods for Computing Inferences in First Order Logic. *Annals of Operations Research*, **43**.

KAGAN, VADIM, NERODE, ANIL, & SUBRAHMANIAN, V. S. 1994. Computing Definite Logic Programs by Partial Instantiation. *Annals of Pure and Applied Logic*, **67**(1–3), 161–182.

LETZ, REINHOLD, SCHUMANN, JOHANN, BAYERL, STEPHAN, & BIBEL, WOLFGANG. 1992. SETHEO: A High-Performance Theorem Prover. *Journal of Automated Reasoning*, **8**(2), 183–212.

PLAISTED, DAVID A., & GREENBAUM, STEVEN. 1986. A Structure-Preserving Clause Form Translation. *Journal of Symbolic Computation*, **2**, 293–304.

RAGO, GABRIELLA. 1994 (Mar.). *Optimization, Hypergraphs and Logical Inference*. Ph.D. thesis, Dipartimento di Informatica, Università di Pisa. Available as Tech Report TD-4/94.

lean*EA*: A Lean Evolving Algebra Compiler

Bernhard Beckert[1] and Joachim Posegga[2]

[1] University of Karlsruhe, Institute for Logic, Complexity and Deduction Systems, 76128 Karlsruhe, Germany; beckert@ira.uka.de

[2] Deutsche Telekom AG, Research Centre, 64276 Darmstadt, Germany; posegga@fz.telekom.de

Abstract. The Prolog program

```
"term_expansion((define C as A with B), (C=>A:-B,!)).
 term_expansion((transition E if C then D),
               ((transition E):-C,!,B,A,(transition _))) :-
        rearrange(D,B,A).
 rearrange((E,F),(C,D),(A,B)) :-
         rearrange(E,C,B), rearrange(F,D,A).
 rearrange(F:=G, ([G]=>*[E],F=..[C|D],D=>*B,A=..[C|B]),
          asserta(A=>E)).
 [G|H]=>*[E|F] :-
        (G=\E; G=..[C|D],D=>*B,A=..[C|B],A=>E), !,H=>*F.
 []=>*[].
 A=?B :- [A,B]=>*[D,C], D==C."
```

implements an efficient and flexible simulator for evolving algebra specifications.

1 Introduction

Evolving algebras (EAs) (Gurevich, 1991; Gurevich, 1995) are abstract machines used mainly for formal specification of algorithms. The main advantage of EAs over classical formalisms for specifying operational semantics, like Turing machines for instance, is that they have been designed to be usable by human beings: whilst the concrete appearance of a Turing machine has a solely mathematical motivation, EAs try to provide a user friendly and natural—though rigorous—specification tool. The number of specifications using EAs is rapidly growing; examples are specifications of the languages ANSI C (Gurevich & Huggins, 1993) and ISO Prolog (Börger & Rosenzweig, 1995), and of the virtual architecture APE (Börger *et al.*, 1994b). EA specifications have also been used to validate language implementations (e.g., Occam (Börger *et al.*, 1994a)) and distributed protocols (Gurevich & Mani, 1995).

When working with EAs, it is very handy to have a simulator at hand for running the specified algebras. This observation is of course not new and implementations of abstract machines for EAs already exist: Angelica Kappel describes a Prolog-based implementation in (Kappel, 1993), and Jim Huggins reports an implementation written in C. Both implementations are quite sophisticated and offer a convenient language for specifying EAs.

In this paper, we describe a new approach to implementing a simulator for evolving algebras; we focus on deterministic, sequential EAs. Our implementation differs from previous approaches in that it emphasizes on simplicity, flexibility and elegance of the implementation, rather than on sophistication. We present a simple, Prolog-based approach for executing EAs. The underlying idea is to compile EA specifications into Prolog programs. Rather than programming a machine explicitly, we turn the Prolog system itself into a virtual machine for EA specifications: this is achieved by changing the Prolog reader, such that the transformation of EAs into Prolog code takes place whenever the Prolog system reads input. As a result, evolving algebra specifications can be treated like ordinary Prolog programs.

The main advantage of our approach, which we call lean*EA*, is its flexibility: the Prolog program[3] we discuss in the sequel can easily be understood and extended to the needs of concrete specification tasks (non-determinism, special handling of undefined functions, etc.). Furthermore, its flexibility allows to easily embed it into, or interface it with other systems.

The paper is organized as follows: Section 2 briefly explains how a deterministic, untyped EA can be programmed in lean*EA*; no mathematical treatment is given in this section, but it is explained what a user has to do in order to use EAs with lean*EA*. The implementation of the basic version of lean*EA* is explained in parallel. This basic version is characterized mathematically in Section 4 by giving the semantics of lean*EA* programs; Subsection 4.6 summarizes the differences to the standard semantics of EAs, as defined in the Lipari Guide (Gurevich, 1995). In Section 5, a number of purely syntactical extensions are added for the sake of programming convenience, and more semantical extensions like including typed algebras, or implementing non-deterministic evolving algebras are discussed. Section 6 introduces modularized EAs, where Prolog's concept of modules is used to structure the specified algebras. Finally, we draw conclusions from our research in Section 7.

Through the paper we assume the reader to be familiar with the basic ideas behind evolving algebras, and with the basics of Prolog (see e.g. (O'Keefe, 1990)).

2 lean*EA*: the Program and its Use

An algebra can be understood as a formalism for describing static relations between things: there is a universe consisting of the objects we are talking about, and a set of functions mapping members of the universe to other members. *Evolving* algebras offer a formalism for describing changes as well: an evolving algebra "moves" from one state to another, while functions are changed. lean*EA* is a programming language that allows to program this behavior. From a declarative point of view, a lean*EA* program is a specification of an EA. In this section, we explain the implementation of lean*EA*, and how it is used to specify EAs.

[3] The program is available on the *World Wide Web*. The URL for the lean*EA* home page is `http://i12www.ira.uka.de/leanea`.

2.1 Overview

lean*EA* is an extension of standard Prolog, thus a lean*EA* program can be treated like any other Prolog program, i.e., it can be loaded (or compiled) into the underlying Prolog system (provided lean*EA* itself has been loaded before).

lean*EA* has two syntactical constructs for programming an EA: these are *function definitions* of the form

define *Location* **as** *Value* **with** *Goal.*

that specify the initial state of an EA, and *transition definitions*

transition *Name* **if** *Condition* **then** *Updates.*

defining the EA's evolving, i.e., the mapping from one state to another.

The syntax of these syntactical constructs is implemented by a couple of Prolog operators as shown in Figure 1, Lines 1–6.[4]

The signature of EAs is in our approach the set of all ground Prolog terms. The (single) universe, that is not sorted, consists of ground Prolog terms, too; it is not specified explicitly.

Furthermore, the final state(s) of the EA are not given explicitly in lean*EA*; a state S is defined to be final if no transition is applicable in S or if a transition fires that uses undefined functions in its updates.

A specified evolving algebra is started by calling the Prolog goal

```
transition _
```

lean*EA* then recursively searches for applicable transitions and executes them until no more transitions are applicable, or an undefined term is evaluated.

2.2 Representation of States in lean*EA*

Before explaining how function definitions set up the initial state of an EA, we consider the lean*EA* internals for representing states: A state is given by the mapping of locations to their values, i.e., elements of the universe. A location $f(u_1, \ldots, u_n)$, $n \geq 0$, consists of a functor f and arguments $u_1, \ldots, u_n$ that are members of the universe.

Example 1. Assume that `f` denotes a partial function mapping a pair of members of the universe to a single element, and that `2` and `3` are members of the universe. The application of `f` to `2` and `3` is denoted by the Prolog term `f(2,3)`. This location either has a value in the current state, or it is undefined.

Technically, this mapping of locations to values is implemented with a dynamic Prolog predicate `=>/2`, (cf. Fig. 1, Line 7) that behaves as follows: The goal "`Loc => Val`" succeeds if `Loc` is bound to a ground Prolog term that is a

[4] Note, that the precedences of operators (those pre-defined by lean*EA* as well as others used in a lean*EA* program) can influence the semantics of Prolog goals included in lean*EA* programs.

```
:- op(1199,fy,(transition)),  op(1180,xfx,(if)),
   op(1192,fy,(define)),      op(1185,xfy,(with)),
   op(1190,xfy,(as)),         op(1170,xfx,(then)),
   op(900,xfx,(=>)),          op(900,xfx,(=>*)),
   op(900,xfx,(:=)),          op(900,xfx,(=?)),
   op(100,fx,(\)).

:- multifile (=>)/2.
:- dynamic (=>)/2.

term_expansion((define Location as Value with Goal),
               ((Location => Value) :- Goal,!)).

term_expansion((transition Name if Condition then Updates),
               (transition(Name) :-
                  (Condition,!,
                   FrontCode,BackCode,transition(_)))) :-
        rearrange(Updates,FrontCode,BackCode).

rearrange((A,B),(FrontA,FrontB),(BackB,BackA)) :-
        rearrange(A,FrontA,BackA),
        rearrange(B,FrontB,BackB).

rearrange((LocTerm := Expr),
          ([Expr] =>* [Val], LocTerm =.. [Func|Args],
           Args =>* ArgVals, Loc =..[Func|ArgVals]),
          asserta(Loc => Val)).

([H|T] =>* [HVal|TVal]) :-
       (   H = \HVal
       ;   H  =.. [Func|Args], Args =>* ArgVals,
           H1 =.. [Func|ArgVals], H1 => HVal
       ),!,
       T =>* TVal.

[] =>* [].

(S =? T) :- ([S,T] =>* [Val1,Val2]), Val1 == Val2.
```

Fig. 1. lean*EA*: the Program

location in the algebra, and if a value is defined for this location; then `Val` is bound to that value. The goal fails if no value is defined for `Loc` in the current state of the algebra.

To evaluate a function call like, for example, `f(f(2,3),3)`, lean*EA* uses `=>*/2` as an evaluation predicate: the relation *t* `=>*` *v* holds for ground Prolog terms *t* and *v* if the value of *t*—where *t* is interpreted as a function call—is *v* (in the current state of the algebra).

In general, the arguments of a function call are not necessarily elements of the universe (contrary to the arguments of a location), but are expressions that are recursively evaluated. For the sake of convenience, one can refer to members of the universe in function calls explicitly: these are denoted by preceding them with a backslash "\"; no evaluation of whatever Prolog term comes after a backslash is performed. We will refer to this as *quoting* in the sequel.

For economical reasons, the predicate `=>*/2` actually maps a *list* of function calls to a list of values. Figure 1, Lines 23–28, shows the Prolog code for `=>*`: if the term to be evaluated (bound to the first argument of the predicate) is preceded with a backslash, the term itself is the result of the evaluation; otherwise, all arguments are recursively evaluated and the value of the term is looked up with the predicate `=>/2`. Easing the evaluation of the arguments of terms is the reason for implementing `=>*` over lists. The base step of the recursion is the identity of the empty list (Line 29). `=>*` fails if the value of the function call is undefined in the current state.

Example 2. Consider again the binary function `f`, and assume it behaves like addition in the current state of the algebra. Then both the goals

`[f(\1,\2)] =>* [X]` and `[f(f(\0,\1),\2)] =>* [X]`

succeed with binding `X` to `3`. The goals

`[f(\f(0,1),\2)] =>* [X]` and `[f(f(0,1),\2)] =>* [X]`

will fail since, in the first case, the term `f(0,1)` is not an integer but a location, and, in the second case, `0` and `1` are undefined constants (0-ary functions).

2.3 Function Definitions

The initial state of an EA is specified by a sequence of function definitions. They define the initial values of locations by providing Prolog code to compute these values. A construct of the form

define *Location* **as** *Value* **with** *Goal*.

gives a procedure for computing the value of a location that matches the Prolog term *Location*: if *Goal* succeeds, then *Value* is taken as the value of this location. Function definitions set up the predicate `=>` (and thus `=>*`) in the initial state. One function definition can specify values for more than one functor of the algebra. It is possible in principle, although quite inconvenient, to define all functors within a single function definition. The value computed for a location may depend on the additional Prolog code in a lean*EA*-program (code besides function and transition definitions), since *Goal* may call any Prolog predicate. If several function definitions define values for a single location, the (textually) first definition is chosen.

lean*EA* translates a function definition into a Prolog clause

(*Location* => *Value*) :- *Goal*,!.

Since each definition is mapped into one such clause, *Goal* must not contain a cut "!"; otherwise, the cut might prevent Prolog from considering subsequent => clauses that match a certain location.

Technically, the translation of define statements to a => clauses is implemented by modifying the Prolog reader as shown in Figure 1, Lines 9–10.[5]

Examples for Function Definitions

Constants The following definition assigns the value 1 to the constant reg1:

```
define reg1 as 1 with true.
```

Prolog Data Types Prolog Data Types are easily imported into the algebra. Here is how to introduce lists:

```
define X as X with X=[]; X=[H|T].
```

This causes all lists to evaluate to themselves; thus a list in a transition refers to the same list in the universe and needs not to be quoted. Similarly,

```
define X as X with integer(X).
```

introduces Prolog's integers.

Evaluating Functions by Calling Prolog Predicates The following example interfaces Prolog predicates with an evolving algebra:

```
define X+Y as Z with Z is X+Y.
define append(X,Y) as Result with append(X,Y,Result).
```

Input and Output Useful definitions for input and output are

```
define read as X with read(X).
define output(X) as X with write(X).
```

Whilst the purpose of read should be immediate, the returning of the argument of output might not be clear: the idea is that the returned value can be used in expressions. That is, an expression of the form f(\1,output(\2)) will print 2 while it is evaluated.

[5] In most Prolog dialects (e.g., SICStus Prolog and Quintus Prolog) the Prolog reader is changed by adding clauses for the term_expansion/2 predicate. If a term t is read, and term_expansion(t,S) succeeds and binds the variable S to a term s, then the Prolog reader replaces t by s.

Necessary Conditions for Function Definitions The design of lean*EA* constrains function definitions in several ways; it is important to understand these restrictions, since they are not checked by lean*EA*. Thus, the programmer of an EA has to ensure that:

1. All computed values are *ground* Prolog terms, and the goals for computing them either fail or succeed (i.e.: terminate) for all possible instantiations that might appear. Prolog exceptions that terminate execution must be avoided as well.[6]
2. The goals do not change the Prolog data base or have any side effects affecting other computations.
3. The goals do not (syntactically) contain a cut "!".
4. The goals do not call the lean*EA* internal predicates **transition/1**, **=>*/2**, and =>/2.

Violating these rules does not necessarily mean that lean*EA* will not function properly; however, unless one is very well aware of what he/she is doing, we strongly recommend against it.

2.4 Transition Definitions

Transitions (called *guarded multi-update instructions* in the Lipari Guide) specify the evolving of an EA. An applicable transition maps one state of an EA to a new state by changing the value of locations. Transitions are specified as:[7]

transition *Name* **if** *Condition* **then** *Updates.*

where

Name is an arbitrary Prolog term (usually an atom).
Condition is a Prolog goal that determines when the transition is applicable. It usually contains calls to the predicate **=?/2** (see Section 2.4 below), and often uses the logical Prolog operators "," (conjunction), ";" (disjunction), "->" (implication), and "\+" (negation).
Updates is a comma-separated sequence of updates of the form

$$f_1(r_{11},\ldots,r_{1n_1}) \texttt{ := } v_1\texttt{,}$$
$$\vdots$$
$$f_k(r_{k1},\ldots,r_{kn_k}) \texttt{ := } v_k$$

[6] Defining + by "**define X+Y as Z with integer(X), integer(Y), Z is X+Y.**" is, for instance, safe in this respect.

[7] Guarded multi-updates (if-then-else constructs that may be nested) make EAs more convenient; lean*EA* can be extended to allow guarded multi-updates by changing the predicate **rearrange** such that it (recursively) translates guarded multi-updates into Prolog's if-then-else.

An update $f_i(r_{i1}, \ldots, r_{in_i}) := v_i$ $(1 \leq i \leq k)$ changes the value of the location that consists of (a) the functor f_i and (b) the elements of the universe that are the values of the function calls $r_{i1}, \ldots, r_{in_i}$; the new value of this location is determined by evaluating the function call v_i. All function calls in the updates are evaluated simultaneously (i.e., in the old state). If one of the function calls is undefined, the assignment fails.[8]

A transition is applicable (fires) in a state, if *Condition* succeeds. For calculating the successor state, the (textually) first applicable transition is selected, and its *Updates* are executed (i.e., several firing transitions are not executed simultaneously, see Sections 3 and 4.6). If no transition fires or if one of the updates of the first firing transition fails, the new state cannot be computed. In that case, the evolving algebra terminates, i.e., the current state is final. Otherwise, the computation continues iteratively with calculating further states of the algebra.

Technically, lean*EA* maps a transition of the above form into a Prolog clause

```
transition(Name) :-
        Condition, !,
        UpdateCode,
        transition(_).
```

Likewise to function definitions, this is achieved by modifying the Prolog reader as shown in Figure 1, Lines 11–15.

Since the updates in transitions must be executed simultaneously, all function calls have to be evaluated before the first assignment takes place. The auxiliary predicate **rearrange/3** (Lines 16–22) serves this purpose: it splits all updates into evaluation code, that uses the predicate `=>*/2`, and into subsequent code for storing the new values by asserting an appropriate `=>/2` clause.[9] The sequential code generated by **rearrange** thus simulates a simultaneous update.

The Equality Relation Besides logical operators, lean*EA* allows in the condition of transitions the use of the pre-defined predicate `=?/2` (Fig. 1, Line 30) implementing the equality relation: the goal "s =? t" succeeds if the function calls s and t evaluate (in the current state) to the same element of the universe. It fails, if one of the calls is undefined or if they evaluate to different elements.

[8] If the left-hand side of an update is quoted by a preceding backslash, the update will have no effect besides that the right-hand side is evaluated, i.e., attempts to change the meaning of the backslash are ignored.

[9] To retract the old value from the database and, thus, reduce the memory usage during run-time, one could insert the line

```
( clause((Loc => _),true),retract(Loc => _) ; true ),
```

between Lines 21 and 22. (Note, that the default values specifying the initial state will not be retracted, since these clauses have a non-empty body.) We favored, however, the smaller and slightly faster version that does not retract old values.

2.5 An Example Algebra

We conclude this section with an example for an evolving algebra: Figure 2 shows a lean*EA* program which is the specification of an EA for computing $n!$. The constant **state** is used for controlling the firing of transitions: in the initial state, only the transition **start** fires and reads an integer; it assigns the input value to **reg1**. The transition **step** iteratively computes the factorial of **reg1**'s value by decrementing **reg1** and storing the intermediate results in **reg2**. If the value of **reg1** is 1, the computation is complete, and the only applicable transition **result** prints **reg2**. After this, the algebra halts since no further transition fires and a final state is reached.

```
define state as initial with true.
define readint as X with read(X), integer(X).
define write(X) as X with write(X).
define X as X with integer(X).
define X-Y as R with integer(X),integer(Y),R is X-Y.
define X*Y as R with integer(X),integer(Y),R is X*Y.

transition step
     if   state =? \running, \+(reg1 =? 1)
     then reg1 := reg1-1,
          reg2 := (reg2*reg1).

transition start
     if   state =? \initial
     then reg1  := readint,
          reg2  := 1,
          state := \running.

transition result
     if   state =? \running, reg1 =? 1
     then reg2  := write(reg2),
          state := \final.
```

Fig. 2. An Evolving Algebra for Computing $n!$ (in lean*EA* Syntax)

3 Some Hints for Programmers

Simultaneous Execution of Transitions. If more than one transition fires in a state, lean*EA* executes only the (textually) first one—in difference to (Gurevich, 1995), where such transitions are executed simultaneously (see Section 4.6). There is, however, an easy way to make sure that in all states only one transition fires and that, therefore, leanEA programs behave according to the semantics as defined in the Lipari Guide: If there are two transitions

```
transition N1 if C1 then Update1.
transition N2 if C2 then Update2.
```

in a leanEA program, where the conditions C_1 and C_2 may both become true in some state of the EA, a new transition

```
transition N0 if (C1,C2) then Update1,Update2.
```

is inserted before N_1 and N_2. In general, for every subset $\mathcal{S} = \{T_1, \ldots, T_k\}$ ($k \geq 2$) of transitions in a program that may all fire simultaneously in some state, a new transition $T_{\mathcal{S}}$ =

```
transition NS if (C1,...,Ck) then Update1,...,Updatek.
```

is added to the program. To make sure that in all states the most general of the new transitions is executed, $T_{\mathcal{S}}$ has to be placed before other new transitions $T_{\mathcal{S}'}$ if $\mathcal{S} \supset \mathcal{S}'$, and before the old transitions $T_i \in \mathcal{S}$.

Final States. The basic version of leanEA does not have an explicit construct for specifying the final state of an EA; instead, the algebra is in a final state if no more transition is applicable. A more declarative way to halt an algebra is to evaluate an undefined expression, like "`stop := stop`".

Tracing Transitions. Programming in leanEA—like in any other programming language—usually requires debugging. For tracing transitions, it is often useful to include calls to `write` or `trace` at the end of conditions: the code will be executed whenever the transition fires and it allows to provide information about the state of the EA.

Tracing the Evaluation of Terms. A definition of the form

```
define f(X) as _ with write(f(X)), fail.
```

will trace the evaluation of functions: if the above function definition precedes the "actual" definition of `f(X)`, it will print the expression to be evaluated whenever the evaluation takes place.

Examining States. All defined values of locations in the current state can be listed by calling the Prolog predicate `listing(=>)`. Note, that this does not show any default values.

4 Semantics

This section formalizes the semantics of leanEA programs, in the sense that it explains in detail which evolving algebra is specified by a concrete leanEA-program.

Definition 1. Let P be a leanEA-program; then $\mathcal{D}_P$ denotes the sequence of function definitions in P (in the order in which they occur in P), $\mathcal{T}_P$ denotes the sequence of transition definitions in P (in the order in which they occur in P), and $\mathcal{C}_P$ denotes the additional Prolog-code in P, i.e., P without $\mathcal{D}_P$ and $\mathcal{T}_P$.

The function definitions $\mathcal{D}_P$ (that may call predicates from $\mathcal{C}_P$) specify the initial state of an evolving algebra, whereas the transition definitions specify how the algebra evolves from one state to another.

The signature of evolving algebras is in our approach the set *GTerms* of all ground Prolog terms. The (single) universe, that is not sorted, is a subset of *GTerms*.

Definition 2. *GTerms* denotes the set of all ground Prolog terms; it is the *signature* of the evolving algebra specified by a lean*EA* program.

We represent the states S of an algebra (including the initial state S_0) by an evaluation function $[\![\,]\!]_S$, mapping locations to the universe. Section 4.1 explains how $[\![\,]\!]_{S_0}$, i.e., the initial state, is derived from the function definitions $\mathcal{D}$. In what way the states evolve according to the transition definitions in $\mathcal{T}$ (which is modeled by altering $[\![\,]\!]$) is the subject of Section 4.3.

The final state(s) are not given explicitly in lean*EA*. Instead, a state S is defined to be final if no transition is applicable in S or if a transition fires that uses undefined function calls in its updates (Def. 8).[10]

4.1 Semantics of Function Definitions

A function definition "`define` F `as` R `with` G." gives a procedure for calculating the value of a location $f(t_1,\ldots,t_n)$ $(n \geq 0)$. Procedurally, this works by instantiating F to the location and executing G. If G succeeds, then R is taken as the value of the location. If several definitions provide values for a single location, we use the first one. Note, that the value of a location depends on the additional Prolog code $\mathcal{C}_P$ in a lean*EA*-program P, since G may call predicates from $\mathcal{C}_P$.

Definition 3. Let $\mathcal{D}$ be a sequence of function definitions and $\mathcal{C}$ be additional Prolog code.

A function definition

$$D \;=\; \texttt{define}\ F\ \texttt{as}\ R\ \texttt{with}\ G.$$

in $\mathcal{D}$ is *succeeding* for $t \in GTerms$ with answer $r = R\tau$, if

1. there is a (most general) substitution σ such that $F\sigma = t$;
2. $G\sigma$ succeeds (possibly using predicates from $\mathcal{C}$);
3. τ is the answer substitution of $G\sigma$ (the first answer substitution if $G\sigma$ is not deterministic).

If no matching substitutions σ exists or if $G\sigma$ fails, D is *failing* for t.

The partial function

$$[\![\,]\!]_{\mathcal{D},\mathcal{C}} \;:\; GTerms \longrightarrow GTerms$$

[10] The user may, however, explicitly terminate the execution of a lean*EA*-program (see Section 3).

is defined by

$$[\![t]\!]_{\mathcal{D},\mathcal{C}} = r \ ,$$

where r is the answer (for t) of the first function definition $D \in \mathcal{D}$ succeeding for t. If no function definition $D \in \mathcal{D}$ is succeeding for t, then $[\![t]\!]_{\mathcal{D},\mathcal{C}}$ is undefined.

The following definition formalizes the conditions function definitions have to meet (see Section 2.3):

Definition 4. A sequence $\mathcal{D}$ of function definitions and additional Prolog code $\mathcal{C}$ are *well defining* if

1. no function definition $D_i \in \mathcal{D}$ is for some term $t \in GTerms$ neither succeeding nor failing (i.e., not terminating), unless there is a definition $D_j \in \mathcal{D}$, $j < i$, in front of D_i that is succeeding for t;
2. if $D \in \mathcal{D}$ is succeeding for $t \in GTerms$ with answer r, then $r \in GTerms$;
3. $\mathcal{D}$ does not (syntactically) contain a cut "!";[11]
4. the goals in $\mathcal{D}$ and the code $\mathcal{C}$
   (a) do not change the Prolog data base or have any other side effects;
   (b) do not call the internal predicates `transition/1`, `=>*/2`, and `=>/2`.

Proposition 5. *If a sequence $\mathcal{D}$ of function definitions and additional Prolog code $\mathcal{C}$ are well defining, then $[\![\,]\!]_{\mathcal{D},\mathcal{C}}$ is a well defined partial function on GTerms (a term mapping).*

A well-defined term mapping $[\![\,]\!]$ is the basis for defining the evaluation function of an evolving algebra, that is the extension of $[\![\,]\!]$ to function calls that are not a location:

Definition 6. Let $[\![\,]\!]$ be a well defined term mapping. The partial function

$$[\![\,]\!]^* \ : \ GTerms \longrightarrow GTerms$$

is defined for $t = f(r_1, \ldots, r_n) \in GTerms$ ($n \geq 0$) as follows:

$$[\![t]\!]^* = \begin{cases} s & \text{if } t = \backslash s \\ [\![f([\![r_1]\!]^*, \ldots, [\![r_n]\!]^*)]\!] & \text{otherwise} \end{cases}$$

4.2 The Universe

A well-defined term mapping $[\![\,]\!]_{\mathcal{D}_P,\mathcal{C}_P}$ enumerates the universe $\mathcal{U}_P$ of the evolving algebra specified by P; in addition, $\mathcal{U}_P$ contains all quoted terms (without the quote) occurring in P:

[11] Prolog-negation and the Prolog-implication "->" are allowed.

Definition 7. If P is a leanEA program, and $[\![]\!]_{\mathcal{D}_P,\mathcal{C}_P}$ is a well defined term mapping, then the universe $\mathcal{U}_P$ is the union of the co-domain of $[\![]\!]_{\mathcal{D}_P,\mathcal{C}_P}$, i.e.,

$$[\![GTerms]\!]_{\mathcal{D}_P,\mathcal{C}_P} = \{[\![t]\!]_{\mathcal{D}_P,\mathcal{C}_P} \ : t \in GTerms, \ [\![t]\!]_{\mathcal{D}_P,\mathcal{C}_P} \downarrow\} \ ,$$

and the set

$$\{t \ : \ t \in GTerms, \ \backslash t \text{ occurs in } P\} \ .$$

Note, that (obviously) the co-domain of $[\![]\!]^*$ is a subset of the universe, i.e.,

$$[\![GTerms]\!]^*_{\mathcal{D}_P,\mathcal{C}_P} \subset \mathcal{U}_P \ .$$

The universe $\mathcal{U}_P$ as defined above is not necessarily decidable. In practice, however, one usually uses a decidable universe, i.e., a decidable subset of *GTerms* that is a superset of $\mathcal{U}_P$ (e.g. *GTerms* itself). This can be achieved by adding function definitions and thus expanding the universe.[12]

4.3 Semantics of Transition Definitions

After having set up the semantics of the function definitions, which constitute the initial evaluation function and thus the initial state of an evolving algebra, we proceed with the dynamic part.

The transition definitions $\mathcal{T}_P$ of a leanEA-program P specify how a state S of the evolving algebra represented by P maps to a new state S'.

Definition 8. Let S be a state of an evolving algebra corresponding to a well defined term mapping $[\![]\!]_S$, and let $\mathcal{T}$ be a sequence of transition definitions.

A transition

transition *Name* **if** *Condition* **then** *Updates*

is said to *fire*, if the Prolog goal *Condition* succeeds in state S (possibly using the predicate =?/2, Def. 10).

Let

$$f_1(r_{11}, \ldots, r_{1n_1}) := v_1$$
$$\vdots$$
$$f_k(r_{k1}, \ldots, r_{kn_k}) := v_k$$

($k \geq 1, n_i \geq 0$) be the sequence *Updates* of the first transition in $\mathcal{T}$ that fires. Then the term mapping $[\![]\!]_{S'}$ and thus the state S' are defined by

$$[\![t]\!]_{S'} = \begin{cases} [\![v_i]\!]^*_S & \text{if there is a smallest } i, \ 1 \leq i \leq k, \\ & \text{such that } t = f_i([\![r_{i1}]\!]^*_S, \ldots, [\![r_{in_i}]\!]^*_S) \\ [\![t]\!]_S & \text{otherwise} \end{cases}$$

If $[\![]\!]^*_S$ is undefined for one of the terms r_{ij} or v_i, $1 \leq i \leq k$, $1 \leq j \leq n_i$ of the first transition in $\mathcal{T}$ that fires, or if no transition fires, then the state S is *final* and $[\![]\!]_{S'}$ is undefined.

Proposition 9. *If* $[\![]\!]_{S'}$ *is a well defined term mapping, then* $[\![]\!]_{S'}$ *(as defined in Def. 8) is well defined.*

[12] It is also possible to change Definition 7; that, in its current form, defines the minimal version of the universe.

4.4 The Equality Relation

Besides "," (and), ";" (or), "\+" (negation), and "->" (implication) lean*EA* allows in conditions of transitions the pre-defined predicate =?/2, that implements the equality relation for examining the current state:

Definition 10. In a state S of an evolving algebra (that corresponds to the well defined term mapping $[\![\,]\!]_S$), for all $t_1, t_2 \in GTerms$, the relation t_1 =? t_2 holds iff

$$[\![t_1]\!]^*_S \downarrow \text{ and } [\![t_2]\!]^*_S \downarrow, \qquad \text{and} \qquad [\![t_1]\!]^*_S = [\![t_2]\!]^*_S .$$

4.5 Runs of lean*EA*-programs

A run of a lean*EA*-program P is a sequence of states $S_0, S_1, S_2, \ldots$ of the specified evolving algebra. Its initial state S_0 is given by

$$[\![\,]\!]_{S_0} = [\![\,]\!]_{\mathcal{D}_P, \mathcal{C}_P}$$

(Def. 6). The following states are determined according to Definition 8 and using

$$S_{n+1} = (S_n)' \qquad (n \geq 0) \ .$$

This process continues iteratively until a final state is reached.

Proposition 11. *lean*EA *implements the semantics as described in this section; i.e., provided* $[\![\,]\!]_{\mathcal{D}_P, \mathcal{C}_P}$ *is well defined,*

1. *in each state S of the run of a lean*EA*-program P the goal* "[t] =>* [X]" *succeeds and binds the Prolog variable* X *to u iff* $[\![t]\!]^*_S = u$;
2. *the execution of P terminates in a state S iff S is a final state;*
3. *the predicate* =? *implements the equality relation.*

4.6 Peculiarities of lean*EA*'s Semantics

The Lipari Guide (Gurevich, 1995) defines what is usually understood as the standard semantics of EAs. Although lean*EA* is oriented at this semantics, there are a couple of details where lean*EA*'s semantics differ. The reason for the differences is not that the standard semantics could not be implemented, but that we decided to compromise for the sake of elegance and clearness of our program.

lean*EA* complies with the semantics given in (Gurevich, 1995) with the following exceptions:

Several Firing Transitions If several transitions fire in a state, lean*EA* executes only the (syntactically) first one, instead of executing all of them simultaneously. Although this makes a significant difference in theory, it is less important in practice, because the firing of more than one transition is usually avoided. Furthermore, the overall expressiveness of EAs is not affected, since the transformation from Section 3 can be applied (this could even be done automatically).

Relations There are no special pre-defined elements denoting true and false in the universe. The value of the relation `=?` (and similar pre-defined relations, see Section 5.2) is represented by succeeding (resp. failing) of the corresponding predicate.

Undefined Function Calls Similarly, there is no pre-defined element **undef** in the universe, but evaluation *fails* if no value is defined. This, however, can be changed by adding as the last function definition:

```
define _ as undef with true.
```

Internal and External Functions In leanEA there is no formal distinction between internal and external functions. Function definitions can be seen as giving default values to functions; if the default values of a function remain unchanged, then it can be regarded external (pre-defined). If no default value is defined for a certain function, it is classically internal. If the default value of a location is changed, this is what is called an external location in (Gurevich, 1995). The relation `=?` (and similar predicates) are static.

Since there is no real distinction, it is possible to mix internal and external functions in function calls.

External functions are reiterated (i.e., evaluated multiply in one state) if they occur multiply in a term being evaluated. If an external function is non-deterministic (an oracle), this can lead to inconsistencies and should be avoided.

Importing and Discarding Elements leanEA does not have constructs for importing or discarding elements. The latter is not needed anyway. If this should be needed for an application, "`import v`" can be simulated by "`v := import`", where `import` is defined by the function definition

```
define import as X with gensym(f,X).
```
[13]

Local Non-determinism If the updates of a firing transition are inconsistent, i.e., several updates define a new value for the same location, the first value is chosen (this is called local non-determinism in (Gurevich, 1995)).

5 Extensions

5.1 The `let` Instruction

It is often useful to use local abbreviations in a transition. The possibility to do so can be implemented by adding a clause

```
rearrange((let Var = Term),
          ([Term] =>* [Val],Var = \Val), true).
```

to leanEA.[14] Then, in addition to updates, instructions of the form

[13] The Prolog predicate `gensym` generates a new atom every time it is called.

[14] And defining the operator `let` by adding "`:- op(910,fx,(let)).`".

`let` x `=` t

can be used in the update part of transitions, where x is a Prolog variable and t a Prolog term. This allows to use x instead of t in subsequent updates (and `let` instructions) of the same transition. A variable x must be defined only once in a transition using `let`. Note, that x is bound to the quoted term $\backslash[\![t]\!]^*$; thus, using an x inside another quoted term may lead to undesired results (see the first part of Example 3).

Example 3. "`let X = \a, reg := \f(X)`" is equivalent to "`reg := \f(\a).`" (which is different from "`reg := \f(a).`").

`let X = \b,`
`let Y = f(X,X),`
`reg1 := g(Y,Y),`
`reg2(X) := X.`
	is equivalent to	`reg1 := g(f(\b,\b),f(\b,\b)),`
		`reg2(\b) := \b.`

Using `let` not only shortens updates syntactically, but also enhances efficiency, because function calls that occur multiply in an update do not have to be re-evaluated.

5.2 Additional Relations

The Prolog predicate `=?`, that implements the equality relation (Def. 10), is the only one that can be used in the condition of a transition (besides the logical operators). It is possible to implement similar relations using the lean*EA* internal predicate `=>*` to evaluate the arguments of the relation:

A predicate $p(t_1, \ldots, t_n)$, $n \geq 0$, is implemented by adding the code

$p(t_1, \ldots, t_n)$ `:- [`$t_1, \ldots, t_n$`] =>* [`$x_1, \ldots, x_n$`],` *Code*.

to lean*EA*.[15] Then the goal "$p(t_1, \ldots, t_n)$" can be used in conditions of transitions instead of $p'(t_1, \ldots, t_n)$ `=? true`", where p' is defined by the function definition

`define` $p'(x_1, \ldots, x_n)$ `as true with` *Code*.

(which is the standard way of implementing relations using function definitions). Note, that p fails, if one of $[\![t_1]\!]^*_S, \ldots, [\![t_n]\!]^*_S$ is undefined in the current state S.

Example 4. The predicate `<>` implements the is-not-equal relation: t_1 `<>` t_2 succeeds iff $[\![t_1]\!]^* \downarrow$, $[\![t_2]\!]^* \downarrow$, and $[\![t_1]\!]^* \neq [\![t_2]\!]^*$. `<>` is implemented by adding the following clause to lean*EA*:

```
(A <> B) :- ([A,B] =>* [Val1,Val2], Val1 \== Val2).
```

[15] $x_1, \ldots, x_n$ must be n distinct and uninstantiated Prolog variables when `=>*` is called. Thus, "`(S =? T) :- ([S,T] =>* [V1,V2]), V1 == V2.`", rather than "`(S =? T) :- ([S,T] =>* [V,V])`" is needed for implementing "`=?`".

5.3 Non-determinism

It is not possible to define non-deterministic EAs in the basic version of lean*EA*. If more than one transition fire in a state, the first is chosen.

This behavior can be changed—such that non-deterministic EAs can be executed—in the following way:

- The cut from Line 13 has to be removed. Then, further firing transitions are executed if backtracking occurs.
- A "retract on backtrack" must be added to the transitions for removing the effect of updates and restoring the previous state if backtracking occurs. Line 22 has to be changed to

```
( asserta(Loc => Val) ; (retract(Loc => Val),fail) ).
```

Now, lean*EA* will enumerate all possible sequences of transitions. Backtracking is initiated, if a final state is reached, i.e., if the further execution of a lean*EA* program fails.

The user has to make sure that there is no infinite sequence of transitions (e.g., by imposing a limit on the length of sequences).

Note, that usually the number of possible transition sequences grows exponentially in their length, which leads to an enormous search space if one tries to find a sequence that ends in a "successful" state by enumerating all possible sequences.

6 Modularized Evolving Algebras

One of the main advantages of EAs is that they allow a problem-oriented formalization. This means, that the level of abstraction of an evolving algebra can be chosen as needed. In the example algebra for computing $n!$ in Section 2.5 for instance, we simply used Prolog's arithmetics over integers and did not bother to specify what multiplication or subtraction actually means. In this section, we demonstrate how such levels of abstraction can be integrated into lean*EA*; the basic idea behind it is to exploit the module-mechanism of the underlying Prolog implementation.

6.1 The Algebra Declaration Statement

In the modularized version of lean*EA*, each specification of an algebra will become a Prolog module; therefore, each algebra must be specified in a separate file. For this, we add an *algebra declaration statement* that looks as follows:

```
algebra Name(In,Out)
      using [Include-List]
      start Updates
      stop Guard.
```

Name is an arbitrary Prolog atom that is used as the name of the predicate for running the specified algebra, and as the name of the module. It is required that *Name*.pl is also the file name of the specification and that the algebra-statement is the first statement in this file.

In, Out are two lists containing the input and output parameters of the algebra. The elements of *Out* will be evaluated if the algebra reaches a final state (see below).

Include-List is a list of names of sub-algebras used by this algebra.

Updates is a list of updates; it specifies that part of the initial state of the algebra (see Section 2.4), that depends on the input *In*.

Guard is a condition that specifies the final state of the evolving algebra. If *Guard* is satisfied in some state, the computation is stopped and the algebra is halted (see Section 2.4).

```
algebra  fak([N],[reg2])
  using  [mult]
  start  reg1 := N,
         reg2 := 1
  stop   reg1 =? 1.

define readint as X with read(X), integer(X).
define write(X) as X with write(X).
define X as X with integer(X).
define X-Y as R with integer(X),integer(Y),R is X-Y.
define X*Y as R with mult([X,Y],[R]).

transition step
     if   \+(reg1 =? 1)
     then reg1 := (reg1-1),
          reg2 := (reg2*reg1).
```

Fig. 3. A Modularized EA for Computing n!

Example 5. As an example consider the algebra statement in Figure 3: an algebra **fak** is defined that computes n!. This is a modularized version of the algebra shown in Section 2.5. The transitions **start** and **result** are now integrated into the algebra statement.

The last function definition in the algebra is of particular interest: it shows how the sub-algebra **mult**, included by the algebra statement, is called. Where the earlier algebra for computing n! in Section 2.5 used Prolog's built-in multiplication, a sub-algebra for carrying out multiplication is called. Its definition can be found in Figure 4.

```
algebra  mult([X,Y],[result])
  using  []
  start  reg1 := X,
         reg2 := Y,
         result := 0
  stop   reg1 =? 0.

define write(X) as X with write(X).
define X as X with integer(X).
define X+Y as R with integer(X),integer(Y),R is X+Y.
define X-Y as R with integer(X),integer(Y),R is X-Y.

transition step
     if   \+(reg1 =? 0)
     then reg1 := (reg1-1),
          result := (result+reg2).
```

Fig. 4. A Modularized EA for Multiplication

6.2 Implementation of Modularized EAs

The basic difference between the basic version of lean*EA* and the modularized version is that the **algebra**-statement at the beginning of a file containing an EA specification is mapped into appropriate **module** and **use_module** statements in Prolog. Since the algebra will be loaded within the named module, we also need an evaluation function that is defined internally in this module. This allows to use functions with the same name in different algebras without interference.

Figure 5 lists the modularized program. It defines four additional operators (**algebra**, **start**, **stop**, and **using**) that are needed for the algebra statement. The first **term_expansion** clause (Lines 9–26) translates such a statement into a Prolog module header, declares **=>/2** to be dynamic in the module, and defines the evaluation predicate **=>*** for this module.[16] The effect of the **term_expansion**-statement is probably best seen when setting an example: the module declaration in Figure 3, for instance, is mapped into

```
:- module(fak,[fak/2]).
fak:(:-use_module([mult])).
:- dynamic fak:(=>)/2.
```

plus the usual definition of **=>*/2**.

[16] This implementation is probably specific for SICStus Prolog and needs to be changed to run on other Prolog systems. The "**Name:**"-prefix is required in SICStus, because a "**:- module(...)**"-declaration becomes effective *after* the current term was processed.

```
:- op(1199,fy,(transition)), op(1180,xfx,(if)),
   op(1192,fy,(define)),     op(1185,xfy,(with)),
   op(1190,xfy,(as)),        op(1170,xfx,(then)),
   op(900,xfx,(=>)),         op(900,xfx,(=>*)),
   op(900,xfx,(:=)),         op(900,xfx,(=?)),
   op(100,fx,(\)),           op(1199,fx,(algebra)),
   op(1190,xfy,(start)),     op(1170,xfx,(stop)),
   op(1180,xfy,(using)).

term_expansion((algebra Head using Include_list
                     start Updates stop Guard),
               [(:- module(Name,[Name/2])),
                Name:(:- use_module(Include_list)),
                (:- dynamic(Name:(=>)/2)),
                Name:(([H|T] =>* [HVal|TVal]) :-
                     (   H = \HVal
                      ;   H  =.. [Func|Args], Args =>* ArgVals,
                      H1 =.. [Func|ArgVals], H1 => HVal),!,
                      T =>* TVal),
                Name:([] =>* []),
                Name:((A =? B) :- ([A,B] =>* [Val1,Val2]),
                                  Val1 == Val2),
                Name:(NewHead :- FrontCode,BackCode,!,
                        (transition _),Out =>* Value),
                Name:(transition(result) :- (Guard,!))]):-
        Head =..[Name,In,Out], NewHead =..[Name,In,Value],
        rearrange(Updates,FrontCode,BackCode).

term_expansion((define Location as Value with Goal),
               ((Location => Value) :- Goal,!)).

term_expansion((transition Name if Condition then Updates),
               (transition(Name) :-
                  (Condition,!,
                   FrontCode,BackCode,transition(_)))) :-
        rearrange(Updates,FrontCode,BackCode).

rearrange((A,B),(FrontA,FrontB),(BackB,BackA)) :-
        rearrange(A,FrontA,BackA),
        rearrange(B,FrontB,BackB).

rearrange((LocTerm := Expr),
          ([Expr] =>* [Val], LocTerm =.. [Func|Args],
           Args =>* ArgVals, Loc =..[Func|ArgVals]),
          asserta(Loc => Val)).
```

Fig. 5. Modularized EAs: the Program

6.3 Running Modularized EAs

In contrast to the basic version of lean*EA*, a modularized EA has a defined interface to the outside world: The algebra-statement defines a Prolog predicate that can be used to run the specified EA. Thus, the user does not need to start the transitions manually. Furthermore, the run of a modularized EA does not end with failure of the starting predicate, but with success. This is the case since a modularized EA has a defined final state. If the predicate succeeds, the final state has been reached.

For the example algebra above (Figure 3), the run proceeds as follows:

```
| ?- compile([leanea,fak]).
{leanea.pl compiled, 190 msec 4768 bytes}
{compiled mult.pl in module mult, 120 msec 10656 bytes}
{compiled fak.pl in module fak, 270 msec 20944 bytes}
yes

| ?- fak(6,Result).
Result = [720] ?
yes
```

After compiling lean*EA*, the EA shown in Figure 3 is loaded from the file `fak.pl`, which in turn loads the algebra for multiplication from `mult.pl`. The algebra is then started and the result of 6! is returned. The computation takes roughly one second on a Sun SPARC 10.[17]

7 Conclusion

We presented lean*EA*, an approach to simulation evolving algebra specifications. The underlying idea is to modifying the Prolog reader, such that loading a specification of an evolving algebra means compiling it into Prolog clauses. Thus, the Prolog system itself is turned into an abstract machine for running EAs. The contribution of our work is twofold:

Firstly, lean*EA* offers an efficient and very flexible framework for simulating EAs. lean*EA* is open, in the sense that it is easily interfaced with other applications, embedded into other systems, or adapted to concrete needs. We believe that this is a very important feature that is often underestimated: if a specification system is supposed to be used in practice, then it must be embedded in an appropriate system for program development. lean*EA*, as presented in this paper, is surely more a starting point than a solution for this, but it demonstrates clearly one way for proceeding.

Second, lean*EA* demonstrates that little effort is needed to implement a simulator for EAs. This supports the claim that EAs are a practically relevant tool, and it shows a clear advantage of EAs over other specification formalisms: these

[17] Recall that all multiplications are carried out within the EA and not by Prolog's internal multiplication predicate.

are often hard to understand, and difficult to deal with when implementing them. EAs, on the other hand, are easily understood and easily used. Thus, lean*EA* shows that one of the major goals of EAs, namely to "bridge the gap between computation models and specification methods" (following Gurevich (1995)), was achieved.

Acknowledgement

We would like to thank an anonymous referee for his helpful comments on an earlier version of this paper.

References

BÖRGER, EGON, & ROSENZWEIG, DEAN. 1995. A Mathematical Definition of Full Prolog. *Science of Computer Programming*, **24**(3), 249–286.

BÖRGER, EGON, DURDANOVIC, IGOR, & ROSENZWEIG, DEAN. 1994a. Occam: Specification and Compiler Correctness. *Pages 489–508 of:* MONTANARI, U., & OLDEROG, E.-R. (eds), *Proceedings, IFIP Working Conference on Programming Concepts, Methods and Calculi (PROCOMET 94)*. North-Holland.

BÖRGER, EGON, DEL CASTILLO, GIUSEPPE, GLAVAN, P., & ROSENZWEIG, DEAN. 1994b. Towards a Mathematical Specification of the APE100 Architecture: The APESE Model. *Pages 396–401 of:* PEHRSON, B., & SIMON, I. (eds), *Proceedings, IFIP 13th World Computer Congress*, vol. 1. Amsterdam: Elsevier.

GUREVICH, YURI. 1991. Evolving Algebras. A Tutorial Introduction. *Bulletin of the EATCS*, **43**, 264–284.

GUREVICH, YURI. 1995. Evolving Algebras 1993: Lipari Guide. *In:* BÖRGER, E. (ed), *Specification and Validation Methods*. Oxford University Press.

GUREVICH, YURI, & HUGGINS, JIM. 1993. The Semantics of the C Programming Language. *Pages 273–309 of: Proceedings, Computer Science Logic (CSL)*. LNCS 702. Springer.

GUREVICH, YURI, & MANI, RAGHU. 1995. Group Membership Protocol: Specification and Verification. *In:* BÖRGER, E. (ed), *Specification and Validation Methods*. Oxford University Press.

KAPPEL, ANGELICA M. 1993. Executable Specifications based on Dynamic Algebras. *Pages 229–240 of: Proceedings, 4th International Conference on Logic Programming and Automated Reasoning (LPAR), St. Petersburg, Russia*. LNCS 698. Springer.

O'KEEFE, RICHARD A. 1990. *The Craft of Prolog*. MIT Press.

A Proof System for Finite Trees

Patrick Blackburn,[1] Wilfried Meyer-Viol[2] and Maarten de Rijke[3]

[1] Computerlinguistik, Universität des Saarlandes, Postfach 1150,
D-66041 Saarbrücken, Germany
patrick@coli.uni-sb.de
[2] Dept. of Computing, Imperial College, 180 Queen's Gate,
London SW7 2BZ, England
wm3@doc.ic.ac.uk
[3] Dept. of Computer Science, University of Warwick,
Coventry CV4 7AL, England
mdr@dcs.warwick.ac.uk

Abstract. In this paper we introduce a description language for finite trees. Although we briefly note some of its intended applications, the main goal of the paper is to provide it with a sound and complete proof system. We do so using standard axioms from *modal provability logic* and *modal logics of programs*, and prove completeness by extending techniques due to Van Benthem and Meyer-Viol (1994) and Blackburn and Meyer-Viol (1994). We conclude with a proof of the EXPTIME-completeness of the satisfiability problem, and a discussion of issues related to complexity and theorem proving.

1 Introduction

In this paper we introduce a modal language for describing the internal structure of trees, provide it with an axiom system which we prove to be complete with respect to the class of all finite trees, and prove the decidability and EXPTIME-completeness of its satisfiability problem. But before getting down to the technicalities, some motivation.

In many applications, finite trees are the fundamental data structure. Moreover, in many of these applications one wishes to specify how the nodes *within a single tree* relate to each other; that is, it is often the *internal* perspective that is fundamental. By way of contrast, most work on logics of trees in the computer science literature takes an *external* perspective on tree structure. For example, in the work of Courcelle (1985) and Maher (1988), variables range over entire trees. This is a natural choice for work on the semantics of programming languages, but unsuitable for the applications mentioned below. And although the internal perspective on trees has been explored in the logical literature (the classic example is Rabin's (1969) monadic second order theory SnS), such explorations have usually been for extremely powerful languages. It is interesting to explore (modal) fragments of these systems, and that is the purpose of the present paper.

Although the work that follows is concerned solely with technical issues, the reader may find it helpful to consider the sort of applications we have in mind.

One has already arisen in theoretical and computational linguistics. In contemporary linguistics, grammars are often considered to be a set of *constraints* (i.e. axioms) which grammatical structures must satisfy. To specify such grammars, it is crucial to have the ability to specify how tree nodes are related to each other and what properties they must possess. Moreover, it is desirable that such specifications be given in a simple, machine implementable system. A substantial body of work already exists which models the most commonly encountered grammatical formalisms using internal logics of trees: we draw the reader's attention to Backofen *et al.* (1995), Blackburn *et al.* (1993, 1994, 1995), Kracht (1993, 1995), and Rogers (1996). Modal logics of the type considered here have been shown to provide an appropriate level of expressivity for this application.

Another possible application is the formal treatment of corrections in graphical user interfaces. Many competing 'undo mechanisms' have been proposed, differing mainly in the way they allow users to jump through the histories of their actions, and in the way they perceive these histories. In multi-user applications where several agents submit commands concurrently such histories are finite trees, and the complexities of the possible action sequences call for simple, yet expressive description languages (see Berlage (1994)). Examination of the literature suggests that modal languages may be an appropriate modeling tool here as well.

2 The Language $\mathcal{L}$

$\mathcal{L}$ is a propositional modal language with eight modalities: $\langle l \rangle$, $\langle r \rangle$, $\langle u \rangle$ and $\langle d \rangle$ explore the left-sister, right-sister, mother-of and daughter-of relations, while $\langle l+ \rangle$, $\langle r+ \rangle$, $\langle u+ \rangle$ and $\langle d+ \rangle$ explore their transitive closures. The formal definition of $\mathcal{L}$'s syntax is as follows. We suppose we have fixed a non-empty, finite or countably infinite, set of atomic symbols A whose elements are typically denoted by p.

$$\phi ::= p \mid \bot \mid \top \mid \neg\phi \mid \phi \wedge \phi \mid \langle x \rangle \phi \mid \langle x+ \rangle \phi$$
$$x ::= l \mid r \mid u \mid d.$$

We sometimes write $\mathcal{L}(\mathrm{A})$ to emphasize the dependence on A. We employ the usual boolean abbreviations.

We interpret $\mathcal{L}(\mathrm{A})$ on *finite ordered trees* whose nodes are *labeled* with symbols drawn from A. We assume that the reader is familiar with finite trees and such concepts as 'daughter-of', 'mother-of', 'sister-of', 'root-node', 'terminal-node', and so on. If a node has no sister to the immediate right we call it a last node, and if it has no sister to the immediate left we call it a first node. Note that the root node is both first and last. A labeling of a finite tree associates a subset of A with each tree node.

Formally, we present finite ordered trees as tuples $\mathbf{T} = (T, R_l, R_r, R_u, R_d)$. Here T is the set of tree nodes and R_l, R_r, R_u and R_d are the left-sister, right-sister, mother-of and daughter-of relations respectively. A pair $(\mathbf{T}, V)$, where $\mathbf{T}$

is a finite tree and $V : A \longrightarrow Pow(T)$, is called a *model*, and we say that V is a *labeling function* or a *valuation*. Let $(R_x)^+$ denote the transitive closure of R_x. Then we interpret $\mathcal{L}(A)$ on models as follows:

Definition 1 (Truth). For any model $\mathbf{M}$ $(= (T, R_l, R_r, R_u, R_d, V))$ define:

$$
\begin{array}{rll}
\mathbf{M}, t \models p & \text{iff} & p \in V(t) \text{ for all } p \in \mathrm{A} \\
\mathbf{M}, t \models \neg\phi & \text{iff} & \mathbf{M}, t \not\models \phi \\
\mathbf{M}, t \models \phi \wedge \psi & \text{iff} & \mathbf{M}, t \models \phi \text{ and } \mathbf{M}, t \models \psi \\
\mathbf{M}, t \models \langle x \rangle \phi & \text{iff} & \exists t' \, (t R_x t' \text{ and } \mathbf{M}, t' \models \phi), \text{ where } x \in \{l, r, u, d\} \\
\mathbf{M}, t \models \langle x{+} \rangle \phi & \text{iff} & \exists t' \, (t (R_x)^+ t' \text{ and } \mathbf{M}, t' \models \phi), \text{ where } x \in \{l, r, u, d\}.
\end{array}
$$

If $\mathbf{M}, t \models \phi$, then we say ϕ is *satisfied* in $\mathbf{M}$ at t. For any formula ϕ, if there is a model $\mathbf{M}$ and a node t in $\mathbf{M}$ such that $\mathbf{M}, t \models \phi$, then we say that ϕ is *satisfiable*. If ϕ is true at all nodes in a model $\mathbf{M}$ then we say it is *valid in the model* $\mathbf{M}$. If a formula ϕ is valid in all models then we say it is *valid* and write $\models \phi$.

The following defined operators will prove useful. First we define *duals* of the basic operators: $[x]\phi := \neg\langle x \rangle \neg\phi$ and $[x{+}]\phi := \neg\langle x{+} \rangle \neg\phi$, for all $x \in \{l, r, u, d\}$. We also define operators for talking about the *reflexive* transitive closure of four basic relations: $\langle x{*} \rangle \phi := \phi \vee \langle x{+} \rangle \phi$ and $[x{*}]\phi := \neg\langle x{*} \rangle \neg\phi$, for all $x \in \{l, r, u, d\}$. Next we define the following constants: *first* $:= [l]\bot$, *last* $:= [r]\bot$, *start* $:= [u]\bot$ and *term* $:= [d]\bot$. Note that *first*, *last*, *start* and *term* are constants true only at left nodes, right nodes, the root node, and terminal nodes, respectively.

3 A Proof System for $\mathcal{L}$

We now introduce a logic called LOFT (Logic Of Finite Trees). LOFT is the smallest set of $\mathcal{L}$ formulas that (a) contains all tautologies, (b) contains all instances of the axiom schemas given below, (c) is closed under modus ponens (if ϕ and $\phi \rightarrow \psi$ belong to LOFT then so does ψ), and (d) is closed under generalisation (if ϕ belongs to LOFT then so do $[l]\phi$, $[r]\phi$, $[u]\phi$, $[d]\phi$, $[l{+}]\phi$, $[r{+}]\phi$, $[u{+}]\phi$, and $[d{+}]\phi$). Note that this is a purely *syntactical* description of LOFT. The completeness theorem proved below shows that LOFT really does deserve its name: LOFT consists of precisely the formulas of $\mathcal{L}$ valid on finite trees.

It remains to specify the axiom schemas. These fall naturally into four groups. The first group is the simplest. Schema 1 is the fundamental schema of normal modal logic. Schemas 2l, 2r, 2u and 2d reflect the fact that both R_l and R_r, and R_u and R_d, are converse pairs of relations (these schemas are basic axioms of temporal logic), while schema 3 (familiar from modal logic) reflects the fact that R_l, R_r and R_u are partial functions.

1. $[x](\phi \rightarrow \psi) \rightarrow ([x]\phi \rightarrow [x]\psi)$ $\qquad (x \in \{l, r, u, d\})$

2l. $\phi \rightarrow [l]\langle r \rangle \phi$

2r. $\phi \rightarrow [r]\langle l\rangle\phi$
2u. $\phi \rightarrow [u]\langle d\rangle\phi$
2d. $\phi \rightarrow [d]\langle u\rangle\phi$
3. $\langle x\rangle\phi \rightarrow [x]\phi$ $\quad (x \in \{l, r, u\})$

The second group are (irreflexive analogs of) the Segerberg schemas used in modal logics of programs; they reflect the fact that the operators $[l+]$, $[r+]$, $[u+]$ and $[d+]$ make use of the transitive closure of the relations for $[l]$, $[r]$, $[u]$ and $[d]$ respectively.

4. $[x+]\phi \leftrightarrow [x][x*]\phi$ $\quad (x \in \{l, r, u, d\})$
5. $[x+](\phi \rightarrow [x]\phi) \rightarrow ([x]\phi \rightarrow [x+]\phi)$ $\quad (x \in \{l, r, u, d\})$.

The third group reflects the fact that we are working only with *finite trees*. Schema 7 (Löb's schema) is the crucial one. It is the key schema of *modal provability logic* and expresses a second-order fact about finite trees: the transitive closure of the 'daughter-of' relation, and of the 'to-the-right-of' relation, are both converse well founded.

6. $\langle u*\rangle \mathit{start} \wedge \langle d*\rangle \mathit{term} \wedge \langle l*\rangle \mathit{first} \wedge \langle r*\rangle \mathit{last}$
7. $[x+]([x+]\phi \rightarrow \phi) \rightarrow [x+]\phi$ $\quad (x \in \{r, d\})$.

The fourth group reflects the links between the vertically and horizontally scanning modalities.

8. $\langle d\rangle\phi \rightarrow [d](\mathit{first} \rightarrow \langle r*\rangle\phi)$
9. $\langle d\rangle\phi \rightarrow \langle d\rangle \mathit{first} \wedge \langle d\rangle \mathit{last}$
10. $\mathit{start} \rightarrow \mathit{first} \wedge \mathit{last}$.

4 Proving Completeness

In this section we prove the completeness of LOFT. (Proving that LOFT is sound with respect to finite trees is straightforward, though readers new to modal logic may find it helpful to refer to Goldblatt (1992) or Smoryński (1985) for further discussion of the Segerberg and Löb schemas.) Our proof uses ideas from provability logic and dynamic logic, and extends techniques used by Van Benthem and Meyer-Viol (1994) and Blackburn and Meyer-Viol (1994). The work falls into three phases. First, we show that LOFT is complete with respect to a certain class of finite pseudo-models. Although pseudo-models are not trees, they embody a great deal of useful information about LOFT, and in the second phase we show how to make use of this: we prove a sufficient condition (the *truth lemma for induced models*) under which pseudo-models induce genuine models on finite trees. In the third stage, the heart of the proof, we show that there is a (finite) inductive method for building induced models.

4.1 Preliminaries

The first notion we need is that of a *closure* of sentences. Recall that a set of formulas Σ is *closed under subformulas* iff for all $\phi \in \Sigma$, every subformula of ϕ is in Σ. Following Fischer and Ladner (1979) we define sets of formulas that are closed under a little more structure than simply subformulahood.

Definition 2 (Closures). Let Σ be a set of formulas. $Cl(\Sigma)$ is the smallest set of sentences containing Σ that is closed under subformulas and satisfies the following additional constraints.

1. If $\langle x+\rangle\phi \in Cl(\Sigma)$, then $\langle x\rangle\phi \in Cl(\Sigma)$, where $x \in \{l, r, u, d\}$.
2. If $\langle x+\rangle\phi \in Cl(\Sigma)$, then $\langle x\rangle\langle x+\rangle\phi \in Cl(\Sigma)$, where $x \in \{l, r, u, d\}$.
3. If $\langle d\rangle\phi \in Cl(\Sigma)$, then $\langle r*\rangle\phi \in Cl(\Sigma)$.
4. $\langle x\rangle\top \in Cl(\Sigma)$ for $x \in \{l, r, u, d\}$.
5. $\langle d\rangle \mathit{first}$, $\langle d\rangle \mathit{last} \in Cl(\Sigma)$.
6. $\langle l*\rangle \mathit{first}$, $\langle r*\rangle \mathit{last}$, $\langle u*\rangle \mathit{start}$, $\langle d*\rangle \mathit{term} \in Cl(\Sigma)$.
7. If $\phi \in Cl(\Sigma)$ and ϕ is not of the form $\neg\psi$, then $\neg\phi \in Cl(\Sigma)$.

$Cl(\Sigma)$ is called the *closure* of Σ. Observe that for every $\phi \in Cl(\Sigma)$ there is a $\psi \in Cl(\Sigma)$ such that ψ is equivalent to $\neg\phi$; we will often pretend that for every $\phi \in Cl(\Sigma)$, $\neg\phi$ is also in $Cl(\Sigma)$.

Lemma 3. *Let Σ be a finite set of formulas. Then $Cl(\Sigma)$ is finite too.*

Definition 4 (Atoms). If Σ is a set of formulas, then $At(\Sigma)$ consists of all the maximal consistent subsets of $Cl(\Sigma)$. In other words, $At(\Sigma)$ consists of all sets $\mathcal{A} \subseteq Cl(\Sigma)$ such that $\mathcal{A}$ is consistent, and if $\mathcal{B}$ is consistent and $\mathcal{A} \subseteq \mathcal{B} \subseteq Cl(\Sigma)$, then $\mathcal{A} = \mathcal{B}$. The elements of $At(\Sigma)$ are called *atoms* (*over* Σ).

Lemma 5 (Atoms exist). *If $\phi \in Cl(\Sigma)$ and ϕ is consistent, then there exists an atom $\mathcal{A} \in At(\Sigma)$ such that $\phi \in \mathcal{A}$.*

Proof. Use the usual Lindenbaum technique together with the observation that $At(\Sigma) = \{\mathcal{M} \cap Cl(\Sigma) \mid \mathcal{M}$ is a maximal consistent set in the usual sense $\}$. ⊣

Lemma 6 (Properties of atoms). *Let Σ be a set of formulas and $\mathcal{A} \in Cl(\Sigma)$.*

1. *If $\phi \in Cl(\Sigma)$, then $\phi \in \mathcal{A}$ iff $\neg\phi \notin \mathcal{A}$.*
2. *If $\phi \wedge \psi \in Cl(\Sigma)$ then $\phi \wedge \psi \in \mathcal{A}$ iff $\phi \in \mathcal{A}$ and $\psi \in \mathcal{A}$*
3. *If $\phi \to \psi \in Cl(\Sigma)$, then $\phi \to \psi$ and $\phi \in \mathcal{A}$ implies $\psi \in \mathcal{A}$.*
4. *If $\langle x+\rangle\phi \in Cl(\Sigma)$, then $\langle x+\rangle\phi \in \mathcal{A}$ iff $\langle x\rangle\phi \in \mathcal{A}$ or $\langle x\rangle\langle x+\rangle\phi \in \mathcal{A}$, where $x \in \{l, r, u, d\}$.*
5. *$\langle u*\rangle \mathit{start}$, $\langle d*\rangle \mathit{term}$, $\langle l*\rangle \mathit{first}$, $\langle r*\rangle \mathit{last}$, $\top \in \mathcal{A}$.*

Lemma 7. *Suppose $At(\Sigma) = \{\mathcal{A}_1, \ldots, \mathcal{A}_n\}$. Then $\vdash \bigwedge \mathcal{A}_1 \vee \cdots \vee \bigwedge \mathcal{A}_n$.*

Proof. Use the propositional tautology $\phi \leftrightarrow ((\phi \wedge \psi) \vee (\phi \wedge \neg\psi))$. ⊣

4.2 Pseudo-models

In this subsection we define a collection of finite pseudo-models with the following property: if ϕ is a consistent formula, then there is a (finite) pseudo-model that satisfies ϕ. Although this result is of interest in its own right (as we shall see at the end of the paper), of equal importance are the definitions and results we encounter along the way, for these will be used throughout.

Definition 8 (Canonical relations). Let $\mathcal{A}, \mathcal{B} \in At(\Sigma)$. For each $x \in \{l, r, u, d, l+, r+, u+, d+\}$ we define the *canonical relations* S_x on $At(\Sigma)$ as follows:

$$\mathcal{A}S_x\mathcal{B} \text{ iff } \bigwedge \mathcal{A} \wedge \langle x \rangle \bigwedge \mathcal{B} \text{ is consistent.}$$

Lemma 9. *Let $\mathcal{A}$ be an atom, $x \in \{l, r, u, d, l+, r+, u+, d+\}$, and $\psi \in Cl(\Sigma)$. If $\bigwedge \mathcal{A} \wedge \langle x \rangle \psi$ is consistent, then there is an atom $\mathcal{B}$ over Σ such that $\psi \in \mathcal{B}$ and $\mathcal{A}S_x\mathcal{B}$.*

Proof. Suppose that $\bigwedge \mathcal{A} \wedge \langle x \rangle \psi$ is consistent. We show how to construct the required atom $\mathcal{B}$ by 'forcing a choice' between the formulas in $At(\Sigma)$. For all formulas χ, $\psi \leftrightarrow (\psi \wedge \chi) \vee (\psi \wedge \neg\chi)$ is a propositional tautology, hence by simple modal reasoning: $\vdash \langle x \rangle \psi \leftrightarrow \langle x \rangle (\psi \wedge \chi) \vee \langle x \rangle (\psi \wedge \neg\chi)$. Hence by propositional logic, either $\bigwedge \mathcal{A} \wedge \langle x \rangle (\psi \wedge \chi)$ or $\bigwedge \mathcal{A} \wedge \langle x \rangle (\psi \wedge \neg\chi)$ is consistent. This observation enables us to construct the desired $\mathcal{B}$ 'behind the modality' $\langle x \rangle$ by working through all the formulas in $Cl(\Sigma)$. $\dashv$

Lemma 10. *Let $\mathcal{A}$ be an atom, $x \in \{l, r, u, d, l+, r+, u+, d+\}$, and $\langle x \rangle \psi \in Cl(\Sigma)$. Then $\langle x \rangle \psi \in \mathcal{A}$ iff there is an atom $\mathcal{B}$ such that $\psi \in \mathcal{A}$ and $\mathcal{A}S_x\mathcal{B}$.*

Proof. For the left to right direction, note that if $\langle x \rangle \psi \in \mathcal{A}$ then $\bigwedge A \wedge \langle x \rangle \psi$ is consistent, and the result follows by the previous lemma. For the right to left direction note that if such a $\mathcal{B}$ exists, then $\bigwedge \mathcal{A} \wedge \langle x \rangle \bigwedge \mathcal{B}$ is consistent, thus so is $\bigwedge \mathcal{A} \wedge \langle x \rangle \psi$. As $\langle x \rangle \psi \in Cl(\Sigma)$, by maximality it belongs to $\mathcal{A}$. $\dashv$

Lemma 11. *Let $\mathcal{A}$ and $\mathcal{B}$ be atoms in $Cl(\Sigma)$. Then for all $x \in \{l, r, u, d\}$, if $\mathcal{A}S_{x+}\mathcal{B}$ then $\mathcal{A}(S_x)^+\mathcal{B}$.*

Proof. Assume that $\mathcal{A}S_{x+}\mathcal{B}$ where x is either l, r u or d. That is, $\bigwedge \mathcal{A} \wedge \langle x+ \rangle \bigwedge \mathcal{B}$ is consistent. Let

$$\sigma := \bigvee \left\{ \bigwedge \mathcal{C} \mid \mathcal{A}(S_x)^+\mathcal{C} \right\},$$

where $(S_x)^+$ is the transitive closure of S_x. Then $\sigma \wedge \langle x \rangle \neg\sigma$ is inconsistent, for otherwise $\sigma \wedge \langle x \rangle \bigwedge \mathcal{C}'$ would be consistent for at least one $\mathcal{C}'$ *not* reachable from $\mathcal{A}$ in finitely many S_x steps; but then $\bigwedge \mathcal{C} \wedge \langle x \rangle \bigwedge \mathcal{C}'$ would be consistent for at least one $\mathcal{C} \in At(\Sigma)$ with $\mathcal{A}(S_x)^+\mathcal{C}$. Hence $\mathcal{A}(S_x)^+\mathcal{C}'$ — a contradiction. Therefore

$$\begin{aligned} \vdash \sigma \wedge \langle x \rangle \neg\sigma \rightarrow \bot &\Rightarrow \vdash \sigma \rightarrow [x]\sigma \\ &\Rightarrow \vdash [x+](\sigma \rightarrow [x]\sigma), \text{ by generalization} \\ &\Rightarrow \vdash [x]\sigma \rightarrow [x+]\sigma, \text{ by axiom 5.} \end{aligned}$$

By simple modal reasoning, we have $\vdash \bigwedge \mathcal{A} \to [x]\sigma$, so $\vdash \bigwedge \mathcal{A} \to [x+]\sigma$. Then, as $\bigwedge \mathcal{A} \wedge \langle x+\rangle \bigwedge \mathcal{B}$ was assumed consistent, $\langle x+\rangle(\bigwedge \mathcal{B} \wedge \sigma)$ is consistent as well, and so $\bigwedge \mathcal{B} \wedge \sigma$ must be consistent. By the definition of σ this means that $\bigwedge \mathcal{B} \wedge \bigwedge \mathcal{C}$ is consistent for at least one atom $\mathcal{C}$ with $\mathcal{A}(S_x)^+\mathcal{C}$. By maximality $\mathcal{B} = \mathcal{C}$, and so $\mathcal{A}(S_x)^+\mathcal{B}$, as required. ⊣

Lemma 12. *Let $\mathcal{A} \in At(\Sigma)$, and let $x \in \{l, r, u, d\}$. Assume that $\langle x+\rangle\psi \in Cl(\Sigma)$. Then $\langle x+\rangle\psi \in \mathcal{A}$ iff for some $\mathcal{B} \in At(\Sigma)$ we have $\mathcal{A}(S_x)^+\mathcal{B}$ and $\psi \in \mathcal{B}$.*

Proof. Suppose $\langle x+\rangle\psi \in \mathcal{A}$. By Lemma 10 there is an atom $\mathcal{B}$ such that $\mathcal{A}S_{x+}\mathcal{B}$, hence by Lemma 11, $\mathcal{A}(S_x)^+\mathcal{B}$.

Conversely, suppose that $\mathcal{A} = \mathcal{A}_1 S_x \cdots S_x \mathcal{A}_k = \mathcal{B}$ and $\psi \in \mathcal{B}$. We show the desired result by induction on k. If $k = 1$, then $\mathcal{A}S_x\mathcal{B}$. We need to show $\langle x+\rangle\psi \in \mathcal{A}$. As $\mathcal{A}S_x\mathcal{B}$, $\langle x\rangle\psi \in \mathcal{A}$. By axiom 4, $\langle x\rangle\psi \to \langle x+\rangle\psi$, hence by maximality $\langle x+\rangle\psi \in \mathcal{A}$. For the induction step, assume that $k > 1$ and $\mathcal{A} = \mathcal{A}_1 S_x \mathcal{A}_2 \cdots S_x \mathcal{A}_k = \mathcal{B}$. By the induction hypothesis, $\langle x+\rangle\psi \in \mathcal{A}_2$. It follows that $\langle x\rangle\langle x+\rangle\psi \in \mathcal{A}_1 = \mathcal{A}$ (this uses the second closure condition on $Cl(\Sigma)$), and hence $\langle x+\rangle\psi \in \mathcal{A}$ by axiom 4. ⊣

Definition 13. Let a finite set of formulas Σ be given. Define the *canonical pseudo-model over* $At(\Sigma)$ to be the structure

$$\mathbf{P} = (At(\Sigma), S_l, S_r, S_u, S_d, (S_l)^+, (S_r)^+, (S_u)^+, (S_d)^+, V),$$

where $V(p) = \{\mathcal{A} \mid p \in \mathcal{A}\}$. We interpret $\mathcal{L}$ in the obvious way on pseudo-models.

Lemma 14 (Truth lemma for pseudo-models). *Let $\mathbf{P}$ be the pseudo-model over $At(\Sigma)$. For all $\mathcal{A} \in At(\Sigma)$ and all $\psi \in Cl(\Sigma)$, $\psi \in \mathcal{A}$ iff $\mathbf{P}, \mathcal{A} \models \psi$.*

Proof. By induction on the structure of ψ. The base case is clear and the boolean cases are trivial. It remains to examine the argument for the modalities.

First, let $x \in \{l, r, u, d\}$ and suppose that $\mathbf{P}, \mathcal{A} \models \langle x\rangle\psi$. This happens iff there is an atom $\mathcal{B}$ such that $\mathcal{A}S_x\mathcal{B}$ and $\mathbf{P}, \mathcal{B} \models \psi$. By the inductive hypothesis, this happens iff there is an atom $\mathcal{B}$ such that $\mathcal{A}S_x\mathcal{B}$ and $\psi \in \mathcal{B}$. By Lemma 10, this happens iff $\langle x\rangle\psi \in \mathcal{A}$, the desired result.

Next, let $x \in \{l+, r+, u+, d+\}$, and suppose that $\mathbf{P}, \mathcal{A} \models \langle x\rangle\psi$. This happens iff there is an atom $\mathcal{B}$ such that $\mathcal{A}(S_x)^+\mathcal{B}$ and $\mathbf{P}, \mathcal{B} \models \psi$. By the inductive hypothesis, this happens iff there is an atom $\mathcal{B}$ such that $\mathcal{A}(S_x)^+\mathcal{B}$ and $\psi \in \mathcal{B}$. By Lemma 12, this happens iff $\langle x\rangle\psi \in \mathcal{A}$, the desired result. ⊣

Theorem 15. LOFT *is complete with respect to the class of finite pseudo-models.*

Proof. Given a LOFT-consistent formula ψ, form the (finite) pseudo-model $\mathbf{P}$ over $At(\{\psi\})$. As ψ is consistent it belongs to some atom $\mathcal{A}$, hence by the above truth lemma $\mathbf{P}, \mathcal{A} \models \psi$. Thus every consistent sentence has a model, and completeness follows. ⊣

This gives us a completeness theorem for LOFT. Unfortunately it's not the one we want, since pseudo-models need not be based on finite trees. (The easiest way to see this is to observe that S_l, S_r, and S_u need not be partial functions.) However, as we shall now see, pseudo-models contain all the information needed to induce genuine models on finite trees.

4.3 Induced Models

In this subsection we prove the following result: if the nodes of a finite tree **T** are *sensibly decorated* with the atoms from some pseudo-model, then the pseudo-model induces a genuine model on **T**.

Definition 16. Let $\mathbf{T} = (T, R_l, R_r, R_u, R_d)$ be a finite tree and Σ any finite set of sentences. A *decoration* of **T** by $At(\Sigma)$ is a function $h : T \longrightarrow At(\Sigma)$, and the *model induced by the decoration* on **T** is the pair $(\mathbf{T}, V)$, where V is the valuation on **T** defined by $t \in V(p)$ iff $p \in h(t)$. Suppose that h is a decoration with the following properties:

1. For all t, $t' \in T$, if tR_dt' then $h(t)S_dh(t')$.
2. For all t, $t' \in T$, if tR_rt' then $h(t)S_rh(t')$.
3. For all $t \in T$, if $\langle d\rangle\psi \in h(t)$ then there is a $t' \in T$ such that tR_dt' and $\psi \in h(t')$.
4. *start* $\in h(t)$ iff $t = root$; *term* $\in h(t)$ (respectively: *first* $\in h(t)$, *last* $\in h(t)$) iff t is a terminal node (respectively: iff t is a first node, iff t is a last node).

Then h is called a *sensible decoration* of **T**. (In short, a sensible decoration is simply a certain kind of order preserving morphism between a finite tree and the pseudo-model over $At(\Sigma)$.)

To prove a truth lemma for induced models, we need some additional facts.

Lemma 17. *Let* $\mathcal{A}$, $\mathcal{B} \in At(\Sigma)$. *Then* $\mathcal{A}S_l\mathcal{B}$ *iff* $\mathcal{B}S_r\mathcal{A}$, *and* $\mathcal{A}S_u\mathcal{B}$ *iff* $\mathcal{B}S_d\mathcal{A}$.

Proof. This is proved using the temporal logic axioms. We show that $\mathcal{A}S_d\mathcal{B}$ iff $\mathcal{B}S_u\mathcal{A}$; the other case is similar. Let $\mathcal{A}S_d\mathcal{B}$ and suppose for the sake of a contradiction that $\bigwedge \mathcal{B} \wedge \langle u\rangle \bigwedge \mathcal{A}$ is inconsistent. Thus $\vdash \bigwedge \mathcal{B} \rightarrow \neg\langle u\rangle \bigwedge \mathcal{A}$. Hence by generalisation $\vdash [d] \bigwedge \mathcal{B} \rightarrow [d]\neg\langle u\rangle \bigwedge \mathcal{A}$. As $\mathcal{A}S_d\mathcal{B}$, $\bigwedge \mathcal{A} \wedge \langle d\rangle \bigwedge \mathcal{B}$ is consistent, thus by simple modal reasoning, so is $\bigwedge \mathcal{A} \wedge \langle d\rangle\neg\langle u\rangle \bigwedge \mathcal{A}$. But by axiom 2d, $\vdash \bigwedge \mathcal{A} \rightarrow [d]\langle u\rangle\mathcal{A}$, therefore $\langle d\rangle(\langle u\rangle\mathcal{A} \wedge \neg\langle u\rangle \bigwedge \mathcal{A})$ is consistent — a contradiction. We conclude that $\mathcal{B}S_u\mathcal{A}$. A symmetric argument (using axiom 2u) establishes the converse, as required. ⊣

Corollary 18. *Let* h *be a sensible decoration of* **T** *and* $x \in \{l, r, u, d\}$. *Then for all nodes* t, t' *in* **T**, tR_xt' *implies* $h(t)S_xh(t')$.

Proof. For r and d this is immediate from the definition of sensible decorations. For l and r it follows from the previous lemma. ⊣

Lemma 19. *For all atoms $\mathcal{A}$ and $\mathcal{B}$ in $Cl(\Sigma)$, and all $x \in \{l, r, u\}$, if $\mathcal{A}S_x\mathcal{B}$ and $\langle x\rangle\psi \in \mathcal{A}$ then $\psi \in \mathcal{B}$.*

Proof. As $\mathcal{A}S_x\mathcal{B}$, $\bigwedge\mathcal{A} \wedge \langle x\rangle \bigwedge\mathcal{B}$ is consistent, hence as $\langle x\rangle\psi \in \mathcal{A}$, $\langle x\rangle\psi \wedge \langle x\rangle \bigwedge\mathcal{B}$ is consistent. It is an easy consequence of axiom 3, the partial functionality axiom, that $\vdash \langle x\rangle\theta \wedge \langle x\rangle\chi \rightarrow \langle x\rangle(\theta \wedge \chi)$; thus it follows that $\langle x\rangle(\psi \wedge \bigwedge\mathcal{B})$ is consistent, and thus so is $\psi \wedge \bigwedge\mathcal{B}$. As $\psi \in Cl(\Sigma)$, by maximality we get $\psi \in \mathcal{B}$. ⊣

Lemma 20 (Effects of the constants). *Let $\mathcal{A} \in At(\Sigma)$. Then*

1. *start $\in \mathcal{A}$ iff no formula of the form $\langle u\rangle\phi$ or $\langle u{+}\rangle\phi$ is in $\mathcal{A}$;*
2. *term $\in \mathcal{A}$ iff no formula of the form $\langle d\rangle\phi$ or $\langle d{+}\rangle\phi$ is in $\mathcal{A}$;*
3. *first $\in \mathcal{A}$ iff no formula of the form $\langle l\rangle\phi$ or $\langle l{+}\rangle\phi$ is in $\mathcal{A}$;*
4. *last $\in \mathcal{A}$ iff no formula of the form $\langle r\rangle\phi$ or $\langle r{+}\rangle\phi$ is in $\mathcal{A}$.*

Proof. For the one step modalities the result is immediate. For the transitive closure modalities, note that by axiom 4, $\vdash \langle x{+}\rangle\phi \leftrightarrow (\langle x\rangle\phi \vee \langle x\rangle\langle x{+}\rangle\phi)$. So, assuming that $\langle x{+}\rangle\phi \in Cl(\Sigma)$, by the first and second closure conditions, we find that $\langle x{+}\rangle\phi$ is in $\mathcal{A}$ iff either $\langle x\rangle\phi$ or $\langle x\rangle\langle x{+}\rangle\phi)$ is in $\mathcal{A}$. This observation reduces the transitive closure case to the case for the one step modalities. ⊣

Lemma 21. *Let $\mathcal{A}, \mathcal{B} \in At(\Sigma)$, let $x \in \{l, r, u, d\}$, and $\mathcal{A}S_x\mathcal{B}$. If $\langle x{+}\rangle\psi \in \mathcal{A}$ then either $\psi \in \mathcal{B}$ or $\langle x{+}\rangle\psi \in \mathcal{B}$.*

Proof. Follows from axiom 4 and the first and second closure conditions. ⊣

Lemma 22 (Truth lemma for induced models). *Let h be a sensible decoration of $\mathbf{T}$ and $\mathbf{M} = (\mathbf{T}, V)$ be the model induced by h on $\mathbf{T}$. Then for all nodes t in $\mathbf{T}$, and all $\psi \in Cl(\Sigma)$, $\mathbf{M}, t \models \psi$ iff $\psi \in h(t)$.*

Proof. By induction on the structure of ψ. The base case is clear by definition, and the boolean cases are trivial. It remains to consider the modalities.

First we treat the case for the one step modalities. Suppose $\mathbf{M}, t \models \langle x\rangle\psi$, where $x \in \{l, r, u, d\}$. Then there is a node t' such that tR_xt' and $\mathbf{M}, t' \models \psi$. As h is a sensible decoration, by Corollary 18 $h(t)S_xh(t')$, and by the inductive hypothesis, $\psi \in h(t')$. By Lemma 10, $\langle x\rangle\psi \in h(t)$ as required.

For the converse, suppose $\mathbf{M}, t \not\models \langle x\rangle\psi$. Then *either* $x = u$ and t is the root node (respectively: $x = d$ and t is a terminal node, $x = l$ and t is a first node, $x = r$ and t is a last node) *or* there is at least one node t' such that tR_xt' but for all such nodes $\mathbf{M}, t' \not\models \psi$. Suppose the former. Then by Lemma 20, $\langle x\rangle\psi \notin h(t)$ for any ψ, the required result. So suppose that there is a t' such that tR_xt' but for all such nodes $\mathbf{M}, t' \not\models \psi$. As h is sensible, $h(t)S_xh(t')$ and by the inductive hypothesis $\psi \notin h(t')$. Now, if $x \in \{l, r, u\}$ then by Lemma 19, $\langle x\rangle\psi \notin h(t)$, the required result. On the other hand, if $x = d$ then we also have that $\langle x\rangle\psi \notin h(t)$, as otherwise we would contradict item 3 in the definition of sensible decorations. Either way, we have the required result.

It remains to treat the transitive closure operators. Suppose $\mathbf{M}, t \models \langle x{+}\rangle\psi$, where $x \in \{l, r, u, d\}$. Then there is a node t' such that $t(R_x)^+t'$; that is, there is a finite sequence of nodes $t = t_1 R_x \cdots R_x t_k = t'$ and $\mathbf{M}, t' \models \psi$. As h is sensible, $h(t) = h(t_1) S_x \cdots S_x h(t_k) = h(t')$, and by the induction hypothesis, $\psi \in h(t')$. Thus by Lemma 12, $\langle x+\rangle\psi \in h(t)$, as required.

Conversely, suppose $\mathbf{M}, t \not\models \langle x+\rangle\psi$. Then for all t' such that $tR_x^+ t'$ we have $\mathbf{M}, t' \not\models \psi$, and hence by the inductive hypothesis, $\psi \notin h(t')$. Suppose for the sake of a contradiction that $\langle x+\rangle\psi \in h(t)$. Then by Lemma 20, the constant corresponding to x (that is, *first*, *last*, *start* and *term* for l, r, u and d respectively) does not belong to $h(t)$. As h is a sensible decoration, this means that t has an R_x successor t_1. By Lemma 21, either ψ or $\langle x+\rangle\psi$ belongs to $h(t_1)$, so as $\psi \notin h(t_1)$, $\langle x+\rangle\psi \in h(t_1)$. We are now in the same position with respect to t_1 that we were in with respect to t, and can repeat the argument as many times as we wish, generating a sequence of nodes $tR_x t_1 R_x t_2 \ldots$ such that $\langle x+\rangle\psi \in h(t_i)$ for all i. But as t lives in a finite tree, it only has *finitely* many successors; hence, for some j, $h(t_j)$ must also contain the constant corresponding to x — but then by Lemma 20, it must also contain $\neg\langle x+\rangle\psi \in h(t_i)$. As atoms are consistent this is impossible. We conclude that $\langle x+\rangle\psi \notin h(t)$, the desired result. ⊣

4.4 Levels and Ranks

The truth lemma for induced models suggests the following strategy for proving completeness: given a consistent sentence ϕ, simultaneously build by induction a suitable finite tree and sensible decoration, and then use the induced model. This is essentially what we shall do, but there is a problem. We need to build a *finite* tree, so we must guarantee that the inductive construction halts after finitely many steps. It is here that the Löb axioms come into play. Roughly speaking, they enable us to assign to each atom two natural numbers: a vertical 'layer', and a horizontal 'rank'. These have the following property: when generating vertically we can always work with atoms of lower level, and when generating horizontally we can always work with atoms of lower rank. This will enable us to devise a terminating construction method. (The reader is warned, however, that these remarks are only intended to give the basic intuition; as we shall see, the real situation is more complex.)

The basic observation on which these ideas rest is the following:

Lemma 23. *Let $x \in \{r, d\}$. If $\langle x+\rangle\phi$ is consistent then so is $\phi \wedge [x][x*]\neg\phi$.*

Proof. The contrapositive of the Löb axiom is $\langle x+\rangle\phi \rightarrow \langle x+\rangle(\phi \wedge [x+]\neg\phi)$. Using the first Segerberg axiom, this can be rewritten as

$$\langle x+\rangle\phi \rightarrow \langle x+\rangle(\phi \wedge [x][x*]\neg\phi).$$

Hence, if $\langle x+\rangle\phi$ is consistent, so are $\langle x+\rangle(\phi \wedge [x][x*]\neg\phi)$ and $\phi \wedge [x][x*]\neg\phi$. ⊣

The following group of definitions and lemmas build on this to show that the set of atoms is 'vertically well behaved'.

Definition 24. S_Σ is the set of all atoms in $At(\Sigma)$ that contain *start*.

Note that S_Σ is non-empty for any choice of $At(\Sigma)$. To see this, note that by axiom 6, $\langle u+\rangle$***start*** is consistent, hence so is ***start***. By our closure conditions, ***start*** $\in Cl(\Sigma)$, hence there is some atom in $At(\Sigma)$ containing ***start***.

Lemma 25. *Suppose* $At(\Sigma)\setminus \mathsf{S}_\Sigma$ *is non-empty, and let* $\mathsf{A} = \{\mathcal{A}_1,\ldots,\mathcal{A}_n\}$ *and* $\mathsf{B} = \{\mathcal{B}_1,\ldots,\mathcal{B}_m\}$ *be disjoint non-empty sets of atoms with* $\mathsf{A}\cup\mathsf{B} = At(\Sigma)\setminus \mathsf{S}_\Sigma$. *Then for some* $\mathcal{A}\in\mathsf{A}$,

$$\bigwedge \mathcal{A} \wedge [d][d+](\bigwedge \mathcal{B}_1 \vee \cdots \vee \bigwedge \mathcal{B}_m)$$

is consistent.

Proof. Let $\mathbf{A}$ be $\bigwedge \mathcal{A}_1 \vee\cdots\vee \bigwedge \mathcal{A}_n$. As any atom is consistent, $\mathbf{A}$ is consistent, and as $\neg$***start*** belongs to every atom in A, $\langle d+\rangle\mathbf{A}$ is consistent. Let S_Σ be enumerated as $\mathcal{S}_1,\ldots,\mathcal{S}_l$ (this is possible, for S_Σ is finite) and let $\mathbf{S}$ be $\bigwedge\mathcal{S}_1 \vee\cdots\vee \bigwedge\mathcal{S}_l$. As $\langle d+\rangle\mathbf{A}$ is consistent, so is $\langle d+\rangle(\mathbf{S}\vee\mathbf{A})$, hence by the previous lemma

$$(\mathbf{S}\vee\mathbf{A}) \wedge [d][d*]\neg(\mathbf{S}\vee\mathbf{A})$$

is consistent too.

Let $\mathbf{B}$ be $\bigwedge \mathcal{B}_1 \vee\cdots\vee \bigwedge\mathcal{B}_m$. As $\mathsf{S}_\Sigma\cup\mathsf{A}\cup\mathsf{B} = At(\Sigma)$, by Lemma 7, $\vdash \mathbf{S}\vee\mathbf{A}\vee\mathbf{B}$, hence $\vdash \neg(\mathbf{S}\vee\mathbf{A}) \rightarrow \mathbf{B}$. Thus $(\mathbf{S}\vee\mathbf{A})\wedge[d][d*]\mathbf{B}$ is consistent, hence $\mathbf{A}\wedge[d][d*]\mathbf{B}$ is consistent, hence for some $\mathcal{A}\in\mathsf{A}$, $\mathcal{A}\wedge[d][d*]\mathbf{B}$ is consistent, which yields the desired result. ⊣

Definition 26 (Levels 1). Let $Cl(\Sigma)$ be a closed set such that $At(\Sigma)\setminus\mathsf{S}_\Sigma$ is non-empty. Then the *levels* on $At(\Sigma)\setminus\mathsf{S}_\Sigma$ are defined as follows. L_0 is defined to be $\{\mathcal{A}\in(At(\Sigma)\setminus\mathsf{S}_\Sigma) \mid \textit{term}\in\mathcal{A}\}$. For $i\geq 0$, V_i is $\bigcup_{0\leq j\leq i} L_j$, and if $At(\Sigma)\setminus V_i$ is non-empty, then L_{i+1} exists and is defined to be

$$\left\{\mathcal{A}\in(At(\Sigma)\setminus\mathsf{S}_\Sigma) \mid \mathcal{A}\notin V_i \text{ and } \bigwedge\mathcal{A}\wedge[d][d*]\bigvee_{\mathcal{B}\in V_i}\bigwedge\mathcal{B} \text{ is consistent}\right\}.$$

On the other hand, if $At(\Sigma)\setminus V_i$ is empty then there is no $i+1$-th level on $At(\Sigma)\setminus\mathsf{S}_\Sigma$.

Lemma 27. *Suppose* $At(\Sigma)\setminus\mathsf{S}_\Sigma$ *is non-empty. Then every atom in* $At(\Sigma)\setminus\mathsf{S}_\Sigma$ *belongs to exactly one level. Furthermore, there is a maximal level* L_{max}.

Proof. It is clear that each atom in $At(\Sigma)\setminus\mathsf{S}_\Sigma$ belongs to at most one level. Further, it follows by induction that no level is non-empty. For the base case let $\mathcal{A}\in At(\Sigma)\setminus\mathsf{S}_\Sigma$. By Lemma 6 item 5, $\langle d*\rangle$*term* $\in\mathcal{A}$. If *term* $\in\mathcal{A}$, then $\mathcal{A}$ belongs to L_0. On the other hand, if *term* $\notin\mathcal{A}$, then $\langle d+\rangle$*term* $\in\mathcal{A}$, and by Lemma 12, there is an atom $\mathcal{B}$ such that *term* $\in\mathcal{B}$ and $\mathcal{A}(S_d)^+\mathcal{B}$. Either way, some atom contains *term* and the base case of the induction is established. To drive through the inductive step of this argument, use Lemma 25. It follows by induction that no level is empty.

As there are only finitely many atoms, there is a maximum level L_{max}. Suppose for the sake of a contradiction that some atom $\mathcal{A}$ belongs to no level. Then $\mathcal{A} \notin V_{max}$, hence $At(\Sigma) \setminus V_{max}$ is non-empty, hence by Lemma 25 L_{max+1} exists and is non-empty; a contradiction. We conclude that every atom belongs to at least one level. ⊣

Definition 28 (Levels 2). For an arbitrary closed set $Cl(\Sigma)$, the *levels* on $At(\Sigma)$ are defined as follows. If $\mathsf{S}_\Sigma = At(\Sigma)$, then all atoms have level 0. On the other hand, if $At(\Sigma) \setminus \mathsf{S}_\Sigma$ is non-empty, then all atoms in $At(\Sigma) \setminus \mathsf{S}_\Sigma$ receive the level assigned by Definition 26, and all atoms in S_Σ are assigned the level L_{max+1}, where L_{max} is the maximum level assigned to an atom in $At(\Sigma) \setminus \mathsf{S}_\Sigma$.

The following lemma tells us that $At(\Sigma)$ really is 'vertically well behaved'.

Lemma 29. *Let $\mathcal{A}, \mathcal{B} \in At(\Sigma)$. Suppose $\mathcal{A} \in L_{i+1}$ where $i \geq 0$ and $\langle d \rangle \phi \in \mathcal{A}$. Then there is an atom $\mathcal{B} \in L_m$, where $m < i+1$, such that $\phi \in \mathcal{B}$ and $\mathcal{A}S_d\mathcal{B}$.*

Proof. Case 1: $\mathcal{A} \in L_{max+1}$. Let $\langle d \rangle \phi \in \mathcal{A}$, and suppose for the sake of a contradiction that there is no atom $\mathcal{B}$ in a lower level such that $\phi \in \mathcal{B}$ and $\mathcal{A}S_d\mathcal{B}$. Now, by Lemma 10 there is at least one atom $\mathcal{C}$ such that $\phi \in \mathcal{C}$ and $\mathcal{A}S_d\mathcal{C}$, hence by our initial supposition $\mathcal{C}$ must be in L_{max+1}, and hence $\mathit{start} \in \mathcal{C}$. As $\mathcal{A}S_d\mathcal{C}$, by Lemma 17, $\mathcal{C}S_u\mathcal{A}$. As $\top \in \mathcal{A}$, $\langle u \rangle \top \in \mathcal{C}$. But by Lemma 20 this contradicts the fact that $\mathit{start} \in \mathcal{C}$. We conclude that an appropriate atom $\mathcal{B}$ in a lower level exists.

Case 2: $\mathcal{A} \in L_{i+1}$ where $i+1 \leq max$. Let $\langle d \rangle \phi \in \mathcal{A}$. Suppose for the sake of a contradiction that for all atoms $\mathcal{B} \in V_i$, $\bigwedge \mathcal{A} \wedge \langle d \rangle \bigwedge \mathcal{B}$ is inconsistent. This means that for all $\mathcal{B} \in V_i$, $\vdash \bigwedge \mathcal{A} \rightarrow [d]\neg \bigwedge \mathcal{B}$. Enumerate all the atoms in V_i as $\{\mathcal{B}_1, \ldots, \mathcal{B}_n\}$, and let $\mathbf{B}$ be $\bigwedge \mathcal{B}_1 \vee \cdots \vee \bigwedge \mathcal{B}_n$. It follows by simple modal reasoning that $\vdash \bigwedge \mathcal{A} \rightarrow [d]\neg\mathbf{B}$. Now, by our definition of levels, $\bigwedge \mathcal{A} \wedge [d]\mathbf{B}$ is consistent, therefore $\bigwedge \mathcal{A} \wedge [d](\mathbf{B} \wedge \neg\mathbf{B})$ is consistent also. But as $\langle d \rangle \phi$ belongs to $\mathcal{A}$, this implies that $\langle d \rangle(\mathbf{B} \wedge \neg\mathbf{B})$ is consistent, which is impossible. We conclude that the required atom $\mathcal{B}$ exists. ⊣

We now turn to a trickier task: ensuring that $At(\Sigma)$ is also 'horizontally well behaved'. We need the auxiliary notion of a downset.

Definition 30 (Downsets). Let $\mathcal{A}_0 \in L_{i+1}$, where $i \geq 0$. Then the *downset* of $\mathcal{A}_0$ is $\{\mathcal{D} \in V_i \mid \mathcal{A}_0 S_d \mathcal{D}\}$, and the *initial segment* of the downset is simply $\{\mathcal{D} \in V_i \mid \mathcal{A}_0 S_d \mathcal{D}$ and $\mathit{first} \in \mathcal{D}\}$.

Lemma 31. *Let $\mathcal{A}_0 \in L_{i+1}$, where $i \geq 0$. Then the downset of $\mathcal{A}_0$, and the initial segment of this downset, are both non-empty.*

Proof. As $\mathcal{A}_0 \in L_{i+1}$, where $i \geq 0$, $\mathit{term} \notin \mathcal{A}_0$. Hence by Lemma 20, there is some formula of the form $\langle d \rangle \psi \in \mathcal{A}_0$. By axiom 9 and the fifth closure condition, $\langle d \rangle \mathit{first} \in \mathcal{A}_0$. By the previous lemma, there is a $\mathcal{D} \in V_i$ such that $\mathit{first} \in \mathcal{D}$ and $\mathcal{A}_0 S_d \mathcal{D}$, thus the initial segment of $\mathcal{A}_0$'s downset is non-empty, and so is $\mathcal{A}_0$'s downset. ⊣

In order to proceed further, we must define a notion of *rank* on downsets. The basic ideas are similar to those underlying our notion of level; in particular, our initial observation concerning the Löb axiom does the real work. As a first step, we prove a horizontal analog of Lemma 25.

Lemma 32. *Let* D *be a downset of some atom* $\mathcal{A}_0$ *belonging to* L_{i+1}*, where* $i \geq 0$*, and let* I *be its initial segment. Suppose* $\mathsf{D} \setminus \mathsf{I}$ *is non-empty, and let* $\mathsf{A} = \{\mathcal{A}_1, \ldots, \mathcal{A}_n\}$ *and* $\mathsf{B} = \{\mathcal{B}_1, \ldots, \mathcal{B}_m\}$ *be disjoint non-empty sets of atoms such that* $\mathsf{A} \cup \mathsf{B} = \mathsf{D} \setminus \mathsf{I}$*. Then for some* $\mathcal{A} \in \mathsf{A}$*,*

$$\bigwedge \mathcal{A} \wedge [r][r+](\bigwedge \mathcal{B}_1 \vee \cdots \vee \bigwedge \mathcal{B}_m)$$

is consistent.

Proof. Let $\mathbf{A}$ be $\bigwedge \mathcal{A}_1 \vee \cdots \vee \bigwedge \mathcal{A}_n$. As any atom is consistent, so is $\mathbf{A}$. By the previous lemma, I is non-empty. Let $\mathbf{I}$ be $\bigwedge \mathcal{I}_1 \vee \cdots \vee \bigwedge \mathcal{I}_l$, where the $\mathcal{I}_j$ $(1 \leq j \leq l)$ are all and only the elements of I. As *first* does not belong to any atom in A, $\langle r+\rangle \mathbf{A}$ is consistent.

Let H (short for 'High') be the set of all atoms in $At(\Sigma) \setminus V_i$. Note that H is non-empty, for by our initial assumption there is at least one atom in L_{i+1}. Define $\mathbf{H}$ to be $\bigwedge \mathcal{H}_1 \vee \cdots \vee \bigwedge \mathcal{H}_p$, where the $\mathcal{H}_j$ $(1 \leq j \leq p)$ are all and only the elements of H. Let L (short for 'Low') be the set of all atoms in $V_i \setminus \mathsf{D}$. Note that it is possible that L is empty. If this is the case, we define $\mathbf{L}$ to be $\perp$, otherwise we define it to be $\bigwedge \mathcal{L}_1 \vee \cdots \vee \bigwedge \mathcal{L}_q$, where the $\mathcal{L}_j$ $(1 \leq j \leq q)$ are all and only the elements of L. Let Ψ be $\mathbf{I} \vee \mathbf{H} \vee \mathbf{L} \vee \mathbf{A}$. As $\langle r+\rangle \mathbf{A}$ is consistent, so is $\langle r+\rangle \Psi$, hence by Lemma 23, $\Psi \wedge [r][r+]\neg\Psi$ is consistent too.

Let $\mathbf{B}$ be $\bigwedge \mathcal{B}_1 \vee \cdots \vee \bigwedge \mathcal{B}_m$. As $At(\Sigma) = \mathsf{I} \cup \mathsf{H} \cup \mathsf{L} \cup \mathsf{A} \cup \mathsf{B}$, it follows from Lemma 7 that

$$\begin{aligned} \vdash \mathbf{I} \vee \mathbf{H} \vee \mathbf{L} \vee \mathbf{A} \vee \mathbf{B} &\Rightarrow \vdash \neg(\mathbf{I} \vee \mathbf{H} \vee \mathbf{L} \vee \mathbf{A}) \rightarrow \mathbf{B} \\ &\Rightarrow \vdash \neg\Psi \rightarrow \mathbf{B} \\ &\Rightarrow \Psi \wedge [r][r+]\mathbf{B} \text{ is consistent} \\ &\Rightarrow \mathbf{A} \wedge [r][r+]\mathbf{B} \text{ is consistent.} \end{aligned}$$

Hence for some $\mathcal{A} \in \mathsf{A}$, $\mathcal{A} \wedge [r][r+]\mathbf{B}$ is consistent, the required result. ⊣

Definition 33 (Ranks 1). Let D be a downset of some atom $\mathcal{A}_0$ belonging to L_{i+1} $(i \geq 0)$ with a non-empty initial segment I. Then the $\mathcal{A}_0$-*ranks* on $\mathsf{D} \setminus \mathsf{I}$ are defined as follows. R_0 is $\{\mathcal{D} \in (\mathsf{D} \setminus \mathsf{I}) \mid \textit{last} \in \mathcal{D}\}$. For $i \geq 0$, H_i is defined to be $\bigcup_{0 \leq j \leq i} R_j$, and if $\mathsf{D} \setminus H_i$ is non-empty then R_{i+1} exists and is defined to be

$$\left\{ \mathcal{D} \in (\mathsf{D} \setminus \mathsf{I}) \mid \mathcal{D} \notin H_i \text{ and } \bigwedge \mathcal{D} \wedge [r][r*] \bigvee_{\mathcal{E} \in H_i} \bigwedge \mathcal{E} \text{ is consistent} \right\}.$$

On the other hand, if $\mathsf{D} \setminus H_i$ is empty then there is no $i+1$-th rank on $\mathsf{D} \setminus \mathsf{S}_{\Sigma}$.

Although the point should be clear, it's probably worth emphasizing that ranks are defined relative to some atom $\mathcal{A}_0$. Levels, on the other hand, were defined in absolute terms.

Next we prove a horizontal analog of Lemma 27.

Lemma 34. *Let* D *be a downset of some atom* $\mathcal{A}_0$ *belonging to* L_{i+1}, *where* $i \geq 0$, *with a non-empty initial segment* I. *Then every atom in* D $\setminus$ I *belongs to exactly one* $\mathcal{A}_0$*-rank. Furthermore, there is a maximal* $\mathcal{A}_0$*-rank* R_{max} *on* D.

Proof. It is clear that each atom in D $\setminus$ I belongs at most one $\mathcal{A}_0$-rank. Further, it follows by induction that no $\mathcal{A}_0$-rank is non-empty. For the base case, note that D is the downset of the atom $\mathcal{A}_0$ in L_{i+1}. At $\mathcal{A}_0$ has a non-empty downset, it contains a formula of the form $\langle d\rangle\psi$. By axiom 9 and the fifth condition on closures, it must also contain $\langle d\rangle$*last*, hence by Lemma 29 there is some atom $\mathcal{D} \in$ D containing *last* and the base case is established. The inductive step follows from Lemma 32, and hence every $\mathcal{A}_0$-rank is non-empty. The remainder of the argument is essentially the same as that for Lemma 27. ⊣

Definition 35 (Ranks 2). For an arbitrary downset D of an atom $\mathcal{A}_0$, the $\mathcal{A}_0$-*ranks* on D are defined as follows. If D $\setminus$ I is empty, then all atoms in D have $\mathcal{A}_0$-rank 0. On the other hand, if D $\setminus$ I is non-empty, then all atoms in D $\setminus$ I receive the $\mathcal{A}_0$-rank assigned by Definition 33, and all atoms in I are assigned the $\mathcal{A}_0$-rank R_{max+1}, where R_{max} is the maximum $\mathcal{A}_0$-rank assigned to an atom in D $\setminus$ I.

Lemma 36. *Suppose* $\mathcal{A}$ *has* $\mathcal{A}_0$*-rank* R_{i+1}, *where* $i \geq 0$ *and* $\langle r\rangle\phi \in \mathcal{A}$. *Then there is a* $\mathcal{B}$ *with* $\mathcal{A}_0$*-rank* R_m, *where* $m < i+1$, *such that* $\phi \in \mathcal{B}$ *and* $\mathcal{A}S_r\mathcal{B}$.

Proof. Essentially identical to the proof of Lemma 29. ⊣

The previous lemma is our first clue that downsets are horizontally well behaved, but we have more work to do. The next definition isolates the key concept required.

Definition 37 (Witnessing paths). Let $\mathcal{A} \in L_{i+1}$ and let D be its downset. A *witnessing path* for $\mathcal{A}$ is non-empty subset $\{\mathcal{D}_1, \ldots, \mathcal{D}_n\}$ of D such that:

1. $\mathcal{D}_i S_r \mathcal{D}_{i+1}$, for for all $i < n$.
2. *first* $\in \mathcal{D}_1$; and for all $i > 1$, *first* $\notin \mathcal{D}_i$.
3. *last* $\in \mathcal{D}_n$; and for all $i < n$, *last* $\notin \mathcal{D}_i$.
4. If $\langle d\rangle\psi \in \mathcal{A}$, then $\psi \in \mathcal{D}_i$ for some $0 \leq i \leq n$.

The reader should compare this definition with the definition of sensible decorations. Witnessing paths are designed to provide the structure demanded by the truth lemma for induced models, and to do so using atoms of lower level. Thus our goal is to prove that enough witnessing paths exist. First, a preliminary lemma.

Lemma 38. *Let $\mathcal{A} \in L_{i+1}$, and let $\mathcal{F}$ be any element of the initial segment of $\mathcal{A}$'s downset. If $\langle d\rangle\psi \in \mathcal{A}$, then $\langle r*\rangle\psi \in \mathcal{F}$.*

Proof. By Lemma 31, the initial segment of $\mathcal{A}$'s downset is non-empty, so such an $\mathcal{F}$ exists. Suppose for the sake of a contradiction that for some $\langle d\rangle\psi \in \mathcal{A}$, $\langle r*\rangle\psi \notin \mathcal{F}$. By the third closure condition, $\neg\langle r*\rangle\psi \in \mathcal{F}$, hence as *first* $\in \mathcal{F}$, *first* $\wedge \neg\langle r*\rangle\psi$ is consistent. Now, as $\mathcal{A}S_d\mathcal{F}$ holds, $\bigwedge \mathcal{A} \wedge \langle d\rangle \bigwedge \mathcal{F}$ is consistent, hence $\bigwedge \mathcal{A} \wedge \langle d\rangle(\mathit{first} \wedge \neg\langle r*\rangle\psi)$ is consistent. As $\langle d\rangle\psi \in \mathcal{A}$,

$$\bigwedge \mathcal{A} \wedge \langle d\rangle\psi \wedge \langle d\rangle(\mathit{first} \wedge \neg\langle r*\rangle\psi)$$

is also consistent. Hence by axiom 8,

$$\bigwedge \mathcal{A} \wedge [d](\mathit{first} \rightarrow \langle r*\rangle\psi) \wedge [d](\mathit{first} \rightarrow \neg\langle r*\rangle\psi)$$

is consistent, thus by simple modal reasoning,

$$\bigwedge \mathcal{A} \wedge [d]((\mathit{first} \rightarrow \langle r*\rangle\psi) \wedge (\mathit{first} \rightarrow \neg\langle r*\rangle\psi))$$

is consistent as well. As $\mathcal{A}$'s downset is non-empty, $\langle d\rangle\mathit{first} \in \mathcal{A}$, hence

$$\langle d\rangle\mathit{first} \wedge [d]((\mathit{first} \rightarrow \langle r*\rangle\psi) \wedge (\mathit{first} \rightarrow \neg\langle r*\rangle\psi))$$

is consistent, hence $\langle d\rangle(\langle r*\rangle\psi \wedge \neg\langle r*\rangle\psi)$ is consistent too — but this is impossible. We conclude that $\langle r*\rangle\psi \in \mathcal{F}$. ⊣

Lemma 39. *Let $\mathcal{A} \in L_{i+1}$ and let* D *be its downset. Then $\mathcal{A}$ has a witnessing path.*

Proof. Choose any element $\mathcal{F}$ of $\mathcal{A}$'s initial segment. We now construct a witnessing path for $\mathcal{A}$ whose first item is $\mathcal{F}$.

Case 1: $\mathcal{F}$ contains no formula of the form $\langle r\rangle\phi$. Suppose $\langle d\rangle\psi \in \mathcal{A}$. By the previous lemma, $\langle r*\rangle\psi \in \mathcal{F}$. As no formula of the form $\langle r\rangle\phi$ is in $\mathcal{F}$, no formula of the form $\langle r+\rangle\phi$ is in $\mathcal{F}$ either, and hence $\psi \in \mathcal{F}$. As a special case of this, note that by axiom 9 and the fifth closure condition, *last* $\in \mathcal{F}$. Hence $\{\mathcal{F}\}$ is a witnessing path for $\mathcal{A}$.

Case 2: $\mathcal{F}$ contains a formula of the form $\langle r\rangle\phi$. By Lemma 36, it is possible to construct a sequence $\mathcal{F} = \mathcal{D}_1 S_r \mathcal{D}_2 \cdots$, where all items in the sequence belong to $\mathcal{A}$'s downset, and such that $\mathcal{D}_i S_r \mathcal{D}_{i+1}$ implies that $\mathcal{D}_{i+1}$ has a strictly lower $\mathcal{A}$-rank than $\mathcal{D}_i$. Construct such a sequence that is closed under S_r successors. As $\langle x\rangle\psi \in \mathcal{F}$, this sequence has length at least 2. Moreover, the sequence must be finite: as each item in the sequence has a strictly lower $\mathcal{A}$-rank than all its predecessors, each item in the sequence is unique. As there are only finitely many atoms in $\mathcal{A}$'s downset, the sequence has length n, for some natural number n.

Clearly *first* $\in \mathcal{F}$. Moreover, for any atom $\mathcal{D}_i$ in the sequence ($2 \leq i \leq n$), $\mathcal{D}_{i-1} S_r \mathcal{D}_i$, hence by Lemma 17 $\mathcal{D}_i S_l \mathcal{D}_{i-1}$. As $\top \in \mathcal{D}_{i-1}$, $\langle l\rangle\top \in \mathcal{D}_i$, hence by Lemma 20, *first* $\notin \mathcal{D}_i$. Next, note that there can be no formula of the form $\langle r\rangle\psi \in \mathcal{D}_n$. If there were, we could apply Lemma 36 to find an atom $\mathcal{D}_{n+1}$ such that $\mathcal{D}S_r\mathcal{D}_{n+1}$. But the sequence is closed under S_r successors, and $\mathcal{D}_n$ is the final item in the sequence, so this is impossible. Thus no formula of the form $\langle r\rangle\psi$ belongs to $\mathcal{D}_n$, hence by Lemma 20, *last* $\in \mathcal{D}_n$. We leave it to the reader to verify (again using Lemma 20) that *last* cannot belong to $\mathcal{D}_i$ for $i < n$.

It remains to verify that $\langle d\rangle\psi \in \mathcal{A}$ implies $\mathcal{A} \in \mathcal{D}_i$ for some $1 \leq i \leq n$. Suppose for the sake of a contradiction that this is not the case; that is, for some $\langle d\rangle\psi \in \mathcal{A}$, $\psi \notin \mathcal{D}_i$ for all $1 \leq i \leq n$. Now, by the previous lemma, $\langle d\rangle\psi \in \mathcal{A}$ implies that $\langle r*\rangle\psi \in \mathcal{F}$. As $\langle r*\rangle\psi \in \mathcal{F}$ and $\psi \notin \mathcal{F}$, we have that $\langle r+\rangle\psi \in \mathcal{F}$. By Lemma 21, for all $1 \leq i < n$, if $\langle r+\rangle\psi \in \mathcal{D}_i$ and $\mathcal{D}_i S_r \mathcal{D}_{i+1}$, then $\psi \in \mathcal{D}_{i+1}$ or $\langle r+\rangle\psi \in \mathcal{D}_{i+1}$. As by assumption ψ belongs to no item in the sequence, $\langle r+\rangle\psi$ belongs to them all, and in particular, $\langle r+\rangle\psi \in \mathcal{D}_n$. By Lemma 20, this means that $\neg$*last* $\in \mathcal{D}_n$, contradicting the fact that *last* $\in \mathcal{D}_n$. We conclude that our original supposition was false, and have the desired result. ⊣

4.5 Constructing and Decorating a Finite Tree

We can now simultaneously construct a finite tree $\mathbf{T}$ and a decoration h of $\mathbf{T}$ by induction. The construction will terminate after finitely many steps, and, as we shall see, results in a *sensible* decoration of $\mathbf{T}$.

So, suppose ψ is LOFT-consistent. Let T be a denumerably infinite set. We will use (finitely many) of its elements as the tree nodes, and decorate them with atoms taken from $At(\{start \wedge \langle d*\rangle\psi\})$.

Stage 1. Choose some $t_1 \in \mathsf{T}$ and an atom $\mathcal{A} \in At(\{start \wedge \langle d*\rangle\psi\})$ that contains $start \wedge \langle d*\rangle\psi$. (As ψ is consistent, so is $start \wedge \langle d*\rangle\psi$, so this is possible.) Define

$$
\begin{aligned}
T^1 &:= \{t_1\}\\
R_r^1 &:= \emptyset\\
R_d^1 &:= \emptyset\\
h^1 &:= \{(t_1, \mathcal{A})\}.
\end{aligned}
$$

Stage n+1. Suppose n stages of the construction have been performed. Call $t \in T^n$ *unsatisfied* if for some $\langle d\rangle\psi \in h^n(t)$ there is no $t' \in T^n$ such that tR_dt' and $\psi \in h^n(t')$.

if there are no unsatisfied nodes
then halt
else choose an unsatisfied node t. As $\langle d\rangle\psi \in h^n(t)$, by Lemma 39 $h^n(t)$ has a witnessing path $\{\mathcal{D}_1, \ldots, \mathcal{D}_k\}$. Let $t_1, \ldots, t_k \in \mathsf{T}\backslash T^n$. Define:

$$
\begin{aligned}
T^{n+1} &= T^n \cup \{t_1, \ldots, t_k\}\\
R_d^{n+1} &= R_d^n \cup \{(t, t_1), \ldots, (t, t_k)\}\\
R_r^{n+1} &= R_r^n \cup \{(t_i, t_{i+1}) \mid 1 \leq i < k\}\\
h^{n+1} &= h^n \cup \{(t_i, \mathcal{D}_i) \mid 1 \leq i \leq k\}.
\end{aligned}
$$

Lemma 40. *The above construction halts after finitely many steps. Moreover the number of nodes adjoined in the course of the construction is finite.*

Proof. Whenever we adjoin new R_d successors to a node t, we adjoin one new node for each element of the chosen witnessing path for $h(t)$. But witnessing paths are finite, thus at each stage we adjoin only finitely many nodes. Moreover, as witnessing paths are subsets of downsets, each element of $h(t)$'s witnessing path belongs to a strictly lower level that $h(t)$. As there are only finitely many levels, we can only adjoin new nodes finitely many times in the course of the construction. ⊣

Let max be the stage at which the construction halts. Define T to be T^{max}, R_d to be R_d^{max}, R_r to be R_r^{max}, and h to be h^{max}. Let R_l and R_u be the converses of R_r and R_d respectively. Let $\mathbf{T}$ be (T, R_l, R_r, R_u, R_d).

Lemma 41. $\mathbf{T}$ *is a finite tree and* h *is a sensible decoration of* $\mathbf{T}$.

Proof. That $\mathbf{T}$ is a finite tree follows straightforwardly from the nature of the inductive construction. To see that h is a sensible decoration of $\mathbf{T}$, argue as follows.

First, suppose the construction halts immediately after stage 1. By construction, $start \in h(t)$. As the construction halted after one step, t_1 was not unsatisfied, so there is no formula of the form $\langle d \rangle \psi \in h(t_1)$ and hence by Lemma 20, $term \in h(t)$. By axiom 10, $first, last \in h(t)$ also. It follows that h is a sensible decoration of $\mathbf{T}$.

So suppose the construction closed after max steps, where $max > 1$. The important point to observe is that because we used witnessing paths to satisfy tree nodes t, h fulfills the first three clauses in the definition of a sensible decoration. The fourth clause in the definition of sensible decorations insists that the constants be 'sensibly distributed'. Now, *first* and *last* are sensibly distributed in all witnessing paths. Further, *start* is sensibly distributed because $start \in h(t)$, where t is the root node in the tree, and thereafter the construction assigns atoms of lower level to tree nodes, and such nodes do not contain *start*. We leave it the reader to verify that *term* is also sensibly distributed. ⊣

Theorem 42. LOFT *is complete with respect to finite trees.*

Proof. Given a consistent formula ϕ, use the inductive construction to build a finite tree $\mathbf{T}$ and a decoration $h : \mathbf{T} \longrightarrow At(\{start \wedge \langle d* \rangle \phi\})$. Let $\mathbf{M}$ be the model induced by h on $\mathbf{T}$. By the previous lemma, h is a sensible decoration of $\mathbf{T}$, hence by the truth lemma for induced models (Lemma 22), $\mathbf{M}$ satisfies $start \wedge \langle d* \rangle \phi$ at the root node, and thus ϕ is true somewhere in this model. ⊣

5 Discussion

To conclude the paper we note some issues concerning complexity and theorem proving raised by this work. As a first step, note that LOFT is decidable. This could be proved by appealing to the results of Rabin (1969), but the completeness result yields it immediately.

Theorem 43. LOFT *is decidable.*

Proof. Because we are only working with finite trees, the set of satisfiable formulas is clearly RE. But the set of non-satisfiable formulas is also RE: by completeness, our axiomatisation recursively enumerates all the valid $\mathcal{L}$ formulas. So if a formula ϕ is not satisfiable on a finite tree, then its negation will eventually be generated.

What is the complexity of LOFT's satisfiability problem? The easiest way to answer this question is to think in terms of pseudo-models. We proved the following completeness theorem: if ϕ is consistent, then, by Lemma 22, it is satisfiable in a pseudo-model, namely, the pseudo-model over $At(\{\phi\})$. (The corresponding soundness theorem is clear: if ϕ is not consistent, it cannot belong to any atom in any closure, hence it cannot be satisfied in any pseudo-model at all.) As we now know that LOFT is the logic of finite trees, the completeness result for pseudo-models takes on a new significance. For a start, as $|At(\{\phi\})|$ is $O(2^{|\phi|})$, it gives an exponential upper bound on the size of pseudo-models needed to establish LOFT-satisfiability. This immediately yields:

Theorem 44. LOFT-*satisfiability is in NEXPTIME.*

But with a little more effort, one can do better.

Theorem 45. LOFT-*satisfiability is EXPTIME-complete.*

Proof. The lower bound is an immediate corollary of Spaan's (1993) analysis of the lower bound result for PDL. She notes that the following fragment of PDL is EXPTIME-hard: formulas of the form $\psi \wedge [a*]\theta$, (where ψ and θ contain only the atomic program a and no embedded modalities) that are satisfiable at the root of a finite binary tree. Trivially, this PDL fragment can be identified with an $\mathcal{L}$ fragment in the modalities $[d*]$ and $[d]$, hence LOFT-satisfiability is also EXPTIME-hard.

The upper bound can be proved by using the methods of Pratt (1979). We sketch what is involved. The reader who consults Pratt's paper will have no difficulty in filling in the details.

Following Pratt, we define $H(\Sigma)$, the set of ***Hintikka sets*** over Σ, to be subsets of $Cl(\Sigma)$ that have all the properties of atoms listed in lemma 6, but that may not be consistent. That is, $At(\Sigma) \subseteq H(\Sigma) \subseteq Cl(\Sigma)$. For $\mathcal{H}, \mathcal{H}' \in H(\Sigma)$ and $x \in \{l, r, u, d\}$, define $\mathcal{H}S'_x\mathcal{H}'$ to hold iff for some atomic formula p, $\langle x \rangle p \in \mathcal{H}$ and $p \in \mathcal{H}'$, and moreover, for all atomic formulas q, $[x]q \in \mathcal{H}$ implies $q \in \mathcal{H}'$. Define

$$\mathbf{D}^0 := (H(\Sigma), \{S'_x, (S'_x)^+\}_{x \in \{l,r,u,d\}}).$$

Given $\mathbf{D}^n$, one forms $\mathbf{D}^{n+1}$ by eliminating all Hintikka sets $\mathcal{H} \in \mathbf{D}^n$ such that $\langle x \rangle \phi \in \mathcal{H}$, but there is no $\mathcal{H}'$ such that $\phi \in \mathcal{H}'$ and $\mathcal{H}S'_x\mathcal{H}'$. The relations for $\mathbf{D}^{n+1}$ are defined by restricting the relations on $\mathbf{D}^n$ to this (smaller) set of Hintikka sets. This process terminates (there are only finitely many Hintikka sets) and yields a model. It is standard work to show that if ϕ is consistent, then this model satisfies ϕ.

From the point of view of complexity, two points are important. First, the process terminates after at most exponentially many steps, as there are only exponentially many Hintikka sets. Second, at each stage it is possible to calculate in polynomial time which Hintikka sets to eliminate. Thus 'elimination of Hintikka sets' is a deterministic EXPTIME-algorithm for LOFT-satisfiability. $\dashv$

However, while interesting in its own right, the above EXPTIME-completeness result for LOFT raises another question. For many applications we are not merely interested in whether or not ϕ is satisfiable: if ϕ is satisfiable, we would like to see a concrete finite tree that satisfies it. (This would be useful for applications in computational linguistics.) By the previous result, this problem is EXPTIME-hard, but at present we do not have tight upper and lower bounds.

Similar considerations apply to theorem proving for LOFT. It is clearly possible to devise tableaux systems for LOFT: working with pseudo-models is essentially the same as working with tableaux, and indeed the completeness result for pseudo-models gives us all that is required to define such systems. But a more interesting question is the following. Is it possible to develop a tableaux system that produces finite trees directly and is reasonably efficient on the formulas typically encountered in applications? Such issues are the focus of our ongoing work.

Acknowledgement. Wilfried Meyer-Viol was partially supported by the Engineering and Physical Sciences Research Counsil (EPSRC) under Grant Reference Number GR/K68776.

Part of the research was carried out while Maarten de Rijke was with CWI, Amsterdam; during this period he was supported by the Netherlands Organization for Scientific Research (NWO), project NF 102/62-356.

References

Backofen, R., Rogers, J., Vijay-Shanker, K.: A first-order axiomatisation of the theory of finite trees. *Journal of Logic, Language and Information*, 4:5–39, 1995.

van Benthem, J., Meyer-Viol, W.: *Logical Semantics of Programming.* Manuscript, 1994.

Berlage, T.: A selective undo mechanism for graphical user interfaces on command objects. *ACM Transactions on Computer-Human Interaction* 1(3):269–294, 1994.

Blackburn, P., Gardent, C., Meyer-Viol, W.: Talking about trees. In *Proceedings of the 6th Conference of the European Chapter of the Association for Computational Linguistics*, pages 21–29, Utrecht, The Netherlands, 1993.

Blackburn, P., Meyer-Viol, W.: Linguistics, logic and finite trees. *Bulletin of the IGPL* 2:2–29, 1994.

Blackburn, P., Gardent, C.: A specification language for lexical functional grammars. In *Proceedings of the 7th Conference of the European Chapter of the Association for Computational Linguistics*, pages 39–44, Dublin, Ireland, 1995.

Courcelle, B.: Fundamental properties of infinite trees. *Theoretical Computer Science* 25:95–169, 1985.

Fischer, M.J., Ladner, R.F.: Propositional dynamic logic of regular programs. *J. Comp. Syst. Sci.* 18:194–211, 1979.

Kracht, M.: Mathematical Aspects of command relations. In *Proceedings of the 6th Conference of the European Chapter of the Association for Computational Linguistics*, pages 240–249, Utrecht, The Netherlands, 1993.

Kracht, M.: Syntactic codes and grammar refinement. *Journal of Logic, Language and Information* 4: 41–60, 1995.

Maher, M.: Complete axiomatisations of the algebras of finite, rational and infinite trees. In *Proceedings of the 3rd International Symposium on Logic in Computer Science*, pages 348–357, Edinburgh, Scotland, 1988.

Goldblatt, R.: *Logics of Time and Computation.* 2nd edition, CSLI Lecture notes 7, Center for the Study of Language and Information, Stanford, 1992.

Pratt, V.: Models of program logics. In *Proceedings of the 20th IEEE Symposium on Foundations of Computer Science*, pages 115-122, 1979.

Rabin, M.: Decidability of second-order theories and automata on infinite trees. *Transactions of the American Mathematical Society* 141:1–35, 1969.

Rogers, J.: *A Descriptive Approach to Language-Theoretic Complexity.* Studies in Logic, Language and Information, CSLI Publications, Stanford, 1996, to appear.

Smoryński, C.: *Self Reference and Modal Logic.* Springer Verlag, 1985.

Spaan, E.: *Complexity of Modal Logics.* PhD thesis, University of Amsterdam, 1993.

Representing Unification in a Logical Framework*

Jason Brown and Lincoln A. Wallen

Oxford University Computing Laboratory,
Wolfson Building,
Parks Road,
Oxford OX1 3QD,
U.K.

1 Introduction

The aim of this paper is three-fold:

- First, to present the search space for unification in $\lambda\Pi$: the dependently typed lambda calculus at the heart of the Edinburgh Logical Framework.
- Secondly, to demonstrate how search spaces for unification in first-order languages can be derived from this system by inspecting the structure of the signature that defines the encoding of the first-order language in the framework.
- Thirdly, to outline the context for this study as an approach to a problem of modularity in environments for machine-assisted proof.

Unification algorithms for $\lambda\Pi$ have been discussed before [8, 9, 21, 22]; our contribution is to present the search space for the unification algorithm as a reduction system following [26]. This presentation has a certain simplicity and it is based on a formal theory of type similarity.[2] However, our main purpose for re-presenting unification in this particular way is to support the second and third aims above.

The rest of this introduction is devoted to a discussion of the motivation for our work.

1.1 A problem of modularity

To manipulate a logic by machine we must have some representation of the terms, and possibly the proofs, of the logic in the machine, and some representation of the methods of manipulation to be used. It is usual for terms to be represented by data structures and methods to be represented by programs. Proofs are variously represented by data structures [7], by programs [11], or by computations [2].

* This research is supported in part by UK EPSRC grant GR/J46616 and an HCM fellowship (ERBCHBG-CT94-0733) at TH Darmstadt, Fachbereich Informatik, Fachgebiet Intellektik, D-64283 Darmstadt, Germany, held by the first author.

[2] This theory is developed fully in [3].

Some important judgements that we wish to make about these representations are

- that the data structures faithfully represent logical notions;
- that the programs perform logically sound manipulations of, or computations over, the data structures;
- that the programs are efficient enough for practical purposes.

Implementing a computational environment for a logic may require a substantial effort, possibly extending over several years. This, together with the recognition that different problem domains require different logical formalisms, has the consequence that it is rare for environments to comprise the most effective methods available at any given time.

In our opinion, what hinders the routine incorporation of the very best developments in automated reasoning into flexible and practical environments for machine-assisted proof is a general *lack of modularity* in the description and implementation of the algorithms themselves.

1.2 Parameterisation via logical frameworks

One approach to this problem of modularity is to achieve a degree of parameterisation in the definition of proof procedures by means of a *logical framework*. A logical framework is a (formal) metalanguage together with a discipline for representing the logical notions common to various classes of logical system. A degree of modularity is achieved by developing machine representations of the terms (and sometimes the proofs) of the *framework* language, and implementing methods for manipulating these items. The terms and proofs of the target logic are then encoded as terms of the framework language and manipulated via the mechanisms implemented for manipulating the framework language itself.[3] Paulson's Isabelle system [19] and Pfenning's Elf system [20] are particularly successful realisations of this approach.

1.3 Limits of parameterisation

While the degree of parameterisation achieved by the systems cited above constitutes a substantial step forwards, the algorithmic methods for manipulating object logics reside, conceptually speaking, within one module, albeit parameterised by the explicit definition of the logical systems of interest. Methods that make direct use of the object languages themselves must still be implemented individually, and would typically involve subverting the typing discipline used to guarantee soundness.

Perhaps this point is best illustrated by an example. Suppose we wish to manipulate (classical) predicate logic within Isabelle; we represent the terms, formulae and inference rules in the type-theoretic metalanguage of the system and manipulate these representations via the impressive suite of tactics available

[3] [14, 15] contain selections of articles on such frameworks.

in the system. Although we may know an efficient unification algorithm for first-order terms [18], or an efficient method of proof-search [17], within Isabelle we will make use of an implementation of higher-order unification, and resolution tactics, that are based on Isabelle's (classical) type-theoretic metalanguage. To do better than this we must resort to direct programming.

It is not this need for programming that we wish to avoid; we see this step as essential. The type of problem we wish to address is how we can smoothly and soundly import algorithmic methods that are formulated directly in terms of the object level language into an environment such as Isabelle. In other words, it is the interface of these object logic specific programs to the environment that we are concerned with. We seek to support the systematic *enhancement* of such systems, not necessarily the *replacement* of any of their existing facilities.

1.4 Procedures and invariants

Our suggestion for increasing the modularity achievable in environments structured along the lines of those mentioned above is to study the use of the framework language not only for specifying the terms (and sometimes the proofs) of object logics, but also for specifying the *algorithms* by which the object logics are to be manipulated.

Procedures for manipulating logical systems are usually decomposable into *inference/reduction systems* that define a *search space*, and *search algorithms* that traverse that space.[4] We shall aim to specify the search space of procedures, leaving the control a private matter for the *search module*. In effect, we aim to specify the *invariants* of procedures: the *states of search* that are inherent in their operation.[5]

1.5 A type-theoretic setting

The setting we choose to work in is the Edinburgh Logical Framework (LF) [12]. It is closely related to the family of AUTOMATH languages [5], all distinguished by their relative (logical) weakness. Forceful arguments for this weakness are made in [6], but the main motivation stems from the fact that logics exhibit a

[4] Such a decomposition arises from the fact that the sets of interest are at best recursively enumerable; Kleene's normal form theorem allows the computation to be organised as a search over a space characterised as the inductive closure of a set of rules—the inference system. Even in the case when the problem of interest is solvable in polynomial time, such as with certain unification problems, the clarity of exposition obtainable by this decomposition makes the method a common one [26].

[5] This is not as great a restriction as it might seem at first sight. Refinements of resolution, for example, are often formulated as distinct inference systems that take advantage of the structure of a search space to prioritise certain constructions over others. Viewed from the point of view of the less efficient search space, the alternative inference system encodes control information in a uniform way. Having set out an improved inference system (eg, hyper-resolution over binary resolution) what is left is a set of generic search methods such as depth-first, iterative deepening etc.

great degree of commonality as far as their linguistic and inferential machinery are concerned, and that this commonality can be captured uniformly by the mechanisms of weak (dependently) typed lambda calculi.

In the LF, a logic is specified by means of a *signature*. This is a typing context for constants intended to represent those items used in the formulation of the logic. To represent first-order logic, for example, constants are introduced to stand for function symbols, predicate constants, connectives and quantifiers, as well as inference rules and the unit of judgement of the logic (truth). A theorem of *adequacy* is then formulated to establish that certain classes of terms are in bijective correspondence with the (mathematically defined) classes of first-order terms, formulae and proofs respectively. Using the adequacy theorems inferential methods over the metalanguage can be interpreted as manipulations of the object language constructs.

As mentioned above, our intention is not to try to implement search methods for the framework language, but to see the descriptions of such methods as a means of specifying the search spaces of procedures working directly over object logics. The specifications are to be achieved by specialising a metatheoretic search space using the information contained in the signature that defines the object logic of interest. In this way we hope to provide a discipline in which algorithms designed specifically for an object logic can be imported into an environment along with their complexities and efficiencies.

1.6 Unification: a first example

The use of abstraction to represent binding in a type-theoretic framework language like the LF means that object level variables are identified with those of the metalanguage. For the class of logical systems encodable in this way the treatment of the metalinguistic variables constitutes a *general theory* of substitution, unification, and the treatment of freeness conditions [23].

If our suggestion is to have any merit at all we would expect the programme to yield sensible results in the field of unification algorithms for encodable object logics. Put simply, we would expect to be able to specify the search space for first-order unification given a specification of the search space for unification in the framework language, together with the signature of a first-order language. The rest of this paper is devoted to showing that this, in fact, can be achieved.

A search space for unification in the LF will be defined via a system of reduction rules, structured in such a way that a specification of an system of reduction rules for unification in an object logic can be *derived* from it, given the signature of that logic. We are not attempting to claim that this derivation can be performed automatically; indeed our experiments with a similar derivation of a system of reduction rules for higher-order unification indicates the need for an extension of the equational theory of the framework [4]. Nevertheless, we believe that the results outlined below show that elegant descriptions of search spaces can be formulated in terms of a type-theoretic framework language and a specification of metatheoretic search spaces.

2 $\lambda\Pi$-Calculus

For completeness of our presentation we first present the $\lambda\Pi$-calculus, originally introduced in [12]. The language has three levels: ***objects***, ***types*** and ***type families***, and ***kinds***. The syntax is specified by the following grammar:

$$
\begin{array}{rll}
K ::= & \mathbf{Type} & \text{types of terms} \\
\mid & \Pi x{:}A.K & \text{type family} \\
A ::= & a & \text{constant} \\
\mid & \Pi x{:}A.B & \text{dept. fun. type} \\
\mid & \lambda x{:}A.B & \text{type fam. form.} \\
\mid & A\,M & \text{type fam. inst.} \\
M ::= & c & \text{constant} \\
\mid & x & \text{variable} \\
\mid & \lambda x{:}A.M & \text{abstraction} \\
\mid & M\,N & \text{application}
\end{array}
$$

Objects are classified by type, types and type families by kinds. The kind **Type** classifies the types; the other kinds classify functions f which yield a type $f M_1 \cdots M_n$ when applied to objects $M_1, \ldots, M_n$ whose types are compatible with the kind of f.

A ***signature***, Σ, is a sequence of pairs associating constants with types or kinds, denoted by $\langle c_1 : A_1, \ldots, c_n : A_n\rangle$. The domain of Σ, $\mathrm{dom}(\Sigma)$, is the set of constants it defines, namely $\{c_1, \ldots, c_n\}$. A ***context***, Γ, is a sequence of pairs associating variables with types only, denoted $[y_1 : A_1, \ldots, y_n : A_n]$. The domain of Γ, $\mathrm{dom}(\Gamma)$, is the set of variables it defines, namely $\{y_1, \ldots, y_n\}$. The syntax of signatures and contexts is given by the following grammar:

$$
\begin{array}{ll}
\Sigma ::= \langle\rangle \mid \Sigma, c{:}K \mid \Sigma, c{:}A & \text{signature} \\
\Gamma ::= \langle\rangle \mid \Gamma, y{:}A & \text{context}
\end{array}
$$

The $\lambda\Pi$-calculus is a formal system over this language for deriving assertions of one of the following forms:

$$
\begin{array}{ll}
\Sigma\ \mathbf{sig} & \Sigma \text{ is a valid signature} \\
\vdash_\Sigma \Gamma & \Gamma \text{ is a valid context in } \Sigma \\
\Gamma \vdash_\Sigma K & K \text{ is a kind in } \Gamma \text{ and } \Sigma \\
\Gamma \vdash_\Sigma A : K & A \text{ has kind } K \text{ in } \Gamma \text{ and } \Sigma \\
\Gamma \vdash_\Sigma M : A & M \text{ has type } A \text{ in } \Gamma \text{ and } \Sigma
\end{array}
$$

The rules of the calculus are presented in table 1. A term is said to be ***well-typed*** in a signature and context if it can be shown to either be a kind, have a kind or have a type in that signature and context. A term is said to be ***well-typable*** if it is well-typed in some signature and context. ***Definitional equality***, denoted by $\equiv$ in table 1, is taken to be $\beta\eta$ conversion (see [24, 10]).

Table 1.: The $\lambda\Pi$ System

Valid Signatures :

$$\frac{}{\langle\rangle \ \mathbf{sig}} \quad \text{(B-EMPTY-SIG)}$$

$$\frac{\Sigma \ \mathbf{sig} \qquad \vdash_\Sigma K \qquad a \notin \mathrm{dom}(\Sigma)}{\Sigma, a\!:\!K \ \mathbf{sig}} \quad \text{(B-KIND-SIG)}$$

$$\frac{\Sigma \ \mathbf{sig} \qquad \vdash_\Sigma A\!:\!\mathbf{Type} \qquad c \notin \mathrm{dom}(\Sigma)}{\Sigma, c\!:\!A \ \mathbf{sig}} \quad \text{(B-TYPE-SIG)}$$

Valid Contexts :

$$\frac{\Sigma \ \mathbf{sig}}{\vdash_\Sigma \langle\rangle} \quad \text{(B-EMPTY-CTX)}$$

$$\frac{\vdash_\Sigma \Gamma \qquad \Gamma \vdash_\Sigma A\!:\!\mathbf{Type} \qquad x \notin \mathrm{dom}(\Gamma)}{\vdash_\Sigma \Gamma, x\!:\!A} \quad \text{(B-TYPE-CTX)}$$

Valid Kinds :

$$\frac{\vdash_\Sigma \Gamma}{\Gamma \vdash_\Sigma \mathbf{Type}} \quad \text{(B-TYPE-KIND)}$$

$$\frac{\Gamma, x\!:\!A \vdash_\Sigma K}{\Gamma \vdash_\Sigma \Pi x\!:\!A.K} \quad \text{(B-PI-KIND)}$$

Valid Families :

$$\frac{\vdash_\Sigma \Gamma \qquad a\!:\!K \in \Sigma}{\Gamma \vdash_\Sigma a\!:\!K} \quad \text{(B-CONST-FAM)}$$

$$\frac{\Gamma, x\!:\!A \vdash_\Sigma B\!:\!\mathbf{Type}}{\Gamma \vdash_\Sigma \Pi x\!:\!A.B\!:\!\mathbf{Type}} \quad \text{(B-PI-FAM)}$$

$$\frac{\Gamma, x\!:\!A \vdash_\Sigma B\!:\!K}{\Gamma \vdash_\Sigma \lambda x\!:\!A.B\!:\!\Pi x\!:\!A.K} \quad \text{(B-ABS-FAM)}$$

$$\frac{\Gamma \vdash_\Sigma A\!:\!\Pi x\!:\!B.K \qquad \Gamma \vdash_\Sigma M\!:\!B}{\Gamma \vdash_\Sigma AM\!:\!K[M/x]} \quad \text{(B-APP-FAM)}$$

$$\frac{\Gamma \vdash_\Sigma A\!:\!K \qquad \Gamma \vdash_\Sigma K' \qquad \Gamma \vdash_\Sigma K \equiv K'}{\Gamma \vdash_\Sigma A\!:\!K'} \quad \text{(B-CONV-FAM)}$$

Valid Objects :

$$\frac{\vdash_\Sigma \Gamma \qquad c\!:\!A \in \Sigma}{\Gamma \vdash_\Sigma c\!:\!A} \quad \text{(B-CONST-OBJ)}$$

$$\frac{\vdash_\Sigma \Gamma \qquad x\!:\!A \in \Gamma}{\Gamma \vdash_\Sigma x\!:\!A} \quad \text{(B-VAR-OBJ)}$$

$$\frac{\Gamma, x\!:\!A \vdash_\Sigma M\!:\!B}{\Gamma \vdash_\Sigma \lambda x\!:\!A.M\!:\!\Pi x\!:\!A.B} \quad \text{(B-ABS-OBJ)}$$

$$\frac{\Gamma \vdash_\Sigma M\!:\!\Pi x\!:\!A.B \qquad \Gamma \vdash_\Sigma N\!:\!A}{\Gamma \vdash_\Sigma MN\!:\!B[N/x]} \quad \text{(B-APP-OBJ)}$$

$$\frac{\Gamma \vdash_\Sigma M\!:\!A \qquad \Gamma \vdash_\Sigma A'\!:\!\mathbf{Type} \qquad \Gamma \vdash_\Sigma A \equiv A'}{\Gamma \vdash_\Sigma M\!:\!A'} \quad \text{(B-CONV-OBJ)}$$

Remark. The canonical form of a type is

$$\Pi x_1 : A_1 . \ldots . \Pi x_n : A_n . a\, M_1 \cdots M_p$$

for $n, p \geq 0$, where A_i $(1 \leq i \leq n)$ are canonical types, a is a constant of kind $\Pi y_1 : B_1 . \ldots \Pi y_p : B_p . \mathbf{Type}$ and M_i $(1 \leq i \leq p)$ are terms of the appropriate type. We shall assume that all types are in canonical form. A result due to Geuvers [10], who noted that once a signature and context are established only judgements of the form $\Gamma \vdash_\Sigma M : A$ with A of kind **Type** need be considered, tells us that the rule (B-ABS-FAM) is admissible. Hence we can take (well-formed) signatures and contexts to be in canonical form; there is no need to form types of the form $\lambda x : A.B$, and consequently we need only consider the contraction of object β- and η-redexes in types (i.e., redexes of the form $(\lambda x : A.B)M$ and $(\lambda x : A.B\, x)$ do not exist).

Definition 1. Consider the object $\lambda x_1 : A_1 \cdots \lambda x_n : A_n (@\, M_1 \cdots M_m)$, where $@$ is an atom—a constant or variable—and the M_i are terms. The sequence: $\lambda x_1 : A_1 \cdots \lambda x_n : A_n$, is called the ***binder*** of the term; this may be written $\lambda(x : A)_n$. Each x_i is called the ***binding occurrence*** of that variable. $(@\, M_1 \cdots M_m)$ is called the ***matrix*** of the term. For brevity we may write $\boldsymbol{M}_m$ for $M_1 \cdots M_m$, or sometimes just $\boldsymbol{M}$. Finally, $\lambda(x : A)_n . @$ is called the ***heading*** and $@$ the ***head*** of the term.

These notions are extended to types and type families in the obvious way.

Definition 2 (Long $\beta\eta$-normal forms). Consider an object $\lambda(x : A)_n . @\, \boldsymbol{M}_m$ in β-normal form and of type $\Pi(x : A)_{n+k} . c\, \boldsymbol{N}_q$. The long $\beta\eta$-normal form of M, denoted $\eta[M]$, is obtained by adding k new variables of the appropriate types to the binder and matrix, and (recursively) applying the same expansion to the subterms to obtain: $\lambda(x : A)_{n+k} . @\, \eta[M_1] \cdots \eta[x_{n+k}]$. Note that if $@$ is a variable, we abbreviate its long $\beta\eta$-normal form to just $@$.

We shall use the following notational conventions: $a, b, c, \ldots$ for constants; f, g, h for variables of function type; w, x, y, z for variables of arbitrary type; $\boldsymbol{w}, \boldsymbol{x}, \boldsymbol{y}, \boldsymbol{z}$ for vectors of variables; $A, B, C, \ldots$ for types; $M, N, P, Q, R, \ldots$ for objects; $\boldsymbol{M}, \boldsymbol{N}, \boldsymbol{P}, \boldsymbol{Q}, \boldsymbol{R}, \ldots$ for vectors of objects; and U, V, W for terms (i.e., either objects or types).

3 $\lambda\Pi$-Unification

In this section we re-present $\lambda\Pi$-unification, first considered independently by Elliott [8, 9] and by Pym [22, 21]. Although our presentation is greatly influenced by this work, we have chosen to define $\lambda\Pi$-unification as search over a space defined by a system of reduction rules, similar in style to Snyder and Gallier's transformation systems [26, 25] for λ-unification (i.e., higher-order unification). This helps to separate the logical aspects from the dynamic ones. In the next section we show that the set of rules for $\lambda\Pi$-unification defines a sound and complete search space.

The presentation is motivated by the role unification plays in proof-search for the $\lambda\Pi$-calculus [23, 21]. For this reason we distinguish a class of variables called *indeterminates*, denoted by lowercase Greek letters α, β ... etc. The syntactic category of $\lambda\Pi$-objects is extended to include indeterminates thus:

$$M ::= c \mid \alpha \mid x \mid \lambda x{:}A.M \mid M\,N$$

and the class of contexts is extended thus:

$$\Gamma ::= \langle\rangle \mid \Gamma, y{:}A \mid \Gamma, \alpha{:}A$$

Notice that indeterminates cannot be bound by λ. By virtue of this extension, entities of all syntactic classes may now contain indeterminates as subterms. When we wish to emphasize that a syntactic entity is free of indeterminates we shall refer to it as being *ground*. A term with an indeterminate as its head will be called *flexible*, otherwise it will be called *rigid*. We use the notation $\mathsf{Ind}(U)$ to denote the set of indeterminates occurring in U.

Definition 3 (Substitution). A substitution is a finite map, σ, from indeterminates to objects together with a pair of contexts, (Δ, Γ), written $\sigma : \Delta \rightarrow \Gamma$ satisfying :

1. $\operatorname{dom}\sigma = \{\alpha \mid \alpha \in \operatorname{dom}(\Gamma)\}$
2. $\Delta \vdash_\Sigma \alpha\sigma{:}A\sigma$, for every $\alpha{:}A \in \Gamma$.

Composition of substitutions is a substitution.

Definition 4. We say that one substitution $\theta{:}\Gamma \rightarrow \Delta$ is *more general than* the substitution $\sigma : \Theta \rightarrow \Delta$, written $\sigma \leq \theta$, just in case there exists a substitution $\eta{:}\Theta \rightarrow \Gamma$ such that $\sigma = \eta \circ \theta$.

It is now possible to give a definition of unification and unifier for terms of the $\lambda\Pi$-calculus.

Definition 5. A *unification problem* over the signature Σ and context Γ is an equation of the form:

$$\Gamma \vdash_\Sigma U{:}V \stackrel{?}{=} U'{:}V'$$

where $\Gamma \vdash_\Sigma U{:}V$ and $\Gamma \vdash_\Sigma U'{:}V'$. A solution to this equation is a substitution $\theta{:}\Theta \rightarrow \Gamma$, called a *unifier*, satisfying

$$\vdash_\Sigma \Theta \qquad \text{(C3.1)}$$

$$\begin{array}{l} \Theta \vdash_\Sigma (U{:}V)\sigma \\ \Theta \vdash_\Sigma (U'{:}V')\sigma \end{array} \qquad \text{(C3.2)}$$

$$\begin{array}{l} U\sigma =_{\beta\eta} U'\sigma \\ V\sigma =_{\beta\eta} V'\sigma \end{array} \qquad \text{(C3.3)}$$

A set of unifiers is complete for a unification problem if all unifiers of the problem are less general than one from the set.

3.1 Pre-Unification

One of the major achievements of the theses of Elliott [9] and Pym [21] was to show that $\lambda\Pi$-unification is semi-decidable by giving sound and complete algorithms for $\lambda\Pi$-unifiability. This was achieved by adapting Huet's method of pre-unification which involves postponing the choice of unifier for flex-flex pairs. The presence of dependent types means that the types of the two terms of a unification problem may be dependent on the solutions to other, possibly postponed, unification problems. The following example will illustrate the difficulties encountered.

Consider the $\lambda\Pi$-unification problem

$$\Gamma \vdash_\Sigma (D\, M\, \alpha) : C \stackrel{?}{=} (D\, M'\, N') : C \tag{4}$$

where

$$\Sigma = \langle A : \mathbf{Type}\ , C : \mathbf{Type}\ , B : A \to \mathbf{Type}\ , D : \Pi x : A.(B\, x) \to C \rangle$$
$$\Gamma = \Gamma_1, \alpha : (BM), \Gamma_2$$

and the terms M, M' and N' are of type A, A and (BM') respectively. Since D is a constant, any solution to (4) does not affect D. Hence finding a solution for (4) requires finding solutions for

$$\Gamma \vdash_\Sigma M : A \stackrel{?}{=} M' : A \tag{5}$$

$$\Gamma \vdash_\Sigma \alpha : (BM) \stackrel{?}{=} N' : (BM') \tag{6}$$

If we only have a pre-unifier, σ, for (5) it may be the case that $(B\, M)\sigma \neq_{\beta\eta} (B\, M')\sigma$. Consequently, the unifiability of two terms that do not have $\beta\eta$-equal types must be countenanced. This is in contrast to the situation in λ-unification where two terms with unequal types are simply not unifiable. However, type inequality is an important measure of potential non-unifiability, so both Pym and Elliott introduce a *meta-notation* that gives a weaker notion of type equality than $=_{\beta\eta}$. Pym calls this weaker equality *similarity* and Elliott defines essentially an equivalent notion via the notion of *approximate well-typedness*, we adopt the former notion. Types are *similar* if they have the same structural shape:

Definition 6 (Similarity). Let A and B be types of kind **Type** , then A and B are *similar*, written $A \sim B$, if

$$A \equiv \Pi x_1 : A_1 \ldots \Pi x_n : A_n.a\, M_1 \ldots M_q$$

$$B \equiv \Pi y_1 : B_1 \ldots \Pi y_n : B_n.a\, N_1 \ldots N_q$$

and $A_i \sim B_i$ for $1 \leq i \leq n$.

Similarity is preserved under substitution. In Brown and Ritter [3] a formal theory of type similarity is defined—the $\lambda\Pi_{\sim}$-calculus—and its terms shown to be Church-Rosser and strongly normalizing. As a consequence, well-typed $\lambda\Pi_{\sim}$-terms have unique normal forms, rather than just unique weak head normal forms; we shall use this fact heavily in the sequel to simplify the presentation of the search space for $\lambda\Pi$-unification. By presenting the search space as a system of reduction rules the dependencies between postponed flex-flex unification problems can be defined in terms of the structure of reduction trees, and the induction required for the soundness proof further simplified.

3.2 $\lambda\Pi$-Pre-Unification: a system of reduction rules

We now present a system of reduction rules for $\lambda\Pi$-pre-unification in the spirit of the transformation systems of Snyder and Gallier [26, 25].

Snyder and Gallier develop transformation systems for first-order and λ-unification, extending those developed by Martelli and Montanari [18]. For these languages, a unification problem is a set of pairs of terms to be simultaneously unified. Transformations are defined that decompose pairs of terms into simpler pairs of terms, a process which is repeated until either a pair of terms is found to be non-unifiable or the set of pairs of terms are all trivially unifiable; in the latter case a unifier can be read off from the pairs of terms. We shall use the same technique but express the transformations as reduction rules on ***sequents***; that reflect the complications arising from the (dependent) typing constraints in $\lambda\Pi$.

We have seen above the necessity of considering unification problems involving terms of similar (and not equal) type. We shall therefore define unification for $\lambda\Pi$ using the $\lambda\Pi_{\sim}$-calculus of [3].

Objects, types, and the notions of reduction for the $\lambda\Pi_{\sim}$-calculus are those of the $\lambda\Pi$. The judgements of the calculus are exactly those for the $\lambda\Pi$-calculus, but with definitional equality defined as similarity. Terms of the $\lambda\Pi_{\sim}$-calculus have both the Church-Rosser and the strong normalization properties [3]; therefore we can simplify the presentation (and any implementation) by assuming that all terms are in long $\beta\eta$-normal form (definition 2).

The sequents of the system are denoted by $\Gamma \Vdash_{\Sigma;\Delta} \langle U : V, U' : V'\rangle$. The additional typing context Δ serves a special purpose in that it contains the variables, both λ and Π bound, of $U:V$ and $U':V'$. The head symbols of U and U' in the sequent are called its ***principal symbols.***

Definition 7 (Flexible and elimination sequents). A sequent with one principal indeterminate α will be called ***flex-rigid for*** α. A sequent with two principal indeterminates, α and β say, will be called ***flex-flex for*** α ***and*** β.

The unification problem $\Gamma \vdash_{\Sigma} M : A \stackrel{?}{=} N : B$ is represented by the initial sequent $\Gamma \Vdash_{\Sigma;\langle\rangle} \langle M : A, N : B\rangle$. Each reduction rule in the system is of the form

$$\frac{\Gamma_1 \Vdash_{\Sigma;\Delta_1} \langle U_1 : V_1, U_1' : V_1'\rangle \quad \cdots \quad \Gamma_n \Vdash_{\Sigma;\Delta_n} \langle U_n : V_n, U_n' : V_n'\rangle}{\Gamma \Vdash_{\Sigma;\Delta} \langle U : V, U' : V'\rangle}$$

Table 2.: $\lambda\Pi$-Preunification Reduction Rules : Types

$$\frac{}{\Gamma \Vdash_{\Delta} \langle a, a \rangle} \qquad \text{(Const-Const-Type)}$$

where $a : \mathbf{Type} \in \Sigma$.

$$\frac{\Gamma \Vdash_{\Delta} \langle M_i : A_i(\boldsymbol{M}_{i-1}), N_i : A_i(\boldsymbol{N}_{i-1}) \rangle \quad (1 \leq i \leq n)}{\Gamma \Vdash_{\Delta} \langle a\,\boldsymbol{M}_n, a\,\boldsymbol{N}_n \rangle} \qquad \text{(Rigid-Rigid-Type)}$$

where $a : \Pi(x : A)_n.\mathbf{Type} \in \Sigma$.

$$\frac{\Gamma \Vdash_{\Delta} \langle A_1, B_1 \rangle \quad \Gamma \Vdash_{\Delta, x:A_1} \langle A, B \rangle}{\Gamma \Vdash_{\Delta} \langle \Pi x : A_1.A, \Pi x : B_1.B \rangle} \qquad \text{(Pi-Pi-Type)}$$

---

with a single conclusion sequent and $n(\geq 0)$ premises. (Pre-)unification problems are solved by constructing (a series of) reduction trees in the system starting from the initial sequent. *Axioms* are rules with no premises. The presence of a flex-rigid sequent for α in a reduction tree determines the value of the pre-unifier on the indeterminate α.

For the remainder of this section we shall assume a fixed signature and so drop the signature subscript on sequents. The reduction rules for $\lambda\Pi$-pre-unification are presented in table 2 and 3. The rules arise from a case analysis on the structure of $\lambda\Pi$-terms and state the conditions required to determine unifiability. In the rule (Flex-Rigid) an object instantiation for the indeterminate α must be chosen that unifies the objects $\alpha\, M_1, \ldots, M_m$ and $@\, N_1, \ldots, N_n$. One option is to substitute for α an object whose head is @. Such an instantiation is known as an *imitation binding.* The second option is to "lift" one of the M_i's whose head is either @ or flexible. This sort of instantiation is known as a *projection binding.* In the case of a projection binding another flexible object is produced requiring further reduction. The matrix of the instantiation will be made up of the most general objects required to render the sequence of M_i's unifiable with the sequence of N_i's. The form of this follows closely its counterpart in λ-unification [26]. Note that the rules (Rigid-Rigid-Type) and (Rigid-Rigid) have n and $p+3$ premises, respectively.

An important property preserved by the reduction rules in table 2 and 3 is type similarity. That is, if the terms of a conclusion sequent of any rule are type similar, then the terms of each premise sequent of that rule are type similar.

In the following definition we identify some properties of reduction trees that will be useful in the sequel.

Definition 8 (Properties of reduction trees). *Reduction trees* are trees regulated by the rules. Such a tree is said to be *fully developed* if no reduction is applicable at any leaf. A fully developed tree is said to be *closed* if all of its leaves are axioms. A reduction tree is said to be *pseudo-ground* if it is closed and

Table 3.: $\lambda\Pi$-Preunification Reduction Rules : Objects

$$\frac{\Gamma \Vdash_{\Delta} \langle A, B\rangle \quad \Gamma \Vdash_{\Delta} \langle A, C\rangle}{\Gamma \Vdash_{\Delta} \langle c\colon A, c\colon B\rangle} \qquad \text{(Const-Const)}$$

where $c\colon C \in \Sigma$.

$$\frac{\Gamma \Vdash_{\Delta} \langle A, B\rangle \quad \Gamma \Vdash_{\Delta} \langle A, C\rangle}{\Gamma \Vdash_{\Delta} \langle x\colon A, x\colon B\rangle} \qquad \text{(Var-Var)}$$

where $x\colon C \in \Gamma \cup \Delta$.

$$\frac{\Gamma \Vdash_{\Delta} \langle M_i\colon C_i(\boldsymbol{M}_{i-1}), N_i\colon C_i(\boldsymbol{N}_{i-1})\rangle\ (1 \le i \le p) \;\; \Gamma \Vdash_{\Delta} \langle A, C(\boldsymbol{M}_p)\rangle \;\; \Gamma \Vdash_{\Delta} \langle B, C(\boldsymbol{N}_p)\rangle}{\Gamma \Vdash_{\Delta} \langle @\,\boldsymbol{M}_p\colon A, @\,\boldsymbol{N}_p\colon B\rangle}$$

(Rigid-Rigid)

where $@\colon \Pi(x\colon C)_p.C \in (\Sigma \cup \Gamma \cup \Delta)$.

$$\frac{\Gamma \Vdash_{\Delta} \langle B_1, B_1'\rangle \quad \Gamma \Vdash_{\Delta} \langle A_1, A_1'\rangle \quad \Gamma \Vdash_{\Delta} \langle A_1, B_1\rangle \quad \Gamma \Vdash_{\Delta, x:A_1} \langle M\colon A', N\colon B'\rangle}{\Gamma \Vdash_{\Delta} \langle \lambda x\colon A_1.M\colon \Pi x\colon A_1'.A', \lambda x\colon B_1.N\colon \Pi x\colon B_1'.B'\rangle}$$

(Lam-Lam)

$$\frac{\Gamma \Vdash_{\Delta} \langle \Pi(x\colon C)_m.C, \Pi(x\colon C)_m.B\rangle \quad \Gamma \Vdash_{\Delta} \langle A, B\rangle}{\Gamma \Vdash_{\Delta} \langle \alpha\,\boldsymbol{x}_m\colon A, N\colon B\rangle} \qquad \text{(Ind-Elim)}$$

where $\alpha\colon \Pi(x\colon C)_m.C \in \Gamma$ and $\Delta = \Delta', (x\colon A)_m$. The binding for α is $\lambda(x\colon C)_n.N$.

$$\frac{\Gamma' \Vdash_{\Delta} \langle \Pi(x\colon C)_m.C, \Pi(x\colon C)_m.D(\boldsymbol{Q}_n)\rangle \quad \Gamma \Vdash_{\Delta} \langle A, B\rangle}{\Gamma \Vdash_{\Delta} \langle \alpha\,\boldsymbol{M}_m\colon A, @\,\boldsymbol{N}_n\colon B\rangle} \qquad \text{(Flex-Rigid)}$$

where $\Gamma = \Gamma_1, \alpha : \Pi(x : C)_m.C, \Gamma_2$ and $\Gamma' = \Gamma_1, \Theta, \alpha : \Pi(x : C)_m.C, \Gamma_2$, furthermore $@\colon \Pi(y\colon D)_n.D \in (\Sigma \cup (\Gamma_1, \Gamma_2))$ where $D_i = \Pi(z\colon E^i)_{p_i}.D_i'$ for some D_i', $p_i > 0$ for $1 \le i \le n$. The binding for α is $\lambda(x\colon C)_m.@\,Q_1 \cdots Q_n$ (an appropriate *imitation/projection* binding with head @ (see [26])) where $Q_i = \lambda(z\colon E^i)_{p_i}.\alpha_i\,\boldsymbol{x}_m\,z_{p_i}$ for $1 \le i \le n$; Θ is the context declaring the types of the indeterminates introduced by this binding, namely $\{\alpha_1, \ldots, \alpha_n\}$.

$$\frac{\Gamma \Vdash_{\Delta} \langle A, B\rangle}{\Gamma \Vdash_{\Delta} \langle \alpha\,\boldsymbol{M}_m\colon A, \beta\,\boldsymbol{N}_n\colon B\rangle} \qquad \text{(Flex-Flex)}$$

where $\alpha, \beta \in \text{dom}(\Gamma)$.

does not contain flex-rigid sequents. If additionally, all the flex-flex sequents of a pseudo-ground reduction tree associate $\beta\eta$-equal objects it shall be referred to as *solved*. A pseudo-ground reduction tree which contains no flex-flex sequents will be called *ground*, and consequently it contains no instances of the rules (Flex-Rigid), (Flex-Flex), (Ind-Elim).

Since indeterminates can occur on different branches of a reduction tree we can either represent the emerging pre-unifier using an environment, or perform instantiation in the tree itself. We adopt the latter approach.

Let π be a fully developed reduction tree and l a flex-rigid sequent for α in π.

Definition 9 (Frontier). Let $\mathcal{F}_\alpha(\pi)$ denote the *α-frontier* of π (cf. [18, 16]), i.e., the subtree of π obtained by removing all sequents that appear above any flex-rigid sequent for α.

Definition 10 (Transformation). Define $\mathcal{T}_l$, a transformation on reduction trees, by

$$\mathcal{T}_l(\pi) = \mathcal{F}_\alpha(\pi)[P/\alpha]$$

where P is the binding defined by the flex-rigid sequent l. Substitution over trees is defined in the obvious way.

Note that the reduction tree that results from such a transformation may no longer be fully developed. Furthermore, note that not all instantiations are well-behaved; we are interested only in those that are potentially well-typed. Following [23], we shall treat contexts as (strict) partially ordered sets. A reduction tree π determines a context Γ_π as follows

$$\Gamma_\pi = \biguplus_{l \in \pi} \Delta_l$$

where Δ_l is the context of sequent l, and $\uplus$ is order preserving union of posets.

Definition 11 (Consistency). Γ_π is said to be *consistent* if it is well-founded. A reduction tree π is said to be consistent if Γ_π is consistent.

The following lemma expresses a fundamental property of the reduction system.

Lemma 12. *The reduction tree resulting from reduction of a leaf of a consistent reduction tree is itself consistent (i.e., reduction preserves consistency).*

Proof. The property follows easily for all rules except (Flex-Rigid), which requires an induction on the structure of the projection or imitation binding.

The next definition identifies a class of indeterminates that are considered to be solved in a reduction tree. In essence an indeterminate is *solved* if it can never become the principle indeterminate of a flex-rigid sequent. As a consequence a solved indeterminate can only occur in flex-flex sequents whose principle indeterminates are solved.

Definition 13 (Solved Indeterminate). An indeterminate α of a reduction tree π is said to be ***solved in*** π whenever

1. There are no flex-rigid sequents for α in π;
2. If α is in a flex-flex sequent for γ, β in π, then one of the following conditions holds
   (a) $\alpha = \beta$ and γ is solved;
   (b) $\alpha = \gamma$ and β is solved;
   (c) β and γ are solved.

Using the definition of solved indeterminates it is possible to identify a class of flex-rigid sequents that can be solved.

Definition 14 (Solvable Flex-Rigid Sequent). Let l be a flex-rigid sequent for α in π. l is said to be ***solvable in*** π whenever

1. The left premise of l is the root of a pseudo-ground reduction, π' say. i.e.,

$$\dfrac{\begin{array}{c}\pi'\\ \vdots\\ \Gamma' \Vdash_{\Delta} \langle \Pi(x:C)_m.C, \Pi(x:C)_m.B\rangle \end{array} \qquad \Gamma \Vdash_{\Delta} \langle A, B\rangle}{\Gamma \Vdash_{\Delta} \langle \alpha\, \boldsymbol{x}_m : A, N : B\rangle}\ \text{(Ind-Elim)}$$

or

$$\dfrac{\begin{array}{c}\pi'\\ \vdots\\ \Gamma' \Vdash_{\Delta} \langle \Pi(x:C)_m.C, \Pi(x:C)_m.D(\boldsymbol{Q}_n)\rangle \end{array} \qquad \Gamma \Vdash_{\Delta} \langle A, B\rangle}{\Gamma \Vdash_{\Delta} \langle \alpha\, \boldsymbol{M}_m : A, @\, \boldsymbol{N}_n : B\rangle}\ \text{(Flex-Rigid)}$$

and
2. Both indeterminates of every flex-flex sequent in π' are solved in π.

The notion of a solvable flex-rigid sequent leads directly to the notion of a solvable indeterminate.

Definition 15 (Solvable Indeterminate). An indeterminate α is ***solvable in*** π if all flex-rigid sequents for α in π are solvable.

It is now possible to define the search space of $\lambda\Pi$-preunification based on reduction trees and their transformations.

Definition 16 (Search Space). A *reduction sequence* of a unification problem

$$\Gamma \vdash_{\Sigma} M:A \stackrel{?}{=} N:B$$

is a sequence of fully developed reduction trees, $\pi_0, \pi_1, \ldots, \pi_n$, satisfying the following:

1. the endsequent of π_0 is $\Gamma \Vdash_{[]} \langle M:A, N:B\rangle$;

2. π_i is closed, for all $i < n$;
3. π_{i+1} is a full development of $\mathcal{T}_{l_i}(\pi_i)$, for exactly one flex-rigid sequent for α, l_i, of π_i, $(i < n)$;
4. $\mathcal{T}_{l_i}(\pi_i)$ is consistent and α is solvable, for all $i < n$.

Each transformation of a reduction tree yields a substitution. A reduction

$$\pi_0 \xrightarrow{\mathcal{T}_{l_1}} \mathcal{T}_{l_1}(\pi_0) \to \pi_1 \xrightarrow{\mathcal{T}_{l_2}} \cdots \xrightarrow{\mathcal{T}_{l_n}} \mathcal{T}_{l_n}(\pi_{n-1}) \to \pi_n$$

determines the substitution

$$\sigma = [P_n/\alpha_n] \circ \cdots \circ [P_1/\alpha_1]$$

where l_i is a flex-rigid sequent for α_i and P_i is the binding defined by l_i, $1 \leq i \leq n$.

A reduction is said to be ***pseudo-ground*** if its last reduction tree is pseudo-ground. In order to show that pseudo-ground reductions determine pre-unifiers, we need to show that all flex-flex sequents in this reduction are solvable. To this end, we need the following lemma, due to Pym [22, 21], regarding the solvability of two flexible $\lambda\Pi$ -objects of $\beta\eta$-equivalent types. It is a simple extension of an analogous result for the simply typed λ-calculus due to Huet [13].

Lemma 17 (Flex-Flex solvability). *Two flexible objects of ($\beta\eta$-)equivalent type have a unifying substitution.*

Theorem 18 (Soundness). *If a unification problem has a pseudo-ground reduction, then it is solvable. Moreover, the final tree of the reduction determines a pre-unifier for the problem.*

Proof (Sketch). Let π be the last reduction tree of the pseudo-ground reduction and τ the substitution determined by the sequence π is itself pseudo-ground and Γ^{π} is consistent.

The tree ordering on π induces a strict ordering on its flex-flex sequents. Each maximal flex-flex sequent is the endsequent of a pseudo-ground subtree π' of π having that flex-flex sequent at its root. The last rule of π' is (Flex-Flex), and the tree above this sequent is solved. The flexible objects of the flex-flex sequent are therefore of $\beta\eta$-equivalent type and hence, by the previous lemma, there is a substitution that solves it. Applying this argument repeatedly to maximal flex-flex sequents yields a substitution θ such that $\pi\theta$ is solved.

Now, if $\Gamma \vdash_{\Sigma} M : A \stackrel{?}{=}_{\beta\eta} N : B$ is the original unification problem and $\sigma = \theta \circ \tau$, $\Gamma\sigma \Vdash_{\langle\rangle} \langle (M : A)\sigma, (N : B)\sigma \rangle$ is the endsequent of $\pi\theta$. Hence σ is a unifier of the unification problem.

Theorem 19 (Completeness). *If a unification problem is solvable, then it has a pseudo-ground reduction.*

Completeness is easily established by inspection of unifiers and the construction of appropriate reductions; the argument is omitted.

4 Specification of First Order Unification

In this section we show how the search space for $\lambda\Pi$ -pre-unification can be used to determine a sound and complete search space for the signature Σ_{FOL}: the encoding of first-order arithmetic (FOA) terms presented in [12]. The language of terms is given by the following abstract syntax:

$$t ::= \alpha \mid 0 \mid \text{succ}(t) \mid t + t \mid t \times t$$

Notice that we have used the syntactic category of indeterminates for the variables of FOA. The syntactic category of first order arithmetic terms is represented in the LF by the type ι (*iota*) of individual. Thus the signature for first order arithmetic terms, Σ_{FOL}, starts with the declaration of this type

$$\iota : \textbf{Type}$$

each term is represented as a constant in the $\lambda\Pi$, thus

$$\begin{aligned} 0 &: \iota \\ \text{succ} &: \iota \longrightarrow \iota \\ + &: \iota \longrightarrow \iota \longrightarrow \iota \\ \times &: \iota \longrightarrow \iota \longrightarrow \iota \end{aligned}$$

Terms of first order arithmetic are encoded in $\lambda\Pi$ by the function ϵ_X, for X a finite set of indeterminates, which maps terms of first order arithmetic with indeterminates in X to $\lambda\Pi$ -terms of type ι relative to signature Σ_{FOL} and context Γ_X, where Γ_X is the context $\alpha_1 : \iota, \ldots, \alpha_n : \iota$. The function ϵ_X is defined inductively on the structure of FOA terms as follows :

$$\begin{aligned} \epsilon_X(\alpha) &= \alpha \\ \epsilon_X(0) &= 0 \\ \epsilon_X(\text{succ}(t)) &= \text{succ}\, \epsilon_X(t) \\ \epsilon_X(t + u) &= + \, \epsilon_X(t)\, \epsilon_X(u) \\ \epsilon_X(t \times u) &= \times \, \epsilon_X(t)\, \epsilon_X(u) \end{aligned}$$

Note that there is no declaration for a type of variables; variables of the object logic are identified with variables of the LF.

Theorem 20 ([12]). *The encoding ϵ_X is a bijection between the terms of first-order arithmetic with free indeterminates in X and the canonical forms of type ι in Σ_{FOL} and Γ_X. Moreover, the encoding is compositional in the sense that for $t[\alpha_1, \ldots, \alpha_n]$ a term with indeterminates in $X = \{\alpha_1, \ldots \alpha_n\}$ and $t_1, \ldots, t_n$ terms with free variables in Y,*

$$\epsilon_Y(t[t_1, \ldots, t_n]) = \epsilon_X(t)[\epsilon_Y(t_1)/\alpha_1, \ldots, \epsilon_Y(t_n)/\alpha_n]$$

Proof. It is easy to see that ϵ_X is injective and maps every term to a canonical terms of type ι in signature Σ_{FOL} and context Γ_X. The function ϵ_X has a left-inverse, $\boldsymbol{\delta}_X$, defined inductively on the structure of canonical forms, thus

$$\begin{aligned}
\boldsymbol{\delta}_X(\alpha) &= \alpha \\
\boldsymbol{\delta}_X(0) &= 0 \\
\boldsymbol{\delta}_X(\mathrm{succ}(M)) &= \mathrm{succ}\,\boldsymbol{\delta}_X(M) \\
\boldsymbol{\delta}_X(+\,M\,N) &= \boldsymbol{\delta}_X(M) + \boldsymbol{\delta}_X(N) \\
\boldsymbol{\delta}_X(\times\,M\,N) &= \boldsymbol{\delta}_X(M) \times \boldsymbol{\delta}_X(N)
\end{aligned}$$

By inspection of the possible canonical forms we see that $\boldsymbol{\delta}_X$ is total and well-defined. It is easy to show that by induction on the structure of t that

$$\boldsymbol{\delta}_X(\epsilon_X(t)) = t$$

The compositionality property is shown by structural induction on the first-order terms.

4.1 First Order Unification

The map ϵ_X encodes first-order terms as canonical $\lambda\Pi$-terms of type ι. Moreover, we have the following property:

Lemma 21. *For any $\lambda\Pi$-type A,*

$$A \sim \iota \textit{ iff } A \equiv \iota\,,$$

where $\equiv$ is the definitional equality of the LF.

Proof. By inspection and the definition of similar types.

Using this lemma with the fact that all reduction rules preserve type similarity we can prove that any reduction tree of a sequent representing a first-order unification problem is of a certain restricted form, as characterised by the following definition.

Definition 22 (First-Order Reduction Tree). A reduction tree π is a *first-order reduction tree* if for every sequent $\Theta \Vdash_{\Sigma_{\text{FOT}}} \langle U_1 : V_1, U_2 : V_2\rangle$ of π, one of the following conditions hold

1. $V_1 = V_2 = \iota$ and
$$\exists t_1, t_2. U_1 = \epsilon_Y(t_1) \text{ and } U_2 = \epsilon_Y(t_2)$$
where t_1, t_2 are first order terms and $Y = \mathrm{dom}(\Theta)$;
2. $U_1 : V_1 = U_2 : V_2 = \iota : \mathbf{Type}$.

The importance of identifying this restricted form of reduction tree is that it will enable us later to observe that a subset of the reduction rules for $\lambda\Pi$-preunification is sufficient for capturing unification of first-order individuals. This is aided by the following lemma.

Lemma 23. *A first-order reduction tree has no instances of the rules* (Pi-Pi-Type), (Rigid-Rigid-Type), (Var-Var) *and* (Lam-Lam).

Proof. This follows trivially by observation of the sequent forms in a first-order reduction tree and the conclusion sequents of reduction rules. None of these reduction rules are applicable to any sequent of a first-order reduction tree.

The following lemma states that the reduction tree of a unification problem for first-order individuals is first-order. The proof makes an essential use of the η-long normal forms of $\lambda\Pi_{\sim}$-terms and the adequacy theorem for the encoding of first-order terms. The normal forms, along with the adequacy theorem, enable one to assert the existence of a first-order term for the terms of a sequent in a reduction tree.

Lemma 24. *If π is a reduction tree of the sequent*

$$\Gamma_X \Vdash_{\Sigma_{\mathrm{FOT}};[]} \langle \epsilon_X(t):\iota, \epsilon_X(s):\iota \rangle$$

representing a first-order unification problem for first-order terms t and s, then π is a first-order reduction tree.

Proof. By induction on the structure of the reduction tree π.

We can prove something stronger than this, which is that all reduction trees in a reduction sequence of a unification problem for first-order individuals are first-order. This will help in the proof of soundness of $\lambda\Pi$-preunification over unification problems of first-order individuals.

Lemma 25. *Every reduction tree in a reduction sequence of a unification problem for first-order individuals is a first-order reduction tree.*

Proof. The proof proceeds by induction on the length of the reduction sequence.

From the previous lemma and lemma 23 we can identify a subset of the reduction rules for $\lambda\Pi$-pre-unification that are particular to unification problems of first-order individuals. The net result is that we obtain the set of rules of table 4 specialising those in table 2 and 3.

Furthermore, the proof of the previous lemma demonstrates that $\lambda\Pi$-pre-unification constructs first-order substitutions. Using these facts will enable us to show the soundness and completeness of $\lambda\Pi$-pre-unification in determining first-order unifiers. Moreover, this tells us that the system of reduction rules in table 4 characterise the search space of unification problems for first-order individuals.

Table 4.: Unification of First-Order Individuals

$$\frac{}{\Gamma \Vdash_{\Sigma_{\mathrm{FOT}}} \langle \iota, \iota \rangle} \qquad \text{(Const-Const-Type)}$$

where $\iota \in \Sigma_{\mathrm{FOT}}$.

$$\frac{\Gamma \Vdash_{\Sigma_{\mathrm{FOT}}} \langle \iota, \iota \rangle}{\Gamma \Vdash_{\Sigma_{\mathrm{FOT}}} \langle c\!:\!\iota, c\!:\!\iota \rangle} \qquad \text{(Const-Const)}$$

where $c\!:\!\iota \in \Sigma_{\mathrm{FOT}}$.

$$\frac{\Gamma \Vdash_{\Sigma_{\mathrm{FOT}}} \langle M_i\!:\!\iota, N_i\!:\!\iota \rangle \,(1 \leq i \leq p) \quad \Gamma \Vdash_{\Sigma_{\mathrm{FOT}}} \langle \iota, \iota \rangle}{\Gamma \Vdash_{\Sigma_{\mathrm{FOT}}} \langle @\,\boldsymbol{M}_p\!:\!\iota, @\,\boldsymbol{N}_p\!:\!\iota \rangle} \qquad \text{(Rigid-Rigid)}$$

where $@\!:(\iota)_p \to \iota \in (\Sigma_{\mathrm{FOT}} \cup \Gamma)$ for some p.

$$\frac{\Gamma \Vdash_{\Sigma_{\mathrm{FOT}}} \langle \iota, \iota \rangle}{\Gamma \Vdash_{\Sigma_{\mathrm{FOT}}} \langle \alpha\!:\!\iota, N\!:\!\iota \rangle} \qquad \text{(Ind-Elim)}$$

where $\alpha\!:\!\iota \in \Gamma$ and the binding for α is N.

$$\frac{\Gamma' \Vdash_{\Sigma_{\mathrm{FOT}}} \langle \iota, \iota \rangle}{\Gamma \Vdash_{\Sigma_{\mathrm{FOT}}} \langle \alpha\!:\!\iota, @\,\boldsymbol{N}_n\!:\!\iota \rangle} \qquad \text{(Flex-Rigid)}$$

where $\alpha\!:\!\iota \in \Gamma$ and $@\,\boldsymbol{\alpha}_n$ is a (partial) binding for α and head $@$ of type $(\iota)_n \to \iota$ and $\alpha_i, 1 \leq i \leq n$ new indeterminates. The context Γ' is the extension of Γ with these new indeterminates introduced by the partial binding.

$$\frac{\Gamma \Vdash_{\Sigma_{\mathrm{FOT}}} \langle \iota, \iota \rangle}{\Gamma \Vdash_{\Sigma_{\mathrm{FOT}}} \langle \alpha\!:\!\iota, \beta\!:\!\iota \rangle} \qquad \text{(Flex-Flex)}$$

where $\alpha, \beta \in \mathrm{dom}(\Gamma)$.

Theorem 26 (Soundness). *Let $t \stackrel{?}{=} s$ be a first-order unification problem for two first-order individuals t and s. If there exists a pseudo-ground reduction sequence of the $\lambda\Pi$ -pre-unification problem*

$$\Gamma_X \vdash_{\Sigma_{\mathrm{FOT}}} \epsilon_X(t)\!:\!\iota \stackrel{?}{=} \epsilon_X(s)\!:\!\iota$$

then $t \stackrel{?}{=} s$ is solvable. Moreover, the final tree of the reduction sequence determines a unifier of the problem $t \stackrel{?}{=} s$.

Theorem 27 (Completeness) . *Let $t \stackrel{?}{=} s$ be a unification problem for two first-order individuals t and s and let θ be a solution. Then, there exists a pseudo-ground reduction sequence of the unification problem*

$$\Gamma_X \vdash_{\Sigma_{\mathrm{FOT}}} \epsilon_X(t) : \iota \stackrel{?}{=} \epsilon_X(s) : \iota$$

such that $\theta \leq \delta_X(\sigma)$, where σ is the substitution determined by the reduction sequence.

Suppose that we use $\langle t, s \rangle$ to denote the sequent corresponding to the first-order unification problem $t \stackrel{?}{=} s$, where t and s are first-order terms. By definition of first-order reduction trees (Definition 22) and by lemma 24 one can identify a correspondence between first-order reduction trees and reduction trees over sequents of first-order unification problems. Let π be a first-order reduction tree, then one can identify a sequent, of π, of the form

$$\Gamma \Vdash_{\Sigma_{\mathrm{FOT}}} \langle U_1 : \iota, U_2 : \iota \rangle$$

with the sequent

$$\langle t, s \rangle$$

where $U_1 = \epsilon_Y(t), U_2 = \epsilon_Y(s)$ and $Y = \mathrm{dom}(\Gamma)$. The existence of t and s is a result of the definition of first-order reduction trees. This identification only provides a mapping from first-order reduction trees to trees over sequents of first-order unification problems. However, this mapping along with lemma 23 results in a correspondence between reduction rules. Consequently the reduction rules of table 5 are in correspondence with the reduction rules of table 4.

The correspondence of reduction rules gives a correspondence between first-order reduction trees and reduction trees over sequents for first-order unification problems. Consequently, by lemma 25 we have a correspondence between reduction sequences. Then by the soundness and completeness theorem (Theorem 26 and 27) for the reduction rules of table 4 we have that the reduction rules of table 5 give a sound and complete characterisation of a first-order unification algorithm.

4.2 An Alternative First-Order Unification Specification

The reduction rules of table 4 and 5 induce search spaces for pre-unification problems of first-order individuals and first-order terms respectively. However, it is possible to reduce the set of reduction rules without loss of completeness [26]. In [26], Snyder and Gallier argue the admissibility of the transformation for imitation binding (reduction rule (Flex-Rigid) here). Multiple applications of such a transformation are replaced by a single application of the variable elimination transformation (reduction rule (Ind-Elim) here). In this way variable elimination *short circuits* [26] these transformations.

Table 5.: First-Order Unification

$$\frac{}{\langle c, c\rangle} \qquad \text{(Const-Const)}$$

$$\frac{\langle M_1, N_1\rangle \quad \cdots \quad \langle M_p, N_p\rangle}{\langle @\boldsymbol{M}_p, @\boldsymbol{N}_p\rangle} \qquad \text{(Rigid-Rigid)}$$

$$\frac{}{\langle \alpha, N\rangle} \qquad \text{(Ind-Elim)}$$

where the binding for α is N.

$$\frac{}{\langle \alpha, @\boldsymbol{N}_n\rangle} \qquad \text{(Flex-Rigid)}$$

where the binding for α is $@\boldsymbol{\alpha}_n$, for new indeterminates $\alpha_i, (1 \leq i \leq n)$.

$$\frac{}{\langle \alpha, \beta\rangle} \qquad \text{(Flex-Flex)}$$

Furthermore, the reduction rules of table 4 and 5 determine ***pre-unifiers*** in that unification problems of the form $\alpha \stackrel{?}{=} \beta$ are left unsolved. Such unification problems are trivially solvable, as demonstrated in the proof of Theorem 26. There are in fact two possible solutions to the unification problem $\alpha \stackrel{?}{=} \beta$, namely $[\alpha/\beta]$ and $[\beta/\alpha]$. Either solution leads to a most general unifier, implying that most general unifiers are in fact not strictly unique [26]. However, in practical applications their difference can essentially be ignored. Consequently variable elimination can be applied to unification problems of the form $\alpha \stackrel{?}{=} \beta$.

Adopting these arguments results in the system of reduction rules of table 6 for unification problems of first-order individuals. Using the analysis from above we get a corresponding system of reduction rules for first-order unification problems. This set of rules is given in table 7.

5 Conclusion

We have given a general argument pointing to the *lack of modularity* in theorem-proving environments and the difficulty in incorporating new and even standard methods into such systems. We have argued that logical frameworks constitute an important step along the way to address this problem as far as linguistic constructs and descriptions of (complete) proofs are concerned. They do this by means of a form of parameterisation on specifications of the logical systems of interest. We have also argued that a further step is required, namely, to provide specifications of the logical properties of the methods used to manipulate the target logics.

Table 6.: Unification of First-Order Individuals (reduced system).

$$\frac{}{\Gamma \Vdash_{\Sigma_{\mathrm{FOT}}} \langle \iota, \iota \rangle} \qquad \text{(Const-Const-Type)}$$

$$\frac{\Gamma \Vdash_{\Sigma_{\mathrm{FOT}}} \langle \iota, \iota \rangle}{\Gamma \Vdash_{\Sigma_{\mathrm{FOT}}} \langle c : \iota, c : \iota \rangle} \qquad \text{(Const-Const)}$$

where $c : \iota \in \Sigma_{\mathrm{FOT}}$.

$$\frac{\Gamma \Vdash_{\Sigma_{\mathrm{FOT}}} \langle M_i : \iota, N_i : \iota \rangle \; (1 \leq i \leq p) \qquad \Gamma \Vdash_{\Sigma_{\mathrm{FOT}}} \langle \iota, \iota \rangle}{\Gamma \Vdash_{\Sigma_{\mathrm{FOT}}} \langle @ \boldsymbol{M}_p : \iota, @ \boldsymbol{N}_p : \iota \rangle} \qquad \text{(Rigid-Rigid)}$$

where $@ : (\iota)_p \to \iota \in (\Sigma_{\mathrm{FOT}} \cup \Gamma)$ for some p.

$$\frac{\Gamma \Vdash_{\Sigma_{\mathrm{FOT}}} \langle \iota, \iota \rangle}{\Gamma \Vdash_{\Sigma_{\mathrm{FOT}}} \langle \alpha : \iota, N : \iota \rangle} \qquad \text{(Ind-Elim)}$$

where $\alpha : \iota \in \Gamma$ and the binding for α is N.

Table 7.: First-Order Unification

$$\frac{}{\langle c, c \rangle} \qquad \text{(Const-Const)}$$

$$\frac{\langle M_1, N_1 \rangle \quad \cdots \quad \langle M_p, N_p \rangle}{\langle @ \boldsymbol{M}_p, @ \boldsymbol{N}_p \rangle} \qquad \text{(Rigid-Rigid)}$$

$$\frac{}{\langle \alpha, N \rangle} \qquad \text{(Ind-Elim)}$$

where the binding for α is N.

As a first step along this path, we have begun the study of unification problems for object logics using a framework language as a metalanguage for stating the invariants (i.e., defining the search spaces) for unification algorithms. To this end we have reconstructed a presentation of unification for a framework language ($\lambda\Pi$) starting from the work of Elliott [9] and Pym [21], but achieving a number of technical advances:

- to strengthen the theory of type similarity [3] so as to obtain a more comprehensive theory of normal forms; based on this
- to present unification as a system of reduction rules following [26]; and subsequently
- to show how unification systems for first-order languages can be specified using the unification system of $\lambda\Pi$ as a template.

In this last contribution, we have achieved a specification which permits the most efficient methods of first-order unification to be imported into an environment and used in a manner that preserves logical soundness (w.r.t. to the encoding of the object logic in the environment).

A system of reduction rules for λ- (or higher-order) unification has been developed in a similar manner (see [4]); the details will be reported elsewhere. The next step is to study other types of standard search algorithm such as resolution, tableau methods and connection methods. In each case we would propose to use the framework language to derive the interface between a module implementing the algorithm directly on the object language, and the environment.

Acknowledgements

The authors gratefully acknowledge many illuminating discussions with Eike Ritter and David Pym which helped them in the formulation of this work and to the referees for their helpful suggestions. Errors and infelicities are, of course, of our own making.

References

1. H. P. Barendregt. *The Lambda Calculus, its syntax and semantics.* North Holland, 1984.
2. R. Boyer and J. Moore. *A Computational Logic.* Academic Pres, 1979.
3. Jason Brown and Eike Ritter. $\lambda\Pi$-calculus with type similarity. Technical Report PRG-TR-1-95, Oxford University Computing Laboratory, January 1995.
4. Jason Brown. *Presentations of Unification in a Logical Framework.* DPhil thesis, University of Oxford, submitted January 1996.
5. N. G. de Bruijn. The mathematical language AUTOMATH, its usage, and some of its extensions. In M. Laudet, editor, *Proceedings of the Symposium on Automatic Demonstration*, pages 29-61, Versailles, France, December 1968. Springer-Verlag LNM 125.
6. N. G. de Bruijn. A plea for weaker frameworks. In G. Huet and G. Plotkin, editors, *Logical Frameworks*, pages 149–181. Cambridge University Press, 1991.
7. R. L. Constable, et al. *Implementing Mathematics with the Nuprl Proof Development System.* Prentice-Hall, Englewood Cliffs, New Jersey, 1986.
8. Conal Elliott. Higher-order unification with dependent type functions. In N. Dershowitz, editor, *Proceedings of the* 3rd *International Conference on Rewriting Techniques and Applications*, volume 355 of *LNCS*, pages 121–136. Springer-Verlag, 1989.
9. Conal Elliott. *Extensions and Applications of Higher-Order Unification.* PhD thesis, School of Computer Science, Carnegie Mellon University, 1990.
10. Herman Geuvers. *Logics and Type Systems.* PhD thesis, Katholieke Universiteit Nijmegen, 1993.
11. M. Gordon, R, Milner and C. Wadsworth. Edinburgh LCF: A Mechanized Logic of Computation. In volume 78 of *LNCS.* Springer-Verlag, 1979.

12. Robert Harper, Furio Honsell, and Gordon Plotkin. A framework for defining logics. *Journal of the ACM*, 40(1):143–184, January 1993.
13. Gérard Huet. A unification algorithm for typed λ-calculus. *Theoretical Computer Science*, 1:27–57, 1975.
14. Gérard Huet and Gordon Plotkin, editors. *Logical Frameworks*. Cambridge University Press, Cambridge, 1991.
15. Gérard Huet and Gordon Plotkin, editors. *Logical Environments*. Cambridge University Press, Cambridge, 1993.
16. D. Jensen and T. Pietrzykowski. Mechanizing ω-order type theory through unification. *Theoretical Computer Science*, 3(1):123–171, 1976.
17. R. Letz, J. Schumann, S. Boyerl and W. Bibel. SETHEO: a high-performance theorem prover. *Journal of Automated Reasoning*, 8(2):183–212, 1992.
18. Alberto Martelli and Ugo Montanari. An efficient unification algorithm. *ACM Transactions on Programming Languages and Systems*, 4(2):258–282, 1982.
19. L. Paulson. Isabelle: The next 700 theorem provers. In P. Odifreddi, editor, *Logic and Computer Science*, pages 361–386. Academic Press, 1990.
20. Frank Pfenning. *Logic Programming in the LF logical framework*. In G. Huet and G. Plotkin, editors, *Logical Frameworks*, pages 149–181. Cambridge University Press, 1991.
21. David Pym. *Proofs, Search and Computation in General Logic*. PhD thesis, Laboratory for the Foundations of Computer Science University of Edinburgh, 1990. Available as technical report no. CST-69-90.
22. David Pym. A unification algorithm for the $\lambda\Pi$-Calculus. *International Journal of Foundations of Computer Science*, 3(3):333–378, 1992.
23. David Pym and Lincoln Wallen. Proof search in the $\lambda\Pi$-calculus. In G. Huet and G. Plotkin, editors, *Logical Frameworks*, pages 309–340. Cambridge University Press, 1991.
24. A. Salvesen. The Church-Rosser property for $\beta\eta$-reduction. Manuscript, 1991. p
25. Wayne Snyder. *A proof theory for general unification*. Birkhauser, 1991.
26. Wayne Snyder and Jean Gallier. Higher-order unification revisited : Complete sets of transformations. *Journal of Symbolic Computation*, 8:101–140, 1989.

Decision Procedures Using Model Building Techniques

Ricardo Caferra and Nicolas Peltier

LIFIA-IMAG
46, Avenue Félix Viallet 38031 Grenoble Cedex FRANCE
{caferra| peltier}@lifia.imag.fr
Phone: (33) 76.57.46.59, Fax: (33) 76 57 46 02

Abstract. Few year ago we have developed an Automated Deduction approach to model building. The method, called RAMC[1] looks simultaneously for inconsistencies and models for a given formula. The capabilities of RAMC have been extended both for model building and for unsatisfiability detection by including in it the use of *semantic strategies*. In the present work we go further in this direction and define more general and powerful semantic rules. These rules are an extension of Slagle's semantic resolution. The robustness of our approach is evidenced by proving that the method is also a decision procedure for a wide range of classes decidable by semantic resolution and in particular by hyperresolution. Moreover, the method *builds models* for satisfiable formulae in these classes, in particular, for satisfiable formulae that do not have any finite model.

1 Introduction

Model building and model checking are extremely important topics in Logic and Computer Science. Few years ago we have developed an Automated Deduction approach to model building. The method, called RAMC, looks simultaneously for inconsistencies and models for a given formula. It is refutationally complete, builds models incrementally and allows a unified view of model building and model checking [CZ92, CP95b]. A particularly interesting feature of the method is that it allows to build *infinite* models as well as finite ones. This feature is particularly interesting when dealing with decidable — but non finitely controllable[2] — classes.

In order to increase the capabilities of RAMC (both for proof search and model building), we introduced in the method the use of *semantic strategies* [CP95a] by modifying some of its key rules. In the present work we go further in this direction by defining more general and more powerful rules. These rules can be seen as an extension of semantic resolution as defined in [SLA67]. Concerning model building, our method can be seen as a procedure transforming partial

[1] standing for Refutation And Model Construction.

[2] A class is said *finitely controllable* iff any satisfiable formula in the class has a finite model.

(even trivial) models into total ones (the trivial models are the interpretations needed for the application of semantic resolution). This feature is especially important in interactive model building.

The study of decidable classes is also an outstanding problem in Logic and Computer Science. Though decidability is strongly related to the existence of models, standard techniques used in the field of decidability are different from those used in model building. In the study of decidable classes a key technique is to show the existence of bounds (say $n \in \mathbb{N}$) such that it is sufficient to expand a formula schema up to a maximum of n Herbrand instances and then test this finite expansion for (in)consistency to decide the validity of the formula (see for example [DG79, BÖR84, LEW79]). A characteristic of this technique is that there is practically *no uniform* treatment of the different classes (for each class the bound n must be found in an ad hoc manner). A first unified approach to treat decidable class — to the best of our knowledge — was the one by the Russian school (Maslov, Zamov)[3]. The first work in this direction in the West seems to be [JOY76] who used resolution as a decision procedure. More recently Fermüller, Leitsch, Tammet and Zamov went further in this direction using resolution as the base calculus, instead of Maslov's inverse method (see [FL92, FLTZ93, TAM91]). They studied strategies for partitioning the Herbrand universe in a finite number of equivalence classes, allowing to generate finite search spaces. In some cases they are also able to extract models from the set of generated Herbrand instances [FL92, TAM91, FL95].

In principle our model building method was not intended to be a unified approach to treat decidable classes. Now, intuitively, a method that looks simultaneously for complementary goals: refutations and models, should "work" as a decision procedure. *Therefore the main aim of this work is to put links between our work on model building and the unified treatment of decidable classes of first order logic.* More precisely, we show in this paper the robustness of our approach by proving that the method is also a decision procedure for a wide range of classes decidable by semantic resolution, and in particular by hyper-resolution. Therefore we capture all the classes decidable by the Fermüller and Leitsch model building method [FL95]. Besides the method *builds models* for all the satisfiable formulae in these classes.

The paper is divided into 6 sections: Section 2 recalls briefly the ideas underlying our method and the notions necessary for the understanding of the paper (in particular some disinference rules). In section 3 two new rules are introduced: the $\mathcal{I}$-resolution and the $\mathcal{I}$-disresolution. It is proven that they are sound and preserve refutational completeness. In section 4, after recalling a very useful rule: the so-called GMPL rule, we show that it increases strictly the power of the method. In section 5, the limits of the method without strategy are shown. A strategy restricting the application of the disinference rules is proposed. Classes of c-clauses for which the method with the new strategy is a decision procedure **and** builds models are identified. Section 6 contains concluding remarks and main lines of future work.

[3] [MIN91], page 397: "One of the aims of the inverse method was to give a unified treatment of decidable cases of the predicates calculus"

2 Preliminaries

RAMC captures the "normal" attitude of a human being faced to a conjecture: he considers simultaneously two possibilities: to *prove* and to *disprove* the conjecture.

The method is based on the use of *constrained clauses* instead of standard clauses. A *constrained clause* (or *c-clause* for short) is a couple noted $[\![C \ : \mathcal{P}]\!]$ where C is a clause (in the standard sense) and $\mathcal{P}$ an equational formula, called the *constraint*.

Constraints denote the range of the variables of the clauses.

Presently, constraints are represented by equational problems [CZ92]. Equational problems are a decidable class of logical formulae quantified in a particular way and using only $=, \neq, \wedge, \vee$. For any equational problem $\mathcal{P}$, $\mathcal{S}(\mathcal{P})$ denotes the set of *solutions* of $\mathcal{P}$, i.e. the set of ground substitutions σ such that $\sigma(\mathcal{P})$ is valid in the Herbrand universe. $\perp$ denote the false problem (i.e. a problem with no solution) and $\top$ denotes the problem always true. (Hence a clause C in the classical sense is equivalent to the c-clause $[\![C \ : \top]\!]$).

The idea of our method is to code the conditions necessary either to the application or the impossibility of application of the inference rules. Consequently two different kinds of rules are considered: the *refutation rules* (or *rc-rules*) and the *model building rules* (or *mc-rules*), called also *disinference rules*. We recall below some of the key rules of the method (for more details see [CZ92]).

Notation: For any term t (resp. clause, formula ...) we note $Var(t)$ the set of variables of t. We note $\bar{t}$ a n-uple of terms.

2.1 Refutation rules (or inference rules).

*The binary c-resolution:*The rule of *binary c-resolution* (abbreviated *bc-resolution*) on c_1 and c_2 upon the complementary literals $P(\bar{s})$ and $\neg P(\bar{t})$ is defined as follows:

$$\frac{[\![\neg P(\bar{t}) \vee c_1' \ : \mathcal{X}]\!] \quad [\![P(\bar{s}) \vee c_2' \ : \mathcal{Y}]\!]}{[\![c_1' \vee c_2' \ : \mathcal{X} \wedge \mathcal{Y} \wedge \bar{t} = \bar{s}]\!]}$$

2.2 Model building rules (or dis-inference rules).

The *model building rules* called also *dis-inference rules* aim at building a model of the initial set of c-clauses.

The unit bc-disresolution: Let S be a satisfiable set of c-clauses. By the unit bc-disresolution rule, it is possible to eliminate from the clause of a c-clause of S those literals falsified by any model of S. Let $c_1 : [\![\neg P(\bar{t}) \ : \mathcal{X}]\!]$ be a unit c-clause and $c_2 : [\![P(\bar{s}) \vee c_2'(\bar{y}) \ : \mathcal{Y}]\!]$ be a c-clause:

The rule of *unit bc-disresolution* (abbreviated *bc-disresolution*) on c_2 with c_1 upon $P(\overline{s})$ is defined as follows (where $\overline{x} = Var(\mathcal{X}) \cup Var(\neg P(\overline{t}))$):

$$\frac{[\![\neg P(\overline{t}) \ : \mathcal{X}]\!] \qquad [\![P(\overline{s}) \vee c_2'(\overline{y}) \ : \mathcal{Y}]\!]}{[\![P(\overline{s}) \vee c_2'(\overline{y}) \ : \mathcal{Y} \wedge \forall \overline{x}.[\neg \mathcal{X} \vee \overline{s} \neq \overline{t}]]\!]}$$

The bc-dissubsumption: The *unit bc-dissubsumption rule* imposes constraints preventing a c-clause from being subsumed by a unit c-clause. It allows the elimination of some c-clauses that are logical consequences of other c-clauses in S, as subsumption does. It is defined as follows (where $\overline{x} = Var(\mathcal{X}) \cup Var(P(\overline{s}))$):

$$\frac{[\![P(\overline{t}) \vee c' \ : \mathcal{Y}]\!] \qquad [\![P(\overline{s}) \ : \mathcal{X}]\!]}{[\![P(\overline{t}) \vee c' \ : \mathcal{Y} \wedge \forall \overline{x}.[\neg \mathcal{X} \vee \overline{s} \neq \overline{t}]]\!]}$$

The *bc-dissubsumption* rule (i.e. both clauses are possibly non unit) is defined in the same way. If C and D are two c-clauses we note $DisSub(C, D)$ the c-clause obtained by dissubsumption between C and D. If $DisSub(C, D) = \top$ (i.e. if the constraints of D are reduced to $\perp$) then we note $C \leq_{sub} D$. If S is a set of c-clauses and $[\![D \ : \mathcal{X}]\!]$ a c-clause we note $S \leq_{sub} D$ iff for all $\theta \in \mathcal{S}(\mathcal{X})$ there exists $C \in S$ such that $C \leq_{sub} \theta(D)$. Similarly, if S and S' are two sets of c-clauses we note $S \leq_{sub} S'$ iff for all $C \in S'$, $S \leq_{sub} C$.

2.3 The underlying semantics

The interpretations built by RAMC are called *peq-interpretation* (for partial interpretation definable by equational problems). The partial interpretation of the predicates is given by the unit c-clauses generated by RAMC: each n-ary predicate P is mapped to two subsets $\mathcal{I}(P)^+$ and $\mathcal{I}(P)^-$ of $\tau(\Sigma)^n$ ($\tau(\Sigma)$ denotes the Herbrand universe) corresponding to the sets of n-tuples of ground terms for which P is respectively evaluated to **True** and to **False**. The interpretation is *partial* because $\mathcal{I}(P)^+ \cup \mathcal{I}(P)^- \subseteq \tau(\Sigma)^n$. If $\mathcal{I}(P)^+ \cup \mathcal{I}(P)^- = \tau(\Sigma)^n$, we have a total interpretation of predicate P[4]. Obviously total interpretations are particular cases of partial interpretations. The sets $\mathcal{I}(P)^+$ and $\mathcal{I}(P)^-$ are presently expressed by equational problems in an equational theory. Therefore a peq-interpretation $\mathcal{I}$ can be represented by a satisfiable set of unit c-clauses: $E = \{[\![L_i(\overline{t_i}) \ : \mathcal{X}_i]\!]\}$, such that, for any ground literal L, L is **true** in $\mathcal{I}$ iff there exists i and $\sigma \in \mathcal{S}(\mathcal{X}_i)$ such that $L = \sigma(L_i(\overline{t_i}))$.

A peq-interpretation $\mathcal{I}$ *validates* a c-clause $[\![C \ : \mathcal{X}]\!]$ (noted $\mathcal{I} \models [\![C \ : \mathcal{X}]\!]$) iff for all ground solution $\sigma \in \mathcal{S}(\mathcal{X})$, there exists a ground literal $L(\overline{t}) \in C\sigma$ (resp. $\neg L(\overline{t})$) such that $\overline{t} \in \mathcal{I}^+(L)$ (resp. $\overline{t} \in \mathcal{I}^-(L)$).

Remark:

- Throughout the paper "interpretation" (resp. "model") will mean "peq-interpretation" (resp. "peq-model").
- The *atomic representations* defined in [FL95] are particular cases of eq-interpretations. Moreover there exists eq-interpretations that cannot be expressed by atomic representations: $S = \{[\![P(x, y) \ : x \neq y]\!], [\![Q(x, x) \ : \top]\!]\}$.

[4] Notice that not to be false in a partial model in not equivalent to be true in it.

3 Extending the method

In [CP95a] we have extended semantic resolution in order to improve the capabilities of RAMC both for model building and for unsatisfiability detection. The idea is to code in the constraints the conditions imposing that at least one of the two c-clauses is false in the model. This extension was focused on *binary* resolution.

In this section we extend these results to resolution applied on 2 or more clauses. More precisely we define the rule of $\mathcal{I}$-c-resolution and we prove its soundness and refutational completeness.

Let $\mathcal{I}$ be an interpretation. $\mathcal{I}$ is represented by a set of unit c-clauses.

$$\mathcal{I} = \{[\![L_1(\overline{s_1}) \ : \mathcal{X}_1]\!], \ldots, [\![L_n(\overline{s_n}) \ : \mathcal{X}_n]\!]\}$$

Let $\overline{y_i} = Var([\![L_i(\overline{s_i}) \ : \mathcal{X}_i]\!])$, and let $C : [\![\bigvee_{i=1}^{m} P_i(\overline{t_i}) \ : \mathcal{X}]\!]$ be a c-clause.
We note $\mathcal{F}_\mathcal{I}(C)$ the formula:

$$\mathcal{F}_\mathcal{I}(C) : \mathcal{X} \wedge \bigvee_{P_j = L_i} (\exists \overline{y_j}.\mathcal{X}_j \wedge \overline{s}_i = \overline{t}_j)$$

Remark: $\mathcal{F}_\mathcal{I}(C)$ codes the set of necessary conditions allowing one of the c-literals in $\mathcal{I}$ to subsume C. The next theorem formalizes this relationship.

Theorem 1. *For any c-clause C, if $\sigma \in \mathcal{S}(\mathcal{F}_\mathcal{I}(C))$ then $\mathcal{I} \models \sigma(C)$. Moreover, if $\mathcal{I}$ is total or if C is irreducible w.r.t. the distautology rule (i.e. if the distautology rule cannot be applied on C), then:*

$$\sigma \in \mathcal{S}(\mathcal{F}_\mathcal{I}(C)) \Leftrightarrow \mathcal{I} \models \sigma(C)$$

Proof. see [CP95a].

The following definition is a straightforward generalisation of the notion of clash in [SLA67] to c-clauses.

Let $\mathcal{I}$ be an interpretation. A *$\mathcal{I}$-c-clash* is a finite sequence of c-clauses: $\{E_1, \ldots, E_q, C\}$ satisfying the following conditions:

- C is of the form: $[\![\bigvee_{i=1}^{q} L_i(\overline{t_i}) \vee R \ : \mathcal{X}]\!]$ (with R possibly empty). C is called the *nucleus* of the c-clash.
- For all i, E_i is of the form: $[\![\neg L_i(\overline{s_i}) \vee R_i \ : \mathcal{X}_i]\!]$ (with R_i possibly empty). The E_i are called the *electrons*.
- $\mathcal{X} \wedge \bigwedge_{i=1}^{q}(\mathcal{X}_i \wedge s_i = t_i \wedge \neg\mathcal{F}_\mathcal{I}(E_i)) \wedge \neg\mathcal{F}_\mathcal{I}(R)$ has at least one solution

The *$\mathcal{I}$-c-resolvent* of $\{E_1, \ldots, E_q, C\}$ is the c-clause: $[\![R \vee \bigvee_{i=1}^{q} R_i \ : \mathcal{Y}_{res}]\!]$ where:

$$\mathcal{Y}_{res} = \mathcal{X} \wedge \bigwedge_{i=1}^{q}(\mathcal{X}_i \wedge s_i = t_i \wedge \neg\mathcal{F}_\mathcal{I}(E_i)) \wedge \neg\mathcal{F}_\mathcal{I}(R)$$

Remark: $\mathcal{Y}_{res}$ codes the condition: "it is possible to apply simultaneously resolution between C and E_i and neither the E_i nor the sub-clause R are true in $\mathcal{I}$".

3.1 Properties of the $\mathcal{I}$-c-resolution: soundness and refutational completeness

Theorem 2 (Soundness). *$\mathcal{I}$-c-resolution is sound.*

Proof. The proof is similar to the one of lemma 3.1 in [CZ92].

The proof of the refutational completeness needs the following two lemmas:

Lemma 3 (Model Extension). *Let $\mathcal{I}$ be a partial interpretation $\mathcal{I}$. Then there exists a total interpretation $\mathcal{I}'$ ($\mathcal{I}'$ is a total extension of $\mathcal{I}$) such that, for all ground clauses C: If $\mathcal{I} \models C$ then $\mathcal{I}' \models C$*

Proof. see [CP95a].

Lemma 4 (Lifting lemma). *Let $E_1, \dots E_n, C$ be c-clauses, $\sigma_1, \dots \sigma_n, \sigma$ be solutions of $\mathcal{X}_1, \dots, \mathcal{X}_n, \mathcal{X}$ respectively, $\mathcal{I}$ an interpretation, $\mathcal{I}'$ the total interpretation defined as in lemma 3, and R_g an $\mathcal{I}'$-resolvent of $\sigma_1(E_1), \dots \sigma_n(E_n), \sigma(C)$.*
There exists a $\mathcal{I}$-c-resolvent R of $E_1, \dots E_n, C$, and a substitution $\theta \in \mathcal{S}(\mathcal{Y}_{res})$, such that: $\theta(R) = R_g$

Proof. The proof is similar to the one of Lemma 2 in [CP95a].

Theorem 5 (Refutational Completeness). *For all interpretation $\mathcal{I}$, and for all unsatisfiable set S of c-clauses, there exists a refutation of S using only $\mathcal{I}$-c-rules.*

Proof. By refutational completeness of semantic resolution [SLA67] there exists a ground $\mathcal{I}'$-refutation of S. By lemma 4 it can be lifted to non ground c-clauses, to obtain an $\mathcal{I}$-c-refutation of S.

The converse of the lifting lemma also holds:

Lemma 6. *Let $\mathcal{I}$ be an interpretation. Let $E_1, \dots E_n, C$ be a clash. Let $[\![R : \mathcal{Y}]\!]$ be a $\mathcal{I}$-c-resolvent of $E_1, \dots E_n, C$. Let $\theta \in \mathcal{S}(\mathcal{Y})$. $\theta(R)$ is a $\mathcal{I}$-resolvent of $\theta(E_1), \dots, \theta(E_n), \theta(C)$.*

We deduce the following:

Corollary 7. *Let $\mathcal{I}$ be an interpretation, S a set of c-clauses and let d be a derivation from S using the $\mathcal{I}$-c-resolution rule. Assume that a corresponding ground derivation $d' = \sigma(d)$ exists. Then d' is a ground semantic derivation from ground instances of c-clauses in S.*

Proof. By induction on the length n of the derivation.

Remark: Corollary 7 proves that any semantic c-derivation corresponds to a semantic ground derivation. It is worth noting than semantic resolution does not have this property (see [CP95a, MH85]). This theorem is a nice side effect of our approach. It shows that it prunes the search space in a *stronger* way than semantic resolution does, *provided that an eq-interpretation is used to guide proof search.*

3.2 Semantic Disresolution (or $\mathcal{I}$-c-disresolution)

We apply the same ideas as in [CZ92], in order to define the *semantic c-disresolution* rule. The principle of this rule is to impose conditions preventing the application of $\mathcal{I}$-c-resolution (keeping refutational completeness). The $\mathcal{I}$-c-disresolution is a *restriction* of the disresolution rule defined in [CZ92].

Let $S = [\![R_1 : \mathcal{X}_1]\!], \ldots, [\![R_n : \mathcal{X}_n]\!]$ be a c-clash and $\overline{x} = Var(S)$. The set of c-disresolvents of S is the set $\bigcup_{i=1}^{n}\{C_i, D_i\}$, where C_i and D_i are defined as follow:

$$C_i : [\![R_i : \forall \overline{y}.\neg \mathcal{Y}_{res} \wedge \mathcal{X}_i]\!] \qquad D_i : [\![R_i : \exists \overline{y}.\mathcal{Y}_{res} \wedge \mathcal{X}_i]\!]$$

where $\overline{y} = \overline{x} \setminus Var([\![R_i : \mathcal{X}_i]\!])$, and $\mathcal{Y}_{res}$ is defined as above.

It is straightforward to see that $[\![R_i : \mathcal{X}_i]\!] \equiv C_i \wedge D_i$. Hence the parent c-clause can be deleted from S and replaced by the two c-clauses C_i and D_i.

Terminology: We shall call RAMC$_{\mathcal{I}}$ the procedure using the $\mathcal{I}$-c-resolution, $\mathcal{I}$-c-disresolution, c-factorization, c-disfactorization, c-dissubsumption, c-distautology rules and constraint solving rules.

Theorem 8. *Let S be a set of c-clauses stable by RAMC$_{\mathcal{I}}$.*[5]*. Let C : $[\![L(t) \vee R : \mathcal{X}]\!]$ be a c-clause in S. Then S is satisfiable iff $S \cup [\![L(t) : \mathcal{X} \wedge \neg \mathcal{F}_{\mathcal{I}}(C)]\!]$ is satisfiable.*

Proof. Assume that $S' : S \cup [\![L(t) : \mathcal{X} \wedge \neg \mathcal{F}_{\mathcal{I}}(C)]\!]$ is unsatisfiable. Then there exists a $\mathcal{I}$-c-refutation of S'. Since $\mathcal{F}_{\mathcal{I}}([\![L(t) \vee R : \mathcal{X} \wedge \neg \mathcal{F}_{\mathcal{I}}(C)]\!]) \equiv \bot$, this refutation can be transformed into a derivation from S of: C : $[\![\sigma_1(R) \vee \ldots \vee \sigma_n(R) : \bigwedge_{i=1}^{n} \sigma_i(\mathcal{X} \wedge \neg \mathcal{F}_{\mathcal{I}}(C)) \wedge \mathcal{Z}]\!]$ where $\mathcal{Z}$ are the constraints introduced by semantic c-resolution.

Since S is stable by $\mathcal{I}$-c-disresolution, $\mathcal{Z}$ is a *renaming* of variables in S. Moreover since C is stable by the **Explosion**[6] rule, C does not contains any disequation. Hence, C is reduced (by factorization) to: $C' = [\![R : \mathcal{X} \wedge \neg \mathcal{F}_{\mathcal{I}}(C)]\!]$. Since S is stable by RAMC$_{\mathcal{I}}$, there exists $C'' \in S$, such that C'' subsumes C. But this is impossible since C' subsumes C and S is stable by dissubsumption.

3.3 Model Building

The results of section 3.2 suggest a procedure for building models, based on *saturation*. This procedure is similar to the one of [FL95].

[5] i.e. all possible applications of the rules do not change S.

[6] The **Explosion** rule allows to express solutions (on a given signature) of disequations: for example, $x \neq a$ on the signature $\Sigma = \{f, a\}$ is equivalent to: $\exists y.x = f(y)$.

Procedure RAMC$_\mathcal{I}$

Input:
A set of c-clauses S
An interpretation $\mathcal{I}$
Output:
A model of S or **unsatisfiable**

begin
while $\Box \notin S$ and S is not stable or contains a non unit
c-clause C not true in $\mathcal{I}$
if a refutation rule or a model building rule ρ can be applied
then apply ρ on S with the strategy
else
choose a literal $L \in C : [\![L \vee R \ : \mathcal{X}]\!] \in S$
$S := S \cup \{[\![L \ : \mathcal{X} \wedge \neg \mathcal{F}_\mathcal{I}(C)]\!]\}$
if $\Box \in S$
then return unsatisfiable
else return S
end

Theorem 9. *If $RAMC_\mathcal{I}$ terminates, then a model of S can be automatically computed.*

Proof. In [CP95a], we proved that the interpretation $\mathcal{I}'$ defined below is a model of S.

For all ground term $\bar{t}$:

$$\mathcal{I}'(L(\bar{t})) = \top \text{ if } \exists [\![L(\bar{s}) \ : \mathcal{X}]\!] \in S \text{ such that } \bar{t} = \bar{s} \wedge \mathcal{X} \not\equiv \bot$$
$$\mathcal{I}'(L(\bar{t})) = \mathcal{I}(L(\bar{t})), \text{ elsewhere}$$

Remark: As pointed out in [CP95a], the model built by RAMC is computed by *modifying* and *extending* the initial interpretation. This allows to perform an incremental model building which is especially useful when dealing with large sets of c-clauses. The method can therefore be seen as a procedure that transforms a partial interpretation into a total model.

4 A very useful rule: The GMPL rule

The procedure RAMC defined above can be very inefficient, and, worse, may lead to non termination.

Indeed all the c-clauses deducible from the initial set of c-clauses have to be generated *before* the model is found. In particular, if this set of c-clauses is infinite, that is to say if we cannot get a stable set of c-clauses, then the above procedure will not terminate even if S has a very simple eq-model. This is the case in the following example.

Example 1. Let S be the set of c-clauses:
1 $[\![\neg P(x) \vee \neg P(f(x)) \ : \top]\!]$
2 $[\![A(x) \vee P(x) \vee P(f(x)) \ : \top]\!]$
3 $[\![A(x) \vee B(x) \ : \top]\!]$
4 $[\![\neg B(x) \vee \neg A(x) \ : \top]\!]$
By inspection of the last two literals of c-clauses 1 and 2, it is easy to see that the c-resolution applied on S generates an infinite number of distinct c-clauses of the form: $[\![\bigvee_{i=0}^{n} A(f^{2i}(x)) \vee P(x) \vee P(f^{2n}(f(x))) \ : \top]\!]$ Hence $\mathcal{I}$-c-resolution (as well as positive or negative hyper-resolution) does not terminate on S.
Nevertheless S has a very simple model $\{\neg P(x), A(x), \neg B(x)\}$

In the above example, one can easily remark that the set $S' = \{\neg P(x), A(x), A(x) \vee B(x), \neg A(x) \vee \neg B(x)\}$ is satisfiable. The two remaining literals of the c-clauses 1 and 2 are irrelevant. Nevertheless these "irrelevant" literals prevent the building of a model, since the application of the c-resolution and c-disresolution rules upon them leads to non termination.

To solve this problem, we have introduced the GMPL[7] rule, that is a natural way to detect models "hidden" in this way. This rule allows to add the set of literals $\{\neg P(x), A(x), \neg B(x)\}$ to the set of c-clauses of example 1, by preserving the satisfiability of the set of c-clauses. GMPL can be seen as an efficient way to detect stable subsets of c-clauses in sets such as S.

The GMPL rule is defined as follows:

GMPL (Generating **M**any **P**ure **L**iterals) :

$$\frac{S}{E}$$

where E is obtained by applying the following system of rules R_S on a c-literal $[\![L(\bar{t}) \ : \mathcal{X}]\!]$ occurring in S.

(Simplification) $E \cup C \rightarrow E \cup C'$
If $C \rightarrow C'$ by a constraint solving rules.

(Extension) $E \rightarrow E \cup \{[\![L(\bar{t}) \ : \mathcal{X}]\!]\}$
if $C = [\![L(\bar{t}) \vee R \ : \mathcal{X}]\!] \in S$

(Reduction) $E : E' \cup [\![L(\bar{t}) \ : \mathcal{X}]\!] \rightarrow E \cup [\![L(\bar{t}) \ : \mathcal{X} \wedge \forall y. \neg \mathcal{Y} \vee \bar{t} \neq \bar{s}]\!]$
$C = [\![\neg L(\bar{s}) \vee R \ : \mathcal{Y}]\!] \in S \wedge DisSub(E, C) \not\equiv \top$

(Clash Elimination) $E \cup [\![L(\bar{t}) \ : \mathcal{X}]\!] \cup [\![\neg L(\bar{s}) \ : \mathcal{Y}]\!] \rightarrow E \cup [\![L(\bar{t}) \ : \mathcal{X}]\!] \cup$
$[\![\neg L(\bar{s}) \ : \mathcal{Y} \wedge \forall x(\neg \mathcal{X} \vee \bar{s} \neq \bar{t})]\!]$

[7] Standing for Generating Many Pure Literals

In [CP95b], we proved that this system of rules terminates on any set of c-clauses, provided that the **Extension** rule is applied a finite number of times on each literal. Moreover, for all satisfiable set of c-clauses S, and for all set of unit c-clauses E stable by R_S, $E \cup S$ is satisfiable.

Remark: there exists sets of c-clauses such that RAMC$_{\mathcal{I}}$ $\cup$ { GMPL } terminates and such that RAMC$_{\mathcal{I}}$ (or the semantic resolution using $\mathcal{I}$) does not terminate, as shown by the following example.

Example 2. Consider the following set of c-clauses S:
1 $[\![P(x,y) \vee Q(x,y) \ : \top]\!]$
2 $[\![-P(x,y) \vee -Q(x,y) \ : \top]\!]$
3 $[\![-P(a,f(x)) \ : \top]\!]$
4 $[\![P(x,x) \ : \top]\!]$
5 $[\![P(x,y) \vee -P(f(x),f(y)) \ : \top]\!]$
6 $[\![-P(x,y) \vee P(f(x),f(y)) \ : \top]\!]$
Let $\mathcal{I} = \emptyset$.
By applying the GMPL rule the following set of c-clauses is obtained:
7 $[\![\neg P(x,y) \ : x \neq y]\!]$
8 $[\![Q(x,y) \ : x \neq y]\!]$
Then all the remaining nonunit c-clauses can be removed by applying the c-dissubsumption rule.

Moreover, it is easy to see that the hyper-resolution rule (resp. negative hyper-resolution) generates an infinite sequence of c-clauses of the form: $[\![Q(f^n(a),f(f^n(x))) \ : \top]\!]$ (resp. $[\![-P(f^n(a),f(f^n(x))) \ : \top]\!]$).

Therefore the GMPL rule *increases* the capabilities of the method (i.e. the classes of formulae for which it terminates and builds model). The GMPL is in particular essential for building models for sets of c-clauses for which the $\mathcal{I}$-c-resolution does not terminate (for example for set of c-clauses that are not decidable by hyper-resolution).

5 Termination

In this section we identify precisely some classes of sets of c-clauses for which our method terminates (**and** builds a model). We show that it is possible to define a particular strategy restricting the application of the $\mathcal{I}$-disresolution rule, in order to insure that RAMC$_{\mathcal{I}}$ terminates *on any set of c-clauses S such that $\mathcal{I}$-c-resolution terminates.* We show that the results of section 3.2 concerning the possibilities of building a model from a set of c-clauses stable by RAMC$_{\mathcal{I}}$ are preserved if the new strategy is used. These results imply that our method is a **decision procedure and is able to compute a model** for all sets of c-clauses S, for which semantic resolution (as in [SLA67]) terminates. Since hyper-resolution is a particular case of semantic resolution (corresponding to the empty interpretation), this implies that our method is a decision procedure for all classes decidable by hyper-resolution.

5.1 The limits of the method without strategy

Example 2 shows that there are sets of clauses for which RAMC$_\mathcal{I}$ can stop and such that hyper-resolution does not terminate. Then a question arises naturally: *do there exist sets of c-clauses for which the semantic resolution (with a given model $\mathcal{I}$) terminates, and such that RAMC$_\mathcal{I}$ (without any particular strategy) does not terminate ?*

The following example answers positively to this question.

Example 3. Let S be the following set of c-clauses:

$c_1 : [\![P(x) \vee P(f(x)) \vee R(x) \ : \top]\!]$
$c_2 : [\![\neg P(f(x)) \vee Q(x) \ : \top]\!]$

It is easy to see that S becomes stable by resolution. This is not the case for disresolution: Using the disresolution rule, we obtain:

$c_3 : [\![P(f(x)) \vee P(f(f(x))) \vee R(f(x)) \ : \top]\!]$
$c_4 : [\![P(a) \vee P(f(a)) \vee R(a) \ : \top]\!]$
$c_5 : [\![\neg P(f(f(x))) \vee Q(f(x)) \ : \top]\!]$
$c_6 : [\![\neg P(f(a)) \vee Q(a) \ : \top]\!]$
$c_7 : [\![P(f(f(x))) \vee P(f(f(f(x)))) \vee R(f(f(x))) \ : \top]\!]$
...

We obtain an infinite number of distinct c-clauses of the form:

$$[\![P(f^n(x)) \vee P(f^{n+1}(x)) \vee R(f^n(x)) \ : \top]\!]$$

Therefore, if we want to increase the capabilities of satisfiability detection of a method based on $\mathcal{I}$-c-resolution and $\mathcal{I}$-c-disresolution, it is necessary to restrict the application of the disresolution rule.

5.2 A d-strategy: a strategy for disinference rules

Let S be a set of c-clauses such that semantic resolution terminates on S. Our aim in this section is to define a restriction strategy on the model building rules such that:

- The restricted model building rules terminate on S.
- The class of formulae for which the method is able to build models is not diminished by using the restriction strategy.

For defining the d-strategy we need the following definitions. Let $\mathcal{I}$ be an interpretation, S be a set of c-clauses, and $C \in S$. We denote by $Cl(C)$ the multiset of sets of c-clauses $S' \subset S$ such that S' is a $\mathcal{I}$-c-clash and $C \in S'$.

Each c-clause $C \in S$ is mapped to a sequence of integers $p(C) = (p_1(C), p_2(C), \ldots, p_n(C), \ldots)$.

We define the integers k, n and the set $E_{k,n}(C)$ as follows:

- Initially $(n, k) = (1, 1)$, $E_{k,n}(C) = Cl(C)$.
- If $E_{k,n}(C) = \emptyset$ then k is increased by 1, $E_{k,n} = Cl(C)$.

- If $\not\exists C \in S/p_n(C) > k$, then n is increased by 1, k is set to 1 and $E_{k,n}$ is set to $Cl(C)$.
- If a the $\mathcal{I}$-c-disresolution is applied on a c-clash S then S is deleted from $E_{k,n}(C)$.

Initially each c-clause C_i in S is mapped to a sequence of the form: $p(C_i) = \{i, 0, \ldots\}$. If a c-clause C is deduced by resolution, or GMPL, then $p(C)$ is mapped to 0. If two c-clauses C_1 and C_2 are deduced from C by $\mathcal{I}$-c-disresolution or $\mathcal{I}$-c-disfactorization, then C_1 and C_2 are respectively mapped to the sequences: $p_1(C), \ldots, p_n(C), max\{p_{n+1}(C)/C \in S\}$ and $p_1(C), \ldots, p_n(C), max\{p_{n+1}(C_1) + 1/C \in S\}$.

Then the rule of disresolution restricted by the d-strategy is:

$$\frac{S : \{[\![R_1 \; : \mathcal{X}_1]\!], \ldots, [\![R_n \; : \mathcal{X}_n]\!]\}}{C_i : [\![R_i \; : \forall \bar{y}. \neg \mathcal{Y} \wedge \mathcal{X}_i]\!] \qquad D_i : [\![R_i \; : \exists \bar{y}. \mathcal{Y} \wedge \mathcal{X}_i]\!]}$$

if: $S \in E_{n,k}$, $p_n([\![R_i \; : \mathcal{X}_i]\!]) = k$.
Moreover, the dissubsumption is applied on C only if $p(C) = 0$.
We also define the following new rule (noted $R_{\mathcal{I}}$):

$$\frac{C : [\![R \; : \mathcal{X}]\!]}{[\![R \; : \mathcal{X} \wedge \neg \mathcal{F}_{\mathcal{I}}(C)]\!] \quad [\![R \; : \mathcal{X} \wedge \mathcal{F}_{\mathcal{I}}(C)]\!]}$$

If $\mathcal{F}_{\mathcal{I}}(C) \neq \bot$.
We shall call $\text{RAMC}'_{\mathcal{I}}$ the procedure using the $\mathcal{I}$-c-rules, $\mathcal{I}$-c-disresolution, $\mathcal{I}$-factorisation, $\mathcal{I}$-c-dissubsumption, $\mathcal{I}$-c-disfactorization, and constraint solving rules, guided by the above strategy.

5.3 Termination and Model Building

Let us define the following two operators R and R_S (they are similar to the operators R_H and R_{HS} defined in [FL95] for hyper-resolution on standard clauses):

Let S be a set of clauses. We note $\rho_{\mathcal{I}}(S)$ the set of all c-resolvents (and c-factors) of c-clauses in S, $simp(S)$, the set of c-clauses obtained by applying the distautology and the dissubsumption rules on c-clauses in S.

Let (R^n) and (R^n_S) be the sequences of set of clauses defined as followed:

- $R^0_S = R^0 = S$
- $R^{n+1} = R^n \cup \rho_{\mathcal{I}}(R^n)$, $R^{n+1}_S = simp(R^n_S \cup \rho_{\mathcal{I}}(R^n_S))$

We note $R^\infty(S) = \bigcup_{i=1}^n R^i(S)$ and $R^\infty_S(S) = \bigcup_{i \geq 0} \bigcap_{j \geq i} R^j_S(S)$.

Remark: it is easy to see that if semantic resolution (in the sense of [SLA67]) using the model $\mathcal{I}$ terminates on S then $R^\infty(S)$ is finite. Similarly, if the semantic resolution with subsumption and deletion of tautologies terminates on S then $R^\infty_S(S)$ is finite. Nevertheless the converse is *not* true: there exists set of c-clauses such that the $\mathcal{I}$-c-resolution terminates and such that the standard semantic resolution using $\mathcal{I}$ does not terminate as in the example below.

Example 4. Consider the following set of clauses:

1 $P(f(x))$ 2 $P(a)$
3 $R(a)$ 4 $P(x) \vee \neg R(x) \vee R(f(x))$

Hyper-resolution generates an infinite number of c-clauses $P(a) \vee \ldots \vee P(f^n(a)) \vee R(f^{n+1}(a))$. Nevertheless clause 4 can be reduced by dissubsumption (with clauses 1 and 2) to: $[\![P(x) \vee \neg R(x) \vee R(f(x)) : x \neq a \wedge \forall y.x \neq f(y)]\!]$, hence to $\top$.

We need the following definitions and lemma:

Let $[\![C : \mathcal{X}]\!]$ and $[\![D : \mathcal{Y}]\!]$ be two c-clauses. We say that $[\![C : \mathcal{X}]\!]$ is a *restriction* of $[\![D : \mathcal{Y}]\!]$, noted $[\![C : \mathcal{X}]\!] \preceq [\![D : \mathcal{Y}]\!]$, iff for all $\sigma \in \mathcal{S}(\mathcal{X})$, there exists $\theta \in \mathcal{S}(\mathcal{Y})$ such that $\sigma(C) = \theta(D)$. A c-clause C is said to be a *variant* of a c-clause D iff $C \preceq D$ and $D \preceq C$ (we note: $C \equiv D$).

A c-literal L is said to be *n-$\mathcal{I}$-reachable* from a set of c-clauses S iff there exists a derivation of length n from S to S' using RAMC$_\mathcal{I}$ rules and a set of c-literals $L_1, \ldots, L_n$ in S' such that:

- $L \equiv L_1 \wedge \ldots \wedge L_n$.
- For all i, there exists a c-clause $[\![P \vee R : \mathcal{X}]\!] \in S'$ such that $L_i \equiv [\![P : \mathcal{X}]\!]$.

A c-literal L is *$\mathcal{I}$-reachable* if it is n-$\mathcal{I}$-reachable for some n. A eq-model $\mathcal{M}$ is said to be *$\mathcal{I}$-reachable* iff all its c-literals are $\mathcal{I}$-reachable.

Lemma 10. *Let S be a set of clauses. If $R^\infty(S)$ is finite, then S has a $\mathcal{I}$-reachable model.*

Proof. (too long to be included here)

The proof is constructive: let S be a set of clauses such that $S = R^\infty(S)$. We show (by induction on the size of S) that there exists a eq-model of S. Then we show that this model is reachable.

An infinite derivation $S_0 \rightarrow \ldots \rightarrow S_n \rightarrow \ldots$ is called *fair* if either there are infinitely many applications of the disresolution and disfactorization rules or there exists j such that S_j is stable under disresolution and for all c-clauses $C \in R^\infty(S)$ there exists $k > 0$ such that $S_k \leq_{sub} C$.

Theorem 11. *Let S be a satisfiable set of c-clauses. If S has a $\mathcal{I}$-reachable eq-model, then any fair application of RAMC$_\mathcal{I}$ terminates on S, provided that the dissubsumption and the GMPL rules are applied as soon as possible.*

Proof. (sketch)

We prove by induction on n the following property: *if there exists a derivation d_n of length n (i.e. with n applications of the disresolution rule) from S to S' using mc-rules, such that there exists k c-clauses $C_1, \ldots, C_k$ occurring in S' such that $C \equiv C_1 \wedge \ldots \wedge C_k$, then there exists j and a set of c-clauses $C'_1, \ldots, C'_m$ of S_j such that $C \equiv \bigwedge_{i=1}^m C'_i$*

Then we consider the following application of GMPL:

- We apply the rule **Extension** only if there exists at least one instance of $[\![L(\bar{t}) \ : \mathcal{X} \wedge \bar{s} = \bar{t} \wedge \mathcal{X}']\!]$ that is true in $\mathcal{I}$.
- We apply the rule **Clash Elimination** and **Reduction** only if $[\![\neg L(\bar{s}) \ : \mathcal{Y}]\!]$ is true in $\mathcal{I}$

It is easy to prove that this application of the GMPL rule generates a non empty set of unit c-clauses. Moreover, if E is irreducible by the restricted application of R_S then E is irreducible by R_S.

Therefore, by applying several times the GMPL rule one can therefore generate a peq-model of S.

Corollary: RAMC$'_{\mathcal{I}}$ is a decision procedure for all classes of formulae such that semantic resolution in the sense of [SLA67] using the model $\mathcal{I}$ terminates.

In particular since hyper-resolution is a particular case of semantic resolution with the model $\mathcal{I}^-(P) = \tau(\Sigma)$, for all P (each positiye atom is false), then our method is a decision procedure for all classes of formulae decidable by hyper-resolution.

Moreover unlike semantic resolution, RAMC$'_{\mathcal{I}}$ is **also** able to build models for satisfiable formulae in this classes.

6 Conclusion and future work

We have presented a powerful extension of our former method for building models for first order formulae. The notion of d-strategy (i.e. strategy for disinference rules) has been introduced. Using a d-strategy restricting the application of the disinference rules, we have shown that our approach captures a wide range of classes decidable by semantic resolution (provided that the interpretation used to guide the search is a eq-interpretation). In particular it captures all classes known to be decidable by hyper-resolution such as the classes PVD$_+$, OCC1N$_+$ ... (see [FLTZ93, LEI93]). It is also able to detect satisfiability of some formula schemata for which decision procedures based on hyper-resolution do not stop. Short term research will be focused on:

- Study of more powerful d-strategies.
- Study of the relationship (comparative power, simulation...) of ordering strategies (in the standard sense) and d-strategies.

Acknowledgements

We thank the referees for their pertinent and valuable comments on the first version of this paper.

References

[BÖR84] Egon BÖRGER. Decision problems in predicate logic. In G. Longo G. Lolli and A. Marcja, editors, *Logic Colloquium'82*, pages 263–301. North-Holland, 1984.

[CP95a] Ricardo CAFERRA and Nicolas PELTIER. Extending semantic resolution via automated model building: applications. In *Proceeding of IJCAI'95*. Morgan Kaufmann, 1995.

[CP95b] Ricardo CAFERRA and Nicolas PELTIER. Model building and interactive theory discovery. In *Proceeding of Tableaux'95*, LNAI 918, pages 154–168. Springer-Verlag, 1995.

[CZ92] Ricardo CAFERRA and Nicolas ZABEL. A method for simultaneous search for refutations and models by equational constraint solving. *Journal of Symbolic Computation*, 13:613–641, 1992.

[DG79] Burton DREBEN and Warren D. GOLDFARB. *The Decision Problem, Solvable Classes of Quantificational Formulas*. Addison-Wesley, 1979.

[FL92] Christian FERMÜLLER and Alexander LEITSCH. Model building by resolution. In *Computer Science Logic, CSL'92*, pages 134–148. Springer-Verlag, LNCS 702, 1992.

[FL95] Christian FERMÜLLER and A. LEITSCH. Hyperresolution and automated model building. *Journal of Logic and Computation*, 1995. To appear.

[FLTZ93] C. FERMÜLLER, A. LEITSCH, T. TAMMET, and N. ZAMOV. *Resolution Methods for the Decision Problem*. LNAI 679. Springer-Verlag, 1993.

[JOY76] W.H. JOYNER. Resolution strategies as decision procedures. *Journal of the ACM*, 23:398–417, 1976.

[LEI93] Alexander LEITSCH. Deciding clause classes by semantic clash resolution. *Fundamenta Informaticae*, 18:163–182, 1993.

[LEW79] Harry LEWIS. *Unsolvable classes of quantificational formulas*. Addison-Wesley, 1979.

[MH85] William McCUNE and Lawrence HENSCHEN. Experiments with semantic paramodulation. *Journal of Automated Reasoning*, 1:231–261, 1985.

[MIN91] Grigori E. MINTS. Proof theory in the USSR 1925-1969. *Journal of Symbolic Logic*, 56(2):385–424, June 1991.

[SLA67] James R. SLAGLE. Automatic theorem proving with renamable and semantic resolution. *Journal of the ACM*, 14(4):687–697, October 1967.

[TAM91] Tanel TAMMET. Using resolution for deciding solvable classes and building finite models. In *Baltic Computer Science*, pages 33–64. Springer-Verlag, LNCS 502, 1991.

A Note on the Relation Between Polynomial Time Functionals and Constable's Class $\mathcal{K}$

P. Clote*
clote@informatik.uni-muenchen.de

Institut für Informatik, Ludwig-Maximilians-Universität München, Oettingenstr. 67, D-80538 München.

Abstract. A result claimed without proof by R. Constable in a STOC73 paper is here corrected: a strictly increasing function f is presented for which Constable's class $K(f)$ is properly contained in $FP(f)$, the collection of functions polynomial time computable in f.

Introduction

In [10] A. Cobham[2] was the first to isolate the notion of polynomial time computable function. There he characterized the class FP of polynomial time computable functions as the smallest function algebra $\mathcal{L}$ containing certain initial functions and closed under composition and a certain variant of primitive recursion called *bounded recursion on notation.* Since Cobham's seminal work, a number of other complexity classes have been characterized by function algebras, such as linear space [18][3], logspace [15], polynomial space [20], exponential time [17], certain general complexity classes [22], AC^0, AC^k, NC [9, 1], $ACC(2)$, $ACC(6)$, TC^0 [7], etc.[4]

One of the first persons to consider type 2 functional computational complexity was R. Constable, who in [11] introduced a type 2 machine model and related programming language, and then studied polynomial time reducibilities between functions. On p. 118 of [11], Constable defined the class $\mathcal{L}(f)$ to be the collection of functions of the form $\lambda \mathbf{x} F(f, \mathbf{x})$, where F is a type 2 polynomial time computable operator; i.e. $\mathcal{L}(f)$ is the collection of all functions polynomial time computable in f. From subsequent work of K. Mehlhorn [16] and especially of B. Kapron and S. Cook [14], it is known that Constable's class $\mathcal{L}(f)$ can alternately be defined in a machine independent manner as the smallest class of functions containing Cobham's initial functions together with f, and closed under composition and bounded recursion on notation.

* Part of this research supported by NSF CCR-9408090 and US-Czech Science and Technology Program 93025.

[2] J. Edmonds [12] independently isolated the notion of *good* (i.e. polynomial time) algorithm.

[3] Ritchie's work was actually prior to that of Cobham.

[4] For a survey, see chapter 10 of [23] or [4].

Drawing on analogy with the Kalmár elementary functions[5] Constable defined $K(f)$ to be the smallest class of functions containing the initial functions $+, \dot{-}, \times, \lfloor x/y \rfloor, f$ and closed under the operations of substitution, explicit transformation, length bounded addition $f(x,\mathbf{y}) = \sum_{i=0}^{|x|} h(i,\mathbf{y})$ and length bounded multiplication $f(x,\mathbf{y}) = \prod_{i=0}^{|x|} h(i,\mathbf{y})$. The class K is defined as previously, but without the initial function f.[6] On page 118 of [11], the following claim is stated as a theorem without proof.

Claim I

(a) For all f, $K(f) \subseteq \mathcal{L}(f)$.
(b) For all non-decreasing f, $K(f) = \mathcal{L}(f)$.

While part (a) is clearly true, the purpose of this note is to present a counterexample to part (b). On the same page of [11], the following claim is stated as a corollary without proof.

Claim II $K = \mathcal{L}$.

Since Cobham [10] had characterized the polynomial time computable functions FP by the function algebra $\mathcal{L}$, this corollary would have given a very elegant characterization of FP. This corollary is unlikely to be true, since by consideration of a binary tree whose inner parent nodes perform the sum [resp. product] of the values associated with the children, it is easy to see that $K \subseteq NC \subseteq FP$. Hence if NC is properly contained in the class FP of polynomial time computable functions, then the claimed corollary is false. Similarly, though our proof procedes slightly differently, it is easy to see that for functions f_L, c_L associated with C. Wilson's oracle separating NC from P, it is the case that

$$K(f_L) = K(c_L) \subseteq \mathcal{F}NC^L \subset \mathcal{F}P^L = \mathcal{L}(f)$$

and hence that $K(f) \subset \mathcal{L}(f)$ for a particular non-decreasing function.[7]

I believe it is worth clarifying the status of these claims (for which no proofs can be found in the literature), since on page 194 of [23], Claim II is stated as Theorem 10.27 again without proof.

R. Constable's work [11] was quite seminal. K. Mehlhorn [16][8] subsequently studied polynomial time reducibility between functions, and (essentially) defined the collection BFF of basic feasible type 2 functionals as the straightforward extension of Cobham's machine-independent characterization of the polynomial

[5] The elementary functions [13] form the smallest class containing certain initial functions including 2^x and closed under composition, bounded addition $g(x,y) = \sum_{i=0}^{x} h(i,y)$, and bounded multiplication $g(x,y) = \prod_{i=0}^{x} h(i,y)$. It is known that this class coincides with those functions computable in time (or space) bounded by a finite stack of 2's topped by the length of the input.

[6] In the terminology of [11], $K(f()) = [+, -, \times, \lfloor x/y \rfloor, f(); Os, \sum_{|x|}, \prod_{|x|}]$.

[7] All unexplained notation is later introduced.

[8] [16] contains results from Mehlhorn's Ph.D. dissertation written under the direction of R. Constable.

time computable functions to type 2.[9] Mehlhorn proved (essentially) that BFF equals the collection of type 2 functionals $F(f,x)$ for which there exists a function oracle Turing machine M such that $M(f,x) = F(f,x)$ for all f,x and the runtime of $M(f,x)$ is bounded by $|G(f,x)|$ where $G \in BFF$. Mehlhorn measured the cost for function oracle calls as 1 (unit cost).

In [14], B. Kapron and S. Cook proved a difficult extension of Mehlhorn's theorem. Their result states that a type 2 functional $F \in BFF$ if and only if there is a Turing machine M computing F, for which the runtime of $M(f,x)$ is bounded by $P(|f|,|x|)$, where P is a *second order polynomial.* B. Kapron, A. Ignjatovic and the author [6] then characterized type 2 AC^0 functionals and gave a characterization of type 2 NC functionals.[10]

The plan of this paper is as follows. In section 1 basic definitions and background results are given. In section 2 we prove that $K(f)$ is properly contained in $\mathcal{L}(f)$ for some increasing f. In section 3 we show K contains TC^0 and ACC, and pose the question whether K contains $ALOGTIME$ and $LOGSPACE$.

1 Definitions

1.1 Oracle Turing machine

In [11], R. Constable introduced a natural programming language including *function oracle calls*, and with respect to this model defined the notion of polynomial time type 2 functional. In [14], B. Kapron and S. Cook defined the notion of *norm* (or length) of a function, and studied polynomial time (function) oracle machines, running in second order polynomial time.

Definition 1. The length of x in binary satisfies $|x| = \lceil log_2(x+1)\rceil$. The *length* or *norm* $|f|$ of function f is

$$|f|(n) = \max_{|x|\leq n} |f(x)|.$$

Let $f_1,\ldots,f_m$ be variables ranging over $\mathbf{N}^N$ and $x_1,\ldots,x_n$ be variables ranging over $\mathbf{N}$. The collection C of second order polynomials $P(f_1,\ldots,f_m,x_1,\ldots,x_n)$ is defined inductively as follows.

(i) for any integer c, $c \in C$,
(ii) for every $1 \leq i \leq n$, $x_i \in C$,
(iii) if $P,Q \in C$ then $P+Q \in C$ and $P \cdot Q \in C$,
(iv) if $P \in C$ then $f_i(P) \in C$ for $1 \leq i \leq m$.

---

[9] Mehlhorn called such functionals polynomial time computable operators. This class of functionals was then studied by M. Townsend [21], who called them $POLY$, and later by B. Kapron and S. Cook [14], who first denoted this class as BFF, the basic feasible functionals of type 2.

[10] The characterization of NC in [6] extended Mehlhorn's approach; the parallel analogue of [14] will appear in the journal version of [6].

In the Kapron-Cook model, a type 2 functional F is ***polynomial time computable*** if there is a second order polynomial P and an oracle Turing machine M, such that $F(f,x) = M(f,x)$, where the runtime of $M(f,x)$ is at most $P(|f|,|x|)$. Here, the cost for a function oracle call $f(y)$ is $|f(y)|$.

The main result of [14] was a characterization of type 2 polynomial time computable functionals — the function algebra BFF of ***basic feasible functionals*** equals the type 2 polynomial time computable functionals. The formal definition of BFF, given in Definition 19, is a straightforward type 2 generalization of Cobham's function algebra $\mathcal{L}$. It immediately follows from [14] that R. Constable's class $\mathcal{L}(f)$ is equal to the function algebra $[0, I, s_0, s_1, \#, f; \text{COMP}, \text{BRN}]$, which is equal to the collection of functions $\lambda \mathbf{x} F(f, \mathbf{x})$, where $F \in BFF$.

1.2 Circuit families

An *oracle boolean circuit* is a directed acyclic graph. Nodes with fan-in 0 are labeled by $x_1, \ldots, x_n, 0, 1$. All other nodes, called ***gates*** are labeled by one of $\wedge$, $\vee$, $\neg$, ?, the latter called an ***oracle gate***. Nodes labeled by $\neg$ have fan-in 1, all other gates have arbitrary fan-in. All nodes except for the unique ***output*** node have arbitrary fan-out; the output node has fan-out 0. The ***size*** $s(\alpha)$ of a circuit α is the number of gates. The ***depth*** $d(\alpha)$ of a circuit is defined recursively as follows.

$$d(\alpha) = \begin{cases} 0 & \text{if } \alpha \text{ is labeled by } x_1, \ldots, x_n, 0, 1 \\ 1 + d(\beta) & \text{if } \alpha \text{ is } \neg\beta \\ 1 + \max_{1 \le i \le m}(d(\beta_i)) & \text{if } \alpha \text{ is } \bigvee_{i=1}^m \beta_i \text{ or } \bigwedge_{i=1}^m \beta_i \\ |m| + \max(d(\beta_1), \ldots, d(\beta_m)) & \text{if } \alpha \text{ is } ?(\beta_1, \ldots, \beta_m) \end{cases}$$

If $A \subseteq \{0,1\}^*$, $x \in \{0,1\}^*$, then an oracle boolean circuit α *computes* on input A, x in the obvious manner. Formally, one defines a function $Eval(\alpha, A, w)$, where

$$Eval(\alpha, A, w) = \begin{cases} \text{label of } \alpha & \text{if } \alpha \text{ is labeled by } x_1, \ldots, x_n, 0, 1 \\ \neg Eval(\beta, A, w) & \text{if } \alpha \equiv \neg\beta \\ \bigvee_{1 \le i \le m} Eval(\beta_i, A, w) & \text{if } \alpha \text{ is } \bigvee_{i=1}^m \beta_i \\ \bigwedge_{1 \le i \le m} Eval(\beta_i, A, w) & \text{if } \alpha \text{ is } \bigwedge_{i=1}^m \beta_i \\ 1 & \text{if } \alpha \equiv ?(\beta_1, \ldots, \beta_m) \\ & \text{and } (\beta_1(w), \ldots, \beta_m(w)) \in A \\ 0 & \text{if } \alpha \equiv ?(\beta_1, \ldots, \beta_m) \\ & \text{and } (\beta_1(w), \ldots, \beta_m(w)) \notin A \end{cases}$$

AC_k^A is the collection of all languages computed by a logtime uniform family $\langle \alpha_n : n \in \mathbf{N} \rangle$ of oracle boolean circuits, where $s(\alpha_n) = n^{O(1)}$ and depth $d(\alpha_n) = O(\log^k(n))$ (see [2]). NC_k^A is similarly defined, but where $\wedge$-gates and $\vee$ gates are restricted to be of fan-in 2. $AC_k^\emptyset$ and $NC_k^\emptyset$ are usually designated by AC^k and NC^k, and $NC = \cup AC^k = \cup NC^k$.[11] Most often in the literature, AC^k,

[11] Here we follow Wilson's convention of defining boolean complexity classes of *languages* rather than functions, as well as his convention of writing AC_k in place of AC^k to allow for an oracle superscript.

NC^k and NC refer to *function classes* rather than classes of relations. Here, we define $\mathcal{F}NC$ to be the class of functions $f(\mathbf{x})$ such that

(i) f is of polynomial growth rate; i.e. there is a multivariable polynomial p such that

$$|f(x_1,\ldots,x_n)| \leq p(|x_1|,\ldots,|x_n|)$$

(ii) the bitgraph $A_f \in NC$, where $A_f(i,\mathbf{x})$ holds iff the i-th bit of $f(\mathbf{x})$ is 1.

Similarly the classes of functions of polynomial growth rate whose bitgraph belongs to AC^k [resp. NC^k] is designated here as $\mathcal{F}AC^k$ [resp.$\mathcal{F}NC^k$]. Finally, $\mathcal{F}NC^L$ [resp. $\mathcal{F}AC^L_k$, $\mathcal{F}NC^L_k$] denotes the class of functions of polynomial growth rate whose bitgraph belongs to the relativized class NC^L [resp. AC^L_k, NC^L_k].

1.3 Function algebras

Definition 2. If $\mathcal{X}$ is a set of functions and OP is a collection of operations, then $[\mathcal{X};\text{OP}]$ denotes the smallest set of functions containing $\mathcal{X}$ and closed under the operations of OP. The set $[\mathcal{X};\text{OP}]$ is called a *function algebra*. The *characteristic function* $c_p(\mathbf{x})$ of a predicate P satisfies

$$c_p(\mathbf{x}) = \begin{cases} 1 & \text{if } P(\mathbf{x}) \\ 0 & \text{else,} \end{cases} \tag{1}$$

where P is often written in place of c_P. If $\mathcal{F}$ is a class of functions, then $\mathcal{F}_*$ is the class of predicates whose characteristic function belongs to $\mathcal{F}$.

Definition 3. The *successor* function $s(x) = x+1$; the *binary successor* functions s_0, s_1 satisfy $s_0(x) = 2{\cdot}x$, $s_1(x) = 2{\cdot}x+1$; the *smash* function $x\#y = 2^{|x|\cdot|y|}$; the n-place projection functions $I^n_k(x_1,\ldots,x_n) = x_k$; I denotes the collection of all projection functions.

Definition 4. The function f is defined by *composition* (COMP) from functions $h, g_1,\ldots,g_m$ if

$$f(x_1,\ldots,x_n) = h(g_1(x_1,\ldots,x_n),\ldots,g_m(x_1,\ldots,x_n)).$$

Definition 5 (A. Cobham [10]). The function f is defined by *bounded recursion on notation* (BRN) from g, h_0, h_1, k if

$$\begin{aligned} f(0,\mathbf{y}) &= g(\mathbf{y}) \\ f(s_0(x),\mathbf{y}) &= h_0(x,\mathbf{y},f(x,\mathbf{y})) \text{ if } x \neq 0 \\ f(s_1(x),\mathbf{y}) &= h_1(x,\mathbf{y},f(x,\mathbf{y})) \end{aligned}$$

provided that $f(x,\mathbf{y}) \leq k(x,\mathbf{y})$ for all $x,\mathbf{y}$. Define the algebras

$$\begin{aligned} \mathcal{L} &= [0,I,s_0,s_1,\#;\text{COMP},\text{BRN}] \\ \mathcal{L}(f) &= [0,I,f,s_0,s_1,\#;\text{COMP},\text{BRN}]. \end{aligned}$$

The class FP consists of the collection of polynomial time computable functions.

Theorem 6 A. Cobham [10]. $FP = \mathcal{L}$.

See [19] for a detailed proof of Cobham's theorem.

Definition 7 (R. Constable [11]). The function f is defined by *weak summation* (WSUM) [resp. *weak product* (WPROD)] from g if $f(x, \mathbf{y})$ equals

$$\sum_{i=0}^{|x|} g(i, \mathbf{y}) \qquad [\text{resp. } \textstyle\prod_{i=0}^{|x|} g(i, \mathbf{y})].$$

Define the algebras

$$K = [0, I, s_0, s_1, +, \dot{-}, \times, \lfloor x/y \rfloor; \text{COMP}, \text{WSUM}, \text{WPROD}]$$
$$K(f) = [0, I, s_0, s_1, +, \dot{-}, \times, \lfloor x/y \rfloor, f; \text{COMP}, \text{WSUM}, \text{WPROD}].$$

Definition 8 (P. Clote [9]). Assume that $h_0(x, \mathbf{y}), h_1(x, \mathbf{y}) \leq 1$. The function f is defined by *concatenation recursion on notation* (CRN) from g, h_0, h_1 if

$$\begin{aligned} f(0, \mathbf{y}) &= g(\mathbf{y}) \\ f(s_0(x), \mathbf{y}) &= s_{h_0(x,\mathbf{y})}(f(x, \mathbf{y})), \text{ if } x \neq 0 \\ f(s_1(x), \mathbf{y}) &= s_{h_1(x,\mathbf{y})}(f(x, \mathbf{y})). \end{aligned}$$

This scheme is written in the abbreviated form

$$\begin{aligned} f(0, \mathbf{y}) &= g(\mathbf{y}) \\ f(s_i(x), \mathbf{y}) &= s_{h_i(x,\mathbf{y})}(f(x, \mathbf{y})). \end{aligned}$$

Definition 9. The function $\text{BIT}(i, x) = \text{MOD2}(\lfloor \frac{x}{2^i} \rfloor)$ yields the coefficient of 2^i in the binary representation of x; $\text{MOD2}(x) = x - 2 \cdot \lfloor \frac{x}{2} \rfloor$. The algebra A_0 is defined to be

$$[0, I, s_0, s_1, \text{BIT}, |x|, \#; \text{COMP}, \text{CRN}].$$

The algebra $A_0(f)$ is defined to be

$$[0, I, s_0, s_1, \text{BIT}, |x|, \#, f; \text{COMP}, \text{CRN}].$$

Definition 10. The function f is defined by *weak bounded recursion on notation* (WBRN) from g, h, k if

$$\begin{aligned} F(0, \mathbf{x}) &= g(\mathbf{x}) \\ F(s_0(n), \mathbf{x}) &= h_0(n, \mathbf{x}, F(n, \mathbf{x})), \text{ if } n \neq 0 \\ F(s_1(n), \mathbf{x}) &= h_1(n, \mathbf{x}, F(n, \mathbf{x})) \\ f(n, \mathbf{x}) &= F(|n|, \mathbf{x}) \end{aligned}$$

provided that $F(n, \mathbf{x}) \leq k(n, \mathbf{x})$ holds for all $n, \mathbf{x}$. The algebra A is defined to be

$$[0, I, s_0, s_1, \text{BIT}, |x|, \#; \text{COMP}, \text{CRN}, \text{WBRN}].$$

The algebra $A(f)$ is defined to be

$$[0, I, s_0, s_1, \text{BIT}, |x|, \#, f; \text{COMP}, \text{CRN}, \text{WBRN}].$$

Part (a) of the following theorem appears in [8]. Part (b) is straightforward from the techniques there developed.

Theorem 11 (P. Clote [8]). (a) $\mathcal{F}NC = A$.
(b) *For all* $L \subseteq \mathbf{N}$, $\mathcal{F}NC^L = A(c_L)$.

2 Main results

Lemma 12. *A is closed under* WSUM.

Proof Let $f(x,\mathbf{y}) = \sum_{i \le |x|} g(i,\mathbf{y})$, where $g \in A$. We must show that $f(x,\mathbf{y}) \in A$. The idea is to formalize using CRN and WBRN the "addition tree", a binary tree where values $g(i,\mathbf{y})$ are placed at the leaves and internal nodes have as values the sum of their two children. To do so, we proceed as follows.

In [9] explicit definitions of a number of functions were given in the algebra A_0. Such functions included $+$, $\dot{-}$, rev, where

$$x \dot{-} y = \begin{cases} x - y & \text{if } x \ge y \\ 0 & \text{else} \end{cases}$$

and $rev(x) = y$ holds if the binary representation of y is the reverse of the binary representation of x. In A_0, define the *bounded exponential* function

$$Exp(a,b) = 2^{\min(a,|b|)} \tag{2}$$

by

$$Exp(x,y) = \lfloor rev(exp0(x,y,s_1(y)))/2 \rfloor$$

where the auxiliary function $exp0$ is defined by

$$\begin{aligned} exp0(x,y,0) &= 1 \\ exp0(x,y,s_i(z)) &= \begin{cases} s_1(exp0(x,y,z)) \text{ if } |z| = x \le |y| \lor |z| = |y| \le x \\ s_0(exp0(x,y,z)) \text{ else.} \end{cases} \end{aligned}$$

Define functions $\ell(x)$ [resp. $n(x)$] whose value is the number of *leaves* [resp. *nodes*] of a full binary tree T_x which will be associated with x:

$$\ell(x) = Exp(||x||, 2 \cdot |x|) \tag{3}$$

$$n(x) = 2 \cdot \ell(x) - 1. \tag{4}$$

Thus $1 \le \ell(x) = 2^{||x||} \le 2 \cdot |x|$ is a power 2 and

$$\begin{aligned} n(x) &= 2 \cdot \ell(x) - 1 < 2 \cdot 2^{||x||} \le 4 \cdot |x| \\ 2^{n(x)} &\le 2^{4 \cdot |x|} \le (2^{|x|})^4 \le (2 \cdot x)^4. \end{aligned}$$

Since $Exp(n(x),(2 \cdot x)^4) = 2^{n(x)}$, we can freely use $2^{n(x)}$ in defining functions in A_0 and A.

Let T_x be the full binary tree having $\ell(x)$ many leaves and altogether $n(x)$ many nodes, whose nodes are labeled as follows: leaves are labeled $0, \dots, \ell(x) - 1$

from left to right, then parents of leaves are labeled $\ell(x), \ldots, \ell(x) + \frac{\ell(x)}{2} - 1$ from left to right, etc.

More formally, define

$$LC(i,x) = n(x) - [2 \cdot (n(x) - i) - 1]$$
$$RC(i,x) = n(x) - [2 \cdot (n(x) - i)].$$

Then $L(i,x)$ [resp. $R(i,x)$] is the left [resp. right] child of i in T_x, provided that $\ell(x) \leq i < n(x)$.

Using the scheme WBRN we will formalize a computation on the tree T_x. Though not used in the formal definition, it is helpful to compare the label of a node in T_x with the label of the same node in the tree U_x, defined as follows. Let U_x be the full binary tree having $\ell(x)$ many leaves, and altogether $n(x)$ many nodes, where the root is labeled 1 and for all internal nodes labeled by ν, the right child is labeled by $2 \cdot \nu$ and the left child is labeled by $2 \cdot \nu + 1$. For example, if $x = 7$ (or $4 \leq x \leq 7$) then $\ell(x) = 2^2 = 4$, $n(x) = 7$, and T_x, U_x are given as follows.

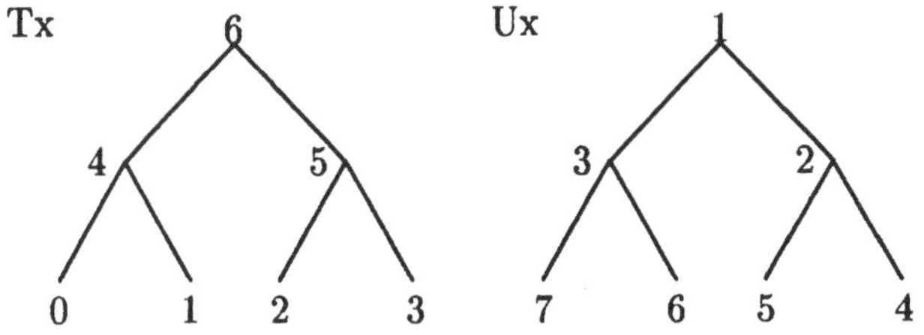

Define

$$f(i,x,\mathbf{y}) = \begin{cases} g(i,\mathbf{y}) & \text{if } i \leq |x| \\ 0 & \text{if } |x| < i < \ell(x) \\ f(LC(i,x),x,\mathbf{y}) + f(RC(i,x),x,\mathbf{y}) & \text{if } \ell(x) \leq i < n(x) \\ 0 & \text{if } n(x) \leq i \end{cases}$$

It is easily verified that

$$f(n(x)-1,x,\mathbf{y}) = \sum_{i=0}^{|x|} g(i,\mathbf{y}) \tag{5}$$

since f assigns values $g(0,\mathbf{y}), \ldots, g(|x|,\mathbf{y})$ to the leaves of T_x and then computes level-by-level the pairwise sums so that $\sum_{i=0}^{|x|} g(i,\mathbf{y})$ is assigned at the root $n(x)-1$ of T_x.

Define a pairing function

$$pair(x,y) = 2^{\max(|x|,|y|)+1} \cdot (2^{\max(|x|,|y|)} + y) + (2^{\max(|x|,|y|)} + x).$$

and its projections

$$left(pair(x,y)) = x$$
$$right(pair(x,y)) = y$$

Following [9], to encode the sequence $(t_1, \ldots, t_n)$, let m be the least power of 2 greater than or equal to $|t_i| + 1$, for $i \leq n$. Then define the sequence number

$$\langle t_1, \ldots, t_n \rangle$$

encoding the sequence to be $pair(t, 2^m)$, where

$$t = \sum_{i=1}^{n} (2^{m-1} + t_i) \cdot 2^{m \cdot (i-1)}.$$

If t encodes a sequence $\langle t_1, \ldots, t_n \rangle$ of length n, then define the β function by $\beta(t, 0) = n$ and for $1 \leq i \leq n$, $\beta(t, i) = t_i$. On p. 166 of [3], the functions $pair$, $left$, $right$, β were shown to belong to A_0. (For a systematic presentation of details, see [4].)

It is then straightforward to show that a sequence concatenation function $\frown$ exists in A_0 for which if $s = \langle s_1, \ldots, s_n \rangle$ and $t = \langle t_1, \ldots, t_m \rangle$ then $s \frown t = \langle s_1, \ldots, s_n, t_1, \ldots, t_m \rangle$. In [9] it is shown that the function $MSP(x, y) = \lfloor x / 2^{|y|} \rfloor$ belongs to A_0.

Now define $F(z, x, \mathbf{y})$ by

$$\begin{aligned} F(0, x, \mathbf{y}) &= \langle \ \rangle \\ F(s_i(z), x, \mathbf{y}) &= H(z, x, \mathbf{y}, F(z, x, \mathbf{y})) \end{aligned}$$

where $H(z, x, \mathbf{y}, u) = F(z, x, \mathbf{y}) \frown \langle h(z, x, \mathbf{y}) \rangle$ and

$$h(z, x, \mathbf{y}) = \begin{cases} g(|z|, \mathbf{y}) & \text{if } |z| < |x| \\ 0 & \text{if } |x| \leq |z| < \ell(x) \\ \beta(F(z, x, \mathbf{y}), LC(|z|, x)) + \beta(F(z, x, \mathbf{y}), RC(|z|, x)) & \text{if } \ell(x) \leq |z| < n(x) \\ 0 & \text{else.} \end{cases}$$

Thus $F(z, x, \mathbf{y}) = \langle f(0, x, \mathbf{y}), \ldots, f(|z|-1, x, \mathbf{y}) \rangle$. Define $G(z, x, \mathbf{y}) = F(|z|, x, \mathbf{y})$. In [7] it was shown that if $g \in A_0$, then the *maximum* function

$$m_g(x, \mathbf{y}) = \max\{g(i, \mathbf{y}) : i \leq |x|\}$$

belongs to A_0. It follows that if $g \in A$, then $m_g \in A$. Hence,

$$\begin{aligned} \sum_{i=0}^{|x|} g(i, \mathbf{y}) &\leq m_g(x, \mathbf{y}) \cdot (|x| + 1) \\ &\leq m_g(x, \mathbf{y}) \# (2 \cdot x) \end{aligned}$$

and so $\sum_{i=0}^{|x|} g(i, \mathbf{y})$ is bounded by a function in A. Thus G is defined by WBRN from functions in A and hence belongs to A. Finally, define K by

$$\begin{aligned} K(x, \mathbf{y}) &= G(2^{n(x)} \dot{-} 1, x, \mathbf{y}) \\ &= F(n(x), x, \mathbf{y}) \\ &= \langle f(0, x, \mathbf{y}), \ldots, f(n(x) - 1, x, \mathbf{y}) \rangle. \end{aligned}$$

It follows from (5) that

$$\beta(K(x,\mathbf{y}),n(x)) = \sum_{i=0}^{|x|} g(i,\mathbf{y})$$

and hence A is closed under WSUM. □

Theorem 13. *$K \subseteq A$. For any f, $K(f) \subseteq A(f)$.*

Proof By replacing sum by product, the proof of the previous lemma can immediately be modified to yield that A is closed under WPROD.[12] The initial functions 0, I, s_0, s_1, $+$, $\times$ of K all belong to A — the first three belong to A by definition; in [9], it was shown that $+ \in A_0 \subseteq A$; $\times$ is known to belong to NC (even NC^1), hence by Theorem 11 belongs to A. The algebra A is closed under composition, and by the previous lemma, under WSUM and WPROD. It follows that $K \subseteq A$. The same proof, in the presence of an additional initial function f, yields the inclusion $K(f) \subseteq A(f)$. □

In [24], C. Wilson relativized the bounded fan-in boolean circuit model to allow oracle gates (see section 1.2), and for this model constructed an oracle L for which the class NC^L is properly contained in polynomial time P^L. Wilson's circuit families were defined to be logspace uniform (logtime uniformity may be assumed), where the logspace machine outputting the blueprint of the circuit does not have access to the oracle. Oracle calls cost $\lfloor \log_2 k \rfloor$ depth, where k is the size of the query x.

Theorem 14 C. Wilson [24]. *There is an oracle $L \subset \mathbf{N}$, for which $NC^L \subset P^L$.*

It easily follows from this theorem that there exists $L \subseteq \mathbf{N}$, such that $\mathcal{F}NC^L \subset FP^L$.

Definition 15. For $L \subseteq \mathbf{N}$, let f_L be defined by

$$f_L(x) = \begin{cases} 2x & \text{if } x \notin L \\ 2x+1 & \text{if } x \in L. \end{cases}$$

$$c_L(x) = \begin{cases} 0 & \text{if } f_L(x) = 2x \\ 1 & \text{if } f_L(x) = 2x+1 \end{cases} \quad f_L(x) = \begin{cases} s_0(x) & \text{if } c_L(x) = 0 \\ s_1(x) & \text{if } c_L(x) = 1 \end{cases}$$

It easily follows from this observation that for any $L \subseteq \mathbf{N}$, $A(f_L) = A(c_L)$ and $FP^L = \mathcal{L}(f_L) = \mathcal{L}(c_L)$. Let L be as in Theorem 14. Putting everything together, we have the following theorem.

[12] In showing that G is definable by WBRN, note that

$$\prod_{i=0}^{|x|} g(i,\mathbf{y}) \leq m_g(x,\mathbf{y})^{|x|+1} \leq m(x,\mathbf{y})\#(2\cdot x).$$

Theorem 16. *There exists a strictly increasing function f such that $K(f)$ is properly contained in $\mathcal{L}(f)$.*

Proof Let $f = f_L$, where L is the oracle from Theorem 14. Then

$$K(f_L) \subseteq A(f_L) = A(c_L) = \mathcal{F}NC^L \subset FP^L = \mathcal{L}(c_L) = \mathcal{L}(f_L).$$

□

3 Complexity classes contained in K

In [2], TC^0 is defined as the class of logtime uniform, constant depth, polynomial size threshold circuits.

Theorem 17. $TC^0 \subseteq K$.

Proof By [7],

$$TC^0 = [0, I, s_0, s_1, |x|, \text{BIT}, \#, \times; \text{COMP}, \text{CRN}].$$

By definition,

$$K = [0, I, s_0, s_1, +, \dot{-}, \times, \lfloor x/y \rfloor; \text{COMP}, \text{WSUM}, \text{WPROD}].$$

We begin by showing that the initial functions of TC^0 can be defined in K.

$$\begin{aligned}
|x| &= (\sum_{i \leq |x|} 1) \dot{-} 1 \\
2^{|x|} &= \lfloor \frac{\prod_{i \leq |x|} 2}{2} \rfloor \\
\overline{sg}(x) &= 1 \dot{-} x = \begin{cases} 1 \text{ if } x = 0 \\ 0 \text{ else} \end{cases} \\
sg(x) &= 1 \dot{-} \overline{sg}(x) = \begin{cases} 0 \text{ if } x = 0 \\ 1 \text{ else} \end{cases} \\
c_{\leq}(x, y) &= sg(x \dot{-} y) = \begin{cases} 1 \text{ if } x \leq y \\ 0 \text{ else} \end{cases} \\
cond(x, y, z) &= \overline{sg}(x) \cdot y + sg(x) \cdot z = \begin{cases} y \text{ if } x = 0 \\ z \text{ else} \end{cases} \\
\min(x, y) &= cond(x \dot{-} y, x, y).
\end{aligned}$$

From these functions, definitions by case are admissible in K. Definitions of the form $f(x, \mathbf{y}) = \sum_{i \leq |x|} h(i, x, \mathbf{y})$ and $f(x, \mathbf{y}) = \prod_{i \leq |x|} h(i, x, \mathbf{y})$ are allowed by WSUM and WPROD. Define

$$Exp(a, b) = 2^{\min(a, |b|)} = \prod_{i \leq |b|} g(i, a, b)$$

where

$$g(i,a,b) = \begin{cases} 2 \text{ if } i < \min(a,|b|) \\ 1 \text{ else.} \end{cases}$$

Further define

$$MSP(x,i) = \lfloor \frac{x}{Exp(i,x)} \rfloor$$

$$\text{BIT}(i,x) = MSP(x,i) \dot{-} 2 \cdot \lfloor \frac{MSP(x,i)}{2} \rfloor$$

$$x \# y = \lfloor \frac{\prod_{i \leq |y|} 2^{|x|}}{2^{|x|}} \rfloor = 2^{|x| \cdot |y|}$$

Thus all the initial functions of TC^0 belong to K.

To show closure of K under CRN, we first show closure under sharply bounded quantifiers and sharply bounded μ-operator. Suppose that $R(x, \mathbf{z})$ is a relation whose characteristic function belongs to K. Then the characteristic function of $(\exists x \leq |y|)R(x, \mathbf{z})$ [resp. $(\forall x \leq |y|)R(x, \mathbf{z})$] is

$$sg(\sum_{x \leq |y|} c_R(x, \mathbf{z})) \qquad [\text{resp. } \overline{sg}(\textstyle\sum_{x \leq |y|} \overline{sg}(c_R(x, \mathbf{z})))].$$

Define $(\mu i < |y|)R(i, \mathbf{z})$ to be the least $i < |y|$ satisfying $R(i, \mathbf{z})$, if such exists, and otherwise 0. Then $(\mu i < |y|)R(i, \mathbf{z})$ can be defined in K by $\sum_{i \leq |y|} g(i, y, \mathbf{z})$, where

$$g(i,y,\mathbf{z}) = \begin{cases} 1 \text{ if } (\forall j \leq |y|)(j \leq i \rightarrow \neg R(j, \mathbf{z})) \\ 0 \text{ else.} \end{cases}$$

Now suppose that the function k is defined from $h_0, h_1 \in K$ by a simple restricted version of CRN as follows.

(6)
$$\begin{aligned} k(0, \mathbf{y}) &= 1 \\ k(s_0(x), \mathbf{y}) &= s_{h_0(x,\mathbf{y})}(k(x, \mathbf{y})) \\ k(s_1(x), \mathbf{y}) &= s_{h_1(x,\mathbf{y})}(k(x, \mathbf{y})). \end{aligned}$$

Then k is definable in K by

$$k(x, \mathbf{y}) = \begin{cases} 1 & \text{if } x = 0 \\ (\mu z < |4 \cdot x|)[\phi(x, \mathbf{y}, z)] & \text{else} \end{cases}$$

where $\phi(x, \mathbf{y}, z)$ is

$$[|z| = |x| + 1 \land (\forall i < |x|)(\text{BIT}(i,z) = h_{\text{BIT}(i,x)}(MSP(x, i+1), \mathbf{y}))].$$

Suppose that f is defined from $g, h_0, h_1 \in K$ by CRN:

$$\begin{aligned} f(0, \mathbf{y}) &= g(\mathbf{y}) \\ f(s_0(x), \mathbf{y}) &= s_{h_0(x,\mathbf{y})}(f(x, \mathbf{y})) \\ f(s_1(x), \mathbf{y}) &= s_{h_1(x,\mathbf{y})}(f(x, \mathbf{y})). \end{aligned}$$

Let k be defined from h_0, h_1 by the simpler version (6) of CRN. We have that $k \in K$ and

$$f(x, \mathbf{y}) = \begin{cases} 2^{|x|} \dot{-} k(x, \mathbf{y}) & \text{if } g(\mathbf{y}) = 0 \\ (g(\mathbf{y}) \dot{-} 1) \cdot 2^{|x|} + k(x, \mathbf{y}) & \text{else.} \end{cases}$$

Thus K contains all the initial functions of TC^0 and is closed under the operations COMP and CRN, hence $TC^0 \subseteq K$. □

Remark. Since modular counting

$$f(x, \mathbf{y}, m) = \Big(\sum_{i \leq |x|} g(i, \mathbf{y})\Big) \bmod m$$

is definable in K, it follows that $ACC \subseteq K$ (see [2] for definition of ACC). Moreover, note that the majority quantifier of [2] is directly definable by $c_{\leq}(\sum_{i \leq |x|} g(i), \frac{x}{2})$.

Question 18. (i) $ALOGTIME \subseteq K$?
(ii) $\mathcal{F}LOGSPACE \subseteq K$?
(iii) To what complexity class does K correspond?[13]

By [3, 7], $ALOGTIME$ and $\mathcal{F}LOGSPACE$ are characterized by function algebras involving respectively *k-bounded recursion on notation*

$$\begin{aligned} f(0, \mathbf{y}) &= g(\mathbf{y}) \\ f(s_0(x), \mathbf{y}) &= h_0(x, \mathbf{y}, f(x, \mathbf{y})) \\ f(s_1(x), \mathbf{y}) &= h_1(x, \mathbf{y}, f(x, \mathbf{y})) \end{aligned}$$

where $f(x, \mathbf{y})$ is bounded by the constant k, and *length bounded recursion on notation*

$$\begin{aligned} f(0, \mathbf{y}) &= g(\mathbf{y}) \\ f(s_0(x), \mathbf{y}) &= h_0(x, \mathbf{y}, f(x, \mathbf{y})) \\ f(s_1(x), \mathbf{y}) &= h_1(x, \mathbf{y}, f(x, \mathbf{y})) \end{aligned}$$

where $f(x, \mathbf{y}) \leq |k(x, \mathbf{y})|$. It does not seem clear how to go about defining either of these schemes using WSUM and WPROD.

---

[13] H.-J. Burtschick (personal correspondence) has suggested a possible relation to uniform, polysize arithmetic circuits.

4 Concluding remarks

In this paper, we have used Wilson's oracle separation of NC from P in order to refute Claim II(b) and cast doubt on Claim I. The area of higher type computational complexity abounds in open problems. Unlike the case where function classes $\mathcal{F}NC$, $\mathcal{F}AC^k$, FP, etc. have functions of the same (polynomial) growth rate, it may be that growth rates may distinguish between type 2 complexity classes. In particular, it would be interesting to know the answers of the questions below.

For economy of space, we refer the reader to [6] for definitions of the functional complexity classes $\mathcal{A}_0$, $\mathcal{A}$ which are respectively the type 2 analogues of A_0, A, as BFF below is the type 2 analogue of FP.

Definition 19 Townsend [21]. F is defined from $H, G_1, \ldots, G_m$ by functional composition if for all $\mathbf{f}, \mathbf{x}$,

$$F(\mathbf{f},\mathbf{x}) = H(\mathbf{f}, G_1(\mathbf{f},\mathbf{x}), \ldots, G_m(\mathbf{f},\mathbf{x}), \mathbf{x}).$$

F is defined from G by expansion if for all $\mathbf{f}, \mathbf{g}, \mathbf{x}, \mathbf{y}$,

$$F(\mathbf{f},\mathbf{g},\mathbf{x},\mathbf{y}) = G(\mathbf{f},\mathbf{x}).$$

F is defined from $G, G_1, \ldots, G_m$ by functional substitution if for all $\mathbf{f}, \mathbf{x}$,

$$F(\mathbf{f},\mathbf{x}) = H(\mathbf{f}, \lambda y.G_1(\mathbf{f},\mathbf{x},y), \ldots, \lambda y.G_m(\mathbf{f},\mathbf{x},y), \mathbf{x}).$$

F is defined from G, H, K by limited recursion on notation (LRN) if for all $\mathbf{f}, \mathbf{x}, y$,

$$F(\mathbf{f},\mathbf{x},0) = G(\mathbf{f},\mathbf{x})$$
$$F(\mathbf{f},\mathbf{x},y) = H(\mathbf{f},\mathbf{x},y,F(\mathbf{f},\mathbf{x},\lfloor \tfrac{y}{2} \rfloor)), \text{ if } y \neq 0.$$

provided that $F(\mathbf{f},\mathbf{x},y) < K(\mathbf{f},\mathbf{x},y)$ holds for all $\mathbf{f}, \mathbf{x}, y$.

The class of basic feasible functionals BFF is the smallest class of type 2 functionals containing $0, s_0, s_1, i_k^n, \#, Ap$ (defined by $Ap(f,x) = f(x)$) and closed under functional composition, expansion, functional substitution, and LRN.

Define the type 2 analogue $\mathcal{K}$ of Constable's K as follows. The functional $F(x,\mathbf{y},\mathbf{f})$ is defined by WSUM [resp. WPROD] from G if $F(x,\mathbf{y},\mathbf{f})$ equals

$$\sum_{i=0}^{|x|} G(i,\mathbf{y},\mathbf{f}) \qquad [\text{resp. } \textstyle\prod_{i=0}^{|x|} G(i,\mathbf{y},\mathbf{f})]$$

Definition 20. The class $\mathcal{K}$ is the smallest class of type 2 functionals containing $0, s_0, s_1, i_k^n, +, \dot{-}, \times, \lfloor x/y \rfloor, Ap$ and closed under functional composition, expansion, functional substitution, WSUM and WPROD.

Recall the following result from [6].

Theorem 21. $\mathcal{A}_0 \subset \mathcal{A} \subset BFF$.

It follows from this paper that $\mathcal{A}_0 \subset \mathcal{K} \subseteq \mathcal{A} \subset BFF$.

Question 22. Does there exist a function f, such that $K(f) \subset A(f) \subset FP(f)$? If so, can f be chosen to be of polynomial growth rate? Is $\mathcal{K}$ properly contained in $\mathcal{A}$?

For classes $\mathcal{F}$, $\mathcal{G}$ of type 2 functionals, let's say that $\mathcal{G}$ *majorizes* $\mathcal{F}$ if for every functional $F \in \mathcal{F}$ there exists $G \in \mathcal{G}$ such that

$$(\forall \mathbf{f}, \mathbf{x})[F(\mathbf{f}, \mathbf{x}) \leq G(\mathbf{f}, \mathbf{x})].$$

Write $\mathcal{F} \leq \mathcal{G}$ when $\mathcal{G}$ majorizes $\mathcal{F}$, and $\mathcal{F} < \mathcal{G}$ when $\mathcal{F} \leq \mathcal{G}$ but not $\mathcal{G} \leq \mathcal{F}$.

Question 23. Is it the case that $\mathcal{A}_0 < \mathcal{K} < \mathcal{A} < BFF$?

I would like to thank Chris Wilson for email correspondence and for sending a copy of [24].

References

1. B. Allen. Arithmetizing uniform NC. *Annals of Pure and Applied Logic*, 53(1):1–50, 1991.
2. D. Mix Barrington, N. Immerman, and H. Straubing. On uniformity in NC^1. *Journal of Computer and System Science*, 41(3):274–306, 1990.
3. P. Clote. Polynomial size frege proofs of certain combinatorial principles. In P. Clote and J. Krajíček, editors, *Arithmetic, Proof Theory and Computational Complexity*, pages 162 – 184. Oxford University Press, 1993.
4. P. Clote. Computation models and function algebras. In E. Griffor, editor, *Handbook of Recursion Theory*. in preparation.
5. P. Clote, B. Kapron, and A. Ignjatovic. Parallel computable higher type functionals. Technical Report BCCS-94-04, Department of Computer Science, Boston College, June 1994.
6. P. Clote, B. Kapron, and A. Ignjatovic. Parallel computable higher type functionals. In *Proceedings of IEEE 34th Annual Symposium on Foundations of Computer Science*, Nov 3–5, 1993. Palo Alto CA. pp. 72–83.
7. P. Clote and G. Takeuti. First order bounded arithmetic and small boolean circuit complexity classes. In P. Clote and J. Remmel, editors, *Feasible Mathematics II*, pages 154–218. Birkhäuser Boston Inc., 1995.
8. Peter Clote and Evangelos Kranakis. Boolean functions, invariance groups and parallel complexity. *SIAM J. Comput.* 20:553-590, 1991.
9. P.G. Clote. Sequential, machine-independent characterizations of the parallel complexity classes $ALOGTIME, AC^k, NC^k$ and NC. In P.J. Scott S.R. Buss, editor, *Feasible Mathematics*, pages 49–70. Birkhäuser, 1990.
10. A. Cobham. The intrinsic computational difficulty of functions. In Y. Bar-Hillel, editor, *Logic, Methodology and Philosophy of Science II*, pages 24–30. North-Holland, 1965.
11. R. Constable. Type 2 computational complexity. In *5th Annual ACM Symposium on Theory of Computing*, 1973. pp. 108–121.
12. J. Edmonds. Paths, trees, flowers. *Canad. J. Math.*, 17:449–467, 1965.

13. L. Kálmar. Egyszerü példa eldönthetetlen aritmetikai problémára. *Mate és Fizikai Lapok*, 50:1–23, 1943. [In Hungarian with German abstract].
14. B. Kapron and S. Cook. A new characterization of Mehlhorn's poly time functionals. In *Proceedings of IEEE 32th Annual Symposium on Foundations of Computer Science*, pages pp. 342–347, 1991. Journal version in *SIAM J. on Comput.*
15. J.C. Lind. Computing in logarithmic space. Technical Report Project MAC Technical Memorandum 52, Massachusetts Institute of Technology, September 1974.
16. K. Mehlhorn. Polynomial and abstract subrecursive classes. *Journal of Computer and System Science*, 12:147–178, 1976.
17. B. Monien. A recursive and grammatical characterization of exponential time languages. *Theoretical Computer Science*, 3:61–74, 1977.
18. R.W. Ritchie. Classes of predictably computable functions. *Trans. Am. Math. Soc.*, 106:139–173, 1963.
19. H. E. Rose. *Subrecursion: Function and Hierarchies*, volume 9 of *Oxford Logic Guides*. Clarendon Press, Oxford, 1984. 191 pages.
20. D.B. Thompson. Subrecursiveness: machine independent notions of computability in restricted time and storage. *Math. Systems Theory*, 6:3–15, 1972.
21. M. Townsend. Complexity for type-2 relations. *Notre Dame Journal of Formal Logic*, 31:241–262, 1990.
22. K. Wagner. Bounded recursion and complexity classes. In *Lecture Notes in Computer Science*, volume 74, pages 492–498. Springer-Verlag, 1979.
23. K. Wagner and G. Wechsung. *Computational Complexity*. Reidel Publishing Co., 1986.
24. C. Wilson. Relativized nc. *Math. Systems Theory*, 20:13–29, 1987.

First Order Logic, Fixed Point Logic and Linear Order

Anuj Dawar*[1], Steven Lindell**[2], Scott Weinstein***[3]

[1] Dept. of Computer Science, Univ. of Wales, Swansea, Swansea SA2 8PP, U.K.
e-mail: a.dawar@swansea.ac.uk
[2] Dept. of Computer Science, Haverford College, Haverford, PA 19041, U.S.A.
e-mail: slindell@haverford.edu
[3] Dept. of Philosophy, Univ. of Pennsylvania, Philadelphia, PA 19104, U.S.A.
e-mail: weinstein@cis.upenn.edu

Abstract. The Ordered conjecture of Kolaitis and Vardi asks whether fixed-point logic differs from first-order logic on every infinite class of finite ordered structures. In this paper, we develop the tool of bounded variable element types, and illustrate its application to this and the original conjectures of McColm, which arose from the study of inductive definability and infinitary logic on proficient classes of finite structures (those admitting an unbounded induction). In particular, for a class of finite structures, we introduce a compactness notion which yields a new proof of a ramified version of McColm's second conjecture. Furthermore, we show a connection between a model-theoretic preservation property and the Ordered Conjecture, allowing us to prove it for classes of strings (colored orderings). We also elaborate on complexity-theoretic implications of this line of research.

1 Introduction

The extensions of first order logic by means of fixed point operators, in particular the least fixed point and partial fixed point operators, have been much studied in recent years in the field of finite model theory. This is in large measure due to their connection with complexity classes. Immerman [Imm86] and Vardi [Var82] showed that the logic LFP, the extension of first order logic with a least fixed point operator, captures the class PTIME on ordered structures. Vardi [Var82] and Abiteboul and Vianu [AV91] showed that the similar extension of first order logic with a partial fixed point operator PFP captures the class PSPACE on ordered structures. Furthermore, Abiteboul and Vianu [AV95] showed that LFP = PFP if, and only if, PTIME = PSPACE, even without the restriction to ordered structures. One of the most important tools in the analysis of the fixed point logics is the bounded variable infinitary logic $L^{\omega}_{\infty\omega}$. Kolaitis and Vardi

* Research supported by EPSRC grant GR/H 81108
** Partially supported by NSF grant CCR-9403447, and the John C. Whitehead faculty research fund at Haverford College
*** Supported in part by NSF CCR-9403447.

[KV92b] showed that, on the class of finite structures, LFP and PFP can be seen as fragments of $L^{\omega}_{\infty\omega}$. Moreover, $L^{\omega}_{\infty\omega}$ has an elegant characterization in terms of pebble games which has proved an extremely useful tool in the analysis of the expressive power of the fixed point logics.

The logics LFP and PFP are both extensions of first order logic, and indeed, they are proper extensions on the class of all finite structures and on the class of ordered finite structures. It also follows from the result of Abiteboul and Vianu that if we can separate these two logics on any class of finite structures $\mathcal{C}$, then we would separate PTIME from PSPACE. On the other hand, one can construct infinite classes of structures on which the logics are equivalent and both of them, indeed even $L^{\omega}_{\infty\omega}$, collapse to first order logic.

Kolaitis and Vardi [KV92a] initiated an investigation of which classes of structures $\mathcal{C}$ have the property that LFP and $L^{\omega}_{\infty\omega}$ collapse to first order logic on $\mathcal{C}$. They proved a conjecture of McColm [McC90], showing that $L^{\omega}_{\infty\omega}$ collapses to FO if, and only if, every positive, first-order induction is bounded. Gurevich, Immerman and Shelah [GIS94] refuted another conjecture due to McColm by constructing a class of structures on which LFP collapses to FO, but $L^{\omega}_{\infty\omega}$ does not. Kolaitis and Vardi [KV92b] conjectured the following weaker version of McColm's conjecture, which remains open:

Conjecture 1 (Kolaitis-Vardi) *On every infinite class of ordered structures, there is a polynomial time computable query that is not first order definable.*

In this paper, we discuss McColm's conjectures, relating them to finite variable element types as introduced in [DLW95], a notion of compactness for classes of finite structures and a preservation property. In particular, we relate this preservation property to Conjecture 1, allowing us to prove it for classes of strings (linear orders with unary relations). We also comment on the complexity theoretic implications of Conjecture 1. Parts of the material in this paper appeared in preliminary form in [Daw93].

Section 2 covers the background material on fixed point logics, infinitary logics and element types. Section 3 relates inductive definitions and McColm's conjectures to bounded variable element types, compactness and preservation properties. Section 4 discusses the relation between the preservation properties and Conjecture 1, while Section 5 relates this conjecture to questions in complexity theory.

2 Background

We assume the standard definitions of a first order language (or signature) and a structure interpreting it. Unless otherwise mentioned, all structures we will be dealing with are assumed to have finite universe and all signatures are assumed to be finite and relational, that is, to consist of finitely many relation symbols. We write $\mathcal{F}_\sigma$ to denote the class of all finite structures of signature σ, and $\mathcal{O}_\sigma$ to denote the class of ordered finite σ–structures, i.e. $\mathcal{O}_\sigma$ is the collection of structures in $\mathcal{F}_{\sigma \cup \{\leq\}}$ which interpret the binary relation symbol $\leq$ as a linear order.

An *n-ary query* over a class of structures $\mathcal{C}$ is a map Q sending each structure $\mathfrak{A} \in \mathcal{C}$ to an n-ary relation over $\mathfrak{A}$ which satisfies the following condition: for all $\mathfrak{A}, \mathfrak{B} \in \mathcal{C}$, if f is an isomorphism from $\mathfrak{A}$ onto $\mathfrak{B}$, then $Q(\mathfrak{B}) = f[Q(\mathfrak{A})]$.

We will write FO, LFP, *etc.* both to denote logics (i.e. sets of formulas) and the classes of queries that are expressible in the respective logics. We say a logic L *collapses to* another logic L' over a class of structures $\mathcal{C}$, if and only if, the collection of restrictions of queries in L to $\mathcal{C}$ is included in the collection of restrictions of queries in L' to $\mathcal{C}$.

2.1 Inductive and Infinitary Logics

Let $\varphi(R, x_1, \ldots, x_k)$ be a first-order formula. On a structure, $\mathfrak{A}$, φ defines the operator, $\Phi_{\mathfrak{A}}(R^{\mathfrak{A}}) = \{\langle a_1, \ldots a_k\rangle | \langle \mathfrak{A}, R^{\mathfrak{A}}\rangle \models \varphi[a_1, \ldots, a_k]\}$. If φ is an R-positive formula, $\Phi_{\mathfrak{A}}$ is monotone. We may view φ as determining an induction on $\mathfrak{A}$ the stages of which are defined as follows: $\varphi^0_{\mathfrak{A}} = \emptyset$; $\varphi^{m+1}_{\mathfrak{A}} = \Phi_{\mathfrak{A}}(\varphi^m_{\mathfrak{A}})$. The *closure ordinal* of φ on $\mathfrak{A}$, denoted $||\varphi||_{\mathfrak{A}}$, is the least m such that $\varphi^m_{\mathfrak{A}} = \varphi^{m+1}_{\mathfrak{A}}$. The mth stage of the induction determined by φ can be uniformly defined over all structures by a first-order formula which we denote by φ^m. The set inductively defined by φ on $\mathfrak{A}$, denoted $\varphi^\infty_{\mathfrak{A}}$, is the least fixed point of the operator $\Phi_{\mathfrak{A}}$, that is, $\varphi^\infty_{\mathfrak{A}} = \varphi^m_{\mathfrak{A}}$, where $m = ||\varphi||_{\mathfrak{A}}$. If s is a k-tuple of elements of $\mathfrak{A}$ and $s \in \varphi^\infty_{\mathfrak{A}}$ we use $|s|_\varphi$ to denote the least m such that $s \in \varphi^m_{\mathfrak{A}}$. The *stage comparison query* for φ, denoted $\leq_\varphi$, is the query which assigns to each structure $\mathfrak{A}$ the $2k$-ary relation defined as follows:

$$s \leq_\varphi s' \iff s \in \varphi^\infty_{\mathfrak{A}} \wedge s' \in \varphi^\infty_{\mathfrak{A}} \wedge |s|_\varphi \leq |s'|_\varphi$$

where s and s' are k-tuples of elements of $\mathfrak{A}$.

We write LFP for the extension of first-order logic with the **lfp** operation which uniformly determines the least fixed point of an R-positive formula. That is, for any R-positive formula φ, $\mathbf{lfp}(R, x_1, \ldots, x_k)\varphi$ is a formula of LFP and $\mathfrak{A} \models \mathbf{lfp}(R, x_1, \ldots, x_k)\varphi[s]$, if and only if, $s \in \varphi^\infty_{\mathfrak{A}}$. We will need the following basic result about inductive definability which is a special case of Moschovakis's Stage Comparison Theorem (see [Mos74]).

Theorem 2 [Mos74]. *Let φ be an R-positive first-order formula. The stage comparison query $\leq_\varphi$ is definable in* LFP.

The stages $\varphi^m_{\mathfrak{A}}$ can be defined for an arbitrary (not necessarily positive) formula φ on a structure $\mathfrak{A}$. If the formula is not positive, these stages are not necessarily increasing, and they may or may not converge to a fixed point. We define the partial fixed point of φ on structure $\mathfrak{A}$ to be $\varphi^m_{\mathfrak{A}}$, for m such that $\varphi^m_{\mathfrak{A}} = \varphi^{m+1}_{\mathfrak{A}}$, if such an m exists and empty otherwise. The logic PFP is then the closure of first order logic under an operation **pfp** uniformly defining the partial fixed point of a formula.

The interest in fixed point logics on finite structures stems largely from their connection with complexity classes, as established by the following results.

Theorem 3 [Imm86, Var82]. *For any signature σ,* LFP = PTIME *on $\mathcal{O}_\sigma$.*

Theorem 4 [Var82, AV91]. *For any signature σ,* PFP = PSPACE *on $\mathcal{O}_\sigma$.*

Theorem 5 [AV95]. LFP = PFP *if and only if* PTIME = PSPACE.

In particular, it follows from Theorem 5 that the separation of LFP and PFP on any class $\mathcal{C}$ of finite structures would yield the separation of PTIME from PSPACE.

Let L^k be the fragment of first–order logic which consists of those formulas whose variables, both free and bound, are among $x_1, \ldots, x_k$. Let $L^k_{\infty\omega}$ be the closure of L^k under the first order operations and the operations of conjunction and disjunction applied to arbitrary (finite or infinite) sets of formulas. $L^\omega_{\infty\omega} = \bigcup_{k\in\omega} L^k_{\infty\omega}$. Kolaitis and Vardi [KV92b] established that on $\mathcal{F}_\sigma$, the fixed point logics LFP and PFP can be viewed as fragments of $L^\omega_{\infty\omega}$. Indeed, they establish the following result concerning the stages of a first-order induction.

Theorem 6 [KV92b]. *Let $\varphi \in L^k$ and let φ^m be the m-th stage of the induction determined by φ. φ^m is uniformly definable in L^{2k} over the class of finite structures. Hence, the least fixed point of φ is uniformly definable in $L^{2k}_{\infty\omega}$ over the class of finite structures.*

The following definition was introduced by McColm [McC90].

Definition 7. A class $\mathcal{C}$ of structures is proficient, if there is some positive formula φ such that $\sup(\{||\varphi||_{\mathfrak{A}} \mid \mathfrak{A} \in \mathcal{C}\}) \geq \omega$.

McColm [McC90] formulated two conjectures, which taken together state that the following three conditions are equivalent for any class of structures $\mathcal{C}$.

1. $\mathcal{C}$ is not proficient;
2. LFP collapses to first order logic on $\mathcal{C}$;
3. $L^\omega_{\infty\omega}$ collapses to first order logic on $\mathcal{C}$.

It is easily seen that condition (1) implies (2), for if φ is a formula such that $\sup(\{||\varphi||_{\mathfrak{A}} \mid \mathfrak{A} \in \mathcal{C}\}) < \omega$, then there is an $m \in \omega$ such that $\varphi^\infty_{\mathfrak{A}} = \varphi^m_{\mathfrak{A}}$ for all $\mathfrak{A} \in \mathcal{C}$. But, by Theorem 6 it follows that φ^m is uniformly defined by a first order formula. McColm [McC90] also showed that condition (3) implies (1). Kolaitis and Vardi [KV92a] showed that (1) implies (3), thereby establishing the equivalence of (1) and (3) and resolving the second of McColm's two conjectures. Gurevich *et al.* [GIS94] construct an example of a class of structures where (2) holds but (1) fails, refuting the first of the two conjectures.

While McColm's first conjecture has been refuted in the general case, it remains open whether it nonetheless holds on classes of ordered structures, i.e. for any class $\mathcal{C}$ that is a subclass of $\mathcal{O}_\sigma$ for some σ. It was conjectured by Kolaitis and Vardi [KV92a] that it does. Since the only implication that is unresolved is the implication (2) $\Rightarrow$ (1), this conjecture is the one stated as Conjecture 1 above.

2.2 Element Types

The following definition introduces the notion of element type which plays a fundamental role in our investigations.

Definition 8. Let $\mathfrak{A}$ be a structure and let $l \leq k$ be natural numbers. For any sequence $s = \langle a_1, \ldots, a_l \rangle$ of elements of $\mathfrak{A}$, the *L^k-type* of s in $\mathfrak{A}$, denoted $\text{Type}_k(\mathfrak{A}, s)$, is the set of formulas, $\varphi \in L^k$ with free variables among $x_1, \ldots, x_l$, such that $\mathfrak{A} \models \varphi[a_1 \ldots a_l]$. τ is an L^k–type, if and only if, it is the L^k–type of some tuple in some (finite or infinite) structure. If τ is an L^k–type we say that the tuple s *realizes* τ *in* $\mathfrak{A}$, if and only if, $\tau = \text{Type}_k(\mathfrak{A}, s)$.

In [DLW95] we established some properties of L^k–types realized in finite structures, among them the following basic result that the L^k–type of a tuple in a finite structure is determined by a single formula of L^k.

Theorem 9 [DLW95]. *For every finite structure $\mathfrak{A}$, for every $l \leq k$ and l-tuple s of elements from $\mathfrak{A}$, there is a formula $\varphi \in$ $\text{Type}_k(\mathfrak{A}, s)$ such that for any structure $\mathfrak{B}$, and l-tuple t of elements $\mathfrak{B}$, if $\mathfrak{B} \models \varphi[t]$, then* $\text{Type}_k(\mathfrak{A}, s) = \text{Type}_k(\mathfrak{B}, t)$.

If φ satisfies the conditions of Theorem 9 we say that φ *isolates* $\text{Type}_k(\mathfrak{A}, s)$.

We write $\langle \mathfrak{A}, s \rangle \equiv^k \langle \mathfrak{B}, t \rangle$ to denote that $\text{Type}_k(\mathfrak{A}, s) = \text{Type}_k(\mathfrak{B}, t)$. Recall that the quantifier rank of a formula is the maximum depth of nesting of quantifiers in the formula. We write $\langle \mathfrak{A}, s \rangle \equiv^{k,n} \langle \mathfrak{B}, t \rangle$ to denote that $\text{Type}_k(\mathfrak{A}, s)$ and $\text{Type}_k(\mathfrak{B}, t)$ agree on all formulas of L^k of quantifier rank $\leq n$. Finally, we write $\langle \mathfrak{A}, s \rangle \equiv^k_{\infty\omega} \langle \mathfrak{B}, t \rangle$ to denote that for every formula $\varphi \in L^k_{\infty\omega}$, $\mathfrak{A} \models \varphi[s]$ if and only if $\mathfrak{B} \models \varphi[t]$.

Notice that by Theorem 9, for every structure $\mathfrak{A}$ and every tuple s of elements of $\mathfrak{A}$ of length $\leq k$, there is an n such that for every tuple of elements s' of $\mathfrak{A}$, if $\langle \mathfrak{A}, s \rangle \equiv^{k,n} \langle \mathfrak{A}, s' \rangle$, then $\langle \mathfrak{A}, s \rangle \equiv^k \langle \mathfrak{A}, s' \rangle$. This observation justifies the following definition.

Definition 10. Let $\mathfrak{A}$ be a structure and s be a tuple of elements of $\mathfrak{A}$ of length $\leq k$. The *Scott rank* of s in $\mathfrak{A}$ with respect to k, denoted $\text{sr}^k_{\mathfrak{A}}(s)$ is equal to the least n such that for every tuple of elements s' of $\mathfrak{A}$, if $\langle \mathfrak{A}, s \rangle \equiv^{k,n} \langle \mathfrak{A}, s' \rangle$, then $\langle \mathfrak{A}, s \rangle \equiv^k \langle \mathfrak{A}, s' \rangle$. The *Scott rank* of a structure $\mathfrak{A}$ with respect to k, denoted $\text{sr}^k(\mathfrak{A})$, is equal to $\sup(\{\text{sr}^k_{\mathfrak{A}}(s) | s \in |\mathfrak{A}|^{\leq k}\})$.

We will make use of Scott ranks in obtaining information about the expressive power of LFP over arbitrary classes of finite structures. The next lemma codifies a simple relation between the Scott rank of a structure $\mathfrak{A}$ and the number of L^k-types of k-tuples realized over $\mathfrak{A}$. The definition which precedes it introduces notation which will be useful here and below.

Definition 11. Let $\mathfrak{A}$ be a structure, let C be a class of structures, and let l, k be natural numbers with $l \leq k$.

1. $S_l^k(\mathfrak{A}) = \{\text{Type}_k(\mathfrak{A}, \langle a_1, \ldots, a_l\rangle) \mid a_1, \ldots, a_l \in |\mathfrak{A}|\}$.
2. $\nu_k(\mathfrak{A}) = \text{card}(S_k^k(\mathfrak{A}))$.
3. $S_l^k(C) = \bigcup_{\mathfrak{A} \in C} S_l^k(\mathfrak{A})$.

Lemma 12. *For all finite structures $\mathfrak{A}$ and $k \in \omega$,*

$$\text{sr}^k(\mathfrak{A}) \leq \nu_k(\mathfrak{A}) - 1.$$

Proof: Note that for each $\mathfrak{A}$, k, and n, $\equiv^{k,n}$ and $\equiv^k$ determine equivalence relations on the set of k-tuples of elements of $\mathfrak{A}$. The collection of equivalence classes determined by $\equiv^k$ corresponds exactly to $S_k^k(\mathfrak{A})$ and thus the number of equivalence classes is $\nu_k(\mathfrak{A})$. For each n, the equivalence relation $\equiv^{k,n+1}$ is a refinement of $\equiv^{k,n}$. Moreover, if $m = \text{sr}^k(\mathfrak{A})$, then the equivalence relation $\equiv^{k,m}$ is identical to $\equiv^k$. The result now follows immediately. ■

The equivalence relations $\equiv^{k,n}$ (and consequently, $\equiv^k$) can be characterized in terms of the following two-player k–pebble game. We have a board consisting of one copy of each of the structures $\mathfrak{A}$ and $\mathfrak{B}$. There is also a supply of pairs of pebbles $\{\langle a_1, b_1\rangle, \ldots, \langle a_k, b_k\rangle\}$. At each move of the game, Player I picks up one of the pebbles (either an unused pebble, or one that is already on the board) and places it on an element of the corresponding structure (i.e. she places a_i on an element of A or b_i on an element of B). Player II then responds by placing the unused pebble in the pair on an element of the other structure. Player II loses if the resulting map, f, from $\mathfrak{A}$ to $\mathfrak{B}$, given by $f(a_j) = b_j, 1 \leq j \leq k$, is not a partial isomorphism. Player II wins the n-move game if she has a strategy to avoid losing in the first n moves, regardless of what moves are made by Player I. Moreover, some of the pebbles may be placed on the board before the start of the game. That is, if s is an l-tuple of elements of $\mathfrak{A}$ and t is an l-tuple of elements of $\mathfrak{B}$, where $l \leq k$, then we say the pebbles are initially placed on s and t if before the start of the game, the pebbles $a_1, \ldots, a_l$ are on the elements of s and the pebbles $b_1, \ldots, b_k$ are on the elements of t. We then have the following characterization:

Theorem 13 [Imm82, Poi82]. *Let $\mathfrak{A}$ and $\mathfrak{B}$ be structures over a fixed signature and let s and t be tuples of elements from the respective structures. Player II wins the n move, k–pebble game on structures $\mathfrak{A}$ and $\mathfrak{B}$ with the pebbles initially on the tuples s and t, if and only if, $\langle\mathfrak{A}, s\rangle \equiv^{k,n} \langle\mathfrak{B}, t\rangle$.*

Kolaitis and Vardi [KV92b] proved that the equivalence relations $\equiv^k$ and $\equiv^k_{\infty\omega}$ coincide when restricted to finite structures.

Theorem 14 [KV92b]. *For finite structures $\mathfrak{A}$ and $\mathfrak{B}$, and tuples s and t of elements from the respective structures, the following are equivalent:*

- $\langle\mathfrak{A}, s\rangle \equiv^k \langle\mathfrak{B}, t\rangle$;
- $\langle\mathfrak{A}, s\rangle \equiv^k_{\infty\omega} \langle\mathfrak{B}, t\rangle$.

The next result characterizes the descriptive complexity of L^k-type equivalence and establishes a further connection between finite variable element types and inductive definability.

Theorem 15 [DLW95]. *Let $l \leq k$ and let σ be a finite, relational signature. There is an R-positive first-order formula ζ such that for any structure $\mathfrak{A}$ of signature σ and any l-tuples s and s', $\mathfrak{A} \models \mathbf{lfp}(R, x_1, \ldots, x_{2l})\zeta[s, s']$, if and only if, s and s' realize distinct L^k-types in $\mathfrak{A}$.*

In sketching a proof of this theorem, we will use the following notion of basic type.

Definition 16. For any structure $\mathfrak{A}$ and elements $a_1, \ldots, a_l \in |\mathfrak{A}|$, where $l \leq k$ the *basic L^k-type* of $a_1, \ldots, a_l$ is the set of *atomic* formulas, φ, of L^k in l free variables such that $\mathfrak{A} \models \varphi[a_1, \ldots, a_l]$.

Note that for a given finite, relational signature, σ, there are only finitely many distinct basic types. Furthermore, each basic type is characterized by a single quantifier free formula of L^k.

Proof of Theorem 15 (Sketch): Let $\alpha_1(x_1, \ldots, x_k), \ldots, \alpha_q(x_1, \ldots, x_k)$ be a fixed enumeration of quantifier free formulas of L^k in k free variables characterizing all the basic types in the signature σ . Then, define φ_0 as follows:

$$\varphi_0(x_1, \ldots, x_k, y_1, \ldots, y_k) \equiv \bigvee_{1 \leq i \neq j \leq q} (\alpha_i(\bar{x}) \wedge \alpha_j(\bar{y}))$$

where $\alpha_i(\bar{y})$ is obtained from $\alpha_i(\bar{x})$ by replacing every x_j by y_j. It should be clear that for any tuples $\bar{a}, \bar{b} \in |\mathfrak{A}|^k$, $\mathfrak{A} \models \varphi_0[\bar{a}\bar{b}]$ if and only if the basic types of $\bar{a}$ and $\bar{b}$ are different.

Now, define ζ as follows:

$$\begin{aligned}\zeta(R, x_1, \ldots, x_k, y_1, \ldots, y_k) \equiv \varphi_0(\bar{x}\bar{y}) &\vee \bigvee_{1 \leq i \leq k} \exists x_i \forall y_i R(x_1, \ldots, x_k, y_1, \ldots, y_k) \\ &\vee \bigvee_{1 \leq i \leq k} \exists y_i \forall x_i R(x_1, \ldots, x_k, y_1, \ldots, y_k)\end{aligned}$$

A k-pebble game argument can now be used to show that the least fixed point of ζ expresses the *inequivalence* of L^k-types. Indeed, the $n+1$-th stage of the induction determined by ζ expresses the inequivalence of L^k-types restricted to formulas of quantifier rank at most n. ∎

The following lemma is a corollary to the proof of the preceding theorem. It relates Scott ranks to the stages of the induction generated by the formula ζ in our proof sketch above.

Lemma 17. *Let $l \leq k$ and let σ be a finite, relational signature. Let ζ be the formula constructed above relative to k and σ. Let $\mathfrak{A}$ be a structure of signature σ, and let s be an l-tuple of elements of $\mathfrak{A}$ with $\mathrm{sr}^k_{\mathfrak{A}}(s) = m$. Then,*

1. *there is an l-tuple s', such that $\mathfrak{A} \not\models \zeta^m[s, s']$ and $\mathfrak{A} \models \zeta^{m+1}[s, s']$.*
2. *for every l-tuple s', if $\mathfrak{A} \models \mathbf{lfp}(R, x_1, \ldots, x_k, y_1, \ldots, y_k)\zeta[s, s']$, then $\mathfrak{A} \models \zeta^{m+1}[s, s']$.*

In consequence, $||\zeta||_{\mathfrak{A}} = \mathrm{sr}^k(\mathfrak{A}) + 1$.

Moreover, a stronger form of Theorem 15 can be shown, namely that the equivalence classes with respect to L^k in a structure $\mathfrak{A}$ can, in some sense, be ordered uniformly by a formula of LFP. This result, stated formally below, is a crucial step in the proof of the result due to Abiteboul and Vianu that LFP = PFP if and only if P=PSPACE.

Theorem 18 [AV95, DLW95]. *For every k and any signature σ, there is an* LFP *formula $\xi(x_1, \ldots, x_{2k})$ such that for any σ-structure $\mathfrak{A}$ and k-tuples s, s' and s'' of elements of $\mathfrak{A}$:*

1. *if $\mathfrak{A} \models \xi[s, s']$ then s and s' realize distinct L^k types in $\mathfrak{A}$;*
2. *it is not the case that $\mathfrak{A} \models \xi[s, s']$ and $\mathfrak{A} \models \xi[s', s]$; and*
3. *if s and s' realize distinct L^k types in $\mathfrak{A}$ then either $\mathfrak{A} \models \xi[s, s']$ or $\mathfrak{A} \models \xi[s', s]$.*
4. *if $\mathfrak{A} \models \xi[s, s']$ and $\mathfrak{A} \models \xi[s', s'']$ then $\mathfrak{A} \models \xi[s, s'']$.*

We will use the symbol $<_k$ to denote the pre-order on k-tuples defined by the formula ξ.

3 Element Types and Inductive Definitions

In this section, we use the machinery of L^k-types developed above to provide a proof of McColm's second conjecture and related results. The definition of proficiency of a class C given in Definition 7 states that there is an inductive definition over C that is unbounded. As we saw in the preceding section, it is possible to think of inductive definitions as computations over bounded variable element types. Intuitively speaking, for C to admit unbounded inductions, it must contain structures with arbitrarily large numbers of types. This motivates a notion of compactness of a class of finite structures, which we define below. The definition of a class C being k-compact is essentially equivalent to McColm's condition for C being k-anti-proficient (see [McC90]).

Definition 19. The class of structures C is *k-compact*, if and only if, $S_k^k(C)$ is finite.

In other words, a class C is k-compact, if and only if, there are only finitely many L^k-types of k-tuples realized in structures in C. Observe that if $S_k^k(C)$ is finite, then $S_l^k(C)$ is finite for all $l \leq k$. The property we have defined is called k-compactness because it is equivalent to C satisfying a certain "compactness condition", as we show next. Recall from Definition 8 that a set of L^k formulas is an L^k-type, if and only if, it is the L^k-type of some tuple in some (finite or infinite) structure.

Theorem 20. *A class of finite structures C is k-compact, if and only if, for every L^k-type τ, if for every finite subset δ of τ, there is a type $\tau' \in S_l^k(C)$ such that $\delta \subseteq \tau'$, then $\tau \in S_l^k(C)$.*

Proof:

$\Rightarrow$ Let $\mathcal{C}$ be k-compact and let $S_l^k(\mathcal{C}) = \{\tau_1, \ldots, \tau_n\}$. We know from Theorem 9 that there are formulas $\varphi_1, \ldots, \varphi_n$ that isolate the types $\tau_1, \ldots, \tau_n$ respectively. Thus, if τ is a type that is not realized in any structure in $\mathcal{C}$, it must be the case that $\neg\varphi_1, \ldots, \neg\varphi_n \in \tau$. But then, $\{\neg\varphi_1, \ldots, \neg\varphi_n\}$ is a finite subset of τ that is not realized in any structure in $\mathcal{C}$.

$\Leftarrow$ Suppose $\mathcal{C}$ is not k-compact. Let $S_k^k(\mathcal{C}) = \{\tau_i \mid i \in \omega\}$ and let $\varphi_i (i \in \omega)$ be an enumeration of formulas such that φ_i isolates τ_i. Let $\Gamma = \{\neg\varphi_i \mid i \in \omega\}$. We show that Γ can be completed to a type τ such that every finite subset of τ is realized in some structure in $\mathcal{C}$. However, it is clear that τ could not be realized in any structure in $\mathcal{C}$.
To construct τ, let $\alpha_i (i \in \omega)$ be a fixed enumeration of all formulas of L^k. We define the sets of formulas δ_n inductively as follows:

$$\delta_0 = \emptyset$$
$$\delta_{n+1} = \begin{cases} \delta_n \cup \{\alpha_n\} & \text{if } \delta_n \cup \{\alpha_n\} \subseteq \tau_i \text{ for infinitely many } i \in \omega; \\ \delta_n \cup \{\neg\alpha_n\} & \text{otherwise.} \end{cases}$$

A simple argument by induction shows that for all n, $\delta_n \subseteq \tau_i$ for infinitely many i. Let $\tau = \Gamma \cup \bigcup_{n\in\omega} \delta_n$. The construction ensures that every finite subset of τ is realized in some structure in $\mathcal{C}$. It then follows from a direct application of the Compactness Theorem that τ is realized in some (possibly infinite) structure. Thus, τ is an L^k-type, and as was observed earlier, it cannot be realized in any structure in $\mathcal{C}$. ■

We motivated the definition of k-compactness with the intuition that inductions are bounded over a class of structures if there is a bound on the number of types that are realized in any structure in the class. However, k-compactness is, on the face of it, a stronger condition. It stipulates that there is a finite number of types realized in the entire class. The next lemma shows that the two notions, indeed, coincide.

Lemma 21. *For any class of finite structures $\mathcal{C}$, the following conditions are equivalent:*

1. *$\mathcal{C}$ is k-compact;*
2. $\sup(\{\nu_k(\mathfrak{A}) \mid \mathfrak{A} \in \mathcal{C}\}) < \omega$; *and*
3. $\sup(\{\mathrm{sr}^k(\mathfrak{A}) \mid \mathfrak{A} \in \mathcal{C}\}) < \omega$.

Proof:

$1 \Rightarrow 2$ It is clear that $\nu_k(\mathfrak{A}) \leq \mathrm{card}(S_k^k(\mathcal{C}))$ for all $\mathfrak{A} \in \mathcal{C}$. Thus, if $S_k^k(\mathcal{C})$ is finite, there is a finite bound on all $\nu_k(\mathfrak{A})$.

$2 \Rightarrow 3$ This follows immediately from Lemma 12.

$3 \Rightarrow 1$ It follows from the definition of Scott rank that every L^k-type realized in $\mathfrak{A}$ is isolated by a formula of L^k of quantifier rank at most $\mathrm{sr}^k(\mathfrak{A})$. Thus if $m = \sup(\{\mathrm{sr}^k(\mathfrak{A}) \mid \mathfrak{A} \in \mathcal{C}\})$, every type in $S_k^k(\mathcal{C})$ is isolated by a formula of quantifier rank at most m. However, for any fixed m, there are, up to logical equivalence, only finitely many formulas of L^k of quantifier rank at most m.[4] Thus, $S_k^k(C)$ must be finite. ∎

We can now relate closure ordinals of formulas and types through the following lemma, which will then allow us to make the connection between proficiency and k-compactness in Theorem 23 below.

Lemma 22. *For every R-positive formula $\varphi \in L^k$ and every finite structure $\mathfrak{A}$, $||\varphi||_{\mathfrak{A}} \leq \nu_{2k}(\mathfrak{A})$.*

Proof:
Each stage φ^m of the iteration of the operator defined by φ is closed under the equivalence relation $\equiv^{2k}$ (see Theorem 6); therefore, it can be viewed as a union of equivalence classes under this relation. Furthermore, since the operator defined by φ is monotone, the number of stages in which it converges must be bounded by the number of equivalence classes. This number is, of course, just $\nu_{2k}(\mathfrak{A})$. ∎

We are now in a position to prove the following theorem.

Theorem 23. *Let C be a class of finite structures of signature σ. C is proficient, if and only if, there is a k such that C is not k-compact.*

Proof:
Suppose C is proficient. Then, there is a k and a formula $\varphi \in L^k$ such that $\sup(\{||\varphi||_{\mathfrak{A}} \mid \mathfrak{A} \in C\} \geq \omega$. But it then follows immediately by Lemmas 22 and 21 that C is not $2k$-compact.

For the other direction, let k be such that C is not k-compact. By Lemma 21, it follows that $\sup(\{\mathrm{sr}^k(\mathfrak{A}) \mid \mathfrak{A} \in C\}) \geq \omega$. From this and Lemma 17 it follows at once that C is proficient. In particular, $\sup(\{||\zeta||_{\mathfrak{A}} \mid \mathfrak{A} \in C\}) \geq \omega$, where ζ is the formula defined above with respect to k and σ. ∎

Having related the notions of k-compactness and proficiency in Theorem 23, we now establish the relationship between k-compactness of a class C and the expressive power of $L^k_{\infty\omega}$ over this class, in the following theorem.

Theorem 24. *Let C be a class of finite structures.*

1. *If C is k-compact, then only finitely many distinct queries are definable in $L^k_{\infty\omega}$ over C. Moreover, each such query is already definable in L^k.*
2. *If C is not k-compact, then 2^ω distinct queries are definable in $L^k_{\infty\omega}$ over C. Hence, some such query is not first-order definable.*

Proof:

1. Suppose C is k-compact. We know from Theorem 9 that there is a list $\varphi_1, \ldots, \varphi_n$ of L^k formulas which isolates each of the L^k-types of k-tuples realized over structures in C. Clearly, every $L^k_{\infty\omega}$ query is equivalent over C to a disjunction of the φ_i's. But there are 2^n such disjunctions and each of them is a formula of L^k.

[4] Recall that we are dealing with purely relational languages. This is not true in languages that include function symbols.

2. Suppose $\mathcal{C}$ is not k-compact. Again we know from Theorem 9 that there is a list $\varphi_i (i \in \omega)$ of formulas of L^k which isolate the countably many distinct types realized over structures in $\mathcal{C}$. Again, each $L^k_{\infty\omega}$ query is equivalent over $\mathcal{C}$ to a (countable) disjunction of the φ_i's. But there are 2^ω such disjunctions (which define distinct queries) and only countably many first-order formulas. ■

We now have the positive solution to McColm's second conjecture as a corollary of Theorems 23 and 24.

Corollary 25 [McC90],[KV92a]. *A class $\mathcal{C}$ of finite structures is proficient, if and only if, there is a query expressible over $\mathcal{C}$ in $L^\omega_{\infty\omega}$ that is not expressible in* FO *on $\mathcal{C}$.*

Indeed, we have also shown a somewhat stronger result. It is a direct consequence of Theorem 24 that for every k, $L^k_{\infty\omega}$ collapses to FO on a class of finite structures $\mathcal{C}$, if and only if, $L^k_{\infty\omega}$ collapses to L^k on $\mathcal{C}$. This is a version of what Kolaitis and Vardi termed the "ramified" version of McColm's conjecture [KV92a].

The proof of Theorem 23 relies on the fact that in any class that is not k-compact, the induction defined by the formula ζ is unbounded. As we see below, we can extract from this fact an LFP definable query that is closed under the relation $\equiv^k$ but is not definable in L^k in any class that is not k-compact. The query is constructed to include exactly one $\equiv^k$–equivalence class in each structure $\mathfrak{A}$. The equivalence class selected will be one of maximal Scott rank in $\mathfrak{A}$. This is formally stated in the lemma below.

Lemma 26. *For any k there is a formula $\chi(x_1, \ldots, x_k)$ of* LFP *with the following properties: for every structure $\mathfrak{A}$,*

1. *$\mathfrak{A} \models \exists x_1, \ldots, x_k \chi$;*
2. *for any two k-tuples s and s' of elements of $\mathfrak{A}$, if $\mathfrak{A} \models \chi[s]$ and $\mathfrak{A} \models \chi[s']$, then $\mathrm{Type}_k(\mathfrak{A}, s) = \mathrm{Type}_k(\mathfrak{A}, s')$;*
3. *χ is equivalent to a formula of $L^k_{\infty\omega}$;*
4. *for every k-tuple s of elements of $\mathfrak{A}$, if $\mathfrak{A} \models \chi[s]$, then $\mathrm{sr}^k_{\mathfrak{A}}(s) = \mathrm{sr}^k(\mathfrak{A})$.*

Proof:
Let $\zeta(R, z_1, \ldots, z_{2k})$ be the formula given by Theorem 15. Consider the stage comparison relation of this formula, $\leq_\zeta$, which is definable in LFP by Theorem 2. Define $\theta(x_1, \ldots, x_k)$ as follows:

$$\theta \equiv \exists y_1, \ldots, y_k \forall z_1, \ldots, z_{2k} (\mathbf{lfp}(R, z_1, \ldots, z_{2k})\zeta(z_1, \ldots, z_{2k}) \rightarrow \langle z_1, \ldots, z_{2k}\rangle \leq_\zeta \langle x_1, \ldots, x_k, y_1, \ldots, y_k\rangle)).$$

Then, by Lemma 17, for any structure $\mathfrak{A}$ and any k-tuple s of elements of $\mathfrak{A}$, $\mathfrak{A} \models \theta[s]$, if and only if, $\mathrm{sr}^k_{\mathfrak{A}}(s) = \mathrm{sr}^k(\mathfrak{A})$. That is θ picks out all the tuples in $\mathfrak{A}$ of maximal Scott rank. Since there must clearly be some such tuples, θ satisfies the first and the fourth conditions. Furthermore, since tuples that realize the same type have the same Scott rank, the query defined by θ is closed under the equivalence relation $\equiv^k$, and therefore it is definable in $L^k_{\infty\omega}$, and it satisfies the third condition. In general, however, it does not satisfy the second condition, since there may be more than one equivalence class of maximal Scott rank in any given structure. To select from among these, we use the ordering on equivalence classes, $<_k$ given by Theorem 18. Now, define the formula $\chi(x_1, \ldots, x_k)$ as follows:

$$\chi \equiv \theta(x_1, \ldots, x_k) \wedge \forall y_1, \ldots, y_k(\theta(y_1, \ldots, y_k) \rightarrow \neg\langle y_1, \ldots, y_k\rangle <_k \langle x_1, \ldots, x_k\rangle).$$

Since χ selects exactly one equivalence class, it satisfies condition 1 and 2, and the equivalence class is selected from among those selected by θ, so it satisfies condition 4. Since the entire equivalence class is chosen (this follows from the definition of the pre-order $<_k$), χ defines a query closed under the equivalence relation $\equiv^k$ and it therefore satisfies condition 3. ∎

It is clear that the formula χ is not equivalent to any formula of L^k in any class $\mathcal{C}$ that is not k-compact. Indeed, suppose it were equivalent to such a formula of quantifier rank m. Then, since $\mathcal{C}$ is not k-compact, it contains a structure $\mathfrak{A}$ with $\mathrm{sr}^k(\mathfrak{A}) > m$, but all tuples s in $\mathfrak{A}$ such that $\mathfrak{A} \models \chi[s]$ are L^k-equivalent, and by the definition of Scott ranks, they cannot be distinguished from all other tuples in $\mathfrak{A}$ by formulas of quantifier rank $\leq m$, yielding a contradiction. This argument enables us to establish the following two theorems:

Theorem 27. *For any class of structures $\mathcal{C}$, the following are equivalent:*

1. *$\mathcal{C}$ is k-compact.*
2. *$L^k_{\infty\omega} \cap \mathrm{LFP} = L^k$ on $\mathcal{C}$.*

Proof:
(1)$\Rightarrow$ (2) follows from Theorem 24. Conversely, if (1) is false, then the formula χ of Theorem 26 witnesses that the separation of $L^k_{\infty\omega} \cap \mathrm{LFP}$ from L^k. ∎

The above can be seen as strengthening Theorem 24 in the sense that it shows that if $\mathcal{C}$ is not k-compact, then not only can we separate $L^k_{\infty\omega}$ from L^k, but the separating query can be chosen to be LFP definable.

Definition 28. A class of structures $\mathcal{C}$ has the *k-preservation property* if every query that is $\equiv^k$-closed over $\mathcal{C}$ and first order definable on $\mathcal{C}$ is definable in L^k over $\mathcal{C}$.

This definition allows us to state a sufficient condition on a class of structures for the separation of LFP and FO.

Theorem 29. *If there is a k such that $\mathcal{C}$ is not k-compact and has the k-preservation property, then* LFP *does not collapse to* FO *on $\mathcal{C}$.*

4 The Ordered Conjecture

Theorem 29 raises the question of which classes of structures $\mathcal{C}$ have the k-preservation property. In this section, we investigate this question for classes of ordered structures. We also show that this is linked to the question of whether the class of all finite structures $\mathcal{F}_\sigma$ has the k-preservation property.

In the case of the class of all structures (finite or infinite), this question is resolved as a direct consequence of a result proved by Immerman and Kozen [IK89], using the compactness theorem. This is stated in the theorem below.

Theorem 30 [IK89]. *The class $\mathcal{S}$ of all structures (finite or infinite) has the k-preservation property, for all k.*

It has been observed that most preservation theorems that hold on the class of all structures fail when we restrict ourselves to finite structures (see [Gur84]). One would expect that this is the case for the above as well. Here, we show that the question of whether such a preservation theorem holds on finite structures is connected to Conjecture 1. To see this, we first establish a technical lemma.

For any signature σ, let the width of σ, denoted $w(\sigma)$, be the maximum arity of any relation symbol in σ. Fix a signature σ and let $m = \max(w(\sigma), 3)$. We then have the following:

Lemma 31. *For any structure $\mathfrak{A}$ in $\mathcal{O}_\sigma$, and any l-tuple $s = \langle a_1, \ldots, a_l \rangle$ of elements in $\mathfrak{A}$, where $l \leq m$, there is a formula φ of L^m such that, for any structure $\mathfrak{B}$ of signature $\sigma \cup \{\leq\}$, $\mathfrak{B} \models \varphi[t]$ if and only if there is an isomorphism $f : \mathfrak{A} \cong \mathfrak{B}$ with $f(s) = t$.*

Proof:
We first show that, for every element a of $\mathfrak{A}$, there is a formula $\beta_a(x)$ of L^2 such that a is the unique element of $\mathfrak{A}$ satisfying $\mathfrak{A} \models \beta_a[a]$. To show this, we inductively define the following class of formulas.

$$\begin{aligned} \alpha_0(x) &\equiv \neg(x = x) \\ \alpha_{n+1}(x) &\equiv \forall y((y \leq x) \rightarrow (x = y \vee \exists x(x = y \wedge \alpha_n(x)))) \end{aligned}$$

It is clear that $\mathfrak{A} \models \alpha_n[a]$ if and only if there are at most n elements less than or equal to a in the linear order $\leq^{\mathfrak{A}}$. Thus, the formula $\beta_n \equiv \neg\alpha_{n-1} \wedge \alpha_n$ identifies the nth element of the order uniquely.

Using these formulas, it is clear that any m-tuple can be uniquely identified by a formula of L^m, and we can therefore construct a sentence $\psi_{\mathfrak{A}}$ of L^m that determines the structure $\mathfrak{A}$ up to isomorphism among structures in $\mathcal{O}_\sigma$. If λ is the sentence of L^3 that asserts that $\leq$ is a linear order, then $\psi_{\mathfrak{A}} \wedge \lambda \wedge \bigwedge_{1 \leq i \leq l} \beta_{a_i}(x_i)$ is the required formula φ. ■

It follows from Lemma 31 that if $\mathcal{C}$ is a class of ordered structures over some signature σ, where $w(\sigma) \leq m$, then every query, of arity at most m, on $\mathcal{C}$ is definable in $L^m_{\infty\omega}$ (assuming m is at least 3). Furthermore, if φ is any first-order formula (with at most k free variables, for any $k \geq m$) in such a signature σ and λ is as above, then it follows easily from Lemma 31 that $\varphi \wedge \lambda$ is equivalent over the class $\mathcal{F}_\sigma$ to a formula of $L^k_{\infty\omega}$. Let σ' denote the signature $\sigma \cup \{\leq\}$. We can now prove the following theorem.

Theorem 32. *If there is a $k \geq m$ such that $\mathcal{F}_{\sigma'}$ has the k-preservation property, then every class $\mathcal{C} \subseteq \mathcal{O}_\sigma$ has the k-preservation property.*

Proof:
Let φ be any first-order formula with free variables among $x_1, \ldots, x_k$. Since $m \leq k$, by the observations above, $\varphi \wedge \lambda$ is equivalent over $\mathcal{F}_{\sigma'}$ to a formula of $L^k_{\infty\omega}$. But then, by the k-preservation property of $\mathcal{F}_{\sigma'}$, there is a formula ψ of L^k that is equivalent to $\varphi \wedge \lambda$ over $\mathcal{F}_{\sigma'}$. Since λ is true in all structures in $\mathcal{C}$, it follows that on $\mathcal{C}$, ψ defines the same query as φ. ■

Theorem 32 shows that a preservation theorem along the lines of Theorem 30 for finite structures would resolve Conjecture 1. This, however, seems an unlikely eventuality, since it seems unlikely that every class of ordered structures has the k-preservation property for some k. This is because, for any class $\mathcal{C} \subseteq \mathcal{O}_\sigma$ and any $k \geq m$, if $\mathcal{C}$ has the k-preservation property, then every first order definable query of arity k or less is definable in L^k. Thus, in particular, every first order sentence is equivalent to one with no more than k variables. Nonetheless, there are interesting classes of structures for which this property holds. The following result is due to Poizat [Poi82] (for another exposition of this result see [IK89]).

Theorem 33 [Poi82]. *If σ contains only unary relation symbols, then every first order formula with at most three free variables is equivalent on $\mathcal{O}_\sigma$ to a formula of L^3.*

As a corollary, we get the following theorem.

Theorem 34. *For any unary signature σ, and any class $\mathcal{C} \subseteq \mathcal{O}_\sigma$, if $\mathcal{C}$ contains arbitrarily large structures, then* LFP *does not collapse to* FO *on $\mathcal{C}$.*

5 Complexity Theoretic Implications

It turns out that a resolution of Conjecture 1, whether positive or negative, would have important implications in complexity theory. Moreover, if the question is resolved by the methods outlined in the previous section, i.e. by showing that the class $\mathcal{O}_\sigma$ has the k-preservation property for some k, then this has some unlikely implications, that follow from the observation contained in the next proposition.

Proposition 35. *If $\mathcal{O}_\sigma$ has the k-preservation property, then every first order definable k-ary query on $\mathcal{F}_\sigma$ is computable in* DTIME$[n^k]$.

Proof:
By the k-preservation property, every first order definable k-ary query is definable by a formula φ of L^k. In such a formula, every sub-formula contains at most k free variables. Since there is a constant number of such sub-formulas, we can evaluate φ in a structure $\mathfrak{A}$ of size n, by enumerating all n^k k-tuples in $\mathfrak{A}$, and

checking whether they satisfy the sub-formulas. It can be verified that such an algorithm runs in time $O(n^k)$. ∎

Taking σ to be the language of graphs, i.e. the signature consisting of just one binary relation, it follows from the above that if there is a k such that $\mathcal{O}_\sigma$ has the k-preservation property, then for every c, the problem of determining whether a graph has a c-clique is solvable in DTIME$[n^k]$. On the other hand, it is difficult to prove that there is no k such that every first order definable Boolean query on $\mathcal{F}_\sigma$ is computable in DTIME$[n^k]$, because such a result would imply the separation of PTIME from PSPACE (see [ST95]).

Moreover, if we could show that Conjecture 1 is false, that would also establish the separation of PTIME and PSPACE. This follows from the result in [DH95] that on any infinite class of ordered structures, there is a PFP query that is not first order definable. Thus, we have the following proposition.

Proposition 36. *If there is an infinite class of ordered structures on which* LFP = FO, *then* PTIME $\neq$ PSPACE.

In order to state the complexity theoretic implications of a positive resolution of Conjecture 1, we introduce some notation. Log-H denotes the logarithmic time hierarchy, i.e. the class of those problems that can be solved in logarithmic time by an alternating machine with a bounded number of alternations. Similarly, Lin-H denotes the linear time hierarchy, i.e. those problems that can be solved by a linear time, bounded depth, alternating machine.

Consider a signature σ including ternary relation symbols $+$ and $\times$. Let $\mathcal{C} \subseteq \mathcal{O}_\sigma$ be the class of structures such that $+$ is interpreted as the addition relation consistent with the order $\leq$, and $\times$ is interpreted as the corresponding multiplication relation. It follows from a result of Barrington *et al.* [BIS90] that FO = Log-H on this class of structures. Now consider the class of structures $\mathcal{D}$ of the form $\langle m, +, \times \rangle$, i.e. containing no relations other than the numerical predicates. This allows us to give a succinct representation of these structures. That is, since the structure is completely determined by the value of m, we can represent it as a binary string of length $\log(m)$. It then follows that on this class, a query is definable in first order logic if, and only if, it is in Lin-H (another way to characterize this class is as the class RUD of rudimentary sets of binary strings, which was shown in [Wra79] to be equivalent to Lin-H). Similarly, a query is definable in LFP on this class if and only if it is computable in DTIME$[2^{O(n)}]$ (note here that $n = \log(m)$ is the length of the binary string). We write ETIME to denote the latter class. Thus, we have the following proposition.

Proposition 37. *If Conjecture 1 holds then* Lin-H $\neq$ ETIME.

The complexity theoretic separation of Proposition 37 can be seen as a linear counterpart to the separation of PH from EXPTIME.

6 Conclusions

To conclude, we present several directions of investigation suggested by the results we have presented. The first is to show that the class of ordered graphs does not have the k-preservation property for any k, or equivalently, to show that there is a class of ordered structures for which FO does not collapse to L^k, for any k. Another direction is to investigate for what classes of ordered structures the sufficient condition provided by Theorem 29 can be used to establish the separation of LFP and FO. That is, for what classes of ordered structures is it the case that there is a k such that FO collapses to L^k? We showed that this is true for all classes of strings (i.e. linear orders with additional unary predicates), but are there other interesting classes of structures for which this holds? Since we do not expect all classes of ordered structures to have this property, it would also be instructive to find other, weaker, sufficient conditions on a class of ordered structures so that LFP $\neq$ FO.

References

[AV91] S. Abiteboul and V. Vianu. Datalog extensions for database queries and updates. *Journal of Computer and System Sciences*, 43:62–124, 1991.

[AV95] S. Abiteboul and V. Vianu. Computing with first-order logic. *Journal of Computer and System Sciences*, 50(2):309–335, 1995.

[BIS90] D.M. Barrington, N. Immerman, and H. Straubing. On uniformity within NC_1. *Journal of Computer and System Sciences*, 41:274–306, 1990.

[Daw93] A. Dawar. *Feasible Computation through Model Theory*. PhD thesis, University of Pennsylvania, 1993.

[DH95] A. Dawar and L. Hella. The expressive power of finitely many generalized quantifiers. *Information and Computation*, 123(2):172–184, 1995.

[DLW95] A. Dawar, S. Lindell, and S. Weinstein. Infinitary logic and inductive definability over finite structures. *Information and Computation*, 119(2):160–175, 1995.

[GIS94] Y. Gurevich, N. Immerman, and S. Shelah. McColm's conjecture. In *Proc. 9th IEEE Symp. on Logic in Computer Science*, 1994.

[Gur84] Y. Gurevich. Toward logic tailored for computational complexity. In M. Richter et al., editors, *Computation and Proof Theory*, pages 175–216. Springer Lecture Notes in Mathematics, 1984.

[IK89] N. Immerman and D. Kozen. Definability with bounded number of bound variables. *Information and Computation*, 83:121–139, 1989.

[Imm82] N. Immerman. Upper and lower bounds for first-order expressibility. *Journal of Computer and System Sciences*, 25:76–98, 1982.

[Imm86] N. Immerman. Relational queries computable in polynomial time. *Information and Control*, 68:86–104, 1986.

[KV92a] Ph. G. Kolaitis and M. Y. Vardi. Fixpoint logic vs. infinitary logic in finite-model theory. In *Proc. 7th IEEE Symp. on Logic in Computer Science*, pages 46–57, 1992.

[KV92b] Ph. G. Kolaitis and M. Y. Vardi. Infinitary logics and 0-1 laws. *Information and Computation*, 98(2):258–294, 1992.

[McC90] G. L. McColm. When is arithmetic possible? *Annals of Pure and Applied Logic*, 50:29–51, 1990.

[Mos74] Y. N. Moschovakis. *Elementary Induction on Abstract Structures*. North Holland, 1974.

[Poi82] B. Poizat. Deux ou trois choses que je sais de L_n. *Journal of Symbolic Logic*, 47(3):641–658, 1982.

[ST95] A. Stolbouskin and M. Taitslin. Is first order contained in an initial segment of PTIME? In *Computer Science Logic 94*, volume 933 of *LNCS*. Springer-Verlag, 1995.

[Var82] M. Y. Vardi. The complexity of relational query languages. In *Proceedings of the 14th ACM Symposium on the Theory of Computing*, pages 137–146, 1982.

[Wra79] C. Wrathall. Rudimentary predicates and relative computation. *SIAM Journal on Computing*, 7(2):194–209, 1979.

Simultaneous Rigid E-Unification Is Undecidable

Anatoli Degtyarev and Andrei Voronkov*

Computing Science Department, Uppsala University, Box 311, S 751 05, Sweden

Abstract. Simultaneous rigid E-unification was introduced in 1987 by Gallier, Raatz and Snyder. It is used in the area of automated reasoning with equality in *extension procedures,* like the tableau method or the connection method. There were several faulty proofs of the decidability of this problem. We prove the undecidability of simultaneous rigid E-unification using reduction of Hilbert's tenth problem. As a consequence, we obtain the undecidability of the $\exists^*$-fragment of intuitionistic logic with equality and representability of recursively enumerable sets by solutions of simultaneous rigid E-unification.

1 Introduction

The simultaneous rigid E-unification problem plays a crucial role in automatic proof methods for first-order logic with equality based on sequent calculi, such as semantic tableaux [8], model elimination [33], the method of matings [1] (also known as the connection method [9]), and a dozen other procedures. All these methods are based on the Herbrand theorem and express the idea that the proof-search can be considered as the problem of checking that every path through a matrix of the goal formula is inconsistent (for this reason these methods are sometimes characterized as *matrix methods*). This idea was originally justified by Prawitz [43]. Instead of generating instances of a quantifier-free formula $M(\bar{x})$, he proposed to search for a substitution σ for $\bar{x}_1, \ldots, \bar{x}_n$ such that every path in $(M(\bar{x}_1) \wedge \ldots \wedge M(\bar{x}_n))\sigma$ becomes complementary (or inconsistent). In the case without equality, the search for such a substitution can be carried out using ordinary (simultaneous) unification. Thus, for a matrix $M(\bar{x}_1) \wedge \ldots \wedge M(\bar{x}_n)$, the problem of the existence of an appropriate substitution is decidable and can be performed by any known unification algorithm. The idea of reducing the provability (or, dually, unsatisfiability) problem to checking paths in matrices for inconsistency can also be used for logic with equality [30, 22], but the search for a suitable substitution σ results in simultaneous rigid E-unification.

Simultaneous rigid E-unification can be formulated as follows. Given term equations $s_i = t_i$ and finite sets of term equations E_i, $i \in \{1, \ldots, n\}$, find a substitution σ such that $\vdash \forall((\bigwedge_{e \in E_i} e\sigma) \supset s_i\sigma = t_i\sigma)$, for all i (here $\vdash$ means

* Anatoli Degtyarev is on leave from Glushkov Institute of Cybernetics, Kiev. He is supported by grants from the Swedish Institute and the Swedish Royal Academy of Sciences. Andrei Voronkov is supported by a TFR grant.

provability in first-order logic with equality). The corresponding instance of the simultaneous rigid E-unification problem is denoted by the system of *rigid equations* $E_i \vdash_\forall s_i = t_i$.

Consider an example. Assume that we want to establish the unsatisfiability of the formula $\forall x h(x) = a \wedge \forall y([h(a) = y \wedge y \neq g(h(y))] \vee [h(b) = f(y) \wedge y \neq g(f(y))])$. We can duplicate the quantifier $\forall x$ creating two copies of the subformula $h(x) = a$. Following [1], we can display the resulting matrix in a two-dimensional format, with disjunctions being displayed horizontally and conjunctions being displayed vertically:

$$\begin{bmatrix} h(x_1) = a \\ h(x_2) = a \\ \begin{bmatrix} h(a) = y \\ y \neq g(h(y)) \end{bmatrix} \bigvee \begin{bmatrix} h(b) = f(y) \\ y \neq g(f(y)) \end{bmatrix} \end{bmatrix}$$

Collecting formulas lying on the two vertical paths in this matrix we obtain the following two rigid equations expressing inconsistency of this set of paths

$$\begin{array}{l} h(x_1) = a, h(x_2) = a, h(a) = y \vdash_\forall y = g(h(y)) \\ h(x_1) = a, h(x_2) = a, h(b) = f(y) \vdash_\forall y = g(f(y)) \end{array}$$

Some solutions of this system of rigid equations are $\{a/x_1, b/x_2, g(h^n(a))/y\}$, for every $n \geq 0$.

Since simultaneous rigid E-unification was introduced by Gallier, Raatz and Snyder [24], there have been a number of publications on simultaneous rigid E-unification itself and its use in theorem proving, for example [22, 25, 23, 3, 7, 21, 10, 4, 5, 29, 41]. Some of these articles were based on the conjecture that simultaneous rigid E-unification is decidable. There were several faulty proofs of the decidability of this problem (e.g. [22, 23, 29]).

The following results on simultaneous rigid E-unification have been known before our first undecidability proof [14]:

1. Non-simultaneous (i.e. the case $n = 1$) rigid E-unification with E_1 ground (i.e. without variables) is NP-complete (Kozen [31]);
2. Non-simultaneous rigid E-unification is NP-complete (Gallier et.al. [22, 23]);
3. For non-simultaneous rigid E-unification there exist finite complete sets of unifiers (Gallier et.al. [22, 23]);
4. The monadic case (the arity of function symbols is ≤ 1) is PSPACE-hard (Gobault [29]);
5. The word equation problem is polynomially reducible to monadic simultaneous rigid E-unification (Matiyasevich and the authors [11, 12]);
6. Simultaneous rigid E-unification in the signature with one unary function symbol and a countable number of constants is decidable (Matiyasevich and the authors [11, 12]). The decidability proof for this case uses deep number-theoretic facts.

In [14] we proved the undecidability of simultaneous rigid E-unification. That first proof used reduction of so called monadic semi-unification whose undecidability was proven by Baaz [2]. A more intuitive proof appeared in [15] using reduction of second-order unification whose undecidability was proven by Goldfarb [28]. Here we give a most elementary proof using reduction of Hilbert's tenth problem. The technique of this proof essentially combines the techniques used by Goldfarb [28] and us [15].

Our paper to CSL'95 was first submitted in May 1995. This version is written in March 1996. In the meantime, several new papers on simultaneous rigid E-unification appeared. They are considered in Section 5.

2 Simultaneous rigid E-unification

Signature in this paper means a finite set of function symbols. *Ground terms* are terms without occurrences of variables. We assume that Σ is a fixed signature containing constants a and $[]$ and a binary function symbol $[\_|\_]$. An *equation* in a signature Δ is an expression of the form $s = t$, where s, t are terms in the signature Δ. The notation $s \approx t$ means that the terms s and t are identical. Variables will always be denoted by x, y, z, u, v, w, maybe with indices.

We assume the standard notion of *substitutions*. Substitutions will be denoted by $\{t_1/x_1, \ldots, t_n/x_n\}$ and mean the operation of the simultaneous replacement of variables x_i by terms t_i. The application of a substitution θ to any expression E (e.g. a term or a set of equations) is denoted by $E\theta$.

For an equation $s = t$ and a set of equations E we write $E \vdash s = t$ to denote that the formula $\forall((\bigwedge_{e \in E} e) \supset s = t)$ is provable in first-order logic with equality. For such formulas provability can be tested by the congruence closure algorithm [44].

Definition 1. A *rigid equation* is an expression of the form $E \vdash_\forall s = t$, where E is a finite set of equations and s, t are terms. Its *solution* is any substitution θ such that $E\theta \vdash s\theta = t\theta$. A substitution θ is a solution of a set S of rigid equations iff θ is a solution of every rigid equation in S. A *system* of rigid equations is a finite set of rigid equations.[2].

The *simultaneous rigid E-unification problem* is the problem of determining whether any system of rigid equations possesses a solution.

Let E be an arbitrary expression. Then $E\{c_1 \leftarrow t_1, \ldots, c_n \leftarrow t_n\}$ will denote the expression obtained from E by the simultaneous replacement of all occurrences of constants c_i by terms t_i.

We shall use the following lemma:

Lemma 2. *Let $c_1, \ldots, c_n$ be pairwise different constants and $s_1, s_2, t_1, \ldots, t_n$ be terms such that c_i does not occur in t_j for all $i, j \in \{1, \ldots, n\}$. Then $c_1 =$*

[2] The term "rigid equation" could be more adequately expressed as "instance of a (non-simultaneous) rigid E-unification problem", but this would be too lengthy.

$t_1, \ldots, c_n = t_n \vdash s_1 = s_2$ *iff* $s_1\{c_1 \leftarrow t_1, \ldots, c_n \leftarrow t_n\} \approx s_2\{c_1 \leftarrow t_1, \ldots, c_n \leftarrow t_n\}$.

We shall use the following notation for some special terms. If $t, t_1, \ldots, t_n$ are terms, then $[t_1, \ldots, t_n \,|\, t]$ denotes the term $[t_1 \,|\, [t_2 \,|\, \ldots [t_n \,|\, t] \ldots]]$. In particular, when $n = 0$ then $[t_1, \ldots, t_n \,|\, t]$ denotes t. If $t_1, \ldots, t_n$ are terms, then $[t_1, \ldots, t_n]$ denotes the term $[t_1 \,|\, [t_2 \,|\, \ldots [t_n \,|\, []] \ldots]]$.

3 Undecidability proof

In this section we reduce Hilbert's tenth problem to simultaneous rigid E-unification.

Let $c \notin \Sigma$ be any constant. A *c-numeral* is any term $[a, \ldots, a \,|\, c]$. Such a c-numeral with k occurrences of a will be denoted by $a^k c$. We shall use it to represent the natural number k.

For any constant $c \notin \Sigma$ and variable x denote by $Num(x, c)$ the rigid equation

$$c = [a \,|\, c] \vdash_\forall x = c$$

Lemma 3. *A substitution θ is a solution of $Num(x, c)$ iff $x\theta$ is a c-numeral.*

Proof. Obvious.

For any pairwise different constants $b, c, d \notin \Sigma$ and variable x denote by $Lst(x, b, c, d)$ the rigid equation

$$b = [a \,|\, b], c = [a \,|\, c], d = [[b, c] \,|\, d] \vdash_\forall x = d$$

Lemma 4. *A substitution θ is a solution of $Lst(x, b, c, d)$ iff $x\theta$ has the form $[t_1, \ldots, t_n \,|\, d]$ for some $n \geq 0$ and t_i of the form $[r_i, s_i]$, where all r_i are b-numerals and all s_i are c-numerals.*

Proof. Similar to that of Lemma 3. QED

In our undecidability proof we shall use reduction of Hilbert's tenth problem. To represent it, we need to represent addition and multiplication on natural numbers. It is done in the following two lemmas.

Let $b, c, d \notin \Sigma$ be pairwise different constants. Denote by $Add(x, y, z, b, c, d)$ the rigid equation

$$d = c, b = y \vdash_\forall z = x$$

Lemma 5. *Let S be the system of rigid equations*

$$\{\, Num(x, b),\ Num(y, c),\ Num(z, d),\ Add(x, y, z, b, c, d)\}$$

A substitution θ is a solution of S iff for some natural numbers k, l, $x\theta \approx a^k b$, $y\theta \approx a^l c$ and $z\theta \approx a^{k+l} d$.

Proof. Suppose θ is a solution of S. By Lemma 3, the terms $x\theta$, $y\theta$ and $z\theta$ have the forms $a^k b$, $a^l c$ and $a^m d$, respectively. Since θ is a solution of the rigid equation $Add(x, y, z, b, c, d)$, we have

$$d = c, b = a^l c \vdash a^m d = a^k b$$

Lemma 2 yields $a^m c \approx a^k a^l c$. Thus, $m = k + l$.

The "only if" direction is similar. QED

The representation of multiplication is more complicated. We give a simplified construction used in [28] for second-order unification. Let $e, c_1, c_2, c_3, d_1, d_2, d_3 \notin \Sigma$ be pairwise different constants. Then $Mult_1(u, v, c_1, c_2, c_3, d_1, d_2, d_3)$ denotes the rigid equation

$$c_1 = d_1, c_2 = d_2, c_3 = d_3 \vdash_\forall u = v$$

Denote by $Mult_2(u, v, x, y, z, e, c_1, c_2, c_3, d_1, d_2, d_3)$ the rigid equation

$$e = d_1, c_1 = x, c_2 = [a \,|\, d_2], d_3 = [[z, y] \,|\, c_3] \vdash_\forall v = [[d_1, d_2] \,|\, u]$$

Lemma 6. *Let S be the system of rigid equations*

$$\begin{aligned}
\{\, & Num(x, e), \\
& Num(y, d_2), \\
& Num(z, d_1), \\
& Lst(u, c_1, c_2, c_3), \\
& Lst(v, d_1, d_2, d_3), \\
& Mult_1(u, v, c_1, c_2, c_3, d_1, d_2, d_3), \\
& Mult_2(u, v, x, y, z, e, c_1, c_2, c_3, d_1, d_2, d_3)\}
\end{aligned}$$

A substitution θ is a solution of S iff for some natural numbers k, l, $x\theta \approx a^k e$, $y\theta \approx a^l d_2$ and $z\theta \approx a^{k \cdot l} d_1$.

Proof. Suppose θ is a solution of S. Since θ is a solution of $Lst(u, c_1, c_2, c_3)$, by Lemma 4, the term $u\theta$ has the form

$$[[a^{p_1} c_1, a^{q_1} c_2], \ldots, [a^{p_n} c_1, a^{q_n} c_2] \,|\, c_3]$$

Since θ is a solution of $Lst(v, d_1, d_2, d_3)$ and $Mult_1(u, v, c_1, c_2, c_3, d_1, d_2, d_3)$, by Lemmas 2 and 4, the term $v\theta$ has the form

$$[[a^{p_1} d_1, a^{q_1} d_2], \ldots, [a^{p_n} d_1, a^{q_n} d_2] \,|\, d_3]$$

Since θ is a solution of $Num(x, e)$, $Num(y, d_2)$ and $Num(z, d_1)$, by Lemma 3, the terms $x\theta$, $y\theta$ and $z\theta$ have the forms $a^k e$, $a^l d_2$ and $a^m d_1$, respectively.

Since θ is a solution of $Mult_2(u, v, x, y, z, e, c_1, c_2, c_3, d_1, d_2, d_3)$ we have

$$e = d_1, c_1 = a^k e, c_2 = [a \,|\, d_2], d_3 = [[a^m d_1, a^l d_2] \,|\, c_3] \vdash v\theta = [[d_1, d_2] \,|\, u\theta]$$

which is equivalent to

$$e = d_1, c_1 = a^k d_1, c_2 = [a \,|\, d_2], d_3 = [[a^m d_1, a^l d_2] \,|\, c_3] \vdash v\theta = [[d_1, d_2] \,|\, u\theta]$$

By Lemma 2,

$$v\theta\{e \leftarrow d_1, c_1 \leftarrow a^k d_1, c_2 \leftarrow [a \,|\, d_2], d_3 \leftarrow [[a^m d_1, a^l d_2] \,|\, c_3]\} \approx$$
$$[[d_1, d_2] \,|\, u\theta]\{e \leftarrow d_1, c_1 \leftarrow a^k d_1, c_2 \leftarrow [a \,|\, d_2], d_3 \leftarrow [[a^m d_1, a^l d_2] \,|\, c_3]\}$$

Substituting for $v\theta$ and $u\theta$, we obtain

$$[[a^{p_1} d_1, a^{q_1} d_2], \ldots, [a^{p_n} d_1, a^{q_n} d_2] \,|\, d_3]$$
$$\{e \leftarrow d_1, c_1 \leftarrow a^k d_1, c_2 \leftarrow [a \,|\, d_2], d_3 \leftarrow [[a^m d_1, a^l d_2] \,|\, c_3]\} \approx$$
$$[[d_1, d_2], [a^{p_1} c_1, a^{q_1} c_2], \ldots, [a^{p_n} c_1, a^{q_n} c_2] \,|\, c_3]$$
$$\{e \leftarrow d_1, c_1 \leftarrow a^k d_1, c_2 \leftarrow [a \,|\, d_2], d_3 \leftarrow [[a^m d_1, a^l d_2] \,|\, c_3]\}$$

Replacing the constants c_1, c_2, d_3 by the corresponding terms, we obtain

$$[[a^{p_1} d_1, a^{q_1} d_2], \ldots, [a^{p_n} d_1, a^{q_n} d_2], [a^m d_1, a^l d_2] \,|\, c_3] \approx$$
$$[[d_1, d_2], [a^{p_1+k} d_1, a^{q_1+1} d_2], \ldots, [a^{p_n+k} d_1, a^{q_n+1} d_2] \,|\, c_3]$$

This implies $p_1 = 0, q_1 = 0, m = p_n + k, l = q_n + 1$ and $p_{i+1} = p_i + k, q_{i+1} = q_i + 1$, for all $i \in \{1, \ldots, n-1\}$. Then for all $j \in \{1, \ldots, n\}$, $p_j = (j-1) \cdot k$ and $q_j = j-1$. This yields $m = n \cdot k$ and $l = n$. Hence, $m = k \cdot l$.

The "only if" direction is similar. QED

Lemma 7. *There is an effective method that reduces Hilbert's tenth problem to simultaneous rigid E-unification.*

Proof. Let $\mathcal{D}$ be any finite set of equations of the forms $x_i = 1$, $x_i \cdot x_j = x_k$ and $x_i + x_j = x_k$, where $i, j, k \in \{1, \ldots, n\}$. Its solution is any assignment of natural numbers to x_i that makes all equations in $\mathcal{D}$ true. Let $c_1, \ldots, c_n, b_1, b_2, b_3, d \notin \Sigma$ be pairwise different constants. It suffices to effectively construct a system of rigid equations $\mathcal{R}$ that is solvable iff $\mathcal{D}$ is solvable.

We shall construct such a system of rigid equations $\mathcal{R}$ using the variables $x_1, \ldots, x_n$ and maybe some extra variables. The system of rigid equations $\mathcal{R}$ will satisfy even stronger conditions on its solutions:

(C1) If θ is a solution of $\mathcal{R}$ then $x_i\theta$ is a c_i-numeral;
(C2) For every solution of $\mathcal{D}$, if this solution assigns numbers p_i to x_i, then there is a solution θ of $\mathcal{R}$ such that $x_i\theta \approx a^{p_i} c_i$, for all $i \in \{1, \ldots, n\}$;
(C3) For every solution θ of $\mathcal{R}$, if $x_i\theta \approx a^{p_i} c_i$, then the assignment of numbers p_i to x_i is a solution of $\mathcal{D}$.

The system $\mathcal{R}$ consists of the following rigid equations:

1. Rigid equations $Num(x_i, c_i)$, for all $i \in \{1, \ldots, n\}$;

2. Rigid equations $\vdash_\forall x_i = [a\,|\,c_i]$ for every equation $x_i = 1$ in $\mathcal{D}$;
3. For every equation $x_i \cdot x_j = x_k$ the rigid equations

$$\begin{aligned}&Lst(u, b_1, b_2, b_3),\\&Lst(v, c_k, c_j, d),\\&Mult_1(u, v, b_1, b_2, b_3, c_k, c_j, d),\\&Mult_2(u, v, x_i, x_j, x_k, c_i, b_1, b_2, b_3, c_k, c_j, d),\end{aligned}$$

   where u, v are some unique variables (different for every different equation $x_i \cdot x_j = x_k$).
4. Rigid equations $Add(x_i, x_j, x_k, c_i, c_j, c_k)$ for every equation $x_i + x_j = x_k$ in $\mathcal{D}$;

Conditions (C1)–(C3) can easily be checked using Lemmas 3, 5 and 6. QED

In our construction we used a countable number of new constants c_i, b_j, d. One can note that the proof can be modified as well so that we use only a finite number of new symbols. The modification is as follows. Let f, g be unary function symbols and b be a constant all foreign to Σ. Replace all new constants c_i, b_j, d used in the proofs by different terms of the form $f(g^m(b))$. The proof remains correct because $f(g^k(b))$ and $f(g^l(b))$ are not subterms of each other when $k \neq l$. This shows that Hilbert's tenth problem is effectively reducible to simultaneous rigid E-unification in the signature $\Sigma \cup \{f, g, b\}$. By the undecidability of tenth Hilbert's problem [35] we obtain

Theorem 8. *Simultaneous rigid E-unification is undecidable.*

Due to our reduction of Hilbert's tenth problem, we can prove that all recursively enumerable predicates are representable in simultaneous rigid E-unification in the following sense:

Theorem 9. *Let S be any recursively enumerable set of natural numbers. Then there is a system of rigid equations $\mathcal{R}$ in the signature $\Sigma \cup \{f, g, b, c\}$ with a variable x such that*

1. *For every solution θ of $\mathcal{R}$, $x\theta$ is a c-numeral;*
2. *For every natural number n, $n \in S$ iff there is a solution θ of $\mathcal{R}$ such that $x\theta \approx a^n c$.*

Proof. Straightforward from the proof of Theorem 8. QED

As noted recently in [45], it is enough to have one binary function symbol and one constant to represent any Turing machine.

4 The undecidability and recursive completeness of the $\exists^*$-fragment of intuitionistic logic with equality

In [23] Gallier et.al. note that "rigid E-unification and Girard's linear logic [26] share the same spirit". In this section we show that simultaneous rigid E-unification is representable already in a very "weak" fragment of intuitionistic logic with equality, thus obtaining the undecidability result for this fragment. The decidability problems for some other fragments of intuitionistic logic with and without equality were studied by Orevkov [38, 40], Mints [36] and Lifschitz [32].

Theorem 10. *The class of formulas provable in intuitionistic logic with equality of the form*

$$\exists x_1 \ldots \exists x_k \Phi$$

where Φ is a quantifier-free formula built from atomic formulas using $\wedge, \supset$, is undecidable.

Proof. We use Theorem 8 on the undecidability of simultaneous rigid E-unification.

Let $E_i \vdash_\forall s_i = t_i,\ \ i \in 1, \ldots, n$ be a system of rigid equations all whose variables are among $x_1, \ldots, x_k$. Consider the formula

$$\exists x_1 \ldots \exists x_k \bigwedge_{i=1}^{n} ((\bigwedge_{e \in E_i} e) \supset s_i = t_i)$$

By the explicit definability property of intuitionistic predicate calculus with equality, this formula is provable iff there are terms $r_1, \ldots, r_k$ such that the formula

$$\bigwedge_{i=1}^{n} ((\bigwedge_{e \in E_i} e) \supset s_i = t_i)\{r_1/x_1, \ldots, r_k/x_k\}$$

is provable. Denote the substitution $\{r_1/x_1, \ldots, r_k/x_k\}$ by σ. It is easy to see that the above formula is provable in intuitionistic logic iff each of the formulas $(\bigwedge_{e \in E_i} e\sigma) \supset s_i\sigma = t_i\sigma$ is provable in intuitionistic logic, which (for this class of formulas) is the same as their provability in classical logic. Provability of all these formulas in classical logic means that σ is a solution of the rigid equations $E_i \vdash_\forall s_i = t_i$. QED

The sequent calculus and the notion of a cut-free proof for intuitionistic logic with equality are standard and can be found in e.g. in [39, 34, 18, 47]. By combining the proofs of Theorems 9 and 10, we obtain

Theorem 11. *Let S be any recursively enumerable set of natural numbers. Then there is a closed formula ψ of the form $\exists x \exists \bar{y} \varphi(x, \bar{y})$ such that*

1. *Every cut-free proof of ψ has the form*

$$\frac{\begin{array}{c}\vdots\\ \rightarrow \exists\bar{y}\varphi(a^n c, \bar{y})\end{array}}{\rightarrow \exists x \exists \bar{y} \varphi(x, \bar{y})}$$

2. *For every natural number n, $n \in S$ iff there is a cut-free proof of ψ of the above form.*

Proof. Straightforward from the proof of Theorem 8. QED

These results are similar to the description of computable functions in the successor arithmetic given by Goad [27], but we do not need any induction axioms.

5 Conclusion

Since our first proof of the undecidability of simultaneous rigid E-unification, other results have been proved. We briefly discuss these results here.

1. Simultaneous rigid E-unification has been originally proposed as a way of handling equality in the method of matings and related methods. It happened that the attractive features of paramodulation-based equality reasoning, such as ordering and basic restrictions, simplification and deletion techniques, are not easy to combine with goal-oriented methods (like semantic tableaux, model elimination or the connection method). In [13, 17, 16] a method not using simultaneous rigid E-unification is introduced for goal-oriented systems. This method of ***equality elimination*** is based on an extension of top-down procedures by a bottom-up equation solver using basic superposition. A similar approach is developed by Moser, Lynch and Steinbach [37].
2. Plaisted [42] proved that simultaneous rigid E-unification is undecidable even when the left-hand sides of rigid equations are ground. He uses a technique considerably different from ours to reduce the Post Correspondence Problem to simultaneous rigid E-unification. This construction is improved by Veanes [45], where it is shown how to simulate arbitrary Turing machines by simultaneous rigid E-unification with ground left-hand sides. Veanes notes that one binary function symbol, one constant and two variables are enough for proving the undecidability. His result implies that the $\exists\exists$-fragment of intuitionistic logic with equality and function symbols is undecidable which improves our Theorem 10. Plaisted [42] also discusses some substitutes for simultaneous rigid E-unification.
3. Voda and Komara [46] study the problem of *Herbrand skeletons:* for a given formula $\exists\bar{x}\varphi(\bar{x})$ of classical logic with equality and a positive integer n, whether the formula $\varphi(\bar{x}_1) \vee \ldots \vee \varphi(\bar{x}_n)$ has a valid instantiation. Our undecidability result for simultaneous rigid E-unification immediately implies

the undecidability of the Herbrand skeleton problem in the same way as in the proof of Theorem 10. Voda and Komara state that for each particular n, the corresponding problem is also undecidable (our result proves the undecidability only for $n = 1$). They use a reduction of Hilbert's tenth problem similar to ours, but we did not check the details of their proof.

4. In [47] the second author considers the problem of automated theorem proving in intuitionistic logic with equality. It is shown that any complete (semi-decision) procedure for intuitionistic logic with equality gives a semi-decision procedure for simultaneous rigid E-unifiability, and vice versa.
5. In [18] simultaneous rigid E-unification is applied to show the decidability of some fragments of intuitionistic logic with equality. In particular, it is shown that the prenex fragment of intuitionistic logic with equality and without function symbols is PSPACE-complete.
6. The results of [11, 46, 42] show that it is also unlikely to find generally useful decidable subsets of simultaneous rigid E-unification. An alternative approach to use decidable substitutes for this problem has been recently proposed by Petermann [41] and Beckert [6]. Their proposals are based on the restriction on solutions of simultaneous rigid E-unification to be *minimal* in some appropriate sense similar to that of Gallier et.a. [21]. It is an open problem whether the use of minimal solutions results in a complete procedure for classical logic with equality. Using instead of minimal solutions the *basic solutions* to rigid E-unification, in [19] we show that an incomplete but terminating procedure for rigid E-unification gives a complete procedure for classical logic with equality much in the style of the original Gallier et.al.'s proposal [24, 21].
7. In [12] we show that simultaneous rigid E-unification with k unary function symbols is decidable iff it is decidable for $k = 2$. The decidability for this case is still an open problem.

Proofs of the undecidability of simultaneous rigid E-unification, including the one presented in this paper, are summarized in [45].

Acknowledgments

We thank Yuri Matiyasevich for many helpful discussions and suggestions. Gerard Becher, Hans Leiß, Gennady Makanin, Leszek Pacholski, Uwe Petermann, Klaus Schulz and Jerzy Tiuryn have given us valuable explanations on rigid E-unification and some related algorithmic problems. We also thank the program committee of the Tableaux'95 Workshop for stimulating our interest in simultaneous rigid E-unification.

References

1. P.B. Andrews. Theorem proving via general matings. *Journal of the Association for Computing Machinery*, 28(2):193–214, 1981.

2. M. Baaz. Note on the existence of most general semi-unifiers. In *Arithmetic, Proof Theory and Computation Complexity*, volume 23 of *Oxford Logic Guides*, pages 20–29. Oxford University Press, 1993.
3. Peter Baumgartner. An ordered theory resolution calculus. In A. Voronkov, editor, *Logic Programming and Automated Reasoning (LPAR'92)*, volume 624 of *Lecture Notes in Computer Science*, pages 119–130, 1992.
4. G. Becher and U. Petermann. Rigid unification by completion and rigid paramodulation. In B. Nebel and L. Dreschler-Fischer, editors, *KI-94: Advances in Artificial Intelligence. 18th German Annual Conference on Artificial Intelligence*, volume 861 of *Lecture Notes in Artificial Intelligence*, pages 319–330, Saarbrücken, Germany, September 1994. Springer Verlag.
5. B. Beckert. A completion-based method for mixed universal and rigid E-unification. In A. Bundy, editor, *Automated Deduction — CADE-12. 12th International Conference on Automated Deduction.*, volume 814 of *Lecture Notes in Artificial Intelligence*, pages 678–692, Nancy, France, June/July 1994.
6. B. Beckert. Are minimal solutions to simultaneous rigid E-unification problems sufficient to adding equality to semantic tableaux. Privately circulated manuscript, 1995.
7. B. Beckert and R. Hähnle. An improved method for adding equality to free variable semantic tableaux. In D. Kapur, editor, *11th International Conference on Automated Deduction (CADE)*, volume 607 of *Lecture Notes in Artificial Intelligence*, pages 678–692, Saratoga Springs, NY, USA, June 1992. Springer Verlag.
8. E.W. Beth. *The Foundations of Mathematics*. North Holland, 1959.
9. W. Bibel. On matrices with connections. *Journal of the Association for Computing Machinery*, 28(4):633–645, 1981.
10. W. Bibel. *Deduction. Automated Logic*. Academic Press, 1993.
11. A. Degtyarev, Yu. Matiyasevich, and A. Voronkov. Simultaneous rigid E-unification is not so simple. UPMAIL Technical Report 104, Uppsala University, Computing Science Department, April 1995.
12. A. Degtyarev, Yu. Matiyasevich, and A. Voronkov. Simultaneous rigid E-unification and related algorithmic problems. To appear in *LICS'96*, 1996.
13. A. Degtyarev and A. Voronkov. Equality elimination for semantic tableaux. UPMAIL Technical Report 90, Uppsala University, Computing Science Department, December 1994. Submitted to a conference.
14. A. Degtyarev and A. Voronkov. Simultaneous rigid E-unification is undecidable. UPMAIL Technical Report 105, Uppsala University, Computing Science Department, May 1995.
15. A. Degtyarev and A. Voronkov. Reduction of second-order unification to simultaneous rigid E-unification. UPMAIL Technical Report 109, Uppsala University, Computing Science Department, June 1995.
16. A. Degtyarev and A. Voronkov. Equality elimination for the inverse method and extension procedures. In C.S. Mellish, editor, *Proc. International Joint Conference on Artificial Intelligence (IJCAI)*, volume 1, pages 342–347, Montréal, August 1995.
17. A. Degtyarev and A. Voronkov. General connections via equality elimination. In M. De Glas and Z. Pawlak, editors, *Second World Conference on the Fundamentals of Artificial Intelligence (WOCFAI-95)*, pages 109–120, Paris, July 1995. Angkor.
18. A. Degtyarev and A. Voronkov. Skolemization and decidability problems for fragments of intuitionistic logic. To appear in *LICS'96*, 1996.

19. A. Degtyarev and A. Voronkov. A complete proof procedure for first-order logic based on an incomplete procedure for rigid E-unification. *Submitted to a conference*, 1996.
20. A. Degtyarev and A. Voronkov. The undecidability of simultaneous rigid E-unification. To appear in *Theoretical Computer Science*, 10 pages, 1996.
21. J. Gallier, P. Narendran, S. Raatz, and W. Snyder. Theorem proving using equational matings and rigid E-unification. *Journal of the Association for Computing Machinery*, 39(2):377–429, 1992.
22. J.H. Gallier, P. Narendran, D. Plaisted, and W. Snyder. Rigid E-unification is NP-complete. In *Logic in Computer Science (LICS'88) (Edinburgh, Scotland)*, pages 338–346. IEEE Computer Society Press, July 1988.
23. J. Gallier, P. Narendran, D. Plaisted, and W. Snyder. Rigid E-unification: NP-completeness and applications to equational matings. *Information and Computation*, 87(1/2):129–195, 1990.
24. J.H. Gallier, S. Raatz, and W. Snyder. Theorem proving using rigid E-unification: Equational matings. In *Logic in Computer Science (LICS'87) (Ithaca, N.Y.)*, pages 338–346. IEEE Computer Society Press, 1987.
25. J.H. Gallier, S. Raatz, and W. Snyder. Rigid E-unification and its applications to equational matings. In H. Aït Kaci and M. Nivat, editors, *Resolution of Equations in Algebraic Structures*, volume 1, pages 151–216. Academic Press, 1989.
26. J.-Y. Girard. Linear logic. *Theoretical Computer Science*, 50(1):1–101, 1987.
27. C.A. Goad. Computational uses of the manipulation of formal proofs. Technical Report TR no. STAN-CS-80-819, Stanford Univ. Department of Computer Science, 1980.
28. W. D. Goldfarb. The undecidability of the second-order unification problem. *Theoretical Computer Science*, 13:225–230, 1981.
29. J. Goubault. Rigid $\bar{E}$-unifiability is DEXPTIME-complete. In *Logic in Computer Science (LICS'94)*. IEEE Computer Society Press, 1994.
30. S. Kanger. A simplified proof method for elementary logic. In J. Siekmann and G. Wrightson, editors, *Automation of Reasoning. Classical Papers on Computational Logic*, volume 1, pages 364–371. Springer Verlag, 1983. Originally appeared in 1963.
31. D. Kozen. Positive first-order logic is NP-complete. *IBM J. of Research and Development*, 25(4):327–332, 1981.
32. V. Lifschitz. Problem of decidability for some constructive theories of equalities (in Russian). *Zapiski Nauchnyh Seminarov LOMI*, 4:78–85, 1967. English Translation in: Seminars in Mathematics: Steklov Math. Inst. 4, Consultants Bureau, NY-London, 1969, p.29–31.
33. D.W. Loveland. Mechanical theorem proving by model elimination. *Journal of the Association for Computing Machinery*, 15:236–251, 1968.
34. S.Yu. Maslov. Invertible sequential variant of constructive predicate calculus (in Russian). *Zapiski Nauchnyh Seminarov LOMI*, 4:96–111, 1967. English Translation in: Seminars in Mathematics: Steklov Math. Inst. 4, Consultants Bureau, NY-London, 1969, p.36–42.
35. Y.V. Matiyasevič. Enumerable sets are Diophantine. *Soviet Mathematical Doklady*, 11(2):354–358, 1970.
36. G.E. Mints. Choice of terms in quantifier rules of constructive predicate calculus (in Russian). *Zapiski Nauchnyh Seminarov LOMI*, 4:78–85, 1967. English Translation in: Seminars in Mathematics: Steklov Math. Inst. 4, Consultants Bureau, NY-London, 1969, p.43–46.

37. M. Moser, C. Lynch, and J. Steinbach. Model elimination with basic ordered paramodulation. Technical Report AR-95-11, Fakultät für Informatik, Technische Universität München, München, 1995.
38. V.P. Orevkov. Unsolvability in the constructive predicate calculus of the class of the formulas of the type $\neg\neg\forall\exists$ (in Russian). *Soviet Mathematical Doklady*, 163(3):581–583, 1965.
39. V.P. Orevkov. On nonlengthening applications of equality rules (in Russian). *Zapiski Nauchnyh Seminarov LOMI*, 16:152–156, 1969. English Translation in: Seminars in Mathematics: Steklov Math. Inst. 16, Consultants Bureau, NY-London, 1971, p.77-79.
40. V.P. Orevkov. Solvable classes of pseudo-prenex formulas (in Russian). *Zapiski Nauchnyh Seminarov LOMI*, 60:109–170, 1976. English translation in: Journal of Soviet Mathematics.
41. U. Petermann. A complete connection calculus with rigid E-unification. In *JELIA'94*, volume 838 of *Lecture Notes in Computer Science*, pages 152–166, 1994.
42. D.A. Plaisted. Special cases and substitutes for rigid E-unification. Technical Report MPI-I-95-2-010, Max-Planck-Institut für Informatik, November 1995.
43. D. Prawitz. An improved proof procedure. In J. Siekmann and G. Wrightson, editors, *Automation of Reasoning. Classical Papers on Computational Logic*, volume 1, pages 162–201. Springer Verlag, 1983. Originally appeared in 1960.
44. R. Shostak. An algorithm for reasoning about equality. *Communications of the ACM*, 21:583–585, July 1978.
45. M. Veanes. Undecidability proofs of simultaneous rigid E-unification. Upmail technical report, Uppsala University, Computing Science Department, 1996. To appear.
46. P.J. Voda and J. Komara. On Herbrand skeletons. Technical report, Institute of Informatics, Comenius University Bratislava, July 1995.
47. A. Voronkov. On proof-search in intuitionistic logic with equality, or back to simultaneous rigid E-Unification. UPMAIL Technical Report 121, Uppsala University, Computing Science Department, January 1996. To appear in *CADE'96*, 15 pages, 1996.

An Evolving Algebra Abstract Machine

Giuseppe Del Castillo[1], Igor Đurđanović[2], Uwe Glässer[1]

[1] Heinz Nixdorf Institut, Universität-GH Paderborn, Fürstenallee 11, 33102 Paderborn, Germany, *{giusp,glaesser}@uni-paderborn.de*

[2] FB Mathematik–Informatik, Universität-GH Paderborn, Warburger Str. 100, 33098 Paderborn, Germany, *igor@uni-paderborn.de*

Abstract. *Evolving algebras (EAs)* as defined by Yuri Gurevich constitute the basis of a powerful and elegant specification and verification method which has successfully been applied to the design and analysis of various kinds of discrete dynamic systems. Aiming at the development of a comprehensive EA-based specification and design environment, we introduce the concept of an *evolving algebra abstract machine (EAM)* as a platform for the systematic development of EA tools; for instance, as required for machine based analysis and execution of EA specifications. We give a formal definition of the EAM ground model in terms of a *universal evolving algebra*, where we validate the correctness of the relation between evolving algebras (their theoretical foundations) and their EAM representation and interpretation. Our approach covers sequential as well as distributed evolving algebras.

Introduction

The notion of *evolving algebra (EA)* as introduced by Yuri Gurevich in [13, 14] constitutes a powerful and elegant concept of mathematical modelling of discrete dynamic systems: it provides an expressive means to specify the operational semantics of a system at a *natural* abstraction level in a direct and essentially coding-free manner [7, 5]. Evolving algebras have been used with considerable success for the specification and verification of various kinds of discrete dynamic systems including architectures, languages, and protocols of sequential, distributed, and real-time systems (see [3, 4, 5] for a comprehensive overview on EA-related work)[3].

From a pragmatic point of view, however, a specification methodology does not meet the requirements imposed by complex systems engineering and design tasks, as long as there is no appropriate tool support. As a first step towards a comprehensive EA-based specification and design environment, we present the formal definition and practical realization of an *evolving algebra abstract machine* (EAM) as a conceptual framework for the development of EA tools. The EAM introduces an intermediate level of abstraction between the one on which

[3] For further information on the WWW see: `http://www.uni-paderborn.de/cs/eas/` or `http://www.eecs.umich.edu/ealgebras/`.

evolving algebras are originally defined and the one which is appropriate for machine based analysis and execution of EA specifications—i.e., for implementing evolving algebras on real machines.

Our mathematical definition of the EAM *ground model*[4] EAM_0, which covers sequential as well as distributed evolving algebras, comes as a *universal evolving algebra*. This model in particular reflects the relation between evolving algebras (their theoretical foundation) and their EAM representation and interpretation; it therefore constitutes the basis upon which we establish the correctness of our implementations.

The remainder of this paper is organized as follows. After introducing a few notational conventions and some basic definitions with respect to the syntax and semantics of *sequential* (or *single-agent*) evolving algebras (Sect. 1), we develop the part of the ground model which is concerned with the static representation of syntactic and semantic objects (Sects. 2.1-2.3). The dynamic behaviour is modeled in terms of two metainterpreters for sequential evolving algebras (Sect. 2.4) and distributed evolving algebras (Sect. 3), where the latter is obtained as an extension of the former. We finish our paper with some references to related works (Sect. 4), as well as a brief conclusion (Sect. 5).

1 Basic Concepts of Evolving Algebras

Section 1.1 introduces a few notational conventions which will be used throughout this paper. In Sects. 1.2 and 1.3 we briefly recall, for the convenience of the reader and for further reference in the sequel of this paper (but with no claim of completeness) the syntax and semantics of sequential evolving algebras. Readers who are familiar with the subject may skip Sects. 1.2 and 1.3. For an exhaustive definition of evolving algebras, however, we refer to the *Lipari Guide* [14].

1.1 Notational Conventions

Function and relation names other than names of *unary* relations are written in small italic letters; unary relation names denote *universes* (or *domains*) and are written in capital italic letters.

The interpretation of a function (or relation) name f in a given algebra S is written as $\mathbf{f}_S$. We write $\mathcal{U}_S$ to refer to the universe of S. In the context of evolving algebras, we often suppress S when no ambiguity arises, for instance, when referring to fixed interpretations of standard functions which are uniquely identified (like **true** for *true*).

[4] In evolving algebras the term *ground model* has a special meaning: the role of the ground model in an attempt to specify some given system S is to provide a reliable basis such that any other more abstract or more concrete model of S can be obtained by coarsening or refining the ground model. The ground model reflects our intuitions about the basic objects and basic operations of S in such a way that we are able to establish its correctness versus our understanding of S (for further detail see [5]).

To refer to the interpretation of a ground term t in S, we write $S(t)$. For a nonground term t containing the free variables $v_1, \ldots, v_k$ assume to have an environment $\rho = [v_1 \mapsto x_1, \ldots, v_k \mapsto x_k]$ defining an assignment of values $x_1, \ldots, x_k \in \mathcal{U}_S$ to the free variables of t. Then the interpretation of t in S with respect to ρ is denoted as $S_\rho(t)$. Finally, the notation $\rho[v \mapsto x]$ refers to the environment obtained by modifying ρ to bind v to x.

1.2 Syntax of Evolving Algebras

We consider here only basic constructs, assuming that all abbreviations and macros (as defined through **let**, **where** and **extend**) are fully expanded: this can easily be handled by a preprocessing step and will not be addressed here any further. In the productions below we denote the various syntactical categories in the following way: f (*function names*), v (*variables*), t (*terms*), G (*guards*), and R (*rules*). In addition, we use U to refer to unary relation names (universes).

Function Names and Terms Terms are defined on a given *vocabulary* (or *signature*) Υ as in first order logic. A vocabulary Υ is a finite collection of function names, each of a fixed arity; function names may further be characterized by marking them as *relation names* or *static names*. Every vocabulary Υ includes an a priori given set of function names, the so-called *basic logic names*[5].

Transition Rules The core of evolving algebras is constituted by the so-called *basic transition rules*, namely: the *update instruction*, the *block constructor* and the *conditional constructor*. In this subset of evolving algebras all terms are ground.

$$R ::= f(t_1, \ldots, t_r) := t$$

$$R ::= R_1 \ \ldots \ R_k$$

$$R ::= \textbf{if } G_0 \textbf{ then } R_0 \textbf{ elseif } G_1 \textbf{ then } R_1 \ldots \textbf{elseif } G_k \textbf{ then } R_k \textbf{ endif}$$

Note that a static function name is not allowed as subject (f in the first production above) of an update instruction. If the last guard G_k in a conditional constructor is *true*, the alternate form "**else** R_k" is also allowed in place of the last **elseif** clause.[6]

Basic transition rules are then extended by further constructs introducing variables, namely: the *import constructor*, the *choose constructor* and the *declaration constructor*. In the so extended evolving algebras terms may contain variables.

---

[5] Basic logic names are the equality sign, the nullary function names *true*, *false*, *undef*, the special universe *RESERVE*, and the names of the usual boolean operations. Except for *RESERVE*, basic logic names are static names; *true*, *false*, and the equality sign are relation names.

[6] In the sequel of this paper, we shall diverge slightly from the syntax described here by writing **elif** instead of **elseif** (for layout reasons) and omitting the explicit delimitation of rules by end... when no ambiguities can arise.

$R ::=$ **import** v R_0 **endimport**

$R ::=$ **choose** v **in** U **satisfying** G R_0 **endchoose**

$R ::=$ **var** v **ranges over** U R_0 **endvar**

The **satisfying** clause of a choose constructor can be omitted: this corresponds to specifying *true* as its condition G. Furthermore, guards of conditional constructs may contain quantifiers with variables ranging over finite domains.

Programs A *program* is a rule without free variables; a *basic program* is a basic rule without free variables. (However, it is often convenient to consider a program P of the form $P = R_1 \ldots R_n$ as a collection of rules $\{R_1, \ldots, R_n\}$).

1.3 Semantics of Transition Rules

Evolving algebras are transition systems over Υ-algebras[7]: they specify computations (*runs*) whose states are algebras (which are also called *static algebras* in this context). The universes of algebras constituting states of a computation of a given evolving algebra are identical with so-called *superuniverse* of the evolving algebra.

A transition leading from an Υ-state S to an Υ-state S' modifies the interpretation of the non-static part of Υ. Such redefinitions of the interpretation of function names are intended to reflect local rather than global changes—the values of a given function may only alter at finite many arguments at a time. In this way, evolving algebras—which can be considered, in a first approximation, as given by a program P together with an initial state S_0—model computations of discrete dynamic systems through finite or infinite *runs*: a run is a sequence of states $S_0 S_1 S_2 \ldots$ such that S_0 refers to some given initial state and S_{i+1} is obtained as the result of firing the program P at S_i (the precise meaning of *firing a transition rule* is defined below, after some preliminary definitions).

Locations, Updates, Update Sets In the following definitions we consider Υ-algebras with a common superuniverse $\mathcal{U}$ (constituting the class of *states* for a given evolving algebra).

A *location* of a state S is a pair $loc = (f, \overline{x})$, where f is a non-static function name in Υ and $\overline{x} \in \mathcal{U}^n$, where n is the arity of f.

An *update* of S is a pair $\delta = (loc, val)$, where $val \in \mathcal{U}$ is the new value to be associated with the location loc of S. To *fire* $\delta = ((f, \overline{x}), val)$ at S means to transform S into a state S' such that $\mathrm{f}_{S'}(\overline{x}) = val$ and all other locations loc' of S, $loc' \neq loc$, are not affected.

An *update set* Δ over S is a set of updates of S. The update set Δ is *consistent* if Δ does not contain any two updates δ, δ' such that $\delta = (loc, x)$ and $\delta' = (loc, y)$ and $x \neq y$. Otherwise, Δ is *inconsistent*. To *fire* a consistent update

[7] The term *algebra*, as it is used here, relates to the notion of *structure* in first-order logic. A regular first-order structure consists of *domains, functions*, and *relations*, while structures without relations are called *algebras*.

set Δ at a state S means to fire all its members at S, i.e. to produce a new state S' such that

$$\mathbf{f}_{S'}(\overline{x}) = \begin{cases} y & \text{if } ((f,\overline{x}),y) \in \Delta \\ \mathbf{f}_S(\overline{x}) & \text{otherwise.} \end{cases}$$

To fire an inconsistent update set means to do nothing (i.e. to produce a state S' such that $S' = S$).

Semantics of Basic Transition Rules The effect of applying a ground rule R on an appropriate state S is defined by means of an update set Updates(R, S): to fire R at S fire Updates(R, S). The update set Updates(R, S) is inductively defined on the structure of R:

- if $R \equiv f(t_1, \ldots, t_n) := t$, then Updates$(R, S) = \{ (loc, S(t)) \}$, where $loc = (f, (S(t_1), \ldots, S(t_n)))$;
- if $R \equiv R_1 \ldots R_k$, then Updates$(R, S) = \bigcup_{i=1}^{k}$ Updates(R_i, S);
- if $R \equiv$ **if** G_0 **then** R_0 **elif** G_1 **then** R_1 ...**elif** G_k **then** R_k **endif**, then Updates(R, S) is defined as

$$\begin{cases} \text{Updates}(R_i, S) & \text{if } \exists i \forall j : j < i \Rightarrow S(G_j) = \mathbf{false} \wedge S(G_i) = \mathbf{true}, \\ \emptyset & \text{otherwise.} \end{cases}$$

Semantics of Non-Ground Rules In addition to basic transition rules, we now consider rules introducing variables, namely: **import** rules, which produce fresh elements; **choose** rules, which perform non-deterministic choices; and **var** rules, which allow a simple form of synchronous parallelism. We restrict to those rules which do not have both bound and free occurrences of the same variables and in which each bound variable is declared at most once (so-called *perspicuous* rules)[8].

In general, for a (possibly non-ground) transition rule R, the effect of applying R on S is defined by an update set of the form Updates(R, S, ρ, ξ), where ρ is an environment which binds the free variables of R, and ξ is a so-called *global choice function* which determines the variable bindings for **import** and **choose** rules. For basic transition rules the meaning of Updates(R, S, ρ, ξ) is obtained by substituting in the definitions above each occurrence of Updates(R, S) by Updates(R, S, ρ, ξ) and each occurrence of $S(t)$ by $S_\rho(t)$; for the other rules, it is defined as below (to simplify the explanation, we first define the semantics of **import** and **choose** rules for programs containing no **var** rules, and then we generalize the definitions to allow arbitrary combinations of rules).

Import and Choose Rules For programs P containing **import** rules, in a given state S, consider an injective *global choice function* ξ : Bound$_{\text{import}}(P) \rightarrow$ **RESERVE**$_S$ which maps all variables bound by **import** constructors in P to different elements of the reserve of S. Then, for **import** rules, the update set Updates(R, S, ρ, ξ) will be defined as follows:

[8] Note that rules can always be transformed into this form by appropriately renaming the variables (as explained in [14]). This can be handled by a preprocessing step.

- if $R \equiv$ **import** v R_0 **endimport**, then

$$\text{Updates}(R, S, \rho, \xi) = \\ \{ ((\mathit{RESERVE}, (\xi(v))), \textbf{false}) \} \cup \text{Updates}(R_0, S, \rho[v \mapsto \xi(v)], \xi),$$

Note that, due to the special properties of the reserve (which is essentially a set without structure—see [14] for details), the choice of ξ is irrelevant: in fact, in the presence of **import** rules, the computed states are unique up to isomorphism.

The semantics of **choose** rules can be defined in a similar way, by fixing (non-deterministically) the global choice function ξ on $\text{Bound}_{\text{choose}}(P)$ so that, for each variable v bound by a "**choose** v **in** U **satisfying** G" occurring in P, $\xi(v) \in A$ if the set $A = \{ y \mid y \in \mathbf{U}_S \wedge S_{[v \mapsto x]}(G) \}$ is not empty, or $\xi(v) = \bot$ otherwise. (The function ξ is not required to be injective on $\text{Bound}_{\text{choose}}(P)$: in fact, there is no correlation between the individual choices[9]). The update set $\text{Updates}(R, S, \rho, \xi)$ will then be defined as follows (so that trying to choose an element in an empty set produces an inconsistency, symbolized by $\bot$):

- if $R \equiv$ **choose** v **in** U **satisfying** G R_0 **endchoose**, then

$$\text{Updates}(R, S, \rho, \xi) = \\ \begin{cases} \text{Updates}(R_0, S, \rho[v \mapsto \xi(v)], \xi) & \text{if } \xi(v) \neq \bot \\ \bot & \text{otherwise.} \end{cases}$$

(The update set definitions for the other rules must be extended in such a way that, for each rule R, $\text{Updates}(R, S, \rho, \xi) = \bot$ whenever $\text{Updates}(R', S, \rho', \xi) = \bot$ for some subrule R' of R).

Var Rules and their Interactions The update set $\text{Updates}(R, S, \rho, \xi)$ for declaration constructs (**var** rules) is defined as follows:

- if $R \equiv$ **var** v **ranges over** U R_0 **endvar**, then

$$\text{Updates}(R, S, \rho, \xi) = \bigcup_{x \in \mathbf{U}_S} \text{Updates}(R_0, S, \rho[v \mapsto x], \xi).$$

Essentially, the effect of a **var** rule is to execute simultaneously an instance of the subrule R_0 for each element of U. When **import** or **choose** rules occur inside the scope of **var** rules, they are expected to import (or choose) an element for each rule instance: this can be reflected by extending the domain of the global choice function to

$$\{ (v, x_1, \ldots, x_{n(v)}) \mid v \in \text{Bound}_{\text{import/choose}}(P), x_i \in \mathbf{U}_S^{\mathbf{v,i}} \}$$

where $U^{v,1}, \ldots, U^{v,n(v)}$ are the ranges of variables $u^{v,1}, \ldots, u^{v,n(v)}$ declared by the $n(v)$ **var** constructs enclosing the **import** (**choose**) which binds v. Additionally, in the definitions of $\text{Updates}(R, S, \rho, \xi)$ for **import** and **choose**, $\xi(v)$ must be substituted by $\xi(v, \rho(u^{v,1}), \ldots, \rho(u^{v,n(v)}))$, so that, for each rule instance, the appropriate values are bound to the variable v.

[9] Note also that G should not contain free variables other than v.

2 The EAM Ground Model

We present here the mathematical definition of the EAM at an abstraction level which is intended to provide a suitable understanding of its *ground model* EAM_0. Besides the overall organization and the internal structure of the EAM, our definition of the EAM ground model in particular does also reflect the relation between evolving algebras (their theoretical foundation) and their EAM representation and interpretation; it therefore constitutes the basis upon which we establish the correctness of our implementations.

Sect. 2.1 outlines the structure of the specification which the EAM expects as input from the user (the *user specification*). Sect. 2.2 describes the EAM internal representation of such specifications. Sect. 2.3 shows how the states of the user specification are embedded into the states of the EAM. Finally, Sect. 2.4 specifies the EAM simulation of the dynamic behaviour of the user specification in terms of an abstract (meta-)interpreter.

The basic EAM_0 model as presented in Sects. 2.2–2.4 for sequential (single-agent) evolving algebras is then extended to multi-agent evolving algebras in Sect. 3.

2.1 The User Specification

The EAM realizes a generic scheme as required in machine based analysis and execution of evolving algebra specifications. Within this framework we introduce the ground model EAM_0 as a *universal evolving algebra*[10] used to run arbitrary (user-defined) evolving algebras. In that sense, the EAM simulates a *user evolving algebra* $\mathcal{A} = (\mathcal{P}, \mathcal{S}_0)$ consisting of a *user program* $\mathcal{P}$ and an *initial state* $\mathcal{S}_0$.[11] To avoid unnecessary complications, we will henceforth require that $\mathcal{P}$ is a syntactically correct program and that $\mathcal{S}_0$ is *appropriate* for $\mathcal{P}$, i.e. $\mathcal{S}_0$ is defined on a vocabulary $\Upsilon_{\mathcal{A}}$ which contains at least all the function names occurring in $\mathcal{P}$.

We assume $\mathcal{S}_0$ to be specified as follows:

1. An implicitly given part of $\mathcal{S}_0$ results from default interpretations of predefined function names identified by some subset Υ_0 of the vocabulary $\Upsilon_{\mathcal{A}}$ such that these functions are considered as built-in functions of the EAM model. Υ_0 contains at least the basic logic names. With exception of *RESERVE*, all function names in Υ_0 are treated as static names.
2. A second (possibly empty) part of the initial state $\mathcal{S}_0$ is explicitly specified through *initial state definitions* belonging to a set of *function definitions* $\mathcal{D}$ provided by the user.

[10] In [2], Blass and Gurevich used the model of a universal evolving algebra for complexity theoretic considerations. Compared to their model the universal evolving algebra employed here is defined at a much more concrete abstraction layer.

[11] From now on, we use calligraphic letters to refer to objects pertaining to the user evolving algebra, while straight letters refer to objects of the EAM.

3. Finally, the vocabulary $\Upsilon_{\mathcal{A}}$ may as well contain a third category of function names referring to so-called *oracle functions*[12] As a conceptual means to specify how the externally represented interpretations of oracle functions are accessed within the EAM model, we assume that $\mathcal{D}$ contains a suitable *interface declaration* for each oracle function name occurring in $\mathcal{A}$.

Note that, if externally alterable functions are involved, $\mathcal{S}_0$ is not uniquely determined through the declarations in $\mathcal{D}$: instead, it is non-deterministically chosen (by an appropriate assignment of values to the external functions) in the class of states satisfying $\mathcal{D}$.

Specification of Static Algebras The language of evolving algebras comes without stipulating any specific expressive means to specify the underlying static algebras (any appropriate formalism can be employed for this purpose). On the other hand, every implementable model of evolving algebras must restrict to some concrete and a priori specified notation for defining domains and functions.

There are well known examples showing us how this could be done; algebraic specification languages, like COLD-K [11] for instance, suggest to have at least the following two options: *constructive definitions*, which uniquely characterize a domain or function in terms of other domains or functions, and *axiomatic definitions*, which introduce a domain or function that is characterized (not necessarily in a unique way) through axioms. As we are interested in executable specifications, we use axioms rather as *integrity constraints* (conditions which must be satisfied in order to ensure a meaningful behaviour of the system) than as definitions.

As a thorough discussion of these issues goes beyond the scope of this paper, we abstract in the EAM ground model from concrete state specifications by considering $\mathcal{D}$ as a set of *abstract function definitions*[13]. We only mention that such definitions are essentially of two kinds:

- *Constructive definitions* come in the form of algorithmic descriptions of (computable) functions which the EAM is able to evaluate. They can be

[12] In contrast to *internally alterable functions*, which are updated by the transition rules of the program $\mathcal{P}$, *oracle functions* cannot be affected by the program (as they do not appear in updates). However, this does not mean that oracle functions need to be static: there are *externally alterable oracle functions* whose values are determined (or at least may be influenced) by an external environment. Finally, there are also functions which are externally and internally alterable at the same time. Such functions are not considered here. For further details see on the classification of functions see [5]. Note also that, in the new classification of [5], the *external functions* defined by the Lipari Guide correspond to *externally alterable oracle functions*: we use both terms interchangeably in this paper.

[13] We do not consider here the specification and representation of user-defined domains. However, it would be easy to extend the state specifications by introducing abstract *domain definitions*, allowing the construction of new domains by combining the EAM predefined domains, along with corresponding declarations of *constructor functions*, denoting elements of the user-defined universes.

employed as initial state definitions which may also include definitions of oracle function for those oracle functions that are either static or do only depend on the state (see the function *Val* defined in Sect. 2.3 for an example of such an oracle function).

- *Interface declarations*, which define externally alterable oracle functions by specifying an interface to the external world[14] (as represented by some *environment* into which the model is supposed to be embedded). Interface declarations usually come in combination with a set of *integrity constraints* expressing requirements on the environment. When executing a specification, external function values can be checked against the integrity constraints at run time. For the purpose of verifying properties of the specification, the integrity constraints can be taken as assumptions (some properties of the system may hold under the condition that the environment satisfies such requirements).

The User Specification The EAM accepts as its input a *user specification* of the form

$$SPEC = (\Upsilon_{SPEC}, \mathcal{D}, \mathcal{P}),$$

where $\mathcal{D}$ is a set of function definitions, $\mathcal{P}$ a program and Υ_{SPEC} a vocabulary containing at least all function names occurring in $\mathcal{D}$ and $\mathcal{P}$.

2.2 Representation of Syntactic Objects

In order to simulate the user evolving algebra, the EAM states (defined on the EAM vocabulary Υ_{EAM}) must hold a representation of both the user program $\mathcal{P}$ and the function definitions $\mathcal{D}$. In this section we describe the general scheme according to which the syntactic objects of the user specification (like terms, rules, and function definitions) are *encoded* into their EAM internal representation. The encoding can be carried out in a direct and straightforward way (using standard compiler techniques and tools) by a preprocessing step, which also performs macro-expansions and renaming of variables (see Sects. 1.2 and 1.3).

As the details of the preprocessing step are irrelevant for the definition of the EAM ground model, we do not address it any further here. Instead, we represent the relation between $\mathcal{P}$ and $\mathcal{D}$ and their EAM-encoding abstractly, by means of a mapping "$[\![\,.\,]\!]$" which yields for each syntactic object of the user specification the corresponding element of the appropriate EAM domain, namely: *function names*, *variables*, *terms*, *transition rules*, and *abstract function definitions* are represented by elements of the EAM universes *FNAME*, *VAR*, *TERM*, *RULE*, and *DEF*, respectively. Below we specify some properties of the mapping, which are necessary conditions for the EAM correctness.

[14] As concrete instances of externally alterable (oracle) functions one could imagine the following examples: some input interactively provided by the user; some values computed by concurrently running evolving algebra modules; some physical quantities registered by a measuring device.

Function Names and Variables For function names f in the vocabulary $\Upsilon_{\mathcal{A}}$ of the user evolving algebra $\mathcal{A}$, the mapping is defined by

$$[\![f]\!] = \psi(f),$$

where ψ is an *injective* function from $\Upsilon_{\mathcal{A}}$ into **FNAME** (so that different function names have different representations).

We assume that the EAM and $\mathcal{A}$ share the same subvocabulary Υ_0 of standard function names, i.e. $\Upsilon_{\mathrm{EAM}} \cap \Upsilon_0 = \Upsilon_{\mathcal{A}} \cap \Upsilon_0 = \Upsilon_0$ (see Sect. 2.1). For each standard function name f in Υ_0, the EAM vocabulary Υ_{EAM} contains an additional nullary function name "f" : $FNAME$ (*quoted* f), such that

$$\text{"}\mathbf{f}\text{"} = \psi(f).$$

Through the quoted names, the EAM can access the representations of standard names occurring in the user specification, and establish a relation between those representations and the objects denoted by the standard names themselves. For example, Υ_{EAM} contains both function names *true* and "*true*": the former refers to the boolean value **true**, the latter to the element $x \in \mathbf{FNAME}$ such that $x = \psi(true) = [\![true]\!]$ (see also Sect. 2.3, in particular the definition of the *val* function).

The relevant signature information associated with the function names of $\Upsilon_{\mathcal{A}}$ is represented by the following EAM functions (with an obvious meaning):

$$arity : FNAME \to N$$
$$relation, static : FNAME \to BOOL.$$

As far as the representation of variables is concerned, the only requirement on the mapping is to be an injective function such that it associates each variable v occurring in the program to the corresponding encoding $[\![v]\!] \in \mathbf{VAR}$. Here we assume the program to be *perspicuous* (see Sect. 1.3) due to the renaming of variables as performed by the preprocessing step.

Terms and Transition Rules For terms and transition rules the mapping $[\![\,.\,]\!]$ is inductively defined on the structure of terms (rules), in such a way that different terms (rules) are mapped to different elements of **TERM** (**RULE**).

With respect to the representation of terms, the individual elements of the domain **TERM** are identified by means of a term constructor function[15]

$$term : (FNAME \times TERM^*) \cup VAR \to TERM.$$

[15] Note that the EAM representation of terms diverges slightly from the usual definition of terms in first-order logic (and evolving algebras). Namely, a nullary function name a is not itself a term: instead, the term a is considered as composed of the function name a with an empty sequence of subterms. Note, however, that this affects only the internal representation of terms but not their syntax (the user will write terms in the usual notation).

A term $f(t_1, \ldots, t_n)$ occurring in the user specification is encoded in the EAM in a canonical way as

$$[\![f(t_1, \ldots, t_n)]\!] = \mathbf{term}([\![f]\!], \langle [\![t_1]\!], \ldots, [\![t_n]\!] \rangle).$$

The representation of transition rules is defined using the same technique, except that there are six different constructor functions, corresponding to the different kinds of rules[16] (see Sect. 1.2):

$$\begin{aligned} \mathit{update\_instr} &: \mathit{TERM} \times \mathit{TERM} \rightarrow \mathit{RULE} \\ \mathit{block\_cons} &: \mathit{RULE}^* \rightarrow \mathit{RULE} \\ \mathit{cond\_cons} &: (\mathit{TERM} \times \mathit{RULE})^* \rightarrow \mathit{RULE} \\ \mathit{import\_cons} &: \mathit{VAR} \times \mathit{RULE} \rightarrow \mathit{RULE} \\ \mathit{choose\_cons} &: \mathit{VAR} \times \mathit{FNAME} \times \mathit{TERM} \times \mathit{RULE} \rightarrow \mathit{RULE} \\ \mathit{var\_cons} &: \mathit{VAR} \times \mathit{FNAME} \times \mathit{RULE} \rightarrow \mathit{RULE} \end{aligned}$$

By means of the above constructors, the mapping of transition rules is defined inductively in the natural way.

Note that, in addition to the constructor functions introduced above, appropriate selector functions are defined which allow extracting the components of each term (or rule). However, to simplify the notation and make the EAM specification more readable, we suppress the explicit use of selector functions by using a simple pattern matching notation.

The Program The EAM can access the (representation of the) user program $\mathcal{P}$ through a nullary function name *prog* : *RULE* with the obvious interpretation

$$\mathbf{prog} = [\![\mathcal{P}]\!].$$

Function Definitions The mapping of function definitions is left abstract since the ground model is not concerned with their concrete representation. It is sufficient to know that the representations of the function definitions in $\mathcal{D}$ are accessible through a unary function *def* : *FNAME* → *DEF* associating to each function name the corresponding definition (or *undef* if $\mathcal{D}$ contains no definition for the given function name).

2.3 Representation of States

In this section we describe the relation between the (Υ_{EAM}-)states of the EAM and the (Υ_{SPEC}-)states induced by the user specification (*user states*)—in particular, we show how the latter are embedded into the former.

---

[16] Obviously, the codomains of the different rule constructors are intended to be pairwise disjoint subsets of **RULE**.

The EAM States The states of the EAM can be seen as composed of the following three parts:

1. Predefined domains and functions provide interpretations for basic logic names and the other standard function names in the subvocabulary $\Upsilon_0 \subset \Upsilon_{\mathrm{EAM}}$. We assume that Υ_{EAM} contains a universe name *VALUE*, interpreted as

$$\mathbf{VALUE} = \mathbf{BOOL} \cup \{\, \mathbf{undef} \,\} \cup \ldots \cup \mathbf{N} \cup \ldots \cup \mathbf{RESERVE}_{\mathbf{S}_0},$$

   i.e., as the union of all predefined domains together with the initial reserve. Note that each nullary function name a in Υ_0 is interpreted as an element $\mathbf{a} \in \mathbf{VALUE}$, and each n-ary function name f in Υ_0 (with $n > 0$) as a function $\mathbf{f} : \mathbf{VALUE}^n \to \mathbf{VALUE}$.
2. Domains and functions constituting the EAM representation of the user specification (*syntactic objects*), as defined in Sect. 2.2. We assume that Υ_{EAM} contains a universe name *SYNTAX*, interpreted as

$$\mathbf{SYNTAX} = \mathbf{FNAME} \cup \mathbf{VAR} \cup \mathbf{TERM} \cup \mathbf{RULE} \cup \mathbf{DEF}.$$

   If we define a subvocabulary $\Upsilon_{\mathrm{SYN}} \subset \Upsilon_{\mathrm{EAM}}$ as containing all function names referring to syntactic objects (see Sect. 2.2), then between Υ_{SYN} and **SYNTAX** holds the same relation as between Υ_0 and **VALUE**.
3. Domains and functions needed for the implementation of the internal workings of the EAM, for instance, the domain *UPDATE* representing the update structure (Sect. 2.4) or the term evaluation function *Val* defined below. (Note that this third part of the EAM state includes essentially all objects which do not fall into any of the above two categories).

If we denote the set of objects used internally by the EAM (part 3 above) by a universe name *MACHINE*, the superuniverse $\mathcal{U}_{\mathrm{EAM}}$ of the EAM is given by

$$\mathcal{U}_{\mathrm{EAM}} = \mathbf{VALUE} \cup \mathbf{SYNTAX} \cup \mathbf{MACHINE}$$

(where **VALUE**, **SYNTAX** and **MACHINE** are pairwise disjoint).

Relation between EAM states and user states As we are in a first-order context, the states of the user evolving algebra (in particular, the initial state) can not be encoded into the EAM in a direct way, i.e., through a function which maps elements of **FNAME** to functions.

Instead, the EAM tries to "reconstruct" such states as the need arises, by using the fixed interpretations of some functions and the information contained in the user specification (also taking into account, for non-initial states, the modifications which may have been effected by state transitions). We shall see that an adequate notion of equivalence between the so reconstructed states and the original states of the user evolving algebra can be formulated by referring to interpretations of ground terms.

First of all, we have to state the following preliminary assumptions:

- The superuniverse $\mathcal{U}$ of the user evolving algebra is assumed to be a proper subset of the EAM superuniverse $\mathcal{U}_{\text{EAM}}$, such that $\mathcal{U} = \mathbf{VALUE}$.[17]
- The interpretation of standard function names in the initial state $\mathcal{S}_0$ of the user evolving algebra coincides with their interpretation in the EAM initial state S_0, i.e., for each f in Υ_0, $\mathbf{f}_{\mathcal{S}_0} = \mathbf{f}_{\mathrm{S}_0}$.[18]

We now introduce the *evaluation function*

$$Val : TERM \to VALUE,$$

which yields the interpretations associated with representations of ground terms, and constitutes the basis of the mechanism which allows to embed user states into EAM states.

To specify the evaluation of ground terms depending on the particular kinds of function names, we introduce following auxiliary functions:

- $g_1, \ldots, g_r$ represent the predefined functions and relations from Υ_0.
- $apply : DEF \times VALUE^* \to VALUE$ is a function which produces values for the user-defined functions, given a function definition and a sequence of arguments. In particular, if the definition is constructive, *apply* computes the result by applying the constructive definition on the arguments; if the definition is an interface declaration, *apply* returns a value provided by the environment, according to the interface information contained in the definition and to the arguments.
- $cont : LOCATION \to VALUE$ is a dynamic function from *locations* to *values*, which holds the (finitely many) updated values of dynamic functions and relations. In the initial state we have $cont(loc) = nil$ for each location loc, indicating that no locations have been updated yet[19] (for all the locations which have not been updated the value obtained by applying the initial state definition must be taken).

The function *Val* is therefore defined, for each f, t_i, with $FNAME(f)$ and $TERM(t_i)$, $i = 1, \ldots, n$, by the equation

$$Val(term(f, \langle t_1, \ldots, t_n \rangle)) = val(\langle f, \langle Val(t_1), \ldots, Val(t_n) \rangle \rangle).$$

---

[17] We do not consider here the possibility of constructing user-defined domains: to allow such construction, the user specification should be extended with appropriate *domain definitions*, in addition to the function definitions introduced in Sect. 2.1.

[18] Intuitively, this means that the user evolving algebra uses the "resources" (predefined domains and functions) available in the EAM—except, of course, for those constituting the representation of the user specification or implementing the internal mechanisms of the EAM.

[19] We introduce and use here the nullary function *nil*, denoting a special element **nil** $\in$ **MACHINE**, to avoid ambiguities which could arise by using *undef* (in particular if the user program updates some location to *undef*).

The auxiliary function $val : (FNAME \times VALUE^*) \rightarrow VALUE$ is defined as follows (with $\overline{x}$ standing for $x_1, \ldots, x_n$):

$$val(\langle f, \langle \overline{x} \rangle \rangle) = \begin{cases} \text{if } f = \text{“}g_1\text{” then } g_1(\overline{x}) \\ \text{else if } f = \text{“}g_2\text{” then } g_2(\overline{x}) \\ \ldots \\ \text{else if } f = \text{“}g_r\text{” then } g_r(\overline{x}) \\ \text{else if } cont(\langle f, \langle \overline{x} \rangle \rangle) \neq nil \text{ then } cont(\langle f, \langle \overline{x} \rangle \rangle) \\ \text{else if } def(f) \neq undef \text{ then } apply(def(f), \langle \overline{x} \rangle) \\ \text{else if } relation(f) \text{ then } false \text{ else } undef \end{cases}$$

The function *Val* can be extended to evaluate terms with quantifiers (which we do not address here) and terms with free variables (which will be discussed in Sect. 2.4). To formulate an equivalence notion between states and their EAM-encodings, the definition of *Val* as given so far is sufficient. This notion of equivalence provides an adequate basis to formalize the intuitive idea of *simulation* of the user evolving algebra by the EAM.

Definition 1 (Equivalence of $\Upsilon_{\mathcal{A}}$-states and Υ_{EAM}-states). An $\Upsilon_{\mathcal{A}}$-state $\mathcal{S}$ and a Υ_{EAM}-state S are *equivalent* if, for each ground term t over $\Upsilon_{\mathcal{A}}$, the following condition holds:

$$\mathbf{Val}_{\mathrm{S}}([\![t]\!]) = \mathcal{S}(t).$$

Assumption 2 (EAM **Initial State).** Let S_0 be the EAM initial state and $\mathcal{S}_0$ the initial state of the user evolving algebra $\mathcal{A}$. Then, for each function name $f \in \Upsilon_{\mathcal{A}} \setminus \Upsilon_0$, and for each combination of arguments $x_1, \ldots, x_n \in \mathbf{VALUE}_{\mathrm{S}_0}$, S_0 is such that

$$\mathbf{apply}_{\mathrm{S}_0}(\mathbf{def}([\![f]\!]), \langle x_1, \ldots, x_n \rangle) = \mathbf{f}_{\mathcal{S}_0}(x_1, \ldots, x_n).$$

Note that: *(i)* if $\mathbf{def}([\![f]\!])$ is a constructive definition, we require that the definition is correct wrt the interpretation $\mathbf{f}_{\mathcal{S}_0}$ of f in $\mathcal{S}_0$; *(ii)* if $\mathbf{def}([\![f]\!])$ is an interface declaration, we require that the values provided by the environment for **f** at S_0 correspond to those of $\mathbf{f}_{\mathcal{S}_0}$.

Proposition 3 (Correctness of the initial state encoding). *If the initial state* S_0 *of the* EAM *satisfies the Assumption 2, then* $\mathcal{S}_0$ *and the* EAM*-state* S_0 *(resulting from the encoding of the user specification into the* EAM*) are equivalent.*

Proof. By induction on the structure of terms (see [8]).

2.4 The Metainterpreter

The last step of the EAM construction is the definition of an evolving algebra program (the *metainterpreter*) which—given the EAM-encoding of the user specification—simulates the execution of the user program.

The execution model given by the metainterpreter reflects the underlying semantic definitions (see Sect. 1.3) in a straightforward and faithful manner; in fact, it is obtained as the result of a direct translation of those definitions into an operational model. It can therefore be taken as the starting point for a sequence of refinement steps, each of which introduces a more restricted computational agent, such that the resulting model is suitable to be executed on real machines.

The metainterpreter operates in two phases: *(i)* in the *collecting phase* the updates forming the update set for the user program $\mathcal{P}$ in the current state $\mathcal{S}$ are computed and collected by traversing the tree structure associated with $\mathcal{P}$; *(ii)* in the *firing phase* the update set computed in the preceeding collecting phase is fired, so that dynamic functions are appropriately modified.

Signature In addition to the function $prog : RULE$, which represents the EAM encoding of $\mathcal{P}$ (introduced in Sect. 2.2), there is a unary relation

$$CLOSURE\_SET : (RULE \times ENV) \rightarrow BOOL$$

which identifies the instances of subrules of $\mathcal{P}$ which are being considered in a given step of the *collecting phase*: such instances are given by a rule together with an environment containing bindings for the free variables occurring in the rule, and are referred to as *closures*. Environments are represented in a universe ENV, and manipulated through operations

$$\begin{aligned} empty\_env &: ENV \\ env\_val &: VAR \times ENV \rightarrow VALUE \\ env\_upd &: (VAR \times VALUE) \times ENV \rightarrow ENV, \end{aligned}$$

which have the expected meaning. Note that the function Val, defined in Sect. 2.3 for ground terms, must be extended to evaluate terms with variables, given an appropriate environment: if $Val^* : TERM^* \times ENV \rightarrow VALUE^*$ is an auxiliary function which evaluates sequences of terms to sequences of values (i.e., such that $Val^*(\langle t_1, \ldots, t_n \rangle, env) = \langle Val(t_1, env), \ldots, Val(t_n, env) \rangle$), then Val is defined by the following equations:

$$\begin{aligned} Val(term(f, t^*), env) &= val(\langle f, Val^*(t^*, env) \rangle) \\ Val(term(v), env) &= env\_val(v, env) \end{aligned}$$

(for $f \in FNAME$, $t^* \in TERM^*$, and $v \in VAR$, respectively). Henceforth we will omit the second argument of Val when referring to the evaluation of ground terms (which does not depend on the environment).

The current content of the incrementally constructed update set is identified by the unary relation

$$UPDATE\_SET : UPDATE \rightarrow BOOL,$$

The (static) universe $UPDATE$ above is defined as $UPDATE = (LOCATION \times VALUE)$, where $LOCATION = (FNAME \times VALUE^*)$, reflecting in a direct way the definitions of Sect. 1.3.

Initialization and Execution In the EAM initial state S_0 the closure set contains the encoding of the user program $\mathcal{P}$ together with an empty environment ($\mathcal{P}$ does not contain free variables), while the update set is empty:

$$\mathbf{CLOSURE\_SET}_{S_0} = \{\, \langle \mathbf{prog}, \mathbf{empty\_env} \rangle \,\}, \qquad \mathbf{UPDATE\_SET}_{S_0} = \emptyset.$$

The actual evolving algebra program of the metainterpreter for basic transition rules consists of two rules, namely: Collect and Fire. The Collect rule is applied repeatedly during the update collecting phase:

$$\begin{array}{l}
\mathsf{Collect} \equiv \mathtt{if}\ \ (\exists r \in \mathit{CLOSURE_SET}) \\
\qquad\qquad \mathtt{then\ var}\ \langle \mathit{rule}, \mathit{env} \rangle\ \mathtt{ranges\ over}\ \mathit{CLOSURE_SET} \\
\qquad\qquad\qquad\qquad \mathit{CLOSURE_SET}(\langle \mathit{rule}, \mathit{env} \rangle) := \mathit{false} \\
\qquad\qquad\qquad\qquad \mathsf{CollectUpdatesInRule}(\mathit{rule}, \mathit{env})
\end{array}$$

The subrule CollectUpdatesInRule specifies the appropriate collection procedure depending on the kind of rule under consideration:

$$\begin{array}{ll}
\mathsf{CollectUpdatesInRule}(\mathit{rule}, \mathit{env}) & \\
\ \equiv\ \mathsf{CaseOfUpdateRule}(\mathit{rule}, \mathit{env}) & \mathsf{CaseOfBlockRule}(\mathit{rule}, \mathit{env}) \\
\quad\ \ \mathsf{CaseOfConditionalRule}(\mathit{rule}, \mathit{env}) & \mathsf{CaseOfImportRule}(\mathit{rule}, \mathit{env}) \\
\quad\ \ \mathsf{CaseOfChooseRule}(\mathit{rule}, \mathit{env}) & \mathsf{CaseOfVarRule}(\mathit{rule}, \mathit{env})
\end{array}$$

In the case of an update instruction, the corresponding update is computed and added to the current update set:

$$\begin{array}{l}
\mathsf{CaseOfUpdateRule}(\mathit{rule}, \mathit{env}) \\
\ \equiv\ \mathtt{if}\ \mathit{update_instr}(\mathit{term}(f, t^*), t) \\
\quad\ \ \mathtt{then\ let}\ \mathit{loc} \equiv \langle f, \mathit{Val}^*(t^*, \mathit{env}) \rangle \\
\qquad\qquad\qquad \mathit{val} \equiv \mathit{Val}(t, \mathit{env}) \\
\qquad\qquad \mathtt{in}\ \mathit{UPDATE_SET}(\langle \mathit{loc}, \mathit{val} \rangle) := \mathit{true}
\end{array}$$

Compound rules which are formed by means of (non-empty) block and conditional constructors are executed by extending *CLOSURE_SET* with the subrules to be considered in the subsequent computation step. According to the semantics of blocks and conditionals this can be done in the following way:

$$\begin{array}{l}
\mathsf{CaseOfBlockRule}(\mathit{rule}, \mathit{env}) \\
\ \equiv\ \mathtt{if}\ \mathit{rule} = \mathit{block_cons}(R_1\ \mathit{rest}) \\
\quad\ \ \mathtt{then}\ \mathit{CLOSURE_SET}(\langle R_1, \mathit{env} \rangle) := \mathit{true} \\
\qquad\qquad \mathit{CLOSURE_SET}(\langle \mathit{block_cons}(\mathit{rest}), \mathit{env} \rangle) := \mathit{true}
\end{array}$$

$$\begin{array}{l}
\mathsf{CaseOfConditionalRule}(\mathit{rule}, \mathit{env}) \\
\ \equiv\ \mathtt{if}\ \mathit{rule} = \mathit{cond_cons}(\langle G_0, R_0 \rangle\ \mathit{rest}) \\
\quad\ \ \mathtt{then\ if}\ \mathit{Val}(G_0, \mathit{env}) \\
\qquad\qquad \mathtt{then}\ \mathit{CLOSURE_SET}(\langle R_0, \mathit{env} \rangle) := \mathit{true} \\
\qquad\qquad \mathtt{else}\ \mathit{CLOSURE_SET}(\langle \mathit{cond_cons}(\mathit{rest}), \mathit{env} \rangle) := \mathit{true}
\end{array}$$

The `import`, `choose` and `var` constructs are implemented by the following rules, which add to *CLOSURE_SET* new closures consisting of the subrule with appropriately extended environments:

CaseOfImportRule(*rule*, *env*)
  ≡ **if** *rule* = *import_cons*(*v*, *R*)
    then import *x*
        CLOSURE_SET(⟨*R*, *env_upd*(⟨*v*, *x*⟩, *env*)⟩) := *true*

CaseOfChooseRule(*rule*, *env*)
  ≡ **if** *rule* = *choose_cons*(*v*, *U*, *G*, *R*)
    then let *acceptable*(*x*) ≡ *val*(⟨*U*, ⟨*x*⟩⟩) ∧ *Val*(*G*, *env_upd*(⟨*v*, *x*⟩, *env*))
        in choose *x* **in** *VALUE* **satisfying** *acceptable*(*x*)
          CLOSURE_SET(⟨*R*, *env_upd*(⟨*v*, *x*⟩, *env*)⟩) := *true*

CaseOfVarRule(*rule*, *env*)
  ≡ **if** *rule* = *var_cons*(*v*, *U*, *R*)
    then var *x* **ranges over** *VALUE*
        if *val*(⟨*U*, ⟨*x*⟩⟩)
        then *CLOSURE_SET*(⟨*R*, *env_upd*(⟨*v*, *x*⟩, *env*)⟩) := *true*

The firing phase consists in the application of the following rule:

Fire ≡ **if** ¬(∃*r* ∈ *CLOSURE_SET*)
    then *CLOSURE_SET*(⟨ *prog*, *empty_env* ⟩) := *true*
      FireUpdates

where the subrule FireUpdates actually carries out the collected updates:

FireUpdates
  ≡ **var** ⟨*loc*, *val*⟩ **ranges over** *UPDATE_SET*
    cont(*loc*) := *val*
    UPDATE_SET(⟨*loc*, *val*⟩) := *false*

Note that the Fire rule updates *CLOSURE_SET*, in order to allow a new collecting phase to begin in the subsequent computation step.

Definition 4 (Significant EAM States). A state S_i of an EAM computation is *significant* if it satisfies the following conditions:

$$\mathbf{UPDATE\_SET}_{S_i} = \emptyset \quad \text{and} \quad \mathbf{CLOSURE\_SET}_{S_i} = \{\langle \mathbf{prog}, \mathbf{empty\_env}\rangle\}.$$

(Note that the EAM initial state S_0 is significant).

Assumption 5 (Steadiness of External Functions). We presuppose that the interpretation of externally alterable oracle functions may only change on significant states, i.e for any non-significant state S_i and for each n-ary external function name $f \in \Upsilon_{\mathcal{A}} \setminus \Upsilon_0$ and $\overline{x} \in \mathbf{VALUE}^n_{S_i}$ the following condition must hold

$$\mathbf{apply}_{S_i}(\mathbf{def}([\![f]\!]), \langle\overline{x}\rangle) = \mathbf{apply}_{S_{i-1}}(\mathbf{def}([\![f]\!]), \langle\overline{x}\rangle).$$

Proposition 6 (Metainterpreter Correctness). *The metainterpreter, when applied to the* EAM-*encoding of a user evolving algebra* $\mathcal{A} = (\mathcal{P}, \mathcal{S}_0)$, *simulates the execution of* $\mathcal{P}$ *on* $\mathcal{S}_0$ *and the resulting state sequence* $\mathcal{S}_0, \mathcal{S}_1, \mathcal{S}_2, \ldots$ *by computing a sequence of states* $S_{g(0)}, S_{g(1)}, S_{g(2)}, \ldots$ *(for some* g *with* $g(0) = 0, g(i) < g(i+1)$ *for all* i*) such that the corresponding states* $\mathcal{S}_i$ *and* $S_{g(i)}$ *are pairwise equivalent.*

Proof. By choosing g such that $S_{g(0)}, S_{g(1)}, S_{g(2)}, \ldots$ is the sequence of all significant states reached by the EAM during its computation (see [8] for details).

3 Execution of Distributed Evolving Algebras

So far we have considered the case of single-agent evolving algebras. In this section we show how the EAM_0 model can be extended, in a simple and elegant way, to simulate multiple-agent evolving algebras as well.

3.1 Distributed Evolving Algebras

We recall here, for the convenience of the reader, the basic ideas and definitions of distributed evolving algebras, as given by [14] (to which we refer for a more extensive discussion) up to slight notational changes. We also restrict here to the deterministic case (i.e., distributed evolving algebras without external functions or **choose** constructs).

A distributed evolving algebra $\mathcal{A}$ contains several computational *agents*, which concurrently execute a number of single-agent programs (called *modules*). Formally, a *distributed evolving algebra* $\mathcal{A}$ consists of:

- A finite indexed set of single-agent programs π_μ (the modules), identified by *module names* μ (which are static nullary function names).
- A vocabulary $\Upsilon_{\mathcal{A}}$ containing all function names occurring in the modules π_μ (except *Self*—see below), as well as a special unary function name *Mod*, representing the relation between agents and modules: an element a is an *agent* at a given state S if there is a module name μ such that $S \models Mod(a) = \mu$ (the corresponding $\mathcal{P}(a) = \pi_\mu$ is the program of a).[20]
- A collection of states of $\mathcal{A}$, called *initial states* of $\mathcal{A}$. (A state of $\mathcal{A}$ is defined as a $\Upsilon_{\mathcal{A}}$-state S such that: *(i)* different module names are interpreted in S as different elements, and *(ii)* there are only finitely many agents at S).

The special nullary function name *Self* (which we regard, for convenience, as a variable) allows the self-identification of agents: *Self* is interpreted as a by each agent a, and can be used, for instance, to model some local state of the agents. We say that an agent a makes a *move* at a given state S if the update set

$$\text{Updates}(a, S) = \text{Updates}(\mathcal{P}(a), S, [Self \mapsto a])$$

is fired at S. Building upon this basic concept of move, different notions of *run* for distributed evolving algebras can be defined, e.g. *sequential* or *quasi-sequential* runs.

[20] Note that the agents—which may be arbitrary elements of the superuniverse of $\mathcal{A}$—are dynamic: they can be created, destroyed and associated with modules at run-time, by updating the function *Mod*.

Definition 7 (Sequential Run). A *sequential run* ρ of a distributed evolving algebra $\mathcal{A}$ is a sequence (S_n) of states of $\mathcal{A}$, where S_0 is an initial state and each S_{n+1} is obtained from S_n by executing a move of an agent.

Definition 8 (Quasi-sequential Run). A *quasi-sequential run* ρ of $\mathcal{A}$ is a sequence (S_n) of states of $\mathcal{A}$, where S_0 is an initial state and each S_{n+1} is obtained from S_n by firing a collection A_n of agents, i.e. by firing the update set $\bigcup_{a \in A_n} \text{Updates}(a, S)$.

However, the most general notion of distributed computation for evolving algebras is given by *partially ordered runs* (also called simply *runs*).

Definition 9 (Partially Ordered Run). A *partially ordered run* ρ of a distributed evolving algebra $\mathcal{A}$ is a triple (M, A, σ) satisfying the following conditions:

1. M is a partially ordered set, where all sets $\{ y \mid y \leq x \}, x \in M$, are finite: elements of M represent *moves* made by various agents during the run.
2. A is a function on M such that every nonempty set $\{ x \mid A(x) = a \}$ is linearly ordered: $A(x)$ is the *agent* performing the move x (the moves of any single agent are supposed to be linearly ordered).
3. σ is a function which assigns a *state* of $\mathcal{A}$ to each initial segment[21] of M, such that $\sigma(\emptyset)$ is an initial state: for each initial segment X of M, $\sigma(X)$ is the state which results from performing all moves in X.
4. The *coherence condition*: if x is a maximal element in a finite initial segment X of M and $Y = X - \{ x \}$, then $A(x)$ is an agent in $\sigma(Y)$ and $\sigma(X)$ is obtained from $\sigma(Y)$ by firing $A(x)$ at $\sigma(Y)$.

A relation between partially ordered runs and sequential runs can be established by considering those sequential runs S_n which are *linearizations* for a given partially ordered run. The following corollary results immediately from the definitions:

Corollary 10. *For partially ordered runs ρ, all linearizations of the same finite initial segment of ρ have the same final state.*

Unfortunately, there is no such simple relation between partially ordered runs and quasi-sequential runs: this fact makes the implementation of a parallel interpreter for distributed evolving algebras very complicated (and probably not convenient).

3.2 A Distributed Version of EAM_0

The basic idea in the realization of a distributed version of the metainterpreter specified in Sect. 2.4 is to have several agents—one for each agent in the user evolving algebra to be simulated—executing an instance of (a slightly modified version of) the sequential interpreter.

[21] An *initial segment* of a partially ordered set P is a substructure X of P such that, if $x \in X$ and $y < x$ in P, then $y \in X$.

Representation of Modules and Agents The representation scheme of Sect. 2 is extended by introducing universes $MNAME \subset FNAME$ and $MODULE \subset RULE$, representing module names and modules of $\mathcal{A}$ respectively, such that

$$\begin{aligned} \mathbf{MNAME} &= \{ \ [\![\mu]\!] \mid \mu \text{ is a module name of } \mathcal{A} \ \}, \\ \mathbf{MODULE} &= \{ \ [\![\pi_\mu]\!] \mid \mu \text{ is a module name of } \mathcal{A} \ \}. \end{aligned}$$

Each module name is associated to the corresponding module by means of a function $which\_module : MNAME \to MODULE$, while the module name assigned to an agent a is given—according to the definition of distributed evolving algebras—by $val(\langle \text{"}Mod\text{"}, \langle a \rangle \rangle)$.[22] The set of agents can then be characterized by the formula

$$AGENT(x) \Leftrightarrow MNAME(val(\langle \text{"}Mod\text{"}, \langle x \rangle \rangle)),$$

and the program of an agent a is given by

$$prog(a) = which\_module(val(\langle \text{"}Mod\text{"}, \langle a \rangle \rangle))$$

(the nullary function *prog* is refined, in the distributed version of the EAM, to a unary function $prog : AGENT \to MODULE$).

Furthermore, it is convenient to identify the agents of the EAM with the representations of the agents of $\mathcal{A}$ as given by the universe $AGENT$ (in fact, there is a one-to-one correspondence between the two sets of agents). However, the agents of the EAM always execute the metainterpreter (which is the only EAM module), i.e., for each a in $AGENT$, $Mod(a) = \text{INTERPRETER}$, where INTERPRETER is the module name of the interpreter.

As we shall see, there are several possible ways of defining such an interpreter, which correspond to different execution models for distributed evolving algebras. A common feature to all of them is to operate in three phases, namely: *selecting*, *collecting*, and *firing*. While the collecting and firing phases have the same function as in the sequential version, the additional selecting phase is needed to determine which agents participate to the next (simulated) computation step[23].

3.3 An Interpreter for Distributed Evolving Algebras

In this section we show how the interpreter for sequential evolving algebras can be modified to execute distributed evolving algebras.

[22] Note that, in the distributed version of the EAM, the vocabulary Υ_{EAM} contains the quoted names "*Self*" and "*Mod*", to refer to the names *Self* and *Mod* occurring in the user modules (see the discussion of quoted names in Sect. 2.2).

[23] Note that, in the sequential version, the (trivial) selecting phase was essentially incorporated in the firing phase (update of $CLOSURE\_SET$ in the Fire rule).

Structures of the Interpreter The execution of multiple agents requires to keep track of several closures at a time. Making use of a special function "*Self*" : *VAR*, the information about the current closures and their respective "owners" can be embedded into the unary relation *CLOSURE_SET* such that the *env* components specify the corresponding bindings for "*Self*". It is convenient to introduce the following abbreviation, expressing the extraction of the "owner agent" from an environment *env*:

$$agent(env) \equiv Val(term(\text{"}Self\text{"}), env).$$

The structure holding the update set is also modified, in order to hold the information about the agent which is performing a given update; this structure (*labeled updated set*) is represented by the unary relation

$$UPDATE\_SET : UPDATE \times AGENT \rightarrow BOOL.$$

Initial State The initial state S_0 satisfies the following conditions:

$$\mathbf{CLOSURE\_SET}_{S_0} = \emptyset, \qquad \mathbf{UPDATE\_SET}_{S_0} = \emptyset.$$

The Program The first phase to be executed by the program is the selecting phase as expressed by the following rule, which will be executed by each agent independently:

Select ≡ **if** *SELECTED_AGENT*(*Self*)
  then *CLOSURE_SET*(⟨*prog*(*Self*), {⟨"*Self*", *Self*⟩}⟩) := *true*
  SELECTED_AGENT(*Self*) := *false*

The unary relation *SELECTED_AGENT* is an oracle function which identifies a subset of *AGENT* whose moves are to be simulated by the EAM in the next simulation cycle (by means of the following collecting and firing phases). We make the following assumptions about *SELECTED_AGENT*:

1. The environment determines a new interpretation for *SELECTED_AGENT* on all the EAM *significant states* (i.e., on all those states S of an EAM run, such that $\mathbf{CLOSURE\_SET}_S = \emptyset$ and $\mathbf{UPDATE\_SET}_S = \emptyset$). In all other states *SELECTED_AGENT* is subject to the updates effected by the interpreter.
2. The sets of agents identified by *SELECTED_AGENT* on significant states are such that the resulting computations actually constitute simulations of runs of the user evolving algebra, in particular in the sense that the coherence condition (see Def. 9) will be satisfied.

Different choices for defining *SELECTED_AGENT* will result in different execution models. For instance, if *SELECTED_AGENT* is such that it always determines sets consisting of only one agent, the EAM will simulate linearizations of the runs of the user evolving algebra (so that, as Corollary 10 implies, the resulting simulations are correct). Other implementations of *SELECTED_AGENT* are possible, but—in order to realize correct parallel implementations—complex global analyses of the state are needed to identify independent agents which can be executed concurrently in a safe way.

After the execution of the selecting phase the set of selected agents becomes empty and the collecting phase will be started. The **Collect** rule is modified—w.r.t. the corresponding rule of the sequential interpreter—so that each agent evaluates and collects exclusively its own updates (this reflects the design intention to have an EAM agent simulating each agent of the user evolving algebra):

$$\begin{aligned}
&\mathsf{Collect} \equiv \texttt{if } \neg(\exists a \in SELECTED_AGENT) \wedge (\exists r \in CLOSURE_SET) \\
&\quad \texttt{then var } \langle rule, env \rangle \texttt{ ranges over } CLOSURE_SET \\
&\quad\quad \texttt{if } agent(env) = Self \\
&\quad\quad \texttt{then } CLOSURE_SET(\langle rule, env \rangle) := false \\
&\quad\quad\quad \mathsf{CollectUpdatesInRule}(rule, env)
\end{aligned}$$

The rule **CaseOfUpdateRule** must be obviously adapted to the structure of the labeled update set by substituting the update

$$UPDATE\_SET(\langle loc, val \rangle) := true$$

with

$$UPDATE\_SET(\langle \langle loc, val \rangle, agent(env) \rangle) := true.$$

The firing phase is implemented by the following **Fire** rule, which differs from the corresponding rule of the sequential version in that it does no longer perform the reinitialization of $CLOSURE\_SET$ needed to allow the beginning of the next collecting phase (as this pertains now to the selecting phase):

$$\begin{aligned}
&\mathsf{Fire} \equiv \texttt{if } \neg(\exists a \in SELECTED_AGENT) \wedge \neg(\exists r \in CLOSURE_SET) \\
&\quad \texttt{then } \mathsf{FireUpdates}
\end{aligned}$$

The **FireUpdates** rule is also modified, so that each agent performs its own updates (see the discussion of the **Collect** rule above):

$$\begin{aligned}
&\mathsf{FireUpdates} \\
&\quad \equiv \texttt{var } \langle \langle loc, val \rangle, agent \rangle \texttt{ ranges over } UPDATE_SET \\
&\quad\quad \texttt{if } agent = Self \\
&\quad\quad \texttt{then } cont(loc) := val \\
&\quad\quad\quad UPDATE_SET(\langle \langle loc, val \rangle, agent \rangle) := false
\end{aligned}$$

4 Related Work

Closely related to the work presented here is [2], which presents a universal evolving algebra for sequential deterministic evolving algebras (without variables).

Also related to our work are various developments of EA interpreters. Ben Harrison and Jim Huggins have implemented a C interpreter for sequential evolving algebras at the EECS Department of the University of Michigan at Ann Arbor. An improved interpreter based on this one, which can also handle distributed EA programs, is currently being developed at the University of Michigan by Raghu Mani. A Prolog interpreter was developed by Angelika Kappel at the

Computer Science Department of Dortmund University [15]. At the Computer Science Department of Karlsruhe University, Bernhard Beckert and Joachim Posegga have implemented a compiler to Prolog for a special subset of evolving algebras, which they call lean *EA* [1]. An interpreter in Scheme was developed by Dag Diesen at the Department of Informatics, University of Oslo [9].

To the best of our knowledge, the concept of using an EA based specification of an abstract EA machine model as a conceptual framework for implementing evolving algebras is new.

5 Conclusions

Our mathematical definition of the EAM, as presented in this paper, covers single-agent as well as distributed evolving algebras and has been shown to be correct with respect to the evolving algebra semantics defined in the Lipari Guide. The conceptual framework of an abstract machine model which is effectively realized by a hierarchy of operational models at different abstraction levels is particularly useful for the development of various kinds of evolving algebra tools—e.g. as required for machine based analysis and execution of EA specifications.

Note that the definition of the ground model EAM_0, for instance, provides a universal EA representation scheme which is not only applicable to interpreters and compilers, but also to analysers and transformation tools. In that respect the work presented here can be considered as a starting point for the development of a comprehensive EA-based specification and design environment into which a variety of tools is integrated by sharing a common view on evolving algebras. As a first step in this direction some EAM-based tools are currently being developed, namely: *(i)* a parser/preprocessor, implemented using the compiler tool system Eli [12, 16], which produces the abstract syntax trees described in Sect. 2.2 from an EAspecification in textual form; *(ii)* various tools for processing EAspecifications in abstract syntac tree form, written in Standard ML [17], including a code generator producing C++ code corresponding to the EAM_1 model (not described in this paper); *(iii)* a C++ kernel implementing the EAM_1 model, which efficiently executes the EAM_1 code produced by the code generator.

Finally, there is another point that should be mentioned: to the best of our knowledge the specification of the EAM is the first attempt to use evolving algebras to design a system from scratch; all other known applications of this method are actually reengineering applications.

Acknowledgments

A special thank to Jim Huggins for his very detailed and helpful comments on an early version of this paper and for the fruitful discussion which followed.

References

1. Bernhard Beckert and Joachim Posegga. lean *EA*: A poor's man's evolving algebra compiler. Internal Report 25/95, Fakultät für Informatik, Universität Karlsruhe, April 1995.
2. Andreas Blass and Yuri Gurevich. Evolving Algebras and Linear Time Hierarchy. In B. Pehrson and I. Simon, editors, Proc. of the IFIP 13th World Computer Congress 1994, Volume I: Technology and Foundations, Elsevier Science Publishers B. V., 1994, pp. 383-390.
3. Egon Börger. Annotated bibliography on evolving algebras. In E. Börger, editor, *Specification and Validation Methods.* Oxford University Press, 1995.
4. Egon Börger, editor. *Specification and Validation Methods.* Oxford University Press, 1995.
5. Egon Börger. On the use of evolving algebras for hardware and software engineering. In *Proc. of SOFSEM'95 (Nov. 25 - Dec. 2, 1995, Bratislava, Czech Republic).* To appear in LNCS.
6. Egon Börger and Igor Đurđanović. Correctness of compiling Occam to Transputer code. Computer Journal, to appear.
7. Egon Börger and Uwe Glässer. Modelling and analysis of distributed and reactive systems using evolving algebras. Technical Report NS-95-4, BRICS, July 1995.
8. G. Del Castillo, I. Đurđanović and U. Glässer. Specification and Design of the EAM (EAM - Evolving Algebra Abstract Machine). Technical Report *tr-rsfb-96-003*, Paderborn University.
9. Dag Diesen. *Specifying Algorithms using Evolving Algebra. Implementation of Functional Programming Languages.* Research Report 199, Department of Informatics, University of Oslo, March 1995.
10. H. Ehrig and B. Mahr, editors. *Fundamentals of Algebraic Specification 1 – Equations and Initial Semantics.* EATCS Monographs on Theoretical Computer Science. Springer-Verlag, 1985.
11. L.M.G. Feijs and H.B.M. Jonkers, editors. *Formal Specification and Design.* Cambridge Tracts in Theoretical Computer Science 35. Cambridge University Press, 1992.
12. R.W. Gray, V.P. Heuring, St.P. Levi, A.M. Sloane, W.M. Waite, *Eli: A Complete, Flexible Compiler Construction System.* Communications of the ACM, Februar 1992, 121ff.
13. Yuri Gurevich. Evolving algebras – a tutorial introduction. *Bulletin of the EATCS,* (43):264-284, February 1991.
14. Yuri Gurevich. Evolving Algebras 1993: Lipari Guide. In E. Börger, editor, *Specification and Validation Methods.* Oxford University Press, 1995.
15. A.M. Kappel. Executable specifications based on dynamic algebras. In A. Voronkov, editor, *Logic Programming and Automated Reasoning,* volume 698 of *LNAI,* pages 229-240. Springer, 1993.
16. U. Kastens, W.M. Waite. *Modularity and Reusability in Attribute Grammars.* Universität-GH Paderborn, Reihe Informatik, Bericht Nr. 102, Juli 1992.
17. R. Milner, M. Tofte and R. Harper. *The Definition of Standard ML.* The MIT Press, 1990.
18. Martin Wirsing. Algebraic specifications. In J. van Leeuwen, editor, *Handbook of Theoretical Computer Science B,* pages 675-788. Elsevier, 1990.

Rewriting with Extensional Polymorphic λ-calculus

Roberto Di Cosmo[1] and Delia Kesner[2]

[1] LIENS (CNRS) - DMI
Ecole Normale Supérieure
45, Rue d'Ulm
75005 Paris - France, E-mail: dicosmo@dmi.ens.fr
[2] CNRS and LRI
Bât 490, Université de Paris-Sud
91405 ORSAY Cedex, France, E-mail: kesner@lri.lri.fr

Abstract. We provide a confluent and strongly normalizing rewriting system, based on expansion rules, for the *extensional* second order typed lambda calculus with product and *unit* types: this system corresponds to the Intuitionistic Positive Calculus with implication, conjunction, quantification over proposition and the constant *True*. This result is an important step towards a new theory of reduction based on expansion rules, and gives a natural interpretation to the notion of second order η-long normal forms used in higher order resolution and unification, that are here just the normal forms of our reduction system.

1 Introduction

Typed lambda calculus provides a convenient framework for studying functional programming and offers a natural formalism to deal with proofs in intuitionistic logic. It comes traditionally equipped with a fundamental computational mechanism, which is the β equality $(\lambda x.M)N = M[N/x]$, and with a minimal tool for reasoning about programs, which is the η *extensional* equality $\lambda x.Mx = M$. This basic calculus can then be extended by adding further types, like products, unit and second order types, each coming with its own computational mechanism and/or its extensional equalities.

This work provides a confluent and strongly normalizing rewriting system for second order lambda calculus equipped with extensionality axioms for the product and for the arrow type, no longer oriented as *contractive* rules, but, according to the now growing practice [Aka93, Dou93, DCK94b, Cub92, DCK94a, DCP95, JG92], as *expansive* rewriting rules.

Using expansive rewrite rules, in a controlled fashion, allows us to obtain a simple canonical system that can be used to decide equality, has the second order Huet's $\beta\eta$-long normal forms as normal forms and is naturally compatible with rules that break confluence when added to systems with contractive rules for extensional equalities. This is the case, for example, of the special *unit* type T and the rule $M : T \longrightarrow * : T$ that one needs to define the extensional first order lambda calculus associated to Cartesian Closed Categories. Another example is the extensional first order lambda calculus enriched with a confluent algebraic rewriting system, where confluence is also broken by contractive rules [DCK94a].

As it has been noticed before, the expansive interpretation of extensional rules is not new, but has been neglected for a long time, so that the theory of lambda calculus with expansion rules is far from being fully developed: even for η-contraction, that has been extensively studied for a long time, a satisfactory treatment has been provided only recently [Geu92].

A first positive result for polymorphic systems is presented in [DCP95], but just for the first order expansive η rule: unfortunately, the proof technique used there, which is based essentially on η postponement, does not extend to polymorphic η expansion nor to expansive surjective pairing.

Here we provide a proof of confluence and normalization for the full polymorphic system with the extensionality of arrow, product and universal types turned into expansive rules. Since the rewriting relation with controlled expansive rules is not a congruence and is not stable by substitution, we cannot use the traditional reducibility proofs, that strongly rely on these properties.

Our proof is based on a *modification* of Girard's reducibility candidates, as first suggested for the first order calculus in [Jay92], that requires some careful reordering of the traditional lemmas in Girard's proof, but works homogeneously for products as well as arrow and polymorphic types. A related approach has been independently taken in [Gha95] for the fragment without products and terminal object: there a different modification of reducibility is introduced, which seems very promising.

It is worth to notice that the expansive interpretation of extensional equalities does not fit the various higher order schemes proposed for example in [Klo80, JO91, Nip90], as those schemes do not allow the left hand side of the reduction rules to be a single higher-order variable.

We also present a simple argument that allows to add in a fully modular way the special rule for the *unit* type to any rewriting system, preserving normalization.

Overall, this provides us with the first canonical rewriting system for the full polymorphic extension of the first order lambda calculus associated to Cartesian Closed Categories, an important step towards a full theory of expansive extensionality.

1.1 Brief Survey

Several proof techniques have been developed to tackle the expansionary interpretation of the extensional equalities, and show that it yields a confluent and normalizing system in the first order case. One idea is to try to separate the expansion rules from the rest of the reduction, and then try to show some kind of modularity of the reduction systems. In [Aka93] this is done by means of the following property:

Lemma 1. *Let S and R be confluent and strongly normalizing reductions, s.t.*

$$\forall M, N \quad (M \stackrel{R}{\Longrightarrow} N) \quad \textit{implies} \quad (M^S \stackrel{R}{\Longrightarrow}{}^{+} N^S)$$

where M^S is the S normal form of M, then $S \cup R$ is also confluent and strongly normalizing.

The lemma applies to S taken as the expansions and R the usual reductions. In [DCK94b], we reduced confluence and strong normalization of the full expansionary system to that of the traditional one without expansions using another modular technique based on a translation.

A different non-modular approach is taken in [JG92] and [Dou93], where the proofs of strong normalization are based on an extension of the traditional techniques of reducibility and allow to handle also the peculiarity of the expansion rules. But that is not all, since one is left to prove weak confluence separately, which is not an easy task in the presence of expansion rules, as the rewrite relation is not a congruence (see [DCK94b] for details).

An even different technique is used in [Cub92], where confluence is shown by a careful study of the residuals in the reduction.

Finally, in [DCP95], one finds a simple general lemma, that appears also in [Ges90], and that is today the most satisfactory tool to handle the addition of expansion rules to first order systems, since it is fully modular and extremely easy to apply.

Lemma 2. *Let $\langle \mathcal{A}, R, S\rangle$ be an Abstract Reduction System, where R-reduction is strongly normalizing. Let the following commutation hold*

$$\forall a, b, c, d \in \mathcal{A} \quad \begin{array}{ccc} a & \xrightarrow{R} & c \\ \downarrow S & & \downarrow S \\ b & \overset{R}{\underset{+}{\dashrightarrow\!\!\!\rightarrow}} & d \end{array}$$

Then S^* and R^+ commute, so, in particular, S^* and R^* commute.

Since the union of two confluent reductions that commute is confluent, by Hindley-Rosen's lemma (see [Bar84]), this lemma gives an easy way of proving confluence modularly: in particular, if we take expansive η and SP as S, and the rest of the system as R, all *first order* systems cited above satisfy the lemma, so confluence comes up immediately from the separate confluence of the expansions alone and of the non expansive subsystems.

As for normalization, if R preserves S normal forms, and S and R are both confluent and normalizing, it is easy to see that commutation also entails the hypothesis of Akama's lemma, so also normalization comes up modularly. This is the case in all first order systems: since the type of any subterm do not evolve during reduction, expansive normal forms are preserved, so one gets immediately strong normalization for the full system.

For these reasons, we can consider that the treatment of expansive rules in first order systems is nowadays fully satisfactory. Unfortunately, in the presence of second order quantification, the type of a subterm *can evolve* during evaluation, and this fact allows us to build very simple examples suggesting that the modular approaches [Aka93, DCK94b, DCP95] cannot be satisfactorily extended to the second order case, and we have to go back and have a better look at reducibility candidates.

Expansions and polymorphism are not modular The following simple example shows that we cannot use the modular techniques developed up to now to separate the complexities introduced by expansion rules and polymorphic typing.

Example 1. Let $M = (\Lambda X.(x[X \rightarrow X])(\lambda y : X.y))[A \times B]$ where $x : \forall Z.(Z \rightarrow A)$ and A and B are base types. Then, the term M is a normal form w.r.t expansion rules, but its immediate β^2 reduct is not:

$$M' = (x[A \times B \rightarrow A \times B])(\lambda y : A \times B.y)$$

In fact, M' reduces to the term

$$M'' = (x[A \times B \rightarrow A \times B])(\lambda y : A \times B.\langle \pi_1(y), \pi_2(y) \rangle)$$

Now, there is no way to reduce M to M'', which is the (η, SP)-normal form of M', without using expansions: this means that the hypothesis of lemma 1 are not satisfied, and we fail to obtain normalization modularly (also lemma 2 alone is no good for normalization).

This same example can be used to show how the use of expansor terms of [DCK94b] is neither viable.

Our approach Since the modular techniques are not viable, we focused on the reducibility predicates defined in [JG92] for the first order calculi with expansion rules, and we adapt the strong normalization proof to handle both second order quantification and expansion rules, by a careful reorganisation of the traditional arguments.

One fundamental difference between the proof for the simply typed and the proof for polymorphic lambda calculus is that one does not work with just one reducibility candidate, but with all reducibility candidates at once. This requires to deal with many subtle points in the second order case that do not appear in the first order case.

The paper is organized as follows: we define the calculus in section 2 and we show weak confluence of the full reduction system in section 3. We then give the proof of strong normalization in section 4, add the Top type in section 5 and we finally conclude with some ideas for further work.

We will use some standard notions from the theory of rewriting system, such as redex, normal form, confluence, weak confluence and strong normalization. See [Bar84] for references.

2 The Calculus

We consider a denumerable set of atomic types and a denumerable set of type variables. The set of types of our calculus can be defined by the following grammar:

$$A ::= \iota \mid X \mid A \times A \mid A \to A \mid \forall X.A$$

where ι ranges over the set of atomic types and X over the set of type variables.

Variables are typed by the following axiom:

$$x_1 : A_1, \ldots, x_n : A_n \vdash x_i : A_i \quad (1 \leq i \leq n)$$

where the x_j's are pairwise distinct.

And terms are typed by the following rules:

$$\frac{\Gamma, x : A \vdash M : B}{\Gamma \vdash \lambda x : A.M : A \to B} \qquad \frac{\Gamma \vdash M : A \to B \quad \Gamma \vdash N : A}{\Gamma \vdash MN : B}$$

$$\frac{\Gamma \vdash M_1 : A_1 \quad \Gamma \vdash M_2 : A_2}{\Gamma \vdash \langle M_1, M_2 \rangle : A_1 \times A_2} \quad \frac{\Gamma \vdash M : B_1 \times B_2}{\Gamma \vdash \pi_1(M) : B_1} \quad \frac{\Gamma \vdash M : B_1 \times B_2}{\Gamma \vdash \pi_2(M) : B_2}$$

$$\frac{\Gamma \vdash M : A \quad \text{X not free in } \Gamma}{\Gamma \vdash \Lambda X.M : \forall X.A} \qquad \frac{\Gamma \vdash M : \forall X.A}{\Gamma \vdash M[B] : A[B/X]}$$

We write $M : A$ is M has type A under some context Γ. The set of free variables of a term M, denoted $FV(M)$ is defined as usual. If M is a term and θ a substitution, $M\theta$ is the term M where each $x \in FV(M)$ is replaced by $\theta(x)$. Substitutions are *typed*, in the sense that the substituted variable and term must have the same type.

We identify terms up to α-conversion, *i.e.* renaming of bound variables. The reduction rules are the following (we refer the interested reader to [DCK94b] for a discussion of the restrictions on the expansion rules):

(β) $(\lambda x : A.M)N \xrightarrow{\beta} M[N/x]$

(β^2) $(\Lambda X.M)[A] \xrightarrow{\beta^2} M[A/X]$

(π_i) $\pi_i\langle M_1, M_2\rangle \xrightarrow{\pi_i} M_i$, for $i = 1, 2$

(δ) $M \xrightarrow{\delta} \langle \pi_1(M), \pi_2(M)\rangle$, if $\begin{cases} M : A \times B \\ M \text{ is not a pair} \end{cases}$

(η) $M \xrightarrow{\eta} \lambda x : A.Mx$, if $\begin{cases} x \notin FV(M) \\ M : A \to C \\ M \text{ is not a } \lambda\text{-abstraction} \end{cases}$

(η^2) $M \xrightarrow{\eta^2} \Lambda X.M[X]$, if $\begin{cases} X \text{ is not free in } M \\ X \text{ is not free in the type of any free variable of } M \\ M : \forall Y.A \\ M \text{ is not a } \Lambda\text{-abstraction} \end{cases}$

The one-step reduction relation between terms, denoted $\Longrightarrow$, is defined as the closure of the reduction rules $\beta, \beta^2, \eta, \eta^2, \pi_1, \pi_2, \delta$ for all the contexts *except* in the application and projection cases, *i.e*:

- If $M \Longrightarrow M'$, then $MN \Longrightarrow M'N$ except in the case $M \xrightarrow{\eta} M'$
- If $M \Longrightarrow M'$, then $M[A] \Longrightarrow M'[A]$ except in the case $M \xrightarrow{\eta^2} M'$
- If $M \Longrightarrow M'$, then $\pi_i(M) \Longrightarrow \pi_i(M')$ except in the case $M \xrightarrow{\delta} M'$

Notation 3 *The transitive and the reflexive transitive closure of* $\Longrightarrow$ *are noted* $\Longrightarrow^+$ *and* $\Longrightarrow^*$ *respectively.*

3 Weak Confluence

Since we already know that the first order fragment of the calculus is confluent [Aka93, DCK94b, JG92, Dou93, Cub92], this task is greatly simplified: we are left to examine only the critical pairs that arise from the use of the second order rules β^2 and η^2.

We first prove a substitution lemma for *types*:

Lemma 4. *If* $Q \Longrightarrow Q'$, *then* $Q[A/X] \Longrightarrow Q'[A/X]$

Proof. By a simple case analysis.

Then, we can proceed to prove the following

Lemma 5 Critical Pairs. *If* $M \longrightarrow M_1$ *and* $M \Longrightarrow M_2$, *there is* M_3 *such that* $M_1 \Longrightarrow^* M_3$ *and* $M_2 \Longrightarrow^* M_3$.

Proof. We analyse only the cases where $M \longrightarrow M_1$ is an $\xrightarrow{\eta^2}$ or $\xrightarrow{\beta^2}$, all the other cases can be found in [DCK94b].

1.

$$\begin{array}{ccc}
(\Lambda X.Q)[A] & \Longrightarrow & (\Lambda X.Q')[A] \\
\beta^2 \big\downarrow & & \big\downarrow \beta^2 \\
Q[A/X] & \underset{\text{by lemma 4}}{\Longrightarrow} & Q'[A/X]
\end{array}$$

2.

$$\begin{array}{ccc}
(\Lambda X.Q)[A] & \xrightarrow{\eta} & \lambda y : B.((\Lambda X.Q)[A])y \\
\beta^2 \big\downarrow & & \big\downarrow \beta^2 \\
Q[A/X] & & \lambda y : B.(Q[A/X])y
\end{array}$$

If $Q[A/X]$ is not a λ-abstraction, then $Q[A/X] \xrightarrow{\eta} \lambda y : B.(Q[A/X])y$, otherwise $Q[A/X] = \lambda z.N$ and we have

$$\lambda y : B.(\lambda z.N)y \xrightarrow{\beta} \lambda y : B.(N[y/z]) =_\alpha \lambda z.N = Q[A/X]$$

3.

$$\begin{array}{ccc}
(\Lambda X.Q)[A] & \xrightarrow{\delta} & \langle \pi_1((\Lambda X.Q)[A]), \pi_2((\Lambda X.Q)[A]) \rangle \\
 & & \big\downarrow \beta^2 \\
\beta^2 \big\downarrow & & \langle \pi_1(Q[A/X]), \pi_2((\Lambda X.Q)[A]) \rangle \\
 & & \big\downarrow \beta^2 \\
Q[A/X] & & \langle \pi_1(Q[A/X]), \pi_2(Q[A/X]) \rangle
\end{array}$$

If $Q[A/X]$ is not a pair, then $Q[A/X] \xrightarrow{\delta} \langle \pi_1(Q[A/X]), \pi_2(Q[A/X]) \rangle$, otherwise $Q[A/X] = \langle N_1, N_2 \rangle$ and we have

$$\langle \pi_1(\langle N_1, N_2 \rangle), \pi_2(\langle N_1, N_2 \rangle) \rangle \xrightarrow{\pi_1} \langle N_1, \pi_2(\langle N_1, N_2 \rangle) \rangle \xrightarrow{\pi_2} \langle N_1, N_2 \rangle = Q[A/X]$$

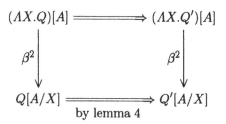

4.

$$\begin{array}{ccc} (\Lambda X.Q)[A] & \xrightarrow{\eta^2} & \Lambda Y.((\Lambda X.Q)[A])[Y] \\ \Big\downarrow \beta^2 & & \Big\downarrow \beta^2 \\ Q[A/X] & & \Lambda Y.(Q[A/X])[Y] \end{array}$$

If $Q[A/X]$ is not a Λ-abstraction, then $Q[A/X] \xrightarrow{\eta^2} \Lambda Y.(Q[A/X])[Y]$, otherwise $Q[A/X] = \Lambda Z.N$ and we have

$$\Lambda Y.(\Lambda Z.N)y \xrightarrow{\beta^2} \Lambda Y.(N[Y/Z]) =_\alpha \Lambda Z.N = Q[A/X]$$

5.

$$\begin{array}{ccc} Q & \Longrightarrow & Q' \\ \Big\downarrow \eta^2 & & \Big\downarrow \eta^2 \\ \Lambda Y.Q[Y] & = \Rightarrow & \Lambda Y.Q'[Y] \end{array}$$

This is because if $Q \Longrightarrow Q'$ is an internal reduction, it is not a root expansion and then $Q[Y] \Longrightarrow Q'[Y]$ which implies also $\Lambda Y.Q[Y] \Longrightarrow \Lambda Y.Q'[Y]$

6.

$$\begin{array}{ccc} (\lambda y.M)N & \xrightarrow{\beta} & M[N/y] \\ \Big\downarrow \eta^2 & & \\ \Lambda Y.((\lambda y.M)N)[Y] & & \end{array}$$

If $M[N/y]$ is not a Λ-abstraction, then $M[N/y] \xrightarrow{\eta^2} \Lambda Y.(M[N/y])[Y]$, otherwise $M[N/y] = \Lambda Z.L$ and we have:

$$\Lambda Y.(\Lambda Z.L)[Y] \xrightarrow{\beta^2} \Lambda Y.L[Y/Z] =_\alpha \Lambda Z.L = M[N/y]$$

Finally, the proof of the weak confluence for the calculus proceeds exactly as in Theorem 4.11 of [DCK94b].

4 Strong normalization

In this section we prove strong normalization for the full system by means of a notion of reducibility modified as in [JG92].

4.1 Definitions

Definition 6 (neutral terms) *A term $t{:}U$ is neutral if it is not a λ-abstraction, a type abstraction or a pair.*

Definition 7 (longest reduction path for a term, or rank) *Let u be a term, then $\nu(u)$ denotes the length of the longest reduction path starting from u. Notice that, by König's Lemma, if u is strongly normalisable then $\nu(u)$ is finite.*

Definition 8 *A reducibility candidate of type U is a set R of terms of type U with the following properties.*

(CR1) *if $t \in R$, then t is strongly normalisable.*
(CR2) *if $t \in R$ and $t \longrightarrow t'$, then $t' \in R$.*
(CR3) *if t is neutral and for all t' s.t. $t \longrightarrow t'$* **other than a basic expansion** *we have that $t' \in R$, then $t \in R$.*

The modification written in bold in CR3 was first suggested in [Jay92] to adapt Girard's reducibility proof for the simply typed λ-calculus with expansion rules.

To discuss its implications, let us recall here the steps that one follows in a traditional reducibility proof for second order calculi. First, one defines the notion of reducibility candidate, remarks that the set of strongly normalizing terms is a reducibility candidate, defines the notion of product and function space for reducibility candidates, and shows that the product and function spaces of any given reducibility candidate is still a reducibility candidate. Then one defines a notion of reducibility candidate *with parameters* $RED[\overrightarrow{R}/\overrightarrow{X}]$ for all types T and shows by induction on the types that any reducibility candidate with parameters is a reducibility candidate. Finally, using a bunch of technical lemmas, one shows by structural induction on the terms that every instance of a term t (and in particular t itself) is reducible, hence strongly normalizable.

In the presence of expansions, we have to alter the order of several lemmas, and it is not evident that the set of strongly normalizing terms form a reducibility candidate in general, while this is trivial with Girard's formulation of CR3.

Fortunately, it will be enough to show that the set of strongly normalizing terms of *atomic or variable types only* are a reducibility candidate.

Proposition 9. *The set of strongly normalizable terms of atomic type or variable type are a reducibility candidate.*

Proof. Just notice that on terms of atomic type or variable type the modified (CR3) condition is equal to Girard's original (CR3) condition, because no root expansion is possible, so the proof goes through as in the usual case without expansions.

Remark. A reducibility candidate R, if it exists, is never empty as CR3 implies that it always contains the variables of type U, because they are neutral and there is no reduction other than basic expansions leaving them.

We will often write in the sequel s.n. for strongly normalizing.

Lemma 10 Normalization lemma.

(i) *If* $t : A \times B$ *is a term such that* $\pi_1(t) : A$ *and* $\pi_2(t)$ *are s. n. then so is* t.
(ii) *If* $t : A \to B$ *is a term and* $x : A$ *is a variable not free in* t *such that* $tx : B$ *is s. n. then* t *is s. n.*
(iii) *If* $t : \forall Y.A$ *is a term and* X *is a type variable not free in* t *such that* $t[X] : A[X/Y]$ *is s. n. then* t *is s. n..*
(iv) *If* $t : A$ *is a s. n. term, then* $\lambda x.t$ *and* $\Lambda X.t$ *are s. n. too.*

Proof. By induction on the maximal reduction lengths of the strongly normalizing terms.

If R and S are reducibility candidates of types U and V, we can define the following sets:

$$t \in R \times S \Longleftrightarrow \pi_1(t) \in U \text{ and } \pi_2(t) \in V \qquad t \in R \to S \Longleftrightarrow \text{ for all } u \in R, tu \in S$$

Lemma 11 Pairing. *Let* R_1 *and* R_2 *be reducibility candidates of types* A_1 *and* A_2 *and let* $u : A_1 \in R_1$ *and* $v : A_2 \in R_2$. *Then* $\pi_i\langle u, v\rangle : A_i \in R_i$.

Proof. By induction on the normalization lengths of u and v, using (CR3), as usual.

Theorem 12. *If* R_1 *and* R_2 *are reducibility candidates of types* U_1 *and* U_2, *then* $R_1 \times R_2$ *is a reducibility candidate of type* $U_1 \times U_2$.

Proof. The proof is still done by induction on the type. It is rather different from the usual one, so we show it in full in the Appendix.

4.2 Reducibility with parameters

Let T be a type, and $\vec{X}$ be a set of type variables that contains at least all the free type variables of T. For $\vec{U}$ a sequence of types of the same length, let $T[\vec{U}/\vec{X}]$ be the type obtained by simultaneous substitution of the X's with the U's, and $\vec{R}$ a sequence of reducibility candidates of corresponding types.

Definition 13 *The set* $RED_T[\vec{R}/\vec{X}]$ *of reducible terms of type* T *is defined by induction on the type* T *as follows (where the* $\vec{R}$ *are reducibility candidates of type* $\vec{U}$ *).*

- if T is atomic, $RED_T[\vec{R}/\vec{X}]$ is the set of s. n. terms of type T
- if T is X_i, $RED_T[\vec{R}/\vec{X}]$ is R_i
- if T is $U \times V$ then $RED_T[\vec{R}/\vec{X}]$ is $RED_U[\vec{R}/\vec{X}] \times RED_V[\vec{R}/\vec{X}]$
- if T is $U \to V$ then $RED_T[\vec{R}/\vec{X}]$ is $RED_U[\vec{R}/\vec{X}] \to RED_V[\vec{R}/\vec{X}]$

- if T is $\forall Y.W$ then $RED_T[\vec{R}/\vec{X}]$ is the set of terms t of type $T[\vec{U}/\vec{X}]$ such that, for every type V and reducibility candidate S of this type, $t[V] \in RED_W[\vec{R}/\vec{U}, S/Y]$

Lemma 14 Universal abstraction. *If for every type V and candidate S, $RED_W[\vec{R}/\vec{X}, S/Y]$ is a reducibility candidate and $v[V/Y] \in RED_W[\vec{R}/\vec{X}, S/Y]$, then $\Lambda Y.v \in RED_{\forall Y.W}[\vec{R}/\vec{X}]$*

Proof. We need to show that $(\Lambda Y.v)[V] \in RED_W[\vec{R}/\vec{X}, S/Y]$ for every type V and candidate S of type V. We can argue by induction on $\nu(v)$, because v is strongly normalizable as $v = v[Y/Y]$ is in $RED_W[\vec{R}/\vec{X}, SN_Y/Y]$, which is a reducibility candidate by hypothesis. Since $(\Lambda Y.v)[V]$ is neutral, we will use CR3 for $RED_W[\vec{R}/\vec{X}, S/Y]$.

Converting a redex of $(\Lambda Y.v)[V]$ without using basic expansions can yield:

- $v[V/Y]$, which is in $RED_W[\vec{R}/\vec{X}, S/Y]$ by hypothesis
- $(\Lambda Y.v')[V]$ with v' one step from v; now, $v[V/Y]$ reduces to $v'[V/Y]$[3], so we can apply induction on $\nu(v)$ and get $(\Lambda Y.v')[V] \in RED_W[\vec{R}/\vec{X}, S/Y]$

The results follows then by CR3 for $RED_W[\vec{R}/\vec{X}]$.

In the following lemma we will talk about *subtypes* of a given type, where the subtypes of $A \to B$ are given by $A \to B$ itself together with the subtypes of A and B, and similarly for $A \times B$, while the subtypes of $\forall X.A$ are given by $\forall X.A$ itself together with the subtypes of A. This notion also provide a natural order over types.

Lemma 15 Abstraction.
Let $x : U$ and $v : V$, and suppose that $RED_W[\vec{R}/\vec{X}]$ is a reducibility candidate for all W subtypes of U or V (inclusive). If for all $u \in RED_U[\vec{R}/\vec{X}]$ we have $v[u/x] \in RED_V[\vec{R}/\vec{X}]$, then $\lambda x.v \in RED_{U \to V}[\vec{R}/\vec{X}]$

Proof. Assume the property is true for all subtypes of U and V.

To show that $\lambda x.v \in RED_{U \to V}[\vec{R}/\vec{X}]$, we need to show that $(\lambda x.v)u \in RED_V[\vec{R}/\vec{X}]$ for all $u \in RED_U[\vec{R}/\vec{X}]$, and we will do so by using CR3 for $RED_V[\vec{R}/\vec{X}]$.

We know that $x : U$ is in $RED_U[\vec{R}/\vec{X}]$ (remark 4.1).

So $v = v[x/x]$ is in $RED_V[\vec{R}/\vec{X}]$, hence strongly normalizable by CR1 and we can argue by induction on $\nu(u) + \nu(v)$ to show that all terms one step from $(\lambda x.v)u$ are reducible.

The term $(\lambda x.v)u$ converts to

[3] Since type substitution does not alter the structure of a term, we can perform on $v[V/Y]$ all the reductions we could perform on v, or maybe more as new expansion redexes can arise, but surely not less.

- $v[u/x]$ that is in $RED_V[\vec{R}/\vec{X}]$ by hypothesis.

- $(\lambda x.v')u$ with v' one step from v. To apply the induction hypothesis using the fact that $\nu(v') < \nu(v)$, and get $(\lambda x.v')u \in RED_V[\vec{R}/\vec{X}]$, we need to show now that $v'[u/x]$ is in $RED_V[\vec{R}/\vec{X}]$. If $v'[u/x]$ is one step from $v[u/x]$, then this comes from CR2 for $RED_V[\vec{R}/\vec{X}]$.

  If $v'[u/x]$ is not one step from $v[u/x]$, then v' is obtained from v by an expansion of an occurrence of x and u is either a pair, a λ-abstraction or a type abstraction. Notice now that if u is a pair, $\langle\pi_1(u), \pi_2(u)\rangle$ is reducible by Lemma 11; if u is an abstraction of type $U = C \to D$ then by definition of $u \in RED_U[\vec{R}/\vec{X}]$, $ut \in RED_D[\vec{R}/\vec{X}]$ for all $t \in RED_C[\vec{R}/\vec{X}]$, and by induction hypothesis on the type we have that $\lambda y.uy \in RED_{C\to D}[\vec{R}/\vec{X}]$; finally, if u is a type abstraction of type $U = \forall X.W$, then by definition of $u \in RED_U[\vec{R}/\vec{X}]$, for every type V and reducibility candidate S of this type, $u[X][V/X] = u[V] \in RED_W[\vec{R}/\vec{U}, S/Y]$, which is a reducibiblity candidate by hypothesis, so we have that $\Lambda X.u[X] \in RED_{\forall X.D}[\vec{R}/\vec{X}]$ by lemma 14.
  Let us now use $\eta(u)$ for either $\langle\pi_1(u), \pi_2(u)\rangle$ with u a pair or $\lambda y.uy$ with u a λ-abstraction or $\Lambda X.u[X]$ with u a type abstraction. What we have just shown means that by hypothesis $v[\eta(u)/x] \in RED_V[\vec{R}/\vec{X}]$, but it is straightforward to see that $\eta(u) \twoheadrightarrow u$, so we can build a reduction sequence $v[\eta(u)/x] \twoheadrightarrow v'[u/x]$, and then use repeatedly CR2 for $RED_V[\vec{R}/\vec{X}]$ to deduce $v'[u/x] \in RED_V[\vec{R}/\vec{X}]$, as neeeded.
- $(\lambda x.v)u'$ with u' one step from u. Then $u' \in RED_U[\vec{R}/\vec{X}]$ by CR2, $\nu(u') < \nu(u)$ and $v[u'/x] \in RED_V[\vec{R}/\vec{X}]$ by repeated applications of CR2, as it is some steps from v[u/x]. So we can apply again the induction hypothesis.

Since $(\lambda x.v)u$ is neutral and it converts to terms in $RED_V[\vec{R}/\vec{X}]$ only, it is in $RED_V[\vec{R}/\vec{X}]$ too. Hence $\lambda x.v$ is in $RED_{U\to V}[\vec{R}/\vec{X}]$ by definition.

Theorem 16. *$RED_T[\vec{R}/\vec{X}]$ is a reducibility candidate of type $T[\vec{U}/\vec{X}]$.*

Proof. We proceed by structural induction on the type T. We show only the cases for the arrow and universal types, which are the ones that change with expansions.

(Arrow types) Let T be $U_1 \to U_2$. We know by induction hypothesis that $RED_{U_1}[\vec{R}/\vec{X}]$, $RED_{U_2}[\vec{R}/\vec{X}]$ and in fact all $RED_W[\vec{R}/\vec{X}]$ for W subtype of the U_i, are reducibility candidates, and we will now show that $RED_{U_1\to U_2}[\vec{R}/\vec{X}] = RED_{U_1}[\vec{R}/\vec{X}] \to RED_{U_1}[\vec{R}/\vec{X}]$ is a reducibility candidate.

- (CR1) if $t \in RED_{U_1}[\vec{R}/\vec{X}] \to RED_{U_2}[\vec{R}/\vec{X}]$, then let x be a variable of type U_1. Since $x \in$ *any* reducibility candidate of type U_1, (remark 4.1), in particular $x \in RED_{U_1}[\vec{R}/\vec{X}]$ and we get that $(tx) \in RED_{U_2}[\vec{R}/\vec{X}]$ by definition, hence (tx) is strongly normalisable by CR1 for $RED_{U_2}[\vec{R}/\vec{X}]$, which is a reducibility candidate by induction hypothesis. This suffices to show that t is strongly normalisable, by lemma 10.

- (CR2) if $t \longrightarrow t'$, we need to show that $(t'u) \in RED_{U_2}[\vec{R}/\vec{X}]$ for all term $u \in RED_{U_1}[\vec{R}/\vec{X}]$. Take $u \in RED_{U_1}[\vec{R}/\vec{X}]$; we have $(tu) \in RED_{U_2}[\vec{R}/\vec{X}]$ by definition of reducibility candidate. If $(tu) \longrightarrow (t'u)$, then $(t'u) \in RED_{U_2}[\vec{R}/\vec{X}]$ by CR2 for $RED_{U_2}[\vec{R}/\vec{X}]$, which is a reducibility candidate by induction hypothesis. Otherwise, $t \longrightarrow \lambda x : U_1.tx$, but $(tu) = (tx)[u/x]$ is in $RED_{U_2}[\vec{R}/\vec{X}]$ for any $u \in RED_{U_1}[\vec{R}/\vec{X}]$ by induction hypothesis, so we can conclude by applying lemma 15.
- (CR3) t is neutral and all t' one step from t other than basic expansions are in $RED_{U_1}[\vec{R}/\vec{X}] \to RED_{U_2}[\vec{R}/\vec{X}]$. In order to show $t \in RED_{U_1}[\vec{R}/\vec{X}] \to RED_{U_2}[\vec{R}/\vec{X}]$, we need to show that $(tu) \in RED_{U_2}[\vec{R}/\vec{X}]$ for all term $u \in RED_{U_1}[\vec{R}/\vec{X}]$.
  By induction hypothesis on $RED_{U_1}[\vec{R}/\vec{X}]$, we get u is strongly normalisable, so we can argue by induction on $\nu(u)$.
  In one step, and without performing basic expansions, (tu) converts to:
  - $(t'u)$ with t' one step from t.
    As $t' \in RED_{U_1}[\vec{R}/\vec{X}] \to RED_{U_2}[\vec{R}/\vec{X}]$, we get $(t'u) \in RED_{U_2}[\vec{R}/\vec{X}]$ by definition.
  - (tu') with u' one step from u.
    By induction hypothesis on $RED_{U_1}[\vec{R}/\vec{X}]$, $u' \in RED_{U_1}[\vec{R}/\vec{X}]$ and $\nu(u') < \nu(u)$, so $(tu') \in RED_{U_2}[\vec{R}/\vec{X}]$ by the induction hypothesis on u.

(Universal types) Let $T = \forall Y.W$.

- (CR1) if $t \in RED_{\forall Y.W}[\vec{R}/\vec{X}]$, then let X be an arbitrary type variable and S be an arbitrary reducibility candidate of type X (for example, the strongly normalizable terms of type X). Then $t[X] \in RED_W[\vec{R}/\vec{X}, S/Y]$ by definition, so by induction hypothesis we know that $t[X]$ is strongly normalizable. Then we can conclude by lemma 10 that t is strongly normalisable.
- (CR2) let $t \longrightarrow t'$; for all types V and reducibility candidate S of this type, we have that $t[V] \in RED_W[\vec{R}/\vec{X}, S/Y]$, so if $t[V] \longrightarrow t'[V]$, then $t'[V] \in RED_W[\vec{R}/\vec{X}, S/Y]$ by induction hypothesis on W.
  Otherwise $t \longrightarrow \Lambda X.t[X] = t'$: we know by inductive hypothesis that for all types V and reducibility candidate S of this type $RED_W[\vec{R}/\vec{X}, S/Y]$ is a reducibility candidate and that $t[Y][V/Y] = t[V] \in RED_W[\vec{R}/\vec{X}, S/Y]$, so we can apply lemma 14 and we get $t' = \Lambda X.t[X] \in RED_{\forall Y.W}[\vec{R}/\vec{X}]$, and finally we get $t'[V] \in RED_W[\vec{R}/\vec{X}, S/Y]$ by definition.
  In any case, $t'[V] \in RED_W[\vec{R}/\vec{X}]$, so by definition $t' \in RED_{\forall Y.W}[\vec{R}/\vec{X}]$.
- (CR3) t is neutral and all t' one step from t other than basic expansions are in $RED_T[\vec{R}/\vec{X}]$. Take V and S: if we apply a conversion other than a basic

expansion to $t[V]$, the only possible result is $t'[V]$ (since t is neutral), and t' cannot be a basic expansion of t (because t is applied). Now, this means that t' is in $RED_T[\overrightarrow{R}/\overrightarrow{X}]$, so by definition $t'[V]$ is in $RED_W[\overrightarrow{R}/\overrightarrow{X}, S/Y]$, and by (CR3) for W we get that $t[V]$ is in $RED_W[\overrightarrow{R}/\overrightarrow{X}, S/Y]$, so we can conclude that $t \in RED_T[\overrightarrow{R}/\overrightarrow{X}]$.

We shall need now one more lemma to deduce reducibility of a term from reducibility of its subterms.

Lemma 17. $RED_{T[V/Y]}[\overrightarrow{R}/\overrightarrow{X}] = RED_T[\overrightarrow{R}/\overrightarrow{X}, RED_V[\overrightarrow{R}/\overrightarrow{X}]/Y]$

Proof. By induction on T.

Lemma 18 Universal application.
If $t \in RED_{\forall Y.W}[\overrightarrow{R}/\overrightarrow{X}]$, *then* $t[V] \in RED_{W[V/Y]}[\overrightarrow{R}/\overrightarrow{X}]$ *for every type* V.

Proof. By hypothesis, $t[V] \in RED_W[\overrightarrow{R}/\overrightarrow{X}, S/Y]$ for every candidate S of type V. Taking $S = RED_V[\overrightarrow{R}/\overrightarrow{X}]$, the result follows by lemma 17.

The reducibility theorem

As in [GLT90], we say here that a term t of type T is *reducible* if it is in $RED_T[\overrightarrow{SN}/\overrightarrow{X}]$, where $\overrightarrow{X}$ are the free type variables of T and SN_i is the set of strongly normalizable terms of type X_i.
In the proof of the theorem, there is the need of a stronger induction hypothesis, from which the strong normalization follows by putting $u_i = x_i$ and $R_i = SN_i$.

Proposition 19. *Let* $t : T$ *be any term, whose free variables are contained in* $x_1 : U_1, \ldots, x_n : U_n$, *and all the free variable of* T, U_1, $\ldots U_n$ *are among* X_1, $\ldots X_m$. *If* R_1, $\ldots R_m$ *are reducibility candidates of types* V_1, $\ldots V_m$, *and* u_1, $\ldots u_m$ *are terms of types* $U_1[\overrightarrow{V}/\overrightarrow{X}]$, $\ldots U_m[\overrightarrow{V}/\overrightarrow{X}]$ *which are in* $RED_{U_1}[\overrightarrow{R}/\overrightarrow{X}]$, $\ldots RED_{U_n}[\overrightarrow{R}/\overrightarrow{X}]$, *then* $t[\overrightarrow{V}/\overrightarrow{X}][\overrightarrow{u}/\overrightarrow{x}] \in RED_T[\overrightarrow{R}/\overrightarrow{X}]$.

Proof. By induction on t as usual.

Theorem 20. $\overset{\beta^2\eta^2\pi *}{\longrightarrow}$ *is strongly normalizing.*

Proof. Let t be any term, and U be its type. All its free variables are in any reducibility candidate by remark 4.1, so that $t = t[\overrightarrow{X}/\overrightarrow{X}][x_1/x_1, \ldots, x_n/x_n] \in RED_{U[\overrightarrow{X}/\overrightarrow{X}]}[\overrightarrow{SN}/\overrightarrow{X}]$ by the previous lemma. Then it is strongly normalizing by CR1.

5 Adding the Top type *modularly*

It is possible to extend the previous reducibility proof to take into account also the special *unit* type T and the Top rule

$$M : T \longrightarrow * : T \qquad (\text{if } M \not\equiv *)$$

that one needs for various systems (see [CDC91], for a discussion of the motivation for the Top rule), but that would not be a wise approach to this rule: indeed, its great simplicity will allow to add it modularly to a given canonical system, without any need to go again through a long proof involving the rest of the calculus.

Without going into much formal details, we want to give here a very simple argument of general applicability that shows how Top preserves strong normalization of left linear reduction relations, and hence also confluence under some additional assumptions. We are quite informal here about the meaning of left linearity for a reduction relation, but this notion can be formalized properly once one choses an appropriate framework for describing the reduction relation (like for example the Combnatory Reduction Systems).

Proposition 21 Preservation of Strong Normalization with Top. *Given a strongly normalizing left-linear reduction relation R, generated by rules that do not contain the special term $*$ in their left hand side, then $R + Top$ is still strongly normalizing.*

Proof. The argument of the proof is indeed very simple: take any infinite reduction Π in $R + Top$, and notice that (since Top alone is clearly strongly normalizing) this reduction must contain infinite R steps. Now, one can easily build an infinite reduction in R alone by using the infinite number of R steps from the Π reduction: it suffices to remark that any Top reduction step followed by an R reduction step in Π $C[M] \xrightarrow{Top} C[*] \xrightarrow{R} M'$ can be postponed as in $C[M] \xrightarrow{R} M'' \xrightarrow{Top}{}^{*} M'$, as the rules on R are left-linear and do not transform $*$ (basically, rules in R can only pass $*$ around untouched, or delete it).

Clearly, if R is also confluent, and Top does not break local confluence, then, as an easy corollary of Newman's Lemma, $R + Top$ is also confluent.

It is then quite immediate to derive the following

Corollary 22. *The second order lambda calculus with expansive rules for products, arrow and universal types, and the Top rule is strongly normalizing and confluent.*

6 Conclusions and future work

We explained why expansion rules and the second order β rule cannot be handled separately in a modular way and we showed how to handle them together by a careful restructuration of the usual reducibility candidate method. This work suggests that the expansionary approach to extensional rules is viable even in a second order context, and is a firm step towards a redesign of the extensional rules in more complex systems like Fω or the Calculus of Constructions. Expansion rules behave better than contractions in the presence of additional axioms (like the one for *unit* or for a fixpoint combinator) and give a natural characterization of the notion of η-long normal forms.

Finally, we would like to suggest that the use of expansion rules for extensional equalities is very promising in order to improve the modularity results on the combination of the lambda calculus with first or higher order algebraic rewriting systems (presented for example in [BTM86, BT88, BTG94] and [JO91]): these works use the traditional contractive interpretation of η, and cannot handle higher order rewrite rules like the one given above for the *unit* type, while such rule is not problematic at all in the presence of expansion rules.

Acknowledgements

We are endebted to Neil Ghani for the fundamental remark that we only need the set of strongly normalizing terms of basic types for the proof to go through.

References

[Aka93] Yohji Akama. On Mints' reductions for ccc-Calculus. In *Typed Lambda Calculus and Applications*, number 664 in LNCS, pages 1–12. Springer Verlag, 1993.

[Bar84] Henk Barendregt. *The Lambda Calculus; Its syntax and Semantics (revised edition)*. North Holland, 1984.

[BT88] Val Breazu-Tannen. Combining algebra and higher-order types. In *Proceedings, Third Annual Symposium on Logic in Computer Science*, pages 82–90, Edinburgh, Scotland, July 5–8 1988. IEEE Computer Society.

[BTG94] Val Breazu-Tannen and Jean Gallier. Polymorphic rewiting preserves algebraic confluence. *Information and Computation*, 114:1–29, 1994.

[BTM86] Val Breazu-Tannen and Albert R. Meyer. Polymorphism is conservative over simple types (preliminary report). In *Proceedings, Symposium on Logic in Computer Science*, pages 7–17, Cambridge, Massachusetts, June 16–18 1986. IEEE Computer Society.

[CDC91] Pierre-Louis Curien and Roberto Di Cosmo. A confluent reduction system for the λ-calculus with surjective pairing and terminal object. In Leach, Monien, and Artalejo, editors, *Intern. Conf. on Automata, Languages and Programming (ICALP)*, volume 510 of *Lecture Notes in Computer Science*, pages 291–302. Springer-Verlag, July 1991.

[Cub92] Djordje Cubric. On free CCC. Distributed on the **types** mailing list, 1992.

[DCK94a] Roberto Di Cosmo and Delia Kesner. Combining first order algebraic rewriting systems, recursion and extensional lambda calculi. In Serge Abiteboul and Eli Shamir, editors, *Intern. Conf. on Automata, Languages and Programming (ICALP)*, volume 820 of *Lecture Notes in Computer Science*, pages 462–472. Springer-Verlag, July 1994.

[DCK94b] Roberto Di Cosmo and Delia Kesner. Simulating expansions without expansions. *Mathematical Structures in Computer Science*, 4:1–48, 1994. A preliminary version is available as Technical Report LIENS-93-11/INRIA 1911.

[DCP95] Roberto Di Cosmo and Adolfo Piperno. Expanding extensional polymorphism. In Mariangiola Dezani-Ciancaglini and Gordon Plotkin, editors, *Typed Lambda Calculus and Applications*, volume 902 of *Lecture Notes in Computer Science*, pages 139–153, April 1995.

[Dou93] Daniel J. Dougherty. Some lambda calculi with categorical sums and products. In *Proc. of the Fifth International Conference on Rewriting Techniques and Applications (RTA)*, 1993.

[Ges90] Alfons Geser. *Relative termination*. Dissertation, Fakultät für Mathematik und Informatik, Universität Passau, Germany, 1990. Also available as: Report 91-03, Ulmer Informatik-Berichte, Universität Ulm, 1991.

[Geu92] Herman Geuvers. The church-rosser property for $\beta\eta$-reduction in typed λ-calculi. In *7thProceedings of the Symposium on Logic in Computer Science (LICS)*, pages 453–460, 1992.

[Gha95] Neil Ghani. Extensionality and polymorphism. University of Edimburgh, Submitted, 1995.

[GLT90] Jean-Yves Girard, Yves Lafont, and Paul Taylor. *Proofs and Types*. Cambridge University Press, 1990.

[Jay92] Colin Barry Jay. Long $\beta\eta$ normal forms and confluence (revised). Technical Report 44, LFCS - University of Edinburgh, August 1992.

[JG92] Colin Barry Jay and Neil Ghani. The Virtues of Eta-expansion. Technical Report ECS-LFCS-92-243, LFCS, 1992. University of Edimburgh, preliminary version of [JG95].

[JG95] Colin Barry Jay and Neil Ghani. The Virtues of Eta-expansion. *Journal of Functional Programming*, 5(2):135–154, April 1995.

[JO91] Jean-Pierre Jouannaud and Mitsuhiro Okada. A computation model for executable higher-order algebraic specification languages. In *Proceedings, Sixth Annual IEEE Symposium on Logic in Computer Science*, pages 350–361, Amsterdam, The Netherlands, July 15–18 1991. IEEE Computer Society Press.

[Klo80] Jan Willem Klop. Combinatory reduction systems. *Mathematical Center Tracts*, 27, 1980.

[Nip90] Tobias Nipkow. A critical pair lemma for higher-order rewrite systems and its application to λ^*. *First Annual Workshop on Logical Frameworks*, 1990.

A Strong normalization

Theorem 12 *If R_1 and R_2 are reducibility candidates of types U_1 and U_2, then $R_1 \times R_2$ is a reducibility candidate of type $U_1 \times U_2$.*

Proof. Assume that R_1 and R_2 are reducibility candidates of type U_1 and U_2, respectively.

- (CR1) if $t \in R_1 \times R_2$, then $\pi_i(t)$ is strongly normalisable by the hypothesis on R_i, since $\pi_i(t) \in R_i$ by definition. Hence t is strongly normalisable by lemma 10.

- (CR2) if $t \longrightarrow t'$ not via a basic expansion, then $\pi_1(t) \longrightarrow \pi_1(t')$ and $\pi_2(t) \longrightarrow \pi_2(t')$.
  As $t \in R_1 \times R_2$, then $\pi_1(t) \in R_1$ and $\pi_2(t) \in R_2$. By hypothesis CR2 for R_1 and R_2 we get $\pi_1(t') \in R_1$ and $\pi_2(t') \in R_2$, hence, by definition, $t' \in R_1 \times R_2$.
  In the case $t \longrightarrow \langle \pi_1(t), \pi_2(t) \rangle$, we must prove that $\pi_i \langle \pi_1(t), \pi_2(t) \rangle \in R_i$. By definition of $R_1 \times R_2$, $\pi_1(t)$ is in R_1 and $\pi_2(t)$ is in R_2, so we can apply lemma 11.
- (CR3) t is neutral and every t' one step from t other than basic expansions are in $R_1 \times R_2$.
  We need to show $\pi_1(t) \in R_1$ and $\pi_2(t) \in R_2$.
  Now notice that applying a one step reduction to $\pi_i(t)$ which is not a basic expansion can only result in some $\pi_i(t')$ as t is neutral. Furthermore, this t' is not a basic expansion of t because it is in an influential position. So, t' is in $R_1 \times R_2$, and then by definition $\pi_1(t') \in R_1$ and $\pi_2(t') \in R_2$. Since the $\pi_i(t)$ are neutral and every term one step from them other than basic expansions is in R_i, the hypothesis for R_1 and R_2 ensure $\pi_1(t) \in R_1$ and $\pi_2(t) \in R_2$. So $t \in R_1 \times R_2$ by definition.

Languages and Logical Definability in Concurrency Monoids*

Manfred Droste and Dietrich Kuske

Abteilung Mathematik, Technische Universität Dresden, D–01062 Dresden, Germany,
E-mail: {droste,kuske}@math.tu-dresden.de

Abstract. Automata with concurrency relations $\mathcal{A}$ are labeled transition systems with a collection of binary relations describing when two actions in a given state of the automaton can occur independently of each other. The concurrency monoid $\mathrm{M}(\mathcal{A})$ comprises all finite computation sequences of $\mathcal{A}$, modulo a canonical congruence induced by the concurrency relations, with composition as monoid operation; its elements can be represented by labeled partially ordered sets. Under suitable assumptions on $\mathcal{A}$, we show that a language L in $\mathrm{M}(\mathcal{A})$ is recognizable iff it is definable by a formula of monadic second order logic. We also investigate the relationship between aperiodic and first-order definable languages in $\mathrm{M}(\mathcal{A})$. This generalizes various recent results in trace theory.

1 Introduction

In the literature, classical logical definability results of recognizable word languages (Büchi [Bü60]) and aperiodic or starfree languages (McNaughton and Papert [MP71]) have been generalized in various directions, including tree languages (*cf.*, *e.g.*, [T90a]) and, recently, languages in trace monoids. For the latter, in particular, it was shown that a trace language is recognizable iff it is definable by a sentence of monadic second order logic ([T90b]), and it is aperiodic iff it is starfree ([GRS92]) iff it is definable by a first-order sentence ([T90b], *cf.* [EM93]). It is the aim of this paper to extend these results to large classes of even more general monoids, called concurrency monoids.

Trace theory (*cf.* [AR88, Di90, DR95] for surveys) provides a mathematical model for the sequential behaviour of a parallel system in which the order of two independent actions is regarded as irrelevant; one considers a set E of actions together with a single binary relation representing the concurrency of two actions. Here, we will consider a more general model consisting of labeled transition systems in which the concurrency relation depends not only on the two arriving actions, but also on the present state of the system. An *automaton with concurrency relations* is a tuple $\mathcal{A} = (Q, E, T, \|)$ where Q is the set of states, E as before the set of events or actions, $T \subseteq Q \times E \times Q$ the transition relation (assumed deterministic), and $\| = (\|_q)_{q \in Q}$ is a collection of concurrency relations $\|_q$ for E, indexed by the possible states $q \in Q$. Similarly as in trace theory, we declare two sequences $(p, a, q)(q, b, r)$ and $(p, b, q')(q', a, r)$ equivalent, if $a \|_p b$. This induces

* Research supported by the German Research Foundation (DFG)

a congruence $\sim$ on the set $\mathrm{CS}(\mathcal{A})$ of all finite computation sequences; thus, intuitively, two computation sequences are equivalent, if they represent "interleaved views" of a single computation. The quotient $\mathrm{M}(\mathcal{A}) = \mathrm{CS}(\mathcal{A}) /\!\sim \cup \{0\}$ is called the *concurrency monoid associated with* $\mathcal{A}$.

Automata with concurrency relations were introduced and studied in [Dr90, Dr92, BD93, BD94]. Their domains of computation sequences are closely related with event domains and dI–domains arising in denotational semantics of programming languages. These automata also generalize asynchronous transition systems ([Sh85, Be87, WN94]). Very recently, a formalization using several independence relations of the operational semantics of Occam was given in [BR94].

Generalizing results of [Oc85, GRS92] in trace theory, a Kleene-type characterization of the recognizable languages in concurrency monoids $\mathrm{M}(\mathcal{A})$ has been given in [Dr94a], and aperiodic and starfree languages were investigated in [Dr94b]. In [BDK96, BDK95], it was shown how to represent elements of $\mathrm{M}(\mathcal{A})$ by certain labeled graphs, or labeled partially ordered sets. There is a multiplication of (isomorphism classes of) such graphs, yielding a monoid which turns out to be isomorphic to the concurrency monoid $\mathrm{M}(\mathcal{A})$. Therefore here we will identify elements of $\mathrm{M}(\mathcal{A})$ with their graph-theoretical representation. The partial order defined on the enumerated occurrences of actions in a computation denotes that a "smaller" event has to occur before a "larger" one, or, in other words, is a necessary condition for the larger event. Here, we introduce logical languages that allow us to make statements on causal dependencies of events and on the initial state of a computation. Because of the representation of computations we can use the canonical logical languages for labeled partial orders. The satisfaction relation is defined via the representation of a computation by a labeled partially ordered set. We let MSO be the corresponding monadic second order language. For the subsequent results, a useful (and almost necessary) assumption is that $\mathcal{A}$ is stably concurrent (see Def. 4). This means that the concurrency relations of $\mathcal{A}$ depend locally (but not globally) on each other. We will show

Theorem 1. *Let $\mathcal{A}$ be a finite stably concurrent automaton and $L \subseteq \mathrm{M}(\mathcal{A})$. Then L is recognizable if and only if it is definable in* MSO.

Next we turn to aperiodic, starfree and first-order definable languages in $\mathrm{M}(\mathcal{A})$. Aperiodic languages are starfree, and the converse was derived in [Dr94b] for a large class of stably concurrent automata $\mathcal{A}$ (it fails in general). Here, we obtain the following; for undefined notions we refer the reader to Sect. 5.

Theorem 2. *Let $\mathcal{A}$ be a finite stably concurrent automaton.*
(a) If $\mathcal{A}$ is counter free, then each aperiodic language in $\mathrm{M}(\mathcal{A})$ is first-order definable.
(b) If $\mathcal{A}$ has no commuting loops or is an automaton with global independence, then each first-order definable language in $\mathrm{M}(\mathcal{A})$ is aperiodic.

Examples show that neither in (a) nor in (b) the additional assumptions on $\mathcal{A}$ can be omitted. However, there are large classes of stably concurrent automata satisfying these various assumptions, or even their conjunctions, and these theorems contain the corresponding results from trace theory as a special case. Counter free automata have been well studied in the literature, *cf.* [MP71]. We note that in an automaton with global independence the concurrency of actions can be described by a single binary relation. These automata are only slight variants of the full trace automata and the asynchronous transition systems of Bednarczyk ([Be87]) and Shields ([Sh85]) and generalize trace alphabets; also, see *e.g.* [S89a, S89b, BCS93, WN94] for further results on this well-studied class of automata. Even in this class, there are proper inclusions between the classes of first-order definable and aperiodic, and between aperiodic and starfree languages. As shown in [Dr94b], in an automaton without commuting loops the aperiodic languages are precisely the starfree ones. However, these automata are complementary to trace alphabets.

The proofs of Thms. 1 and 2 rest on a detailed analysis of the partial order structure of the representation of elements of $M(\mathcal{A})$ as well as on Büchi's and McNaughton and Papert's classical results for (finite) words; the use of particular accepting devices sometimes employed in the trace theoretic setting (*e.g.* asynchronous automata in [T90b]) is avoided. An extension of the present results to monadically definable languages of infinite computations of stably concurrent automata has recently been achieved in [DK96].

2 Preliminaries

Definition 3. An *automaton with concurrency relations* is a quadruple $\mathcal{A} = (Q, E, T, \|)$ such that

1. Q and E are finite sets of *states* and *events* or *actions*, respectively.
2. $T \subseteq Q \times E \times Q$ is a set of *transitions* assumed deterministic, *i.e.* whenever $(p, a, q), (p, a, r) \in T$, then $q = r$.
3. $\| = (\|_q)_{q \in Q}$ is a collection of irreflexive, symmetric binary relations on E; it is required that whenever $a \|_p b$, then there exist transitions (p, a, q), (p, b, q'), (q, b, r) and (q', a, r) in T.

Note that we consider only *finite* automata $\mathcal{A}$. A transition $\tau = (p, a, q)$ intuitively represents a potential computation step in which event a happens in state p of $\mathcal{A}$ and $\mathcal{A}$ changes from state p to state q. We write $\text{ev}(\tau) = a$, the event of τ. The concurrency relations $\|_p$ describe the concurrency information for pairs of events at state p. The last requirement can be seen as in the diagram:

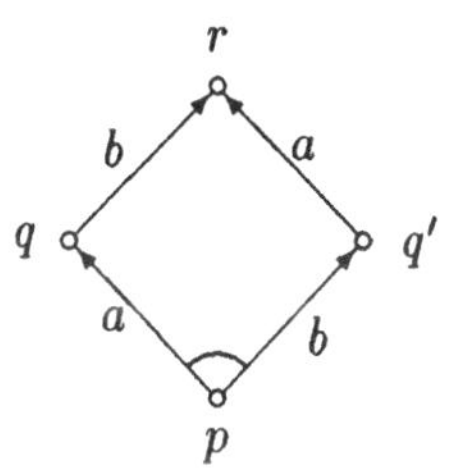

The angle at p indicates that $a \parallel_p b$ holds.

A *computation sequence* in $\mathcal{A}$ is either empty (denoted by ϵ), or a finite sequence $\gamma = \sigma_1 \ldots \sigma_n$ of transitions σ_i of the form $\sigma_i = (q_{i-1}, a_i, q_i)$ for $i = 1 \ldots n$; it can be depicted as

$$q_0 \xrightarrow{a_1} q_1 \xrightarrow{a_2} \ldots \xrightarrow{a_n} q_n.$$

We call q_0 the *domain* of γ, denoted by $\operatorname{dom}\gamma$, q_n the *codomain*, denoted by $\operatorname{cod}\gamma$, and n the length $|\gamma|$ of γ. The sequence $a_1 a_2 \ldots a_n$ is called *event sequence of* γ, denoted by $\operatorname{evseq}\gamma$. Also, for $w \in E^\star$ and $q \in Q$, we write $q.w = r$ if there exists a computation sequence γ with $\operatorname{dom}\gamma = q$, $\operatorname{evseq}\gamma = w$ and $\operatorname{cod}\gamma = r$. Otherwise, $q.w$ is undefined. We let $\mathrm{CS}(\mathcal{A})$ denote the set of all computation sequences of $\mathcal{A}$. The *composition* $\gamma\delta$ is defined in the natural way by concatenating γ and δ if $\operatorname{cod}\gamma = \operatorname{dom}\delta$. Formally we put $\gamma\epsilon = \epsilon\gamma = \gamma$.

Now we want the concurrency relations of $\mathcal{A}$ to induce an equivalence relation on $\mathrm{CS}(\mathcal{A})$ so that equivalent computation sequences are not differentiated by the order in which concurrent events appear. For this, we let $\sim$ be the smallest congruence with respect to composition on $\mathrm{CS}(\mathcal{A})$ making all computation sequences $p \xrightarrow{a} q \xrightarrow{b} r$ and $p \xrightarrow{b} q' \xrightarrow{a} r$ with $a \parallel_p b$ equivalent. We let $[\gamma]$ denote the equivalence class of γ with respect to $\sim$. Also, we let $1 := [\epsilon]$. Defining $\mathrm{M}(\mathcal{A}) = \mathrm{CS}(\mathcal{A}) /\!\sim \cup \{0\}$, we now obtain the *monoid* $\mathrm{M}(\mathcal{A})$ *of computations associated with* $\mathcal{A}$, where 0 is an additional symbol. That is, for $\gamma, \delta \in \mathrm{CS}(\mathcal{A})$ we have $[\gamma] \cdot [\delta] = [\gamma\delta]$ if $\operatorname{cod}\gamma = \operatorname{dom}\delta$ and $[\gamma] \cdot [\delta] = 0$ otherwise. Also, $x \cdot 0 = 0 \cdot x = 0$ and $x \cdot 1 = 1 \cdot x = x$ for any $x \in \mathrm{M}(\mathcal{A})$. Clearly, with this operation $\mathrm{M}(\mathcal{A})$ is a monoid with 1 as unit (and with 0 as zero).

Next we show why these automata and their monoids provide a generalization of trace alphabets and trace monoids. A trace alphabet [Ma77, Ma86, Ma88] is a pair (E, D) where E is a nonempty finite set and $D \subseteq E \times E$ a reflexive, symmetric dependence relations on E. The congruence with respect to (E, D) on the free monoid $E^\star$ is the smallest congruence $\sim$ that identifies ab and ba whenever $(a, b) \notin D$. Then $\mathcal{A} = (Q, E, T, \|)$ with $Q = \{q\}$, $T = Q \times E \times Q$ and $\parallel_q = (E \times E) \setminus D$ is an automaton with concurrency relations. This automaton will be called *automaton induced by* (E, D). Obviously, $\operatorname{evseq} : \mathrm{CS}(\mathcal{A}) \longrightarrow E^\star$ is a bijection. Moreover, for $\gamma, \delta \in \mathrm{CS}(\mathcal{A})$ we have $\gamma \sim \delta$ iff $\operatorname{evseq}\gamma \sim \operatorname{evseq}\delta$ with respect to (E, D). Hence, evseq induces a monoid-isomorphism from $\mathrm{M}(\mathcal{A}) \setminus \{0\}$ onto $M(E, D)$. Thus, automata with concurrency relations generalize trace alphabets.

Here, we will investigate recognizable and aperiodic languages in $\mathrm{M}(\mathcal{A})$. A language $L \subseteq \mathrm{M}(\mathcal{A})$ is *recognizable* if there exists a finite $\mathrm{M}(\mathcal{A})$-automaton that recognizes L, or, equivalently, if there are only finitely many sets $x^{-1}L := \{y \in \mathrm{M}(\mathcal{A}) \mid x \cdot y \in L\}$ $(x \in \mathrm{M}(\mathcal{A}))$. Furthermore, a recognizable language $L \subseteq \mathrm{M}(\mathcal{A})$ is *aperiodic* if there exists $n \in \mathbb{N}$ such that $x \cdot y^n \cdot z \in L$ iff $x \cdot y^{n+1} \cdot z \in L$ for any $x, y, z \in \mathrm{M}(\mathcal{A})$. The smallest natural number n that meets this requirement is the *index* of L.

Now we recall basic definitions, constructions and results from [BDK95, BDK96].

Let $\mathcal{A}$ be an automaton with concurrency relations, and let $\gamma \in \mathrm{CS}(\mathcal{A})$. Analogously to trace theory we define a dependence order on those events that appear in γ. This order should reflect that a "smaller" event has to appear before a "larger" one, i.e. the "smaller" event is a necessary condition for the "larger" one. If two events are incomparable they can appear in any order or even in parallel. Since an event a can appear several times in γ we have to distinguish between the first, the second, ... appearance of a. For $a \in E$ let $|\gamma|_a$ denote the number of transitions σ in γ with $\mathrm{ev}\,\sigma = a$, i.e. the number of a's in the word $\mathrm{evseq}\,\gamma \in E^\star$. We abbreviate $a^i = (a,i)$ for $a \in E$ and $i \in \mathbb{N}$. The precise definition of the dependence order of γ can now be given as follows. Let $\mathrm{O}(\gamma) = \{a^i \mid a \in \mathrm{ev}\,\gamma,\ 1 \le i \le |\gamma|_a\}$. Then, obviously, $|\mathrm{O}(\gamma)| = |\gamma|$. For $a^i, b^j \in \mathrm{O}(\gamma)$ let $a^i \sqsubseteq_\gamma b^j$ iff the i-th appearance of a in γ occurs before the j-th appearance of b, i.e., formally, there are words $u, v, w \in E^\star$ with $\mathrm{evseq}\,\gamma = uavbw$, $|u|_a = i - 1$ and $|uav|_b = j - 1$. Then $\sqsubseteq_\gamma$ is a linear order on $\mathrm{O}(\gamma)$. Since for equivalent computation sequences γ and δ we always have $\mathrm{O}(\gamma) = \mathrm{O}(\delta)$, a partial order on $\mathrm{O}(\gamma)$ can be defined by:

$$\sqsubseteq := \bigcap \{\sqsubseteq_\delta \mid \delta \sim \gamma\}.$$

Hence, $a^i \sqsubseteq b^j$ if and only if the i-th a appears before the j-th b in *any* computation sequence equivalent with γ. For $a \in E$, let E_a comprise all elements of $\mathrm{O}(\gamma)$ of the form a^i. Then $\mathrm{DO}(\gamma) = (\mathrm{O}(\gamma), \sqsubseteq, (E_a)_{a \in E}, \mathrm{dom}\,\gamma)$ is a relational structure with one constant from Q. We call $\mathrm{DO}(\gamma)$ the *dependence order associated with* γ. A sequence $A = (x_1, x_2, \ldots, x_n)$ with $x_i \in \mathrm{O}(\gamma)$ is an *order-preserving enumeration of* $\mathrm{DO}(\gamma)$ if it is an enumeration of $\mathrm{O}(\gamma)$ and $x_i \sqsubseteq x_j$ implies $i \le j$. Then a computation sequence δ is the *linearisation of* $\mathrm{DO}(\gamma)$ *induced by* A if $\mathrm{dom}\,\gamma = \mathrm{dom}\,\delta$ and $\mathrm{evseq}\,\delta = a_1 a_2 \ldots a_n$ with $x_i \in E_{a_i}$ for $i = 1, 2, \ldots, n$. There may exist order-preserving enumerations of $\mathrm{DO}(\gamma)$ that do not induce any linearisation. But, since $\mathcal{A}$ is deterministic, any order-preserving enumeration induces at most one linearisation. We call δ *a linearisation of* $\mathrm{DO}(\gamma)$ if it is the linearisation induced by some order-preserving enumeration. Let $\mathrm{Lin}\,\mathrm{DO}(\gamma)$ comprise all linearisations of $\mathrm{DO}(\gamma)$. Then it is easy to see that $[\gamma] \subseteq \mathrm{Lin}\,\mathrm{DO}(\gamma)$ for any automaton with concurrency relations (*cf.* [BDK96, BDK95]). To prove the converse of this inclusion, we need further assumptions on the underlying automaton:

Definition 4. Let $\mathcal{A}$ be an automaton with concurrency relations. $\mathcal{A}$ is called *stably concurrent automaton*, if for all $q \in Q$ and all $a, b, c \in E$ the following equivalence holds:

$$a \parallel_q b,\ b \parallel_q c \text{ and } a \parallel_{q.b} c \iff a \parallel_q c,\ b \parallel_{q.a} c \text{ and } a \parallel_{q.c} b$$

The equivalence in this definition is depicted by Fig. 1.

The requirement of the implication "$\Rightarrow$" has also been called cube axiom, and the implication "$\Leftarrow$" is called the inverse cube axiom. In various forms, these axioms arose several times in the literature, see *e.g.* [S89a, PSS90, Dr90, Dr92, Ku94a, Ku94b, Dr94a, Dr94b]. In [Dr94a, Dr94b] the recognizable and the aperiodic languages in $\mathrm{M}(\mathcal{A})$ for $\mathcal{A}$ stably concurrent have been characterized. In [Ku94b] it has been shown that stably concurrent automata precisely generate

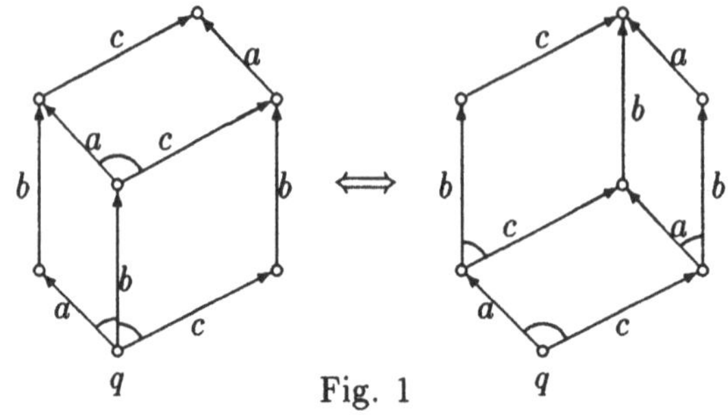

Fig. 1

dI-domains [Cu93] via their domains of finite and infinite computations. This distributivity is the basis for the proofs in [BDK96, BDK95]

Observe that the automaton induced by a trace alphabet is always stably concurrent.

Let $(P, \leq)$ be a partially ordered set and $x \in P$. Then $x\uparrow$ denotes the subset of P comprising all elements y with $x \leq y$. Similarly, $x\downarrow = \{y \in P \mid y \leq x\}$. A subset $M \subseteq P$ is *downward closed* iff $x\downarrow \subseteq M$ for each $x \in M$.

The following proposition is central in the proofs in [BDK96, BDK95] and will be used here, too. Let $\mathcal{A}$ be an automaton with concurrency relations, $\gamma \in \mathrm{CS}(\mathcal{A})$ and $M = \{a_1^{n_1}, a_2^{n_2}, \ldots, a_k^{n_k}\} \subseteq \mathrm{O}(\gamma)$ with $a_i^{n_i} \sqsubseteq_\gamma (a_{i+1})^{n_{i+1}}$. Then $\gamma(M)$ denotes the word $a_1 a_2 \ldots a_k \in E^\star$.

Proposition 5 [BDK96]. *Let $\mathcal{A}$ be a stably concurrent automaton and $\gamma \in \mathrm{CS}(\mathcal{A})$. Let $M \subseteq \mathrm{O}(\gamma)$ be downward closed in $(\mathrm{O}(\gamma), \sqsubseteq)$. Then $q = (\mathrm{dom}\,\gamma).\gamma(M)$ is defined. Suppose furthermore $x, y \in \mathrm{O}(\gamma)$ with $x \in E_a$, $y \in E_b$ and $(x\downarrow \cup y\downarrow) \setminus \{x, y\} \subseteq M \subseteq \mathrm{DO}(\gamma) \setminus (x\uparrow \cup y\uparrow)$ (where $\downarrow$ and $\uparrow$ are to be understood in $(\mathrm{O}(\gamma), \sqsubseteq)$). Then x and y are incomparable with respect to $\sqsubseteq$ if and only if $a \parallel_q b$.*

In [BDK95] the following is proved.

Theorem 6 [BDK95]. *Let $\mathcal{A}$ be a stably concurrent automaton and $\gamma \in \mathrm{CS}(\mathcal{A})$. Then $[\gamma] = \mathrm{Lin}(\mathrm{DO}(\gamma))$. Furthermore, any order-preserving enumeration of $\mathrm{DO}(\gamma)$ induces a linearisation of $\mathrm{DO}(\gamma)$.*

Hence, we have the following equivalences for a stably concurrent automaton $\mathcal{A}$ and computation sequences $\gamma, \delta \in \mathrm{CS}(\mathcal{A})$:

$$\mathrm{DO}(\gamma) = \mathrm{DO}(\delta) \iff \gamma \sim \delta \iff \delta \in \mathrm{Lin}(\mathrm{DO}(\gamma)).$$

This result enables us to represent computations, *i.e.* elements of $\mathrm{M}(\mathcal{A}) \setminus \{0, 1\}$, by dependence orders. To include 0 and 1, formally we put $\mathrm{dom}\,0 = \bot$ and $\mathrm{dom}\,1 = \top$ where $\bot$ and $\top$ are additional symbols not belonging to Q, and, using this, define $\mathrm{DO}(0)$ and $\mathrm{DO}(1)$ similarly as before. Since dependence orders are relational structures, we can define a logical language to describe properties of these dependence orders. The corresponding first-order language FO has variables $x, y, \ldots$ for elements of $\mathrm{O}(\gamma)$. The atomic formulas are $x \leq y$, $E_a(x)$ for

$a \in E$, and constants D_q for $q \in Q \cup \{\bot, \top\}$. Then formulas are built up from atomic formulas by the connectives $\neg$ and $\vee$ and the quantor $\exists$. In the monadic second-order language, also set variables $X, Y, \ldots$, quantification of them and atomic formulas $X(x)$ are admitted. Also, we will use several abbreviations like $x < y$, $x = y$, $\phi \to \psi$, $\forall x\, \phi$ etc. with the usual interpretation. Additionally, $x \parallel y$ stands for $\neg(x \leq y) \wedge \neg(y \leq x)$. This monadic second-order logic is denoted by MSO. A sentence of MSO is a formula without free variables. The satisfaction relation $\mathrm{DO}(\gamma) \models \phi$ between dependence orders and sentences is defined as usually: $x \leq y$ is satisfied iff $x \sqsubseteq y$, $E_a(x)$ iff x is of the form a^i, D_q iff $\operatorname{dom}\gamma = q$ and $X(x)$ iff $x \in X$. Now let ϕ be a sentence of MSO. Then $L(\phi)$ denotes the set of all $[\gamma] \in \mathrm{M}(\mathcal{A})$ such that $\mathrm{DO}(\gamma) \models \phi$. Since $\gamma \sim \delta$ implies $\mathrm{DO}(\gamma) = \mathrm{DO}(\delta)$, the language $L(\phi)$ is welldefined. For a language $L \subseteq \mathrm{M}(\mathcal{A})$ and a sentence ϕ of MSO, we say ϕ *defines* L if $L = L(\phi)$. The language L is *definable in* MSO if there exists a sentence ϕ in MSO that defines L. In the following two sections, we will prove the two implications of

Theorem 1. *Let $\mathcal{A}$ be a finite stably concurrent automaton and $L \subseteq \mathrm{M}(\mathcal{A})$. Then L is recognizable if and only if it is definable in* MSO.

Suppose, $\mathcal{A}$ is the automaton induced by the trace alphabet (E, D). Then the monoids $\mathrm{M}(\mathcal{A}) \setminus \{0\}$ and $M(E, D)$ are isomorphic. Hence, Thm. 1 generalizes the result of [T90b].

3 Definability implies recognizability

In all of this section *let $\mathcal{A}$ be a stably concurrent automaton.* Furthermore, let ϕ be a sentence of MSO and $L = L(\phi) \subseteq \mathrm{M}(\mathcal{A})$ a definable language. We will show that L is recognizable. To prove this, we show that $L^T := \{\gamma \in \mathrm{CS}(\mathcal{A}) \mid [\gamma] \in L\}$ is definable in a monadic second-order language in $T^\star$ where words are considered as finite linear orders. Hence, by [Bü60], L^T is recognizable in $T^\star$. This implies that L is recognizable in $\mathrm{M}(\mathcal{A})$.

Therefore, we need another monadic second-order language to describe properties of words over T. Let $\gamma = \sigma_1\sigma_2\ldots\sigma_n$ be a word over T (not necessarily a computation sequence). We will identify the word γ with the structure $(\mathrm{O}(\gamma), \sqsubseteq_\gamma, (T_t)_{t\in T})$ where $x \in T_t$ iff for some i, x is the i-th element in the finite linear order $(\mathrm{O}(\gamma), \sqsubseteq_\gamma)$ and $\sigma_i = t$. To describe properties of such structures we use the monadic second-order language MSO_T with atomic formulas $x \leq y$, $X(x)$ and $T_t(x)$ for $t \in T$ where x and y are first-order variables and X is a second-order variable. To become familiar with the language MSO_T consider the following sentence :

$$\mathrm{CompSeq} = \forall x \forall y \bigwedge_{t \in T} [(T_t(x) \wedge \mathrm{next}(x,y)) \to \bigvee_{\substack{t' \in T \\ \operatorname{dom} t' = \operatorname{cod} t}} T_{t'}(y))]$$

where $\mathrm{next}(x, y)$ denotes the formula $(x < y) \wedge \forall z((x \leq z \wedge z < y) \to x = z)$. Then $\gamma \in T^\star$ satisfies CompSeq (denoted by $\gamma \models \mathrm{CompSeq}$) iff $\gamma \in \mathrm{CS}(\mathcal{A})$, *i.e.* $\mathrm{CS}(\mathcal{A})$ can be defined by a sentence of the first-order fragment of MSO_T. This sentence CompSeq will be used later again.

Lemma 7. *Let $r \in Q$. Then there exists a formula Cod_r in MSO_T with a free monadic variable such that for any $\gamma \in \mathrm{CS}(\mathcal{A})$ and any $N \subseteq \mathrm{O}(\gamma)$ the following are equivalent:*

1. $(\mathrm{dom}\,\gamma).\gamma(N) = r$.
2. $\gamma \models Cod_r(N)$.

Proof The idea behind the following formula is that X_q comprises all elements $x \in N$ for which the elements of N before x change the state of $\mathcal{A}$ from $\mathrm{dom}\,\gamma$ to q; clearly, these sets X_q ($q \in Q$) are pairwise disjoint. We write $\mathrm{ev}(x) = a$ as abbreviation for $\bigvee_{t=(p,a,q)\in T} T_t(x)$ and $\mathrm{dom}(y) = q$ as abbreviation for $\bigvee_{t=(q,a,r)\in T} T_t(y)$. For $x, y \in N$ we say that y is the successor of x in N, if $x < y$ and there is no $z \in N$ with $x < z < y$; in this case, if $x \in X_p$ and $\mathrm{ev}(x) = a$, then $y \in X_{p.a}$. Now let $Q = \{q_1, q_2, \ldots, q_n\}$ and Cod_r be the following (informally described) formula:

$$
\begin{aligned}
\exists X_{q_1}, \ldots, X_{q_n}\ [\ & (\bigwedge_{i\neq j} X_{q_i} \text{ and } X_{q_j} \text{ are disjoint}) \\
& \wedge \bigwedge_{q\in Q} (\text{the minimal element } y \text{ of } (O(\gamma), \sqsubseteq_\gamma) \text{ satisfies } \mathrm{dom}(y) = q \\
& \qquad \longrightarrow \text{the minimal element } x \text{ of } N \text{ satisfies } X_q(x)) \\
& \wedge \forall x \forall y (y \text{ is the successor of } x \text{ in } N \\
& \qquad \longrightarrow \bigvee_{(p,a,q)\in T} (X_p(x) \wedge \mathrm{ev}(x) = a \wedge X_q(y))) \\
& \wedge \bigvee_{(p,a,r)\in T} (\text{the maximal element } x \text{ of } N \text{ satisfies} \\
& \qquad\qquad X_p(x) \wedge \mathrm{ev}(x) = a)]
\end{aligned}
$$

This can be easily translated into the formal language MSO_T, and the result follows. □

The following lemma characterizes downward closed subsets of $\mathrm{DO}(\gamma)$. For this characterization, if $M \subseteq \mathrm{O}(\gamma)$, $x = a^i \in M$ and $y = b^j \in \mathrm{O}(\gamma) \setminus M$, let $M(x, y) := \{z \in \mathrm{O}(\gamma) \mid z \sqsubset_\gamma y\} \cup \{z \in M \mid z \sqsubset_\gamma x\}$.

Lemma 8. *Let $\gamma \in \mathrm{CS}(\mathcal{A})$ and $M \subseteq \mathrm{O}(\gamma)$. Then the following are equivalent:*

1. *M is downward closed in $\mathrm{DO}(\gamma)$.*
2. *Whenever $x = a^i \in M$, $y = b^j \in \mathrm{O}(\gamma) \setminus M$, $y \sqsubset_\gamma x$ and $r = (\mathrm{dom}\,\gamma).\gamma(M(x, y))$, then $a \parallel_r b$.*

Proof Let M be downward closed in $\mathrm{DO}(\gamma)$, $x \in M$ and $y \in \mathrm{O}(\gamma) \setminus M$ with $y \sqsubset_\gamma x$. Then x and y are incomparable in $\mathrm{DO}(\gamma)$. Hence, $M(x, y)$ is downward closed in $\mathrm{DO}(\gamma)$ with $(x\!\downarrow \cup y\!\downarrow) \setminus \{x,y\} \subseteq M(x,y) \subseteq \mathrm{DO}(\gamma) \setminus (x\!\uparrow \cup y\!\uparrow)$. This implies $a \parallel_r b$ by Prop. 5.

Conversely assume the second statement. Let $x \in M$. We claim that $x\!\downarrow \subseteq M$. We may assume that $x'\!\downarrow \subseteq M$ for all $x' \in M$ with $x' \sqsubset_\gamma x$. Suppose there exists $y' \in \mathrm{O}(\gamma) \setminus M$ with $y' \sqsubset x$. Then there exists an element x' of $\mathrm{O}(\gamma)$ with $y' \sqsubseteq x' \sqsubset x$ such that there are no elements between x' and x, *i.e.* x is a direct cover of x'. If $x' \in M$ then $y' \in M$ by our assumption. Hence $Y = \{x' \in \mathrm{O}(\gamma) \setminus M \mid x \text{ is a direct cover of } x'\}$ is not empty. Let y be the maximum of Y with respect to the linear ordering $\sqsubseteq_\gamma$. We show that this leads to a contradiction.

First we show that $M(x,y)$ is downward closed in $\mathrm{DO}(\gamma)$: Suppose $z \in M(x,y)$, $z' \in \mathrm{O}(\gamma)$ and $z' \sqsubset z$. If $z \sqsubset_\gamma y$, we obtain $z' \sqsubset_\gamma y$ showing $z' \in M(x,y)$. Otherwise, $z \in M$ and $z \sqsubset_\gamma x$. By our assumption, this implies $z' \in M$ showing $z' \in M(x,y)$.

Now suppose $z \in \mathrm{O}(\gamma)$ and $z \sqsubset x$. For $z \in M$ we immediately have $z \in M(x,y)$. Otherwise there exists $x' \in Y$ with $z \sqsubseteq x' \sqsubseteq_\gamma y$ since $y = \max(Y, \sqsubseteq_\gamma)$. Hence $z \in M(x,y)$. Thus, we have $(x\!\downarrow \cup y\!\downarrow) \setminus \{x,y\} \subseteq M(x,y)$.

The inclusion $M(x,y) \subseteq \mathrm{DO}(\gamma) \setminus (x\!\uparrow \cup y\!\uparrow)$ follows from the construction of $M(x,y)$ by $\sqsubseteq \subseteq \sqsubseteq_\gamma$. Choose $a,b \in E$ with $x \in E_a$, $y \in E_b$, and put $r = (\mathrm{dom}\,\gamma).\gamma(M(x,y))$. By Prop. 5 we can conclude that $a \parallel_r b$ does not hold, contradicting the assumption. □

Next we characterize the partial order relation of the dependence order $\mathrm{DO}(\gamma)$ by an MSO_T-formula for $\gamma \in \mathrm{CS}(\mathcal{A})$. In Sect. 5 we will see that this is, in general and in contrast to trace theory, not possible using first-order formulas.

Proposition 9. *There exists a formula LE (for "Less or Equal") in* MSO_T *with two free variables such that for any* $\gamma \in \mathrm{CS}(\mathcal{A})$ *and any* $x, y \in \mathrm{O}(\gamma)$ *the following are equivalent:*

1. $x \sqsubseteq y$ *in* $\mathrm{DO}(\gamma)$.
2. $\gamma \models LE(x,y)$.

Proof By Lemmas 8 and 7 we find a formula DC in MSO_T with one free monadic variable such that $M \subseteq \mathrm{O}(\gamma)$ is downward closed in $\mathrm{DO}(\gamma)$ iff $\gamma \models \mathrm{DC}(M)$. Now let $\mathrm{LE} = \forall M(M(y) \wedge \mathrm{DC}(M) \to M(x))$. Clearly, this formula meets the requirements. □

Now we are able to prove that any language definable in MSO is recognizable.

Theorem 10. *Let* ϕ *be a sentence of* MSO. *Then* $L = L(\phi)$ *is recognizable in* $\mathrm{M}(\mathcal{A})$.

Proof We may assume that $0 \notin L$. In a first step we show that $L^T = \{\gamma \in \mathrm{CS}(\mathcal{A}) \mid [\gamma] \in L\}$ is definable in MSO_T. In the sentence ϕ replace all subformulas "$x \leq y$" by "$\mathrm{LE}(x,y)$", "$E_a(x)$" by "$\bigvee_{\substack{t \in T \\ ev(t)=a}} T_t(x)$" and "$D_q$" (for

$q \in Q$) by "$\exists x (\forall y\, x \leq y \wedge \bigvee_{\substack{t \in T \\ \mathrm{dom}\, t = q}} T_t(x))$". Also, replace "$D_T$" by "$\neg\exists x(x \leq x)$" and "$D_\perp$" by "$\neg$CompSeq". Denote this new formula by $\bar{\phi}$. Clearly, $\bar{\phi}$ is a sentence of MSO_T. For $\gamma \in \mathrm{CS}(\mathcal{A})$ we have $\gamma \models \bar{\phi}$ iff $\mathrm{DO}(\gamma) \models \phi$, *i.e.* iff $\gamma \in L^T$. Hence, $\phi^T = \bar{\phi} \wedge \mathrm{CompSeq}$ defines L^T in $T^\star$. Thus, L^T is recognizable in $T^\star$ by [Bü60]. By $0 \notin L$, we have $L^T = [.]^{-1}(L)$, and since the morphism $[.] : T^\star \longrightarrow \mathrm{M}(\mathcal{A})$ has either $\mathrm{M}(\mathcal{A})$ or $\mathrm{M}(\mathcal{A}) \setminus \{0\}$ as its image, L is recognizable in $\mathrm{M}(\mathcal{A})$. □

4 Recognizability implies definability

In this section, we need a monadic second order language to describe properties of words over E. This language MSO_E is defined similarly to MSO_T. A word $w = a_1 a_2 \ldots a_n$ in $E^\star$ is identified with the structure $(\mathrm{O}(w), \sqsubseteq_w, (E_a)_{a \in E})$ where $x \in E_a$ iff for some i, x is the i-th element in the finite linear order $(\mathrm{O}(w), \sqsubseteq_w)$ and $a = a_i$. Therefore, the language MSO_E has the following atomic formulas: $x \leq y$, $X(x)$ and $E_a(x)$ with first-order variables x and y, second-order variable X and $a \in E$. The first-order fragment of MSO_E is defined as usual and denoted by FO_E.

Also, we will use the lexicographic normal form of a computation sequence of $\mathcal{A}$. Throughout this section, let $\preceq$ be a fixed linear order on E. Let $\gamma \in \mathrm{CS}(\mathcal{A})$. Then $\mathrm{evseq}([\gamma]) := \{\mathrm{evseq}\,\delta \mid \delta \sim \gamma\}$ contains a smallest element w with respect to the lexicographic order on $E^\star$ induced by $\preceq$. The *lexicographic normal form* of γ is defined to be the computation sequence $\delta \sim \gamma$ with $\mathrm{evseq}\,\delta = w$. Let $\mathrm{CS}_{\min}(\mathcal{A})$ comprise all computation sequences that are lexicographic normal forms.

Again, let $\gamma \in \mathrm{CS}(\mathcal{A})$ and $A = (x_1, x_2, \ldots, x_n)$ be the order-preserving enumeration of $\mathrm{DO}(\gamma)$ that induces γ. Let X_i comprise all minimal elements of $\mathrm{O}(\gamma) \setminus \{x_1, x_2, \ldots, x_i\}$ with respect to $\sqsubseteq$ for $i = 0, 1, \ldots, n-1$. Then $x_{i+1} \in X_i$. Since X_i is an antichain in $\mathrm{DO}(\gamma)$, the elements of X_i carry mutually different actions, *i.e.* $a^j, a^k \in X_i$ imply $j = k$, as can be derived from Prop. 5. Using Thm. 6, it is easy to see that γ is a lexicographic normal form iff x_{i+1} carries the smallest action with respect to $\preceq$ in X_i for any $i = 0, 1, \ldots, n-1$. This observation will be used in this section.

Lemma 11. *For any $\gamma \in \mathrm{CS}_{\min}(\mathcal{A})$ and any $a^i, b^j \in \mathrm{O}(\gamma)$, the following are equivalent:*

1. *$a^i \sqsubseteq_\gamma b^j$.*
2. *$a^i \sqsubseteq b^j$ or there exists $c^k \in \mathrm{O}(\gamma)$ with $a \prec c$ such that $a^i \sqsubseteq_\gamma c^k \sqsubseteq b^j$.*

Proof The second statement implies in particular $a^i \sqsubseteq_\gamma b^j$.

Conversely suppose $a^i \sqsubseteq_\gamma b^j$. Let $A = (x_1, x_2, \ldots, x_n)$ be the order-preserving enumeration of $\mathrm{DO}(\gamma)$ that induces γ, *i.e.* $x_k \sqsubseteq_\gamma x_l \iff k \leq l$. Then there exists l with $a^i = x_l$. Let M denote the set of all minimal elements with respect to $\sqsubseteq$ of $O(\gamma) \setminus \{x_1, x_2, \ldots, x_{l-1}\}$. Since A is order-preserving, a^i is an element of M. Since A induces γ which is the lexicographic normal form, a is the minimal action occurring in M. Since $a^i \sqsubseteq_\gamma b^j$ and A induces γ, the event b^j is not contained in $\{x_1, x_2, \ldots, x_{l-1}\}$. Hence there exists c^k in M with $c^k \sqsubseteq b^j$. Since M is an antichain with respect to $\sqsubseteq$ it contains events with mutually different actions. So, if $c = a$ we get $a^i = c^k \sqsubseteq b^j$. Otherwise we have $a \prec c$ since a is minimal in M with respect to $\prec$. Hence $a^i \sqsubseteq_\gamma c^k$. □

To simplify the notation, let $E = \{1, 2, \ldots, r\}$ with $\preceq$ the usual linear order. Now, we define inductively a class of first-order formulas for $s = 1, 2, \ldots, r-1$ with two free variables x and y as follows:

$$\psi_r = (x \leq y)$$

$$\psi_s = (x \leq y) \vee \exists z \left(\bigvee_{\substack{d,c \in E \\ d \prec c}} (E_d(x) \wedge E_c(z)) \wedge \neg\psi_{s+1}(z, x) \wedge z \leq y \right)$$

Note that the formula ψ_1 contains $|E| - 1$ quantifiers. Furthermore, since the existential quantifier in $\psi_{s+1}(z, x)$ occurs in the scope of the negation, the prenex normal form has an alternating sequence of existential and universal quantifiers. Hence ψ_1 is a formula in $\Sigma_{|E|-1}$.

Proposition 12. *For any* $\gamma \in \mathrm{CS}_{\min}(\mathcal{A})$, *any* $a^i, b^j \in O(\gamma)$ *and any* $s \leq a$ *the following are equivalent:*

1. $a^i \sqsubseteq_\gamma b^j$
2. $\mathrm{DO}(\gamma) \models \psi_s(a^i, b^j)$

Proof The proof is done by induction on a.

So let $a = r$ and $s \leq r$. Then by Lemma 11 $a^i \sqsubseteq_\gamma b^j$ iff $a^i \sqsubseteq b^j$ since a is the maximal action with respect to $\preceq$. Because of this maximality, the disjunction in the scope of "$\exists z$" in the second part of ψ_s cannot hold for $x = a^i$. Thus, for $a = r$ we showed the equivalence for any $s \leq r$.

Now suppose we have $c^k \sqsubseteq_\gamma d^l \iff \mathrm{DO}(\gamma) \models \psi_s(c^k, d^l)$ for any $c^k, d^l \in O(\gamma)$ with $a \prec c$ and $s \leq c$. Let $a^i, b^j \in O(\gamma)$ and $s \leq a$.

By Lemma 11, $a^i \sqsubseteq_\gamma b^j$ implies $a^i \sqsubseteq b^j$ or there exists $c^k \in O(\gamma)$ with $a \prec c$ such that $a^i \sqsubseteq_\gamma c^k \sqsubseteq b^j$. Thus in case a^i and b^j are comparable we have $\mathrm{DO}(\gamma) \models \psi_s(a^i, b^j)$. Now let a^i and b^j be incomparable. Then there exists $c^k \in O(\gamma)$ with $a \prec c$ such that $a^i \sqsubseteq_\gamma c^k \sqsubseteq b^j$. Since $s \leq a \prec c$ we have $s+1 \leq c$ and therefore the induction hypothesis yields $\mathrm{DO}(\gamma) \models \neg\psi_{s+1}(c^k, a^i)$. Thus we get $\mathrm{DO}(\gamma) \models \psi_s(a^i, b^j)$. Conversely, suppose $\mathrm{DO}(\gamma) \models \psi_s(a^i, b^j)$. If $a^i \sqsubseteq b^j$ we have immediate $a^i \sqsubseteq_\gamma b^j$. Otherwise there exists c^k in $O(\gamma)$ with $a \prec c$, $\mathrm{DO}(\gamma) \models \neg\psi_{s+1}(c^k, a^i)$ and $c^k \leq b^j$. By the induction hypothesis, we obtain $a^i \sqsubseteq_\gamma c^k$ and therefore $a^i \sqsubseteq_\gamma b^j$. □

Now we can prove that any recognizable language in $\mathrm{M}(\mathcal{A})$ is definable by a sentence of MSO.

Theorem 13. *Let* L *be a recognizable language in* $\mathrm{M}(\mathcal{A})$. *Then there exists a sentence* ϕ *of* MSO *such that* $L = L(\phi)$.

Proof Since $\{0\}$ and $\{1\}$ are definable, we may assume that $0, 1 \notin L$. Let $q \in Q$, $L_q^E = \{\mathrm{evseq}\,\gamma \mid [\gamma] \in L \text{ and } \mathrm{dom}\,\gamma = q\}$ and $x \in E^\star$. If $x^{-1}L_q^E \neq \emptyset$ then there exists a uniquely determined computation sequence $\gamma \in \mathrm{CS}(\mathcal{A})$ with $\mathrm{dom}\,\gamma = q$ and $\mathrm{evseq}\,\gamma = x$. Furthermore, $z \in x^{-1}L_q^E$ iff there exists $\delta \in \mathrm{CS}(\mathcal{A})$ with $\mathrm{evseq}\,\delta = z$ and $[\gamma\delta] \in L$. Hence, $x^{-1}L_q^E = \{\mathrm{evseq}\,\delta \mid [\delta] \in [\gamma]^{-1}L\}$. Since L is recognizable, there are only finitely many sets $[\gamma]^{-1}L$. Hence, $\{x^{-1}L_q^E \mid x \in E^\star\}$ is finite, *i.e.* L_q^E is recognizable in the free monoid $E^\star$.

By [Bü60] there exists a sentence ϕ_q^E of MSO_E such that $L_q^E = \{w \in E^\star \mid w \models \phi_q^E\}$. We construct a sentence ϕ_q^1 of MSO from ϕ_q^E by replacing all subformulas of the form "$x \leq y$" by "$\psi_1(x, y)$". Then put $\phi_q = \phi_q^1 \wedge D_q$.

We show that ϕ_q defines $L_q = \{[\gamma] \in L \mid \mathrm{dom}\,\gamma = q\}$: Let $\gamma' \in \mathrm{CS}(\mathcal{A})$ and γ be the lexicographic normal form of γ', *i.e.* $\gamma \sim \gamma'$ and $\gamma \in \mathrm{CS}_{\min}(\mathcal{A})$. Then, using Prop. 12, we have the following equivalences:

$$\begin{aligned} \mathrm{DO}(\gamma') \models \phi_q &\iff \mathrm{DO}(\gamma) \models \phi_q \\ &\iff \mathrm{evseq}\,\gamma \models \phi_q^E \text{ and } \mathrm{dom}\,\gamma = q \\ &\iff \mathrm{evseq}\,\gamma \in L_q^E \text{ and } \mathrm{dom}\,\gamma = q \\ &\iff [\gamma] \in L_q \iff [\gamma'] \in L_q. \end{aligned}$$

Now clearly the sentence $\bigvee_{q \in Q} \phi_q$ of MSO defines $L = \bigcup_{q \in Q} L_q$. □

Now Thm. 1 is immediate by Thm. 10 and Thm. 13.

5 First-order definable and aperiodic languages

In [T90b, EM93] it has been shown that a language in a trace monoid is definable by a first-order formula iff it is aperiodic. By [GRS92], it is aperiodic iff it is starfree. As shown in [Dr94b], any aperiodic language in a concurrency monoid is starfree, but not necessarily conversely. Here we give examples of concurrency monoids that contain aperiodic languages which are not first-order definable, and vice versa. Hence, the classes of aperiodic, starfree and first-order definable languages are in general mutually different in a concurrency monoid. As a positive result, we formulate a sufficient condition on $\mathcal{A}$ such that any aperiodic language in $\mathrm{M}(\mathcal{A})$ is first-order definable. Also, we describe two classes of automata where any first-order definable language is aperiodic. For one of these classes, the aperiodic and the starfree languages coincide ([Dr94b]). Hence we can describe a class of automata where aperiodic, starfree and first-order definable languages coincide. This class contains, besides others, automata with only one state. Since these are precisely the automata induced by a trace alphabet, our result generalizes the result of [T90b] and that of [EM93] on finite traces.

We start with a simple example of a language that is aperiodic but not first-order definable.

Example 1. Consider the stably concurrent automaton $\mathcal{A}$ with $Q = \{p, q\}$, $E = \{a\}$ and transitions $s = (p, a, q)$ and $t = (q, a, p)$. The reader may check that the language $L = (s \cdot \mathrm{M}(\mathcal{A}) \cdot t \cup t \cdot \mathrm{M}(\mathcal{A}) \cdot s) \setminus \{0\} = \{[\gamma] \in \mathrm{M}(\mathcal{A}) \mid \mathrm{dom}\,\gamma = \mathrm{cod}\,\gamma\}$ is aperiodic with index 2. Clearly, for any $\gamma \in \mathrm{CS}(\mathcal{A})$, $(\mathrm{O}(\gamma), \leq)$ is a linear order with $|\gamma|$ elements. Hence, $[\gamma] \in L$ iff $\mathrm{O}(\gamma)$ has an even number of elements. But a first-order formula cannot distinguish between linear orders of even and of odd length. Hence, L is not definable in FO.

The automaton of this example is not counter free as defined below.

Definition 14. An automaton with concurrency relations $\mathcal{A}$ *is counter free* if $q.w^n = q$ implies $q.w = q$ for any $q \in Q$, $w \in E^\star$ and any natural number $n > 0$.

Obviously, any automaton with precisely one state is counter free. Hence these automata generalize trace alphabets. Now, let $\mathcal{A}$ be a counter free automaton, $w \in E^\star$ and $q \in Q$. Since Q is finite, there exist natural numbers m and $n > 0$ with $q.w^m = q.w^{m+n}$. Suppose m is minimal with this property. Thus, the elements of $\{q.w^k \mid k \leq m\}$ are mutually different. Hence, $m \leq |Q|$. Because of $(q.w^m).w^n = q.w^m$ we obtain by the assumption on $\mathcal{A}$ $q.w^{m+1} = q.w^m$. Thus, we have $q.w^{|Q|} = q.w^{|Q|+1}$ for any $q \in Q$ and $w \in E^\star$. Suppose conversely that this holds in a stably concurrent automaton $\mathcal{A}$. Let $q \in Q$, $w \in E^\star$ and $n > 0$ with $q.w^n = q$. Then we have $q = q.(w^n)^{|Q|} = q.w^{n|Q|}$. This equals $q.w^{n|Q|+1}$ since $n|Q| \geq |Q|$. Hence, $q = (q.w^{n|Q|}).w = q.w$, *i.e.* $\mathcal{A}$ is counter free, too.

Thus, an automaton with concurrency relations is counter free iff $q.w^{|Q|} = q.w^{|Q|+1}$ for any $q \in Q$ and any $w \in E^\star$.

Proposition 15. *Let $\mathcal{A}$ be a counter free stably concurrent automaton. Let $L \subseteq \mathrm{M}(\mathcal{A})$ be an aperiodic language with index k. Then, for any state $q \in Q$, $L_q^E = \{\mathrm{evseq}\,\delta \mid [\delta] \in L, \mathrm{dom}\,\delta = q\}$ is aperiodic in $E^\star$ with index at most $2 \cdot \max(k, |Q|)$.*

Proof Let $n = \max(k, |Q|)$. Suppose $uv^{(2n)}w \in L_q^E$. Then there exist $\gamma, \delta, \eta \in \mathrm{CS}(\mathcal{A})$ with $\mathrm{evseq}\,\gamma = u$, $\mathrm{evseq}\,\delta = v^{2n}$, $\mathrm{evseq}\,\eta = w$ and $[\gamma\delta\eta] \in L$. Also, δ can be written as $\delta_1\delta_2\delta_3$ with $\mathrm{evseq}\,\delta_1 = v^n$, $\mathrm{evseq}\,\delta_2 = v$ and $\mathrm{evseq}\,\delta_3 = v^{n-1}$. Let p denote the codomain of γ. Then we have $\mathrm{cod}\,\delta_1 = p.v^n = p.v^{n+1} = \mathrm{cod}\,\delta_2$ since $\mathcal{A}$ is counter free and $n \geq |Q|$. Hence $\mathrm{dom}\,\delta_2 = \mathrm{dom}\,\delta_3$ and therefore $\delta_2\delta_3 = \delta_2^n$. This implies $[\gamma\delta_1\delta_2^{n+1}\eta] \in L$ since $n \geq k$, the index of L. Now we have $uv^{2n+1}w = uv^n v^{n+1} w \in L_q^E$.

Conversely suppose $uv^{2n+1}w \in L_q^E$. We find $\gamma, \delta_1, \delta_2, \eta \in \mathrm{CS}(\mathcal{A})$ with $\mathrm{evseq}\,\gamma = u$, $\mathrm{dom}\,\gamma = q$, $\mathrm{evseq}\,\delta_1 = v^n$, $\mathrm{evseq}\,\delta_2 = v^{n+1}$, $\mathrm{evseq}\,\eta = w$ and $[\gamma\delta_1\delta_2\eta] \in L$. Again, let p denote the codomain of γ. Since $\mathcal{A}$ is counter free, we have $\mathrm{cod}\,\delta_1 = p.v^n = p.v^{n+1} = p.v^{n+2} = \ldots$ Therefore, we find $\delta \in \mathrm{CS}(\mathcal{A})$ with $\mathrm{dom}\,\delta = \mathrm{cod}\,\delta = p.v^n$ and $\mathrm{evseq}\,\delta = v$ such that $\delta_2 = \delta^{n+1}$. Because of

$[\gamma\delta_1\delta^{n+1}\eta] \in L$ and $n \geq k$, we obtain $[\gamma\delta_1\delta^n\eta] \in L$, *i.e.* $uv^{2n}w = uv^nv^nw \in L_q^E$.

□

Now we can show that in this case all aperiodic languages are definable by FO.

Theorem 16. *Let $\mathcal{A}$ be a counter free stably concurrent automaton. Let $L \subseteq$ M($\mathcal{A}$) be an aperiodic language. Then there exists a sentence ϕ of* FO *such that $L = L(\phi)$.*

Proof Let $q \in Q$. By Prop. 15, L_q^E is aperiodic. By [MP71], there exists a sentence ϕ_q^E of FO_E with $L_q^E = L(\phi_q^E)$. Now, the proof proceeds similarly to the proof of Thm. 13. □

Now, we give an example of a language that can be defined by FO but is not aperiodic.

Example 2. Let $\mathcal{A}$ be the following stably concurrent automaton with $a \parallel_p b$ and $b \parallel_q c$.

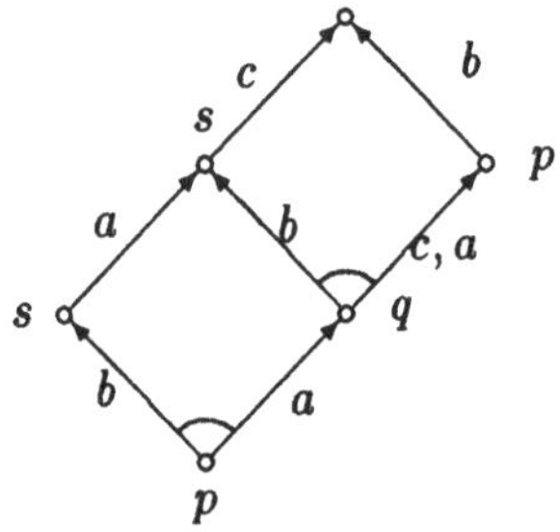

Note that $s.a = s$, $p.a^{2n} = p$, $p.ac = p$ and that b is concurrent with both a and c in state q. We consider the following language

$$L = \{[\gamma] \mid \operatorname{dom}\gamma = p \text{ and } \exists n \in \mathbb{N} : \operatorname{evseq}\gamma = ba^{2n}c\}$$

that is not aperiodic. For $w \in E^\star$ let $w@p$ denote the computation sequence δ with $\operatorname{dom}\delta = p$ and $\operatorname{evseq}\delta = w$ (if it exists). Let $\gamma = bac@p$. Then $\gamma \sim abc@p \sim acb@p$. Hence, b^1 and c^1 are incomparable in $\mathrm{DO}(\gamma)$. Now consider $\gamma = baac@p$. Then we have $[\gamma] = \{baac@p, abac@p, aabc@p\}$. Hence $b^1 \sqsubseteq c^1$ in $\mathrm{DO}(\gamma)$. By induction we can show that a natural number k is even iff $b^1 \sqsubseteq c^1$ in $\mathrm{DO}(ba^kc@p)$. Hence, L can be defined by FO.

Additionally, the example shows that the dependence order $\mathrm{DO}(\gamma)$ cannot be defined by a first-order formula from $\gamma \in \mathrm{CS}(\mathcal{A})$: Suppose there exists a formula LE in FO_T that satisfies Prop. 9. Then, in the example above, $ba^kc@p$ satisfies $LE(b^1, c^1)$ iff k is even. Hence, by [MP71], the language $\{ba^{2n}c@p \mid n \in \mathbb{N}\} \subseteq T^\star$ is aperiodic. But this is not the case.

Lemma 17. *Let $\mathcal{A}$ be a stably concurrent automaton such that a formula LE in FO_T exists with the properties of Prop. 9. Then any first-order definable language in* M($\mathcal{A}$) *is aperiodic.*

Proof Let ϕ be a sentence of FO and $L = L(\phi)$. Following the proof of Thm. 10 we find that L^T can be defined by a sentence of FO_T. By [MP71], L^T is aperiodic in $T^\star$. Hence, L is aperiodic with the same index. □

Thus to show that any first-order definable language is aperiodic, it suffices to show that there exists a formula LE of FO_T that expresses the dependence order. Therefore, we determine two classes of automata that meet this requirement (Def. 18 and 20).

Definition 18. An automaton with concurrency relations $\mathcal{A}$ is an *automaton with global independence* if whenever $a \parallel_p b$ and $q.ab$ is defined then $a \parallel_q b$ for any $a, b \in E$ and $p, q \in Q$.

Note that any automaton induced by a trace alphabet has global independence. It is possible to check that any automaton with global independence is stably concurrent.

Together with Lemma 17, the following proposition implies that for an automaton $\mathcal{A}$ with global independence any first-order definable language in $\mathrm{M}(\mathcal{A})$ is aperiodic.

Proposition 19. *Let $\mathcal{A}$ be an automaton with global independence. Then there exists a formula LE in FO_T with two free variables such that for any $\gamma \in \mathrm{CS}(\mathcal{A})$ and any $x, y \in \mathrm{O}(\gamma)$ the following are equivalent:*

1. $x \sqsubseteq y$ *in* $\mathrm{DO}(\gamma)$.
2. $\gamma \models LE(x, y)$.

Proof Let $I := \bigcup\{\parallel_q \mid q \in Q\}$. Then $(E, E^2 \setminus I)$ is a trace alphabet. Let $\gamma \in \mathrm{CS}(\mathcal{A})$. One can show that, since $\mathcal{A}$ is an automaton with global independence, the dependence graph of evseq γ with respect to $(E, E^2 \setminus I)$ and the partially ordered set $(\mathrm{O}(\gamma), \sqsubseteq)$ coincide. But it is well known that the dependence graph can be defined by the following first-order formula LE:

$$\bigvee_{\substack{\{a_1,\ldots,a_n\} \subseteq E \\ (a_i, a_{i+1}) \notin I}} \exists x_1, \ldots, x_n \left[\bigwedge_{i \leq n} E_{a_i}(x_i) \wedge \bigwedge_{i \leq n-1} x_i < x_{i+1} \wedge (x_1 = x) \wedge (x_n = y) \right].$$

□

[Dr94b, Example 3.1] shows that there exists an automaton with global independence $\mathcal{A}$ and a starfree language in $\mathrm{M}(\mathcal{A})$ that is not aperiodic. In this automaton, it is possible to define a language similar to that of Example 1 that is aperiodic but not first-order definable. Now we define a class of automata where a language is aperiodic iff it is starfree ([Dr94b]) and show that furthermore any first-order definable language is aperiodic.

Let $\mathcal{A}$ be a stably concurrent automaton, $w = a_1 a_2 \ldots a_n \in E^\star$, $q \in Q$ and $a \in E$. We say *a and w commute in q* (denoted by $a \parallel_q w$) if $q.w$ is defined and $a \parallel_{q.a_1 a_2 \ldots a_i} a_{i+1}$ for $i = 0, 1, \ldots, n-1$.

Definition 20. A stably concurrent automaton $\mathcal{A}$ *has no commuting loops* if $a \parallel_q w$ implies $q.w \neq q$ for any $q \in Q$, $w \in E^\star$ and $a \in E$.

Suppose $a \in E$, $w \in E^\star$, $q \in Q$ such that $a \parallel_q w$ and $q.w = q$. Then, there exists a prefix uv of w of length at most $|Q|$ such that $q.uv = q.u$. Let $p := q.u$. Now $a \parallel_p v$ is immediate. Hence, to check whether a stably concurrent automaton has a commuting loop it suffices to consider words w of length at most $|Q|$. Note that if $\mathcal{A}$ is the automaton induced by a trace alphabet (E, D), thus has only one state, and has no commuting loops, then $D = E \times E$. Thus the class of automata without commuting loops forms a model for concurrent systems complementary to trace alphabets.

To show that for a stably concurrent automaton without commuting loops there exists a first-order formula describing the dependence order we need the following lemma which describes when two elements of the dependence order $\mathrm{DO}(\gamma)$ are incomparable. It is valid for any stably concurrent automaton.

Lemma 21. *Let $\mathcal{A}$ be a stably concurrent automaton, $\sigma_x, \sigma_y \in T$, $\gamma_i \in \mathrm{CS}(\mathcal{A})$ for $i = 1, 2, 3$, $\gamma = \gamma_1\sigma_x\gamma_2\sigma_y\gamma_3 \in \mathrm{CS}(\mathcal{A})$, $\mathrm{ev}\,\sigma_x = a$, $\mathrm{ev}\,\sigma_y = b$, $|\gamma_1|_a = i - 1$ and $|\gamma_1\sigma_x\gamma_2|_b = j - 1$. Then $x = a^i$ and $y = b^j$ are incomparable in $\mathrm{DO}(\gamma)$ iff there exist computation sequences δ_1 and δ_2 with $\gamma_2 \sim \delta_1\delta_2$, $a \parallel_{\mathrm{cod}\,\gamma_1} (\mathrm{evseq}\,\delta_1)b$ and $b \parallel_{\mathrm{dom}\,\delta_2} \mathrm{evseq}\,\delta_2$.*

Proof Suppose that x and y are incomparable. Let $w_i = \mathrm{evseq}\,\gamma_i$ for $i = 1, 2, 3$. There exists an order-preserving enumeration

$$A = (x_1, x_2, \ldots, x_k, x, y_1, y_2, \ldots, y_l, y, z_1, z_2, \ldots, z_m)$$

of $\mathrm{DO}(\gamma)$ that induces γ. Let $(y'_1, y'_2, \ldots, y'_n)$ denote the subsequence of $(y_1, y_2, \ldots, y_l)$ comprising all elements y_i with $y_i \leq y$ and let $(y'_{n+1}, \ldots, y'_l)$ denote the remaining subsequence of $(y_1, y_2, \ldots, y_l)$. For $i \leq n$ we have $x \parallel y'_i$, hence $y'_i \notin E_a$. Similarly, for $i > n$, we have $y \parallel y'_i$, implying $y'_i \notin E_b$. Hence

$$B = (x_1, x_2, \ldots, x_k, x, y'_1, y'_2, \ldots, y'_l, y, z_1, z_2, \ldots, z_m),$$
$$C = (x_1, x_2, \ldots, x_k, x, y'_1, y'_2, \ldots, y'_n, y, y'_{n+1}, \ldots, y'_l, z_1, z_2, \ldots, z_m) \text{ and}$$
$$D = (x_1, x_2, \ldots, x_k, y'_1, y'_2, \ldots, y'_n, y, x, y'_{n+1}, \ldots, y'_l, z_1, z_2, \ldots, z_m)$$

are order-preserving enumerations of $\mathrm{DO}(\gamma)$. Let u_1 denote the sequence of actions of $(y'_1, y'_2, \ldots, y'_n)$ and u_2 that of $(y'_{n+1}, \ldots, y'_l)$. Then B induces a computation sequence with event sequence $w_1au_1u_2bw_3$. Hence, there exist computation sequences δ_1 and δ_2 with $\mathrm{evseq}\,\delta_i = u_i$ and $\gamma_2 \sim \delta_1\delta_2$. The enumeration C induces a computation sequence with event sequence $w_1au_1bu_2w_3$. Since $y'_i \notin E_b$ for $i > n$, the word u_2 does not contain any b. Therefore, $b \parallel_p u_2$ with $p = (\mathrm{dom}\,\gamma).w_1au_1 = \mathrm{dom}\,\delta_2$. Finally, D induces a computation sequence with event sequence $w_1u_1bau_2w_3$. Since $y'_i \notin E_a$ for $i \leq n$, and since $a \neq b$, the word u_1b does not contain any a. This implies $a \parallel_q u_1b$ with $q = (\mathrm{dom}\,\gamma).w_1 = \mathrm{cod}\,\gamma_1$.

Suppose, conversely, there exist δ_1 and δ_2 with the properties described above. Then $\gamma \sim \gamma_1\delta'_1\sigma'_y\sigma'_x\delta'_2\gamma_3 =: \delta$ with $\mathrm{evseq}\,\delta_i = \mathrm{evseq}\,\delta'_i$ $(i = 1, 2)$, $\mathrm{ev}\,\sigma_x = \mathrm{ev}\,\sigma'_x$

and ev σ_y = ev σ'_y. By $a \parallel_{\mathrm{cod}\,\gamma_1}$ (evseq δ_1)b, we obtain $|\delta'_1\sigma'_y|_a = |\delta_1|_a + |\sigma_y|_a = 0$. Similarly, $b \parallel_{\mathrm{dom}\,\delta_2}$ evseq δ_2 implies $|\delta'_2|_b = |\delta_2|_b = 0$. Hence $|\gamma_1\delta'_1\sigma'_y|_a = i-1$ and $|\gamma_1\delta'_1|_b = |\gamma_1|_b + |\delta_1|_b = |\gamma_1\sigma_x\delta_1\delta_2|_b = j-1$. Hence $y \sqsubseteq_\delta x$ which implies that x and y are incomparable in DO(γ). □

Now, the following proposition implies that for stably concurrent automata without commuting loops any first-order definable language in M($\mathcal{A}$) is aperiodic.

Proposition 22. *Let $\mathcal{A}$ be a stably concurrent automaton without commuting loops. Then there exists a formula LE in* FO_T *with two free variables such that for any $\gamma \in$ CS($\mathcal{A}$) and any $x, y \in$ O(γ) the following are equivalent:*

1. $x \sqsubseteq y$ *in* DO(γ).
2. $\gamma \models LE(x, y)$.

Proof Let $x = a^i$ and $y = b^j$. Clearly, $x \sqsubseteq_\gamma y$ is a necessary condition for $x \sqsubseteq y$. Therefore, suppose $x \sqsubseteq_\gamma y$. Then there exist $\gamma_1, \gamma_2, \gamma_3 \in$ CS($\mathcal{A}$) and $\sigma_x, \sigma_y \in T$ satisfying the assumptions of Lemma 21. Hence, x and y are incomparable in DO(γ) iff there exist $\delta_1, \delta_2 \in$ CS($\mathcal{A}$) with the properties described in Lemma 21. Since $\mathcal{A}$ has no commuting loops, this implies $|\delta_1| < |Q| - 1$ and $|\delta_2| < |Q|$, hence $|\gamma_2| < 2|Q| - 1$. Since $\mathcal{A}$ is finite, there are only finitely many computation sequences of length less than $2|Q| - 1$. Hence it is possible to express by a first-order formula LE that $x \sqsubseteq y$ in DO(γ) holds. □

Summarizing Prop. 19 and 22 and Lemma 17, we obtain:

Theorem 23. *Let $\mathcal{A}$ be either a stably concurrent automaton without commuting loops, or an automaton with global independence. Then each first-order definable language in* M($\mathcal{A}$) *is aperiodic.*

Now Thm. 2 given in the introduction is immediate by Thms. 16 and 23.

Acknowledgment

The authors want to thank V. Diekert whose idea for lexicographic normal forms of traces improved Prop. 12 remarkably. Originally, the authors had a formula with $|E|^2$ quantifiers. He suggested the one given here with only $|E|-1$ quantifiers (*cf.* [DM96]).

References

[AR88] AALBERSBERG, I.J. and G. ROZENBERG: *Theory of traces.* Theor. Comp. Science 60 (1988), 1-82.

[Be87] BEDNARCZYK, M.: *Categories of asynchronous systems.* Ph.D. thesis, University of Sussex, 1987.

[Be78] BERRY, G.: *Stable models of typed λ-calculi.* In: 5th ICALP, Lect. Notes in Comp. Science vol. 62, Springer, 72-89, 1978.

[BCS93] BOLDI, P., F. CARDONE and N. SABADINI: *Concurrent automata, prime event structures and universal domains*, In: *Semantics of Programming Languages and Model Theory* (M. Droste, Y. Gurevich, eds.), Gordon and Breach Science Publ., OPA Amsterdam, 1993, pp. 89-108.

[BR94] BÖRGER, E. and D. ROSENZWEIG: *Occam: Specification and compiler correctness. Part I: Simple mathematical interpreters.* To appear.

[BD93] BRACHO, F. and M. DROSTE: *From domains to automata with concurrency.* In: 20th ICALP, Lecture Notes in Computer Science vol. 700, Springer, 1993, pp. 669-681.

[BD94] BRACHO, F. and M. DROSTE: *Labelled domains and automata with concurrency.* Theor. Comp. Science 135 (1994), 289-318.

[BDK95] BRACHO, F., M. DROSTE and D. KUSKE: *Dependence orders for computations of concurrent automata.* In: STACS'95, Lecture Notes in Computer Science vol. 900, Springer 1995, 467-678.

[BDK96] BRACHO, F., M. DROSTE and D. KUSKE: *Representation of computations in concurrent automata by dependence orders.* Theor. Comp. Science, 1996, to appear.

[Bü60] BÜCHI, J.R.: *Weak second-order arithmetic and finite automata.* Z. Math. Logik Grundlagen Math. 6 (1960), 66-92.

[Cu93] CURIEN, P.L.: *Categorical Combinators, Sequential Algorithms and Functional Programming.* Progress in Theoretical Computer Science, Birkhäuser, Boston, 1993.

[Di90] DIEKERT, V.: *Combinatorics on Traces.* Lecture Notes in Computer Science vol. 454, Springer, 1990.

[DM96] V. DIEKERT and Y. MÉTIVIER: *Partial commutation and traces.* In: G. Rozenberg and A. Salomaa: Handbook on Formal Languages vol. 3, Springer, to appear, 1996.

[DR95] DIEKERT, V. and G. ROZENBERG: *The Book of Traces.* World Scientific Publ. Co., 1995.

[Dr90] DROSTE, M.: *Concurrency, automata and domains.* In: *17th ICALP*, Lecture Notes in Computer Science vol. 443, Springer, 1990, pp. 195-208.

[Dr92] DROSTE, M.: *Concurrent automata and domains.* Intern. J. of Found. of Comp. Science 3 (1992), 389-418.

[Dr94a] DROSTE, M.: *A Kleene theorem for recognizable languages over concurrency monoids.* In: 21st ICALP, Lecture Notes in Computer Science vol. 820, Springer 1994, pp. 388-399.
Full version: *Recognizable languages in concurrency monoids*, Theor. Comp. Science 150 (1996), pp. 77-109.

[Dr94b] DROSTE, M.: *Aperiodic languages over concurrency monoids.* Information and Computation, 1996, to appear.

[DK96] DROSTE, M. and D. KUSKE: *Recognizable and logically definable languages of infinite computations in concurrency monoids.* Technical report, Inst. für Algebra, TU Dresden, 1995, submitted.

[EM93] EBINGER, W. and A. MUSCHOLL: *Logical definability on infinite traces.* In: 20th ICALP, Lecture Notes in Computer Science vol. 700, Springer, 1993, pp. 335-346.

[GRS92] GUAIANA, G., A. RESTIVO and S. SALEMI: *Star-free trace languages.* Theor. Comp. Science 97 (1992), 301-311.

[Ku94a] KUSKE, D.: *Modelle nebenläufiger Prozesse – Monoide, Residuensysteme und Automaten.* Dissertation, Universität GH Essen, 1994.

[Ku94b] KUSKE, D.: *Nondeterministic automata with concurrency relations.* Colloquium on Trees in Algebra and Programming, Lecture Notes in Computer Science vol. 787, Springer, 1994, 202-217.

[Ma77] MAZURKIEWICZ, A.: *Concurrent program schemes and their interpretation.* DAIMI Report PB-78, Aarhus University, Aarhus, 1977.

[Ma86] MAZURKIEWICZ, A.: *Trace theory.* In: *Advanced Course on Petri Nets*, Lecture Notes in Computer Science, Springer, 1986, pp. 279-324.

[Ma88] MAZURKIEWICZ, A.: *Basic notions of trace theory.* In: *Linear Time, Branching Time and Partial Order in Logics and Models for Concurrency* (J.W. de Bakker, W.-P. de Roever, G. Rozenberg), Lecture Notes in Computer Science vol. 354, Springer, 1988, pp. 285-363.

[MP71] MCNAUGHTON, R. and S. PAPERT: *Counter-free Automata.* MIT-Press, Cambridge, USA, 1971.

[Oc85] OCHMANSKI, E.: *Regular behaviour of concurrent systems*, Bull. Europ. Assoc. for Theoret. Comp. Science 27 (1985), 56-67.

[PSS90] PANANGADEN, P., V. SHANBHOGUE and E.W. STARK: *Stability and sequentiability in dataflow networks.* In: *17th ICALP*, Lecture Notes in Computer Science vol. 443, Springer, 1990, pp. 308-321.

[Sh85] SHIELDS, M.W.: *Concurrent machines.* Computer Journal 28 (1985), 449-465.

[S89a] STARK, E.W.: *Connections between a concrete and an abstract model of concurrent systems.* In: *Proceedings of the 5th Conf. on the Mathematical Foundations of Programming Semantics*, Lecture Notes in Computer Science vol. 389, Springer, 1989, pp. 52-74.

[S89b] STARK, E.W.: *Compositional relational semantics for indeterminate dataflow networks.* In: Proc. Category Theory and Computer Science, Lecture Notes in Computer Science vol. 389, Springer, 1989, pp. 52-74.

[T90a] THOMAS, W.: *Automata on Infinite Objects.* In: *Handbook of Theoretical Computer Science* (J. van Leeuwen, ed.), Elsevier Science Publ. B.V., 1990, pp. 133-191.

[T90b] THOMAS, W.: *On logical definability of trace languages.* In: Proc. of the workshop Algebraic Methods in Computer Science, Kochel am See, FRG (1989) (V. Diekert, ed.). Report TUM-I9002, TU Munich, 1990, pp. 172-182.

[WN94] WINSKEL, G. and M. NIELSEN: *Models for concurrency.* In: *Handbook of Logic in Computer Science* (S. Abramsky, D.M. Gabbay, T.S.E. Maibaum, eds.), to appear.

Generalized Implicit Definitions on Finite Structures

Stéphane Grumbach[*1] and **Zoé Lacroix**[**2] and **Steven Lindell**[***3]

[1] University of Toronto and INRIA
[2] Université de Paris-Sud and INRIA
[3] Haverford College

Abstract. We propose a natural generalization of the concept of implicit definitions over finite structures, allowing non-determinism at an intermediate level of a (deterministic) definition. These generalized implicit definitions offer more expressive power than classical implicit definitions. Moreover, their expressive power can be characterized over unordered finite structures in terms of the complexity class NP ∩ co-NP. Finally, we investigate a subclass of these where the non-determinism is restricted to the choice of a unique relation with respect to an implicit linear order, and prove that it captures UP ∩ co-UP also over the class of all finite structures. These results shed some light on the expressive power of non-deterministic primitives.

1 Introduction

Let I be a structure over a vocabulary σ, with R a relation symbol not in σ. A first-order sentence $\varphi(R)$ over $\sigma \cup \{R\}$ *implicitly defines* a relation on I if there is a unique relation R satisfying $\varphi(R)$ on I. On the other hand, a relation R is *explicitly definable* on I if there is a first-order formula $\varphi(\bar{x})$ over σ, which defines it in the ordinary sense: $R = \{\bar{a} \in \mathrm{I}^k : I \models \varphi(\bar{a})\}$. Explicit definitions express a property of the tuples in the relation, whereas implicit definitions express a property of entire relation.

Beth's definability theorem [Bet53] states that if a global relation is implicitly definable over the class of *all* σ-structures, then it is explicitly definable. However, it is well known that this result fails when restricted to specific classes of models. In particular, this failure was illustrated by Gurevich for the class of finite structures [Gur84]. Implicit definitions over finite structures were then further investigated by Kolaitis, where their expressive power as definitions of

* I.N.R.I.A. Rocquencourt, Domaine de Voluceau BP 105, 78153 Le Chesnay, France – E-mail: stephane.grumbach@inria.fr – Work supported in part by an EC-NSF grant DEUS EX MACHINA, and an NSERC fellowship in Canada.

** L.R.I., Université de Paris Sud, 91405 Orsay, France – E-mail: zoe@lri.fr – Work done in the Verso Project at INRIA.

*** Department of Computer Science, Haverford College, Haverford, PA 19041-1392 – E-mail: slindell@haverford.edu – Work partially supported by NSF grant CCR-9403447 and the John C. Whitehead faculty research fund at Haverford College.

queries was studied [Kol90]. A sentence $\varphi(R)$ over $\sigma \cup \{R\}$ implicitly defines a *query* on a class of σ-structures $\mathcal{K}$, if for every structure I in $\mathcal{K}$, there is a unique relation R^I, such that $I \models \varphi(R^I)$.

More generally, Kolaitis introduced the class IMP of queries which use a vector of implicit relations. A k-ary query Q is definable in IMP on $\mathcal{K}$ if there exists a sentence $\varphi(R_1, \ldots, R_n)$ over $\sigma \cup \{R_1, \ldots, R_n\}$ where $R_1, \ldots, R_n$ are relation symbols not in σ and R_1 is of arity k, such that on any σ-structure $I \in \mathcal{K}$, there is a unique sequence of relations $\langle R_1^I, \ldots, R_n^I \rangle$, such that $I \models \varphi(R_1^I, \ldots, R_n^I)$ and $Q(I) = R_1^I$. It was shown in [Kol90] that fixpoint queries [CH82] can be expressed implicitly, as soon as the definition is based on *two* implicitly defined relations. Implicit definitions based on only one relation symbol provide less expressive power. On the other hand, it is easy to show that every implicit query can be expressed by only two implicitly defined relations, the output, R, and some other relation, S, by a first-order sentence $\varphi(R, S)$ over $\sigma \cup \{R, S\}$, such that $\varphi(R, S)$ implicitly defines R and S. That is, for each $I \in \mathcal{K}$,

$$I \models \exists! R \, \exists! S \; \varphi(R, S).$$

The relation S can be seen as an *intermediate relation* used as the "working area", necessary to get the full expressive power of IMP. The assumption that the intermediate relation is itself unique seems rather restrictive and unjustified. So we propose a generalization of the concept of an implicit query, by allowing non-determinism at the level of the intermediate relation S, provided the output relation R is still deterministic. We do this by means of a sentence $\varphi(S)$ satisfied by all intermediate relations, and a formula $\psi(S, \bar{x})$ which is S-invariant with respect to φ, and defines the (unique) output relation explicitly. This relaxation of the strict uniqueness of classical implicit relations was first considered in [Lin87], where it was shown to be always equivalent to Δ_1^1 definability. We call this class of *generalized implicit queries*, GIMP.

This results in a strict increase in expressive power, i.e. IMP $\subset$ GIMP. As an example, the query true if the cardinality of the domain is even can be expressed in GIMP, while it is not definable in IMP. In fact, it is easy to verify directly that every PTIME query is definable in GIMP. Using the inductive definition of PTIME [Imm86], it suffices to first guess an order on the domain, and then implicitly specify the fixed-point (and its negation). For further details consult [Lin87].

The use of non-determinism to compute deterministic queries has also been studied by Abiteboul, Simon and Vianu [ASV90]. For a non-deterministic language $\mathcal{L}$, they introduce two different deterministic semantics, the *possibility* semantics, and the *certainty* semantics. In the *possibility* semantics, each formula of $\mathcal{L}$ defines the set of tuples satisfying the formula for at least one of the non-deterministic choices. In the *certainty* semantics, each formula of $\mathcal{L}$ defines the set of tuples satisfying the formula for all choices. Generalized implicit definitions are related to these semantics in the following way. Queries in GIMP are those such that on every finite σ-structure the *possibility* and *certainty* semantics coincide.

In this paper, we prove the general (non-boolean) case of the theorem in [Lin87].

Theorem 4.1 GIMP = NP ∩ co-NP, on the class of all finite structures.

We then go on to investigate in more detail the precise expressive power resulting from the non-determinism allowed in the intermediate relation. In GIMP, it is possible to "guess" a linear order on the domain of a finite structure, and it is well known that the order relation plays a fundamental role in the characterization of complexity classes below NP by logical formalisms [Var82, Imm86]. We consider a natural restriction, LIMP, of GIMP, where the non-determinism is restricted to the choice of some order relation on the finite domain, and prove our main theorem.

Theorem 5.2 LIMP = UP ∩ co-UP, on the class of all finite structures,

where UP denotes the class of queries computed by *unambiguous* Turing machines, i.e. NP machines with at most one accepting computation on every input [Val76].

This last theorem generalizes a similar result [Kol90] IMP = UP ∩ co-UP which applies only on the more restrictive class of all *ordered* structures. So the relative expressive power of various non-deterministic primitives is linked with difficult open problems in complexity theory.

2 Preliminaries

A *vocabulary* σ is a finite sequence $\{P_1, \ldots, P_s\}$ of relation symbols of fixed arities. A *σ-structure* I is a set I, called the *universe*, along with a mapping associating for all $i \in \{1, \ldots, s\}$ a relation P_i^I over I with the same arity as P_i. A σ-structure is finite if its universe I is a finite set. $\mathcal{K}$ denotes a class of σ-structures, $\mathcal{F}$ the class of all finite σ-structures, and $\mathcal{O}$ the class of finite ordered σ-structures. Let $\mathcal{L}$ be a logic language.

For k a non-negative integer, let a *k-ary query* (often called a *global relation*) Q on $\mathcal{K}$ be a mapping that associates to each σ-structure $I \in \mathcal{K}$ a k-ary relation $Q(I)$ on the universe I such that for all σ-structures I and J and isomorphisms f with $f(I) = J$, tuple $\langle a_1, \ldots, a_k \rangle \in Q(I)$ iff $\langle f(a_1), \ldots, f(a_k) \rangle \in Q(J)$. If $k = 0$, then Q is called a *boolean query*, because $Q(I) \subseteq I^0 = \{\langle\,\rangle\}$ means Q is either $1 = \{\langle\,\rangle\}$ or $0 = \emptyset$. So Q determines the characteristic function of a subclass of $\mathcal{K}$ given by $\{I \in \mathcal{K} : Q(I) = 1\}$. The complement of a k-ary query Q is $\neg Q$ such that for each σ-structure I, $\neg Q(I) = \mathrm{I}^k - Q(I)$.

Definition 2.1 A k-ary query Q ($k \geq 0$) is *explicitly defined* in $\mathcal{L}$ on $\mathcal{K}$ if there is a formula of $\mathcal{L}$ $\varphi(x_1, \ldots, x_k)$ with k free variables such that for each $I \in \mathcal{K}$, $Q(I) = \{\bar{a} \in \mathrm{I}^k : I \models \varphi(\bar{a})\}$.

Generally, when a query is said to be definable in the logic $\mathcal{L}$, it means *explicitly* definable in $\mathcal{L}$. In the following, we often omit the term *explicit* when referring to queries (explicitly) definable in: FO (first-order logic); FP (fixed-point logic); Σ_1^1 (existential second-order logic); and UΣ_1^1 (unique existential second-order logic).

Definition 2.2 A k-ary query Q ($k \geq 0$) is definable in Σ_1^1 if there exists a first-order formula $\varphi(S, x_1, \ldots, x_k)$ over $\sigma \cup \{S\}$ with k free variables such that for each $I \in \mathcal{K}$, $Q(I) = \{\bar{a} \in \mathrm{I}^k : I \models \exists S\varphi(S, a_1, \ldots, a_k)\}$.

A query Q is definable in Π_1^1 if $\neg Q$ is definable in Σ_1^1.

A query Q is definable in Δ_1^1 if both Q and $\neg Q$ are definable in Σ_1^1.

There is a strong correspondence between computational complexity classes and these logics. A logic $\mathcal{L}$ is said to capture a complexity class $\mathcal{C}$ if:

- for any formula φ of $\mathcal{L}$, the set MOD(φ) of the models of φ (the set of structures that satisfy φ) is recognizable in $\mathcal{C}$,
- for all class $\mathcal{K}$ of sets recognizable in $\mathcal{C}$ that is closed under isomorphisms, there exists a formula φ in $\mathcal{L}$ such that $\mathcal{K}$ = MOD(φ).

Fagin's theorem [Fag74] shows that the logic Σ_1^1 captures the computational complexity class NP. Valiant considered a subclass of NP called UP, which denotes the class of queries computed by *unambiguous* Turing machines, i.e. NP machines with at most one accepting computation on every input [Val76]. The corresponding logic UΣ_1^1, a subclass of Σ_1^1, was introduced by Kolaitis such that for any tuple that satisfies the formula there exists a unique relational witness [Kol90].

Definition 2.3 A k-ary query Q ($k \geq 0$) is definable in UΣ_1^1 if there exists a first-order formula $\varphi(S, x_1, \ldots, x_k)$ over $\sigma \cup \{S\}$ with k free variables such that for each $I \in \mathcal{K}$, $Q(I) = \{\bar{a} \in \mathrm{I}^k : I \models \exists S\varphi(S, a_1, \ldots, a_k)\}$ and $I \models \forall \bar{x}[\exists S\varphi(S, x_1, \ldots, x_k) \rightarrow \exists! S\varphi(S, x_1, \ldots, x_k)]$ (where $\exists! S$ means "there is exactly one relation S").

A query Q is definable in UΠ_1^1 if $\neg Q$ is definable in UΣ_1^1.

A query Q is definable in UΔ_1^1 if both Q and $\neg Q$ are definable in UΣ_1^1.

Remark : The set Σ_1^1 is a recursively enumerable set of formulas. In contrast, UΣ_1^1 is a co-recursively enumerable set, because the condition $I \models \forall \bar{x} \exists! S\varphi(S, \bar{x})$ is expressible in Π_1^1 : $I \models \forall \bar{x} \forall S \forall T(\varphi(S, \bar{x}) \wedge \varphi(T, \bar{x}) \rightarrow \forall \bar{y}(S\bar{y} \leftrightarrow T\bar{y}))$. In other words, a sentence $\exists S\varphi(S, \bar{x}) \notin$ UΣ_1^1 iff $\exists \bar{x} \exists S \exists T \varphi(S, \bar{x}) \wedge \varphi(T, \bar{x}) \wedge \exists \bar{y}(S\bar{y} \wedge \neg T\bar{y})$ is finitely satisfiable.

On the class $\mathcal{O}$, UP is characterized by the logic UΣ_1^1. Notice that a built-in order is required to get the correspondence, because it is not possible to postulate a unique order in general.

3 Implicit Definability

In this section we present the notion of an individual global relation being implicitly definable, to be followed by the natural generalization to a sequence of such relations (as described in [Kol90]).

An individual global relation Q of arity k is said to be ***implicitly defined*** on a class of σ-structures $\mathcal{K}$ if there exists a first-order sentence $\varphi(S)$ over $\sigma \cup \{S\}$, where S is a new relation symbol of arity k, such that for each I in $\mathcal{K}$, $Q(I)$ is the unique relation that satisfies φ on I. The global implicit definition of Q over $\mathcal{K}$ is a k-ary query. Let us use IMP_1 to denote the class of individual implicitly definable queries.

Note that an explicitly defined (FO) query is also implicitly definable. Generally, the converse is not true. On the class of *all* σ-structures, Beth's theorem says that explicit and implicit definability coincide [Bet53]. However, this fails on $\mathcal{K} = \mathcal{F}$ as illustrated by Gurevich [Gur84].

Consider the following example of an IMP_1 query.

Example 3.1 Let σ be a vocabulary containing only one binary relation symbol $<$. The unary query Q consisting of the set of even elements with respect to $<$, if $<$ is a linear order on the domain (and the empty set, otherwise), is implicitly defined by the first-order sentence $\varphi(S)$ where S is a new unary relation symbol.

$$\varphi(S) \equiv [\theta(<) \rightarrow \phi(S)] \wedge [\neg\theta(<) \rightarrow \forall x \neg Sx]$$

Here, $\theta(<)$ asserts that $<$ is a linear order, and

$$\phi(S) \equiv \forall x[Sx \rightarrow \exists y < x] \wedge \forall x \forall y[(x < y \wedge \neg\exists z \; x < z < y) \rightarrow (Sx \leftrightarrow \neg Sy)]$$

says that S is the set of even elements with respect to the linear order $<$. More succinctly, if the domain is $\{1, \ldots, n\}$, $\phi(S)$ says $\neg S(1) \wedge (\forall x < n)[\neg S(x) \leftrightarrow S(x+1)]$. Q is not explicit since if there was a first-order formula $\alpha(x)$ defining Q on finite total orders, then $\forall x[\forall y \neg x < y \rightarrow \alpha(x)]$ would determine if the cardinality of the domain was even, and it is easy to show this is not FO (e.g. by 0/1 laws [Fag76], or Ehrenfeucht-Fraïssé games [Fra54, Ehr61]).

It is easy to see that IMP_1 is closed under complementation: If $\varphi(S)$ is an implicit definition of a query Q, then $\varphi'(T)$ obtained from $\varphi(S)$ by replacing each occurrence of $S\bar{u}$ by $\neg T\bar{u}$ is an implicit definition of $\neg Q$. But the disjunction (resp. conjunction) of two such implicit definitions is not necessarily implicit (unless they define the same query). Moreover, it is impossible to individually define an implicit *boolean* query without making it explicit.

This leads us to generalize the notion of an implicit definition of an individual relation to an implicit definition of a *sequence of relations*. A sequence of global relations $\langle R_1, \ldots, R_m \rangle$ is implicitly defined on a class of σ-structures $\mathcal{K}$ by the sentence $\varphi(S_1, \ldots, S_m)$, where each $S_i \notin \sigma$ is of the same arity as R_i, if for each I in $\mathcal{K}$, $\langle R_1, \ldots, R_m \rangle$ is the unique sequence of relations that satisfies φ on I. A query Q of arity k is implicitly definable in a sequence if it can be taken to be the first global relation in such a sequence. The class of all such queries over a class of structures $\mathcal{K}$ is called $\text{IMP}_m(\mathcal{K})$ [Kol90], where m is the number of relations defined in the sequence. Letting IMP= $\bigcup \text{IMP}_m$, we get that IMP is closed under all first-order operations: complementation, conjunction, disjunction, and quantification.

It is possible to reduce the sequence to just two relations. Let Q be the query implicitly defined in the sequence determined by a sentence $\varphi(S_1, \ldots, S_m)$ such that if $\langle S_1^I, \ldots, S_m^I \rangle$ is the unique sequence of relations that satisfies φ on a structure I, then $Q(I) = S_1^I$. Then there exists an equivalent implicit definition given by $\varphi'(S, T)$ obtained from $\varphi(S_1, \ldots, S_m)$, by replacing each occurrence of $S_1 \bar{u}$ by $S\bar{u}$, and using T to encode the Cartesian product of $S_2, \ldots, S_m$. Since a sequence of two relations suffices, IMP = IMP_2. The following are elaborations of an example in [Kol90], which illustrate that IMP_1 is not as powerful.

Fact : The transitive-closure of a binary relation, TC, is not in IMP_1. Suppose that TC was implicitly definable by $\psi(S)$ where S is a relation symbol of arity 2. Then ψ', obtained from $\psi(S)$ by replacing each occurrence of Sxy by $x = x \wedge y = y$, would be an explicit definition of connectivity (a graph is connected iff its transitive closure is the Cartesian product of the domain). But connectivity is not first-order definable [Fag75].

Example 3.2 Let σ be a vocabulary consisting of one binary relation E. Then the binary query TC, which is the transitive closure of E, has an implicit definition via $\varphi(S, \preceq)$, where S is of arity two and $\preceq$ of arity four. More precisely, $\varphi(S, \preceq)$ defines implicitly the sequence $\langle TC, \leq_\psi \rangle$ where $\psi(S, x, y) \equiv Exy \vee \exists z(Exz \wedge Szy)$ is the least-fixed-point formula defining TC and $\leq_\psi$ is similar to the *stage comparison preorder* defined in [Mos74]: for all binary tuples (a, b) and (a', b'), $(a, b) \leq_\psi (a', b')$ iff $d(a, b) \leq d(a', b')$, where $d(a, b)$ measures the distance from a to b, and is taken to be infinite is there is no path from a to b. It then remains to combine these positive fixed-point definitions uniquely as outlined in [Kol90].

More generally, on the class $\mathcal{F}$, FP $\subset$ IMP. The inclusion was proved in [Kol90]. Dawar, Hella and Kolaitis, showed that on the class $\mathcal{F}$, there exist implicit queries which are not fixed-point definable [DHK95]. But simple polynomial-time queries such as *Evenness* are not expressible in IMP. In fact, over $\mathcal{F}$, IMP is a complete co-recursively enumerable set of formulas. The problem to tell whether or not a first-order formula $\varphi(S)$ over $\sigma \cup \{S\}$, where $S \notin \sigma$ of arity k, is in IMP is not decidable [Kol90]. IMP is co-r.e. since for each sentence $\varphi(S)$, we can enumerate (up to isomorphism) all finite σ-structures I, and check if there is is no R^I such that $I \models \varphi(R^I)$ or if there are at least two different relations which satisfy $\varphi(S)$ on I.

The arity of the implicitly defined relation has a greater impact on the expressive power than the number of implicitly defined relations. We illustrate this by showing that the full expressive power of IMP (two or more implicitly defined relations) can be obtained in IMP_1 (one implicitly defined relation) followed by an explicit first-order transformation.

Proposition 3.1 A k-ary query Q ($k \geq 0$) is definable in IMP iff it has a definition of the form $\exists U\ \Psi(U) \wedge \varphi(U, \bar{x})$, where $\Psi(U)$ is a sentence in IMP_1 over $\sigma \cup \{U\}$, and $\varphi(U, \bar{x})$ is a formula with k free variables.

To obtain this normal form for IMP, encode a sequence of relations into a Cartesian product defined by $\psi(U)$, and make $\varphi(U, \bar{x})$ project out the first relation in the sequence. In the following, this normal form motivates our generalized implicit definitions.

4 Generalized Implicit Definitions

In this section, we extend the notion of an implicit definition. Instead of requiring a sentence to have a unique solution, we only require the uniqueness of solutions "modulo" another formula. Given a sentence $\psi(S)$ and a formula $\varphi(S, \bar{x})$, we require that on each structure, $\psi(S)$ always has at least one solution S^I, and that for any such solution, $\varphi(S^I, \bar{x})$ is unique. In a sense, S is being used as a non-deterministic "working area" for the purpose of defining a deterministic query. We call these *generalized* implicit definitions, and the class of queries they define, GIMP.

A definition of a k-ary query Q, $k \geq 0$, in GIMP is split into two successive steps:

(i) *non-deterministic*: the choice of a *solution* S^I that satisfies the sentence $\psi(S)$,
(ii) *deterministic*: the evaluation of the formula $\varphi(S, \bar{x})$ with k free variables at S^I.

We say that $\varphi(S, \bar{x})$ mod $\psi(S)$ defines a generalized implicit query if for every finite σ-structure, there is a solution which makes $\psi(S^I)$ true, and for each such solution $\varphi(S^I, \bar{x})$ determines the same relation.

Notice that although non-determinism is involved in defining the semantics of a query in GIMP, each query in GIMP has a deterministic semantics. The use of non-determinism to compute deterministic queries has been studied in [ASV90, Sch90, SZ90, GSZ95]. For a non-deterministic logical language $\mathcal{L}$, Abiteboul, Simon and Vianu introduce two different deterministic semantics, the *possibility* semantics, and the *certainty* semantics [ASV90]. In the *possibility* semantics, each formula of $\mathcal{L}$ defines the set of tuples satisfying that formula for at least one of the non-deterministic choices. That is, the semantics is defined as the union of the possible non-deterministic outputs of the formula. In the *certainty* semantics, each formula of $\mathcal{L}$ defines the set of tuples satisfying that formula for every non-deterministic choice. That is, the semantics is defined as the intersection of the possible non-deterministic outputs of the formula.

Generalized implicit definitions are related to these semantics in the following way. $\varphi(S, \bar{x})$ mod $\psi(S)$ defines a GIMP query iff the possibility semantics, $\{\bar{a} \in \mathrm{I}^k : I \models \exists S \psi(S) \wedge \varphi(S, \bar{a})\}$, and the certainty semantics, $\{\bar{a} \in \mathrm{I}^k : I \models \forall S(\psi(S) \rightarrow \varphi(S, \bar{a}))\}$, coincide for every finite σ-structure I. This leads to a new *Possible-is-Certain* deterministic semantics defined as follows.

Definition 4.1 For a non-deterministic language $\mathcal{L}$, a formula of $\mathcal{L}$ has the *Possible-is-Certain* semantics if the set of tuples satisfying the formula for at least one of the non-deterministic choices coincides with the set of tuples satisfying the formula for all non-deterministic choices.

However, it is important to note that not every pair admits a Possible-is-Certain semantics, and that GIMP is precisely the queries defined by pairs which admit such a semantics. More formally, we define GIMP queries as follows.

Definition 4.2 A GIMP k-ary query Q over a class $\mathcal{K}$ of σ-structures, $S \notin \sigma$, is given by $\varphi(S, \bar{x})$ mod $\psi(S)$ where $\psi(S)$ is a sentence such that

(i) $\models_{\mathcal{K}} \exists S \psi(S)$

and $\varphi(S, \bar{x})$ is a formula with k free variables such that

(ii) $\psi(S) \models_{\mathcal{K}} \forall \bar{x}\ \varphi(S, \bar{x}) \leftrightarrow Q(\bar{x})$.

Remark : Condition (ii) implies the S-invariance of $\varphi(S, \bar{x})$ with respect to $\psi(S)$, that is:
(ii') $\psi(S), \psi(S') \models_{\mathcal{K}} \forall \bar{x}\ \varphi(S, \bar{x}) \leftrightarrow \varphi(S', \bar{x})$.

Example 4.1 The *Evenness* query (true on a finite structure $\mathcal{B}$ iff the cardinality of $\mathcal{B}$ is even) is in GIMP. Let S be a relation symbol of arity 2 that is not in the vocabulary. The formula $\psi(S)$ will define a maximal pairing of the domain as follows:

$$\begin{aligned} \psi(S) \equiv\ & \forall x\ \neg Sxx && (1) \\ & \wedge \forall xy\ (Sxy \rightarrow Syx) && (2) \\ & \wedge [\forall x \exists! y\ Sxy \vee \exists z [\forall y \neg Szy \wedge \forall x (x \neq z \rightarrow \exists! y Sxy)]] && (3) \end{aligned}$$

The first two expressions say that S is a simple graph, and the final expression says that S pairs off the elements with the possible exception of one. Finally,

$$\varphi(S) \equiv \forall x \exists y Sxy$$

says that there is no element left unpaired by S, and hence $\varphi(S)$ mod $\psi(S)$ is a definition of *Evenness* in GIMP.

It is easy to see that GIMP generalizes IMP_1 by choosing $\varphi(S, \bar{x}) \equiv S\bar{x}$. GIMP generalizes IMP since a definition in normal form $\psi(U) \wedge \varphi(U, \bar{x})$ of a query in IMP introduced in section 3 gives $\varphi(U, \bar{x})$ mod $\psi(U)$ in GIMP. Moreover, GIMP is closed under complementation, union, intersection, and projection. The expressive power of GIMP admits a precise characterization in terms of complexity classes. We prove the following result.

Theorem 4.1 On the class $\mathcal{F}$ of all finite structures, GIMP = NP $\cap$ co-NP.

Proof: We first show the easy direction. Consider a query Q in GIMP, given by $\varphi(S,\bar{x})$ mod $\psi(S)$. Observe that on each finite σ-structure I,

$$Q(I) = \{\bar{a} \in \mathrm{I}^k : I \models \exists S\, \psi(S) \wedge \varphi(S,\bar{a})\} = \{\bar{a} \in \mathrm{I}^k : I \models \forall S(\psi(S) \rightarrow \varphi(S,\bar{a}))\}.$$

Hence, Q is included in both Σ^1_1 and Π^1_1. Therefore GIMP $\subseteq \Delta^1_1$. By Fagin's result [Fag74], NP is characterized by Σ^1_1 on finite structures, so the queries computable in NP $\cap$ co-NP are exactly those that have a Δ^1_1 definition. In fact, our proof will show that over any class of structures, GIMP is precisely Δ^1_1.

Conversely, let Q be a k-ary query definable in Δ^1_1. Without loss of generality, we can assume that there exist formulas $\exists S\, \phi(S,\bar{x})$ and $\exists T\, \theta(T,\bar{x})$, where ϕ and θ are first-order formulas with relations S and T of the same arity n, respectively defining Q and $\neg Q$ in Σ^1_1.

Let I be a finite σ-structure with domain I. For all $\bar{a} \in \mathrm{I}^k$, $\bar{a} \in Q(I)$ (respectively $\bar{a} \notin Q(I)$) iff there exists a relation $S_{\bar{a}}$ (respectively $T_{\bar{a}}$) such that $I \models \phi(S_{\bar{a}},\bar{a})$ (respectively $I \models \theta(T_{\bar{a}},\bar{a})$). Therefore, $I \models \forall\bar{x}\, [\exists S\, \phi(S,\bar{x}) \vee \exists T\, \theta(T,\bar{x})]$. Since the relation symbols S and T do not belong to σ, and are of the same arity, we can identify them to obtain $I \models \forall\bar{x}\, \exists S\, [\phi(S,\bar{x}) \vee \theta(S,\bar{x})]$.

Let S' be a new relation symbol of arity $(n+k)$, that intuitively encodes the skolemized dependency of S relatively to $\bar{x}$, interpreted by one of the sets $\{(\bar{a},\bar{b}) : \bar{a} \in Q(I)$ and $\bar{b} \in S_{\bar{a}}$, or $\bar{a} \notin Q(I)$ and $\bar{b} \in T_{\bar{a}}\}$. If we let $\psi(S')$ be the sentence $\forall\bar{x}[\phi'(S',\bar{x}) \vee \theta'(S',\bar{x})]$, where $\phi'(S',\bar{x})$ (resp. $\theta'(S',\bar{x})$) is obtained from $\phi(S,\bar{x})$ (resp. $\theta(S,\bar{x})$) by replacing each occurrence of $S(\bar{u})$ by $S'(\bar{x},\bar{u})$, then we can see that $I \models \exists S' \psi(S')$.

To conclude we claim that $\phi'(S',\bar{x})$ mod $\psi(S')$ defines Q in GIMP. Let I be a finite σ-structure and S_0 any relation of arity $(n+k)$ such that $I \models \psi(S_0)$. We will show that $I \models \phi'(S_0,\bar{a}) \Leftrightarrow \bar{a} \in Q(I)$. Indeed, $I \models \phi'(S_0,\bar{a}) \Rightarrow I \models \phi(\{\bar{b} : (\bar{a},\bar{b}) \in S_0\},\bar{a}) \Rightarrow \bar{a} \in Q(I)$ by the Σ^1_1 definition of Q. For the other direction, $I \not\models \phi'(S_0,\bar{a}) \Rightarrow I \models \theta'(S_0,\bar{a}) \Rightarrow I \models \theta(\{\bar{b} : (\bar{a},\bar{b}) \in S_0\},\bar{a}) \Rightarrow \bar{a} \notin Q(I)$ by the Σ^1_1 definition of $\neg Q$. The proof is now complete. □

Like IMP or Δ^1_1, GIMP is not a recursively enumerable class of queries. The question whether or not $\varphi(S,\bar{x})$ mod $\psi(S)$ is a correct definition in GIMP is clearly co-recursively enumerable. And indeed it is co-recursively enumerable complete since the validity problem of first-order sentences over finite structures can be reduced to it. For each first-order sentence θ over a vocabulary σ containing some binary relation symbol, we consider $\neg Sx$ mod $(\theta \wedge \forall x Sx) \vee (\neg\theta \wedge \exists x Sx)$ which is a correct implicit definition in GIMP on the class of finite structures (of cardinality at least 2) iff θ is valid. Trakhtenbrot's theorem asserts that the set of first-order sentences that are finitely valid is a complete co-recursively enumerable set [Tra50].

The question of whether there exists a recursively enumerable logic for GIMP is connected with the existence of a complete problem for NP $\cap$ co-NP. Gurevich [Gur88] showed that if there exists a logic that captures NP $\cap$ co-NP then NP $\cap$ co-NP has a complete problem with respect to polynomial time reducibility. Since our correspondence is constructive, a recursively enumerable logic for GIMP would testify to the existence of a complete problem for NP $\cap$ co-NP. Gurevich conjectures that if that were the case, something drastic would happen (like NP $\cap$ co-NP = P).

In addition to closure under all first-order operations and composition, GIMP also enjoys closure under the further construction of implicit definitions [Lin87].

Proposition 4.2 Let $\psi(S)$ be a FO definition and $\mathcal{K}$ a class a finite σ-structures such that $\mathcal{K} \models \exists S\psi(S)$. Let $\mathcal{Q}$ be a k-ary query which has a definition in GIMP over $\sigma \cup \{S\}$ such that $\mathcal{Q}$ is S-invariant with respect to $\psi(S)$ on $\mathcal{K}$. Then $\mathcal{Q}$ has a definition in GIMP over σ.

5 Generalized Implicit Definitions with Order

The generalized implicit definitions of GIMP proposed in Section 4 give a logical characterization of NP $\cap$ co-NP over finite structures. In this section, we examine what happens if we restrict the general non-determinism to the choice of a total order, while retaining the classical (unique) implicit definitions for any other further implicitly defined relations. We'll call this LIMP, a restriction of GIMP and a generalization of IMP, where the choice consists of a linear order $\prec$ over the domain of the finite structure and a unique relation S on $\prec$. More formally, we define LIMP queries as follows.

Definition 5.1 A k-ary query Q over the class $\mathcal{F}$ of finite σ-structures, with $\prec, S \notin \sigma$, is in LIMP if it can be defined by $\varphi(\prec, S, \bar{x})$ mod $\psi(\prec, S)$ where $\psi(\prec, S)$ is a sentence such that for each total linear order $\prec$ on $I \in \mathcal{F}$ there exists a unique S_0 such that

(*i*) $I \models \psi(\prec, S_0)$,

and $\varphi(\prec, S, \bar{x})$ is a formula with k free variables satisfying the following for each finite σ-structure I, linear order $\prec$ on I and S satisfying $\psi(\prec, S)$ on I,

(*ii*) $I \models \forall \bar{x}\ \varphi(\prec, S, \bar{x}) \leftrightarrow Q(\bar{x})$.

It is easy to see that LIMP $\subseteq$ GIMP by encoding together the order $\prec$ and the relation S into a new relation symbol U. The *Evenness* query has a definition in LIMP, since its non-deterministic part consists of the choice of a linear order $\prec$ and the (unique) set of even elements with respect to $\prec$.

Example 5.1 The *Evenness* query, true on a finite structure $\mathcal{B}$ iff the cardinality of $\mathcal{B}$ is even, has a definition in LIMP. Let S be a relational symbol of arity 1 that is not in the vocabulary. The formula $\psi(\prec, S)$ defines the set S of even elements with respect to the chosen order $\prec$.

$$\psi(S) \equiv \forall x[Sx \rightarrow \exists y\ y \prec x] \wedge \forall x \forall y[(x \prec y \wedge \neg\exists z\ x \prec z \prec y) \rightarrow (Sx \leftrightarrow \neg Sy)]$$

Then $\forall x[\forall y\ \neg x \prec y \rightarrow Sx]$ mod $\psi(\prec, S)$ is a definition of *Evenness* in LIMP.

The decision problem of whether a first-order formula $\varphi(\prec, S, \bar{x})$ mod $\psi(\prec, S)$, defines a semantically correct query in LIMP over finite σ-structures is undecidable. This is proved by an easy reduction from the validity of first-order sentences on finite structures. Let α be a first-order sentence over σ (containing some binary relation symbol), then consider $\varphi(\prec, x) \equiv (\neg\alpha \wedge \forall y \neg y \prec x) \wedge (\alpha \wedge x = x)$. $\varphi(\prec, x)$ mod $\prec$ is in LIMP iff $\models_{\mathcal{F}} \alpha$. Furthermore, there is a first-order $\sigma \cup \{<\}$-sentence φ such that the decision problem whether φ is order invariant on a σ-structure I is co-NP complete [Gur88].

The presence of an order has an important impact on definability because it rigidifies a finite structure. Since a definition in LIMP consists of the non-deterministic choice of a linear order, followed by an order-invariant part, it is natural to consider a one-one map from the class of queries $\mathcal{Q}$ over finite structures to the class of queries $\mathcal{Q}^*$ over finite ordered structures that are *order-invariant*. For each finite σ-structure I of size n, let $I_1^*, \ldots, I_{n!}^*$ be the $n!$ extensions of I over $\sigma \cup \{<\}$. For each finite $\sigma \cup \{<\}$-structure I^*, let I be its restriction to σ, i.e. the finite σ-structure I with the same domain I and the same interpretation of the symbols in σ.

For any k-ary query Q over the class of finite σ-structures, there exists a k-ary Q^* over finite $\sigma \cup \{<\}$-structures where $<$ is interpreted by a linear order, such that, for each finite σ-structure I of size n, $Q(I) = Q^*(I_1^*) = \cdots = Q^*(I_{n!}^*)$. It is clear that such a Q^* is order-invariant. Conversely, for each query Q^* on finite $\sigma \cup \{<\}$-structures that is *order-invariant* there is a query Q over finite σ-structures such that for all finite $\sigma \cup \{<\}$-structures I^*, $Q(I) = Q^*(I^*)$. An interesting example of an order invariant query that is not first-order definable without the order relation is presented in ([AHV94], Exercise 17.27, page 462).

If $\mathcal{Q}$ is a class of queries on finite ordered structures, then let $\text{Inv}_<(\mathcal{Q})$ be the class of order-invariant queries in $\mathcal{Q}$. The following lemma says that an order-invariant query Q^* is in LIMP iff it is computable in UP $\cap$ co-UP on finite ordered structures.

Lemma 5.1 On the class $\mathcal{O}$ of finite ordered structures,

$$\text{Inv}_<(\text{LIMP}) = \text{Inv}_<(\text{U}\Delta_1^1) = \text{Inv}_<(\text{UP} \cap \text{co-UP}).$$

Proof: We first prove that $\text{Inv}_<(\text{LIMP}) = \text{Inv}_<(\text{U}\Delta_1^1)$ on the class of finite structures ordered by $<$. Consider a k-ary query Q^* in $\text{Inv}_<(\text{LIMP})$ defined by $\varphi(\prec, S, \bar{x})$ mod $\psi(\prec, S)$ over $\sigma \cup \{<\}$. The Σ_1^1 formula $\exists S \psi(<, S) \wedge \varphi(<, S, \bar{x})$, where $\psi(<, S)$ and $\varphi(<, S, \bar{x})$ are obtained from $\psi(\prec, S)$ and $\varphi(\prec, S, \bar{x})$ by replacing each occurrence of $\prec$ by $<$, also defines Q^* on the class of $\sigma \cup \{<\}$-structures ordered by $<$. By definition of LIMP, we know that for any $\sigma \cup \{<\}$-structure I^*, there exists a unique relation S_0^* such that $I^* \models \psi(<, S_0^*)$. Hence, for all $\bar{a} \in Q^*(I^*)$, $I^* \models \exists! S \psi(<, S) \wedge \varphi(<, S, \bar{a})$. Therefore, Q^* has a definition in $\text{U}\Sigma_1^1$. Since LIMP is closed under complementation, Q^* is definable in $\text{U}\Delta_1^1$. Recall that Q^* was order-invariant, so $Q^* \in \text{Inv}_<(\text{U}\Delta_1^1)$.

In the other direction, let Q^* be a k-ary query in $\text{Inv}_<(\text{U}\Delta_1^1)$. So Q^* has a definition in $\text{U}\Delta_1^1$ that does not depend on the order. From [Kol90], we know that IMP = $\mathrm{U}\Delta_1^1$ on any class of structures. So Q^* has a definition in IMP. Since LIMP is a generalization of IMP, it follows that $\mathrm{Inv}_<(\mathrm{IMP}) \subseteq \mathrm{Inv}_<(\mathrm{LIMP})$. Again, since Q^* is order-invariant, $Q^* \in \mathrm{Inv}_<(\mathrm{LIMP})$.

The second equality $\mathrm{Inv}_<(\mathrm{U}\Delta_1^1) = \mathrm{Inv}_<(\mathrm{UP} \cap \text{co-UP})$ comes from the fact that on finite ordered structures, UP=$\mathrm{U}\Sigma_1^1$ [Kol90]. It follows that UP ∩ co-UP = $\mathrm{U}\Sigma_1^1 \cap \text{co-U}\Sigma_1^1$, and hence that $\mathrm{Inv}_<(\mathrm{U}\Delta_1^1) = \mathrm{Inv}_<(\mathrm{UP} \cap \text{co-UP})$. □

The following theorem shows more generally that LIMP also characterizes a complexity class on finite structures.

Theorem 5.2 On the class $\mathcal{F}$ of all finite structures, LIMP = UP ∩ co-UP.

Proof: Using the previous definitions, we first show that a query Q on finite structures is definable in LIMP iff its (order-invariant) extension Q^* on finite ordered structures is definable in LIMP. The following are equivalent: *(i)* $Q \in$ LIMP over σ, and *(ii)* $Q^* \in \mathrm{Inv}_<(\mathrm{LIMP})$ over $\sigma \cup \{<\}$.

(i) ⇒ *(ii)* is immediate.

(ii) ⇒ *(i)* Let Q^* be an order-invariant query defined by $\varphi(\prec, S, \bar{x})$ mod $\psi(\prec, S)$ over $\sigma \cup \{<\}$. Its restriction Q has a definition $\varphi'(\prec, S, \bar{x})$ mod $\psi'(\prec, S)$ in LIMP over σ obtained from $\varphi(\prec, S, \bar{x})$ mod $\psi(\prec, S)$ by replacing each occurrence of $<$ by $\prec$.

Next we show that an order-invariant query Q^* is computable in UP ∩ co-UP iff its restriction Q is in UP ∩ co-UP. The following are equivalent: *(iii)* $Q \in$ UP ∩ co-UP over σ, and *(iv)* $Q^* \in \mathrm{Inv}_<(\mathrm{UP} \cap \text{co-UP})$ over $\sigma \cup \{<\}$.

(iii)⇒(iv) is immediate.

(iv)⇒(iii) Let Q^* be a query in $\mathrm{Inv}_<(\mathrm{UP} \cap \text{co-UP})$ over $\sigma \cup \{<\}$. Let $\mathcal{M}^*$ be an unambiguous Turing machine that computes Q^*. Let $\mathcal{M}$ be a machine whose input is a linear encoding of a σ-structure I that first uses the order of entrance of the elements of I to determine an order and then follows exactly the same transitions as $\mathcal{M}^*$. $\mathcal{M}$ is unambiguous (the encoding of the order is deterministic and the following computation is done by $\mathcal{M}^*$) and computes Q. The same method gives an unambiguous machine that computes $\neg Q$. It follows that $Q \in$ UP ∩ co-UP over σ.

The result now follows from Lemma 5.1. □

6 Conclusion

We have studied two natural extensions of first-order implicit definitions, and show that they characterize well known complexity classes, even over *unordered* finite structures. These extensions are based on the ability to choose non-deterministically an (intermediate) relation R satisfying a sentence $\phi(R)$, and use it to compute (deterministically) a query, independent of the particular choice of R. The first extension GIMP, in which an arbitrary relation is non-deterministically chosen, captures NP ∩ co-NP. The second extension LIMP, in which only an order relation on the domain is non-deterministically chosen, captures UP ∩ co-UP.

It might seem that the non-deterministic choice of an order relation should be enough to capture the full expressive power of GIMP (since it rigidifies the structure), and that maybe the definitions of LIMP could be seen as a normal form for GIMP queries. Nevertheless, it follows from the results presented here that the non-determinism can be reduced to the choice of an order relation if and only if UP ∩ co-UP = NP ∩ co-NP.

Acknowledgments : The authors wish to thank Phokion Kolaitis, Richard Lassaigne, Michel de Rougemont and Victor Vianu for their suggestions and helpful discussions.

References

[AG89] M. Ajtai and Y. Gurevich. Datalog vs. first-order logic. In *30th IEEE Symp. on Foundations of Computer Science*, pages 142–146, 1989.

[AHV94] S. Abiteboul, R. Hull, and V. Vianu. *Foundations of Databases*. Addison-Wesley, 1994.

[ASV90] S. Abiteboul, E. Simon, and V. Vianu. Non-deterministic languages to express deterministic transformations. In *Proc. 9th ACM Symp. on Principles of Database Systems*, 1990.

[Bet53] E. W. Beth. On Padoa's method in the theory of definition. *Indag. Math.*, 15:330-339, 1953.

[CH82] A. Chandra and D. Harel. Structure and Complexity of Relational Queries. *Journal of Computer and System Sciences*, 25(1):99–128, Aug. 1982.

[DHK95] A. Dawar, L. Hella and Ph.G. Kolaitis. Implicit definability and infinitary logic in finite model theory. Proc. 22nd International Colloquium on Automata, Languages and Programming - ICALP 95, Lecture Notes in Computer Science, Springer-Verlag, to appear.

[Ehr61] A. Ehrenfeucht. An application of games to the completness problem for formalized theories. Fund. Math. 49: 129–141, 1961.

[Fag74] R. Fagin. Generalized first-order spectra and polynomial-time recognizable sets. *Complexity of Computations, SIAM-AMS Proceedings 7*, pages 43–73, 1974.

[Fag75] R. Fagin. Monadic generalized spectra. Zeitschrift für Math. Logik 21: 89–96, 1975.

[Fag76] R. Fagin. Probabilities on finite models. Journal of Symbolic Logic 41: 50–58, 1976.

[Fra54] R. Fraïsse. Sur quelques classifications des systèmes de relations. Publications Scientifiques de l'Université d'Alger, Série A 1: 35–182, 1954.

[Gur84] Y. Gurevich. *Computation and Proof Theory (M. Richter et al. Ed.)*, chapter Towards Logic tailored for Computational Complexity, pages 175–216. Lecture Notes in Mathematics, 1104, 1984.

[Gur88] Y. Gurevich. *Current Trends in Theoretical Computer Science, E. Borger Ed.*, chapter Logic and the Challenge of Computer Science, pages 1–57. Computer Science Press, 1988.

[GSZ95] S. Greco and D. Saccà and C. Zaniolo. DATALOG Queries with Stratified Negation and Choice: from P to D^P. In *Proc. ICDT'95*, Springer Lecture Notes in Computer Science 893, 82–96, 1995.

[Imm86] N. Immerman. Relational queries computable in polynomial time. *Inf. and Control*, 68:86–104, 1986.

[Kol90] P. Kolaitis. Implicit definability on finite structures and unambiguous computations. In *Proc. 5th Symp. of Logic in Computer Science*, 1990.

[Lin87] S. Lindell. The Logical Complexity of Queries on Unordered Graphs. Ph.D. thesis, University of California at Los Angeles, 1987.

[Mos74] Y. N. Moschovakis. *Elementary Induction on Abstract Structures.* North Holland, 1974.

[Tra50] B. A. Trakhtenbrot. Impossibility of an algorithm for the decision problem in finite classes. *Doklady Akademii Nauk SSSR*, 70:569–572, 1950.

[Sch90] J.S. Schlipf. The Expressive Powers of the Logic Programming Semantics. In *Proc. 9th ACM Symp. on Principles of Database Systems*, 196–204, 1990.

[SZ90] D. Saccà and C. Zaniolo. Stable Models and Non-Determinism in Logic Programs with Negation. In *Proc. 9th ACM Symp. on Principles of Database Systems*, 205–217, 1990.

[Val76] L. Valiant. Relative complexity of checking and evaluating. *Information Processing*, 5:20–23, 1976.

[Var82] M. Vardi. The complexity of relational query languages. In *Proc. 14th ACM Symp. on Theory of Computing*, pages 137–146, 1982.

The Railroad Crossing Problem: An Experiment with Instantaneous Actions and Immediate Reactions

Yuri Gurevich* and James K. Huggins*

EECS Department, University of Michigan, Ann Arbor, MI, 48109-2122, USA

Abstract. We give an evolving algebra solution for the well-known railroad crossing problem and use the occasion to experiment with agents that perform instantaneous actions in continuous time and in particular with agents that fire at the moment they are enabled.

1 Introduction

The well-known railroad crossing problem has been used as an example for comparing various specification and validation methodologies; see for example [6, 7] and the relevant references there. The evolving algebras (EA) methodology has been used extensively for specification and validation for real-world software and hardware systems; see the EA guide [3] and the EA bibliography [1]. The merits of using "toy" problems as benchmarks are debatable; not every methodology scales well to real-world problems. Still, toy problems are appropriate for experimentation. Here we present an evolving algebra solution for the railway crossing problem and use the opportunity for experimentation with instantaneous actions and reactions in real time.

In Sect. 2, we describe a version of the railroad crossing problem. It is not difficult to generalize the problem (e.g. by relaxing our assumptions on trains) and generalize the solution respectively. An interested reader may view that as an exercise.

In Sect. 3, we give a brief introduction to evolving algebras (in short, ealgebras), in order to make this paper self-contained. We omit many important aspects of ealgebras and refer the interested reader to a fuller definition in the EA guide [3]. In Sect. 4, experimenting with instantaneous actions in real time, we define special distributed real-time ealgebras appropriate to situations like that of the railroad crossing problem.

In Sect. 5 and Sect. 6, we give a solution for the railroad crossing problem which is formalized as an ealgebra. The program for the ealgebra is given in Sect. 5. The reader may wish to look at Sect. 5 right away; the notation is self-explanatory to a large extent. In Sect. 6, we define regular runs (the only relevant runs) of our ealgebra and analyze those runs. Formally speaking, we have to prove

* Partially supported by NSF grant CCR-95-04375 and ONR grant N00014-94-1-1182.

the existence of regular runs for every possible pattern of trains; for technical reasons, we delay the existence theorem until later.

In Sect. 7, we prove the safety and liveness properties of our solution. In Sect. 8 we prove a couple of additional properties of our ealgebra. In Sect. 9, we take advantage of the additional properties and prove the existence theorem for regular runs and analyze the variety of regular runs.

The ealgebra formalization is natural and this allows us to use intuitive terms in our proofs. One may have an impression that no formalization is really needed. However, a formalization is needed if one wants a mathematical verification of an algorithm: mathematical proofs are about mathematical objects. Of course, we could avoid intuitive terms and make the proofs more formal and pedantic, but this paper is addressed to humans and it is so much harder to read pedantic proofs. It is a long standing tradition of applied mathematics to use intuitive terms in proofs. Let us notice though that more formal and pedantic proofs have their own merits; if one wants to check the details of our proofs by machine, it is useful to rewrite the proofs in a pedantic way. In any case, we see a great value in the naturality of formalization. No semantical approach makes inherent difficulties of a given problem go away. At best, the approach does not introduce more complications and allows one to deal with the inherent complexity of the given problem.

Acknowledgments. Raghu Mani participated in an initial stage of the work [5]. During the final stage of the work, the first author was a CNRS[2] visitor in the Laboratoire Informatique Theoretique et Programmation, Paris, France [4].

2 The Railroad Crossing Problem

Imagine a railroad crossing with several train tracks and a common gate, such as the one depicted in Fig. 1. Sensors along every track detect oncoming and departing trains. Let us consider one of the tracks, shown in Fig. 2. It has four sensors at points L1, L2, R1 and R2. Sensor L1 detects trains coming from the left, and sensor L2 detects when those trains leave the crossing. Similarly sensor R1 detects trains coming from the right, and sensor R2 detects when those trains leave the crossing. Based on signals from these sensors, an automatic controller signals the gate to open or close.

The problem is to design a controller that guarantees the following requirements.

Safety If a train is in the crossing, the gate is closed.
Liveness The gate is open as much as possible.

Several assumptions are made about the pattern of train movement. For example, if a train appears from the left, it leaves the crossing to the right. It is easiest to express those assumptions as a restriction on possible histories of train motion on any given track.

[2] Centre National de la Recherche Scientifique

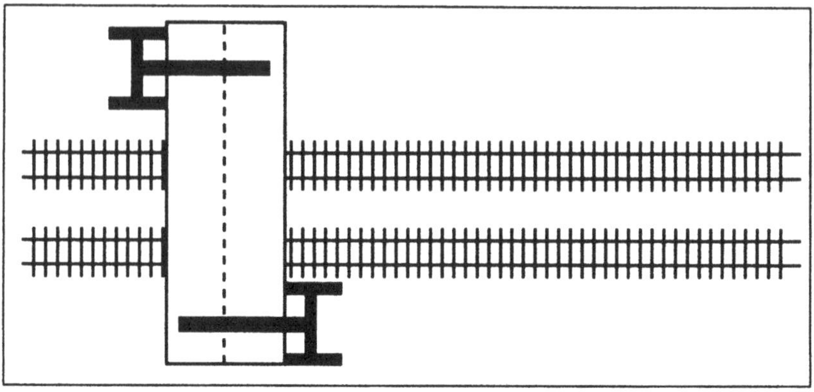

Fig. 1. A railroad crossing.

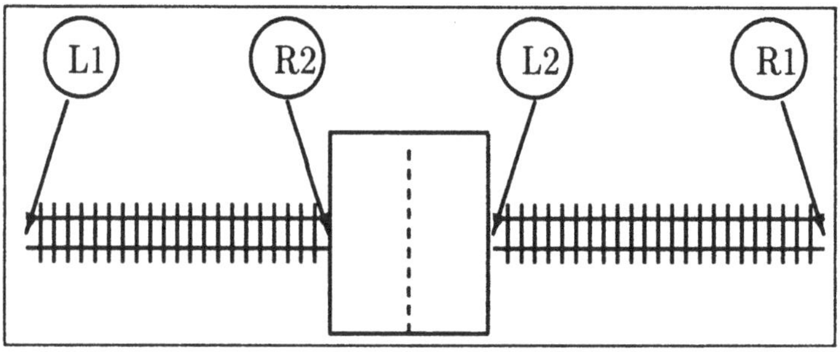

Fig. 2. Placement of sensors along a railroad track.

Assumptions Regarding Train Motion. For any given track, there is a finite or infinite sequence of moments

$$t_0 < t_1 < t_2 < t_3 < \dots$$

satisfying the following conditions.

Initial State The moment t_0 is the initial moment. The observed part $[L1, R1]$ of the track is empty at t_0.

Train Pattern If t_{3i+1} appears in the sequence then t_{3i+3} appears in the sequence and we have that

- at t_{3i+1}, one oncoming train is detected at L1 or R1,
- at t_{3i+2} the train reaches the crossing, and
- at t_{3i+3} the train is detected to have left the crossing at L2 or R2 respectively.

Completeness There are no other trains.

Additional Assumptions. From the moment that an oncoming train is detected, it takes time between d_{min} and d_{max} for the train to reach the crossing. In terms of the sequence $\langle t_0 < t_1 < t_2 < t_3 < \ldots \rangle$ above, this assumption can be stated as follows:

1 Every difference $t_{3i+2} - t_{3i+1}$ belongs to the interval $[d_{\text{min}}, d_{\text{max}}]$.

Further, the gate closes within time d_{close} and opens within time d_{open}. This does not necessarily mean that if the controller signals the gate to close (respectively open) at moment t then the gate closes (respectively opens) by time $t + d_{\text{close}}$ (respectively $t + d_{\text{open}}$). Let us state the assumption more precisely as a restriction on possible histories.

2 There is no interval $I = (t, t + d_{\text{close}})$ (respectively $I = (t, t + d_{\text{open}})$) during which the signal to close (respectively to open) is in force but the gate is not closed (respectively opened) at any moment in I.

It is easy to see that the controller cannot guarantee the safety requirement is satisfied if $d_{\text{min}} < d_{\text{close}}$. We ignore the case $d_{\text{min}} = d_{\text{close}}$ and assume that

3 $d_{\text{close}} < d_{\text{min}}$.

Finally, we will assume that actions are performed instantaneously. Of course, real actions take time and the use of instantaneous actions is an abstraction. But this may be a useful abstraction. For example, in our case, it is natural to ignore the time taken by the controller's actions. It is not natural at all to view closing and opening of the gate as instantaneous actions, and we will not do that. Let us stress that the evolving algebra methodology does not require that actions are necessarily instantaneous. See for example [2] where an instantaneous action ealgebra is refined to a prolonged-action ealgebra.

The design part of the railway crossing problem is not difficult, especially because the problem has been addressed in a number of papers. What remains is to formalize the design in a specification language, in our case as an evolving algebra, and prove the safety and liveness requirements are satisfied.

3 Evolving Algebras Reminder

We give a brief reminder on evolving algebras based on the EA guide [3]. We present only what is necessary here and ignore many important features.

3.1 Static Algebras

Static algebras are essentially logicians' structures except that a tiny bit of meta-mathematics is built into it. They are indeed algebras in the sense of the science of universal algebra.

A *vocabulary* is a collection of function symbols; each symbol has a fixed arity. Some function symbols are tagged as relation symbols (or predicates). It is supposed that every vocabulary contains the following *logic symbols*: nullary symbols *true*, *false*, *undef*, a binary symbol =, and the symbols of the standard propositional connectives.

A *static algebra* (or a *state*) A *of vocabulary* Υ is a nonempty set X (the *basic set* or *superuniverse* of A), together with interpretations of all function symbols in Υ over X (the *basic functions* of A). A function symbol f of arity r is interpreted as an r-ary operation over X (if $r = 0$, it is interpreted as an element of X). The interpretations of predicates (*basic relations*) and the logic symbols satisfy some obvious requirements stated below.

Remark on notations and denotations. A symbol in Υ is a name or notation for the operation that interprets it in A, and the operation is the meaning or denotation of the symbol in A. In English, a word "spoon" is a name of a familiar table utensil, and one says "I like that spoon" rather than a more cumbersome "I like that utensil named 'spoon'". Similarly, when a state is fixed, we may say that f maps a tuple $\bar{a}$ to an element b rather than that the interpretation of f maps a tuple $\bar{a}$ to an element b.

On the interpretations of logic symbols and predicates. Intuitively, (the interpretations of) *true* and *false* represent truth and falsity respectively. Accordingly, the symbols *true* and *false* are interpreted by different elements. These two elements are the only possible values of any basic relation. The Boolean connectives behave in the expected way over these two elements, and the equality function behaves in the expected way over all elements.

Universes and typing. Formally speaking, a static algebra is one-sorted. However, it may be convenient to view it as many-sorted; here we describe a standard way to do this. Some unary basic relations are designated as universes (or sorts) and their names may be called universe symbols. One thinks about a universe U as a set $\{x : U(x) = \mathit{true}\}$. Basic functions are assigned universes as domains. For example, the domain of a binary function f may be given as $U_1 \times U_2$ where U_1 and U_2 are universes. If f is a relation, this means that $f(a_1, a_2) = \mathit{false}$ whenever $a_1 \notin U_1$ or $a_2 \notin U_2$. Otherwise this means that $f(a_1, a_2) = \mathit{undef}$ whenever $a_1 \notin U_1$ or $a_2 \notin U_2$, so that f is intuitively a partial function.

Remark on the built-in piece of meta-mathematics. In first-order logic, an assertion about a given structure does not evaluate to any element of the structure. For technical convenience, in evolving algebras truth and falsity are represented internally and many assertions can be treated as terms. This technical modification does not prevent us from dealing with assertions directly. For example, let f, g be nullary function symbols and P a binary function symbol. Instead of saying that $P(f, g)$ evaluates to *true* (respectively *false*) at a state A, we may say $P(f, g)$ holds (respectively fails) at A. In some cases, we may even omit "holds"; for example, we may assert simply that $f \neq g$. Admittedly, this is not very pedantic, but we write for humans, not machines.

3.2 Updates

Alternatively, a state can be viewed as a kind of memory. A *location* ℓ of a state A of vocabulary Υ is a pair $\ell = (f, \bar{a})$ where f is a symbol in Υ of some arity

r and $\bar{a}$ is an r-tuple of elements of A (that is, of the superuniverse of A). The element $f(\bar{a})$ is the *content* of location ℓ in A.

An *update* of state A is a pair (ℓ, b), where ℓ is some location $(f, \bar{a})$ of A and b is an element of A; it is supposed that b is (the interpretation of) *true* or *false* if f is a predicate. This update is *trivial* if b is the content of ℓ in A. An update can be performed: just replace the value at location ℓ with b. The vocabulary, the superuniverse and the contents of other locations remain unchanged. The state changes only if the update is nontrivial.

Call a set $S = \{(\ell_1, b_1), \ldots, (\ell_n, b_n)\}$ of updates of a state A *consistent* if the locations are distinct. In other words, S is *inconsistent* if there are i, j such that $\ell_i = \ell_j$ but $b_i \neq b_j$. In the case that S is consistent it is performed as follows: replace the content of ℓ_1 with b_1, the content of ℓ_2 with b_2 and so on. To perform an inconsistent update set, do nothing.

A pedantic remark. The equality used in the previous paragraph is not the built-in equality of A but rather the equality of the meta language. One could use another symbol for the built-in equality, but this is not necessary.

A remark to theoreticians. At the point that updates are introduced, some people, in particular Robin Milner [8], raise an objection that an update may destroy algebraic properties. For example, an operation may lose associativity. That is true. So, in what sense are static algebras algebraic? They are algebraic in the sense that the nature of elements does not matter and one does not distinguish between isomorphic algebras. A standard way to access a particular element is to write a term that evaluates to that element. Coming back to algebraic properties like associativity (and going beyond the scope of this paper), let us note that, when necessary, one can guarantee that such a property survives updating by declaring some functions static or by imposing appropriate integrity constraints or just by careful programming.

3.3 Basic Rules

In this subsection we present the syntax and semantics of basic rules. Each rule R has a vocabulary, namely the collection of function symbols that occur in R. A rule R is applicable to a state A only if the vocabulary of A includes that of R. At each state A of sufficiently rich vocabulary, R gives rise to a set of updates. To execute R at such a state A, perform the update set at A.

A *basic update rule* R has the form

$$f(e_1, \ldots, e_r) := e_0$$

where f is an r-ary function symbol (the *head* of R) and each e_i is a ground term, that is, a term without any variables. (In programming languages, terms are usually called expressions; that motivates the use of letter e for terms.) To execute R at a state A of sufficiently rich vocabulary, evaluate all terms e_i at A and then change f accordingly. In other words, the update set generated by R at A consists of one update (ℓ, a_0) where $\ell = (f, (a_1, \ldots, a_r))$ and each a_i is the value of e_i at A.

For example, consider an update rule $f(c_1 + c_2) := c_0$ and a state A where $+$ is interpreted as the standard addition function on natural numbers and where c_1, c_2, c_0 have values $3, 5, 7$ respectively. To execute the rule at A, set $f(8)$ to 7.

There are only two basic rule constructors. One is the *conditional constructor* which produces rules of the form:

if g **then** R_1 **else** R_2 **endif**

where g is a ground term (the *guard* of the new rule) and R_1, R_2 are rules. To execute the new rule in a state A of sufficiently rich vocabulary, evaluate the guard. If it is true, then execute R_1; otherwise execute R_2. (The "**else**" clause may be omitted if desired.)

The other constructor is the *block constructor* which produces rules of the form:

block
    R_1
    $\vdots$
    R_k
endblock

where $R_1, \ldots, R_k$ are rules. (We often omit the keywords "**block**" and "**endblock**" for brevity and use indentation to eliminate ambiguity.) To execute the new rule in a state A of sufficiently rich vocabulary, execute rules $R_1, \ldots, R_k$ simultaneously. More precisely, the update set generated by the new rule at A is the union of the update sets generated by the rules R_i at A.

A *basic program* is simply a basic rule.

In this paper we say that a rule R is *enabled* at a state A of sufficiently rich vocabulary if the update set generated by R at A is consistent and contains a non-trivial update; otherwise R is *disabled* at A. (The notion of being enabled has not been formalized in the EA guide.) Rules will be executed only if they are enabled, so that the execution changes a given state. This seems to be a very pedantic point. What harm is done by executing a rule that does not change a given state? It turns out that the stricter notion of being enabled is convenient in real-time computational theory; see Lemma 7 in this connection.

3.4 Parallel Synchronous Rules

Generalize the previous framework in two directions. First, permit terms with variables and generalize the notion of state: in addition to interpreting some function names, a generalized state may assign values to some variables. (Notice that a variable cannot be the head of an update rule.)

Second, generalize the notion of guards by allowing bounded quantification. More formally, we define *guards* as a new syntactical category. Every term $P(e_1, \ldots, e_r)$, where P is a predicate, is a guard. A Boolean combination of guards is a guard. If $g(x)$ is a guard with a variable x and U is a universe symbol then the expression $(\forall x \in U)g(x)$ is also a guard.

The semantics of guards is quite obvious. A guard $g(\bar{y})$ with free variables $\bar{y}$ holds or fails at a (generalized) state A that assigns values to all free variables of g. The least trivial case is that of a guard $g(\bar{y}) = (\forall x \in U)g'(x, \bar{y})$. For every element b of U in A, let A_b be the expansion of A obtained by assigning the value b to x. Then $g(\bar{y})$ holds at A if $g'(x, \bar{y})$ holds at every A_b; otherwise it fails at A.

Now consider a generalized basic rule $R(x)$ with a variable x and let U be a universe symbol. Form the following rule R^*:

var x **ranges over** U
        $R(x)$
endvar

Intuitively, to execute R^*, one executes $R(x)$ for every $x \in U$. To make this more precise, let A be a (generalized) state that interprets all function names in the vocabulary of $R(x)$ and assigns values to all free variables of $R(x)$ except for x. For each element b of the universe U in A, let A_b be the expansion of A obtained by assigning the value b to x, and let E_b be the update set generated by $R(x)$ at A_b. Since x does not appear as the head of any update instruction in $R(x)$, each E_b is also a set of updates of A. The update set generated by R^* at A is the union of the update sets E_b.

Call the new rule a *parallel synchronous rule* (or a *declaration rule*, as in the EA guide). A *parallel synchronous program* is simply a parallel synchronous rule without free variables. Every occurrence of a variable should be bound by a declaration or a quantifier.

3.5 Special Distributed Programs

For our purposes here, a *distributed program* Π is given by a vocabulary and a finite set of basic or parallel synchronous programs with function symbols from the vocabulary of Π. The constitutent programs are the *modules* of $\mathcal{A}$. A *state* of Π is a state of the vocabulary of Π. Intuitively, each module is executed by a separate agent.

This is a very restricted definition. For example, the EA guide allows the creation of new agents during the evolution.

Intuitively, it is convenient though to distinguish between a module (a piece of syntax) and its executor, and even think about agents in anthropomorphic terms. But since in this case agents are uniquely defined by their programs, there is no real need to have agents at all, and we may identify an agent by the name of its program.

4 Special Distributed Real-Time Ealgebras

A program does not specify a (distributed) ealgebra completely. We need to define what constitutes a computation (or a run) and then to indicate initial states and maybe a relevant class of runs. In this section, we define a restricted class of distributed real-time evolving algebras by restricting attention to static algebras of a particular kind and defining a particular notion of run.

We are interested in computations in real time that satisfiy the following assumptions.

I1 Agents execute instantaneously.
I2 Enviromental changes take place instantaneously.
I3 The global state of the given distributed ealgebra is well defined at every moment.

Let us stress again that the three assumptions above are not a part of the evolving algebra definition. The prolonged-action ealgebra [2], mentioned in Sect. 2, satisfies none of these three assumptions.

Vocabularies and Static Structures. Fix some vocabulary Υ with a universe symbol Reals and let Υ^+ be the extension of Υ with a nullary function symbol CT; it is supposed of course that Υ does not contain CT. Restrict attention to Υ^+-states where the universe Reals is the set of real numbers and CT evaluates to a real number. Intuitively, CT gives the current time.

4.1 Pre-runs

Definition 1. A *pre-run* R of vocabulary Υ^+ is a mapping from the interval $[0, \infty)$ or the real line to states of vocabulary Υ^+ satisfying the following requirements where $\rho(t)$ is the reduct of $R(t)$ to Υ.

Superuniverse Invariability The superuniverse does not change during the evolution; that is, the superuniverse of every $R(t)$ is that of $R(0)$.
Current Time At every $R(t)$, CT evaluates to t.
Discreteness For every $\tau > 0$, there is a finite sequence $0 = t_0 < t_1 < \ldots < t_n = \tau$ such that if $t_i < \alpha < \beta < t_{i+1}$ then $\rho(\alpha) = \rho(\beta)$. □

Remarks. Of course, we could start with an initial moment different from 0, but without loss of generality we can assume that the initial moment is 0. Our discreteness requirement is rather simplistic (but sufficient for our purposes in this paper). One may have continuous time-dependent basic functions around (in addition to CT); in such cases, the discreteness requirement becomes more subtle.

In the rest of this section, R is a pre-run of vocabulary Υ^+ and $\rho(t)$ is the reduct of $R(t)$ to Υ.

The notation $\rho(t+)$ and $\rho(t-)$ is self-explanatory; still, let us define it precisely. $\rho(t+)$ is any state $\rho(t+\varepsilon)$ such that $\varepsilon > 0$ and $\rho(t+\delta) = \rho(t+\varepsilon)$ for all positive $\delta < \varepsilon$. Similarly, if $t > 0$ then $\rho(t-)$ is any state $\rho(t-\varepsilon)$ such that $0 < \varepsilon \leq t$ and $\rho(t-\delta) = \rho(t-\varepsilon)$ for all positive $\delta < \varepsilon$.

Call a moment t *significant* for R if (i) $t = 0$ or (ii) $t > 0$ and either $\rho(t) \neq \rho(t-)$ or $\rho(t) \neq \rho(t+)$.

Lemma 2. *For any moment t, $\rho(t+)$ is well defined. For any moment $t > 0$, $\rho(t-)$ is well defined. If there are infinitely many significant moments then their supremum equals ∞.*

Proof. Obvious. □

Recall that a set S of nonnegative reals is *discrete* if it has no limit points. In other words, S is discrete if and only if, for every nonnegative real τ, the set $\{t \in S : t < \tau\}$ is finite. The discreteness requirement in the definition of pre-runs means exactly that the collection of the significant points of R is discrete.

We finish this subsection with a number of essentially self-evident definitions related to a given pre-run R. Let e be a term of vocabulary Υ^+. If e has free variables then fix the values of those variables, so that e evaluates to a definite value in every state of vocabulary Υ^+. (Formally speaking e is a pair of the form (e', ξ) where e' is a term and ξ assigns elements of $R(0)$ to free variables of e'.)

The value e_t of e at moment t is the value of e in $R(t)$. Accordingly, e *holds* (respectively *fails*) at t if it does so in $R(t)$. Likewise, a module is *enabled* (respectively *disabled*) at t if it is so in $R(t)$. In a similar vein, we speak about a time interval I. For example, e *holds over I* if it holds at every $t \in I$.

If e has the same value over some nonempty interval $(t, t+\varepsilon)$, then this value is *the value e_{t+} of e at $t+$* (respectively *at $t-$*). Similarly, if $t > 0$ and e has the same value over some nonempty interval $(t-\varepsilon, t)$, then this value is *the value e_{t-} of e at $t-$*. Define accordingly when e holds, fails at $t+, t-$ and when an agent is enabled, disabled at $t+, t-$.

Further, *e is set to* a value a (or simply *becomes a*) at t if either (i) $e_{t-} \neq a$ and $e_t = a$, or else (ii) $e_t \neq a$ and $e_{t+} = a$. Define accordingly when an agent becomes enabled, disabled at t.

4.2 Runs

Now consider a distributed program Π with function symbols from vocabulary Υ^+. Runs of Π are pre-runs with some restrictions on how the basic functions evolve. Depending upon their use, the basic functions of Π fall into the following three disjoint categories.

Static These functions do not change during any run. The names of these functions do not appear as the heads of update rules in Π.

Internal Dynamic These functions may be changed only by agents. The names of these functions appear as the heads of update rules and the functions are changed by executing the modules of Π. For brevity, we abbreviate "internal dynamic" to "internal".

External Dynamic These functions may be changed only by the environment. The names of these functions do not appear as the heads of update rules; nevertheless the functions can change from one state to another. Who changes them? The environment. Some restrictions may be imposed on how these functions can change. For brevity, we abbreviate "external dynamic" to "external".

Remark. It may be convenient to have functions that can by changed both by agents and the environment. The EA guide allows that, but we do not need that generality here.

Before we give the definition of runs, let us explain informally that one should be cautious with instantaneous actions. In particular, it may not be possible to assume that agents always fire at the moment they become enabled. Consider the following two interactive scenarios.

Scenario 1 The environment changes a nullary external function f at moment t. This new value of f enables an agent X. The agent fires immediately and changes another nullary function g.

What are the values of f and g at time t, and at what time does X fire? If f has its old value at t then X is disabled at t and fires at some time after t; thus X does not fire immediately. If g has its new value already at t then X had to fire at some time before t; that firing could not be triggered by the change of f. We arrive at the following conclusions: f has its new value at t (and thus f_t differs from f_{t-}), X fires at t, and g has its old value at t (and thus g_t differs from g_{t+}).

Scenario 2 At time t, an agent X changes a function g and in so doing enables another agent Y while disabling himself.

When does Y fire? Since X fires at t, it is enabled at t and thus g has its old value at t. Hence Y is disabled at t and fires at some time after t. Thus Y cannot react immediately.

The following definition is designed to allow immediate agents.

Definition 3. A pre-run R of vocabulary Υ^+ is a *run* of Π if it satisfies the following conditions where $\rho(t)$ is the reduct of R to Υ.

1. If $\rho(t+)$ differs from $\rho(t)$ then $\rho(t+)$ is the Υ-reduct of the state resulting from executing some modules $M_1, \ldots, M_k$ at $R(t)$. In such a case we say t is *internally significant* and the executors of $M_1, \ldots, M_k$ *fire* at t. All external functions with names in Υ have the same values in $\rho(t)$ and $\rho(t+)$.
2. If $i > 0$ and $\rho(\tau)$ differs from $\rho(\tau-)$ then they differ only in the values of external functions. In such a case we say τ is *externally significant*. All internal functions have the same values in $\rho(t-)$ and $\rho(t)$. □

Remark. Notice the global character of the definition of firing. An agent fires at a moment t if $\rho(t+) \neq \rho(t)$. This somewhat simplified definition of firing is sufficient for our purposes in this paper.

In the rest of this section, R is a run of Π and $\rho(t)$ the reduct of $R(t)$ to Υ. Let e be a term e with fixed values of all its free variables. A moment t is *significant for* e if, for every $\varepsilon > 0$, there exists a moment α such that $|\alpha - t| < \varepsilon$ and $e_\alpha \neq e_t$. Call e *discrete* (in the given run R) if the collection of significant moments of e is discrete. In other words, e is discrete if and only, for every $t > 0$, there is a finite sequence

$$0 = t_0 < t_1 < \ldots < t_n = t$$

such that if $t_i < \alpha < \beta < t_{i+1}$ then $e_\alpha = e_\beta$.

Lemma 4 (Discrete Term Lemma). *If a term e is discrete then*

1. *For every t, e has a value at t+.*
2. *For every $t > 0$, e has a value at t−.*

Proof. Obvious. □

Lemma 5 (Preservation Lemma). *Suppose that a term e with fixed values of its free variables does not contain CT. Then e is discrete. Furthermore,*

1. *If e contains no external functions and $t > 0$ then $e_t = e_{t-}$.*
2. *If e contains no internal functions then $e_{t+} = e_t$.*

Proof. This is an obvious consequence of the definition of runs. □

It may be natural to have agents that fire the instant they are enabled.

Definition 6. An agent is *immediate* if it fires at every state where it is enabled. □

Lemma 7 (Immediate Agent Lemma).

1. *The set of moments when an immediate agent is enabled is discrete.*
2. *If the agent is enabled at some moment t then it is disabled at t+ and, if $t > 0$, at t−.*

Proof.

1. If the agent is enabled at a moment t, it fires at t and therefore (according to our notion of being enabled) changes the state; it follows that t is a significant moment of the run. By the discreteness condition on pre-runs, the collection of significant moments of a run is discrete. It remains to notice that every subset of a discrete set is discrete.
2. Follows from 1. □

Recall the scenario S2. There agent Y cannot be immediate. Nevertheless, it may make sense to require that some agents cannot delay firing forever.

Definition 8. An agent X is *bounded* if it is immediate or there exists a bound $b > 0$ such that there is no interval $(t, t + b)$ during which X is continuously enabled but does not fire. □

Notice that it is not required that if a bounded agent X becomes enabled at some moment α, then it fires at some moment $\beta < \alpha + b$. It is possible a priori that X becomes disabled and does not fire in that interval.

5 The Ealgebra for Railroad Crossing Problem

We present our solution for the railroad crossing problem formalized as an evolving algebra $\mathcal{A}$ of a vocabulary $\Upsilon^+ = \Upsilon \cup \{\text{CT}\}$. In this section, we describe the program and initial states of $\mathcal{A}$; this will describe the vocabulary as well. The relevant runs of $\mathcal{A}$ will be described in the next section.

The program of $\mathcal{A}$ has two modules GATE and CONTROLLER, shown in Fig. 3.

```
GATE
    if Dir = open then GateStatus := open endif
    if Dir = close then GateStatus := closed endif

CONTROLLER
    var x ranges over Tracks
        if TrackStatus(x) = coming and Deadline(x) = ∞ then
            Deadline(x) := CT+ WaitTime
        endif
        if CT =Deadline(x) then Dir := close endif
        if TrackStatus(x) = empty and Deadline(x) < ∞ then
            Deadline(x) := ∞
        endif
    endvar
    if Dir=close and SafeToOpen then Dir := open endif
```

Fig. 3. Rules for GATE and CONTROLLER.

Here WaitTime abbreviates the term $d_{\text{min}} - d_{\text{close}}$, and SafeToOpen abbreviates the term

$$(\forall x \in \text{Tracks})[\text{TrackStatus}(x) = \text{empty} \ \text{ or } \ \text{CT} + d_{\text{open}} < \text{Deadline}(x)].$$

We will refer to the two constituent rules of GATE as OpenGate, CloseGate respectively. We will refer to the three constituent rules of CONTROLLER's parallel synchronous rule as SetDeadline(x), SignalClose(x), ClearDeadline(x), respectively, and the remaining conditional rule as SignalOpen.

Our GateStatus has only two values: opened and closed. This is of course a simplification. The position of a real gate could be anywhere between fully closed and fully opened. (In [6], the position of the gate ranges between 0° and 90°.) But this simplification is meaningful. The problem is posed on a level of abstraction where it does not matter whether the gate swings, slides, snaps or does something else; it is even possible that there is no physical gate, just traffic lights. Furthermore, suppose that the gate is opening and consider its position as it swings from 0° to 90°. Is it still closed or already open at 75°? One may say that it is neither, that it is opening. But for the waiting cars, it is still closed.

Accordingly GateStatus is intended to be equal to closed at this moment. It may change to opened when the gate reaches 90°. Alternatively, in the case when the crossing is equipped with traffic lights, it may change to opened when the light becomes green. Similarly, it may change from opened to closed when the light becomes red. If one is interested in specifying the gate in greater detail, our ealgebra can be refined by means of another ealgebra.

The program does not define our evolving algebra $\mathcal{A}$ completely. In addition, we need to specify a collection of *initial states* and relevant runs.

Initial states of $\mathcal{A}$ satisfy the following conditions:

1. The universe Tracks is finite. The universe ExtendedReals is an extension of the universe Reals with an additional element ∞. The binary relation $<$ and the binary operation $+$ are standard; in particular ∞ is the largest element of ExtendedReals.
2. The nullary functions close and open are interpreted by different elements of the universe Directions. The nullary functions closed and opened are interpreted by different elements of the universe GateStatuses. The nullary functions empty, coming, in_crossing are different elements of the universe TrackStatuses.
3. The nullary functions $d_{\text{close}}, d_{\text{open}}, d_{\text{max}}, d_{\text{min}}$ are positive reals such that

$$d_{\text{close}} < d_{\text{min}} \leq d_{\text{max}}.$$

   One may assume for simplicity of understanding that these four reals are predefined: that is, they have the same value in all initial state. This assumption is not necessary.
4. The unary function TrackStatus assigns (the element called) empty to every track (that is, to every element of the universe Tracks). The unary function Deadline assigns ∞ to every track.

It is easy to see that, in any run, every value of the internal function Deadline belongs to ExtendedReals.

6 Regular Runs

The following definition takes into account the assumptions of Sect. 2.

6.1 Definitions

Definition 9. A run R of our evolving algebra is *regular* if it satisfies the following three conditions.

Train Motion For any track x, there is a finite or infinite sequence

$$0 = t_0 < t_1 < t_2 < t_3 < \dots$$

of so-called *significant moments of track x* such that

- TrackStatus(x) = empty holds over every interval $[t_{3i}, t_{3i+1})$;
- TrackStatus(x) = coming holds over every interval $[t_{3i+1}, t_{3i+2})$, and $d_{\min} \le (t_{3i+2} - t_{3i+1}) \le d_{\max}$;
- TrackStatus(x) = in_crossing holds over every interval $[t_{3i+2}, t_{3i+3})$; and
- if t_k is the final significant moment in the sequence, then k is divisible by 3 and TrackStatus(x) = empty over $[t_k, \infty)$.

Controller Timing Agent CONTROLLER is immediate.

Gate Timing Agent GATE is bounded. Moreover, there is no time interval $I = (t, t + d_{\text{close}})$ such that [Dir=close and GateStatus = opened] holds over I. Similarly there is no interval $I = (t, t + d_{\text{open}})$ such that [Dir=open and GateStatus = closed] holds over I. □

In the rest of this paper, we restrict attention to regular runs of $\mathcal{A}$. Let R be a regular run and ρ be the reduct of R to Υ.

6.2 Single Track Analysis

Fix a track x and let $0 = t_0 < t_1 < t_2 < \dots$ be the significant moments of x.

Lemma 10 (Deadline Lemma).

1. *Deadline(x) = ∞ over $(t_{3i}, t_{3i+1}]$, and Deadline(x) = t_{3i+1} + WaitTime over $(t_{3i+1}, t_{3i+3}]$.*
2. *Let $D_{close} = d_{close} + (d_{max} - d_{min}) = d_{max} -$ WaitTime. If TrackStatus(x) $\neq$ in_crossing over an interval (α, β), then Deadline(x) $\geq \beta - D_{close}$ over (α, β).*

Proof.

1. A quite obvious induction along the sequence

$$(t_0, t_1], (t_1, t_3], (t_3, t_4], (t_4, t_6], \dots.$$

The basis of induction. We prove that Deadline(x) = ∞ over $I = (t_0, t_1)$; it will follow by Preservation Lemma that Deadline(x) = ∞ at t_1. Initially, Deadline(x) = ∞. Only SetDeadline(x) can alter that value of Deadline(x), but SetDeadline(x) is disabled over (t_0, t_1). The induction step splits into two cases.

Case 1. Given that Deadline(x) = ∞ at t_{3i+1}, we prove that Deadline(x) = t_{3i+1} + WaitTime over $I = (t_{3i+1}, t_{3i+3})$; it will follow by Preservation Lemma that Deadline(x) = t_{3i+1} + WaitTime at t_{3i+3}. SetDeadline(x) is enabled and therefore fires at t_{3i+1} setting Deadline(x) to t_{3i+1} + WaitTime. ClearDeadline(x) is the only rule that can alter that value of Deadline(x) but it is disabled over I because TrackStatus(x) $\neq$ empty over I.

Case 2. Given that Deadline(x) $< \infty$ at t_{3i} where $i > 0$, we prove that Deadline(x) $= \infty$ over $I = (t_{3i}, t_{3i+1})$; it will follow by Preservation Lemma that Deadline(x) $= \infty$ at t_{3i+1}. ClearDeadline(x) is enabled and therefore fires at t_{3i} setting Deadline(x) to ∞. Only SetDeadline(x) can alter that value of Deadline(x) but it is disabled over I because TrackStatus(x) $=$ empty $\neq$ coming over I.

2. By contradiction suppose that Deadline(x) $< \beta - D_{\text{close}}$ at some $t \in (\alpha, \beta)$. By 1, there is an i such that $t_{3i+1} < t \leq t_{3i+3}$ and Deadline(x) $= t_{3i+1} +$ WaitTime at t. Since (α, β) and the in_crossing interval $[t_{3i+2}, t_{3i+3})$ are disjoint, we have that $t_{3i+1} < t < \beta \leq t_{3i+2}$. By the definition of regular runs, $d_{\max} \geq t_{3i+2} - t_{3i+1} \geq \beta - t_{3i+1}$, so that $t_{3i+1} \geq \beta - d_{\max}$. We have

$$\begin{aligned}\beta - D_{\text{close}} > \text{Deadline}(x) \text{ at t} &= t_{3i+1} + \text{WaitTime} \\ \geq \beta - d_{\max} + \text{WaitTime} &= \beta - D_{\text{close}}\end{aligned}$$

which is impossible. □

Corollary 11 (Three Rules Corollary).

1. *SetDeadline(x) fires exactly at moments t_{3i+1}, that is exactly when TrackStatus(x) becomes coming.*
2. *SignalClose(x) fires exactly at moments t_{3i+1} + WaitTime.*
3. *ClearDeadline(x) fires exactly at moments t_{3i} with $i > 0$, that is exactly when TrackStatus(x) becomes empty.*

Proof. Obvious. □

Let $s(x)$ be the quantifier-free part

$$\text{TrackStatus}(x) = \text{empty} \quad \text{or} \quad \text{CT} + d_{\text{open}} < \text{Deadline}(x).$$

of the term SafeToOpen with the fixed value of x.

Lemma 12 (Local SafeToOpen Lemma).

1. *Suppose that WaitTime $> d_{open}$. Then $s(x)$ holds over intervals $[t_{3i}, t_{3i+1} +$ WaitTime $- d_{open})$ (the* maximal positive intervals of $s(x)$*) and fails over intervals $[t_{3i+1} +$ WaitTime $- d_{open}, t_{3i+3})$.*
2. *Suppose that WaitTime $\leq d_{open}$. Then $s(x)$ holds over intervals $[t_{3i}, t_{3i+1}]$ (the* maximal positive intervals of $s(x)$*) and fails over intervals (t_{3i+1}, t_{3i+3}).*
3. *The term $s(v)$ is discrete.*
4. *$s(x)$ becomes true exactly at moments t_{3i} with $i > 0$, that is exactly when TrackStatus(x) becomes empty.*
5. *If $[\alpha, \beta)$ or $[\alpha, \beta]$ is a maximal positive interval of $s(x)$, then SignalClose(x) is disabled over $[\alpha, \beta]$ and at $\beta+$.*

Proof.

1. Over $[t_{3i}, t_{3i+1})$, TrackStatus(x) = empty and therefore $s(x)$ holds. At t_{3i+1}, Deadline(x) $= \infty$ and therefore $s(x)$ holds. SetDeadline(x) fires at t_{3i+1} and sets Deadline(x) to t_{3i+1} + WaitTime. Over $(t_{3i}, t_{3i+1} + \text{WaitTime} - d_{\text{open}})$,

$$\begin{aligned} \text{CT} + d_{\text{open}} &< (t_{3i+1} + \text{WaitTime} - d_{\text{open}}) + d_{\text{open}} \\ &= t_{3i+1} + \text{WaitTime} = \text{Deadline}(x) \end{aligned}$$

   and therefore $s(x)$ holds. Over the interval $[t_{3i+1} + \text{WaitTime} - d_{\text{open}}, t_{3i+3})$, TrackStatus($x$) $\neq$ empty and $\text{CT} + d_{\text{open}} \geq t_{3i+1} + \text{WaitTime} = \text{Deadline}(x)$ and therefore $s(x)$ fails.
2. The proof is similar to that of 1.
3. This follows from 1 and 2.
4. This follows from 1 and 2.
5. We consider the case when WaitTime $> d_{\text{open}}$; the case when WaitTime $\leq d_{\text{open}}$ is similar. By 1, the maximal open interval of $s(x)$ has the form $[\alpha, \beta) = [t_{3i}, t_{3i+1} + \text{WaitTime} - d_{\text{open}})$ for some i. By Three Rules Corollary, SignalClose(x) fires at moments t_{3j+1} + WaitTime. Now the claim is obvious. □

6.3 Multiple Track Analysis

Lemma 13 (Global SafeToOpen Lemma).

1. *The term SafeToOpen is discrete.*
2. *If SafeToOpen holds at $t+$ then it holds at t.*
3. *If SafeToOpen becomes true at t then some TrackStatus(x) becomes empty at t.*
4. *If SafeToOpen holds at t then t belongs to an interval $[\alpha, \beta)$ (a* maximal positive interval of *SafeToOpen) such that SafeToOpen fails at $\alpha-$, holds over $[\alpha, \beta)$ and fails at β.*

Proof.

1. Use part 3 of Local SafeToOpen Lemma and the fact that there are only finitely many tracks.
2. Use parts 1 and 2 of Local SafeToOpen Lemma.
3. Use parts 1 and 2 of Local SafeToOpen Lemma.
4. Suppose that SafeToOpen holds at t. By parts 1 and 2 of Local SafeToOpen Lemma, for every track x, t belongs to an interval $[\alpha_x < \beta_x)$ such that $s(x)$ fails at α_x-, holds over $[\alpha_x, \beta_x)$ and fails at β_x. The desired $\alpha = \max_x \alpha_x$, and the desired $\beta = \min_x \beta_x$. □

Lemma 14 (Dir Lemma). *Suppose that $[\alpha, b)$ is a maximal positive interval of SafeToOpen.*

1. *Dir = close at α.*
2. *Dir = open over $(\alpha, \beta]$ and at $\beta+$.*

Proof.

1. By Global SafeToOpen Lemma, some TrackStatus(x) becomes empty at t. Fix such an x and let $0 = t_0 < t_1 < t_2 < \ldots$ be the significant moments of TrackStatus(x). Then $\alpha = t_{3i+3}$ for some i. By Three Rules Corollary, SetDeadline(x) fires at t_{3i+1} + WaitTime setting Dir to close. By Local SafeToOpen Lemma, $s(x)$ fails over $I = (t_{3i+1} + \text{WaitTime}, t_{3i+3}]$. Hence SafeToOpen fails over I and therefore every SignalClose(y) is disabled over I. Thus Dir remains close over I.
2. By 1, SignalOpen fires at α setting Dir to open. By part 5 of Local SafeToOpen Lemma, every SignalClose(x) is disabled over $[\alpha, \beta]$ and at $\beta+$. Hence Dir remains open over $(\alpha, \beta]$ and at $\beta+$. □

Corollary 15 (SignalOpen Corollary). *SignalOpen fires exactly when SafeToOpen becomes true. SignalOpen fires only when some TrackStatus(x) becomes true.*

Proof. Obvious. □

We have proved some properties of regular runs of our ealgebra $\mathcal{A}$, but the question arises if there any regular runs. Moreover, are there any regular runs consistent with a given pattern of trains? The answer is positive. In Sect. 8, we will prove that every pattern of trains gives rise to a regular run and will describe all regular runs consistent with a given pattern of trains.

7 Safety and Liveness

Recall that we restrict attention to regular runs of our ealgebra $\mathcal{A}$.

Theorem 16 (Safety Theorem). *The gate is closed whenever a train is in the crossing. More formally, GateStatus = closed whenever TrackStatus(x) = in_crossing for any x.*

Proof. Let $t_0 < t_1 < \ldots$ be the significant moments of some track x. Thus, during periods $[t_{3i+2}, t_{3i+3})$, TrackStatus(x) = in_crossing. We show that GateStatus = closed over $[t_{3i+2}, t_{3i+3}]$ and even over $[t_{3i+1} + d_{\min}, t_{3i+3}]$. (Recall that $d_{\min} \leq t_{3i+2} - t_{3i+1} \leq d_{\max}$ and therefore $t_{3i+1} + d_{\min} \leq t_{3i+2}$.)

By Three Rules Corollary, SetDeadline(x) fires at t_{3i+1} setting Deadline(x) to $\alpha = t_{3i+1}$ + WaitTime. If Dir_α = open then SignalClose(x) fires at α setting Dir to close; regardless, $\text{Dir}_{\alpha+}$ = close. By Local SafeToOpen Lemma, $s(x)$ fails over $I = (\alpha, t_{3i+3})$. Hence, over I, SafeToOpen fails, SignalOpen is disabled, Dir = close, and OpenGate is disabled.

By the definition of regular runs, GateStatus = closed at some moment t such that $\alpha < t < \alpha + d_{\text{close}} = t_{3i+1} + \text{WaitTime} + d_{\text{close}} = t_{3i+1} + d_{\min}$. Since OpenGate is disabled over I, GateStatus remains closed over I and therefore over the interval $[t_{3i+1} + d_{\min}, t_{3i+3})$. By Preservation Lemma, GateStatus = closed at t_{3i+3}. □

Let $D_{\text{close}} = d_{\text{close}} + (d_{\max} - d_{\min}) = d_{\max} - \text{WaitTime}$.

Theorem 17 (Liveness Theorem). *Assume $\alpha + d_{open} < \beta - D_{close}$. If the crossing is empty in the open time interval (α, β), then the gate is open in $[\alpha + d_{open}, \beta - D_{close}]$. More formally, if every TrackStatus(x) $\neq$ in_crossing over (α, β), then GateStatus = opened over $[\alpha + d_{open}, \beta - D_{close}]$.*

Proof. By Deadline Lemma, every Deadline(x) $\geq \beta - D_{\text{close}} > \alpha + d_{\text{open}}$ over (α, β). By the definition of SafeToOpen, it holds at α. If Dir_α = close then SignalOpen fires at α; in any case $\text{Dir}_{\alpha+}$ = open.

By Deadline Lemma, every Deadline(x) $\geq \beta - D_{\text{close}} > CT$ over $(\alpha, \beta - D_{\text{close}})$. Hence, over $(\alpha, \beta - D_{\text{close}})$, every SignalClose($x$) is disabled, Dir remains open, and StartClose is disabled.

By the definition of regular runs, GateStatus = opened at some moment $t \in (\alpha, \alpha + d_{\text{open}})$. Since StartClose is disabled over $(\alpha, \beta - D_{\text{close}})$, GateStatus remains opened over $(t, \beta - D_{\text{close}})$ and therefore is opened over $[\alpha + d_{\text{open}}, \beta - D_{\text{close}})$. By Preservation Lemma, GateStatus = opened at $b - D_{\text{close}}$. □

The next claim shows that, in a sense, Liveness Theorem cannot be improved.

Claim 18.

1. *Liveness Theorem fails if d_{open} is replaced with a smaller constant.*
2. *Liveness Theorem fails if D_{close} is replaced with a smaller constant.*

Proof. The first statement holds because the gate can take time arbitrarily close to d_{open} to open. The second statement holds for two reasons. Recall that $D_{\text{close}} = d_{\text{close}} + (d_{\max} - d_{\min})$. The term $(d_{\max} - d_{\min})$ cannot be reduced; to be on the safe side, the controller must act as if every oncoming train is moving as fast as possible, even if it is moving as slow as possible. The term d_{close} cannot be reduced either; the gate can take arbitrarily short periods of time to close. Now we give a more detailed proof.

Part 1. Given some constant $c_{\text{open}} < d_{\text{open}}$, we construct a regular run of our ealgebra $\mathcal{A}$ and exhibit an open interval $I = (\alpha, \beta)$ such that the crossing is empty during I but the gate is not opened during a part of interval $(\alpha + c_{\text{open}}, \beta - D_{\text{close}})$.

We assume that $d_{\text{open}}, D_{\text{close}} < 1$ (just choose the unit of time appropriately) and that there is only one track.

The traffic. Only one train goes through the crossing. It appears at time 100, reaches the crossing at time $100 + d_{\max}$ and leaves the crossing at time $110 + d_{\max}$, so that Dir should be changed only twice: set to close at $100 + \text{WaitTime}$ and set to open at $110 + d_{\max}$.

The run. We don't care how quickly the gate closes, but we stipulate that the time Δ that the gate takes to open belongs to $(c_{\text{open}}, d_{\text{open}})$.

The interval I: $(110 + d_{\max}, 110 + d_{\max} + d_{\text{open}})$.

Since the only train leaves the crossing at $110 + d_{\max}$, the crossing is empty during I. However the gate takes time $\Delta > c_{\text{open}}$ to open and thus is not opened during the part $(110 + d_{\max} + c_{\text{open}}, 110 + d_{\max} + \Delta)$ of I.

Part 2. Given some constant $C_{\text{close}} < D_{\text{close}}$, we construct a regular run of our ealgebra $\mathcal{A}$ and exhibit an open interval $I = (\alpha, \beta)$ such that the crossing is empty during I but the gate is not opened (even closed) during a part of interval $(\alpha + d_{\text{open}}, \beta - C_{\text{close}})$.

We assume that $d_{\text{open}}, C_{\text{close}} < 1$, and that there is only one track with the same traffic pattern as in part 1.

The run. This time we don't care how quickly the gate opens, but we stipulate that the time Δ that the gate takes to close satisfies the following condition:

$$0 < \Delta < \min\{d_{\text{close}}, D_{\text{close}} - C_{\text{close}}\}.$$

The interval I is $(0, 100 + d_{\max})$, so that $\alpha = 0$ and $\beta = 100 + d_{\max}$.

Since the only train reaches the crossing at $100 + d_{\max}$, the crossing is empty during I. The gate is closed by $100 + \text{WaitTime} + \Delta$ and is closed during the part $(100 + \text{WaitTime} + \Delta, 100 + \text{WaitTime} + (D_{\text{close}} - C_{\text{close}}))$ of interval $(\alpha + d_{\text{open}}, \beta - C_{\text{close}})$. Let us check that $(100 + \text{WaitTime} + \Delta, 100 + \text{WaitTime} + (D_{\text{close}} - C_{\text{close}})$ is indeed a part of $(\alpha + d_{\text{open}}, \beta - C_{\text{close}})$. Clearly, $\alpha + d_{\text{open}} < 0 + 1 < 100 + \text{WaitTime} + \Delta$. Further:

$$\begin{aligned} & 100 + \text{WaitTime} + \Delta \\ < {} & 100 + \text{WaitTime} + (D_{\text{close}} - C_{\text{close}}) \\ = {} & 100 + (d_{\min} - d_{\text{close}}) + [(d_{\text{close}} + d_{\max} - d_{\min}) - C_{\text{close}}] = \beta - C_{\text{close}}. \end{aligned}$$

□

8 Some Additional Properties

Theorem 19 (Uninterrupted Closing Theorem). *The closing of the gate is never interrupted. More formally, if Dir is set to close at some moment α, then Dir = close over the interval $I = (\alpha, \alpha + d_{close})$.*

Recall that, by the definition of regular runs, GateStatus = closed somewhere in I if Dir = close over I.

Proof. Since Dir is set to close at α, some SignalClose(x) fires at α. Fix such an x and let $t_0 < t_1 < \ldots$ be the significant moments of track x. By Three Rules Corollary, there is an i such that $\alpha = t_{3i+1} + \text{WaitTime} = t_{3i+1} + d_{\min} - d_{\text{close}}$. Then $\alpha + d_{\text{close}} = t_{3i+1} + d_{\min} \leq t_{3i+2}$. By the definition of regular runs, TrackStatus(x) = coming over I. By Deadline Theorem, Deadline(x) = α over I, so that $\text{CT} + d_{\text{open}} > \text{CT} > \text{Deadline}(x)$ over I. Because of this x, SafeToOpen fails over I and therefore SignalOpen is disabled over I. Thus Dir = close over I.

Theorem 20 (Uninterrupted Opening Theorem). *Suppose WaitTime $\geq d_{open}$; that is, $d_{min} \geq d_{close} + d_{open}$. Then the opening of the gate is not interrupted; in other words, if Dir is set to open at some moment α, then Dir = open over the interval $I = (\alpha, \alpha + d_{open})$.*

Recall that, by the definition of regular runs, GateStatus = opened somewhere in I if Dir = open over I.

Proof. It suffices to prove that every SignalClose(x) is disabled over I. Pick any x and let $t_0 < t_1 < \ldots$ be the significant moments of track x. Since Dir is set to open at α, SignalOpen fires at α, SafeToOpen holds at α, and $s(x)$ holds at α. We have two cases.

Case 1. $\alpha + d_{\text{open}} <$ Deadline$(x)_\alpha < \infty$. Since Deadline$(x)_\alpha < \infty$, $\tau_{3i+1} < \alpha \leq t_{3i+3}$ and Deadline$(x)_\alpha = t_{3i+1} +$ WaitTime for some i (by Deadline Lemma). We have

$$\alpha + d_{\text{open}} < \text{Deadline}(x)_\alpha = t_{3i+1} + \text{WaitTime} < t_{3i+1} + d_{\text{min}} \leq t_{3i+2} < t_{3i+3}.$$

By Deadline Lemma, Deadline(x) does not change in I, so that CT remains $<$ Deadline(x) in I and therefore SignalClose(x) is disabled over I.

Case 2. $\alpha + d_{\text{open}} \geq \text{Deadline}_\alpha(x)$ or $\text{Deadline}_\alpha(x) = \infty$.

We check that $t_{3i} \leq \alpha \leq t_{3i+1}$ for some i. Indeed, if TrackStatus$(x)_\alpha$ = empty then $t_{3i} \leq \alpha < t_{3i+1}$ for some i. Suppose that TrackStatus$(x)_\alpha \neq$ empty. Since $s(x)$ holds at a, $\alpha + d_{\text{open}} < \text{Deadline}_\alpha(x)$. By the condition of Case 2, Deadline$(x)_\alpha = \infty$. Recall that TrackStatus(x) $\neq$ empty exactly in intervals $[t_{3i+1}, t_{3i+3}$ and Deadline(x) $= \infty$ exactly in periods $(t_{3i}, t_{3i+1}]$. Thus $\alpha = t_{3i+1}$ for some i.

The first moment after α that SignalClose(x) is enabled is $t_{3i+1} +$ WaitTime. Thus it suffices to check that $\alpha + d_{\text{open}} \leq t_{3i+1} +$ WaitTime. Since $d_{\text{min}} \geq d_{\text{close}} + d_{\text{open}}$, we have

$$\alpha + d_{\text{open}} \leq t_{3i+1} + d_{\text{open}} \leq t_{3i+1} + (d_{\text{min}} - d_{\text{close}}) = t_{3i+1} + \text{WaitTime}.\square$$

Corollary 21 (Dir and GateStatus Corollary). *Assume $d_{min} \geq d_{close} + d_{open}$.*

1. *If the sequence $\gamma_1 < \gamma_2 < \gamma_3 < \ldots$ of positive significant moments of Dir is infinite, then the sequence $\delta_1 < \delta_2 < \delta_3 < \ldots$ of positive significant moments of GateStatus is infinite and each $\delta_i \in (\gamma_i, \gamma_{i+1})$.*
2. *If the positive significant moments of Dir form a finite sequence $\gamma_1 < \gamma_2 < \ldots < \gamma_n$, then the positive significant moments of GateStatus form a sequence $\delta_1 < \delta_2 < \ldots < \delta_n$ such that $\delta_i \in (\gamma_i, \gamma_{i+1})$ for all $i < n$ and $\delta_n > \gamma_n$.*

Proof. We prove only the first claim; the second claim is proved similarly.

Since Dir = open and GateStatus = opened initially, GateStatus does not change in $(0, \gamma_1)$. Suppose that we have proved that if $\gamma_1 < \ldots < \gamma_j$ are the first j positive significant moments of Dir, then there are exactly $j - 1$ significant moments $\delta_1 < \ldots < \delta_{j-1}$ of GateStatus in $(0, g_j]$ and each $\delta_i \in (\gamma_i, \gamma_{i+1})$. We restrict attention to the case when j is even; the case of odd j is similar. Since j is even, Dir is set to open at γ_j. If γ_j is the last significant moment of Dir, then the gate will open at some time in $(\gamma_j, \gamma_j + d_{\text{open}})$ and will stay open forever after that. Otherwise, let $k = j + 1$. By Uninterrupted Opening Theorem, the gate opens at some moment $\delta_j \in (\gamma_j, \gamma_k)$. Since Dir remains open in (δ_j, γ_k), GateStatus = opened holds over (δ_j, γ_k). By Preservation Lemma, GateStatus = opened at γ_k. □

9 Existence of Regular Runs

We delayed the existence issue in order to take advantage of Sect. 8. For simplicity, we restrict attention to an easier but seemingly more important case when $d_{\text{min}} \geq d_{\text{close}} + d_{\text{open}}$. The Existence Theorem and the two Claims proved in this section remain true in the case $d_{\text{min}} < d_{\text{close}} + d_{\text{open}}$; we provide remarks explaining the necessary changes.

Let $\Upsilon_1 = \Upsilon - \{\text{GateStatus}\}$, and $\Upsilon_0 = \Upsilon_1 - \{\text{Deadline}, \text{Dir}\}$. For $i = 0, 1$, let $\Upsilon_i^+ = \Upsilon_i \cup \{\text{CT}\}$.

Theorem 22 (Existence Theorem). *Let P be a pre-run of vocabulary Υ_0 satisfying the train motion requirement in the definition of regular runs, and let A be an initial state of $\mathcal{A}$ consistent with $P(0)$. There is a regular run R of $\mathcal{A}$ which starts with A and agrees with P.*

Proof. Let the significant moments of P be $0 = \alpha_0 < \alpha_1 < \ldots$. For simplicity, we consider only the case where this sequence is infinite. The case when the sequence is finite is similar. Our construction proceeds in two phases. In the first phase, we construct a run Q of module CONTROLLER (that is of the corresponding one-module evolving algebra of vocabulary Υ_1^+) consistent with A and P. In the second phase, we construct the desired R by extending Q to include the execution of module GATE.

Phase 1: Constructing Q from P. Let $\beta_0 < \beta_1 < \ldots$ be the sequence that comprises the moments α_i and the moments of the form t + WaitTime where t is a moment when some TrackStatus(x) becomes coming. By Three Rule and SignalOpen Corollaries, these are exactly the significant moments of the desired Q. We define the desired Q by induction on β_i. It is easy to see that $Q(T)$ is uniquely defined by its reduct $q(t)$ to Υ_1.

$Q(0)$ is the appropriate reduct of A. Suppose that Q is defined over $[0, \beta_j]$ and $k = j + 1$. Let γ range over (β_j, β_k). If CONTROLLER does not execute at β_j, define $q(\gamma) = q(\beta_j)$; otherwise let $q(\gamma)$ e the state resulting from executing CONTROLLER at $q(\beta_j)$. Define $q(\beta_k)$ to agree with $q(\gamma)$ at all functions except TrackStatus, where it agrees with $P(\beta_k)$.

Clearly Q is a pre-run. It is easy to check that Q is a run of CONTROLLER and that CONTROLLER is immediate in Q.

Phase 2: Constructing R from Q. We construct R by expanding Q to include GateStatus. Let $\gamma_1 < \gamma_2 < \ldots$ be the sequence of significant moments of Q at which Dir changes. Thus Dir becomes close at moments γ_i where i is odd, and becomes open at moments γ_i where i is even.

There are many possible ways of extending Q depending on how long it takes to perform a given change in GateStatus. Chose a sequence $a_1, a_2, \ldots$ of reals such that (i) $a_i < \gamma_{i+1} - \gamma_i$ and (ii) $a_i < d_{\text{close}}$ if i is odd and $a_i < d_{\text{open}}$ if i is even. The idea is that GATE will delay executing OpenGate or CloseGate for time a_i.

The construction proceeds by induction on γ_i. After i steps, GateStatus will be defined over $[0, g_i]$, and GateStatus_{g_i} will equal opened if i is odd and will equal closed otherwise.

Set GateStatus = opened over $[0, \gamma_1]$. Suppose that GateStatus is defined over $[0, \gamma_i]$ and let $j = i + 1$. We consider only the case when i is even. The case of odd i is similar.

By the induction hypothesis, GateStatus = closed at γ_i. Since i is even, Dir is set to open at γ_i. Define GateStatus = closed over $(\gamma_i, \gamma_i + a_i]$ and opened over $(\gamma_i + a_i, \gamma_j]$.

It is easy to see that R is a regular run of $\mathcal{A}$. □

Remark. If the assumption $d_{\text{min}} \geq d_{\text{close}} + d_{\text{open}}$ is removed, Phase 1 of the construction does not change but Phase 2 becomes more complicated. After i steps, GateStatus is defined over $[0, g_i]$, and GateStatus_{g_i} = closed if i is even; it cannot be guaranteed that GateStatus_{g_i} = opened if i is odd. The first step is as above. For an even i, we have three cases.

Case 1: $a_i < \gamma_j - \gamma_i$. Define GateStatus over $(g_i, g_j]$ as in the Existence Theorem Proof.

Case 2: $a_i > \gamma_j - \gamma_i$. Define GateStatus = closed over $(g_i, g_j]$.

Case 3: $a_i = \gamma_j - \gamma_i$. Define GateStatus = closed over $(g_i, g_j]$ as in sub-case 2 but also mark g_j (to indicate that OpenGate should fire at γ_j).

For an odd i, we have two cases.

Case 1: Either GateStatus = opened at γ_i or else GateStatus = closed at g_i but g_i is marked. Define GateStatus over $(g_i, g_j]$ as in the Existence Theorem Proof.

Case 2: GateStatus = closed at γ_i and γ_i is not marked. Ignore a_i and define GateStatus = closed over $(g_i, g_j]$.

Claim 23 (Uniqueness of Control). *There is only one run of* CONTROLLER *consistent with A and P.*

Proof. Intuitively, the claim is true because the construction of Q was deterministic: we had no choice in determining the significant moments of Q. More formally, assume by reductio ad absurdum that Q_1, Q_2 are runs of CONTROLLER consistent with A and P and the set $D = \{t : Q_1(t) \neq Q_2(t)\}$ is non-empty. Let $\tau = \inf(D)$. Since both Q_1 and Q_2 agree with A, $\tau > 0$. By the choice of τ, Q_1 and Q_2 agree over $[0, \tau)$. Since both Q_1 and Q_2 agree with A and P, they can differ only at internal functions; let q_1, q_2 be reductions of Q_1, Q_2 respectively to the internal part of the vocabulary. By Preservation Lemma, q_1 and q_2 coincide at τ. But the values of internal functions at $\tau+$ are completely defined by the state at t. Thus q_1 and q_2 coincide at $\tau+$ and therefore Q_1, Q_2 coincide over some nonempty interval $[\tau, \tau+\varepsilon)$. This contradicts the definition of τ. □

Claim 24 (Universality of Construction). *Let R' be any regular run of the ealgebra consistent with A and P. In the proof of Existence Theorem, the sequence $a_1, a_2, \ldots$ can be chosen in such a way that the regular run R constructed there coincides with R'.*

Proof. By Uniqueness of Control Claim, the reducts of R and R' to Υ_1^+ coincide. The moments $\gamma_1 < \gamma_2 < \ldots$ when Dir changes in R are exactly the same moments when Dir changes in R'. We have only to construct appropriate constants a_i.

Let $\delta_1 < \delta_2 < \ldots$ be the significant moments of GateStatus in R'. With respect to Dir and GateStatus Corollary, define $a_i = \delta_i - \gamma_i$. It is easy to check that $R = R'$. □

Remark. If the assumption $d_{\text{min}} \geq \text{close} + d_{\text{open}}$ is removed, the proof of Uniqueness of Control Claim does not change but the proof of Universality of Construction Claim becomes slightly complicated. Let $j = i + 1$. For an even i, we have two cases.

Case 1: $\delta_i \leq \gamma_j$. Define $a_i = \delta_i - \gamma_i$.

Case 2: $\delta_i > \gamma_j$. In this case $\gamma_j - \gamma_i < d_{\text{open}}$. The exact value of a_i is irrelevant; it is only important that $a_i \in (\gamma_j - \gamma_i, d_{\text{open}})$. Choose such an a_i arbitrarily.

For an odd i, we also have two cases.

Case 1: In R', either GateStatus = opened at γ_i or else GateStatus = closed at γ_i but OpenGate fires at γ_i. Define $a_i = \delta_i - \gamma_i$.

Case 2: In R', GateStatus = closed at γ_i. The exact value of a_i is irrelevant; it is only important that $a_i < d_{\text{close}}$. Choose such an a_i arbitrarily.

References

1. Egon Börger, Annotated Bibliography on Evolving Algebras, in "Specification and Validation Methods", ed. E. Börger, Oxford University Press, 1995, 37–51.
2. Egon Börger, Yuri Gurevich and Dean Rosenzweig: The Bakery Algorithm: Yet Another Specification and Verification, in "Specification and Validation Methods", ed. E. Börger, Oxford University Press, 1995.
3. Yuri Gurevich, "Evolving Algebra 1993: Lipari Guide", in "Specification and Validation Methods", Ed. E. Börger, Oxford University Press, 1995, 9–36.
4. Yuri Gurevich and James K. Huggins, "The Railroad Crossing Problem: An Evolving Algebra Solution," LITP 95/63, Janvier 1996, Centre National de la Recherche Scientifique Paris, France.
5. Yuri Gurevich, James K. Huggins, and Raghu Mani, "The Generalized Railroad Crossing Problem: An Evolving Algebra Based Solution," University of Michigan EECS Department Technical Report CSE-TR-230-95.

6. Constance Heitmeyer and Nancy Lynch: The Generalized Railroad Crossing: A Case Study in Formal Verification of Real-Time Systems, Proc., Real-Time Systems Symp., San Juan, Puerto Rico, Dec., 1994, IEEE.
7. Ernst-Rüdiger Olderog, Anders P. Ravn and Jens Ulrik Skakkebaek, "Refining System Requirements to Program Specifications", to appear.
8. Robin Milner. A private discussion, Aug. 1994.

A Logical Aspect of Parametric Polymorphism *

Ryu Hasegawa

Oxford University Computing Laboratory, Wolfson Building,
Parks Road, Oxford OX1 3QD, England

Abstract

The system of formal parametric polymorphism has the same theory as second order Peano arithmetic with regard to the provable equality of numerical functions.

1 Introduction

We show that two numerical functions are provably equal in system R of parametric polymorphism [1] exactly when they are provably equal in second order Peano arithmetic. This may be regarded as an extension of the following well-known result: a numerical function is representable as a closed term of type $\mathbb{N} \Rightarrow \mathbb{N}$ in system F if and only if it is provably total in second order Peano arithmetic [6, 8]. However, the formal equality between terms of system F is the $\beta(\eta)$-equality, and thus for example two functions $\lambda xy.\, x+y$ and $\lambda xy.\, y+x$ are not formally equal, while they are evidently equal in second order arithmetic. Furthermore the translations of terms of system F to numerical functions and the other way round are not the inverse of each other.

Apart from the logical point of view, the other way to look at system F is by the notion of *parametricity*, which was the motivation of the independent invention of system F by Reynolds [17]. Later he proposed relational parametricity [18] in order to provide a method to mathematically denote the parametricity captured by system F. This notion of relational parametricity was able to give rich structures to the models of system F. Namely every parametric model has a lot of universal categorical data types, containing products and a natural number object, all definable as types of system F [2, 10, 11]. Several systems were proposed to get the relational parametricity again in formal systems [16, 1]. In this paper, we consider system R [1] (slightly modified) and show that it compensates the logical part lost by the translation from second order arithmetic to system F.

System R has the assertions consisting of three rows as

$$\begin{array}{c} \sigma \\ R \\ \sigma' \end{array} \qquad \text{and} \qquad \begin{array}{c} M : \sigma \\ R \\ M' : \sigma' \end{array} \quad .$$

* This work is supported by EPSRC GR1J97366.

The first asserts that R is a binary relation between two types σ and σ', and the second that two terms M and M' are related by the binary relation R. Each type σ has an identity relation denoted also by σ and therefore in system R we can assert the equality of numerical functions in the following form:

$$\begin{array}{c} M : \mathbb{N} \Rightarrow \mathbb{N} \\ \mathbb{N} \Rightarrow \mathbb{N} \\ M' : \mathbb{N} \Rightarrow \mathbb{N} \end{array}$$

The main theorem in this paper is stated as follows: let D_f denote the closed term of type $\mathbb{N} \Rightarrow \mathbb{N}$ in system F associated to a recursive function f that is provably total in second order Peano arithmetic with full comprehension PA^2, and ξ_M the recursive function associated to a closed term $M : \mathbb{N} \Rightarrow \mathbb{N}$ of system F (these will be defined in later sections). Then the following hold:

$$(1) \qquad \mathrm{PA}^2 \vdash \forall x.\, f(x) = g(x) \qquad \text{implies} \qquad \vdash_R \begin{array}{c} D_f : \mathbb{N} \Rightarrow \mathbb{N} \\ \mathbb{N} \Rightarrow \mathbb{N} \\ D_g : \mathbb{N} \Rightarrow \mathbb{N} \end{array} .$$

$$(2) \qquad \vdash_R \begin{array}{c} M : \mathbb{N} \Rightarrow \mathbb{N} \\ \mathbb{N} \Rightarrow \mathbb{N} \\ N : \mathbb{N} \Rightarrow \mathbb{N} \end{array} \qquad \text{implies} \qquad \mathrm{PA}^2 \vdash \forall x.\, \xi_M(x) = \xi_N(x) .$$

In addition, the following hold:

$$(3) \qquad \mathrm{PA}^2 \vdash \forall x.\, \xi_{D_f}(x) = f(x) .$$

$$(4) \qquad \vdash_R \begin{array}{c} D_{\xi_M} : \mathbb{N} \Rightarrow \mathbb{N} \\ \mathbb{N} \Rightarrow \mathbb{N} \\ M : \mathbb{N} \Rightarrow \mathbb{N} \end{array} .$$

Here f and g range over PA^2-provably total recursive functions and M and N over closed terms of type $\mathbb{N} \Rightarrow \mathbb{N}$ in system F. The first two assertions say that if two numerical functions are provably equal in second order arithmetic then they are equal in system R, and vice versa. The last two say that the translations between PA^2-provably total recursive functions and closed terms of type $\mathbb{N} \Rightarrow \mathbb{N}$ in system F are the inverse of each other.

So system R (i.e., system F plus parametricity) has the same logical power as second order Peano arithmetic. Therefore we view *system R as the decomposition of second order logic into the computation part and the specification part.* These two are clearly separated in the syntax of system R, in contrast, for example, to the calculus of constructions. Among three rows of the assertions the upper and the lower carry the computational part and the middle is the specification in the form of a binary relation. This fact could be an advantage of system R. If we argue in usual intuitionistic logic, the separation of programs from the specifications is not clear only from the expression of the formulas. If we argue in constructive type theory such as the calculus of constructions, the programs contain all proofs within them and the overhead sometimes makes the programs unfeasible.

Among the main results (1) through (4) mentioned above, (2) and (3) are rather easy, since PA^2 is strong and flexible enough to formalise our naive intuition. The manipulation of (1) and (4) is more delicate because system R is lack of some usual constructs, especially first order quantifiers. In order to detour this defect, we use the Dialectica interpretation, which is first defined on first order arithmetic by Gödel [9, 23, 12] and extended to higher order arithmetic by Girard [6]. The essence of the Dialectica interpretation is that all quantifiers are pushed forward so that the formulas become prenex Σ_2 forms $\exists y^\sigma \forall z^\tau . \phi(y, z)$ where ϕ is primitive recursive. We interpret y as a term of system F, z as a free variable, and $\phi(y, z)$ as a binary relation of system R.

In addition to technical merits, our Dialectica interpretation in system R gives a new insight to the controversial feature of the validity of Dialectica interpretation (see Section 3). We show also that with respect to numerical functions the Dialectica interpretation and the first order erasure [22, 14, 8] gives terms that are provably equal in system R. Furthermore, as corollaries of our main theorem, we show that (i) the theory of system R is Σ^0_1-complete; (ii) if two closed terms M and M' of type $\mathbb{N} \Rightarrow \mathbb{N}$ have the same type erasure as untyped lambda terms then they are provably equal in system R, giving an answer to a special case of an open problem posed in [1]. (Remark: the results mentioned above can all be extended to k-ary functions, $k > 1$, and also to other types of free universal algebras [4], since they are embeddable into the type of natural numbers.)

2 Formal parametric polymorphism

System R of formal parametric polymorphism was introduced in [1] to formalise the general semantical argument of parametric polymorphism. We modify the original system in [1] by symmetrising the graph relations. In the original system, if we have a term M of function type $\sigma \Rightarrow \tau$, then we are given a binary relation $\langle M \rangle$ from σ to τ that represents the graph of the function M. In this paper, we extend the graph relation to the wedge relation $\langle M \rangle\, R\, \langle M' \rangle^{\mathrm{op}}$, which is well-defined if $M : \sigma \Rightarrow \tau$, $M' : \sigma' \Rightarrow \tau'$, and R is a binary relation from τ to τ', in which case the wedge relation $\langle M \rangle\, R\, \langle M' \rangle^{\mathrm{op}}$ is from σ to σ'. We substitute the following two rules for the corresponding rules for the graph relations in [1].

$$\Gamma \vdash \begin{array}{c} MN : \tau \\ R \\ M'N' : \tau' \end{array} \quad \Rightarrow \quad \Gamma \vdash \begin{array}{c} N : \sigma \\ \langle M \rangle\, R\, \langle M' \rangle^{\mathrm{op}} \\ N' : \sigma' \end{array}$$

$$\Gamma \vdash \begin{array}{c} N : \sigma \\ \langle M \rangle\, R\, \langle M' \rangle^{\mathrm{op}} \\ N' : \sigma' \end{array} \quad \Rightarrow \quad \Gamma \vdash \begin{array}{c} MN : \tau \\ R \\ M'N' : \tau' \end{array}$$

where M and M' have the type $\sigma \Rightarrow \tau$ and $\sigma' \Rightarrow \tau'$. We believe our extension is natural, and some forms of wedge relations seem to be naturally required for the argument on the systems of third order or more [11]. In this paper, the argument in section 5 relies on the use of wedge relations. Furthermore, as far as composition of relations is concerned, the wedge relation is intuitionistically allowable composition since if L and L' are related by $\langle M \rangle\, R\, \langle M' \rangle$ then we can effectively find the intermediating elements by LM and $L'M'$.

The wedge relations serve to increase the definability of binary relations. For example, we can define a total relation $\top$ from σ to σ' by the wedge relation $\langle \downarrow_\sigma \rangle\, \mathbf{1}\, \langle \downarrow_{\sigma'} \rangle^{\mathrm{op}}$ where $\mathbf{1}$ is the identity relation for the terminal type $\mathbf{1} = \forall X. X \Rightarrow X$, and $\downarrow_\sigma$ is the canonical term (indeed unique up to provable equality) of type $\sigma \Rightarrow \mathbf{1}$. The original graph relation may be regarded as the special case that R is an identity relation and M' is an identity map.

2.1 Remark

We can define a category Ω syntactically from system R by the following data: the objects are closed types and the homset $\Omega(\sigma, \tau)$ is the set of all closed terms of type $\sigma \Rightarrow \tau$ divided by the provable equality in system R. Then the category Ω is a cartesian closed category with finite coproducts. Moreover, every functor definable in system F has initial and terminal fixed points.

The category Ω is at this moment a unique parametric model that is not extensional. To see this, note that the equational theory of system R is Σ^0_1 (in fact, Σ^0_1-complete; Theorem 6.3), while the extensional equality of terms of type $\mathbb{N} \Rightarrow \mathbb{N}$ is Π^0_1-complete, and hence the provable equality of system R cannot be extensional. This fact about non-extensionality may be interesting, since in the general theory in [5, 10] the extensionality was extensively used. System R may be regarded as an axiomatisation in place of extensionality (i.e., well-pointedness), as foreseen in [5]. □

Regarding the previous remark, we put the following question: what is the appropriate definition of models of system R?

3 Dialectica interpretation in system R

In this section we prove the assertion (1) in the introduction. That is to say, for PA^2-provably recursive functions f and g,

$$(1) \qquad \mathrm{PA}^2 \vdash \forall x.\, f(x) = g(x) \qquad \text{implies} \qquad \vdash_R \begin{array}{c} D_f : \mathbb{N} \Rightarrow \mathbb{N} \\ \mathbb{N} \Rightarrow \mathbb{N} \\ D_g : \mathbb{N} \Rightarrow \mathbb{N} \end{array} .$$

Here D_f is a closed term of system F extracted from a PA^2-proof that f is a total recursive function (see Definition 3.4 and Remark 3.5).

First of all we can assume that we deal with intuitionistic second order Heyting arithmetic $\mathrm{HA}^2_{\mathrm{CA}}$ with full comprehension, by application of the double negation transformation. To see this, note that we are concerned with totality and equality of recursive functions, and that these are represented by at most Π_2-formulas, whose provability does not change in classical and intuitionistic systems.

The method used here to extract the term D_f is the Dialectica interpretation [9], which was first defined for first order intuitionistic arithmetic. This interpretation consists of two steps. The first step is to translate each formula to a Σ_2-form $\exists y^\sigma \forall z^\rho. A[y,z]$ where σ and ρ are types of system T [8]. The second step is to validate this Σ_2-form. The first step is well-established, while the second step allows several ways for the validation. We need certain justifications to assert if the Σ_2-form is correct. For example, the approach in [23, 24] defines a quantifier-free arithmetic in all finite types, and shows that if the original formula is provable in Peano arithmetic then the translated Σ_2-form is provable in the quantifier-free arithmetic. Another approach [12] (due to Sanchis) is to write the Σ_2-form in the shape $t[y,z] \rhd \overline{0}$ where t is a term of system T and $\rhd$ is a certain reduction. We can show that, if the original formula is provable in Peano arithmetic, then there is a closed term M of type σ such that, for every closed term N of type ρ, the substituted term $t[M,N]$ is contracted to $\overline{0}$. (Remark: This interpretation is not robust, since equality on closed terms does not imply equality as functionals in the full standard model on natural numbers [3]. However, this ensures equality as effective operators in Myhill-Shepherdson's HEO, as derived from the results proved in [15].)

As to higher order arithmetic, Spector used bar recursion to extend the Dialectica interpretation to full finite order analysis [21]. In this setting, there exists a term in a system having bar recursion such that the validity of the translated formulas is proved in a certain equational logic (called Σ_4) for arithmetic with bar recursion. Girard used system F_ω to give another version of Dialectica interpretation for full finite order analysis [6]. There he introduced the notion of validity *VIF*, which is a combination of the validity in models with a certain form of induction.

So there is a need to give a natural, canonical way to validate the Dialectica interpretation. We use system R as the logic to this purpose. The advantage of our approach is that everything necessary to validate the Dialectica interpretation is derived from a single principle, *parametricity*. The notion of parametricity [17] is a purely computational point of view to system F. Our results below shows that this computational aspect of system F is strong enough to validate the Dialectica interpretaion and to induce some logical consequences from that.

For the moment we consider the second order Heyting arithmetic $\mathrm{HA}^2_{\mathrm{CA}}$ with full comprehension. Each formula A of $\mathrm{HA}^2_{\mathrm{CA}}$ is translated into the Σ_2-form $\exists y^\sigma \forall z^\rho. t_A[y,z]$ where σ and ρ are types of system F and $t_A[y,z]$ is a term of type $\mathsf{Bool} = \forall X. X \Rightarrow X \Rightarrow X$. We show that if A is proved in $\mathrm{HA}^2_{\mathrm{CA}}$ then there is a term $M : \sigma$ of system F such that

$$z : \rho \vdash \begin{array}{c} t_A[M,z] : \mathsf{Bool} \\ \mathsf{Bool} \\ \mathsf{true} : \mathsf{Bool} \end{array}$$

is derivable in system R (where true is the term $\Lambda X \lambda x^X \lambda y^X. x$ of type Bool), or equivalently

$$\begin{array}{c} M:\sigma \\ z:\rho \vdash \langle \lambda y^{\sigma}.\, t_A[y,z] \rangle \ \mathsf{Bool}\ \langle \mathsf{true} \rangle^{\mathrm{op}}. \\ *:\mathbf{1} \end{array}$$

The last form gives us an observation that M is an extracted program from the proof of formula A, and the relation $\langle \lambda y.t_A[y,z] \rangle$ Bool $\langle \mathsf{true} \rangle^{\mathrm{op}}$ is the specification that should be satisfied with M.

We follow the Dialectica interpretation in [6], but there is a single point to notice. For the interpretation, every type must be inhabited, and hence in [6] system OF_ω was used where every type has a constant 0. As the second step, these constants are removed by a syntactic translation of types. This approach does not work in the case of system R, since if we assumed the type $\forall X.\, X$ is inhabited then the system would be inconsistent. The solution to this problem is simple: just do both steps at the same time.

We use the standard encodings of types $\mathbf{1}$, Bool, $\mathbb{N}$, direct product $\sigma \times \tau$, and existential quantification $\exists X.\, \sigma$, as well as the standard encodings of the terms such as $*:\mathbf{1}$, $\mathsf{true}:\mathsf{Bool}$, $\mathsf{false}:\mathsf{Bool}$, $\bar{0}:\mathbb{N}$, $S:\mathbb{N} \Rightarrow \mathbb{N}$, $\pi:\sigma \times \tau \Rightarrow \sigma$, $\pi':\sigma \times \tau \Rightarrow \tau$, and $\langle \cdot,\cdot \rangle : \sigma \Rightarrow \tau \Rightarrow \sigma \times \tau$. Moreover $VX.\, M : (\exists X.\sigma) \Rightarrow \tau$ if M is of type $\sigma \Rightarrow \tau$ where X is not a free variable in τ. Each n-ary set variable in arithmetic is associated to a triple (Y, Z, f) of fresh variables where Y and Z are type variables and f is a term variable of type $\mathbb{N}^n \Rightarrow Y \Rightarrow Z \Rightarrow \mathsf{Bool}$. We write the last type $\tau_X[Y,Z]$. We also assume canonically chosen variables $i^Y : Y$ and $i^Z : Z$.

Suppose $A[X,x]$ is a formula of $\mathrm{HA}^2_{\mathrm{CA}}$, where for simplicity we assume there are only one set variable X and one number variable x. We associate two types $\sigma_A[Y,Z]$, $\rho_A[Y,Z]$ and one term $t_A[Y,Z,f,x;\, y,z]$ of type Bool, which we write in the form

$$\exists y^{\sigma_A[Y,Z]}\, \forall z^{\rho_A[Y,Z]}.\ t_A[Y,Z,f,x;\, y,z]\ .$$

At the same time, we give canonical terms $\iota_A : \sigma[Y,Z]$ and $\bar{\iota}_A : \rho[Y,Z]$, whose free variables are in $\{i^Y, i^Z\}$. Also the term t_A may contain i^Y, i^Z if the corresponding set variables occur freely in A, though we do not display them. The translation of a formula $\forall X.\, A[X]$ is

$$\begin{array}{l} \exists y^{\forall Y,Z.\, Y \Rightarrow Z \Rightarrow \tau_X[Y,Z] \Rightarrow \sigma_A[Y,Z]} \\ \forall z^{\exists Y,Z.\, Y \times Z \times \tau_X[Y,Z] \times \rho_A[Y,Z]} \\ \quad (VY,Z.\, \lambda \langle i,i,f,r \rangle^{Y \times Z \times \tau_X[Y,Z] \times \rho_A[Y,Z]} \\ \qquad\qquad t_A[Y,Z,f;\, y_{YZ} i^Y i^Z f, r])(z) \end{array}$$

and $\iota_{\forall X.A[X]}$ and $\bar{\iota}_{\forall X.A[X]}$ are defined by $\Lambda Y,Z.\, \lambda i^Y i^Z f^{\tau_X[Y,Z]}.\ \iota_A[i^Y, i^Z]$ and $I_{1,1}\langle *, *, \mathsf{true}, \bar{\iota}_A[*,*] \rangle$. Note that the type $\sigma_{\forall X.A[X]}$ of y has the part $Y \Rightarrow Z \Rightarrow \cdots$, which ensures that the type is inhabited. The translation for the first-order connectives is standard and referred to standard texts [23, 12, 6, 7].

The following theorem asserts that if a formula is provable in $\mathrm{HA}^2_{\mathrm{CA}}$, then its Dialectica interpretation is provable in system R. We write simply X and $x : \sigma$, and later $M[x^{\sigma}]\ R\ M'[x'^{\sigma'}]$ in environments in place of

$$\begin{array}{lclcl} X & & x:\sigma & & x:\sigma \\ W & \text{and} & \sigma & \text{, and} & \langle \lambda x^{\sigma}.\, M[x]\rangle \, R \, \langle \lambda x'^{\sigma'}.\, M'[x']\rangle^{\mathrm{op}} \\ X' & & x':\sigma & & x':\sigma' \end{array}$$

where, in the first two, X', W and x' are dummy variables that are not used in the right hand side of turnstile. We also write $M\, R\, M'$ in place of

$$\begin{array}{ccc} M:\sigma & & *:\mathbf{1} \\ R & \text{or} & \langle \lambda v^{\mathbf{1}}.\, M\rangle \, R \, \langle \lambda v^{\mathbf{1}}.\, M'\rangle^{\mathrm{op}} \\ M':\sigma' & & *:\mathbf{1} \end{array},$$

or other equivalent judgements. For simplicity the theorem is asserted in the case that a formula has a single n-ary set variable and a single number variable. It is immediate to give the assertion of the theorem for the general case.

3.1 Theorem
Let $A[X,x]$ be a formula of second order arithmetic and $\exists y^{\sigma_A[Y,Z]}\forall z^{\rho_A[Y,Z]}.\, t_A[Y,Z,f,x;\, y,z]$ its Dialectica translation.

If the formula $A[X,x]$ is provable in $\mathrm{HA}^2_{\mathrm{CA}}$, then there is a term $M = M[Y,Z,f,x]$ of type σ_A such that $\Gamma \vdash (t_A[Y,Z,f,x;M,z])$ Bool true is provable in system R, where Γ is the environment $Y,\ Z,\ f:\tau_X[Y,Z],\ x:\mathbb{N},\ z:\rho_A[Y,Z]$. □

The proof goes as usual by induction on the proof tree of $A[X,x]$. What we require in the proof is that $\mathsf{Bool}, \mathbb{N}, \sigma\times\tau, \exists X.\sigma$ behave as universal categorical data types. The validity *VIF* in [6] is designed so that this requirement is met. In our setting, the universality follows from the simple principle of parametricity [1, 10, 11]:

3.2 Proposition
The following are valid for system R:

(i) *(Universality of Boolean type) If $\Gamma \vdash M[\mathsf{true}]\ R\ M'[\mathsf{true}]$ and $\Gamma \vdash M[\mathsf{false}]\ R\ M'[\mathsf{false}]$ are derivable, then $\Gamma,\ x:\mathsf{Bool} \vdash M[x]\ R\ M'[x]$ is derivable.*

(ii) *(Induction principle) If $\Gamma, \vdash M[\overline{0}]\ R\ M'[\overline{0}]$ and $\Gamma,\ M[x^{\mathbb{N}}]\ R\ M'[x'^{\mathbb{N}}] \vdash M[Sx]\ R\ M'[Sx']$ are derivable, then $\Gamma,\ x:\mathbb{N} \vdash M[x]\ R\ M'[x]$ is derivable.* □

Note that the involved parameters cannot occur in the relation R. For example, in the induction principle the parameter $x:\mathbb{N}$ may occur in M and M' but not in R. For the equality predicate $=$ in arithmetic, we have a natural term $\doteq$ of type $\mathbb{N} \Rightarrow \mathbb{N} \Rightarrow \mathsf{Bool}$, for which by this proposition we can show the following lemma:

3.3 Lemma
Let x, y be variables of type $\mathbb{N}$. The following holds: $\Gamma \vdash (x \doteq y)$ Bool true if and only if $\Gamma \vdash x\ \mathbb{N}\ y$. $\square$

We use Theorem 3.1 to prove (1) presented at the beginning of this section. So we suppose we are given two $\mathrm{HA}^2_{\mathrm{CA}}$-provably recursive functions f and g and suppose $\mathrm{HA}^2_{\mathrm{CA}}$ proves $\forall x.\, f(x) = g(x)$, or pedantically

$$\begin{aligned}\mathrm{HA}^2_{\mathrm{CA}} \ \vdash\ & \forall x, y, y', z, z'.\\ & \quad T(\ulcorner f \urcorner, x, y)\ \&\ U(y) = z\ \&\\ & \quad T(\ulcorner g \urcorner, x, y')\ \&\ U(y') = z'\\ & \qquad \rightarrow z = z'\end{aligned}$$

where T and U are Kleene's T-predicate and U-function, which are both primitive recursive [13]. Using these symbols, the function f being $\mathrm{HA}^2_{\mathrm{CA}}$-provably recursive means $\mathrm{HA}^2_{\mathrm{CA}} \vdash \forall x \exists y, z.\, T(\ulcorner f \urcorner, x, y)\ \&\ U(y) = z$.

3.4 Definition
Let f be an $\mathrm{HA}^2_{\mathrm{CA}}$-provably recursive function.

A closed term $D_f : \mathbb{N} \Rightarrow \mathbb{N}$ of system F is defined by applying Theorem 3.1 to the proof $\mathrm{HA}^2_{\mathrm{CA}} \vdash \forall x \exists y, z.\, T(\ulcorner f \urcorner, x, y)\ \&\ U(y) = z$, so that, together with another term $C_f : \mathbb{N} \Rightarrow \mathbb{N}$, system R proves the following judgement: $x : \mathbb{N} \vdash (T(\ulcorner f \urcorner, x, C_f x)\ \dot{\&}\ U(C_f x) \doteq D_f x)$ Bool true. $\square$

We apply Theorem 3.1 also to the proof of $\forall x.\, f(x) = g(x)$. Then, using the judgement in Definition above, we have $x : \mathbb{N} \vdash (D_f x \doteq D_g x)$ Bool true, from which $\vdash D_f\ (\mathbb{N} \Rightarrow \mathbb{N})\ D_g$ follows (use Lemma 3.3). Therefore the assertion (1) at the beginning of this section has been proved.

3.5 Remark
To be precise, D_f depends on the proof, not only the function f. However, if we have two different extracted terms for D_f, then they must be provably equal in system R by the uniqueness of the output produced by the T-predicate and U-function (in fact, this is used in the proof of Theorem 6.1). Hence the notation is not so misleading. $\square$

4 Parametric per model in arithmetic

In this section we prove the assertion (2) of Introduction. Namely given two closed terms $M, N : \mathbb{N} \Rightarrow \mathbb{N}$ of system F, the following holds:

$$(2) \qquad \vdash_R \begin{array}{c} M : \mathbb{N} \Rightarrow \mathbb{N} \\ \mathbb{N} \Rightarrow \mathbb{N} \\ N : \mathbb{N} \Rightarrow \mathbb{N} \end{array} \qquad \text{implies} \qquad \mathrm{PA}^2 \vdash \forall x.\, \xi_M(x) = \xi_N(x)$$

where ξ_M is the recursive function generated from the term M as defined later. In any case, we must encode the entities in system R in terms of natural numbers in order to argue in arithmetic. But this process has already appeared in the literature: the parametric per model [2, 1] does it. So all we have to show is that the soundness of system R in the parametric per model is provable in second order arithmetic. In the following proposition, we use the symbol $\models$ for the validity in the parametric per model. The formalisation of the validity and the proof are left to the reader.

4.1 Proposition

(i) *If* $\Gamma \vdash \begin{array}{c}\sigma\\ R\\ \sigma'\end{array}$ *is derived in system* R, *then* PA^2 *proves* $\Gamma \models \begin{array}{c}\sigma\\ R\\ \sigma'\end{array}$.

(ii) *If* $\Gamma \vdash \begin{array}{c}M:\sigma\\ R\\ M':\sigma'\end{array}$ *is derived in system* R, *then* PA^2 *proves* $\Gamma \models \begin{array}{c}M:\sigma\\ R\\ M':\sigma'\end{array}$. □

4.2 Remark

In (ii) of the preceding proposition, the derivation of system R must be given at the meta-level. In fact, we can show $\mathrm{PA}^2 \nvdash (\Gamma \vdash M:\sigma \rightarrow \Gamma \models M:\sigma)$. Suppose we have a proof, for contradiction. Then, since every PA^2-provably recursive function is encodable as a term of system F whose well-definedness is easily checked in elementary arithmetic, we have a universal function for PA^2-provably recursive functions, which is itself PA^2-provably recursive. This induces contradiction by the standard diagonalisation argument. □

What remains is to fill the gap between the set ω of natural numbers and the interpretation $[\![\mathrm{N}]\!]$ of the natural number type. In the parametric per model, however, they are isomorphic, provable in PA^2:

4.3 Proposition

Let ω *be the per whose domain is the set of all natural numbers and whose equivalence relation is the ordinary equality between numbers. Then* PA^2 *proves* $[\![\mathrm{N}]\!] \cong \omega$. □

For the proof, it suffices to observe that the proof in [2] is formalisable in PA^2. Alternatively the proof easily follows from the fact that $[\![\mathrm{N}]\!]$ is a natural number object in the category of pers, this fact being provable in PA^2 (since it is provable in system R). We will need a closer inspection of the proof afterwards. For the moment, however, this remark would be enough.

4.4 Definition

Let $q : \omega \rightarrow [\![\mathrm{N}]\!]$ and $q' : [\![\mathrm{N}]\!] \rightarrow \omega$ be the recursive functions which give the isomorphism of Proposition 4.3. A recursive function ξ_M is associated to each closed term $M : \mathbb{N} \Rightarrow \mathbb{N}$ by the composition of recursive functions as follows:

$$\xi_M \;:=\; \omega \xrightarrow{q} [\![\mathbb{N}]\!] \xrightarrow{[\![M]\!]} [\![\mathbb{N}]\!] \xrightarrow{q'} \omega \qquad \square$$

Now our aim (2) immediately follows from Propositions 4.1 and 4.3.

5 Going and returning

We show that two translations studied in the last two sections are the inverse of each other up to provable equality. Namely D_{-} and ξ_{-} are inverse:

(3) $\quad \mathrm{PA}^2 \vdash \forall x.\, \xi_{D_f}(x) = f(x)$

(4) $\quad \vdash_R \begin{array}{c} D_{\xi_M} : \mathbb{N} \Rightarrow \mathbb{N} \\ \mathbb{N} \Rightarrow \mathbb{N} \\ M : \mathbb{N} \Rightarrow \mathbb{N} \end{array}\;.$

For (3), there are few problems and the proof is left to the reader. We give a sketch of the proof of (4). First of all, since the program extraction by the Dialectica interpretation is complicated, it is preferable to reduce the problem to that of the first-order erasure method [22, 14, 8], which is easier to manipulate. So we give a comparison result between the Dialectica interpretation and the first-order erasure, which we hope to be interesting in its own right. In particular, the terms extracted from a proof of totality of a recursive function by these two ways become equivalent in system R.

For the first-order erasure, we refer the reader to [8, 15.2.2]. We denote by ϕ_A the type associated to a formula A. However, the remark in section 3 about empty types in system R applies here, too. Hence we must have modified the translation of second-order quantified formula $\forall X.\, A[X]$. We also modified the translation of first-order quantified formulas so that the comparison with the Dialectica translation becomes simple. The lower row in Table 1 provides the translation.

If we have a proof Π of $\mathrm{HA}^2_{\mathrm{CA}} \vdash A[X, x]$, then there is a term $F_\Pi[X, x]$ of type $\phi_A[X]$ in system F. See [8] for the details. Since we modified the translation of first-order quantified formulas, accordingly some modifications should be applied. For example, if Π is the logical rule $(\forall x.\, A[x]) \to A[t]$, then the extracted term F_Π of type $(\mathbb{N} \Rightarrow \phi_A) \Rightarrow \phi_A$ is defined by $\lambda z^{\mathbb{N} \Rightarrow \phi_A}.\, zt$. In this respect, we do not completely erase the first-order part (hence $F_\Pi[X, x]$ depends also on x).

To give a comparison between the Dialectica interpretation and the first-order erasure, we define a binary relation $K_A[W]$ from $\sigma_A[Y, Z]$ to $\phi_A[X]$ for each formula A, where the relation variable W is from Y to X. The definition is listed in Table 1. In the case of $\forall X.\, A[X]$, we use j that is an obvious term of type $(\forall X.\, X \Rightarrow \phi_A) \Rightarrow (\forall X, Z'.\, X \Rightarrow \mathbf{1} \Rightarrow \mathbf{1} \Rightarrow \phi_A)$ (here Z' is dummy). This is an isomorphism provable in system R. Moreover V is a dummy relation variable and $\top$ is the total relation defined in section 2.

Formulas
σ_A
DEFINITION: K_A
ϕ_A

$t = u$
$\mathbf{1}$
$\mathbf{1}$
$\mathbf{1}$

$Xt_1 \cdots t_n$
Y
W
X

$A \,\&\, B$
$\sigma_A \times \sigma_B$
$K_A \times K_B$
$\phi_A \times \phi_B$

$A \to B$
$(\sigma_A \Rightarrow \sigma_B) \times (\sigma_A \Rightarrow \rho_B \Rightarrow \rho_A)$
$\langle \pi \rangle \, (K_A \Rightarrow K_B) \, \langle id \rangle^{\mathrm{op}}$
$\phi_A \Rightarrow \phi_B$

$\forall x.\, A[x]$
$\mathbb{N} \Rightarrow \sigma_A$
$\mathbb{N} \Rightarrow K_A$
$\mathbb{N} \Rightarrow \phi_A$

$\exists x.\, A[x]$
$\mathbb{N} \times \sigma_A$
$\mathbb{N} \times K_A$
$\mathbb{N} \times \phi_A$

$\forall X.\, A[X]$
$\forall Y, Z.\, Y \Rightarrow Z \Rightarrow \tau_X[Y, Z] \Rightarrow \sigma_A[Y, Z]$
$\langle id \rangle \, (\forall W, V.\, W \Rightarrow \top \Rightarrow \top \Rightarrow K_A[W]) \, \langle j \rangle^{\mathrm{op}}$
$\forall X.\, X \Rightarrow \phi_A[X]$

(See the text for j)

Table 1: Definition of ϕ_A and K_A

For the moment, let us denote by $D_\Pi[Y, Z, f, x]$ the term of type $\sigma_A[Y, Z]$ extracted from a proof Π of $A[X, x]$ by the Dialectica interpretation. Then the term D_Π is related by K_A to the term F_Π extracted by the first-order erasure, as the following theorem shows:

5.1 Theorem
Suppose Π is an $\mathrm{HA}^2_{\mathrm{CA}}$-proof of a formula $A[X, x]$. Then system R proves

$$\Gamma \vdash \begin{array}{c} D_\Pi : \sigma_A \\ K_A \\ F_\Pi : \phi_A \end{array}, \text{ where the environment } \Gamma \text{ is } \begin{array}{c} Y \\ W \\ X \end{array}, \begin{array}{c} Z \\ V \\ Z' \end{array}, \begin{array}{c} i^Y \\ W \\ i^X \end{array}, \begin{array}{c} i^Z \\ \top \\ * \end{array}, \begin{array}{c} f \\ \top \\ * \end{array}, x : \mathbb{N} \qquad \square$$

Here we used $*$ for a dummy variable of type $\mathbf{1}$. In particular, if A is the formula $\forall x \exists y, z.\, T(\ulcorner f \urcorner, x, y) \,\&\, U(y) = z$, then σ_A, ϕ_A, and K_A are all isomorphic to $\mathbb{N} \Rightarrow \mathbb{N} \times \mathbb{N}$ (by discarding $\mathbf{1}$). For each PA^2-provably recursive function f, we set F_f to be the term of type $\mathbb{N} \Rightarrow \mathbb{N}$ obtained by the first-order erasure. Then the next corollary follows:

5.2 Corollary
For each $\mathrm{HA}^2_{\mathrm{CA}}$*-provably total recursive function* f*, the Dialectica translation and the first-order erasure give the terms that are provably equal in system* R*. That is to say,*

$$\vdash \begin{array}{c} D_f : \mathbb{N} \Rightarrow \mathbb{N} \\ \mathbb{N} \Rightarrow \mathbb{N} \\ F_f : \mathbb{N} \Rightarrow \mathbb{N} \end{array} . \quad \square$$

Therefore our problem (4) is reduced to showing that M and F_{ξ_M} are provably equal in system R as terms of type $\mathbb{N} \Rightarrow \mathbb{N}$. Namely

$$\vdash_R \begin{array}{c} F_{\xi_M} : \mathbb{N} \Rightarrow \mathbb{N} \\ \mathbb{N} \Rightarrow \mathbb{N} \\ M : \mathbb{N} \Rightarrow \mathbb{N} \end{array} .$$

The idea to solve this problem is to observe that, for each derivation $\Gamma \vdash M : \sigma$ of system F, there is a natural deduction $\mathrm{HA}^2_{\mathrm{CA}}$-proof of the validity $\Gamma \models M : \sigma$ so that this proof simulates the original derivation.

Suppose given a derivation $\Gamma \vdash M : \sigma$, we construct a natural deduction proof

$$\Pi_M \quad = \quad \begin{array}{c} Hyp_\Gamma \\ \vdots \\ ([\![M]\!]\eta_\Gamma,\ [\![M]\!]\eta'_\Gamma) \in [\![\sigma]\!]\eta^0_\Gamma \end{array}$$

where Hyp_Γ is the open hypothesis corresponding to the environment Γ. Specifically, for each type variable X, we associate three predicate variables P, P', Q and the first-order formula asserting that P and P' are pers and Q is a saturated binary relation from P to P' [1]; for each term variable $x : \sigma$, we associate two number variables z, z' together with a formula asserting that z and z' are related by the per that is the interpretation of the type σ. The assignment η_Γ, η'_Γ, and η^0_Γ are the mappings assigning $x \mapsto z$, $x \mapsto z'$, and $X \mapsto Q$ respectively.

Then the proof Π_M is translated back by the first-order erasure to a derivation in system F, which we denote by $\Gamma' \vdash (\!|M|\!) : (\!|\sigma|\!)$. The type $(\!|\sigma|\!)$ is given by the upper rows in Table 2, where $C[P, P', Q]$ is the type obtained by the first-order erasure from the formula asserting that P, P' are pers and Q is a saturated binary relation from P to P'. Observe that $(\!|\sigma|\!)$ is similar to σ, though annotated with additional structures.

The term $(\!|M|\!) : (\!|\sigma|\!)$ can be compared with the original term M by the binary relation defined in Table 2. There h is an obvious term of type $(\forall X.\sigma) \Rightarrow (\forall Y, Y', X.\, \mathbf{1} \Rightarrow \mathbf{1} \Rightarrow \mathbf{1} \Rightarrow \mathbf{1} \Rightarrow \sigma)$, which is an isomorphism provably in system R (the type variables Y, Y' are dummy). If σ has a free term variable X, then L_σ has a free relation variable W from Q to X (note that $(\!|\sigma|\!) = (\!|\sigma|\!)[Q]$).

Type σ
DEFINITION: $\begin{array}{c} (\!\vert\sigma\vert\!) \\ L_\sigma \\ \sigma \end{array}$

X
$\begin{array}{c} Q \\ W \\ X \end{array}$

$\sigma \Rightarrow \tau$
$\begin{array}{c} \mathbb{N} \times (\!\vert\sigma\vert\!) \Rightarrow \mathbb{N} \times (\!\vert\tau\vert\!) \\ \langle\pi'\rangle\ L_\sigma\ \langle id\rangle^{\mathrm{op}} \Rightarrow \langle\pi'\rangle\ L_\tau\ \langle id\rangle^{\mathrm{op}} \\ \sigma \Rightarrow \tau \end{array}$

$\forall X.\sigma$
$\begin{array}{c} \forall P, P', Q.\ P \Rightarrow P' \Rightarrow Q \Rightarrow C[P, P', Q] \Rightarrow (\!\vert\sigma\vert\!) \\ \langle id\rangle(\forall V, V', W.\ \top \Rightarrow \top \Rightarrow \top \Rightarrow \top \Rightarrow L_\sigma)\langle h\rangle^{\mathrm{op}} \\ \forall X.\sigma \end{array}$

(See the text for h)

Table 2: Definition of $(\!\vert\sigma\vert\!)$ and L_σ

5.3 Proposition

For each $\Gamma \vdash M : \sigma$ in system F, the following holds:

$$L_\Gamma \vdash \begin{array}{c} (\!\vert M\vert\!) : (\!\vert\sigma\vert\!) \\ L_\sigma \\ M : \sigma \end{array}$$

where L_Γ is the environment consisting of

$$\begin{array}{c} P \\ V \\ Y \end{array}, \begin{array}{c} P' \\ V' \\ Y' \end{array}, \begin{array}{c} Q \\ W \\ X \end{array}, \begin{array}{c} k : C[P, P', Q] \\ \top \\ * \end{array} \qquad \textit{for each type variable } X \textit{ in } \Gamma;$$

$$\begin{array}{c} z : \mathbb{N} \\ \top \\ * \end{array}, \begin{array}{c} z' : \mathbb{N} \\ \top \\ * \end{array}, \begin{array}{c} y : (\!\vert\tau\vert\!) \\ L_\tau \\ x : \tau \end{array} \qquad \textit{for each term variable } x : \tau \textit{ in } \Gamma. \quad \square$$

As a special case of this proposition, for each closed term $M : \mathbb{N} \Rightarrow \mathbb{N}$, the following holds:

$$\vdash \begin{array}{c} (\!\vert M\vert\!) : (\!\vert\mathbb{N} \Rightarrow \mathbb{N}\vert\!) \\ L_{\mathbb{N}\Rightarrow\mathbb{N}} \\ M : \mathbb{N} \Rightarrow \mathbb{N}\,. \end{array}$$

Both $(\!|M|\!)$ and F_{ξ_M} are obtained by the first order erasure. The difference is that the former is extracted from the proof of $[\![M]\!] \in dom([\![\mathbb{N} \Rightarrow \mathbb{N}]\!])$, while the latter from $q' \circ [\![M]\!] \circ q : \omega \to \omega$ where $q : \omega \to [\![\mathbb{N}]\!]$ and $q' : [\![\mathbb{N}]\!] \to \omega$ witness the isomorphism $\omega \cong [\![\mathbb{N}]\!]$ in the category of pers. Hence if we put $I : \mathbb{N} \Rightarrow \mathbb{N} \times (\!|\mathbb{N}|\!)$ and $I' : \mathbb{N} \times (\!|\mathbb{N}|\!) \Rightarrow \mathbb{N}$ for the terms extracted from $q : \omega \to [\![\mathbb{N}]\!]$ and $q' : [\![\mathbb{N}]\!] \to \omega$, we have $F_{\xi_M} = I' \circ (\!|M|\!) \circ I$.

To show that F_{ξ_M} equals M, we analyse the terms I and I'. We claim the following:

$$\text{(i)} \qquad \begin{array}{l} Ix \ : \ \mathbb{N} \times (\!|\mathbb{N}|\!) \\ \langle \pi' \rangle \, L_{\mathbb{N}} \, \langle id \rangle^{\mathrm{op}} \\ x : \mathbb{N} \, . \end{array}$$

$$\text{(ii)} \qquad \begin{array}{l} y' \ : \ \mathbb{N} \times (\!|\mathbb{N}|\!) \\ \langle \pi' \rangle \, L_{\mathbb{N}} \, \langle id \rangle^{\mathrm{op}} \\ y \ : \ \mathbb{N} \end{array} \qquad \text{implies} \qquad \begin{array}{l} I'y' \ : \ \mathbb{N} \\ \mathbb{N} \\ y \ : \ \mathbb{N} \, . \end{array}$$

The proof is by a detailed analysis of Proposition 4.3, and is omitted here. From these two claims, if we note that $(\!|\mathbb{N} \Rightarrow \mathbb{N}|\!) = \mathbb{N} \times (\!|\mathbb{N}|\!) \Rightarrow \mathbb{N} \times (\!|\mathbb{N}|\!)$ and $L_{\mathbb{N} \Rightarrow \mathbb{N}} = \langle \pi' \rangle \, L_{\mathbb{N}} \, \langle id \rangle^{\mathrm{op}} \Rightarrow \langle \pi' \rangle \, L_{\mathbb{N}} \, \langle id \rangle^{\mathrm{op}}$, we can easily derive

$$\begin{array}{l} F_{\xi_M} \ : \ \mathbb{N} \Rightarrow \mathbb{N} \\ \mathbb{N} \Rightarrow \mathbb{N} \\ M \ : \ \mathbb{N} \Rightarrow \mathbb{N} \end{array} \qquad \text{from} \qquad \begin{array}{l} (\!|M|\!) \ : \ (\!|\mathbb{N} \Rightarrow \mathbb{N}|\!) \\ L_{\mathbb{N} \Rightarrow \mathbb{N}} \\ M \ : \ \mathbb{N} \Rightarrow \mathbb{N} \, . \end{array}$$

By the remark after Corollary 5.2, we finish the proof of (4) given at the beginning of this section.

5.4 Remark

In [16], another logic of parametric polymorphism is defined. We call this logic LP. Similar results to our main theorem (1) through (4) in the introduction are available to the logic LP, replacing the assertion

$$\vdash_R \begin{array}{l} M : \mathbb{N} \Rightarrow \mathbb{N} \\ \mathbb{N} \Rightarrow \mathbb{N} \\ N : \mathbb{N} \Rightarrow \mathbb{N} \end{array} \qquad \text{by} \qquad \mathrm{LP} \vdash M =_{\mathbb{N} \Rightarrow \mathbb{N}} N.$$

To see this, let us notice that there is a straightforward interpretation of system R in LP. So the clauses (1) and (4) to system R imply the corresponding results to LP. We can directly check (2) to the logic LP. For (3), there is nothing to add. □

6 Applications

In this section, we give two simple applications of the results so far. The first is a partial answer to the problem on the provable equality of terms having the same type-erasure. The second is the complexity of the equational theory of system R.

In [1] (see also [16]), the following question was posed: given two terms M and M' of the same type, if M and M' have the same type-erasure as untyped lambda terms, then are M and M' provably equal in system R? We give a positive answer to the special case that M and M' are closed terms of type $\mathbb{N} \Rightarrow \mathbb{N}$. A proof is immediate from (1) and (4), since the parametric per model interprets the terms having the identical type-erasure as the *same* partial recursive function.

6.1 Theorem

Let M and M' be closed terms of type $\mathbb{N} \Rightarrow \mathbb{N}$.

If the type-erasures of M and M' are identical as untyped lambda terms, then system R proves

$$\vdash \begin{array}{c} M : \mathbb{N} \Rightarrow \mathbb{N} \\ \mathbb{N} \Rightarrow \mathbb{N} \\ M' : \mathbb{N} \Rightarrow \mathbb{N} \end{array} \qquad \square$$

Next we show that the equational theory of system R is Σ_1^0-complete (thus undecidable). The equational theory Eq_R is defined as follows:

6.2 Definition

We define Eq_R as the collection of (Γ, M, M') where M and M' are two terms of the same type and Γ is the environment under which the terms and the type are defined, these satisfying

$$\Gamma \vdash \begin{array}{c} M : \sigma \\ \sigma \\ M' : \sigma \end{array} . \qquad \square$$

The clauses (1) through (4) in the introduction implies that system R is conservative over PA^2 with respect to equational theory. Namely, if $t = u$ is provable in PA^2 then $t\,\mathbb{N}\,u$ is derivable in system R. Since the equational theory of PA^2 is Σ_1^0-complete (see [20] for closely related results), we have the following:

6.3 Theorem

The equational theory Eq_R of system R is Σ_1^0-complete. $\square$

7 Extension to higher order

There are few problems to extend the results so far to all finite order arithmetic and all finite order polymorphic lambda calculus. The Dialectica interpretation of all finite order full arithmetic is given in [6]. Also we can define system R_ω, as a system of parametric polymorphism for system F_ω, this R_ω defined by adding binary relation between constructors of the same kind, on the top of system R. The arguments in the earlier sections extend to finite order in a straightforward manner.

7.1 Theorem

The clauses (1) through (4) in the introduction hold also for PA^{ω} *and system* R_{ω}. □

7.2 Remark

As in the case of second order, we can define an indexed category $(\mathcal{K}, \Omega)$ from system R_{ω}. Here $\mathcal{K}$ is the category whose set of objects is the set of all kinds $\mathbf{K}$ and whose homset $\mathcal{K}(\mathbf{K}, \mathbf{L})$ is the set of all constructors of kind $\mathbf{L}^{\mathbf{K}}$ divided by $\beta\eta$-equality. The category $\Omega^{\mathbf{K}}$ of $\mathbf{K}$-indexed families is the category whose set of objects is the set of all constructors of kind $\Omega^{\mathbf{K}}$ (where Ω is the kind of types) and whose homset $\Omega^{\mathbf{K}}(\sigma, \tau)$ is the set of terms of type $\forall X^{\mathbf{K}}.\sigma X \Rightarrow \tau X$ divided by provable equality in system R_{ω}.

Then $(\mathcal{K}, \Omega)$ is an indexed cartesian closed category with indexed finite coproducts. Each $\Omega^{\mathbf{K}}$ has initial and terminal fixed points for all syntactically definable functors with universal strength. Furthermore, right Kan extension $\mathrm{Ran}_K T$ and left Kan extension $\mathrm{Lan}_K T$ exist for all constructors K and T (not necessarily functors). In particular, $(\mathcal{K}, \Omega)$ is a PL category [19]. All these can be derived from the general argument in [11]. Although extensionality is used there, we can instead argue in appropriate environments of system R_{ω} to avoid extensionality. □

References

1. M. Abadi, L. Cardelli, and P.-L. Curien, Formal parametric polymorphism, *Theoret. Comput. Sci.* **121** (1993) 9–58.
2. E. S. Bainbridge, P. J. Freyd, A. Scedrov, and P. J. Scott, Functorial polymorphism, *Theoret. Comput. Sci.* **70** (1990) 35–64; Corrigendum, **71** (1990) 431.
3. H. P. Barendregt, *The lambda calculus, Its syntax and semantics*, revised edition, (North-Holland, 1984).
4. C. Böhm and A. Berarducci, Automatic synthesis of typed Λ-programs on term algebras, *Theoret. Comput. Sci.* **39** (1985) 135–154.
5. P. Freyd, Structural polymorphism, *Theoret. Comput. Sci.* **115** (1993) 107–129.
6. J.-Y. Girard, *Interprétation Fonctionnelle et Élimination des Coupures de l'Arithmétique d'Ordre Supérieur*, Thèse d'Etat, Université Paris VII (1972).
7. J.-Y. Girard, *Proof Theory and Logical Complexity*, Volume I, Studies in Proof Theory, (Bibliopolis, 1987).
8. J.-Y. Girard, P. Taylor and Y. Lafont, *Proofs and Types*, (Cambridge University Press, 1989).
9. K. Gödel, Über eine bisher noch nicht benützte Erweiterung des finiten Standpunktes, *Dialectica* **12** (1958) 280–287; English translation in *J. Philosophical Logic* **9** (1980) 133–142; reprinted in *Kurt Gödel, Collected Works*, Volume II, Publications 1938–1974, S. Feferman et al., eds., (Oxford University Press, 1990) pp. 240–251.
10. R. Hasegawa, Categorical data types in parametric polymorphism, *Math. Struct. Comput. Sci.* **4** (1994) 71–109.
11. R. Hasegawa, Relational limits in general polymorphism, *Publ. Research Institute for Mathematical Sciences* **30** (1994) 535–576.
12. J. R. Hindley and J. P. Seldin, *Introduction to Combinators and λ-Calculus*, (London Math. Soc., 1986).

13. S. C. Kleene, *Introduction to Metamathematics*, (North-Holland, 1964).
14. D. Leivant, Reasoning about functional programs and complexity classes associated with type disciplines, in: *IEEE 24th Annual Symp. on Foundations of Computer Science*, (IEEE, 1983) pp. 460–469.
15. R. Loader, Models of linear logic and inductive datatypes, Mathematical Institute, Oxford University, preprint (1994).
16. G. Plotkin and M. Abadi, A logic for parametric polymorphism, in: *Typed Lambda Calculi and Applications*, M. Bezem, J. F. Groote, eds., 1993, Utrecht, The Netherlands, Lecture Notes in Computer Science 664, (Springer, 1993) 361–375.
17. J. C. Reynolds, Towards a theory of type structure, in: B. Robinet ed., *Programming Symposium*, Paris, Lecture Notes in Computer Science 19 (Springer, 1974) pp. 408–425.
18. J. C. Reynolds, Types, abstraction, and parametric polymorphism, in: *Information Processing 83*, R. E. A. Mason, ed., (North-Holland, 1983) pp. 513–523.
19. R. A. G. Seely, Categorical semantics for higher order polymorphic lambda calculus, *J. Symbolic Logic* **52** (1987) 969–989.
20. R. M. Smullyan, *Theory of Formal Systems*, Annals of Mathematics Studies 47, (Princeton University Press, 1961).
21. C. Spector, Provably recursive functionals of analysis: A consistency proof of analysis by an extension of principles formulated in current intuitionistic mathematics, in: *Recursive Function Theory*, J. C. E. Dekker, ed., Proceedings of Symposia in Pure Mathematics, Volume V, (AMS, 1962) pp. 1–27.
22. R. Statman, Number theoretic functions computable by polymorphic programs (extended abstract), in: IEEE 22nd Annual Symp. on Foundations of Computer Science, Los Angels, 1981 (IEEE, 1981) pp. 279–282.
23. A. S. Troelstra, *Mathematical Investigations of Intuitionistic Arithmetic and Analysis*, Lecture Notes in Mathematics 344, (Springer, 1973).
24. A. S. Troelstra, Introductory note to 1958 and 1972, in: *Kurt Gödel, Collected Works*, Volume II, Publications 1938–1974, S. Feferman et al., eds., (Oxford University Press, 1990) pp. 217–241.

On the Modal Logic K Plus Theories

Alain Heuerding*, Stefan Schwendimann*

Institut für Informatik und angewandte Mathematik,
Universität Bern, Switzerland

Abstract. $\mathsf{K} + T$ is the propositional modal logic K with the elements of the finite set T as additional axioms.
We develop a sequent calculus that is suited for proof search in $\mathsf{K} + T$ and discuss methods to improve the efficiency. An implementation of the resulting decision procedure is part of the Logics Workbench LWB.
Then we show that – in contrast to K, KT, S4 – there are theories T and formulas A where a counter-model must have a superpolynomial diameter in the size of T plus A.
In the last part we construct an embedding of S4 in $\mathsf{K} + T$.

1 Introduction

A Hilbert-style calculus for (propositional) $\mathsf{K} + T$ is obtained from the usual Hilbert-style calculus for the modal logic K by adding the formulas of T as additional axioms. There is also a natural characterization of $\mathsf{K} + T$ from the point of view of Kripke structures: We restrict ourselves to Kripke structures whose worlds satisfy T.
One application of $\mathsf{K} + T$ is the proof of the equivalence of propositional normal modal logics ([5]). Another application is the well-known wise men puzzle, which can be solved with the multimodal variant of $\mathsf{K} + T$, whereas the multimodal variant of K alone is not sufficient. However, in many systems that offer decision procedures for modal logics, e.g. HLM [9] or Tableaux [1], as well as in discussions of methods for proof search in modal logics, e.g. [14], modal logics plus theories are not considered.
In the first part we develop a sequent calculus that ensures the termination of proof search. Making use of the fact that most rules are invertible and by adding rules for $\leftrightarrow$, the search tree can be considerably reduced. A further non-elementary improvement is obtained by eliminating useless branchings.
The length of the branches of the search tree plays an important role in proof search (see also the multiplicity problem in [14]) and in complexity questions ([8]), but also in the construction of embeddings ([3]). In the case of proof search for the formula A in K, KT or S4, it is possible to give a polynomial upper bound in the size of A. Such a polynomial bound (in the size of A plus T) does not exist for $\mathsf{K} + T$. In our main theorem we prove that this is not a defect of our sequent

* Work supported by the Swiss National Science Foundation, SPP 5003-34279.

calculus, but that sometimes all counter-models must have a superpolynomial diameter in the size of A plus T.
In the last part we construct an embedding of S4 in $\mathsf{K}+T$. The transitivity of the accessibility relation in the Kripke-structures that is present in S4 but not in K is simulated by an appropriate theory T. The existence of such a natural embedding indicates that $\mathsf{K}+T$ is considerably more expressive than K.

2 Notation

Definition 1.
Var $:= \{p_0, p_1, p_2, \ldots\}$ is the set of the variables. The set Fml of the (modal) formulas is inductively defined: If $P \in$ Var, then $P \in$ Fml and $\neg P \in$ Fml; if $A, B \in$ Fml, then $(\Box A), (\Diamond A), (A \wedge B), (A \vee B) \in$ Fml.
If $A, B \in$ Fml, then $A \equiv B$ means that A and B are syntactically equal.
If $A, B \in$ Fml, then: $(\neg(\neg A)) :\equiv A$, $(\neg(\Box A)) :\equiv (\Diamond(\neg A))$, $(\neg(\Diamond A)) :\equiv (\Box(\neg A))$, $(\neg(A \wedge B)) :\equiv ((\neg A) \vee (\neg B))$, $(\neg(A \vee B)) :\equiv ((\neg A) \wedge (\neg B))$, and $(A \rightarrow B) :\equiv ((\neg A) \vee B)$, $(A \leftrightarrow B) :\equiv ((A \rightarrow B) \wedge (B \rightarrow A))$.
A theory is a finite set of formulas.

Usually we omit the outermost brackets. The unary connectives have the highest priority, followed by $\wedge$, $\vee$, $\rightarrow$, and $\leftrightarrow$. $\wedge$, $\vee$, and $\leftrightarrow$ are left associative.
Example: $p_2 \wedge p_0 \wedge p_1 \vee (p_2 \rightarrow p_3)$ stands for $(((p_2 \wedge p_0) \wedge p_1) \vee (p_2 \rightarrow p_3))$.

We use meta-variables as follows: P, Q, R for variables, A, B, C for formulas, Γ, Σ for (perhaps empty) multisets of formulas, T for theories, n for natural numbers (including 0).

Definition 2.
If Γ is the multiset $A_1, \ldots, A_n$, then $\Diamond\Gamma$ is the multiset $\Diamond A_1, \ldots, \Diamond A_n$.
$\Box^0 A :\equiv A$, $\Box^{n+1} A :\equiv \Box \Box^n A$.

Definition 3.
The length $|A|$ of a formula A is the number of variables and connectives in A.
$|T| := \sum_{A \in T} |A|$. (Note that theories are always finite.)
Example: $|p_0 \wedge (\neg p_1 \vee p_0)| = 6$.

Definition 4. $A\{B_1/P_1, \ldots, B_n/P_n\}$ is the formula obtained from A by simultaneously substituting P_1 by B_1, ..., P_n by B_n.

Definition 5. CPC $\vdash A$ means that $\Box$ and $\Diamond$ do not occur in the formula A and that A is provable in classical propositional logic.

Definition 6. $\langle x_0, \ldots, x_n \rangle$ is the $n+1$ tuple with the elements $x_0, \ldots, x_n$.

3 K: syntax and semantics

Definition 7. $\mathsf{K}_{\mathcal{H}}$ is the following Hilbert-style calculus:

$$A\{B_1/P_1,\dots,B_n/P_n\} \quad \text{if CPC} \vdash A$$
$$\Box(A \to B) \to \Box A \to \Box B$$

$$\frac{A \quad A \to B}{B}\,(\text{mp}) \qquad\qquad \frac{A}{\Box A}\,(\Box)$$

Definition 8. The corresponding one-sided sequent calculus $\mathsf{K}_{\mathcal{S}}$ is defined as follows:

$$P, \neg P \qquad\qquad \frac{\Gamma}{A, \Gamma}\,(\text{weak})$$

$$\frac{A, B, \Gamma}{A \lor B, \Gamma}\,(\lor) \qquad\qquad \frac{A, \Gamma \quad B, \Gamma}{A \land B, \Gamma}\,(\land)$$

$$\frac{A, \Gamma}{\Box A, \Diamond\Gamma}\,(\Box)$$

Note 9. We use multisets of formulas, so there is no contraction hidden in $\mathsf{K}_{\mathcal{S}}$.

Definition 10. A Kripke-structure $\mathcal{M}$ is a triple $\langle W_{\mathcal{M}}, \mathcal{R}_{\mathcal{M}}, I_{\mathcal{M}} \rangle$, where $W_{\mathcal{M}}$ is a non-empty set, $\mathcal{R}_{\mathcal{M}} \subset {W_{\mathcal{M}}}^2$, and $I_{\mathcal{M}} : W_{\mathcal{M}} \times \text{Var} \to \{0,1\}$. We call the elements of $W_{\mathcal{M}}$ the worlds of $\mathcal{M}$.

Usually we omit the subscript $_{\mathcal{M}}$. We use $\mathcal{M}$ as a meta-variable for Kripke-structures.

Definition 11. Let $\mathcal{M}$ be a Kripke-structure. For all $w \in W$ the relation $w \models A$ is inductively defined:

$w \models P \;:\Leftrightarrow\; I(w, P) = 1, \quad w \models \neg P \;:\Leftrightarrow\; I(w, P) = 0$
$w \models \Box A \;:\Leftrightarrow\; \forall w' \in W : (w\mathcal{R}w' \Rightarrow w' \models A)$
$w \models \Diamond A \;:\Leftrightarrow\; \exists w' \in W : (w\mathcal{R}w' \text{ and } w' \models A)$
$w \models A \land B \;:\Leftrightarrow\; w \models A \text{ and } w \models B, \quad w \models A \lor B \;:\Leftrightarrow\; w \models A \text{ or } w \models B$
$\mathcal{M} \models A \;:\Leftrightarrow\; \forall w \in W : w \models A$
$\models A$ iff for all Kripke-structures $\mathcal{M}$ we have $\mathcal{M} \models A$.

Theorem 12.

$$K_{\mathcal{H}} \vdash A \quad\Leftrightarrow\quad \models A \quad\Leftrightarrow\quad K_{\mathcal{S}} \vdash A$$

Proof. Left equivalence: see e.g. [12]; right equivalence: see e.g. [2] or [4].

Definition 13. $\langle w_0, \dots, w_n \rangle \in W^{n+1}$ is a path in $\mathcal{M}$ iff

$$\forall i \in \{0, \dots, n-1\} : w_i\mathcal{R}w_{i+1} \text{ and } \forall i, j \in \{0, \dots, n\} : (i \neq j \Rightarrow w_i \neq w_j)$$

Definition 14.
$|w, w'| := \min\{n + 1 | \langle w_0, \dots, w_n \rangle \text{ path in } \mathcal{M}, w_0 = w, w_n = w'\}$ $(\forall w, w' \in W)$.
$\text{diam}(\mathcal{M}) := \max\{|w, w'| \mid w, w' \in W\}$. We call $\text{diam}(\mathcal{M})$ the diameter of $\mathcal{M}$.

4 $\mathsf{K}+T$: syntax and semantics

Definition 15. The Hilbert-style calculus $(\mathsf{K}+T)_{\mathcal{H}}$ is the calculus $\mathsf{K}_{\mathcal{H}}$ plus for all $B \in T$ the axiom B.

Definition 16. The one-sided sequent calculus $(\mathsf{K}+T)_{\mathcal{S}}$ is the calculus $\mathsf{K}_{\mathcal{S}}$ plus for all $B \in T$ the rule

$$\frac{\neg B, \Gamma}{\Gamma}\ (\text{th})$$

Example 1. $T := \{p_1, \Box(p_1 \to p_0)\}$. Then $\Box p_0$ is provable in $(\mathsf{K}+T)_{\mathcal{H}}$ and in $(\mathsf{K}+T)_{\mathcal{S}}$.

$$\dfrac{\dfrac{p_1}{\Box p_1}\ (\Box) \qquad \dfrac{\Box(p_1 \to p_0) \quad \Box(p_1 \to p_0) \to \Box p_1 \to \Box p_0}{\Box p_1 \to \Box p_0}\ (\text{mp})}{\Box p_0}\ (\text{mp})$$

$$\dfrac{\dfrac{\dfrac{\dfrac{\dfrac{p_1, \neg p_1}{p_0, p_1, \neg p_1}\ (\text{weak})}{p_0, p_1}\ (\text{th}) \qquad p_0, \neg p_0}{p_0, p_1 \wedge \neg p_0}\ (\wedge)}{\Box p_0, \Diamond(p_1 \wedge \neg p_0)}\ (\Box)}{\Box p_0}\ (\text{th})$$

Definition 17.
$T \models A \ :\Leftrightarrow\ \forall \mathcal{M} : (\mathcal{M} \models T \Rightarrow \mathcal{M} \models A)$.
$\mathcal{M} \not\models \langle T, A\rangle \ :\Leftrightarrow\ (\mathcal{M} \models T$ and $\mathcal{M} \not\models A)$.
If $\mathcal{M} \not\models \langle T, A\rangle$, then we call $\mathcal{M}$ a counter-model of $\langle T, A\rangle$.

Theorem 18.

$$(K+T)_{\mathcal{H}} \vdash A \quad \Leftrightarrow \quad T \models A \quad \Leftrightarrow \quad (K+T)_{\mathcal{S}} \vdash A$$

Proof. Left equivalence: see e.g. [12]; right equivalence: see e.g. [2].

In the following we write $\mathsf{K}+T \vdash A$ instead of $(\mathsf{K}+T)_{\mathcal{H}} \vdash A$.

Theorem 19. *If* $T = \{B_1, \ldots, B_n\}$, $C :\equiv B_1 \wedge \ldots \wedge B_n$, *then*

$$K+T \vdash A \quad \Leftrightarrow \quad \exists k \in I\!N : K \vdash \Box^0 C \wedge \Box^1 C \wedge \ldots \wedge \Box^k C \to A$$

Proof. See [3].

Remark. With $\Box^0 C \wedge \Box^1 C \wedge \ldots \wedge \Box^k C$ we express that the formulas in T must be satisfied in the actual world and in the following k worlds. The same mechanism is used in the (th) rule of $(\mathsf{K}+T)_{\mathcal{S}}$, however without the limit k.

Note 20. $\mathsf{K} \nvdash \Diamond(p_0 \vee \neg p_0)$, but $\mathsf{K} + \{\Diamond p_1\} \vdash \Diamond(p_0 \vee \neg p_0)$.
It is surprising that $\Diamond p_1$ can help to prove a formula with p_0 as its only variable. If we do backward proof search in $(\mathsf{K}+T)_{\mathcal{S}}$, then $\Diamond p_1$ enables the backward application of ($\Box$). From the point of view of Kripke semantics, $\Diamond(p_0 \vee \neg p_0)$ does not hold for worlds without successor; the addition of $\Diamond p_1$ ensures the existence of successors.

5 Proof search in sequent calculi

Although we consider only finite theories, the backward proof search in $(\mathsf{K}+T)_{\mathcal{S}}$ does not terminate in general, since the (th) rule is always applicable.

Because $(\mathsf{K}+T)_{\mathcal{S}}$ enjoys the subformula property, and $(K+T)_{\mathcal{S}} \vdash A, \Gamma$ iff $(K+T)_{\mathcal{S}} \vdash A, A, \Gamma$, backward proof search can be restricted such that only a finite number of sequents occurs. Consequently each branch either loops or ends in an axiom.

The calculus $(\mathsf{K}+T)_{\mathcal{S},2}$ uses a variant of this restriction. A built-in loop check ensures the termination of the backward proof search. A sequent in $(\mathsf{K}+T)_{\mathcal{S},2}$ consists of a multiset and the history H. H is a set of pairs of a formula and a multiset. Such a pair represents a sequent on which the ($\Box$) rule has already been applied.

Definition 21. $(\mathsf{K}+T)_{\mathcal{S},2}$

$T = \{B_1, \ldots, B_n\}$, Δ contains no duplicate elements

$$P, \neg P, \Gamma; H$$

$$\frac{A, B, \Gamma; H}{A \vee B, \Gamma; H}\,(\vee) \qquad\qquad \frac{A, \Gamma; H \quad B, \Gamma; H}{A \wedge B, \Gamma; H}\,(\wedge)$$

$$\frac{A, \Delta, \neg B_1, \ldots, \neg B_n; H \cup \{\langle A; \Delta\rangle\}}{\Box A, \Diamond\Delta, \Sigma; H}\,\langle A; \Delta\rangle \notin H \qquad (\Box)$$

Note 22. The weakening rule is now integrated in ($\Box$) and in the axioms.

Theorem 23. *If* $T = \{B_1, \ldots, B_n\}$, *then*

$$(K+T)_{\mathcal{S},2} \vdash A, \neg B_1, \ldots, \neg B_n; \emptyset \quad \Leftrightarrow \quad (K+T)_{\mathcal{S}} \vdash A$$

Proof. From the invertibility of the ($\vee$) and ($\wedge$) rules of $\mathsf{K} + T_{\mathcal{S}}$ we can conclude that it is enough to apply (th) backwards right after applying ($\Box$) backwards in $(\mathsf{K}+T)_{\mathcal{S}}$. The equivalence follows with an induction on proof length.

Note 24. From the point of view of Kripke semantics, the combination of the rules ($\Box$) and (th) of $\mathsf{K}_{\mathcal{S}}$ to one rule means: Add the theory only after moving to a new world.

If we do backward proof search in $(\mathsf{K}+T)_{\mathcal{S},2}$, we first apply the invertible rule $(\vee)$ as often as possible, and then the invertible rule $(\wedge)$. Afterwards we have to apply $(\Box)$ backwards in all possible ways until the provability is established or all these possibilities failed. Of course we always choose Σ as small as possible.

In this article we use $\leftrightarrow$ only as an abbreviation, what produces sometimes a superfluous blow up of the formula (consider e.g. the formulas $p_0 \leftrightarrow p_1 \leftrightarrow \ldots \leftrightarrow p_n \leftrightarrow p_0 \leftrightarrow p_1 \leftrightarrow \ldots \leftrightarrow p_n$ of [13]). Using a two-sided sequent calculus with special rules for $\leftrightarrow$ solves this problem.

A serious problem is the superfluous backward application of $(\wedge)$. Consider the following example of backward proof search in $(\mathsf{K}+\{P\vee Q\})_{\mathcal{S},2}$ (we omit the history in the sequents):

$$
\dfrac{\dfrac{\dfrac{\dfrac{P,Q,R,\neg P \quad P,Q,R,\neg Q}{P,Q,R,\neg P\wedge\neg Q}(\wedge)}{P\vee Q\vee R,\neg P\wedge\neg Q}(\vee),(\vee)}{\Box(P\vee Q\vee R),\neg P}(\Box) \qquad \dfrac{\dfrac{\dfrac{P,Q,R,\neg P \quad P,Q,R,\neg Q}{P,Q,R,\neg P\wedge\neg Q}(\wedge)}{P\vee Q\vee R,\neg P\wedge\neg Q}(\vee),(\vee)}{\Box(P\vee Q\vee R),\neg Q}(\Box)}{\Box(P\vee Q\vee R),\neg P\wedge\neg Q}(\wedge)
$$

The right subproof is almost equal to the left subproof, because the subformulas of the main formula $\neg P\wedge\neg Q$ of the first backward application of $(\wedge)$ disappear unused. However, we cannot do without the two remaining applications of $(\wedge)$.

Of course this problem also occurs in classical propositional logic (see e.g. [10]), but in the case of $(\mathsf{K}+T)_{\mathcal{S},2}$ the problem is more serious since the formulas of the theory are added again and again. The so-called use-checking proposed in [11] for intuitionistic propositional logic can be modified such that it fits $\mathsf{K}+T$.

Theorem 25. *If $\mathcal{P}$ is a proof of the sequent $A,\Gamma;H$ in $(K+T)_{\mathcal{S},2}$, and no subformula of A is the main formula of an axiom or of a $(\Box)$ application in $\mathcal{P}$, then $(K+T)_{\mathcal{S},2}\vdash A\wedge B,\Gamma;H$ for all $B\in Fml$.*

Proof. Induction on proof length of $\mathcal{P}$.

For the formula $\Box^n(p_0\vee p_1\vee p_2)$, use-checking leads to an exponential speed-up of backward proof search in $(\mathsf{K}+T)_{\mathcal{S},2}$.

6 Sometimes counter-models must have large diameter

An important property of a calculus is the length of the branches resp. loops that can occur. If backward proof search fails in $(\mathsf{K}+T)_{\mathcal{S},2}$ then a counter-model can be directly derived from the search tree. Each application of $(\Box)$ corresponds to a world in the counter-model or, if a loop occurs, to a connection with an already existing world.

In the case of the sequent calculi for K, KT, S4 (cf. section 7), the diameter of the resulting counter-model is limited by a polynomial in $|A|$. These polynomial bounds immediately show that these decision problems are solvable in PSPACE (see [8] for details).

It is easy to obtain an exponential upper bound for diam($\mathcal{M}$). We know that $(\mathsf{K}+T)_{\mathcal{S},2} \vdash A, \Gamma$ iff $(\mathsf{K}+T)_{\mathcal{S},2} \vdash A, A, \Gamma$, and $(\mathsf{K}+T)_{\mathcal{S},2}$ satisfies the subformula property. Since the number of different subformulas in A and T is at most $|A| + |T|$, the following lemma holds:

Lemma 26. *If $\mathsf{K}+T \not\vdash A$, then there is a Kripke-structure $\mathcal{M}$ such that $\mathcal{M} \not\models \langle T, A\rangle$ and* $\operatorname{diam}(\mathcal{M}) \leq 2^{|A|+|T|}$.

In this section we show that there is no polynomial upper bound for diam($\mathcal{M}$) in the size of A plus T.

Definition 27. If $m, b_1, \ldots, b_m \in \{2, 3, \ldots\}$ and $P, Q_1, \ldots, Q_m, R$ are different variables, then $\forall i \in \{1, \ldots, m\} : \forall j \in I\!N : A_{ij} :\equiv \Box^j Q_i \wedge \bigwedge_{k=1}^{j-1} \Box^k \neg Q_i$ and

$$T_{\langle b_1,\ldots,b_m\rangle} := \{\Diamond R, \neg Q_1 \vee A_{1,b_1}, \ldots, \neg Q_m \vee A_{m,b_m}, P \vee A_{1,b_1} \wedge \ldots \wedge A_{m,b_m}\}$$

Example 2. $m = 2$, $b_1 = 3$, $b_2 = 5$.
Then $\langle\{w_0, \ldots, w_{15}, \mathcal{R}, I\rangle$, where $w_0 \mathcal{R} w_1$, …, $w_{14} \mathcal{R} w_{15}$, $w_{15} \mathcal{R} w_1$, and where I is given by the following table, is a typical counter-model of $\langle T_{\langle 3,5\rangle}, P\rangle$. (A '?' in the table means that the value does not matter.)

I	w_0	w_1	w_2	w_3	w_4	w_5	w_6	w_7	w_8	w_9	w_{10}	w_{11}	w_{12}	w_{13}	w_{14}	w_{15}
P	0	1	1	1	1	1	1	1	1	1	1	1	1	1	1	1
Q_1	?	0	0	1	0	0	1	0	0	1	0	0	1	0	0	1
Q_2	?	0	0	0	0	1	0	0	0	0	1	0	0	0	0	1
R	?	1	1	1	1	1	1	1	1	1	1	1	1	1	1	1

Because of the formula $\Diamond R$ there must always exist a successor world. In a counter-model of $\langle T_{\langle 3,5\rangle}, P\rangle$ there must be a world where P is false, called w_0 in this example. The formula $P \vee A_{1,3} \wedge A_{2,5}$ at the beginning and afterwards the formulas $\neg Q_1 \vee A_{1,3}$ resp. $\neg Q_2 \vee A_{2,5}$ effect that Q_1 is exactely true in every third world resp. that Q_2 is exactely true in every fifth world. This leads to a loop of $3 \cdot 5$ different worlds.

Lemma 28. *If $m, b_1, \ldots, b_m \in \{2, 3, \ldots\}$, then $T_{\langle b_1,\ldots,b_m\rangle} \not\vdash P$.*

Proof. It is always possible to construct a counter-model of $\langle T_{\langle b_1,\ldots,b_m\rangle}, P\rangle$ analogous to the one in the example above.

Note 29. $T_{\langle b_1,\ldots,b_m\rangle} \cup \{\neg Q_1 \vee \ldots \vee \neg Q_m\} \vdash P$.

Definition 30. If $m, b_1, \ldots, b_m \in \{2, 3, \ldots\}$, then $G(b_1, \ldots, b_m)$ stands for

$$\forall i, j \in \{1, \ldots, m\} : (i < j \rightarrow \gcd(b_i, b_j) = 1)$$

Lemma 31. *If* $m, b_1, \ldots, b_m \in \{2,3,\ldots\}$ *and* $G(b_1,\ldots,b_m)$, *then:*

$$\mathcal{M} \not\models \langle T_{\langle b_1,\ldots,b_m\rangle}, P\rangle \quad \Rightarrow \quad \mathrm{diam}(\mathcal{M}) \geq \prod_{i=1}^{m} b_i$$

Proof. Assume that $\mathcal{M} \models T_{\langle b_1,\ldots,b_m\rangle}$ (*), $\mathcal{M} \not\models P$.

(1) $\mathcal{M} \models T_{\langle b_1,\ldots,b_m\rangle} \Rightarrow \forall w \in W : w \models \Diamond R \Rightarrow \forall w \in W : \exists w' \in W : w\mathcal{R}w'$.

(2) $\mathcal{M} \not\models P \Rightarrow \exists w_0 \in W : w_0 \models \neg P$
$\overset{(*)}{\Rightarrow} \exists w_0 \in W : w_0 \models \neg P \wedge (P \vee A_{1,b_1} \wedge \ldots \wedge A_{m,b_m})$
$\Rightarrow \exists w_0 \in W : w_0 \models A_{1,b_1} \wedge \ldots \wedge A_{m,b_m}$.

(3) Assume $w, w' \in W$ and $d_1 \in \{1,\ldots,b_1\}$, ..., $d_m \in \{1,\ldots,b_m\}$ such that $w\mathcal{R}w'$ and $w \models A_{1,d_1} \wedge \ldots \wedge A_{m,d_m}$.
Then we have for all $i \in \{1,\ldots,m\}$:
- $d_i > 1$: $w \models A_{i,d_i} \Rightarrow w \models \Box^{d_i} Q_i \wedge \bigwedge_{k=1}^{d_i-1} \Box^k \neg Q_i$
$\Rightarrow w' \models \Box^{d_i-1} Q_i \wedge \bigwedge_{k=1}^{d_i-2} \Box^k \neg Q_i \Rightarrow w' \models A_{i,d_i-1}$.
- $d_i = 1$: $w \models A_{i,d_i} \Rightarrow w \models \Box Q_i \Rightarrow w' \models Q_i$
$\overset{(*)}{\Rightarrow} w' \models Q_i \wedge (\neg Q_i \vee A_{i,b_i}) \Rightarrow w' \models A_{i,b_i}$.

(4) Assume $w \in W$, $i \in \{1,\ldots,m\}$ and $d_i, d_i' \in \{1,\ldots,b_i\}$, $d_i \leq d_i'$ such that $w \models A_{i,d_i}$ and $w \models A_{i,d_i'}$.
If $d_i < d_i'$, then $w \models \Box^{d_i} Q_i$ and $w \models \Box^{d_i} \neg Q_i$. With (1) follows $\exists w' \in W$: ($w' \models Q_i$ and $w' \models \neg Q_i$). Contradiction.
Thus $d_i = d_i'$.

Conclusion:
We define $c := \prod_{i=1}^{m} b_i$. Because of (1), (2) there are $w_0, w_1, \ldots, w_{c-1} \in W$ such that $w_0\mathcal{R}w_1\mathcal{R}\ldots\mathcal{R}w_{c-1}$ and $w_0 \models A_{1,b_1} \wedge \ldots \wedge A_{m,b_m}$.
With (2),(3),(4) together with $G(b_1,\ldots,b_m)$ follows that $\langle w_0,\ldots,w_{c-1}\rangle$ is a path in $\mathcal{M}$ and that there are no short-cuts, i.e. $|w_0, w_{c-1}| = c$, thus $\mathrm{diam}(\mathcal{M}) \geq c$.

Lemma 32. $\forall e \in \{1,2,\ldots\} : \exists m, b_1, \ldots, b_m \in \{2,3,\ldots\}$ *with* $b_1 < \ldots < b_m$ *such that:*

$$b_m \geq 7 \quad \textit{and} \quad G(b_1,\ldots,b_m) \quad \textit{and} \quad \prod_{i=1}^{m} b_i > {b_m}^{4e}$$

Proof. Let prim_i be the ith prime number ($\mathrm{prim}_1 = 2$) and choose $m := 8e$.
$a := \prod_{i=1}^{m} \mathrm{prim}_i$, $\forall i \in \{1,\ldots,m\} : b_i := a + \mathrm{prim}_i$.
Assume c prim, $c|b_i$, $c|b_j$, where $i,j \in \{1,\ldots,m\}$ and $i < j$.
Then: $c|((a+\mathrm{prim}_j) - (a+\mathrm{prim}_i)) \Rightarrow c|(\mathrm{prim}_j - \mathrm{prim}_i) \Rightarrow c < \mathrm{prim}_j \Rightarrow c|a$.
With $c|b_j$ follows $c|\mathrm{prim}_j$, and since $c < \mathrm{prim}_j$ we have $c = 1$. Contradiction.
Thus $G(b_1,\ldots,b_m)$ is satisfied.
$\prod_{i=1}^{m} b_i > a^m = (a^2)^{\frac{m}{2}} > (2a)^{4e} > (a + \mathrm{prim}_m)^{4e} = {b_m}^{4e}$.

Lemma 33. *If* $m, b_1, \ldots, b_m \in \{2,3,\ldots\}$, $b_m \geq 7$, $b_1 < \ldots < b_m$, $G(b_1,\ldots,b_m)$, *then* $|T_{\langle b_1,\ldots,b_m\rangle}| + |P| < {b_m}^4$.

Proof. $|T_{\langle b_1,\ldots,b_m\rangle}| + |P|$
$= 2 + \sum_{i=1}^{m}(3 + |A_{i,b_i}|) + (1 + \sum_{i=1}^{m}(1 + |A_{i,b_i}|)) + 1$
$< 4+4m+2m|A_{m,b_m}| = 4+m({b_m}^2+7b_m-4) < b_m+b_m({b_m}^2+{b_m}^2) < {b_m}^4.$

Theorem 34. $\forall e \in I\!N : \exists T, A$ *with* $T \not\vdash A$:

$$(\mathcal{M} \models T \text{ and } \mathcal{M} \not\models A) \quad \Rightarrow \quad \mathrm{diam}(\mathcal{M}) \geq (|T| + |A|)^e$$

Proof. We combine the lemmas 28, 31, 32 and 33.

7 Embeddings

Because the accessibility relation in the Kripke structures of S4 is transitive, $\Box B$ means that B is true in the actual world and in all the worlds in the future. This leads to the following theorem:

Theorem 35.

$$S4 + \{B_1, \ldots, B_n\} \vdash A \quad \Leftrightarrow \quad S4 \vdash \Box B_1 \wedge \ldots \wedge \Box B_n \to A$$

Proof. See e.g. [2].

Definition 36. $\mathsf{KT}_\mathcal{S}$ (resp. $(\mathsf{KT} + T)_\mathcal{S}$) is the calculus $\mathsf{K}_\mathcal{S}$ (resp. $(\mathsf{K} + T)_\mathcal{S}$) plus the rule

$$\frac{A, \Diamond A, \Gamma}{\Diamond A, \Gamma}\ (\Diamond)$$

Definition 37. $\mathsf{S4}_\mathcal{S}$ is the calculus $\mathsf{KT}_\mathcal{S}$ with the rule $(\Box)$ replaced by

$$\frac{A, \Diamond\Gamma}{\Box A, \Diamond\Gamma}\ (\Box)$$

We extend the notation for substitution:

Definition 38. Let A be a formula, $Q_1, \ldots, Q_n$ pairwise different variables that do not occur in A, and $B_1, \ldots, B_n$ subformulas of A.
We construct a function $\pi : \{1, \ldots, n\} \to \{1, \ldots, n\}$ such that $\pi(i) < \pi(j)$ implies $|B_{\pi(i)}| \geq |B_{\pi(j)}|$. First we substitute in A the variable $Q_{\pi(1)}$ for $B_{\pi(1)}$, in the result we substitute the variable $Q_{\pi(2)}$ for $B_{\pi(2)}, \ldots$, and finally the variable $Q_{\pi(n)}$ for $B_{\pi(n)}$ (in this order, not in parallel!). We write $A\{Q_1/B_1, \ldots, Q_n/B_n\}$ for the result.
Example: If $A \equiv \Diamond(p_0 \vee \Diamond\Box p_1) \wedge \Diamond\Box p_1$, $B_1 \equiv \Diamond\Box p_1$, $B_2 \equiv \Diamond(p_0 \vee \Diamond\Box p_1)$. Then $\pi(1) = 2$, $\pi(2) = 1$, $A\{Q_1/B_1, Q_2/B_2\} \equiv Q_2 \wedge Q_1$ (i.e. $A\{Q_1/B_1, Q_2/B_2\} \not\equiv \Diamond(p_0 \vee Q_1) \wedge Q_1$).

Theorem 39. *If A is a formula, $\Diamond C_1, \ldots, \Diamond C_n$ are the $\Diamond$ subformulas of A, $Q_1, \ldots, Q_n$ are variables that do not occur in A,*
for all $i \in \{1, \ldots n\} : C'_i :\equiv C_i\{Q_1/\Diamond C_1, \ldots, Q_n/\Diamond C_n\}$,
$A' :\equiv A\{Q_1/\Diamond C_1, \ldots, Q_n/\Diamond C_n\}$,
$T' := \{Q_1 \vee \neg(\Diamond Q_1 \vee \Diamond C'_1), \ldots, Q_n \vee \neg(\Diamond Q_n \vee \Diamond C'_n)\}$,
then:

$$\mathsf{S4} \vdash A \quad \Leftrightarrow \quad \mathsf{KT} + T' \vdash A'$$

Proof.
'$\Rightarrow$': Let $\mathcal{P}$ be a proof of A in $\mathsf{S4}_{\mathcal{S}}$. We construct a proof $\mathcal{P}'$ of A' in $(\mathsf{KT} + T)_{\mathcal{S}}$. The root of $\mathcal{P}'$ is A'. An application of a rule in $\mathcal{P}$ becomes in $\mathcal{P}'$ an application of the corresponding rule of $(\mathsf{KT} + T)_{\mathcal{S}}$.
If Q_i occurs in a sequent in $\mathcal{P}'$, then we insert just above this sequent the part

$$\dfrac{\dfrac{Q_i, \neg Q_i}{Q_i, \neg Q_i, \Gamma}\,(\text{weak}) \qquad \dfrac{\dfrac{\dfrac{\Diamond Q_i, \Diamond C'_i, \Gamma}{Q_i, \Diamond Q_i, \Diamond C'_i, \Gamma}\,(\text{weak})}{Q_i, \Diamond Q_i \vee \Diamond C'_i, \Gamma}\,(\vee)}{}}{\dfrac{Q_i, \neg Q_i \wedge (\Diamond Q_i \vee \Diamond C'_i), \Gamma}{Q_i, \Gamma}\,(\text{th})}\,(\wedge)$$

The inserted part has two purposes:

- If $\Diamond C_i$ occurs for the first time on a branch in $\mathcal{P}$ (seen from the root), then it makes sure that $\Diamond C'_i$ occurs in the corresponding sequent in $\mathcal{P}'$.
- In contrast to $\mathsf{S4}_{\mathcal{S}}$, a backward application on $(\Box)$ in $(\mathsf{KT} + T)_{\mathcal{S}}$ destroys leading $\Diamond$ connectives. The inserted part regenerates them by 'replacing' Q_i by $\Diamond Q_i$.

Thus we know that if $\Diamond C_i$ occurs in a sequent in $\mathcal{P}$, then $\Diamond C'_i$ occurs in the corresponding sequent in $\mathcal{P}'$, i.e. we can continue with the construction.

'$\Leftarrow$': Let $\mathcal{P}'$ be a proof of A' in $(\mathsf{KT} + T)_{\mathcal{S}}$. We construct a proof $\mathcal{P}$ of A in $\mathsf{S4}_{\mathcal{S}}$. The root of $\mathcal{P}$ is A.
Because the rules (th), $(\Diamond)$, $(\wedge)$, $(\vee)$ of $(\mathsf{KT} + T')_{\mathcal{S}}$ are invertible, we can assume that the (th) rule is applied in $\mathcal{P}'$ only in the context displayed above. (If a $(\Box)$ rule is used on the left branch, then the (th) application in $\mathcal{P}'$ is superfluous.) These parts can be omitted in $\mathcal{P}$. Applications of $(\Diamond)$ with the main formula $\Diamond Q_i$ in $\mathcal{P}'$ can be omitted in $\mathcal{P}$ as well.
Axioms of the form $Q_i, \neg Q_i$ can only occur in the situation displayed above, since there is no negative occurrence of Q_i in A' and only one positive occurrence of Q_i in T'. The remaining rules resp. axioms in $\mathcal{P}'$ are replaced by the corresponding rules resp. axioms of $\mathsf{S4}_{\mathcal{S}}$.

Example 3. $A \equiv \Diamond(p_0 \vee \Box \Diamond \neg p_0) \wedge p_0$.
Thus $n = 2$, $C_1 \equiv p_0 \vee \Box \Diamond \neg p_0$, $C_2 \equiv \neg p_0$. We choose $Q_1 \equiv p_1$, $Q_2 \equiv p_2$.
$C'_1 \equiv p_0 \vee \Box Q_2$, $C'_2 \equiv \neg p_0$.
$A' \equiv Q_1 \wedge p_0$.
$T' = \{Q_1 \vee \neg(\Diamond Q_1 \vee \Diamond C'_1), Q_2 \vee \neg(\Diamond Q_2 \vee \Diamond C'_2)\}$.

The accessibility relation of the Kripke structures of KT must be reflexive, thus $\Diamond A$ is also satisfied if A is satisfied in the actual world. The embedding k used in [3] simulates this interpretation. We extend it to theories.

Definition 40. $\mathrm{k}(P) :\equiv P$, $\mathrm{k}(\neg P) :\equiv \neg P$, $\mathrm{k}(\Box A) :\equiv \Box\mathrm{k}(A)$, $\mathrm{k}(\Diamond A) :\equiv \mathrm{k}(A) \vee \Diamond\mathrm{k}(A)$, $\mathrm{k}(A \wedge B) :\equiv \mathrm{k}(A) \wedge \mathrm{k}(B)$, $\mathrm{k}(A \vee B) :\equiv \mathrm{k}(A) \vee \mathrm{k}(B)$.
If $T = \{B_1, \ldots, B_n\}$, then $\mathrm{k}(T) := \{\neg\mathrm{k}(\neg B_1), \ldots, \neg\mathrm{k}(\neg B_n)\}$.

Theorem 41.

$$\begin{aligned} K \vdash k(A) \quad &\Leftrightarrow \quad KT \vdash A \\ K + k(T) \vdash k(A) \quad &\Leftrightarrow \quad KT + T \vdash A \end{aligned}$$

Proof. Induction on proof length.

Note 42. In spite of the simple definition, $|\mathrm{k}(A)|$ can be much longer than $|A|$, for example $|\mathrm{k}(\Diamond^n p_0)| > 2^n$. This problem is diminished if structure sharing is used (provided that $\Box$, $\Diamond$, $\neg$, $\wedge$, $\vee$ are the only connectives of the language).

The same ideas that lead to lemma 26 immediately give an – of course very inefficient – embedding of $\mathsf{K} + T$ in K.

Theorem 43. If T is finite, C is the conjunction of the elements of T, then:

$$K + T \vdash A \Leftrightarrow K \vdash C \wedge \Box C \wedge \ldots \wedge \Box^{2^{|A|+|T|}} C \rightarrow A$$

Summary:

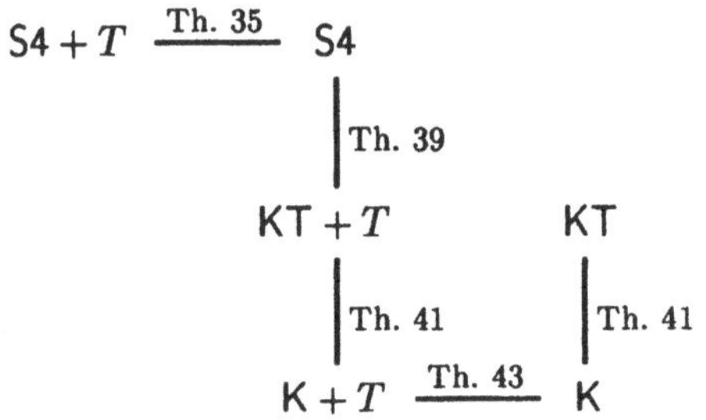

8 Implementation

Decision procedures for K, $\mathsf{K} + T$, KT, $\mathsf{KT} + T$, S4, and $\mathsf{S4} + T$ are implemented in the Logics Workbench LWB ([7]). These decision procedures were intensively used in [5] to prove the equivalence of propositional normal modal logics.
It is possible to use these decision procedures via WWW. Start a WWW browser, open `http://lwbwww.unibe.ch:8080/LWBinfo.html` and choose the item `run a session`.
If you want to run the example from section 4, type

```
load(k);
provable(box p0, [p1, box(p1 -> p0)]);
```

and press the `send` button. After a while you obtain the result.

9 Conclusion

After discussing methods for efficient backward proof search in $\mathsf{K}+T$, we proved that in $K+T$ the construction of a counter-model and therefore backward proof search is (in a certain sense) harder than in K. We did not investigate the complexity of $\mathsf{K}+T$. (From [8] one obtains the lower bound PSPACE, and from [6] the upper bound EXPTIME.)
Another sign of a considerable expressiveness of $\mathsf{K}+T$ is the existence of the natural embedding of S4 in $\mathsf{K}+T$ we constructed in the last section.

To typeset the proof trees we used a macro package by Dirk Roorda. Thanks to Wolfgang Heinle and Werner Wolff for some helpful remarks.

References

1. Laurent Catach. Tableaux: A general theorem prover for modal logics. *Journal of Automated Reasoning*, 7:489–510, 1991.
2. Melvin Fitting. *Proof Methods for Modal and Intuitionistic Logics*. Reidel, Dordrecht, 1983.
3. Melvin Fitting. First-order modal tableaux. *Journal of Automated Reasoning*, 4:191–213, 1988.
4. Rajeev Goré. Tableau methods for modal and temporal logics. Technical report, TR-15-95, Automated Reasoning Project, Australian National University, Canberra, Australia, 1995. To appear in Handbook of Tableau Methods, Kluwer, 199?
5. Rajeev Goré, Wolfgang Heinle, and Alain Heuerding. Relations between propositional normal modal logics: an overview. Submitted.
6. Joseph Y. Halpern and Yoram Moses. A guide to completeness and complexity for modal logics of knowledge and belief. *Artificial Intelligence*, 54:319–379, 1992.
7. Alain Heuerding, Gerhard Jäger, Stefan Schwendimann, and Michael Seyfried. Propositional logics on the computer. In *Theorem Proving with Analytic Tableaux and Related Methods*, LNCS 918, 1995.
8. Richard E. Ladner. The computational complexity of provability in systems of modal propositional logic. *SIAM Journal on Computing*, 6(3):467–480, 1977.
9. Ilkka Niemelä and Heikki Tuominen. Helsinki logic machine: A system for logical expertise. Technical report, Digital Systems Laboratory, Department of Computer Science, Helsinki University of Technology, 1987.
10. F. Oppacher and E. Suen. Harp: A tableau-based theorem prover. *Journal of Automated Reasoning*, 4:69–100, 1988.
11. Dan Sahlin, Torkel Franzén, and Seif Haridi. An intuitionistic predicate logic theorem prover. *Journal of Logic and Computation*, 2(5):619–656, 1992.
12. Kurt Schütte. *Vollständige Systeme modaler und intuitionistischer Logik*. Springer, 1968.
13. Alasdair Urquhart. Complexity of proofs in classical propositional logic. In Yiannis N. Moschovakis, editor, *Logic from Computer Science*, pages 597–608. Springer, 1992.
14. Lincoln Wallen. *Automated Proof Search in Non-Classical Logics*. M.I.T. Press, Cambridge, Massachusetts, 1990.

Improved Decision Procedures for the Modal Logics K, T and S4

Jörg Hudelmaier

WSI, Universität Tübingen Sand 13, D72076 Tübingen
Tel. (49)7071 297361
joerg@logik.informatik.uni-tuebingen.de

Abstract. We propose so called contraction free sequent calculi for the three prominent modal logics K, T, and S4. Deduction search in these calculi is shown to provide more efficient decision procedures than those hitherto known. In particular space requirements for our logics are lowered from the previously established bounds of the form n^2, n^3 and n^4 to $n \log n$, $n \log n$, and $n^2 \log n$ respectively.

1 Introduction

Modal logics are extensions of classical propositional logic by the necessity operator $\Box$. Different properties of necessity give rise to various such logics. Here we consider three logics K, T, and S4. For all these logics basic properties required of the necessity operator are validity of the so called necessitation rule

$$(\mathrm{N}) \quad \frac{a}{\Box a}$$

and of the axiom (K) $\Box(a \to b) \to (\Box a \to \Box b)$. For the logic T we need in addition to (N) and (K) the axiom (T) $\Box a \to a$ and for S4 we need besides (N), (K), and (T) the axiom (4) $\Box a \to \Box\Box a$. Semantics for all these logics are based on so called Kripke models, i.e. sets of possible worlds with binary accessibility relations on them. Validity of a formula is then defined as validity in all suitable Kripke models, where suitability of a model for a given logic is described in terms of properties of the accessibilty relation. So for the logic K any Kripke model is suitable, whereas for T only Kripke models with reflexive accessibilty are suitable and for S4 only models with reflexive and transitive accessibility are suitable. Validity of a formula in a given Kripke model m is defined recursively over the structure of the formula, where the Boolean cases coincide with the definition of classical validity and a formula $\Box a$ is valid in m, iff it is valid in all worlds accessible from m.

It has been shown that validity of formulas for any of these three logics is PSPACE complete, even for their Horn fragments [4] and for formulas with only one propositional variable [6]. In particular Ladner in the 1970s has given decision procedures using Kripke models for the modal logics K, T, and S4 of space complexity respectively n^2, n^3 and n^4 [1]. Now instead of Kripke models most systems designed for actual theorem proving in modal logic (cf. [5], [8]) use so called sequent calculi [3]. These calculi are, however, built on formalized search for counter examples in Kripke models. Thus they can not provide smaller space bounds. Moreover building theorem provers for such calculi is made difficult by the fact that depth first search is not guaranteed to terminate. Thus more sophisticated search procedures have to be applied, e.g. procedures using loop checking. In contrast to this it has recently been shown that for intuitionistic propositional logic so called contraction free sequent calculi, i.e. calculi for which there is a measure such that for each rule of the calculus the measure of all its premisses is smaller than the measure of its conclusion, yield more efficient decision procedures [2]. Thus it was natural to try to extend this approach to modal logic. However it turned out that contraction free calculi could not be obtained directly from these calculi; most notably for the logics T and S4 a new connective had to be added to the language, in order to be able to define a suitable measure function for the contraction free calculus.

2 Basic Clausal Calculi

As our basic language we consider arbitrary modal formulas built up from propositional variables by means of the connectives $\neg$, $\vee$ and $\Box$ and modal clauses, i.e. formulas of the form $\Box\ldots\Box(a_1 \vee \ldots \vee a_l)$ $(1 \leq l \leq 3)$ or $\Box\ldots\Box(a_1 \vee \Box b)$ or $\Box\ldots\Box(a_1 \vee \neg\Box b)$, where the a_i are propositional variables or negations of propositional variables and b is a propositional variable. These clauses we write in the form $\Box^s[c_1, \ldots, c_n]$. Ordinary sequents are pairs of multisets of arbitrary formulas and clausal sequents are multisets of modal clauses.

We start from an often used family of sequent calculi $\mathrm{F_0(K)}$, $\mathrm{F_0(T)}$ and $\mathrm{F_0(4)}$ for deducing ordinary sequents. All these calculi have axioms of the form $M, v \Rightarrow v, N$, where v is a propositional variable and Boolean rules

$$(\mathrm{EB}\neg_0)\ \frac{M \Rightarrow N, v}{M, \neg v \Rightarrow N} \qquad (\mathrm{IB}\neg_0)\ \frac{M, v \Rightarrow N}{M \Rightarrow N, \neg v}$$

$$(\mathrm{EB}\vee_0)\ \frac{M, u \Rightarrow N \quad M, v \Rightarrow N}{M, u \vee v \Rightarrow N} \qquad (\mathrm{IB}\vee_0)\ \frac{M \Rightarrow N, u, v}{M \Rightarrow N, u \vee v}$$

Moreover $\mathrm{F_0(K)}$ has the modal rule

$$(\mathrm{IK}\Box_0)\ \frac{M \Rightarrow v}{L, \Box M \Rightarrow N, \Box v}$$

$\mathrm{F_0(T)}$ has the rule $\mathrm{IK}\Box_0$ and the rule

$$(\mathrm{ET}\Box_0)\ \frac{M, \Box v, v \Rightarrow N}{M, \Box v \Rightarrow N}$$

and $F_0(4)$ has the rule $ET\Box_0$ and the rule

$$(I4\Box_0) \quad \frac{\Box M \Rightarrow v}{L, \Box M \Rightarrow N, \Box v}$$

It is well known that $F_0(K)$ formalizes the modal logic K, $F_0(T)$ formalizes T and $F_0(4)$ formalizes S4 (cf. [3]). Thus in particular for every one of these calculi all the structural rules are admissible, i.e. if a sequent $M \Rightarrow N$ is deducible, then so are the sequents $v, M \Rightarrow N$ and $M \Rightarrow N, v$ (weakening), if a sequent $M, v, v \Rightarrow N$ resp. $M \Rightarrow N, v, v$ is deducible, then so is the sequent $M, v \Rightarrow N$ resp. $M \Rightarrow N, v$ (contraction), and if two sequents $M, v \Rightarrow N$ and $M, \neg v \Rightarrow N$ are deducible, then so is $M \Rightarrow N$ (cut).
We call two sequents s and t equideducible for one of our calculi iff deducibility of s in this calculus implies deducibility of t and vice versa. Then the calculi F_0 allow reduction of sequents to clausal form according to the

Lemma 1. *Let p be a propositional variable which only occurs at the indicated positions. Then the following holds:*

a) These pairs of sequents are equideducible for all calculi F_0*:*

$M \Rightarrow a, N$	*and*	$M, \neg a \Rightarrow N$
$M, \Box^s[A, a \vee b] \Rightarrow N$	*and*	$M, \Box^s[A, a, b] \Rightarrow N$
$M, \Box^s[A, \neg\neg a] \Rightarrow N$	*and*	$M, \Box^s[A, a] \Rightarrow N$
$M, \Box^s[A, \neg(a \vee b)] \Rightarrow N$	*and*	$M, \Box^s[A, \neg p], \Box^s[p, \neg a], \Box^s[p, \neg b] \Rightarrow N$
$M, \Box^s[A, \neg\Box a] \Rightarrow N$	*and*	$M, \Box^s[A, \neg\Box p], \Box^{s+1}[p, \neg a] \Rightarrow N$
$M, \Box^s[A, \Box a] \Rightarrow N$	*and*	$M, \Box^s[A, \Box p], \Box^{s+1}[\neg p, a] \Rightarrow N$
$M, \Box^s[A, B] \Rightarrow N$	*and*	$M, \Box^s[A, p], \Box^s[\neg p, B] \Rightarrow N$

b) The sequents $M, a \Rightarrow N$ and $M, p, \Box[\neg p, \neg a] \Rightarrow N$ are equideducible for $F_0(T)$ *and* $F_0(4)$.
c) The sequents $M, \Box\Box a \Rightarrow N$ and $M, \Box a \Rightarrow N$ are equideducible for $F_0(4)$. □

This lemma is well known (cf. [7]) and using it we may reduce any sequent u to a sequent $CF_K(u)$ of the form $c_1, \ldots, c_n \Rightarrow$, such that u and $CF_K(u)$ are equideducible for $F_0(K)$ and such that the c_i are formulas of the form $\Box^s[a_1, \ldots, a_l]$, $0 \leq s$, $1 \leq l \leq 3$ or $\Box^s[a_1, b]$, where the a_i are propositional variables or negated propositional variables and b is a formula of the form $\Box a$ or $\neg\Box a$, where a is a propositional variable. Moreover we may reduce u to a sequent $CF_T(u)$ of the form $c_1, \ldots, c_n \Rightarrow$ such that u and $CF_T(u)$ are equideducible for $F_0(T)$ and such that the c_i are either propositional variables or formulas of the form $\Box^s[a_1, \ldots, a_l]$ or $\Box^s[a_1, b]$, $1 \leq s$, $1 \leq l \leq 3$. Finally we may reduce u to a sequent $CF_4(u)$ such that u and $CF_4(u)$ are equideducible for $F_0(4)$ and such that the c_i are either propositional variables or formulas of the form $\Box[a_1, \ldots, a_l]$, $1 \leq l \leq 3$ or $\Box[a_1, b]$. In all three cases the number of connectives of the sequents $CF(u)$ is linearly bounded by the length of u.

The Boolean rules of the calculi F_0 are clearly invertible in the sense that any deduction of a conclusion of such a rule may be converted into a deduction of its premiss(es) of smaller or equal length. Therefore the following family F_1 of calculi is complete for deriving clausal sequents:

Axioms of all calculi F_1 are the sequents of the form $M, a, \neg a \Rightarrow$. In addition $F_1(K)$ has the rule

$$(\mathrm{EK}\vee_1) \quad \frac{M, v_1 \Rightarrow \quad \ldots M, v_n \Rightarrow}{M, [v_1, \ldots, v_n] \Rightarrow}$$

and the rule

$$(\mathrm{IK}\Box_1) \quad \frac{M, \neg v \Rightarrow}{L, \Box M, \neg\Box v \Rightarrow}$$

$F_1(T)$ has this latter rule and the rules

$$(\mathrm{ET}\Box_1) \quad \frac{M, \Box\Box v, \Box v \Rightarrow}{M, \Box\Box v \Rightarrow}$$

and

$$(\mathrm{E4}\Box_1) \quad \frac{M, \Box[v_1, \ldots, v_n], v_1 \Rightarrow \quad \ldots \quad M, \Box[v_1, \ldots, v_n], v_n \Rightarrow}{M, \Box[v_1, \ldots, v_n] \Rightarrow}$$

Finally $F_1(4)$ has the rule $\mathrm{E4}\Box_1$ and the rule

$$(\mathrm{I4}\Box_1) \quad \frac{\Box M, \neg v \Rightarrow}{L, \Box M, \neg\Box v \Rightarrow}$$

Now we consider a further calculus $F_2(T)$ which instead of the two rules $\mathrm{ET}\Box_1$ and $\mathrm{E4}\Box_1$ of $F1(T)$ has only a single rule

$$(\mathrm{ET}\Box_2) \quad \frac{M, \Box^s[v_1, \ldots, v_n], v_1 \Rightarrow \quad \ldots \quad M, \Box^s[v_1, \ldots, v_n], v_n \Rightarrow}{M, \Box^s[v_1, \ldots, v_n] \Rightarrow}$$

The rule $\mathrm{E4}\Box_1$ is just a special case of this rule. Thus in order to show that $F_1(T)$ and $F_2(T)$ are equivalent, it suffices to show that the rule $\mathrm{ET}\Box_1$ is admissible, i.e.

Lemma 2. *If a sequent* $M, \Box^{s+1}v, \Box^{s}v \Rightarrow$ *is deducible by* $F_2(T)$, *then so is* $M, \Box^{s+1}v \Rightarrow$.

Proof. If s is 0, then this is rule $ET\Box_2$. Otherwise suppose our sequent is an axiom $M, \Box^{s+1}v, \Box^{s}v, \neg\Box^{s+1}v \Rightarrow$. Then $M, \Box^{s+1}v, \neg\Box^{s+1}v \Rightarrow$ is also an axiom. If it is an axiom of the form $M, \Box^{s+1}v, \Box^{s}v, \neg\Box^{s}v \Rightarrow$, then we obtain the required sequent from the axiom $v, \neg v \Rightarrow$ by one application of $ET\Box_2$ leading to $\Box v, \neg v \Rightarrow$ and s consecutive applications of $IK\Box_1$ leading to $\Box^{s+1}v, \neg\Box v \Rightarrow$ and finally using admissibility of weakening to introduce M.
If our sequent is neither an axiom nor the conclusion of an $IK\Box_1$- inference nor the conclusion of an $ET\Box_2$-inference with prinicipal formula $\Box^{s+1}v$ or $\Box^{s}v$, then these two formulas are present in every premiss and by the induction hypothesis the latter formula may be dropped. Applying the same inference on the transformed premisses therefore results in a deduction of the required sequent. If our sequent is of the form $L, \Box M, \Box^{s+1}v, \Box^{s}v, \neg\Box w \Rightarrow$ and it is the conclusion of an $IK\Box_1$-inference, then its premiss is of the form $M, \Box^{s}v, \Box^{s-1}v, w \Rightarrow$, where $s - 1 \geq 0$. Thus by the induction hypothesis the sequent $M, \Box^{s}v, w \Rightarrow$ is deducible and by an application of $IK\Box_1$ we obtain the required sequent. If $M, \Box^{s+1}v, \Box^{s}v \Rightarrow$ is the conclusion of an application of $ET\Box_2$ with principal formula $\Box^{s+1}v$ or $\Box^{s}v$, then its premisses are of the form $M, \Box^{s+1}v, \Box^{s}v, a_i \Rightarrow$ and by the induction hypothesis we may deduce the sequents $M, \Box^{s+1}v, a_i \Rightarrow$. From these we obtain the sequent $M, \Box^{s+1}v \Rightarrow$ by an application of $ET\Box_2$. □

The rule $EK\vee_1$ of $F_1(K)$ is also just a special case of $ET\Box_2$. Therefore it suffices to show parts b) and c) of the

Lemma 3. *a) There is a transformation converting every* $F_1(K)$*-deduction of a given sequent into another deduction of the same sequent such that in the new deduction every premiss* $M, \neg\Box b \Rightarrow$ *of an* $EK\vee_1$*-inference with principal formula* $[a, \neg\Box b]$ *is the conclusion of an* $IK\Box_1$*-inference with principal formula* $\Box b$.
b) There is a transformation converting every $F_2(T)$*-deduction of a given sequent into another deduction of the same sequent such that in the new deduction every premiss* $M, \Box[a, \neg\Box b], \neg\Box b \Rightarrow$ *of an* $ET\Box_2$*- inference is the conclusion of an* $IK\Box_1$*- inference with principal formula* $\Box b$.
c) There is a transformation converting every $F_1(4)$*-deduction of a given sequent into another deduction of the same sequent such that in the new deduction every premiss* $M, \Box[a, \neg\Box b], \neg\Box b \Rightarrow$ *of an* $E4\Box_1$*- inference is the conclusion of an* $I4\Box_1$*- inference with principal formula* $\Box b$.

Proof. b) For every such premiss P of $ET\Box_2$ we consider the number $n(P)$ which is the maximal number of sequents preceding P in which $\Box b$ appears and for a given deduction d we let $n(d)$ be the sum of all $4^{n(P)} - 1$ for all such premisses P in d. If this number is 0, then all these premisses are conclusions of an application of $IK\Box_1$. But if the principal formula of such an $IK\Box_1$-inference I is different from $\Box b$, then we may drop the $ET\Box_2$-inference and derive its conclusion directly

from the premiss of I by means of IK$\Box_1$. Thus we arrive at a deduction having the required property.
If $n(d)$ is greater than 0, then we consider a maximal application of ET$\Box_2$ with a premiss of this form which is not the conclusion of an IK$\Box_1$- inference, w.l.o.g. a situation of the form

$$\dfrac{K, a \Rightarrow \qquad \dfrac{K, \neg\Box b, c \Rightarrow \qquad \dfrac{M, \Box^{s-1}[a, \neg\Box b], \Box^{t-1}[c, \neg\Box d], e \Rightarrow}{K, \neg\Box b, \neg\Box d \Rightarrow}\,\mathrm{IK}\Box_1}{K, \neg\Box b \Rightarrow}\,\mathrm{ET}\Box_2}{K \Rightarrow}\,\mathrm{ET}\Box_2$$

where K abbreviates $L, \Box M, \Box^s[a, \neg\Box b], \Box^t[c, \neg\Box d]$. If e equals d, then we replace this by

$$\dfrac{\mathrm{ET}\Box_2\,\dfrac{K, c, a \Rightarrow \qquad K, c, \neg\Box b \Rightarrow}{K, c \Rightarrow} \qquad \dfrac{M, \Box^{s-1}[a, \neg\Box b], \Box^{t-1}[c, \neg\Box d], d \Rightarrow}{K, \neg\Box d \Rightarrow}\,\mathrm{IK}\Box_1}{K \Rightarrow}\,\mathrm{ET}\Box_2$$

Here the deduction of the sequent $K, c, a \Rightarrow$ is obtained from the deduction of $K, a \Rightarrow$ by weakening (which obviously does not increase $n(d)$). Thus one premiss P of measure $n(P)$ is replaced by atmost 3 new premisses each of measure atmost $n(P) - 1$ and therefore the measure n of the new deduction has decreased.
If e is different from d, then $\neg\Box e$ is in K and we may replace this series of inferences by a single IK$\Box_1$-inference with principal formula $\neg\Box e$.
c) is proved in the same way, just dropping the superscripts from the $\Box$ and placing a $\Box$ in front of the M at appropriate places. $\Box$

This result implies that the family C$_0$ of calculi is complete for clausal sequents where all the calculi C$_0$ have the usual axioms and moreover C$_0$(K) has the only rule

$$(\mathrm{CK}\Box_0)\quad \dfrac{L, \Box M, a_1 \Rightarrow \quad \dots \quad L, \Box M, a_m \Rightarrow \quad M, \neg b \Rightarrow}{L, \Box M, v \Rightarrow}$$

C$_0$(T) has the only rule

$$(\mathrm{CT}\Box_0)\quad \dfrac{L, \Box M, \Box^s v, a_1 \Rightarrow \quad \dots \quad L, \Box M, \Box^s v, a_m \Rightarrow \quad M, \Box^{s-1} v, \neg b \Rightarrow}{L, \Box M, \Box^s v \Rightarrow}$$

and C$_0$(4) has the rule

$$(\mathrm{C4}\Box_0)\quad \dfrac{L, \Box M, \Box v, a_1 \Rightarrow \quad \dots \quad L, \Box M, \Box v, a_m \Rightarrow \quad \Box M, \Box v, \neg b \Rightarrow}{L, \Box M, \Box v \Rightarrow}$$

where in all rules the rightmost premiss is only present, when v is of the form $[a_1, \neg\Box b]$. Note that in the C_0-calculi any deduction of a clausal sequent consists entirely of clausal sequents.

Now for the rule $CK\Box_0$ all premisses have less connectives than the conclusion. Therefore the length of every $C_0(K)$-deduction of a given sequent is bounded by the number of connectives of its endsequent.

3 Extended Clausal Calculi

For $C_0(T)$, however, the premisses of $CT\Box_0$ of the form $L, \Box M, \Box^s v, a_i \Rightarrow$ in general have more connectives than the conclusion. Therefore we extend our language by a new connective $\circ$ and we consider the calculus $C_1(T)$ consisting of the usual axioms, additional axioms of the form $M, \circ a, \neg a \Rightarrow$ and the rule $(CT\Box_1)$:

$$(CT\Box_1)\;\frac{\begin{array}{c}K,\circ L,\Box M,\circ^s u,a_1 \Rightarrow\\ \cdots\\ K,\circ L,\Box M,\circ^s u,a_l \Rightarrow\end{array}}{K,\circ L,\Box M,\Box^s u \Rightarrow}\quad\frac{\begin{array}{c}K,\circ L,\Box M,\circ^s v,a_1 \Rightarrow\\ K,\circ L,\Box M,\circ^s v,\circ b \Rightarrow\end{array}}{K,\circ L,\Box M,\Box^s v \Rightarrow}\quad\frac{\begin{array}{c}K,\circ L,\Box M,\circ^s w,a_1 \Rightarrow\\ L,M,\Box^{s-1}w,\neg c \Rightarrow\end{array}}{K,\circ L,\Box M,\Box^s w \Rightarrow}$$

where $u = [a_1, \dots, a_l]$, $v = [a_1, \Box b]$, and $w = [a_1, \neg\Box c]$ and $\circ^s v$ stands for $\circ\Box^{s-1}v$.
For $C_1(T)$ we call the premisses of the form $K, \circ L, \Box M, \Box^s v, a_i \Rightarrow$ α-premisses, those of the form $K, \circ L, \Box M, \circ^s v, \circ b \Rightarrow$ β-premisses and those of the form $L, M, \Box^{s-1}v, \neg c \Rightarrow$ γ-premisses.

Lemma 4. *a) If $L, \circ M \Rightarrow$ is deducible by $C_1(T)$, then $L, \Box M \Rightarrow$ is deducible by $C_0(T)$.*
b) If $M, v, v \Rightarrow$ is deducible by $C_1(T)$, where v is either a propositional variable or $v = \circ w$ or $v = \neg w$ and w is a propositional variable, then $M, v \Rightarrow$ is deducible by $C_1(T)$.
c) Weakening is an admissible rule for $C_1(T)$.

Proof. a) If our sequent is an axiom $M, \circ a, \neg a \Rightarrow$, then $M, \Box a, \neg a \Rightarrow$ is deducible by $C_0(T)$. If it is the conclusion of a $CT\Box_1$-inference, then the α- and β- premisses contain $\circ^s v$ which by the induction hypothesis may be changed to $\Box v$, whereas the γ-premiss contains $\Box^{s-1}v$. Hence all premisses necessary for an inference leading to $M, \Box v \Rightarrow$ are deducible and therefore this sequent is deducible, too.
b) For axioms this is obvious. But if our sequent $M, v, v \Rightarrow$ is the conclusion of a $CT\Box_1$- inference, then v cannot be its principal formula, so in the α- and β-premisses both v's are present and in the γ- premiss either both or none of them is present. Thus by the induction hypothesis all these double occurrences may be contracted in the premisses and by the same $CT\Box_1$-inference the required sequent $M, v \Rightarrow$ is deducible.
c) is trivial. □

This implies:

Lemma 5. *a) If $M, v \Rightarrow$ is deducible, where v is a propositional variable, then so is $M, \bigcirc v \Rightarrow$.*
b) $M, \Box v \Rightarrow$, where v is a propositional variable is deducible iff $M, \bigcirc v \Rightarrow$ is.
c) If $M, \Box^s[A, v], v \Rightarrow$ is deducible, then so is $M, \bigcirc^s[A, v], v \Rightarrow$.

Proof. a) For axioms this is obvious. If $M, v \Rightarrow$ is the conclusion of a $\mathrm{CT}\Box_1$-inference, then in the α- and β-premisses v occurs and by the induction hypothesis it may be replaced by $\bigcirc v$, but in the γ-premiss v disappears and may be reintroduced by weakening. Thus all premisses of a $\mathrm{CT}\Box_1$-inference leading to $M, \bigcirc v \Rightarrow$ are deducible and so is this latter sequent.
b) If $M, \Box v \Rightarrow$ is an axiom or the conclusion of an inference with principal formula different from $\Box v$, then this is obvious. Otherwise the only premiss of the final $\mathrm{CT}\Box_1$-inference is $M, \bigcirc v, v \Rightarrow$. By a) this may be changed to $M, \bigcirc v, \bigcirc v \Rightarrow$ and from this by part b) of the preceding lemma we obtain $M, \bigcirc v \Rightarrow$.
c) Case 1: v is a propositional variable or of the form $\neg w$, where w is a propositional variable:
If $\Box^s[A, v]$ is the principal formula of the final inference of the given deduction, then one of its premisses is $M, \bigcirc^s[A, v], v, v \Rightarrow$ and from this sequent we obtain $M, \bigcirc^s[A, v], v \Rightarrow$ by an application of the preceding lemma. If $M, \Box^s[A, v], v \Rightarrow$ is the conclusion of an application of $\mathrm{CT}\Box_1$ with principal formula different from $\Box^s[A, v]$, then in the α- and β-premisses both $\Box^s[A, v]$ and v occur, whence $\Box^s[A, v]$ may be changed to $\bigcirc^s[A, v]$ by the induction hypothesis and in the γ-premiss only $\Box^{s-1}[A, v]$ occurs. Thus all the premisses for an application of $\mathrm{CT}\Box_1$ leading to $M, \bigcirc^s[A, v], v \Rightarrow$ are deducible.
Case 2: v is of the form $\Box w$, where w is a propositional variable:
If $\Box^s[A, v]$ is the principal formula of the final inference of the given deduction, then one of its premisses is $M, \bigcirc^s[A, v], \bigcirc w, \Box w \Rightarrow$ and from this sequent by b) we obtain $M, \bigcirc^s[A, v], \bigcirc w, \bigcirc w \Rightarrow$ and by the preceding lemma we obtain $M, \bigcirc^s[A, v], \bigcirc w \Rightarrow$ and again by b) $M, \bigcirc^s[A, v], v \Rightarrow$. If $\Box^s[A, v]$ is not the principal formula of the last inference, then as in case 1 the induction hypothesis applies. □

This immediately implies:

Lemma 6. *The rule* $\mathrm{CT}\Box_0$ *is admissible for* $\mathrm{C}_1(\mathrm{T})$. □

Thus $\mathrm{C}_0(\mathrm{T})$ and $\mathrm{C}_1(\mathrm{T})$ coincide on sequents without $\bigcirc$. Now for $\mathrm{C}_1(\mathrm{T})$ the parameter

> $d(s) :=$ the number of connectives of a sequent s plus twice the number of $\Box$ of s

decreases under backwards application of the rule $\mathrm{CT}\Box_1$. Thus every deduction of a sequent s has length at most $d(s)$.

For $C_0(4)$ we also use the connective $\bigcirc$, and we start from the calculus $C_1(4)$ which has the usual axioms and a rule

$$(C4\Box_1)\ \frac{K, \bigcirc L, \Box M, \Box v, a_1 \Rightarrow \ \ldots\ K, \bigcirc L, \Box M, \Box v, a_m \Rightarrow \quad \bigcirc L, \Box M, \Box v, \neg b \Rightarrow}{K, \bigcirc L, \Box M, \Box v \Rightarrow}$$

Thus $C_4\Box_1$ results from $C_4\Box_0$ by simply adding parameters $\bigcirc L$ in premisses and conclusion. Therefore the following holds trivially:

Lemma 7. *$M \Rightarrow$ is deducible by $C_0(4)$ iff $\bigcirc L, M \Rightarrow$ is deducible by $C_1(4)$.* □

Thus the cut rule in the form

$$(\text{Cut})\quad \frac{M, v \Rightarrow \qquad M, \neg v \Rightarrow}{M \Rightarrow}$$

is admissible for $C_1(4)$, where $\neg v$ is an abbreviation for the set of clauses resulting from the negation of v.

Next we consider the calculus $C_2(4)$ with the usual axioms and two rules

$$(C4\Box_2\sigma)\ \frac{\begin{array}{c} K, \bigcirc L, \Box M, \bigcirc u, a_1 \Rightarrow \\ \ldots \\ K, \bigcirc L, \Box M, \bigcirc u, a_l \Rightarrow \end{array}}{K, \bigcirc L, \Box M, \Box u \Rightarrow} \qquad \frac{\begin{array}{c} K, \bigcirc L, \Box M, \bigcirc v, a_1 \Rightarrow \\ K, \bigcirc L, \Box M, \Box b \Rightarrow \end{array}}{K, \bigcirc L, \Box M, \Box v \Rightarrow}$$

where u and v are *shallow* formulas, i.e. either the form $[a_1, \ldots, a_l]$ or of the form $[a_1, \Box b]$, and

$$(C4\Box_2\delta)\quad \frac{K, \Box L, \Box M, \Box a_1, a_1 \Rightarrow \qquad \Box L, \Box M, \Box v, \neg b \Rightarrow}{K, \bigcirc L, \Box M, \Box v \Rightarrow}$$

where v is a *deep* formula, i.e. of the form $[a_1, \neg\Box b]$. We call the two types of premisses of the $C4\Box_2\sigma$-rule $\alpha\sigma$- and β-premisses respectively and the two premisses of the $C4\Box_2\delta$ -rule we call $\alpha\delta$- and γ-premisses. The following lemma shows that the rule $C4\Box_1$ is admissible for $C_2(4)$:

Lemma 8. *a) If $M, v, v \Rightarrow$ is deducible by* $\mathrm{C}_2(4)$*, where v is a propositional variable or v is of the form $\neg w$ or $\bigcirc w$, where w is a propositional variable, then $M, v \Rightarrow$ is deducible, too.*
b) If $M, \Box v, a_i \Rightarrow$ is deducible, where v is shallow, then so is $M, \bigcirc v, a_i \Rightarrow$.
c) If $M, \Box[A, v] \Rightarrow$ or $M, \bigcirc[A, v] \Rightarrow$ is deducible, then so is $M, \Box A \Rightarrow$.
d) If $M, \Box v, \Box v \Rightarrow$ is deducible, where v is a propositional variable, then $M, \Box v \Rightarrow$ is deducible, too.
e) If $M, \Box[A, \Box v] \Rightarrow$ is deducible, then so is $M, \Box v \Rightarrow$.

Proof. a) is trivial. b) If $M, \Box v, a_i \Rightarrow$ is an axiom, then so is $M, \bigcirc v, a_i \Rightarrow$. If it is the conclusion of an inference with principal formula $\Box v$, then one of the premisses is $M, \bigcirc v, a_i, a_i \Rightarrow$. From this we obtain the required sequent by a). If it is the conclusion of a $\mathrm{C4}\Box_2\sigma$-inference with principal formula different from $\Box v$, then both $\Box v$ and a_i occur in all premisses and $\Box v$ may thus be changed to $\bigcirc v$ by the induction hypothesis. If it is the conclusion of a $\mathrm{C4}\Box_2\delta$-inference, then the $\alpha\delta$- and γ- premisses leading to a conclusion with $\bigcirc v$ are the same as those for $\Box v$. Therefore in this case, too, $M, \bigcirc v, a_i \Rightarrow$ may be derived.
c) If $M, \Box[A, v] \Rightarrow$ or $M, \bigcirc[A, v] \Rightarrow$ is an axiom, then so is $M, \Box A \Rightarrow$. If it is the conclusion of a $\mathrm{C4}\Box_2\sigma$-inference with principal formula $\Box[A, v]$, then by the induction hypothesis $\bigcirc[A, v]$ in the $\alpha\sigma$- and β-premisses may be changed to $\bigcirc A$ and with these new premisses the given inference yields a deduction of $M, \Box A \Rightarrow$. If it is the conclusion of a $\mathrm{C4}\Box_2\delta$-inference with principal formula $\Box[A, v]$, then either A is a propositional variable or a negated propositional variable and v is of the form $\neg\Box b$ with b a propositional variable or vice versa. In the first case the formula $\Box A$ is shallow and by b) we may change the $\alpha\delta$-premiss of this inference to $M, \bigcirc A, A \Rightarrow$ and from this sequent by an application of $\mathrm{C4}\Box_2\sigma$ we arrive at the desired sequent $M, \Box A \Rightarrow$. In the second case the formula $\Box[A, v]$ occurs in the γ-premiss and by the induction hypothesis may be changed to $\Box A$ and from this new γ-premiss by an application of $\mathrm{C4}\Box_2\delta$ we arrive at the desired sequent. Finally if our sequent is the conclusion of an inference with principal formula different from $\Box[A, v]$, then this formula occurs in every premiss and by the induction hypothesis it may be replaced by $\Box A$.
d) If $M, \Box v, \Box v \Rightarrow$ is not the conclusion of an inference with principal formula $\Box v$, then this is trivial. Otherwise this sequent has a single premiss $M, \bigcirc v, v, \Box v \Rightarrow$. Thus by b) we obtain from this the sequent $M, \bigcirc v, v, \bigcirc v \Rightarrow$ and by a) we obtain $M, \bigcirc v, v \Rightarrow$. From this we obtain $M, \Box v \Rightarrow$ by an application of $\mathrm{C4}\Box_2\sigma$.
e) If $M, \Box[A, \Box v] \Rightarrow$ is not the conclusion of an inference with principal formula $\Box[A, v]$, then by the induction hypothesis this formula may be changed to $\Box v$ in all premisses. Otherwise the required sequent is the β-premiss. □

From this follows:

Lemma 9. *The rule* $\mathrm{C4}\Box_1$ *is admissible for* $\mathrm{C}_2(4)$.

Proof. For suppose we are given sequents $\ldots\ M, \Box v, a_i \Rightarrow, \ldots,\quad M, \Box v, \Box b \Rightarrow$, where v is shallow, then by b), e) and d) of the preceding lemma we obtain the

sequents ... $M, \bigcirc v, a_i \Rightarrow$ ..., $M, \Box b \Rightarrow$, i.e. the premisses of an application of C4$\Box_2\sigma$ leading to the sequent $M, \Box v \Rightarrow$.
If we have sequents ... $L, \Box M, \Box v, a_i \Rightarrow, \ldots,$ $L, \Box M, \Box v, \neg b \Rightarrow$, where v is deep, then by c), e), and d) of the preceding lemma we obtain ... $L, \Box M, \Box a_i, a_i \Rightarrow, \ldots,$ $\Box M, \Box v, \neg b \Rightarrow$ and from these by an application of C4$\Box_2\delta$ we obtain $L, \Box M, \Box v \Rightarrow$. □

On the other hand the rules C4$\Box_2$ are also admissible for $C_1(4)$. This is seen by successive cuts with some $C_1(4)$-deducible sequent. For the C4$\Box_2\sigma$-rule this is obvious and for the C4$\Box_2\delta$-rule we cut the first premiss and the sequent $\Box L, \Box M, \Box v, \neg\Box b \Rightarrow$ obtained from the second premiss by an application of C4$\Box_1$ with the $C_1(4)$- deducible sequent

$$\Box[a, \neg\Box b], \neg(\Box a \wedge a), \neg(\Box[a, \neg\Box b] \wedge \neg\Box b) \Rightarrow$$

and obtain the required conclusion. Thus the calculi $C_1(4)$ and $C_2(4)$ are equivalent.

Now we call a formula $\Box v$ distant in a $C_2(4)$-deduction d iff below any conclusion of an inference with principal formula $\Box v$ there is an $\alpha\delta$-, β- or γ-premiss. Using this definition one observes

Lemma 10. *If there is a $C_2(4)$-deduction of a sequent $M, \Box v \Rightarrow$ in which $\Box v$ is distant, then the sequent $M, \bigcirc v \Rightarrow$ is deducible by $C_2(4)$.*

Proof. Since $\Box v$ has to be distant, this sequent can neither be an axiom nor the conclusion of an inference with principal formula $\Box v$. So if the last inference of this deduction is by an application of C4$\Box_2\sigma$, then $\Box v$ is distant in all deductions of the $\alpha\sigma$-premisses and by the induction hypothesis it may be changed to $\bigcirc v$. From the transformed $\alpha\sigma$-premisses together with the β-premiss we therefore obtain the sequent $M, \bigcirc v \Rightarrow$. But if the last inference is by an application of C4$\Box_2\delta$, then the premisses of $M, \bigcirc v \Rightarrow$ are the same as those of $M, \Box v \Rightarrow$. □

Lemma 11. *There is a transformation sending every deduction of a sequent into another deduction of the same sequent such that in the new deduction for every deep formula $\Box v$ and every $\alpha\sigma$-premiss $M, \Box v \Rightarrow$ the formula $\Box v$ is distant in the deduction of $M, \Box v \Rightarrow$.*

Proof. To every $\alpha\sigma$-premiss P in a deduction d we assign a number $n(P)$, i.e. the maximal number of conclusions of C4$\Box_2\delta$ on a branch of d ending in P which only contains $\alpha\sigma$- and γ-premisses. Then we let $n(d)$ be the sum of all $4^{n(P)} - 1$ for all such premisses P in d.
If this number is 0, then all the $n(P)$ are 0 and for every $\alpha\sigma$-premiss Q of the form $M, \Box v \Rightarrow$ and every path ending in Q which contains the conclusion R of a C4$\Box_2\delta$- inference with principal formula $\Box v$, there is some sequent S between Q and R which is neither an $\alpha\sigma$-premiss nor a γ-premiss. Therefore $\Box v$ is distant in the deduction of $M, \Box v \Rightarrow$.

If this number is greater than 0, then w.l.o.g. there is in d some maximal pair of inferences of the form

$$\dfrac{\dfrac{L,\Box M,\Box v,a,\Box c,c\Rightarrow \qquad \Box M,\Box v,\Box w,\neg d\Rightarrow}{L,\Box M,\bigcirc v,a,\Box w\Rightarrow} \qquad L,\Box M,\Box b,\Box w\Rightarrow}{L,\Box M,\Box v,\Box w\Rightarrow}$$

where $v=[a,\Box b]$ and $w=[c,\neg\Box d]$. We may change this pair of inferences to

$$\dfrac{\dfrac{L,\Box M,\bigcirc v,a,\Box c,c\Rightarrow \qquad L,\Box M,\Box b,\Box c,c\Rightarrow}{L,\Box M,\Box v,\Box c,c\Rightarrow} \qquad \Box M,\Box v,\Box w,\neg d\Rightarrow}{L,\Box M,\Box v,\Box w\Rightarrow}$$

where the deduction of the sequent $L,\Box M,\bigcirc v,a,\Box c,c\Rightarrow$ results from the deduction of $L,\Box M,\Box v,a,\Box c,c\Rightarrow$ by lemma 8 and the deduction of $L,\Box M,\Box b,\Box c,c\Rightarrow$ results from the deduction of $L,\Box M,\Box b,\Box w\Rightarrow$ by the same lemma and by weakening. Thus one $\alpha\sigma$-premiss P of measure $n(P)$ is replaced by atmost 3 new $\alpha\sigma$-premisses each of measure at most $n(P)-1$ and therefore the induction parameter has decreased. $\Box$

The preceding two lemmas show that the following calculus $\mathrm{C}_3(4)$ is complete which consists of the usual axioms, the rule $\mathrm{C4}\Box_3\delta=\mathrm{C4}\Box_2\delta$ and the rule

$$(\mathrm{C4}\Box_3\sigma)\quad \dfrac{\begin{array}{c}J,\bigcirc K,\bigcirc L,\Box M,\bigcirc u,a_1\Rightarrow\\ \cdots\\ J,\bigcirc K,\bigcirc L,\Box M,\bigcirc u,a_l\Rightarrow\end{array}}{J,\bigcirc K,\Box L,\Box M,\Box u\Rightarrow}\qquad \dfrac{\begin{array}{c}J,\bigcirc K,\bigcirc L,\Box M,\bigcirc v,a_1\Rightarrow\\ J,\Box K,\Box L,\Box M,\Box b\Rightarrow\end{array}}{J,\bigcirc K,\Box L,\Box M,\Box v\Rightarrow}$$

where u is $[a_1,\ldots,a_l]$ and v is $[a_1,\Box b]$ and all formulas of L are deep.

Now we observe:

Lemma 12. *In a* $\mathrm{C}_3(4)$*-deduction* d *of a sequent without* $\bigcirc$ *any subdeduction of* d *ending in a* $\mathrm{C4}\Box_3\delta$*-inference has an endsequent without* $\bigcirc$. $\Box$

This means that the calculus $\mathrm{C}_4(4)$ is complete which has the usual axioms, the rule $\mathrm{C4}\Box_4\sigma=\mathrm{C4}\Box_3\sigma$ and the rule

$$(\mathrm{C4}\Box_4\delta)\quad \dfrac{K,\Box L,\Box M,\Box a,a\Rightarrow \qquad \bigcirc L,\Box M,\Box v,\neg b\Rightarrow}{K,\bigcirc L,\Box M,\Box v\Rightarrow}$$

where v is $[a,\neg\Box b]$. (Note that the sequence L is always empty!)

Now we call a formula $\Box v$ distant in a $\mathrm{C}_4(4)$-deduction d iff below any inference with principal formula $\Box v$ in d there is an $\alpha\delta$-, $\alpha\sigma$-, or β-premiss. Then from lemma 10 follows

Lemma 13. *If there is a* $C_4(4)$*-deduction of a sequent* $M, \Box v \Rightarrow$, *where* v *is deep and* $\Box v$ *is distant, then the sequent* $M, \bigcirc v \Rightarrow$ *is deducible by* $C_4(4)$. □

From this follows:

Lemma 14. *A sequent* $\Box M, \Box[a, \neg\Box b], \neg b \Rightarrow$ *is deducible by* $C_4(4)$ *iff the sequent* $\Box M, \bigcirc[a, \neg\Box b], \neg b \Rightarrow$ *is.*

Proof. This is proved by induction on the maximal number of successive γ-premisses preceding $\Box M, \Box[a, \neg\Box b], \neg b \Rightarrow$. If it is 0, then our sequent is either an axiom or it is the conclusion of an application of $C4\Box_4\sigma$. The first case is trivial, and in the second case the α-premisses already have $\bigcirc[a, \neg\Box b]$ and the β- premiss is the same for both $\Box[a, \neg\Box b]$ and $\bigcirc[a, \neg\Box b]$. Thus the same inference applied to the transformed premisses yields the required deduction. If this number is greater than 0, then we distinguish cases according to whether one of these successive $C4\Box_4\delta$- inferences has principal formula $\Box[a, \neg\Box b]$ or not. In the latter case $\Box[a, \neg\Box b]$ is distant, and we may replace it by $\bigcirc[a, \neg\Box b]$. In the former case the induction hypothesis applies to the γ-premisses of this inference, and by repeating the following inferences with the transformed formula we obtain the required deduction of $\Box M, \bigcirc[a, \neg\Box b], \neg b \Rightarrow$. □

This finally shows that the calculus $C_5(4)$ is complete which consists of the usual axioms, the rule $C4\Box_5\sigma = C4\Box_4\sigma$ and the rule

$$(C4\Box_5\delta) \quad \frac{K, \Box L, \Box M, \Box a, a \Rightarrow \qquad \bigcirc L, \Box M, \bigcirc v, \neg b \Rightarrow}{K, \bigcirc L, \Box M, \Box v \Rightarrow}$$

Now for $C_5(4)$ we observe that for the measure

> $d(s)$ =(the total number of connectives of the sequent s times (the number of □ plus the number of ○)) minus the number of ○

and for both rules the measure of the conclusions is greater than the measure of all premisses. Therefore every deduction of a given sequent is bounded in length by some quadratically growing function of the number of connectives of its endsequent.

4 Space Bounds for the Calculi

In order to obtain space bounds for the decision procedures resulting from backwards application of the rules of our calculi $C_0(K)$, $C_1(T)$, and $C_5(4)$ we consider the set of subclauses $sc(s)$ of a given sequent s:
For the logic K we let $sc(\Box^s v)$ be $\{v, a_1, \ldots, a_m, \neg b_1\}$, where v is $[a_1, \ldots, a_m, \neg\Box b]$ and for T we let $sc(\Box^s v)$ be $\{v, a_1, \ldots, a_l, b, \neg c\}$, where v is $[a_1, \ldots, a_l, \Box b, \neg\Box c]$ and for S4 we let $sc(\Box v)$ be $\{v, [a_1, \ldots, a_l, \Box b], a_1, \ldots, a_l, b, \neg c\}$ for the same v. Then it is obvious that in any deduction of a given sequent s all the occurring

formulas are of the form $\Box^s v$ or $\bigcirc^s v$, where v is a subclause of one of the formulas of s. Therefore we may denote any sequent in such a deduction by a string of numbers shorter than twice the greatest exponent in s which has one entry for every subclause of s: If the entry corresponding to a certain subclause v is 0, then this subclause does not occur in the respective sequent; if it is $2(n+1)$, then the formula $\Box^n v$ occurs, and if it is $2(n+1)+1$, then the formula $\bigcirc^n v$ occurs. Thus given any string of this form which denotes a premiss of one of our inferences together with the principal formula of this inference we may obtain both its conclusion and the next premiss. Therefore we need not store whole branches of our deductions but only one sequent string at a time together with a list of the principal formulas on the current branch. Since the number of subclauses of a sequent s is linear in the number of connectives of s we need space $n \log n$ to store this one sequent string. Moreover to store the list of principal formulas we need space $\log n$ times the maximal length of a deduction of s. Thus for K and T we arrive at a decision procedure which requires space $n \log n$ and for S4 we need space $n^2 \log n$, where n is the number of connectives of the endsequent which is in clausal form. But in reducing any given sequent to clausal form we add linearly many connectives; therefore we arrive at the

Theorem 15. *Provability in the modal logics K and T is in the complexity class SPACE($n \log n$) and provability in the modal logic S4 is in SPACE($n^2 \log n$).*

5 Conclusion

We have presented so called contraction free sequent calculi for the three prominent PSPACE complete modal logics K, T, and S4. Using these calculi we have demonstrated how to define decision procedures for these logics which both admit simpler implementation, relying entirely on depth first search, and require less space than conventional decision procedures. Thus we could lower space bounds for the logic K from the previously known bound of n^2 to $\log n$ and for the logic T from n^3 to $n \log n$ and for S4 from n^4 to $n^2 \log n$.

References

1. Ladner, R. E.: The computational complexity of provability in systems of modal propositional logic. Siam Journal of Computing **6** (1977) 467–480
2. Hudelmaier, J.: An $n \log n$-SPACE decision procedure for intuitionistic propositional logic. Journal of Logic and Computatation **3** (1993) 63–75
3. Fitting, M.: Proof Methods for Modal and Intuitionistic Logics. Reidel Publ. Co 1983
4. Chen, C. C. & I. P. Lin: The computational complexity of satisfiability of modal Horn clauses for modal propositional logics. Theoretical Computer Science **129** (1994) 95–121
5. Ognjanovic, Z.: A tableau-like proof procedure for normal modal logics. Theoretical Computer Science **129** (1994) 167–186

6. Halpern, J. Y.: The effect of bounding the number of primitive propositions and the depth of nesting on the complexity of modal logic. Artificial Intelligence **75** (1995) 361–372
7. Mints, G. E.: Gentzen-type systems and resolution rules. In: P. Martin-Löf, G. Mints (eds.): COLOG-88 (Springer LNCS 417) 198–231
8. Wallen, L.: Automated proof search in nonclassical logics. MIT Press 1990

A Fully Abstract Denotational Model for Observational Precongruence

Anna Ingólfsdóttir[1] and Andrea Schalk*

[1] **BRICS** *** Dep. of Computer Science, Aalborg University, Denmark†
[2] Computer Laboratory, University of Cambridge, Cambridge, United Kingdom‡2

Abstract. A domain theoretic denotational model is given for a simple sublanguage of CCS extended with divergence operator. The model is derived as an abstraction on a suitable notion of normal forms for labelled transition systems. It is shown to be fully abstract with respect to observational precongruence.

1 Introduction

In describing the semantics of communicating processes the notion of bisimulation, [Par81, Mil83], has became standard in the literature. In this setting two processes are considered to be behaviourally equivalent if they can simulate each other's behaviour. It is standard practice to distinguish between strong bisimulation, where the silent τ-moves are considered visible, and weak bisimulation, which abstracts away from them. Weak bisimulation equivalence turns out not to be a congruence with respect to some of the standard operators found in process algebras, e.g. the choice operator of CCS, and therefore the notion of weak bisimulation congruence, often called observational congruence, has been introduced.

One of the main characteristics of weak bisimulation equivalence, and of the associated congruence, is the fact that it allows for the abstraction from divergence, i.e. infinite sequences of internal computations, in process behaviours. Semantic theories for processes based on the bisimulation idea which take divergence into account have also been considered in the literature, see, e.g., [Wal90, AH92]. In those studies, bisimulation equivalence is extended to a bisimulation preorder, usually referred to as *prebisimulation*. Intuitively if a process p is smaller than a process q with respect to the bisimulation preorder, then the two processes are bisimilar, but p may diverge more often than q.

For a further understanding and justification of the idea of bisimulation, many researchers have presented more abstract formal descriptions for it, using different theoretical tools to analyse in depth the nature of the concept. Examples

* Partly supported by an EC Human Capital and Mobility Grant

*** Basic Research in Computer Science, Centre of the Danish National Research Foundation.

† **email**: annai@iesd.auc.dk

‡ **email**: Andrea.Schalk@cl.cam.ac.uk

of such alternative descriptions are characterizations of bisimulation by means of modal logics, [Sti87, Mil89], sound and complete axiomatizations, [Hen81, Wal90, AH92], and fully abstract denotational models, [Hen81, Abr91, AH92]. The denotational models are usually given in terms of Σ-domains, where Σ is a signature, i.e. a set of syntactic operators. Typically this is the set of operators which are allowed in the language one wants to model. A Σ-domain is an ω-algebraic cpo endowed with a continuous Σ-algebra structure, i.e. a collection of continuous functions, one for each syntactic operator in Σ.

The existence of a fully abstract model in terms of a Σ-domain has the consequence that the behavioural preorder one is trying to model has to be finitary. Intuitively this means that the behavioural preorder is completely induced by finite observations of process behaviours. This is, in general, not the case for bisimulation as shown in, e.g., [Abr91]. For this reason, studies on mathematical models for such relations usually focus on providing denotational models for *finitary* versions of the bisimulation preorders [Hen81, Abr91, AH92].

There is a natural connection between sound and complete axiomatizations of behavioural preorders and fully abstract denotational models. Denotational models are often given in terms of initial Σ-domains satisfying a set of inequations [Hen88a]. In this kind of models the interpretation of a term is simply the set of terms which can be proved equal to it by the proof system. This type of denotational models is usually referred to as term models in the literature. Examples of such models may be found in, e.g., [Hen81], where the author defines a fully abstract term model for strong prebisimulation on a simple extension of SCCS, and in [AH92], where the authors give a fully abstract term model for observational congruence over an extension of the standard CCS.

Term models have been criticized for not giving much more insight into the semantics than the proof system already does. It is true that the existence of a fully abstract model for a behavioural preorder in terms of an algebraic cpo does imply that the behavioural preorder must be finitary, but usually this property has to be proven first anyway to prove the full abstractness of such a model. On the other hand by giving a syntax free representation of the term model we may gain some insight into the properties of the semantics we want to model. One way of obtaining such a syntax free representation, which is fully abstract with respect to a finitary behavioural preorder, is to investigate the preorder on the process graphs, that define the operational semantics. By investigating this preorder for finite processes we may gain enough information to be able to predict the behaviour for infinite processes. This is typically done by introducing some notion of semantic normal form for process graphs which contains enough information about the behavioural preorder. This kind of semantic normal forms will then induce a poset which coincides with the kernel of the behavioural preorder for finite processes. If all processes in the language can be turned into syntactic normal forms (i.e process terms whose process graph is in semantic normal form) in a sound way, i.e. preserving the behavioural semantics, it is sometimes possible to obtain a fully abstract model by taking the unique algebraic cpo which has the poset derived from semantic normal forms as representation of its compact elements. A similar approach occurs in Hennessy's model for testing equivalence based on finite acceptance trees which basically is a syntax free representation of the syntactic normal forms he defines, [Hen85, Hen88b].

Yet another, and maybe the most mathematically elegant, way of defining a denotational model is to define it as the initial solution to a recursive domain equation. The normal forms may now occur in the description of the compact elements derived from this definition. In [Abr91] Abramsky defines a fully abstract model for the finitary part of strong prebisimulation for SCCS. The domain theoretic constructions he uses are a variant of the Plotkin power construction and a notion of infinite sum. The poset of compact elements of the model may, roughly speaking, be represented as finite convex closed sets of finite synchronization trees ordered by the strong bisimulation preorder.

To give a short summary of the existing denotational models for bisimulation we have: For strong ω-prebisimulation on SCCS a fully abstract term model is given in [Hen81] and a fully abstract syntax free model in [Abr91]. For the ω-version of observational precongruence a fully abstract term model is given in [AH92] for an extension of CCS.

In this paper we will contribute to the investigation in a denotational setting of bisimulation preorders by defining a syntax free model for the ω-observational precongruence. Our aim is therefore to define a Σ-domain which is initial in the class of Σ-domains satisfying the set of equation that characterizes the ω-observational congruence and which does not mention terms or equations. Our approach is based on the idea of normal forms and ideal closure as described above. Thus we introduce semantic normal forms which are simply the process graphs derived from the syntactic normal forms introduced by Walker in [Wal90] ordered by *strong* bisimulation preorder. These normal forms may be represented as restricted form for finite synchronization trees ordered by the Egli-Milner preorder and can therefore be compared to Abramsky's model in [Abr91]. Our hope was to, instead of using equivalence classes as the elements of our model, to represent the equivalence classes by some canonical elements, i.e. the normal forms. Unfortunately our approach did not work quite as well as we had hoped. All the equations turn out to be sound in this model apart from the equation

$$\mu.\tau.x = \mu.x \tag{1}$$

which turns out to be difficult to model. Therefore our model is structured on two levels: on the first level we define the normal synchronization trees as described above whereas we obtain the second level by factoring out equation (1). We show the full abstractness of our model with respect to ω-observational precongruence.

We will focus on much simpler language than the one studied in [AH92] as the signature we consider only consists of action prefixing, the choice operator and the operators *nil* for the convergent inactive operator and Ω for the inactive divergent operator. Thus we only consider a language describing trees, finite or infinite which leaves are either *nil* or Ω. All the aspects we are interested in investigating are captured by this simple language. (Most of the results we obtain may be easily extended to full CCS or similar languages with divergence added to them.) In our study we make an extensive use of properties already proven in the literature, e.g. in the definition of the existing models for bisimulation preorders. Thus we may assume the soundness and completeness of the proof system used to define the term model in [AH92] which of course is simplified and modified according to the different language. In the same reference it is also proved that the ω-observational precongruence is finitary. From [Wal90] we borrow a suitable notion of normal forms and a corresponding normalization theorem. Furthermore we also get from that reference an alternative characterization of the observational precongruence which turns out to be useful in our studies.

The structure of the paper is as follows: In Section 2 we give a short review of labelled transition systems with divergence and the diverse notions of prebisimulation and observational precongruence; in the same section we introduce the notion of normal forms and give an alternative characterization of the observational precongruence on these. In Section 3 we define the language *Trees* and give a short summary of existing results for this: a sound and complete axiomatization of the observational preorder and a normalization theorem for finite trees. In Section 4 we give a short overview over the domain theory we need whereas Section 5 is devoted to the definition of our domain and a proof of a full abstractness with respect to observational precongruence. We finish the paper by giving some concluding remarks.

2 Labelled Transition Systems with Divergence

The operational semantics of the languages considered in this paper will be given in terms of a variation on the notion of labelled transition systems [Kel76] that takes divergence information into account. We refer the interested readers to, e.g., [Hen81, Mil81, Wal90] for motivation and more information on (variations of) this semantic model for reactive systems.

Definition 1. [Labelled Transition Systems with Divergence] A *labelled transition system with divergence (lts)* is a quadruple $(P, Lab, \rightarrow, \uparrow)$, where:

- P is a set of *processes* or *states*, ranged over by s, s', s_i;
- Lab is a set of *labels*, ranged over by ℓ;
- $\rightarrow \subseteq P \times Lab \times P$ is a *transition relation*. As usual, we shall use the more suggestive notation $s \xrightarrow{\ell} s'$ in lieu of $(s, \ell, s') \in \rightarrow$;
- $\uparrow \subseteq P$ is a *divergence predicate*, notation $s \uparrow$.

We let Λ range over all lts's. A *process graph* is a pair of the form (s_0, Λ) where $s_0 \in \mathsf{P}$ is the *initial state* and P is the set of processes in Λ.

We write $s \downarrow$, read "s converges globally", iff it is not the case that $s \uparrow$. The *lts* $\Lambda = (P, Lab, \rightarrow, \uparrow)$ is said to be a *finite state* lts if P is finite and *acyclic* if its derived graph does not contain cycles; it is said to be *finite* if it is a finitely branching finite state lts. A *finite tree lts* is defined in the obvious way. We note here that each acyclic finite lts may be turned into a finite tree lts by making one copy of each state for each incoming arc where the outgoing arcs and their descendants are the same as from the original state. We note that the resulting lts is not graph isomorphic to the original one as in general it has more states. On the other hand it is strongly bisimilar to the original one in the sense to be defined later in this section. In our semantic theory the operational semantics for a process s, is given by a process graph with the process as the initial state. Intuitively, a process graph is an lts with a pointer to the initial state. If the underlying lts Λ is fixed we write s instead of the process graph (s, Λ). A finite tree lts Λ, has a canonical initial state, namely the root of the tree, $root(\Lambda)$. Therefore, if Λ is a finite tree lts, we often refer to the process graph $(root(\Lambda), \Lambda)$ as Λ. In this study we will follow this practice without further explanations.

We define the following operators on process graphs:

1. Action prefixing:
   $l : (s, (P, \longrightarrow, \uparrow)) = (l : s, (\mathsf{P} \cup \{l : s\}, \mathsf{Lab} \cup \{l\}, \longrightarrow \cup \{(l : s, l, s)\}, \uparrow))$ where $l : s \notin \mathsf{P}$ is a new state.
2. Finite sum:
   $\sum_{i \leq N}(s_i, (\mathsf{P}_i, \mathsf{Lab}_i, \longrightarrow_i, \uparrow_i)) = (s', (\mathsf{P}', \mathsf{Lab}', \longrightarrow', \uparrow'))$ where
   (a) $N > 0$,
   (b) $s' = \sum_{i \leq N} s_i \notin \bigcup_{i \leq N} \mathsf{P}_i$ is a new state,
   (c) $\mathsf{P}' = \{s'\} \cup \bigcup_{i \leq N}(\mathsf{P}_i \setminus \{s_i\})$,
   (d) $\mathsf{Lab}' = \bigcup_{i \leq N} \mathsf{Lab}_i$,
   (e) $\longrightarrow' = \bigcup_{i \leq N}(\longrightarrow_i \setminus \{(s_i, l, s_i') \mid (s_i, l, s_i') \in \longrightarrow_i\}$
   $\cup \{(s', l, s_i') \mid (s_i, l, s_i') \in \longrightarrow_i\})$,
   (f) $\uparrow' = \bigcup_{i \leq N} \uparrow_i \cup \{s' \mid \exists j. s_j \in \uparrow_j\}$.

We use the infix notation $\oplus$ for the sum over two lts's. We assume that $\mu : \_$ has priority over $\oplus$. The finite tree lts's may be represented as the set of finite synchronization trees over a set of labels Lab, denoted by ST(Lab). These are the sets generated by the following inductive definition:

1. $\emptyset, \{\perp\} \in \mathsf{ST}(\mathsf{Lab})$,
2. $\ell_i \in \mathsf{Lab}, t_i \in \mathsf{ST}(\mathsf{Lab})$ for $i \leq N$ implies $\{\langle \ell_i, t_i \rangle \mid i \leq N\}[\cup\{\perp\}] \in \mathsf{ST}(\mathsf{Lab})$,

where the notation $[\cup\{\perp\}]$ means optional inclusion of $\perp$. The divergence predicate and the transition relation are defined as follows:

- $t \uparrow$ iff $\perp$ is in t, and
- $t \xrightarrow{\ell_i} t_i$ iff $\langle \ell_i, t_i \rangle$ is in t.

We let t range over $ST(\mathsf{Lab})$.

We note that the process graph operators also apply to $ST(\mathsf{Lab})$; in this representation we have $\mu : t = \{\langle \mu, t \rangle\}$ and $\oplus = \cup$. Furthermore we often write μ instead of $\{\langle \mu, \emptyset \rangle\}$ or $\mu : \emptyset$. This will simplify our notation considerably later on. (The reader should keep in mind that in this case $t_1 \oplus t_2$ and $l : t$ are synchronization trees and therefore sets.)

The following norm on $ST(\mathsf{Lab})$ will be needed in this study.

The depth of a synchronization tree, $d : ST(\mathsf{Lab}) \longrightarrow Nat$ is defined by
1. $d(\emptyset) = d(\{\bot\}) = 0$
2. $d(\{\langle \mu, t\rangle\}) = 1 + d(t)$
3. $(\{\langle \mu_i, t_i\rangle | i \leq N\}[\oplus\{\bot\})] = \max\{d(\{\langle \mu_i, t_i\rangle\} | i \leq N\})$

We extend the function d to $d : ST(\mathsf{Lab}) \times ST(\mathsf{Lab}) \longrightarrow Nat$ by $d(t_1, t_2) = d(t_1) + d(t_2)$.

In what remains of this section we let $\Lambda = (P, Lab, \rightarrow, \uparrow)$ be a fixed lts. Furthermore we let $Rel(P)$ denote the set of binary relations over P. The behavioural relations over processes that we shall study in this paper are those of *prebisimulation* [Mil81, Hen81, Wal90]. (also known as *partial bisimulation* [Abr91]).

Definition 2 Strong Prebisimulation. Define the functional $\mathcal{F}_s : Rel(P) \rightarrow Rel(P)$ (s stands for "strong") by:

Given $\mathcal{R} \in \mathsf{Rel(P)}$, $s_1 \mathcal{F}_s(\mathcal{R}) s_2$ iff, for each $l \in Act_\tau$,
1. If $s_1 \stackrel{l}{\longrightarrow} s_1'$ then, for some s_2', $s_2 \stackrel{l}{\longrightarrow} s_2'$ and $s_1' \mathcal{R} s_2'$.
2. If $s_1 \downarrow$ then
   (a) $s_2 \downarrow$ and
   (b) if $s_2 \stackrel{l}{\longrightarrow} s_2'$ then, for some s_1', $s_1 \stackrel{l}{\longrightarrow} s_1'$ and $s_1' \mathcal{R} s_2'$.

The strong prebisimulation preorder (over Λ), $\precsim_\Lambda$ is defined as the largest fixed-point for $\mathcal{F}_s$. If Λ is known from the context we write $\precsim$ instead of $\precsim_\Lambda$.

The relation $\precsim$ is a preorder over P and its kernel will be denoted by $\sim$, i.e., $\sim = \precsim \cap \precsim^{-1}$. Intuitively, $s_1 \precsim s_2$ if s_2's behaviour is at least as specified as that of s_1, and s_1 and s_2 can simulate each other when restricted to the part of their behaviour that is fully specified. A divergent state s with no outgoing transition is a least element with respect to $\precsim$ and intuitively corresponds to a process whose behaviour is totally unspecified — essentially an operational version of the bottom element $\bot$ in Scott's theory of domains [SS71, Plo81].

The preorder $\precsim$ (and other similar relations) is extended to process graphs by

$$(s_1, \Lambda_1) \precsim (s_2, \Lambda_2) \text{ if and only if } s_1 \precsim_{\Lambda_1 \uplus \Lambda_2} s_2,$$

where $\Lambda_1 \uplus \Lambda_2$ is the standard disjoint union of Λ_1 and Λ_2. Processes from different lts's are compared in this way where we usually write only $s_1 \precsim s_2$. In the sequel, this will be done without further comment. (We will often need to compare states in an lts with finite synchronization trees.)

In this study, we shall be interested in relating the notion of prebisimulation to a preorder on processes induced by a denotational semantics given in terms of an algebraic domain [Plo81]. As such preorders are completely determined by how they act on *finite processes*, we shall be interested in comparing them with the "finitely observable", or *finitary*, part of the bisimulation in the sense of, e.g., [Gue81, Hen81]. The following definition is from [Abr91].

Definition 3. Let $\mathcal{R} \in \mathsf{Rel(P)}$. The *finitary part of* $\mathcal{R}$, $\mathcal{R}^F$, is defined on any lts by

$$s \mathcal{R}^F s' \Leftrightarrow \forall t \in ST(Lab).\ t \mathcal{R} s \Rightarrow t \mathcal{R} s' \ .$$

An alternative method for using the functional $\mathcal{F}_s$ to obtain a behavioural preorder is to apply it inductively as follows:

- $\sqsubseteq_0 = \mathsf{P} \times \mathsf{P}$,
- $\sqsubseteq_{n+1} = \mathcal{F}_s(\sqsubseteq_n)$,

and finally $\sqsubseteq_\omega = \bigcap_{n \geq 0} \sqsubseteq_n$. Intuitively, the preorder $\sqsubseteq_\omega$ is obtained by restricting the prebisimulation relation to observations of finite depth. The preorders $\sqsubseteq$, $\sqsubseteq_\omega$ and $\sqsubseteq^F$ are, in general, related thus:

$$\sqsubseteq \; \subseteq \; \sqsubseteq_\omega \; \subseteq \; \sqsubseteq^F .$$

Moreover the inclusions are, in general, strict. The interested reader is referred to [Abr91] for a wealth of examples distinguishing these preorders, and a very deep analysis of their general relationships and properties. Here we simply state the following useful result, which is a simple consequence of [Abr91, Lem. 5.10]:

Lemma 4. *For every $t \in \mathsf{ST}(\mathsf{Lab})$, $s \in \mathsf{P}$, $t \sqsubseteq s$ iff $t \sqsubseteq_\omega s$.*

Next we define the weak version of the prebisimulation and the derived observational precongruence. Following the standard practice we assume that the set of labels Lab has the form $Act_\tau = Act \cup \{\tau\}$ where Act is a set of observable actions and $\tau \notin Act$ is an unobservable action. We let a range over Act and μ over Act_τ. We let $\overset{\mu}{\Longrightarrow}$ denote $(\overset{\tau}{\longrightarrow})^* \cdot \overset{\mu}{\longrightarrow} \cdot (\overset{\tau}{\longrightarrow})^*$. So $s_1 \overset{\mu}{\Longrightarrow} s_2$ means that s_1 may evolve to s_2 performing the action μ and possibly invisible actions. We will also use the relation $\overset{\varepsilon}{\Longrightarrow}$, defined as $(\overset{\tau}{\longrightarrow})^*$.

For any s, let $Sort(s) = \{\mu \in Act_\tau \mid \exists \sigma \in Act_\tau^*, s' \in P : s \overset{\sigma\mu}{\longrightarrow} s'\}$, where, for $\sigma \in Act_\tau^*$, $\overset{\sigma}{\longrightarrow}$ is defined in the natural way. In this study we only deal with lts's which are sort finite, that is where $Sort(s)$ is finite for each $s \in \mathsf{P}$. Some of our results will depend on this fact.

Processes that can perform an infinite sequence of τ-actions are weakly divergent, which brings us to a definition of a weak divergence predicate. Let $\Downarrow$ be the least predicate over P which satisfies

$$s_1 \downarrow \text{ and (for each } s_2,\ s_1 \overset{\tau}{\longrightarrow} s_2 \text{ then } s_2 \Downarrow) \text{ imply } s_1 \Downarrow .$$

$s \Uparrow$ means that $s \Downarrow$ is not the case. In the semantic preorder to be defined we will use versions of $\Downarrow$ which are parameterized by actions:

$$s_1 \Downarrow \mu \text{ if } s_1 \Downarrow \text{ and , for each } s_2,\ s_1 \overset{\mu}{\Longrightarrow} s_2 \text{ implies } s_2 \Downarrow .$$

We use the standard notation $\hat{\mu}$ where $\hat{\tau}$ stands for ε and $\hat{a}$ stands for a. The following definition is taken directly from [Wal90].

Definition 5. Given $\mathcal{R} \in \mathsf{Rel}(\mathsf{P})$, $s_1 \mathcal{F}_w(\mathcal{R}) s_2$ (w for "weak") iff, for each $\mu \in Act_\tau$,

1. if $s_1 \overset{\mu}{\longrightarrow} s_1'$ then, for some s_2', $s_2 \overset{\hat{\mu}}{\Longrightarrow} s_2'$ and $s_1' \mathcal{R} s_2'$
2. if $s_1 \Downarrow \mu$ then

(a) $s_2 \Downarrow \mu$
(b) if $s_2 \xrightarrow{\mu} s_2'$ then, for some s_1', $s_1 \xRightarrow{\hat{\mu}} s_1'$ and $s_1' \mathcal{R} s_2'$

The weak bisimulation preorder $\sqsubseteq_{\approx}$ is defined as the largest fixed-point for $\mathcal{F}_w$. The weak ω-bisimulation preorder $\sqsubseteq_{\approx\omega}$ is defined by

- $\sqsubseteq_{\approx 0} = \mathsf{P} \times \mathsf{P}$ (the top element in the lattice $(\mathsf{Rel}(\mathsf{P}), \subseteq)$)
- $\sqsubseteq_{\approx n+1} = \mathcal{F}_w(\sqsubseteq_{\approx n})$

and finally $\sqsubseteq_{\approx\omega} = \bigcap_{n \geq 0} \sqsubseteq_{\approx n}$.

Obviously $\sqsubseteq_{\approx} = \sqsubseteq_{\approx\omega}$ when restricted to finite acyclic process graphs. The following result is proved in [AH92].

Lemma 6. *For all $t \in \mathsf{ST}(Act_\tau)$ and $s \in \mathsf{P}$, $t \sqsubseteq_{\approx\omega} s$ iff $t \sqsubseteq_{\approx} s$.*

The set Act_τ is assumed to be fixed throughout the paper and from now on we write ST instead of $ST(Act_\tau)$.

As it is well know from the literature, [Mil83, Mil89, Wal90], the preorder $\sqsubseteq_{\approx}$ is not a precongruence with respect to some of the standard operators, e.g. the choice operator $+$ of CCS. In terms of process graphs this is also the case. Thus the notion of observational precongruence is introduced. This will be done in the following:

For any $\mathcal{R} \in \mathsf{Rel}(\mathsf{P})$ we define the new relation $\mathcal{R}^c$ by:

$$s_1 \mathcal{R}^c s_2 \text{ if, for every context } C[\cdot],\ C[s_1] \mathcal{R} C[s_2].$$

where a context for process graphs has the obvious meaning. Then $\mathcal{R}$ is said to be closed with respect to contexts if $\mathcal{R} = \mathcal{R}^c$. The observational precongruence is defined as $\sqsubseteq_{\approx}^c$ and may be described as the least precongruence contained in weak bisimulation preorder. In [Wal90] Walker gives an operational characterization of $\sqsubseteq_{\approx}^c$. In order to obtain this he defines the operator $\_^*$ on $\mathsf{Rel}(\mathsf{P})$ as follows:

Definition 7. For all $\mathcal{R} \in \mathsf{Rel}(\mathsf{P})$ we let $s_1 \mathcal{R}^* s_2$ iff

1. if $s_1 \xrightarrow{a} s_1'$ then, for some s_2', $s_2 \xRightarrow{a} s_2'$ and $s_1' \mathcal{R} s_2'$,
2. if $s_1 \xrightarrow{\tau} s_1'$ then
   (a) if $s_1' \Downarrow$ then there exists s_2' such that $s_2 \xRightarrow{\tau} s_2'$ and $s_1' \mathcal{R} s_2'$,
   (b) if $s_1' \Uparrow$ then there exists s_2' such that $s_2 \xRightarrow{\varepsilon} s_2'$ and $s_1' \mathcal{R} s_2'$,
3. if $s_1 \Downarrow \mu$ then
   (a) $s_2 \Downarrow \mu$,
   (b) if $s_2 \xrightarrow{\mu} s_2'$ then, for some s_1', $s_1 \xRightarrow{\mu} s_1'$ and $s_1' \mathcal{R} s_2'$.

The following lemma is proved in [Wal90].

Lemma 8. $\sqsubseteq_{\approx}^c = \sqsubseteq_{\approx}^*$ *and* $\sqsubseteq_{\approx\omega}^c = \sqsubseteq_{\approx\omega}^*$.

The following definition of normal forms for synchronization trees is also borrowed from [Wal90] with an obvious adaption to process graphs.

Definition 9. (Normal Forms) An element $n = \{\langle\mu_1, n_1\rangle, \ldots, \langle\mu_l, n_l\rangle\}[\cup\{\bot\}] \in ST$ (where $\cup\{\bot\}$ is optional) is a normal form if

1. n_i is a normal form for $i \leq l$,
2. if $\mu_i = \tau$ then $n_i \Downarrow$,
3. if $n \Downarrow$ and $n \Uparrow a$ then $\langle a, \{\bot\}\rangle \in n$,
4. if $n \stackrel{\mu}{\Longrightarrow} n'$ then $\langle \mu, n'\rangle \in n$.

Note that if n is a normal form then $n \Uparrow$ iff $n \uparrow$ iff $\bot \in n$. This property will play an important role in our investigation of the preorder $\sqsubseteq_{\approx}^{*}$ on normal forms. Now we will give a simple characterization of the normal forms as a subset of ST. For this purpose we introduce the following operators on ST:

Definition 10. We define μ_{NST} by:

$$\tau_{NST}.t = t \cup \{\langle\tau, t\rangle | \bot \not\in t\}$$
$$a_{NST}.t = \{\langle a, t\rangle\} \cup \{\langle a, t'\rangle | \langle\tau, t'\rangle \in t\} \cup \{\langle a, \{\bot\}\rangle | \bot \in t\}$$

Now we define the subset NST of ST as follows:

Definition 11. We define the set NST as the smallest set which satisfies:

1. $\{\bot\}, \emptyset \in NST$.
2. $n \in NST$ and $\mu \in Act_\tau$ implies $\mu_{NST}.n \in NST$.
3. $n_1, n_2 \in NST$ implies $n_1 \oplus n_2 \in NST$.

We have the following lemma:

Lemma 12.

1. *$\mu_{\mathsf{NST}}.\_$ and $\oplus$ preserve $\sqsubseteq_{\approx}$.*
2. *If $n = \sum_{i \leq N} \mu_i : n_i[\oplus\{\bot\}]$ is a normal form then $n = \sum_{i \leq N} \mu_{i\,\mathsf{NST}}.n_i[\oplus\{\bot\}]$.*
3. *The set* NST *is exactly the subset of normal forms of* ST.

Proof.

1. Straight forward and is left to the reader.
2. Let $m = \sum_{i \leq N} \mu_{i\,NST}.n_i[\oplus\{\bot\}]$. We will prove that $n = m$ where "=" is set equality. The inclusion $n \subseteq m$ is obvious. To prove that $m \subseteq n$, assume that $\langle\mu, m'\rangle \in m$. We will prove that $\langle\mu, m'\rangle \in n$. We know that $\langle\mu, m'\rangle \in \mu_{i\,NST}.n_i$ for some i. If $\langle\mu, m'\rangle = \langle\mu_i, n_i\rangle$ we are done so assume this is not the case. We have the following two cases:
   $\mu_i = \tau$: Then either $\tau_{NST}.n = n$ or $\tau_{NST}.n = \{\langle\tau, n\rangle\} \cup n$. As by assumption $\langle\mu, m'\rangle \neq \langle\tau, n\rangle$ this implies $\langle\mu, m'\rangle \in n$.
   $\mu_i = a \in Act$: Then

$$\mu_{i\,NST}.n_i = a : n_i \cup \{\langle a, n_i'\rangle | \langle\tau, n_i'\rangle \in n_i\} \cup [\{\langle a, \{\bot\}\rangle | \bot \in n_i\}].$$

   Now either $\langle\mu, m'\rangle = \langle a, n_i'\rangle$ for some n_i' where $\langle\tau, n_i'\rangle \in n_i$ or $\langle\mu, m'\rangle = \langle a, \{\bot\}\rangle$ where $\bot \in n_i$. In both cases, by definition of normal forms, $\langle\mu, m'\rangle \in n$.

3. Let ST_N denote the subset of normal forms in ST. We will prove that $ST_N = NST$. By a simple induction on the definition of NST we may prove that $NST \subseteq ST_N$. To prove that $ST_N \subseteq NST$, let

$$n = \sum_i \mu_i : n_i[\oplus\{\bot\}] \in ST_N.$$

By part 2. of the lemma

$$n = \sum_i \mu_{i\,NST}.n_i[\oplus\{\bot\}],$$

which in turn implies that $n \in NST$.

In the following we define a finer version of a preorder originally defined in [Wal90]. (In the set of normal forms these two definitions coincide.) It gives a simplified characterization of the preorders $\underset{\approx}{\sqsubset}$ and $\underset{\approx}{\sqsubset}^*$ on NST.

Definition 13.

1. We define $\mathcal{F}^g_w : \mathsf{Rel(P)} \longrightarrow \mathsf{Rel(P)}$ (where g stands for "global convergence") by: Given $\mathcal{R} \in \mathsf{Rel(P)}$, $s_1\mathcal{F}^g_w(\mathcal{R})s_2$ iff, for each $a \in Act$,
   (a) if $s_1 \overset{a}{\longrightarrow} s_1'$ then, for some s_2', $s_2 \overset{a}{\longrightarrow} s_2'$ and $s_1'\mathcal{R}s_2'$,
   (b) if $s_1 \overset{\tau}{\longrightarrow} s_1'$ then, for some s_2', $s_2 \overset{\varepsilon}{\Longrightarrow} s_2'$ and $s_1'\mathcal{R}s_2'$,
   (c) if $s_1 \downarrow$ then the following holds:
      i. $s_2 \downarrow$,
      ii. if $s_2 \overset{a}{\longrightarrow} s_2'$ then, for some s_1', $s_1 \overset{a}{\longrightarrow} s_1'$ and $s_1'\mathcal{R}s_2'$,
      iii. if $s_2 \overset{\tau}{\longrightarrow} s_2'$ then, for some s_1', $s_1 \overset{\varepsilon}{\Longrightarrow} s_1'$ and $s_1'\mathcal{R}s_2'$.

   We define $\underset{\approx}{\sqsubset}_g$ to be the largest fixed point of $\mathcal{F}^g_w$.
2. We define the preorder $\underset{\approx}{\sqsubset}^{\diamond}_g$ by: $s_1 \underset{\approx}{\sqsubset}^{\diamond}_g s_2$ iff, for each $\mu \in Act_\tau$,
   (a) if $s_1 \overset{\mu}{\longrightarrow} s_1'$ then, for some s_2', $s_2 \overset{\mu}{\longrightarrow} s_2'$ and $s_1' \underset{\approx}{\sqsubset}_g s_2'$,
   (b) if $s_1 \downarrow$ then
      i. $s_2 \downarrow$ and
      ii. if $s_2 \overset{\mu}{\longrightarrow} s_2'$ then, for some s_1', $s_1 \overset{\mu}{\longrightarrow} s_1'$ and $s_1' \underset{\approx}{\sqsubset}_g s_2'$.

In [Wal90] the author shows that in general $\underset{\approx}{\sqsubset}_g$ is strictly finer than the weak bisimulation preorder $\underset{\approx}{\sqsubset}$. However it turns out that for normal forms these two preorders and their derived preorders, $\underset{\approx}{\sqsubset}^*$ and $\underset{\approx}{\sqsubset}^{\diamond}_g$, coincide. This is the content of the following theorem.

Theorem 14. *For all $n_1, n_2 \in$ NST, $n_1 \underset{\approx}{\sqsubset} n_2$ iff $n_1 \underset{\approx}{\sqsubset}_g n_2$ and $n_1 \underset{\approx}{\sqsubset}^* n_2$ iff $n_1 \underset{\approx}{\sqsubset}^{\diamond}_g n_2$.*

Proof. See Appendix A.

We observe that the characterization $\underset{\approx}{\sqsubset}^{\diamond}_s$ of the preorder $\underset{\approx}{\sqsubset}^*$ on normal forms looks very much like the definition for the strong prebisimulation preorder $\underset{\sim}{\sqsubset}$. The only difference is that on lower levels a τ transition may be matched by an empty transition. The following example shows that with the definition of normal forms we have chosen the preorders $\underset{\approx}{\sqsubset}^*$ and $\underset{\sim}{\sqsubset}$ do indeed not coincide.

Example 1. Let $n_1 = \tau : (\tau : a \oplus a \oplus a : \{\perp\}) \oplus \tau : a \oplus a \oplus a : \{\perp\}$ and $n_2 = \tau : a \oplus a$. Then $n_1 \sqsubseteq^*_{\approx} n_2$ but $n_1 \not\sqsubseteq_{\approx} n_2$. The reason for this is that the left hand side can perform a sequence of two τs to start with while the left hand side only can perform a sequence of τ-transitions of length one. On the other hand if we add $\tau : (\tau : a \oplus a)$ (adding only $\tau : \tau : a$ would not preserve the normal form property) to the right hand side the τ-depth is balanced and we get that $n_1 \sqsubseteq_{\approx} n_2 \oplus \tau : (\tau : a \oplus a)$. Furthermore $n_2 \approx^* n_2 \oplus \tau : (\tau : a \oplus a)$ (where $\approx^*$ is the kernel of $\sqsubseteq^*_{\approx}$).

The example above illustrates that the preorders $\sqsubseteq^*_{\approx}$ and $\sqsubseteq_{\approx}$ do not coincide on *NST*. But at the same time it also suggests that if $n \sqsubseteq^*_{\approx} m$ then by performing a simple balancing operation on n and m, which is sound with respect to $\approx^*$ we may get a pair of normal forms, n' and m', where $n' \sqsubseteq_{\approx} m'$. In our attempt to give a simple characterization of the preorder $\sqsubseteq^*_{\approx}$ on normal forms this would be a useful result. In the next section we will therefore formalize this informal statement and prove that it holds.

2.1 The Characterization Theorem for Observational Precongruence

In the proof for the characterization result for $\sqsubseteq^*_{\approx}$ on *NST* outlined above we suggested a transformations on normal forms which is sound with respect to $\sqsubseteq^*_{\approx}$. To formalize this idea we introduce a notion of equivalence on *NST* meaning that two elements are equivalent if they can be transformed into the same terms applying the balancing operation described above. As we need to be able to apply the transformation mentioned above recursively on the structure of the normal form we want the equivalence to be a congruence with respect to the graph operators. On the other hand the operator $\mu : \_$ does not preserve normal forms whereas the operator μ_{NST} does. Also the operator $\oplus$ preserves normal forms. Furthermore we know from Lemma 12 that for normal forms

$$\sum_{i \leq N} \mu_i : n_i[\oplus\{\perp\}] = \sum_{i \leq N} \mu_{i\,NST}.n_i[\oplus\{\perp\}].$$

Keeping this in mind we only require the equivalence to be a congruence with respect to the operators $\mu_{NST}.\_$ and $\oplus$. To define the equivalence suggested above we introduce the equation

$$\tau 1 \qquad\qquad \mu.\tau.x = \mu. \tag{2}$$

This equation is interpreted over *NST* with respect to the operators $\mu_{NST}.\_$ above. Now we let $=_{\tau 1}$ denote the least congruence over *NST* with respect to $\mu_{NST}.\_$ and $\oplus$ generated by the equation $\tau 1$ in (2). It is easy to see that this equation is sound with respect to $\approx^*$ on *NST*, i.e. that $=_{\tau 1} \subseteq \approx^*$ on *NST*.

Furthermore we need the following general theorem which is a slight modification of a similar theorem proved in [AH92].

Theorem 15 Hennessy's Theorem. *For all $t_1, t_2 \in \mathsf{ST}$ the following holds:*

$$t_1 \sqsubseteq_{\approx} t_2 \text{ iff } t_1 \sqsubseteq^*_{\approx} t_2 \text{ or } t_1 \sqsubseteq^*_{\approx} \tau_{\mathsf{NST}}.t_2 \text{ or } \tau_{\mathsf{NST}}.t_1 \sqsubseteq^*_{\approx} t_2.$$

The Characterization Theorem is now stated as follows:

Theorem 16 The Characterization Theorem. *Let $n, m \in$ NST. Then $n \sqsubseteq^*_{\approx} m$ if and only if there exist some $n', m' \in$ NST such that $n' \sqsubseteq_{\approx} m'$, $n =_{T1} n'$ and $m =_{T1} m'$.*

Proof. The "if" part follows immediately. To prove the "only" part assume $n \sqsubseteq^*_{\approx} m$. We proceed by induction on the combined depth of n and m, $d(n,m)$.

$d(n,m) = 0$: The only possible combinations are the following:

1. $n = m = \emptyset$,
2. $n = \{\bot\}$ and $m = \emptyset$, and
3. $n = m = \{\bot\}$.

All three cases are obvious.

$d(n,m) = k+1$: Assume

$$n = \sum_{i \leq N} \mu_{i\,NST}.n_i[\oplus\{\bot\}] \text{ and } m = \sum_{i \leq M} \gamma_{j\,NST}.m_j[\oplus\{\bot\}].$$

By Lemma 12 we get

$$n = \sum_{i \leq N} \mu_i : n_i[\oplus\{\bot\}] \text{ and } m = \sum_{i \leq M} \gamma_j : m_j[\oplus\{\bot\}].$$

First let us assume that $\bot \notin n$ and therefore $\bot \notin m$. Now we recall that if $n \xrightarrow{\mu} n'$ then $m \xrightarrow{\mu} m'$ for some m' where $n' \sqsubseteq_{\approx} m'$ and vice versa. We may therefore assume that $N = M$ and that $\mu_i = \gamma_i$ and $n_i \sqsubseteq_{\approx} m_i$ for $i \leq N$. (We may have to rearrange the summands and/or duplicate some of them as well to obtain this.) By Hennessy's Theorem 15, for each i one of the following holds:

Case 1: $n_i \sqsubseteq^*_{\approx} m_i$: By induction there are $n'_i, m'_i \in NST$ such that $n_i =_{T1} n'_i$, $m_i =_{T1} m'_i$ and $n'_i \sqsubseteq_{\approx} m'_i$. Furthermore $\mu_{i\,NST}.n_i =_{T1} \mu_{i\,NST}.n'_i$ and $\mu_{i\,NST}.m_i =_{T1} \mu_{i\,NST}.m'_i$.

Case 2: $n_i \sqsubseteq^*_{\approx} \tau_{NST}.m_i$: By induction there are $n'_i, m'_i \in NST$ such that $n_i =_{T1} n'_i$, $\tau_{NST}.m_i =_{T1} m'_i$ and $n'_i \sqsubseteq_{\approx} m'_i$. Furthermore $\mu_{i\,NST}.n_i =_{T1} \mu_{i\,NST}.n'_i$ and $\mu_{i\,NST}.m_i =_{T1} \mu_{i\,NST}.\tau_{NST}.m_i =_{T1} \mu_{i\,NST}.m'_i$.

Case 3: $\tau_{NST}.n_i \sqsubseteq^*_{\approx} m_i$: By induction there are $n'_i, m'_i \in NST$ such that $\tau_{NST}.n_i =_{T1} n'_i$, $m_i =_{T1} m'_i$ and $n'_i \sqsubseteq_{\approx} m'_i$. Furthermore $\mu_{i\,NST} n_i =_{T1} \mu_{i\,NST}.\tau_{NST}.n_i =_{T1} \mu_{i\,NST}.n'_i$ and $\mu_{i\,NST}.m_i =_{T1} \mu_{i\,NST}.m'_i$.

We let

$$n' = \sum_{i \leq N} \mu_{i\,NST}.n'_i$$

and

$$m' = \sum_{i \leq N} \mu_{i\,NST}.m'_i$$

which both are normal forms. Obviously $n =_{\tau 1} n'$ and $m =_{\tau 1} m'$. Furthermore by Lemma 12,

$$n' = \sum_{i \leq N} \mu_i : n'_i$$

and

$$m' = \sum_{i \leq N} \mu_i : m'_i.$$

It is now easy to see that $n' \lessapprox m'$.

Next assume that $\perp \in n$. The case when it is the only element is obvious, so assume this is not the case. Now we recall that if $n \xrightarrow{\mu} n'$ then there is an m' such that $m \xrightarrow{\mu} m'$ and $n' \lessapprox m'$. By a similar reasoning as in the previous case we may now assume that

$$n = \sum_{i \leq N} \mu_i : n_i \oplus \{\perp\} \text{ and } m = \sum_{i \leq N} \mu_i : m_i \oplus m'$$

where $n_i \lessapprox m_i$ for $i \leq N$. We may also assume that $\sum_{i \leq N} \mu_i : m_i$ and m' are normal forms. Now the proof may proceed as in the previous case but now using the fact that $\{\perp\} \lessapprox m'$.

3 The Language

In this section we will give a short survey of the theory of observational precongruence for a simple sublanguage of *CCS* extended with the divergence operator. The language *Trees* is a language that denotes trees, finite and infinite, and only contains the operators *nil*, $+$ and $\mu.\_$ which all have the standard meaning [Mil80], plus the nullary operator Ω, which stands for the inactive divergent process [Hen81, Wal90]. Infinite processes are given in the standard way by means of the construction $\mathbf{rec}x.\_$ where x is a process variable.

Definition 17. Let Var be a countable set of process variables, ranged over by $x, y \ldots$ and Act_τ have the same meaning as in the previous section, ranged over by μ. The syntax of the language *TreeTerms* is defined by

$$u ::= nil \mid \Omega \mid \mu.u \mid u + u \mid x \mid \mathbf{rec}x.u.$$

We let *Trees* denote the set of closed terms in *TreeTerms* and *FinTrees* the set of recursion free elements of *Trees*. We let u range over *TreeTerms*, p, q over *Trees* and d over *FinTrees*.

The operational semantics in terms of a transition relation and a convergence (and divergence) predicate is also defined in the standard way (see e.g. [Hen81, Wal90, AH92]).

Definition 18.

1. Let $\downarrow$ be the smallest subset of $Trees$ which satisfies
   (a) $nil \downarrow, \mu.p \downarrow$,
   (b) $p \downarrow$ and $q \downarrow$ implies $(p+q) \downarrow$,
   (c) $t[\mathtt{rec}x.t/x] \downarrow$ implies $\mathtt{rec}x.t \downarrow$.
   We say that $p \uparrow$ iff $p \downarrow$ is not true.
2. For each $\mu \in Act_\tau$, let $\xrightarrow{\mu}$ be the least binary relation on $Trees$ which satisfies the following axioms and rules:
   (a) $\mu.p \xrightarrow{\mu} p$,
   (b) $p \xrightarrow{\mu} p'$ implies $p+q \xrightarrow{\mu} p'$ and $q+p \xrightarrow{\mu} p'$,
   (c) $t[\mathtt{rec}x.t/x] \xrightarrow{\mu} p'$ implies $\mathtt{rec}x.t \xrightarrow{\mu} p'$.

This definition generates an lts, $\Lambda_{Tree} = (Trees, Act_\tau, \longrightarrow, \uparrow)$ which obviously is sort finite, as we do not have any relabelling as a construction in the language. The operational semantics for a $p \in Trees$ is defined as the process graph (p, Λ_{Tree}). For $d \in FinTrees$ the process graph that gives its semantics may be represented as an element of $\mathcal{ST}$. Thus the operational semantics for d is given by $\mathcal{G}(d)$ obtained by the following recursive definition:

1. $\mathcal{G}(nil) = \emptyset$,
2. $\mathcal{G}(\Omega) = \{\bot\}$,
3. $\mathcal{G}(\mu.d) = \mu : \mathcal{G}(d)$,
4. $\mathcal{G}(d_1 + d_2) = \mathcal{G}(d_1) \oplus \mathcal{G}(d_2)$.

Of course the definitions of $\sqsubseteq_{\sim}$, $\sqsubseteq_{\approx}$, $\sqsubseteq_{\approx}^{c}$ and $\sqsubseteq_{\approx}^{*}$ and their ω-versions apply for the lts Λ_{Tree} and as before we have that $\sqsubseteq_{\approx}^{c} = \sqsubseteq_{\approx}^{*}$ and $\sqsubseteq_{\approx\omega}^{c} = \sqsubseteq_{\approx\omega}^{*}$.

In [Wal90] and [AH92] the preorder $\sqsubseteq_{\approx\omega}^{*}$ is given an equational characterizations in terms of equationally based proof systems. In Figures 1 and 2 we define such a proof system for $Trees$, which is a slight modification of the proof systems in the afore mentioned references. The proof system consists of a set of inequations, Figure 1, and a set of inference rules, Figure 2. We refer to the full proof system as E_{rec} but the sub-system where the rules (ω) and (rec) are omitted we call E. We write $\sqsubseteq_{E_{rec}}$ and $\sqsubseteq_E$ for the induced preorders. The syntactic approximations p^n, that occur in the rule (ω), are also standard (see e.g. [Hen88b]) and are defined inductively as follows:

Definition 19. (Finite Syntactical Approximations)

1. $u^0 = \Omega$ for all $u \in TreeTerms$.
2. (a) $nil^{n+1} = nil$, $\Omega^{n+1} = \Omega$ and $x^{n+1} = x$ for $x \in \mathtt{Var}$,
   (b) $(u_1 + u_2)^{n+1} = u_1^{n+1} + u_2^{n+1}$,
   (c) $(\mu.u)^{n+1} = \mu.(u^{n+1})$,
   (d) $(\mathtt{rec}x.u)^{n+1} = u^{n+1}[(\mathtt{rec}x.u)^n/x]$.

Here we note that if $p \in Trees$ then $p^n \in FinTrees$. We get the following soundness and completeness result as a special case of the more general soundness and completeness theorem in [AH92].

A1 $x + y = y + x$	**Ω1** $\Omega \sqsubseteq x$
A2 $x + (y + z) = (x + y) + z$	**Ω2** $\tau.(x + \Omega) \sqsubseteq x + \Omega$
A3 $x + x = x$	**τ1** $\mu.\tau.x = \mu.x$
A4 $x + nil = x$	**τ2** $\tau.x + x = \tau.x$
	τ3 $\mu.(x + \tau.y) = \mu.(x + \tau.y) + \mu.y$

Fig. 1. The Inequations

$(ref)\ p \sqsubseteq p$ $\qquad$ $(trans)\ \dfrac{p \sqsubseteq q,\ q \sqsubseteq r}{p \sqsubseteq r}$

$(pre)\ \dfrac{p \sqsubseteq q}{\mu.p \sqsubseteq \mu.q}$ $\qquad$ $(sum)\ \dfrac{p_1 \sqsubseteq p_2, q_1 \sqsubseteq q_2}{p_1 + q_1 \sqsubseteq p_2 + q_2}$

$(rec)\ \dfrac{}{\mathbf{rec}P.p = p[\mathbf{rec}P.p/P]}$ $\qquad$ $(\omega)\ \dfrac{p^{(n)} \sqsubseteq q \text{ for all } n}{p \sqsubseteq q}$

$(inst)\ \dfrac{}{p \sqsubseteq q}$ $p \sqsubseteq q$ is a closed instantiation of the inequations in E

Fig. 2. The Proof system E_{rec}

Theorem 20. *The proof system E_{rec} is sound and complete for Trees with respect to the preorder $\sqsubseteq^c_{\approx_\omega}$.*

From [Wal90] we borrow the following notion of *syntactic normal forms.*

Definition 21. (Syntactic Normal Forms) We say that $\eta \in FinTrees$ is a normal form if $\eta = \sum_i \mu_i.\eta_i[+\Omega]$ and

1. each η_i is a syntactic normal form,
2. if $\mu_i = \tau$ then $\eta_i \Downarrow$
3. if $\eta \Downarrow$ and $\eta \Uparrow a$ then $a.\Omega$ is a summand of η.
4. if $\eta \stackrel{\mu}{\Longrightarrow} \eta'$ then $\eta \stackrel{\mu}{\longrightarrow} \eta'$.

We denote the set of syntactic normal forms by NF ranged over by η.

The following lemma gives the relationship between the syntactic and the semantic normal forms.

Lemma 22. *$\eta \in NF$ iff $\mathcal{G}(\eta) \in \mathsf{NST}$.*

Proof. Follows from a simple structural induction on η.

The following result is proved in [Wal90].

Theorem 23 Normalization Theorem. *For all $d \in FinTree$ there is $\eta \in NF$ such that $d =_E \eta$.*

4 Preliminaries on Algebraic Semantics

In this section, we review the basic notions of algebraic semantics and domain theory that will be needed in the remainder of this study. We assume that the reader is familiar with the basic notions of ordered and continuous algebras (see, e.g., [Gue81, Hen88a, AJ95]); however, in what follows we give a quick overview of the way a denotational semantics can be given to a recursive language like *Trees* following the standard lines of algebraic semantics [Gue81]. The interested reader is invited to consult [Hen88a] for an explanation of the theory.

In what follows, we let Σ denote a signature, i.e. a set of syntactic operators provided with a function, *arity*: $\Sigma \longrightarrow Nat$ which gives the number of arguments the operator takes. A Σ-algebra is a pair $(\mathcal{A}, \Sigma_\mathcal{A})$, where $\mathcal{A}$ is the *carrier* set and $\Sigma_\mathcal{A}$ is a set of *semantic operators* $f_\mathcal{A} : \mathcal{A}^l \rightarrow \mathcal{A}$, where $f \in \Sigma$ and $l = arity(f)$. We call $f_\mathcal{A}$ the *interpretation* of the syntactic operator f in $\mathcal{A}$. Let $(\mathcal{A}, \Sigma_\mathcal{A})$ and $(\mathcal{B}, \Sigma_\mathcal{B})$ be Σ-algebras. A mapping $\varphi : \mathcal{A} \rightarrow \mathcal{B}$ is a *Σ-homomorphism* if it preserves the Σ-structure, i.e. if for every $f \in \Sigma$ and vector $\overline{a}$ of elements of $\mathcal{A}$ of the length *arity*(f):

$$\varphi(f_\mathcal{A}(\overline{a})) = f_\mathcal{B}(\varphi(\overline{a})) \ .$$

The *term algebra* $T(\Sigma)$ is the *initial* Σ-algebra, i.e., if $(\mathcal{A}, \Sigma_\mathcal{A})$ is a Σ-algebra then there is a unique Σ-homomorphism $\iota_\mathcal{A} : T(\Sigma) \rightarrow \mathcal{A}$. We refer to this homomorphism as the *interpretation* of $T(\Sigma)$ in $\mathcal{A}$. We write $T(\Sigma, \mathtt{Var})$ for the term algebra that contains the set of variables $\mathtt{Var}$ as operators of arity 0 and $T^{rec}(\Sigma, \mathtt{Var})$ if it also allows the recursion construction $\mathtt{rec}x.t$.

The obvious idea is to model a language like that of *Trees* by a Σ-algebra where Σ is the set of finite term-forming operations (in the example mentioned, we get $\Sigma = \{\Omega, nil, +\} \cup \{\mu.\_ \mid \mu \in Act_\tau\}$). However, this is not sufficient to model operations like recursion. For that, we need to consider a slightly more sophisticated concept.

A *Σ-domain* $(\mathcal{A}, \sqsubseteq_\mathcal{A}, \Sigma_\mathcal{A})$ is a Σ-algebra whose carrier $(\mathcal{A}, \sqsubseteq_\mathcal{A})$ is an algebraic complete partial order (cpo) (see e.g. [Plo81]) and whose operators in $\Sigma_\mathcal{A}$ are continuous. The notion of *Σ-poset* (respectively *Σ-preorder*) may be defined in a similar way by requiring that $(\mathcal{A}, \sqsubseteq_\mathcal{A})$ is a partially ordered (resp. preordered) set and that the operators are monotonic. The notion of Σ-homomorphism extends to the ordered Σ-structures in the obvious way by requiring that such maps preserve the underlying order-theoretic structure as well as the Σ-structure. Any

Σ-preorder induces a unique Σ-poset which we refer to as its kernel. For any Σ-algebra, $\mathcal{A}$, ordered or not, the set ($\mathtt{Var} \to \mathcal{A}$) of $\mathcal{A}$-environments will be denoted by $\mathrm{ENV}_{\mathcal{A}}$, and ranged over by the meta-variable ρ. The (unique) interpretation of $T(\Sigma, \mathtt{Var})$ in $\mathcal{A}$ is the mapping $\mathcal{A}[\![\cdot]\!] : T(\Sigma, \mathtt{Var}) \to (\mathrm{ENV}_{\mathcal{A}} \to \mathcal{A})$ defined recursively by:

$$\mathcal{A}[\![x]\!]\rho \triangleq \rho(x),$$
$$\mathcal{A}[\![f(p_1, \ldots, p_l)]\!]\rho \triangleq f_{\mathcal{A}}(\mathcal{A}[\![p_1]\!]\rho, \ldots, \mathcal{A}[\![p_l]\!]\rho).$$

If $\mathcal{A}$ is a Σ-domain the interpretation extends to the term algebra $T^{rec}(\Sigma, \mathtt{Var})$ by setting

$$\mathcal{A}[\![\mathtt{rec}x.u]\!]\rho \triangleq \mathsf{Y}\lambda a.\, \mathcal{A}[\![u]\!]\rho[x \to a]$$

where Y denotes the least fixed-point operator. As usual, $\rho[x \to a]$ denotes the environment which is defined as follows:

$$\rho[x \to a](y) \triangleq \begin{cases} a & \text{if } x = y \\ \rho(y) & \text{otherwise.} \end{cases}$$

Note that, for each closed recursive term $p \in T^{rec}(\Sigma, \mathtt{Var})$, $\mathcal{A}[\![p]\!]\rho$ does not depend on the environment ρ. The denotation of a closed term, p, will be denoted by $\mathcal{A}[\![p]\!]$. For recursion free closed terms the mapping $\mathcal{A}[\![\_]\!]$ coincides with $\iota_{\mathcal{A}}$.

It is worth pointing out that the initial Σ-algebra for a set of generators, $\mathtt{Var}$, does indeed exist. Actually, more than just that is true: We can also require a set of equations to hold on the resulting Σ-algebra (such as $x + x = x$, for example). The initial Σ-algebra for a set of generators satisfying a given set of equations is constructed from the term-model by defining an equivalence relation on terms. The operations are well defined with respect to the equivalence classes so that the resulting quotient is again a Σ-algebra.

To find the initial ordered Σ-algebras, we have to say how to construct them. For posets, the process is very much like that of constructing the initial Σ-algebra - only this time one can actually start with a poset of generators, and the order for the resulting Σ-poset is then defined recursively on the terms such that the operations become monotonic. We can even do more in that case: instead of giving a set of equations which we want to hold, we can now deal with a set of inequalities. A typical inequality that one wants to hold in models for languages like ours is $\Omega \leq x$ which can thus be built in. We are, however, not interested in the initial Σ-poset for a set of generators and inequalities but in the initial Σ-domain. These two, however, are closely related: The initial Σ-domain can be obtained as the ideal completion of the corresponding Σ-poset - the operations are the unique continuous extensions of the corresponding operators for the Σ-poset. Similarly any Σ-preorder induces a unique Σ-domain; the ideal completion of its kernel. For more details on how this works, see Chapter 6 in [AJ95].

5 A Fully Abstract Denotational Model for *Trees*

In this section we will define a Σ-domain (where Σ consists of the operators nil, Ω, $+$ and $\mu.\_, (\mu \in Act_\tau)$) in such a way that the derived denotational semantics for $Trees$ is fully abstract with respect to observational precongruence. In particular this means that the operator Ω has to be interpreted as the bottom element of the domain as it is a least element with respect to the observational precongruence.

We show the the full abstractness of the model by showing that it is the initial Σ-algebra with respect to the operations in our language plus the inequations in E. We obtain this by proving that the proof system E, interpreted in the model, is sound and complete with respect to the preorder of the model. The full abstractness then follows from the fact that the proof system is sound and complete with respect to the observational precongruence as stated in Theorem 20.

The domain is obtained as an abstraction on the preorder $(NST, \sqsubseteq_{\approx}^{*})$ as explained in the Introduction.

Definition 24. We define the Σ-preorder $(NST, \sqsubseteq_{NST}, \Sigma_{NST})$ as follows:

1. The preorder $\sqsubseteq_{NST}$ is defined as the least binary relation over NST satisfying:

$$\begin{aligned} n \sqsubseteq_{NST} m \text{ if } & (1)\ \langle \mu, n' \rangle \in n \Rightarrow \exists \langle \mu, m' \rangle \in m.\ n' \sqsubseteq_{NST} m' \text{ and} \\ & (2)\ \bot \in m \Rightarrow \bot \in n \text{ and} \\ & (3)\ \langle \mu, m' \rangle \in m \Rightarrow (\bot \in n \text{ or } \exists \langle \mu, n' \rangle \in n.\ n' \sqsubseteq_{NST} m') \end{aligned}$$

2. The structure Σ_{NST} is defined as follows:
   (a) $\Omega_{NST} = \{\bot\}$,
   (b) $nil_{NST} = \emptyset$,
   (c) μ_{NST}: (compare Definition 10)

$$\tau_{NST}.n = \begin{cases} n & \text{if } \bot \in n \\ \{\langle \tau, n \rangle\} \cup n & \text{if } \bot \notin n \end{cases}$$

$$a_{NST}.n = \begin{cases} \{\langle a, n \rangle\} \cup \{\langle a, n' \rangle | \langle \tau, n' \rangle \in n\} & \text{if } \bot \notin n \\ \{\langle a, n \rangle\} \cup \{\langle a, n' \rangle | \langle \tau, n' \rangle \in n\} \cup \{\langle a, \bot \rangle\} & \text{if } \bot \in n \end{cases}$$

   (d) $+_{NST}$: $n_1 +_{NST} n_2 = n_1 \cup n_2$

Now we have:

Lemma 25.

1. *The preorders* $\sqsubseteq_{\mathsf{NST}}$ *and* $\sqsubseteq$ *coincide on* NST.
2. $(\mathsf{NST}, \sqsubseteq_{\mathsf{NST}}, \Sigma_{\mathsf{NST}})$ *is a* Σ*-preorder.*
3. *For all* $\eta \in NF$, $\mathsf{NST}[\![\eta]\!] = \mathcal{G}(\eta)$.

Proof.

1. Is proved in [Abr91].

2. Follows directly from Lemma 12.1.
3. Follows by Lemma 12.2 and a simple structural induction on η.

Part 3. of the lemma above says that the denotational interpretation in *NST* of a normal form is exactly its operational semantics, i.e. the process graph that is generated by the rules for the operational semantics for the language *Trees*.

Unfortunately the equation (τ**1**) is not sound in *NST* as the following example shows. (To ease the notational complexity we use the notation $\mu : n$ to denote $\{\langle \mu, n\rangle\}$ in what follows as explained in Section 2.)

Example 2. Let $n = \emptyset$. Then

$$\tau_{NST}.\emptyset = \tau : \emptyset \cup \emptyset = \tau : \emptyset$$

and therefore

$$\tau_{NST}.\tau_{NST}.\emptyset = \tau : \tau : \emptyset \cup \tau : \emptyset.$$

It is easy to see that

$$\tau_{NST}.\tau_{NST}.\emptyset \not\sim \tau_{NST}.\emptyset.$$

However we have the following partial soundness result and a completeness result. Let F denote the proof system E minus the equation (τ**1**). Then we have:

Lemma 26. *The proof system F is sound and complete for* $(\mathsf{NST}, \sqsubseteq_{\mathsf{NST}}, \Sigma_{\mathsf{NST}})$.

Proof. The soundness of the inequations (***A*1**)–(***A*4**) and (***Ω*1**)–(***Ω*2**) is obvious. The soundness of the inference rules follows from the fact that $(NST, \sqsubseteq_{NST}, \Sigma_{NST})$ is a Σ-preorder. What remains to prove is the soundness of (τ**2**) and (τ**3**). We proceed as follows:

(τ**2**): Assume that $n \in NST$. We will prove that

$$\tau_{NST}.n +_{NST} n =_{NST} n.$$

The case when $\bot \in n$ is obvious so we may assume that $\bot \notin n$. Then we have

$$\tau_{NST}.n +_{NST} n = (\tau : n \cup n) \cup n = \tau : n \cup n = \tau_{NST}.n.$$

(τ**3**) Assume that $n_1, n_2 \in NST$, we will show that

$$\mu_{NST}.(n_1 +_{NST} \tau_{NST}.n_2) =_{NST} \mu_{NST}.(n_1 +_{NST} \tau_{NST}.n_2) + \mu_{NST}.n_2$$

We have the two possible cases: $\mu = \tau$ and $\mu \neq \tau$. We proceed as follows:

$\mu = \tau$: The case when $\bot \in n_1 \cup n_2$ is straight forward and is left to the reader. Next let us assume that $\bot \notin n_1 \cup n_2$. Then

$$\begin{aligned}
&\tau_{NST}.(n_1 +_{NST} \tau_{NST}.n_2)\\
&= \tau : (n_1 \cup \tau : n_2 \cup n_2) \cup (n_1 \cup \tau : n_2 \cup n_2)\\
&= \tau : (n_1 \cup \tau : n_2 \cup n_2) \cup (n_1 \cup \tau : n_2 \cup n_2) \cup (\tau : n_2 \cup n_2)\\
&= \tau_{NST}.(n_1 +_{NST} \tau_{NST}.n_2) +_{NST} \tau_{NST}.n_2.
\end{aligned}$$

$\mu = a \in Act$: Again we have two possible sub-cases: $\perp \in n_2$ and $\perp \notin n_2$.
$\perp \in n_2$: First we note that

$$\perp \in n_2 \text{ implies } n_2 \sqsubseteq_{NST} n_1 \cup n_2. \tag{3}$$

Now we have the following:

$$\begin{aligned}
& a_{NST}.(n_1 +_{NST} \tau_{NST}.n_2) \\
= \quad & a : (n_1 \cup n_2) \cup \bigcup \{a : n' | \tau : n' \in n_1 \cup n_2\} \cup a : \{\perp\} \\
=_{NST} & \, a : (n_1 \cup n_2) \cup \bigcup \{a : n' | \tau : n' \in n_1 \cup n_2\} \cup a : \{\perp\} \cup \\
& a : n_2 \cup \bigcup \{a : n_2' | \tau : n_2' \in n_2\} \cup a : \{\perp\} \\
& \quad (\text{ as } a : \{\perp\} \sqsubseteq_{NST} a : n_2 \sqsubseteq_{NST} a : (n_1 \cup n_2) \text{ by (3)}) \\
= \quad & a_{NST}.(n_1 +_{NST} \tau_{NST}.n_2) +_{NST} a_{NST}.n_2
\end{aligned}$$

$\perp \notin n_2$: We proceed as follows:

$$\begin{aligned}
& a_{NST}.(n_1 +_{NST} \tau_{NST}.n_2) \\
&= a_{NST}.(n_1 \cup \tau : n_2 \cup n_2) \\
&= a : (n_1 \cup \tau : n_2 \cup n_2) \cup \bigcup \{a : n' | \tau : n' \in n_1 \cup n_2\} \cup \\
&\quad a : n_2 \cup \{a : \{\perp\} | \perp \in n_1\} \\
&= a : (n_1 \cup \tau : n_2 \cup n_2) \cup \bigcup \{a : n' | \tau : n' \in n_1 \cup n_2\} \cup \\
&\quad a : n_2 \cup \{a : \{\perp\} | \perp \in n_1\} \cup \\
&\quad a : n_2 \cup \bigcup \{a : n' | \tau : n' \in n_2\} \\
&= a_{NST}.(n_1 +_{NST} \tau_{NST}.n_2) +_{NST} a_{NST}.n_2.
\end{aligned}$$

Here we note that $=_{NST}$ appears only once in the sequence of the proof above. All the other equalities are set equalities.

The completeness may be easily proved by induction on the combined depth of n and m using Lemma 12. (In fact we do not need the $\boldsymbol{\tau 2}$,$\boldsymbol{\tau 3}$ and $\boldsymbol{\Omega 2}$ at all to prove the completeness as the preorder $\sqsubseteq_{NST}$ coincides with the strong bisimulation preorder $\sqsubseteq$.)

To obtain a Σ-preorder where the equation $\boldsymbol{\tau 1}$ is sound, we follow the suggestion after Example 1. This leads to the following definition (where $=_{\tau 1}$ has the same meaning as in Section 2).

Definition 27. We define $(K, \sqsubseteq_K, \Sigma_K)$ as follows:

1. $K = \{[n] \mid [n] = \{n' \in NST | n' =_{\tau 1} n\}\}$.
2. $\sqsubseteq_K$ is defined by

$$[n_1] \sqsubseteq_K [n_2] \text{ iff } \exists n_1', n_2' \in NST. n_1' =_{\tau 1} n_1, n_2' =_{\tau 1} n_2 \text{ and } n_1' \sqsubseteq_{NST} n_2'.$$

3. Σ_K is defined by
   (a) $nil_K = [\emptyset] = \{\emptyset\}$,
   (b) $\Omega_K = [\{\bot\}] = \{\{\bot\}\}$,
   (c) $[n_1] +_K [n_2] = [n_1 +_{NST} n_2]$,
   (d) $\mu_K.[n] = [\mu_{NST}.n]$.

Here we would like to point out that this model is not a term model as the elements are not equivalence classes over syntactic terms but process graphs. Furthermore the model K is not obtained by simply factoring out equations but involves operational reasoning as well. Now we have the following lemma:

Lemma 28.

1. *For all $n_1, n_2 \in \mathsf{NST}$, $[n_1] \sqsubseteq_K [n_2]$ iff $n_1 \sqsubseteq^*_{\approx} n_2$.*
2. *$(K, \sqsubseteq_K, \Sigma_K)$ is a Σ – preorder.*
3. *The proof system E is sound and complete on $(K, \sqsubseteq_K, \Sigma_K)$.*

Proof. It is easy to see that $\sqsubseteq_K$ is well defined this way, i.e. is independent of the representants for the classes $[n_1]$ and $[n_2]$. As $\sqsubseteq_{NST} = \sqsubseteq_{\approx}$ on NST the first statement follows from the Characterization Theorem 16, and the fact that $=_{\mathcal{T}1} \subseteq \approx^*$. This in turn ensures that $\sqsubseteq_K$ is a preorder. To prove statement 2. it only remains to prove that the operators in Σ_K are well defined and monotonic. This is an easy consequence of the way they are defined and the fact that $=_{\mathcal{T}1}$ is preserved by the operators in NST. What remains to proof is therefore statement 3., the soundness and the completeness of the proof system E on $(K, \sqsubseteq_K, \Sigma_K)$. To prove this we proceed as follows:

Soundness: The only non trivial case is the soundness of $\boldsymbol{\tau 1}$. So assume $n \in NST$ and we will prove that $\mu_K.\tau_K.[n] =_K \mu_K.[n]$. We recall that by definition of $=_{\mathcal{T}1}$,

$$\mu_{NST}.\tau_{NST}.n =_{\mathcal{T}1} \mu_{NST}.n.$$

This implies

$$\mu_K.\tau_K.[n] =_K [\mu_{NST}.(\tau_{NST}.n)] =_K$$

$$[\mu_{NST}.n] =_K \mu_K.[n].$$

Completeness: First we note that $=_{\mathcal{T}1} \subseteq =_E$. Next let $n_1, n_2 \in NST$ and we have the following:

$$[n_1] \sqsubseteq_K [n_2]$$

implies $\exists n_1', n_2' \in NST.\ n_1 =_{\mathcal{T}1} n_1' \sqsubseteq_{NST} n_2' =_{\mathcal{T}1} n_2$ (by definition)

implies $\exists n_1', n_2' \in NST.\ n_1 =_E n_1' \sqsubseteq_E n_2' =_E n_2$ (by Lem. 26)

implies $n_1 \sqsubseteq_E n_2$.

We have the following result:

Lemma 29.

1. *For all $d \in FinTree$, $K[\![d]\!] = [\mathsf{NST}[\![d]\!]]$.*
2. *For each $k \in K$ there is an $\eta \in NF$ such that $K[\![\eta]\!] = k$.*

Proof.

1. The mapping $[NST[\![\_]\!]]$ is an interpretation of *FinTrees* in K. The result follows by uniqueness of such mappings.
2. By definition of K, $k = [n]$ for some $n \in NST$. By a simple induction on the depth of n we may show that there exists an $\eta \in NF$ such that $NST[\![\eta]\!] = n$. By part 1. we get
$$K[\![\eta]\!] = [NST[\![\eta]\!]] = k.$$

5.1 Soundness, Completeness and Full Abstractness for *Trees*

We complete the construction of the the full domain by taking $(\overline{K}, \sqsubseteq_{\overline{K}}, \Sigma_{\overline{K}})$ to be the unique Σ-domain generated by $(K, \sqsubseteq_K, \Sigma_K)$ as described in Chapter 4. The following theorem is standard and is proved in e.g. [Hen88b].

Theorem 30. *For all $p \in Trees$, $\overline{K}[\![p]\!] = \bigsqcup_n \overline{K}[\![p^n]\!]$.*

Now we have the following equivalence result:

Theorem 31. *For all $p_1, p_2 \in Trees$*
$$\overline{K}[\![p_1]\!] \sqsubseteq_{\overline{K}} \overline{K}[\![p_2]\!] \text{ iff } p_1 \sqsubseteq_{E_{rec}} p_2 \text{ iff } p_1 \mathrel{\underset{\approx}{\sqsubseteq}^*} p_2.$$

Proof. That $p_1 \sqsubseteq_{E_{rec}} p_2$ iff $p_1 \mathrel{\underset{\approx}{\sqsubseteq}^*} p_2$ is the content of Theorem 20. Therefore we only have to prove that $\overline{K}[\![p_1]\!] \sqsubseteq_{\overline{K}} \overline{K}[\![p_2]\!]$ iff $p_1 \sqsubseteq_{E_{rec}} p_2$, i.e. that the proof system E_{rec} is sound and complete with respect to the denotational model.

Soundness: The soundness of the (ω)-rule is the content of Theorem 30 whereas the soundness of the (rec)-rule follows from the definition of the semantics of $\mathtt{rec}.p$ as the least fixed point. It remains to prove the soundness of E. To prove this we first prove by a simple induction on the depth of the proof for $p \sqsubseteq_E q$ that
$$p \sqsubseteq_E q \Rightarrow \forall n. p^n \sqsubseteq_E q^n. \tag{4}$$
Then we note that the soundness of E over *FinTrees* with respect to K follows directly from the soundness of E in K. To prove the general result, i.e. the soundness of E over *Trees* with respect to $\overline{K}$, we may proceed as follows. Assume $p \sqsubseteq_E q$. Then, by (4), $p^n \sqsubseteq_E q^n$ for all n. As $p^n, q^n \in$ *FinTrees*, the soundness of E with respect to K implies
$$K[\![p^n]\!] \sqsubseteq_K K[\![q^n]\!] \text{ for all } n,$$
or equivalently
$$\overline{K}[\![p^n]\!] \sqsubseteq_{\overline{K}} \overline{K}[\![q^n]\!] \text{ for all } n.$$
Finally Theorem 30 implies
$$\overline{K}[\![p]\!] \sqsubseteq \overline{K}[\![q]\!].$$

Completeness: Again we reduce the proof to proving that E is complete over $FinTrees$ with respect to K. We first note that Theorem 30 and the ω-algebraicity of the model imply

$$\begin{array}{ll} \overline{K}[\![p]\!] \sqsubseteq_{\overline{K}} \overline{K}[\![q]\!] & \text{implies} \\ \forall n.\overline{K}[\![p^n]\!] \sqsubseteq_{\overline{K}} \overline{K}[\![q]\!] & \text{implies} \\ \forall n \exists m.\overline{K}[\![p^n]\!] \sqsubseteq_{\overline{K}} \overline{K}[\![q^m]\!] & \text{implies} \\ \forall n \exists m.K[\![p^n]\!] \sqsubseteq_K K[\![q^m]\!]. & \end{array} \tag{5}$$

If E is complete over $FinTrees$ with respect to K then

$$K[\![p^n]\!] \sqsubseteq_K K[\![q^m]\!] \text{ implies } p^n \sqsubseteq_E q^m. \tag{6}$$

Now $q^m \sqsubseteq_{E_{rec}} q$ may easily be shown so (5), (6) and the ω-rule give

$$\overline{K}[\![p]\!] \sqsubseteq_{\overline{K}} \overline{K}[\![q]\!] \text{ implies } \forall n.p^n \sqsubseteq_{E_{rec}} q \text{ implies } p \sqsubseteq_{E_{rec}} q.$$

So it only remains to prove the completeness of E over $FinTrees$ with respect to K. Furthermore, by the the normalization Theorem 23, it is sufficient to prove the completeness over normal forms. To prove this completeness result we proceed as follows:
Assume $\eta_1, \eta_2 \in NF$. By Lemma 25 and Lemma 29

$$K[\![\eta_i]\!] = [NST[\![\eta_i]\!]] = [\mathcal{G}(\eta_i)]$$

for $i = 1, 2$. Therefore we have:

$$\begin{array}{lll} & K[\![\eta_1]\!] \sqsubseteq_K K[\![\eta_2]\!] & \\ \text{iff} & [\mathcal{G}(\eta_1)] \sqsubseteq_K [\mathcal{G}(\eta_2)] & \\ \text{iff} & \mathcal{G}(\eta_1) \lessapprox^* \mathcal{G}(\eta_2) & \text{by Lem. 28} \\ \text{iff} & \eta_1 \lessapprox^* \eta_2 & \text{by definition of the op. sem.} \\ \text{iff} & \eta_1 \sqsubseteq_E \eta_2 & \text{as } E \text{ is complete wrt. } \lessapprox^*. \end{array}$$

6 Conclusion and Future Work

Regarding the picture being drawn in the introduction about ways of getting fully abstract denotational models for concurrent languages with an observational preorder, we have obtained the following: By giving a set of inequations, we have found a way of having a term model. Also, we have constructed a syntax free model which is the ideal completion of a preordered set whose elements are finite synchronization trees like the ones that appear in the representation of Abramsky's model for strong bisimulation preorder. These trees are a representation of transition graphs in normal forms which in turn are derived as the operational semantics for syntactic normal forms in the sense of [Wal90]. By defining the operators in a suitable way we obtained a Σ-preorder. Unfortunately the Σ-domain obtained directly as an ideal closure of this Σ-preorder does not satisfy the set of equations that characterize the ω-observational congruence as the equation $\mu.\tau.x = \mu.x$ is not sound in this domain. We obtain a fully abstract model as a further abstraction of this model; roughly speaking we factor out the missing equation and obtain a fully abstract model with respect to the behavioural preorder we had in mind.

What is still missing, is the last part: Finding a mathematical description of the model which does not mention equations at all. This has proved to be more difficult than we first expected. To illustrate the kind of difficulties one runs into, let us consider a related successful attempt of doing something like this. In [Abr91], Abramsky defines a fully abstract denotational model for synchronization trees with respect to strong bisimulation precongruence. It is given as the solution of the recursive domain equation

$$D \cong \mathcal{P}(\sum_{\mu \in Act_\tau} D)$$

where $\mathcal{P}$ is a variant of the Plotkin (or convex) power construction (including the empty set) and $\sum$ is a lifted disjoint union. His proof that this is indeed a fully abstract model for the feature in question uses a sophisticated mathematical machinery that also produces a logic to reason about the model. There is however a shortcut to convince oneself that this is what one wants: Strong bisimulation precongruence for the language we consider can be characterized in terms of the equations **A1** to **A4** which say that + is idempotent, symmetric, associative and has a unit. There are no (in)equations concerning prefixing and in particular no (in)equations connecting prefixing with +. It is then not hard to see that the initial solution to the above domain equation is exactly the free Σ-domain for the empty set of generators where the equations **A1** to **A4** hold and where the set of operators Σ contains + as well as a unary operator for every element of Act_τ. The fact that this Σ-domain can be presented in such an appealing way crucially depends on the simplicity of the equations describing the modelled precongruence.

Since the domain we are looking for is the free Σ-domain for the same set of actions but with the additional inequations $\boldsymbol{\Omega 1}$, $\boldsymbol{\Omega 2}$ and $\boldsymbol{\tau 1}$ to $\boldsymbol{\tau 3}$, the domain we are looking for is a quotient of the one given by Abramsky (the mathematical details of this process can be found in [AJ95]). The domain we give as a model is an improvement over just taking the quotient of Abramsky's, since the only thing we have to take extra trouble over is inequality $\boldsymbol{\tau 1}$. However, it is not quite what we had in mind as forming quotients of this kind is a somewhat obscure process. It is our aim to find another way of presenting this Σ-domain, if possible also as the solution of a recursive domain equation.

A Appendix

In what follows we will prove Theorem 14. For this purpose we need the following definition.

Definition 32 [Wal90]. Given $\mathcal{R} \in \mathsf{Rel(P)}$ we define $s_1 \mathcal{R}^{\diamond} s_2$ by:
$s_1 \mathcal{R}^{\diamond} s_2$ iff

1. if $s_1 \xrightarrow{\mu} s_1'$ then, for some s_2', $s_2 \xrightarrow{\mu} s_2'$ and $s_1' \mathcal{R} s_2'$
2. if $s_1 \downarrow$ then
   (a) $s_2 \downarrow$
   (b) if $s_2 \xrightarrow{\mu} s_2'$ then, for some s_1', $s_1 \xrightarrow{\mu} s_1'$ and $s_1' \mathcal{R} s_2'$

Theorem 14 is a direct consequence of the following Lemma.

Lemma 33. *For all* $n_1, n_2 \in \mathsf{NST}$

1. $n_1 \underset{\approx}{\sqsubset} n_2 \;\Leftrightarrow\; n_1 \underset{\approx}{\sqsubset}_g n_2$,
2. $n_1 \underset{\approx}{\sqsubset}^{*} n_2 \;\Leftrightarrow\; n_1 \underset{\approx}{\sqsubset}_g^{\diamond} n_2$,

Proof.

1. The "$\Longleftarrow$" part is proved in [Wal90, Lemma 7]. Therefore we only have to concentrate on proving the "$\Longrightarrow$" part, i.e that $\underset{\approx}{\sqsubset} \subseteq \underset{\approx}{\sqsubset}_g$. By definition

$$\underset{\approx}{\sqsubset}_g = \bigcup \{\mathcal{R} \mid \mathcal{R} \subseteq \mathcal{F}_w^g(\mathcal{R})\}.$$

   It is therefore sufficient to prove that $\underset{\approx}{\sqsubset} \subseteq \mathcal{F}_w^g(\underset{\approx}{\sqsubset})$. First we recall that for a normal form n, $n \overset{a}{\Longrightarrow} n'$ iff $n \xrightarrow{a} n'$ and $n \Downarrow$ iff $n \downarrow$. Now we proceed as follows: Assume $m_1 \underset{\approx}{\sqsubset} m_2$. As $\underset{\approx}{\sqsubset}$ is a fixed point to $\mathcal{F}_w$ then $m_1 \mathcal{F}_w(\underset{\approx}{\sqsubset}) m_2$. We will prove that $m_1 \mathcal{F}_w^g(\underset{\approx}{\sqsubset}) m_2$.
   (a) If $m_1 \xrightarrow{a} m_1'$, then there is a m_2' such that $m_2 \xrightarrow{a} m_2'$ and $m_1' \underset{\approx}{\sqsubset} m_2'$. Similarly if $m_1 \xrightarrow{\tau} m_1'$, then there is an m_2' such that $m_2 \overset{\varepsilon}{\Longrightarrow} m_2'$ and $m_1' \underset{\approx}{\sqsubset} m_2'$.
   (b) Assume $m_1 \downarrow$, then $m_2 \downarrow$ as $m_1 \underset{\approx}{\sqsubset} m_2$.
   (c) Assume that $m_1 \downarrow$, $m_2 \downarrow$ and $m_2 \xrightarrow{a} m_2'$. We have the following cases:
      $m_1 \Downarrow a$: As $m_1 \underset{\approx}{\sqsubset} m_2$ then $m_2 \Downarrow a$ and $m_1 \xrightarrow{a} m_1'$ for some m_1' such that $m_1' \underset{\approx}{\sqsubset} m_2'$.
      $m_1 \Uparrow a$: As $m_1 \downarrow$ this implies that $\langle a, \{\bot\}\rangle \in m_1$. Therefore $m_1 \xrightarrow{a} \{\bot\}$ where $\{\bot\} \underset{\approx}{\sqsubset} m_2'$.
   (d) Finally assume $m_1 \downarrow$, $m_2 \downarrow$ and $m_2 \xrightarrow{\tau} m_2'$. Then there exists a m_1' such that $m_1 \overset{\varepsilon}{\Longrightarrow} m_1'$ and $m_1' \underset{\approx}{\sqsubset} m_2'$.
2. By part 1 it is sufficient to prove that

$$n_1 \underset{\approx}{\sqsubset}_g^{*} n_2 \;\Leftrightarrow\; n_1 \underset{\approx}{\sqsubset}_g^{\diamond} n_2$$

   We only prove the "$\Longleftarrow$" part as the "$\Longrightarrow$" part may be proved in the same way as the "$\Longrightarrow$" part for the previous case, part 1. Assume $n_1 \underset{\approx}{\sqsubset}_g^{\diamond} n_2$.

(a) Assume $n_1 \xrightarrow{a} n_1'$. As $n_1 \mathrel{\sqsubseteq^{\diamond}_{\approx g}} n_2$, there is an n_2' such that $n_2 \xrightarrow{a} n_2'$ and $n_1' \mathrel{\sqsubseteq_{\approx g}} n_2'$.

(b) Next assume $n_1 \xrightarrow{\tau} n_1'$. As n_1 is a normal form, $n_1 \Downarrow \varepsilon$. Furthermore $n_2 \stackrel{\varepsilon}{\Longrightarrow} n_2'$ for some n_2' such that $n_1' \mathrel{\sqsubseteq_{\approx g}} n_2'$.

(c) i. If $n_1 \Downarrow \tau$ then $n_2 \Downarrow \tau$ by definition of $\sqsubseteq^{\diamond}_{\approx g}$ and as $\downarrow$ and $\Downarrow \tau$ coincide on *NST*.

ii. Next assume that $n_1 \Downarrow \tau$, $n_2 \Downarrow \tau$ and $n_2 \xrightarrow{\tau} n_2'$. By definition of $\sqsubseteq^{\diamond}_{\approx g}$, $n_1 \xrightarrow{\tau} n_2'$ for some n_1' where $n_1' \mathrel{\sqsubseteq_{\approx g}} n_2'$.

(d) i. Assume $n_1 \Downarrow a$. We will prove that $n_2 \Downarrow a$. As $n_1 \Downarrow$ then $n_2 \Downarrow$. So assume $n_1 \Downarrow$, $n_2 \Downarrow$ and $n_1 \Downarrow a$ but that $n_2 \Uparrow a$. This implies that $\langle a, \{\bot\}\rangle$ is an element in n_2 but not in n_1. It is easy to see that this contradicts the fact that $n_1 \mathrel{\sqsubseteq^{\diamond}_{\approx g}} n_2$ and that n_1 and n_2 are normal forms.

ii. Next assume that $n_1 \Downarrow a$, $n_2 \Downarrow a$ and $n_2 \xrightarrow{a} n_2'$. Now $n_1 \mathrel{\sqsubseteq^{\diamond}_{\approx g}} n_2$, $n_1 \downarrow$ and $n_2 \downarrow$ and hence $n_1 \xrightarrow{a} n_1'$ for some n_1' such that $n_1 \mathrel{\sqsubseteq_{\approx g}} n_1'$.

References

[Abr91] S. Abramsky. A domain equation for bisimulation. *Information and Computation*, 92:161–218, 1991.

[AH92] L. Aceto and M. Hennessy. Termination, deadlock and divergence. *Journal of the ACM*, 39(1):147–187, January 1992.

[AJ95] S. Abramsky and A. Jung. Domain theory. In *Handbook of Logic in Computer Science*. Oxford University Press, 1994.

[Gue81] I. Guessarian. *Algebraic Semantics*, volume 99 of *Lecture Notes in Computer Science*. Springer-Verlag, 1981.

[Hen81] M. Hennessy. A term model for synchronous processes. *Information and Computation*, 51(1):58–75, 1981.

[Hen85] M. Hennessy. Acceptance trees. *Journal of the ACM*, 32(4):896–928, 1985.

[Hen88a] M. Hennessy. *Algebraic Theory of Processes*. MIT Press, Cambridge, Massachusetts, 1988.

[Hen88b] M. Hennessy. Axiomatising finite concurrent processes. *SIAM Journal on Computing*, 17(5):997–1017, 1988.

[Kel76] R.M. Keller. Formal verification of parallel programs. *Communications of the ACM*, 19(7):371–384, 1976.

[Mil80] R. Milner. *A Calculus of Communicating Systems*, volume 92 of *Lecture Notes in Computer Science*. Springer-Verlag, 1980.

[Mil81] R. Milner. Modal characterisation of observable machine behaviour. In G. Astesiano and C. Bohm, editors, *Proceedings CAAP 81*, volume 112 of *Lecture Notes in Computer Science*, pages 25–34. Springer-Verlag, 1981.

[Mil83] R. Milner. Calculi for synchrony and asynchrony. *Theoretical Computer Science*, 25:267–310, 1983.

[Mil89] R. Milner. *Communication and Concurrency*. Prentice-Hall International, Englewood Cliffs, 1989.

[Par81] D.M.R. Park. Concurrency and automata on infinite sequences. In P. Deussen, editor, 5th *GI Conference*, volume 104 of *Lecture Notes in Computer Science*, pages 167–183. Springer-Verlag, 1981.

[Plo81] G.D. Plotkin. Lecture notes in domain theory, 1981. University of Edinburgh.

[SS71] D.S. Scott and C. Strachey. Towards a mathematical semantics for computer languages. In *Proceedings of the Symposium on Computers and Automata*, volume 21 of *Microwave Research Institute Symposia Series*, 1971.

[Sti87] C. Stirling. Modal logics for communicating systems. *Theoretical Computer Science*, 49:311–347, 1987.

[Wal90] D.J. Walker. Bisimulation and divergence. *Information and Computation*, 85(2):202–241, 1990.

On Sharply Bounded Length Induction

Jan Johannsen

Universität Erlangen-Nürnberg, Germany
email: johannsen@informatik.uni-erlangen.de

Abstract. We construct models of the theory $L_2^0 := BASIC + \Sigma_0^b$-$LIND$: one where the predecessor function is not total and one not satisfying Σ_0^b-$PIND$, showing that L_2^0 is strictly weaker that S_2^0. The construction also shows that S_2^0 is not $\forall\Sigma_0^b$-axiomatizable.

Introduction

First we recall the definitions of the theories S_2^i and T_2^i of Bounded Arithmetic introduced by S. Buss [1]: The language of these theories is the language of Peano Arithmetic extended by symbols for the functions $\lfloor \frac{1}{2}x \rfloor$, the binary length $|x| := \lceil \log_2(x+1) \rceil$ and $x\#y := 2^{|x|\cdot|y|}$. The presence of $\#$ allows to express polynomial length bounds: if $|x| \leq p(|y|)$ for some polynomial p, then there is a term t containing $\#$ such that $x \leq t(y)$.

A quantifier of the form $\forall x \leq t$, $\exists x \leq t$ with x not occurring in t is called a *bounded quantifier*. Furthermore, a quantifier of the form $\forall x \leq |t|$, $\exists x \leq |t|$ is called *sharply bounded*. A formula is called sharply bounded if all quantifiers in it are sharply bounded.

The class of sharply bounded formulae is denoted Σ_0^b or Π_0^b. For $i \in \mathbb{N}$, let Σ_{i+1}^b (resp. Π_{i+1}^b) be the least class containing Π_i^b (resp. Σ_i^b) and closed under conjunction, disjunction, sharply bounded quantification and bounded existential (resp. universal) quantification. In the standard model, Σ_i^b-formulae describe exactly the sets in Σ_i^P, the ith level of the Polynomial Time Hierarchy, and likewise for Π_i^b-formulae and Π_i^P, for $i \geq 1$.

The theory T_2^i is defined by a finite set $BASIC$ of quantifier-free axioms specifying the interpretation of the language, plus the induction scheme for Σ_i^b-formulae (Σ_i^b-IND). S_2^i is defined by the $BASIC$ axioms plus the scheme of *polynomial induction*

$$\varphi(0) \wedge \forall x\, (\varphi(\lfloor \frac{1}{2}x \rfloor) \rightarrow \varphi(x)) \;\rightarrow\; \forall x \varphi(x)$$

for every Σ_i^b-formula $\varphi(x)$ (Σ_i^b-$PIND$). By the main result of [1], a function f with Σ_i^b-graph is provably total in S_2^i iff $f \in FP^{\Sigma_{i-1}^P}$, for $i \geq 1$.

Now let L_2^i denote the theory given by the $BASIC$ axioms and the scheme of *length induction*

$$\varphi(0) \wedge \forall x\, (\varphi(x) \rightarrow \varphi(Sx)) \;\rightarrow\; \forall x \varphi(|x|)$$

for each Σ_i^b-formula $\varphi(x)$ (Σ_i^b-$LIND$). Then for $i \geq 1$, we have $L_2^i = S_2^i$ (see [3] for a proof).

The proof of the inclusion $L_2^i \subseteq S_2^i$ is fairly easy and also works for $i = 0$: to prove $LIND$ for a formula $\varphi(x)$, apply $PIND$ to $\varphi(|x|)$. The proof of the opposite inclusion rests mainly on the definability of certain functions in L_2^1, and thus can only be applied to the case $i = 0$ if the language is extended by symbols for these functions and axioms on them.

Therefore, in case $i = 0$, have $L_2^0 \subseteq T_2^0$, which is trivial, and $L_2^0 \subseteq S_2^0$. Furthermore the first inclusion is proper since Takeuti [6] showed that the following theorem of T_2^0

$$\forall x\,(x = 0 \vee \exists y\ x = Sy)$$

is unprovable in S_2^0 and hence in L_2^0. This shows that the predecessor and hence the modified subtraction function $\dot{-}$ cannot be provably total in either of these theories.

Note that $L_2^0 = S_2^0$ would imply that S_2^0 is (properly) contained in T_2^0, but it is not ruled out yet that these latter two theories are incomparable w.r.t. inclusion.

As the main result of this paper, we shall show below that $L_2^0 \subsetneqq S_2^0$. The question about the relationship between S_2^0 and T_2^0 remains unresolved. We also show that S_2^0 is not equivalent to any set of $\forall\Sigma_0^b$-axioms, i.e. axioms that are universal closures of sharply bounded formulae.

A Model-Theoretic Property of Σ_0^b-formulae

A property of sharply bounded formulae that we shall need is their absoluteness w.r.t. a certain class of extensions of models:

Definition. Let M and N be models of $BASIC$, M a substructure of N. Then we say M is *length-initial* in N, written $M \subseteq_\ell N$, if for all $a \in M$ and $b \in N$ with $b < |a|$ already $b \in M$ holds.

In the following, barred letters will always denote tuples of variables or elements whose length is either irrelevant or clear from the context.

Proposition 1. *If $M \subseteq_\ell N$, then sharply bounded formulae are absolute between M and N, i.e. for every Σ_0^b-formula $\varphi(\bar{x})$ and $\bar{a} \in M$*

$$M \models \varphi(\bar{a}) \text{ iff } N \models \varphi(\bar{a})\ .$$

Proof. This is proved easily by induction on the complexity of the formula $\varphi(\bar{x})$. The crucial case is $\varphi(\bar{x}) \equiv \forall y \leq |t(\bar{x})|\, \theta(\bar{x}, y)$, where we have

$$\begin{aligned} & M \models \forall y \leq |t(\bar{a})|\, \theta(\bar{a}, y) \\ & \leftrightarrow \text{for all } b \in M \text{ with } b \leq |t(\bar{a})|\ N \models \theta(\bar{a}, b) \\ & \leftrightarrow N \models \forall y \leq |t(\bar{a})|\, \theta(\bar{a}, y)\ . \end{aligned}$$

The first equivalence holds by the induction hypothesis, and the second one by $M \subseteq_\ell N$. □

Now over the *BASIC* axioms, Σ_0^b-*LIND* is equivalent to the following scheme

$$\forall a\ [\varphi(0) \wedge \forall x < |a|\ (\varphi(x) \rightarrow \varphi(Sx)) \rightarrow \varphi(|a|)]\ ,$$

for every sharply bounded formula $\varphi(x)$. Therefore L_2^0 is $\forall\Sigma_0^b$-axiomatizable, and hence from Proposition 1 we get

Corollary 2. *If $N \models L_2^0$ and $M \subseteq_\ell N$, then $M \models L_2^0$.*

A model of L_2^0 with a partial predecessor function

We already know from Takeuti's result for S_2^0 mentioned above and the inclusion $L_2^0 \subseteq S_2^0$, that the existence of predecessors is independent from L_2^0. We shall now construct a model witnessing this independence.

Let $M \models S_2^1$. An element $a \in M$ is called *small*, if $a \leq |b|$ for some $b \in M$, and *large* otherwise. Define

$$M_0 := \{\, a \in M\ ;\ a \text{ is small}\,\} \cup \{\, 1\#a\ ;\ a \in M\,\}\,.$$

Hence M_0 contains all small elements of M, plus a prototypical large element of each length. Let $\hat{M}$ be the closure of M_0 under addition and multiplication. We imagine $\hat{M}$ being built in stages: for $i \in \mathbb{N}$ we define

$$M_{i+1} := \{\, a + b\ ;\ a, b \in M_i\,\} \cup \{\, a \cdot b\ ;\ a, b \in M_i\,\}$$

and $\hat{M} := \bigcup_{i \in \mathbb{N}} M_i$.

Proposition 3. *$\hat{M}$ is closed under $|.|$, $\lfloor \frac{1}{2} \rfloor$ and $\#$.*

Proof. Closure under $|.|$ is clear since all small elements of M are in M_0 and hence in $\hat{M}$. Closure under $\#$ is also easy: for every $a, b \in M$, $a\#b$ is equal to $1\#\lfloor \frac{1}{2}a\#b \rfloor$, since both are powers of two of the same length, and thus $a\#b \in M_0$.

Now for closure under $\lfloor \frac{1}{2} \rfloor$: We first show that M_0 is closed under $\lfloor \frac{1}{2} \rfloor$. This follows from the fact that $\lfloor \frac{1}{2}a \rfloor$ is small iff a is small, and $\lfloor \frac{1}{2}(1\#a) \rfloor = 1\#\lfloor \frac{1}{2}a \rfloor$.

Now suppose that for every $a \in M_i$ $\lfloor \frac{1}{2}a \rfloor \in \hat{M}$, and let $b \in M_{i+1}$. Then there are $b_1, b_2 \in M_i$ such that $b = b_1 + b_2$ or $b = b_1 \cdot b_2$. Now we can calculate

$$\lfloor \frac{1}{2}(b_1 + b_2) \rfloor = \begin{cases} \lfloor \frac{1}{2}b_1 \rfloor + \lfloor \frac{1}{2}b_2 \rfloor & \text{if } b_1 \cdot b_2 \text{ is even} \\ \lfloor \frac{1}{2}b_1 \rfloor + \lfloor \frac{1}{2}b_2 \rfloor + 1 & \text{else} \end{cases}$$

$$\lfloor \frac{1}{2}(b_1 \cdot b_2) \rfloor = \begin{cases} \lfloor \frac{1}{2}b_1 \rfloor \cdot b_2 & \text{if } b_1 \text{ is even} \\ \lfloor \frac{1}{2}b_1 \rfloor \cdot b_2 + \lfloor \frac{1}{2}b_2 \rfloor & \text{else} \end{cases}$$

and see that in either case $\lfloor \frac{1}{2}b \rfloor \in \hat{M}$. □

In particular, $\hat{M}$ is a substructure of M, and from the definition we see that $\hat{M} \subseteq_\ell M$, since $\hat{M}$ contains all small elements of M. Therefore $\hat{M} \models L_2^0$.

Lemma 4. *If there is $b \in \hat{M}$ with $Sb = 1\#a$, then a is bounded by $t(\bar{c})$ for some term $t(\bar{x})$ and some small $\bar{c} \in M$.*

Proof. Recall from [1] that in S_2^1 the function $Bit(x,i)$ giving the value of the ith bit in the binary expansion of x and the operation of *length bounded counting* can be defined. Hence we can talk about the number of bits set in an element of M.

We shall show below that for every $b \in \hat{M}$, the number of bits set is very small, i.e. $\sharp i < |b|\,(Bit(b,i) = 1) \leq p(||\bar{c}||)$ for some polynomial p and $\bar{c} \in M$. On the other hand, if $Sb = 1\#a$, then $\sharp i < |b|\,(Bit(b,i) = 1) = |a|$, so we get $|a| \leq p(||\bar{c}||)$, and thus $a \leq t(|\bar{c}|)$ for some term $t(\bar{x})$.

We prove the above claim by induction, using the above defined M_i. If $b \in M_0$, then either b is small, or $b = 1\#d$ for some $d \in M$. In the first case, $|b| \leq ||c||$, and therefore $\sharp i < |b|\,(Bit(b,i) = 1) \leq |b| \leq ||c||$ for some $c \in M$. In the second case, $\sharp i < |b|\,(Bit(b,i) = 1) = 1$.

Now let $b \in M_{i+1}$, and suppose the claim holds for all elements in M_i. Then there are $b_1, b_2 \in M_i$ such that $b = b_1 + b_2$ or $b = b_1 \cdot b_2$. Let

$$\sharp i < |b_j|\,(Bit(b_j,i) = 1) \leq p_j(||\bar{c}_j||)$$

for $j = 1, 2$. Then if $b = b_1 \circ b_2$,

$$\sharp i < |b|\,(Bit(b,i) = 1) \leq p_1(||\bar{c}_1||) \circ p_2(||\bar{c}_2||)$$

for $\circ \in \{+, \cdot\}$. Thus the claim follows. □

Recall the axioms Ω_2 stating that the function $x \#_3 y := 2^{|x|\#|y|}$ is total, which can be expressed in the language of S_2^1 as $\forall x \exists y |x|\#|x| = |y|$, and exp saying that exponentiation is total and hence there are no large elements. The consistency of the theory $S_2^1 + \Omega_2 + \neg exp$ follows from Parikhs Theorem, see e.g. [5]. Lemma 4 then yields

Theorem 5. *If* $M \models S_2^1 + \Omega_2 + \neg exp$*, then* $\hat{M} \models L_2^0 + \exists x\,(x \neq 0 \wedge \forall y\, Sy \neq x)$.

Proof. Since $M \models \Omega_2$, the small numbers are closed under $\#$, hence if there is $b \in \hat{M}$ with $Sb = 1\#a$, then Lemma 4 shows that a is small. But since $M \models \neg exp$, there are large elements in M and hence in $\hat{M}$. □

The independence of Σ_0^b-*PIND*

Let again $M \models S_2^1 + \Omega_2 + \neg exp$. From this model M, we construct a model $\tilde{M} \models L_2^0$ that does not satisfy S_2^0.

For $x \in M$ and $n \in \mathbb{N}$ we define $x^{\#n}$ inductively by $x^{\#0} := 1$, $x^{\#1} := x$ and $x^{\#(n+1)} := x^{\#n}\#x$ for $n \geq 1$. Choose a large $a \in M$. Then we define

$$\tilde{M} := \{\, b \in M\ ;\ b^{\#n} < a \text{ for all } n \in \mathbb{N} \,\} \cup \{\, b \in M\ ;\ b > a^{\#n} \text{ for all } n \in \mathbb{N} \,\}$$

We call the first set in the union the *lower part* of $\tilde{M}$ and the second set in the union the *upper part*. Note that the upper part is nonempty since $M \models \Omega_2$, for there must be an element b with $|b| = |a|\#|a|$. But then $b > a^{\#n}$ for every n since $b \leq a^{\#n}$ implies that $|b|$ is bounded by a polynomial in $|a|$.

Proposition 6. *$\tilde{M}$ is closed under* $|.|$, $\lfloor\frac{1}{2}\rfloor$, $+$, $\cdot$ *and* $\#$.

Proof. Since $M \models \Omega_2$, all small elements of M are in the lower part, since otherwise a would be small. Hence $\tilde{M}$ is closed under $|.|$.

If b is in the lower part, then of course $\lfloor\frac{1}{2}b\rfloor$ is in the lower part. On the other hand, the upper part is closed under $\lfloor\frac{1}{2}\rfloor$ since if $\lfloor\frac{1}{2}b\rfloor \leq a^{\#n}$, then $b \leq a^{\#(n+1)}$.

If at least one of b, c is in the upper part, then $b \circ c$ is in the upper part, for $\circ \in \{+, \cdot, \#\}$.

Finally, the lower part is closed under $\#$, and thus under $+$ and $\cdot$. To see this, let b and c be in the lower part. Then for every $n \in \mathbb{N}$, $(b\#c)^{\#n} \leq \max(b,c)^{\#2n} < a$, hence $b\#c$ is in the lower part. □

So $\tilde{M}$ is a substructure of M, and moreover $\tilde{M} \subseteq_\ell M$ since all small elements of M are in $\tilde{M}$, and thus $\tilde{M} \models L_2^0$. We show that there is a small element in $\tilde{M}$ that is not the length of any other element of $\tilde{M}$.

Proposition 7. $\tilde{M} \models L_2^0 + \exists x, y\, (x < |y| \wedge \forall z \leq y\, |z| \neq x)$.

Proof. We shall show the following: If b is in the lower part of $\tilde{M}$, then $|b| < |a|$, and if b is in the upper part of $\tilde{M}$, then $|b| > |a|$. Hence the element $|a| \in \tilde{M}$ is small, but there is no $b \in \tilde{M}$ with $|b| = |a|$.

So suppose $|b| \geq |a|$ for some b in the lower part. Then in particular $b\#b < a$, hence $|b\#b| \leq |a|$. But $|b\#b| = |b|^2 + 1 \leq |a| \leq |b|$ leads to a contradiction.

Dually, suppose $|b| \leq |a|$ for some b in the upper part. Then $a\#a < b$, hence $|a\#a| = |a|^2 + 1 \leq |b| \leq |a|$, which is likewise impossible. □

On the other hand, S_2^0 proves that every small element is the length of some other element.

Proposition 8. $S_2^0 \vdash \forall x, y\, (x \leq |y| \rightarrow \exists z \leq y\, |z| = x)$.

Proof. Consider the following case of Σ_0^b-$PIND$:

$$|0| < Sa \wedge \forall x\, (|\lfloor\frac{1}{2}x\rfloor| < Sa \rightarrow |x| < Sa) \rightarrow |b| < Sa$$

By taking the contrapositive of it and using the fact that $Sa \leq 0$ is refutable, we obtain

$$a < |b| \rightarrow \exists x\, (|\lfloor\frac{1}{2}x\rfloor| \leq a \wedge S|\lfloor\frac{1}{2}x\rfloor| > a)$$

and hence $a < |b| \rightarrow \exists x\, (|\lfloor\frac{1}{2}x\rfloor| = a)$, which implies $a < |b| \rightarrow \exists z\, |z| = a$. But if $|z| = a < |b|$, then $z < b$, so the existential quantifier can be bounded by b.

On the other hand, $a = |b| \rightarrow \exists z \leq b\, |z| = a$ is trivial, and combining these, we get

$$a \leq |b| \rightarrow \exists z \leq b\, |z| = a$$

as required. □

From Propositions 7 and 8 we immediately obtain our main result:

Theorem 9. *$L_2^0 \not\vdash \Sigma_0^b$-PIND, hence $L_2^0 \subsetneq S_2^0$.*

This shows that the schemes of polynomial induction and length induction are not necessarily equivalent in all contexts; their equivalence depends on the class of formula they can be applied to and the surrounding theory. Furthermore the proof shows

Corollary 10. *S_2^0 is not axiomatizable by a set of $\forall\Sigma_0^b$-sentences.*

Proof. By the above results $\tilde{M}$ cannot be a model of S_2^0. If S_2^0 were $\forall\Sigma_0^b$-axiomatizable, $M \models S_2^0$ and $\tilde{M} \subseteq_\ell M$ would imply $\tilde{M} \models S_2^0$. □

Acknowledgements: The present paper was somehow inspired by work of Fernando Ferreira [4]. Sam Buss [2] used a model construction remotely similar to ours for a different purpose.

References

1. S. R. Buss. *Bounded Arithmetic.* Bibliopolis, Napoli, 1986.
2. S. R. Buss. A note on bootstrapping intuitionistic bounded arithmetic. In P. Aczel, H. Simmons, and S. S. Wainer, editors, *Proof Theory*, pages 149–169. Cambridge University Press, 1992.
3. S. R. Buss and A. Ignjatović. Unprovability of consistency statements in fragments of bounded arithmetic. *Annals of Pure and Applied Logic*, 74:221–244, 1995.
4. F. Ferreira. Some notes on subword quantification and induction thereof. Typeset Manuscript.
5. P. Hájek and P. Pudlák. *Metamathematics of First-Order Arithmetic.* Springer Verlag, Berlin, 1993.
6. G. Takeuti. Sharply bounded arithmetic and the function $a \dot{-} 1$. In *Logic and Computation*, volume 106 of *Contemporary Mathematics*, pages 281–288. American Mathematical Society, Providence, 1990.

Effective Strategies for Enumeration Games

Martin Kummer and Matthias Ott*

Institut für Logik, Komplexität und Deduktionssysteme
Universität Karlsruhe, D-76128 Karlsruhe, Germany
Email: {kummer; m_ott}@ira.uka.de

Abstract. We study the existence of effective winning strategies in certain infinite games, so called enumeration games. Originally, these were introduced by Lachlan (1970) in his study of the lattice of recursively enumerable sets. We argue that they provide a general and interesting framework for computable games and may also be well suited for modelling reactive systems. Our results are obtained by reductions of enumeration games to regular games. For the latter effective winning strategies exist by a classical result of Büchi and Landweber. This provides more perspicuous proofs for several of Lachlan's results as well as a key for new results. It also shows a way of how strategies for regular games can be scaled up such that they apply to much more general games.

1 Introduction

Infinite games have been studied for a long time in many areas of mathematical logic. In recent years they also appeared in computer science as a framework for modelling reactive systems (see [Tho95] for a recent survey). Here the basic issue is the question of *effective determinacy*, i.e., which of the players has a computable winning strategy and how to determine such a strategy effectively from the description of the game? A central tool for answering this question is the effective determinacy result for regular games of Büchi and Landweber [BL69] which has been restated by McNaughton in a more applicable form concerning infinite games on finite graphs [McN93].

In recursion theory the game theoretic point of view is an important heuristic: Priority arguments can often be visualized as winning strategies in certain infinite games. This was first noticed by Lachlan in his influential paper [Lac70]. In this paper he also introduced the formal framework of *enumeration games* and proved an effective determinacy result for an interesting class of such games. In an enumeration game there are two players who enumerate sets of natural numbers in successive rounds. The winning condition is given by an open formula in the language of the lattice of recursively enumerable (r.e.) sets. Player I wins iff the formula is satisfied by the enumerated sets. Lachlan's determinacy result yields a decision procedure for the $\forall\exists$-formulae that are *uniformly* valid in the lattice of r.e. sets modulo finite sets.

* Supported by the Deutsche Forschungsgemeinschaft Graduiertenkolleg "Beherrschbarkeit komplexer Systeme" (DFG Vo 287/5-5).

In the present paper we give some illustrative examples which show that enumeration games may be useful for modelling aspects of reactive systems. In the main part we study to what extend enumeration games can be reduced to McNaughton's graph games. It turns out that this can be done for interesting subclasses of the games considered by Lachlan. The reductions are of increasing complexity. In the easiest cases there is a one-to-one correspondence between the moves in the enumeration game and the graph game. In a more difficult reduction it happens that some of the moves in the graph game are never transferred to the enumeration game. A priority queue is used to guarantee that sufficiently many moves are transferred.

The original framework of enumeration games can be generalized in two directions, by changing the language of winning conditions (the "specification language"), or by changing the rules for enumeration. In the basic case there is just the predicate $Finite(U)$ stating that U is a finite set. More generally we consider other Σ_2-predicates P and show that effective determinacy still holds for all Σ_2-predicates which are complete w.r.t. extensional m-reductions. However, we also provide a natural example where the corresponding game is not effectively determined.

Finally, we present a class of enumeration games where the rules for enumeration are suitably modified and the original language of Lachlan is extended by cardinality predicates. In our version both players successively extend initial segments of the characteristic functions of their sets. Effective determinacy can again be shown by reductions to graph games and yields as a corollary that the $\forall\exists$-formulae which are uniformly valid in the boolean algebra of recursive sets are decidable.

This paper is based on [Ott95] where additional details can be found.

2 Notation and Definitions

The recursion theoretic notation follows the books [Odi89, Soa87]. ω denotes the set of all natural numbers. We write X^C for the complement of the set $X \subseteq \omega$ in ω. R_1 is the set of all recursive functions. $\{\varphi_i\}_{i\in\omega}$ is a Gödel numbering of the partial recursive functions and $W_i = dom(\varphi_i)$ is the i-th recursively enumerable set. Σ_n and Π_n are the classes of the arithmetical hierarchy.

The notation for handling infinite objects follows [Tho90]. Σ^ω is the set of all ω-sequences over the alphabet Σ. ω-sequences are written in the form $\rho = \rho_0\rho_1 \ldots$. We use $(\exists^\omega i)$ as an abbreviation for "there exists infinitely many i".

We consider two-person-games of infinite duration, i.e., the plays consist of ω many moves. The players are called player I and II. A *strategy* for a player is a function which yields the next move for the player, given all the previous moves. For studying *effective* strategies we assume some effective coding of the finite sequences of moves. σ and τ denote strategies for the players I and II, respectively.

In an *enumeration game* of size n each of the two players enumerates n sets [Lac70]. Player I enumerates the sets $U_1, \ldots, U_n$ and player II the sets $V_1, \ldots, V_n$. A play of an enumeration game proceeds in stages. At stage $t = 0$ all sets are empty. At stages $t = 1, 3, \ldots$ player I can enumerate an element x into a set U_i, which is denoted by $\mu_t = \langle i, x \rangle$. He is also allowed to pass. In this case we write $\mu_t = 0$. At stages $t = 2, 4, \ldots$ player II moves analogously. U_i^t and V_i^t are the sets produced after stage t for $i = 1, \ldots, n$. We stipulate (for technical reasons) that the players do not repeat any move except possibly 0, i.e., no element is enumerated twice into the same set.

The winning condition of enumeration games are *winning formulas* over the sets (set variables) $U_1, \ldots, U_n, V_1, \ldots, V_n$. Winning formulas are chosen from a *specification language*. Different specification languages lead to different classes of games. In particular, we consider specification languages in which formulas are built from the predicate *Infinite*, cardinality predicates $Card_k$ for $k = 0, 1, \ldots$, set operations $\cap$, $\cup$ and ^{C}, and the logical operations $\wedge$, $\vee$ and $\neg$. $Infinite(X)$ is *true* iff X contains infinitely many elements. We write $Finite(X)$ for $\neg Infinite(X)$. $Card_k(X)$ is *true* iff X contains exactly k elements. Specification languages of this type were introduced by Lachlan [Lac70].

Player I wins a play in the enumeration game of size n with winning formula F if F is satisfied by the enumerated sets $U_1, \ldots, U_n, V_1, \ldots, V_n$. Otherwise player II wins the play. A strategy σ is a *winning strategy* for player I, if player I wins every play in which he follows σ. Winning strategies for player II are defined analogously.

A class of (enumeration) games is *effectively determined*, if in every game of the class one player has a computable winning strategy and, moreover, this player and his winning strategy can be computed from a description of the game. A description of an enumeration game is a pair (n, F), where n is the size and F the winning formula of the game.

3 Some Examples

The idea of modelling infinite behaviours of systems with infinite games is widespread in the literature, among others in [BL69, ALW89, Mos89, PR89, WD91, NYY92, NY92, TW94, MPS95]. Infinite games are mainly used to solve Church's problem [Chu63] of synthesizing processes (or automata) from a specification of the infinite input-output behaviour.

We give some examples for the application of enumeration games in reactive systems. It is demonstrated how aspects of the infinite behaviour of our sample systems can be expressed in the specification language of enumeration games.

We do not want to give examples which can only be solved by our theorems. For the given examples the effective determinacy theorem of regular games would suffice (Fact 4). Instead, our emphasis lies in illustrating enumeration games and their connection to reactive systems.

3.1 Printer-Spooler

The origin of our first example is [Gur89]. The reactive system of interest is a printer spooler (player I). The spooler has an input-queue in which the user (player II) can insert print-jobs. From time to time, depending on the environment like printer-status, network-status etc., the spooler takes the first job from the input-queue and sends it to the printer. An event in the system consists of an action a at time t. With each event we associate an identifier.

When the user (player II) inserts an job into the queue, in our model he enumerates the associated identifier into his set V_1. The event of removing and sending a print-job is interpreted as the spooler (player I) enumerates the associated identifier into the set U_1.

Gurevich's specification of the system was that of *fairness*: Every job inserted into the input-queue should eventually be sent to the printer. This requirement is fulfilled if the spooler (player I) wins the game with winning formula

$$F_1 := [\mathit{Infinite}(V_1) \rightarrow \mathit{Infinite}(U_1)].$$

Obviously, there is an effective winning strategy for player I in the game of size 1 with winning formula F_1.

We develop this example further. Instead of one printer there are now $2m$ printers. The printers $P_1, P_3, \ldots, P_{2m-1}$ are the main-printers and the printers $P_2, P_4, \ldots, P_{2m}$ are standby-printers. If printer P_{2i-1} fails, the spooler may sent jobs to P_{2i} instead of sending them to P_{2i-1}, for $i = 1, \ldots, m$. Sending jobs to Printer P_i means enumerating the associated event-identifier into the set U_i for $i = 1, \ldots, 2m$.

We stepwise specify the desired infinite behaviour of the spooler. First we require that the spooler should distribute the jobs equally among the main-printers in infinity:

$$\mathit{Infinite}(V_1) \rightarrow \bigwedge_{i=1,\ldots,m} \mathit{Infinite}(U_{2i-1}).$$

We introduce the possibility of sending jobs to the standby-printers:

$$\mathit{Infinite}(V_1) \rightarrow \bigwedge_{i=1,\ldots,m} (\mathit{Infinite}(U_{2i-1}) \vee \mathit{Infinite}(U_{2i})).$$

This formula has to be improved. When should the main-printers and when the standby-printers get infinitely many jobs? This depends on the error-quota of the main-printers. For handling error-messages we introduce sets E_i for $i = 1, \ldots, 2m$. If printer P_i sends an error-message, the associated event-identifier is enumerated into E_i. We assume that the printers send repeatedly error-messages as long as they are not ready to print. So, receiving no error message from a printer during a period Δt of time implies the printer is okay now. The sets E_i are sets of player II. Thus, player II now comprises the user and the printers, i.e., *all* agents of the environment which are relevant for the spooler-specification.

If there are only finitely many error-messages of printer P_{2i-1} then only finitely many jobs should be sent to the standby-printer P_{2i}.

Jobs can get lost. This can happen when the spooler sends a job to a printer at which an error occurred. There may be a period of time between the occurrence of an error and the arrival of the error-message at the spooler. So the spooler may send jobs to a faulty printer assuming that this printer is okay. We only want to lose finitely many jobs in this way. Therefore, we specify that if there are infinitely many error-messages from printer P_{2i-1}, then only finitely many jobs should be sent to this printer:

$$F_2 := [\mathit{Infinite}(V_1) \rightarrow \bigwedge_{i=1,\ldots,m} [(\mathit{Finite}(E_{2i-1}) \wedge \mathit{Infinite}(U_{2i-1}) \wedge \mathit{Finite}(U_{2i})) \vee (\mathit{Infinite}(E_{2i-1}) \wedge \mathit{Finite}(U_{2i-1}) \wedge \mathit{Infinite}(U_{2i}))]].$$

But in the game with winning formula F_2 player II has a winning strategy. Every time, when player I enumerates a new element in U_{2i-1}, player II extends E_{2i-1} in one of the next moves. Additionally, player II enumerates infinitely many elements in V_1. Consequently, the premise *Infinite*(V_1) of F_2 is fulfilled, but the sets E_{2i-1} and U_{2i-1} either remain both finite or become both infinite for all $i = 1, \ldots, m$. Hence, the desired spooler is not realizable. The requirements on the spooler have to be reduced, e.g. by removing the atoms *Finite*(U_{2i-1}) in the second parts of the disjunctions. Then player I has an effective winning strategy.

Formula F_2 is a good example for a specification, where one gets additional insights by viewing the specification as a winning formula of a game.

How can one check, if a given specification is realizable or not? It follows from Theorem 6 that this can be done automatically for the used specification language. Furthermore, in the case of realizability an implementation can be determined effectively from the specification.

A further requirement on the spooler is that the standby-printers should only be used, if there occurs at least one error at the main printers. This can be expressed by the predicate Card_0 in an additional requirement

$$\bigwedge_{i=1,\ldots,m} (\mathit{Card}_0(E_{2i-1}) \rightarrow \mathit{Card}_0(U_{2i})).$$

The underlying extended specification language is covered by Theorem 7.

3.2 Access-Control-System

As an example for the use of set operations in specifications, we consider an access-control-system. Users can prove their rights for using a particular resource by delivering a *capability* to the access-control-system. (Of course, in such a system security is an issue and has to be achieved by cryptographic methods. But this is not relevant in our context.) With respect to the received capabilities the access-control-system grants or refuses access to the protected resources.

Because of efficiency, capabilities are valid for a period of time, i.e., a user may deliver a capability once and can use the appropriate resource as long as this capability is valid. Thus, one requirement on the access-control-system is that when the delivering of capabilities stops, the system must eventually stop granting access to the appropriate resource.

There are resources which may only be used by groups. If user i delivers a capability for the resource j at day d, the value d is enumerated into the set $V_{i,j}$. Access to the resource j is only granted (for a period of time) if two of the three users 1, 2, 3 deliver a capability at the same day. Granting access to resource j is modeled by enumerating the associated event-identifier into the set U_j. Thus, our requirement is

$$F_3 := [Finite(V_{1,j} \cap V_{2,j}) \wedge Finite(V_{1,j} \cap V_{3,j}) \wedge Finite(V_{2,j} \cap V_{3,j}) \rightarrow Finite(U_j)].$$

Theorem 8 deals with the appropriate kind of specification language. Of course, there are other reasonable premises instead of the premise in formula F_3. Indeed, every formula built from $Finite, \cap, \wedge, \vee$ is in principle a reasonable premise.

4 Reductions to Infinite Graph Games

In [Lac70] A. H. Lachlan stated the following fact:

Fact 1 (Lachlan). *The enumeration games with predicate* Infinite *and the set operations* $\cap$, $\cup$ *and* ^{C} *are effectively determined.*

As a consequence the uniform $\forall\exists$-theory of $\mathcal{E}^*$, the lattice of r.e. sets modulo finite sets, is decidable: An $\forall\exists$-sentence

$$S = (\forall V_1 \ldots \forall V_n)(\exists U_1 \ldots \exists U_n)F[V_1, \ldots, V_n, U_1, \ldots, U_n]$$

with matrix F is called *uniformly* valid in $\mathcal{E}^*$ if there is an effective procedure to compute from indices $i_1, \ldots, i_n$ of the V_i's indices $j_1, \ldots, j_n$ of the U_j's such that $F[W_{i_1}, \ldots, W_{i_n}, W_{j_1}, \ldots, W_{j_n}]$ holds. The following folklore proposition connects the existence of effective winning strategies in enumeration games with uniform validity.

Proposition 2. *An $\forall\exists$-sentence S is uniformly valid iff player I has an effective winning strategy in the enumeration game with winning formula S.*

Proof. Let $S = (\forall V_1 \ldots \forall V_n)(\exists U_1 \ldots \exists U_n)F[V_1, \ldots, V_n, U_1, \ldots, U_n]$ be any given $\forall\exists$-sentence.
($\Leftarrow$) : Given $i_1, \ldots, i_n$ simulate the winning strategy of player I against an opponent who enumerates $W_{i_1}, \ldots, W_{i_n}$. This defines n sets with indices say $j_1, \ldots, j_n$ (obtained from the s-m-n theorem) such that $F[W_{i_1}, \ldots, W_{i_n}, W_{j_1}, \ldots, W_{j_n}]$ holds.

($\Rightarrow$) : We show the contraposition. Assume that player I does not have an effective winning strategy in the enumeration game specified by S. Then, by effective determinacy, player II has an effective winning strategy. Now suppose for a contradiction that the recursive function f witnesses the uniform validity of S. Using f, the recursion theorem, and the winning strategy of player II one can construct indices $i_1, \ldots, i_n$ such that $f(i_1, \ldots, i_n) = (j_1, \ldots, j_n)$ and $F[W_{i_1}, \ldots, W_{i_n}, W_{j_1}, \ldots, W_{j_n}]$ does not hold, a contradiction. □

Lachlan [Lac70, Section 3] gave a very brief sketch of how to prove Fact 1. But this sketched proof is rather difficult.

We now introduce a method for proving the effective determinacy of enumeration games. This method is suitable for a subclass of the games in Fact 1 (the games where the set operation ^{C} is excluded) and for many other classes of enumeration games.

4.1 Infinite Graph Games

The method is based on a result of McNaughton [McN93]. He introduced *infinite graph games*. These two person games are played on a finite graph. At any time of a play a marker is on one node of the graph. The players move this marker alternately from node to node along the edges of the graph. A play consists of ω many moves beginning with a move of player I. The winner of an (infinite) play is determined by the set of nodes, which were visited infinitely often by the marker.

The formal definition of graph games contains some restrictions, which is to some extent for technical reasons only.

Definition 3. An *infinite graph game* $\mathcal{G}$ is an ordered sextuple (Q, Q_{I}, Q_{II}, E, q_0, Ω), where (Q, E) is a finite bipartite directed graph, Q_{I}, Q_{II} are the set of nodes to which players I, II may move, respectively, q_0 is the initial node and $\Omega \subseteq 2^Q$ is the set of winning subsets of Q. We postulate $Q_{\text{I}} \cup Q_{\text{II}} = Q \neq \emptyset$, $Q_{\text{I}} \cap Q_{\text{II}} = \emptyset$ and that for each $e \in E$ there exist $p \in Q_{\text{I}}$ and $q \in Q_{\text{II}}$ such that either $e = (p, q)$ or $e = (q, p)$. Furthermore, for each $p \in Q$ there must be a node $q \in Q$ with $(p, q) \in E$.

A play of a graph game $\mathcal{G} = (Q, Q_{\text{I}}, Q_{\text{II}}, E, q_0, \Omega)$ is a sequence $\rho \in Q^\omega$ such that $\rho_0 = q_0$ and $(\rho_t, \rho_{t+1}) \in E$ for all $t \in \omega$.

$$\text{In}(\rho) := \{q \in Q \colon (\exists^\omega t)[\rho_t = q]\}$$

is the set of nodes, which were visited infinitely often during the play ρ. Player I wins the play ρ if $\text{In}(\rho)$ is an element of Ω, otherwise player II wins the play.

McNaughton proved the following fact:

Fact 4 (McNaughton). *Infinite graph games are effectively determined.*

Actually McNaughton showed a stronger result (Theorem 4.1 in [McN93]). Especially he proved that one can always construct an *LVR-strategy* for the winner. This is a strategy, which needs only finite memory capacity. The name LVR ("latest visitation record") originates in the way of book-keeping the visited nodes. The complexity of the decision procedure and the size of the resulting winning strategies were investigated in [McN93, Les95]. Fact 4 is not really new. It is rather a reformulation of an older result by Büchi and Landweber [BL69]. The games solved there are called *finite-state games* or *regular games*.

4.2 Reductions for Games with Predicate *Infinite*

In this section we prove that the enumeration games with predicate *Infinite* are effectively determined. The proof is by reductions to infinite graph games. The idea of the reductions is to associate an infinite graph game with each enumeration game. In the associated graph game we can effectively compute a winning strategy for one player by Fact 4. This winning strategy is translated into the enumeration game.

Suppose w.l.o.g. that player I has a winning strategy $\sigma_{\mathcal{G}}$ in the graph game. Player I simulates a play in the graph game in parallel to the play in the enumeration game. He has to translate the moves of player II from the enumeration game into the graph game. In the graph game he follows his winning strategy and retranslates the resulting moves into the enumeration game.

Assume that the size n of an enumeration game is given. We now construct the graph game with sets of nodes $Q^n_{\mathrm{I}} = \{U_0, U_1, \ldots, U_n\}$, $Q^n_{\mathrm{II}} = \{V_0, V_1, \ldots, V_n\}$, $Q_n := Q^n_{\mathrm{I}} \cup Q^n_{\mathrm{II}}$ and the edges $E_n := (Q^n_{\mathrm{I}} \times Q^n_{\mathrm{II}}) \cup (Q^n_{\mathrm{II}} \times Q^n_{\mathrm{I}})$. A visit on a node U_i (V_i) in the graph game shall correspond to an extension of the set U_i (V_i) in the enumeration game for $i = 1, \ldots, n$. The nodes U_0 and V_0 of the graph game represent passes in the enumeration game.

At the beginning ($t = 0$) the marker is put on the node V_0 (an arbitrary node from Q^n_{II} would suffice).

In stage $t+1 = 2s+1$ it is player I's turn to move. He computes $q_{t+1} := \sigma_{\mathcal{G}}(q_0 \ldots q_t)$ according to his winning strategy $\sigma_{\mathcal{G}}$. If $q_{t+1} = U_0$ then player I passes in the enumeration game in stage $t+1$, i.e., he chooses $\mu_{t+1} = 0$. Otherwise $q_{t+1} = U_i$ for an $i \in \{1, \ldots, n\}$. In this case player I enumerates a new element into the set U_i by choosing $\mu_{t+1} = \langle i, 1 + \max U_i \rangle$.

In stage $t+1 = 2s+2$ it is player II's turn to move. Player I observes the move μ_{t+1} of player II in the enumeration game. If player II passes, then the marker is put on the node V_0 of the graph. Otherwise $\mu_{t+1} = \langle i, x \rangle$ for an $i \in \{1, \ldots, n\}$. We stipulated that the players perform no repeating moves. So we can conclude $V_i^t \subset V_i^{t+1}$. In this case player I simulates the move of player II by moving the marker on the node V_i of the graph game.

Let $\rho = q_0 q_1 q_2 \ldots$ be the produced play in the graph game. It turns out that every node U_i (V_i) is in $\mathrm{In}(\rho)$ iff the set U_i (V_i) is infinite in the play of the enumeration game (*).

The given construction depends only on the size n of the given enumeration game, but not on the winning formula F. We fix the size n. With each winning formula F we can associate a winning set $\Omega(F)$ by induction on the structure of F:

$$\Omega(\mathit{Infinite}(U_i)) := \{\pi \subseteq Q\colon\ U_i \in \pi\} \text{ for i=1,\dots,n},$$

$$\Omega(\mathit{Infinite}(V_i)) := \{\pi \subseteq Q\colon\ V_i \in \pi\} \text{ for i=1,\dots,n},$$

$$\Omega(F_1 \wedge F_2) := \Omega(F_1) \cap \Omega(F_2),$$

$$\Omega(\neg F_1) := 2^Q - \Omega(F_1).$$

We show that by this definition for each winning formula F of the enumeration game of size n the following Lemma holds:

Lemma 5. *F is valid in the enumeration game* $\Longleftrightarrow$ $In(\rho) \in \Omega(F)$.

Proof. The proof is by induction on the structure of F. For atomic formulas the statement follows directly from (*). In the induction step one only makes use of the analogy between the propositional logic operators and the set operations. □

Lemma 5 says that the plays in both games have the same winner, if player I plays according to the above translation.

We can now prove the following theorem:

Theorem 6. *The enumeration games with predicate* Infinite *are effectively determined by reductions to graph games.*

Proof. For a given enumeration game of size n with winning formula F we construct the graph game $\mathcal{G} = (Q_n, Q_{\mathrm{I}}^n, Q_{\mathrm{II}}^n, E_n, V_0, \Omega(F))$. By Fact 4 we can effectively determine the winner and an effective winning strategy from $\mathcal{G}$. If player I has an effective winning strategy $\sigma_{\mathcal{G}}$ in $\mathcal{G}$ we translate it into a strategy σ for player I in the enumeration game by the described algorithm.

If player I follows σ in the enumeration game he wins the associated play in the graph game, since $\sigma_{\mathcal{G}}$ is an winning strategy for player I. By Lemma 5 player I also wins the play in the enumeration game. Hence σ is a winning strategy for player I in the enumeration game. Since $\sigma_{\mathcal{G}}$ is an effective strategy and all constructions are effective, the strategy σ is also effective.

If player II has a winning strategy in $\mathcal{G}$, this strategy can be analogously translated into an winning strategy for player II in the enumeration game. □

One may argue that the above proof for the games with predicate *Infinite* is somewhat circumstantial. Actually there are more succinct formulations. But the given formulation is for demonstrating the method of reductions to graph games. In more difficult games the above proof scheme is also applicable and turned out to be very helpful.

A slight modification of the given proof yields the result that the games with the predicate "*is superset of A*", for an arbitrary but fixed infinite r.e. set A, are effectively determined. If A is finite this predicate is a Σ_1-predicate (see the introduction of Section 5).

4.3 Predicates *Infinite* and $Card_k$

At first we extend the class of enumeration games of Theorem 6 by allowing cardinality predicates besides the predicate *Infinite*:

Theorem 7. *The enumeration games with the predicates* Infinite *and* Card_k *for* $k \in \omega$ *are effectively determined by reductions to graph games.*

Proof. The proof is similar to that for games with predicate *Infinite* only. But now we additionally attach to each node of the game graph a *counter* $\gamma : \{U_1, \ldots, U_n, V_1, \ldots, V_n\} \to \{1, \ldots, k_1\}$. k_1 is a number such that for all atomic formulas $Card_k(W)$ occurring in the given winning formula F the value of k is less than k_1. Formally we choose as set of nodes

$$Q_{\mathrm{I}}^n := \{(U_i, \gamma) \colon i = 0, \ldots, n \text{ and } \gamma \text{ is a counter}\},$$

$$Q_{\mathrm{II}}^n := \{(V_i, \gamma) \colon i = 0, \ldots, n \text{ and } \gamma \text{ is a counter}\}.$$

The edges are defined in such a way that the cardinality of the sets U_i and V_i are counted in the appropriate γ. But we only increment the counters until the bound k_1 is reached. That is for all $i, j \in \{0, \ldots, n\}$ and all counters δ, γ we take the edge $((U_i, \delta), (V_j, \gamma))$ in the set E_n iff

$$\begin{aligned}
&(j = 0 \land \delta = \gamma) \lor \\
&(j \neq 0 \land \\
&\gamma(V_j) = \min\{\delta(V_j) + 1, k_1\} \land \\
&(\forall W \neq V_j)[\gamma(W) = \delta(W)]).
\end{aligned}$$

The edges $((V_i, \delta), (U_j, \gamma))$ are defined analogously. The translation of a strategy from such a graph game into the enumeration game is performed in an obvious manner. The winning sets are defined by structural induction on the formulas F such that all atomic subformulas $Card_k(W)$ of F satisfy $k < k_1$. We only give the definitions for the sets U_i, $i = 1, \ldots, n$. The definitions for V_i are symmetric.

$$\Omega(\mathit{Infinite}(U_i)) := \{\pi \subseteq Q_n \colon (\exists \gamma)[(U_i, \gamma) \in \pi]\},$$

$$\Omega(\mathit{Card}_k(U_i)) := \{\pi \subseteq Q_n \colon (\forall (W, \gamma) \in \pi)[\gamma(U_i) = k]\} \text{ for } k < k_1.$$

The definition for non-atomic formulas is the same as in Section 4.2. With this definition one can prove the analogous statement to Lemma 5. The remainder of the proof is identical with that of Theorem 6. □

4.4 Predicate *Infinite* and Set Operations ∩ and ∪

In this subsection we extend the specification language of Theorem 6 by introducing the set operations ∩ and ∪ while *Infinite* remains the only allowed predicate.

Theorem 8. *The enumeration games with predicate* Infinite *and the set operations* ∩ *and* ∪ *are effectively determined by reductions to graph games.*

Proof. Because of the distributivity and associativity laws each term built from sets with the operations ∩ and ∪ can be represented in the form

$$\bigcup_{i \in M} \bigcap_{j \in M_i} A_j .$$

But for arbitrary sets $B_1, \ldots, B_m$ we have

$$Infinite(\bigcup_{i=1}^{m} B_i) \iff \bigvee_{i=1}^{m} Infinite(B_i). \tag{1}$$

Hence we can restrict ourselves to the games with atoms

$$Infinite(\bigcap_{W \in M} W)$$

for nonempty sets $M \subseteq \{U_1, \ldots, U_n, V_1, \ldots, V_n\}$.

The idea of the reduction is to introduce graph nodes for each subset $M \subseteq \{U_1, \ldots, U_n, V_1, \ldots, V_n\}$. A node with $M = \emptyset$ represents a pass in the enumeration game. A visit of a graph node marked with a subset $M \neq \emptyset$ shall correspond to an extension of the set

$$S(M) := \bigcap_{W \in M} W - \bigcup_{W \notin M} W.$$

But there is only hope that player I (II) can extend this set, when at least one U_i (V_i) is a member of M. This leads one to the following definitions:

$$Q_{\mathrm{I}}^n := \{(\mathrm{I}, M) : M \subseteq \{U_1, \ldots, U_n, V_1, \ldots, V_n\} \text{ and } (M = \emptyset \text{ or } M \cap \{U_1, \ldots, U_n\} \neq \emptyset)\},$$

$$Q_{\mathrm{II}}^n := \{(\mathrm{II}, M) : M \subseteq \{U_1, \ldots, U_n, V_1, \ldots, V_n\} \text{ and } (M = \emptyset \text{ or } M \cap \{V_1, \ldots, V_n\} \neq \emptyset)\}.$$

Again, we connect the two sets completely:

$$E_n := (Q_{\mathrm{I}}^n \times Q_{\mathrm{II}}^n) \cup (Q_{\mathrm{II}}^n \times Q_{\mathrm{I}}^n).$$

We consider the translation of a strategy for player I from the graph game into the enumeration game. If player II in stage $t+1$ enumerates the new element x into V_i^{t+1}, we determine the set

$$M := \{U_i : x \in U_i^t\} \cup \{V_i : x \in V_i^t\}$$

and move the marker to the node $(\mathrm{II}, M \cup \{V_i\})$.

The other direction is a little bit more complicated. Consider the graph move $q_{t+1} = (\mathrm{I}, M)$ of player I. Now player I wants to enumerate a new element into the set $S(M)$. This is easy if $M = \{U_i\}$. If $|M| > 1$ then he has to find a $U_i \in M$ such that the set $S(M - \{U_i\})$ contains at least one element. But it is possible that all of these sets are empty.

The solution is to put all graph moves into a *buffer* and to translate them later when the moves are *executable*. The buffer is organized as a (horizontal) queue, that is new moves are inserted from the right and executable moves are searched from the left. This secures that all moves which are executable infinitely often will eventually be translated. For technical reasons we must allow player I to perform moves in the enumeration game as long as there are executable ones in the buffer *without* any move of player II in-between. I.e., player I is allowed to perform finitely many moves at each stage. Otherwise player II could hinder player I making $U_1 \cap U_2$ infinite by answering every move of x into U_1 or U_2 with enumerating x also into V_1 in the subsequent move. This generalization does not affect the question of effective determinacy.

Let us now construct the winning sets of the graph game such that all plays in both games have the same winner. A set $\bigcap_{W \in M} W$ becomes infinite iff there is an $N \supseteq M$ such that the set $S(N)$ is extended infinitely often during the play. One can show that this is the case iff either

- (I, N) or (II, N) is visited infinitely often in the graph game and $|N| = 1$ or
- (I, N) is visited infinitely often and there is $U_i \in N$ such that $N - \{U_i\} \neq \emptyset$ and $S(N - \{U_i\})$ is infinite or
- (II, N) is visited infinitely often and there is $V_i \in N$ such that $N - \{V_i\} \neq \emptyset$ and $S(N - \{V_i\})$ is infinite.

Let $D_{\mathrm{I}} := \{U_1, \ldots, U_n\}$ and $D_{\mathrm{II}} := \{V_1, \ldots, V_n\}$. We first define a relation $\mathit{Consistent}(q, \pi)$ for $\pi \subseteq Q_n$ and $q = (\Lambda, N) \in \pi$ as the smallest relation with the following properties:

- $|N| = 1 \implies \mathit{Consistent}(q, \pi)$
- $(\exists \Lambda' \in \{\mathrm{I}, \mathrm{II}\})(\exists W \in D_\Lambda)[\mathit{Consistent}((\Lambda', N - \{W\}), \pi)]$
  $\implies \mathit{Consistent}(q, \pi)$.

For each $M \subseteq \{U_1, \ldots, U_n, V_1, \ldots, V_n\}$, $M \neq \emptyset$ we define

$$\Omega(\mathit{Infinite}(\bigcap_{W \in M} W)) := \{\pi \subseteq Q_n : (\exists (\Lambda, N) \in \pi)[M \subseteq N \wedge \mathit{Consistent}((\Lambda, N), \pi)]\}.$$

The remainder of the proof follows the outline of the previous determinacy proofs. □

The method of reductions to graph games fails if one extends the specification language of Theorem 8 by the set operation ^{C}. This is because set expressions with complement behave non-monotonic. Moreover, the arithmetical hierarchy indicates that the problem with complement is more difficult. The index set $\{i\colon W_i^C \text{ is finite}\}$ is Σ_3-complete while $\{i\colon W_i \text{ is finite}\}$ is only a Σ_2-complete set.

5 Specifications by Σ_2-Predicates

We call a predicate P on the recursively enumerable sets a Σ_n-predicate if the index set $M := \{i : P(W_i)\}$ is in the class Σ_n of the arithmetical hierarchy. Because in the language of winning formulas negation is allowed, the following considerations cover also the case $M \in \Pi_n$.

By use of the Rice-Shapiro theorem Σ_1-predicates can be extended unambiguously to the domain 2^ω. It is easy to show that the enumeration games with such an extended Σ_1-predicate are effectively determined. This can be proved directly by reduction to a finite game.

We now consider games for Σ_2-predicates. First we show for a special kind of such predicates that the corresponding games are effectively determined. Then we give an example for a game with a Σ_2-predicate such that none of the players has an effective winning strategy.

5.1 Σ_2-Complete Predicates with Extensional m-Reductions

In general it is not clear how Σ_n-predicates for $n > 1$ should be extended to the domain 2^ω. So we restrict the rules of enumeration games by requiring that both players have to play according to *effective* strategies. Hence, all sets enumerated during a play are always recursively enumerable. This restriction is only valid for this subsection.

A Σ_2-predicate P is called Σ_2-complete if the index set $M := \{i\colon P(W_i)\}$ is Σ_2-complete. The predicate *Finite* is an example of a Σ_2-complete predicate, because Fin $:= \{i\colon W_i \text{ is finite}\}$ is a Σ_2-complete index set. So, for every Σ_2-complete set M there are recursive functions $f, g \in R_1$ (so-called m-reductions) such that for all i:

$$(i \in \text{Fin} \iff f(i) \in M) \text{ and } (i \in M \iff g(i) \in \text{Fin}).$$

A recursive function $f \in R_1$ is *extensional* if for all i, j:

$$W_i = W_j \implies W_{f(i)} = W_{f(j)}.$$

We consider extensional m-reductions because for these reductions the Theorem of Myhill-Shepherdson is applicable:

Theorem 9 (Myhill-Shepherdson). *If $f \in R_1$ is extensional, then there exists an enumeration operator $\Phi\colon 2^\omega \to 2^\omega$ with $\Phi(W_i) = W_{f(i)}$ for all $i \in \omega$.*

The definition of an enumeration operator can be found e.g. in the book [Rog67], as well as Theorem 9 and Lemma 10. We don't state this definition because we only need one property of enumeration operators here, the continuity:

Lemma 10. *Every enumeration operator $\Phi : 2^\omega \to 2^\omega$ is continuous. I.e., for each increasing sequence $(A_s)_{s\in\omega}$ of subsets of ω:*

$$\Phi(\bigcup_{s\in\omega} A_s) = \bigcup_{s\in\omega} \Phi(A_s).$$

We are now ready for proving the following result:

Theorem 11. *Let P be a predicate such that $M := \{i\colon P(W_i)\}$ is Σ_2-complete and there are extensional m-reductions between M and Fin. Then the enumeration games with predicate P in which both players follow effective strategies are effectively determined.*

Proof. We will reduce the games with predicate P to the games with predicate *Finite*, which are effectively determined by Theorem 6. $U_1, \dots, U_n, V_1, \dots, V_n$ denote the sets which are enumerated in the games with predicate P, and $\tilde{U}_1, \dots, \tilde{U}_n, \tilde{V}_1, \dots, \tilde{V}_n$ denote the sets of the games with predicate *Finite*. Let F be the winning formula of a game with predicate P. Then $\tilde{F}$ is the winning formula of the game with predicate *Finite* built by replacing all occurrences of $P(U_i)$, $P(V_i)$ with $Finite(\tilde{U}_i)$, $Finite(\tilde{V}_i)$, respectively.

Assume w.l.o.g. that player I has an effective winning strategy in the game with winning formula $\tilde{F}$. We translate this winning strategy into the game with winning formula F.

Let Φ_f and Φ_g denote the corresponding enumeration operators from Theorem 9:

$$(\forall j)[\Phi_f(W_j) = W_{f(j)}] \text{ and } (\forall j)[\Phi_g(W_j) = W_{g(j)}].$$

Because f and g are m-reductions we have:

$$(\forall j \in \omega)[Finite(W_j) \iff P(\Phi_f(W_j))], \tag{2}$$

$$(\forall j \in \omega)[P(W_j) \iff Finite(\Phi_g(W_j))]. \tag{3}$$

In the translation we use the operators Φ_f and Φ_g to transform the enumerated sets between the two games:

1 **Translation from $\tilde{F}$ to F**
For all $i \in \{1, \dots, n\}, t \in \omega$ compute an index $\tilde{h}(i,t)$ with $\tilde{U}_i^t = W_{\tilde{h}(i,t)}$ and enumerate the set $W_{f(\tilde{h}(i,t))}$ into U_i (by *dovetailing*).

2 **Translation from F to $\tilde{F}$**
For all $i \in \{1, \dots, n\}, t \in \omega$ compute an index $h(i,t)$ with $V_i^t = W_{h(i,t)}$ and enumerate the set $W_{g(h(i,t))}$ into $\tilde{V}_i$ (by *dovetailing*).

The indices $h(i,t)$ and $\tilde{h}(i,t)$ can be computed because the sets $\tilde{U}_i^t$ and V_i^t are finite. By Lemma 10 we get for all $i = 1, \ldots, n$:

$$U_i = \bigcup_{t \in \omega} W_{f(\tilde{h}(i,t))} = \bigcup_{t \in \omega} \Phi_f(\tilde{U}_i^t) = \Phi_f(\bigcup_{t \in \omega} \tilde{U}_i^t) = \Phi_f(\tilde{U}_i),$$

$$\tilde{V}_i = \bigcup_{t \in \omega} W_{g(h(i,t))} = \bigcup_{t \in \omega} \Phi_g(V_i^t) = \Phi_g(\bigcup_{t \in \omega} V_i^t) = \Phi_g(V_i).$$

Because both players follow effective strategies (by hypothesis) the sets $\tilde{U}_i$ and V_i are all recursively enumerable. Hence the sets U_i and $\tilde{V}_i$ are recursively enumerable, too. From (2) and (3) it follows that the formula F is fulfilled iff the formula $\tilde{F}$ is fulfilled. Since player I follows an effective winning strategy in the game with winning formula $\tilde{F}$, he also wins the game with winning formula F. Thus, we have constructed an effective winning strategy for player I in the game with winning formula F. □

5.2 A Game which is not Effectively Determined

It can be shown that Theorem 11 does not hold if the hypothesis 'extensional' is omitted [Ott95]. However, the counterexample looks somewhat contrived.

We now present a more natural example of a specification which is not effectively determined (however, in this case the Σ_2-predicate is not m-complete).

It is well-known that for every r.e. set A the index set $\{i : W_i \not\subseteq A\}$ belongs to Σ_2.

Theorem 12. *There is a recursively enumerable set A such that the enumeration game with winning formula*

$$F := [U_1 \subseteq A \leftrightarrow (V_1 \subseteq A \vee V_2 \subseteq A)]$$

in which both players follow effective strategies is not effectively determined.

Proof sketch. For every A, player I has a winning strategy recursive in A: As long as V_1^t and V_2^t are subsets of A, player I does nothing. If for the first time $V_1^t \not\subseteq A \wedge V_2^t \not\subseteq A$, then player I chooses an $x \in V_1^t - A$ and puts x into U_1^{t+1}.

Now it is easy to see that for every strategy τ of player II there is an effective strategy of player I which wins against τ.

The r.e. sets A for which player I has an effective winning strategy can be characterized as follows.

Claim: Player I has an effective winning strategy in the enumeration game with winning formula

$$F := [U_1 \subseteq A \leftrightarrow (V_1 \subseteq A \vee V_2 \subseteq A)]$$

iff there is a recursive function f such that for all x, y:

$$W_{f(x,y)} \subseteq A \iff (x \in A \ \vee \ y \in A).$$

Using a finite injury priority argument one can construct an r.e. set A which does not satisfy the condition of the claim. Thus, for the corresponding game neither player I nor player II has an effective winning strategy. □

6 Enumeration Games on Recursive Sets

We now consider enumeration games in which the players enumerate characteristic functions instead of sets. Consequently, if both players follow effective strategies the enumerated games are recursive. Therefore we call them *games on recursive sets.*

In his moves player II defines the values of the characteristic functions $\chi_{V_1}(x), \ldots, \chi_{V_n}(x)$ successively for $x = 0, 1, 2, \ldots$, i.e., in each move he chooses an element from the alphabet $\{0,1\}^n$. Player I is allowed to define the values of $\chi_{U_1}(x), \ldots, \chi_{U_n}(x)$ for an x such that $\chi_{V_1}(x), \ldots, \chi_{V_n}(x)$ are already defined, i.e., he extends the corresponding move $b \in \{0,1\}^n$ from player II with a vector $a \in \{0,1\}^n$ and produces the word ba. Player I is also allowed to pass in his moves. But he must extend all moves from player II exactly once during a play. In this case we call the play *complete.* However, for each move of player II he can wait arbitrary long until he extends it. By convention player I loses all incomplete plays. We let player II do the first move.

In the above definition the options of player I and player II are asymmetric. However, this is just what is needed to decide the uniformly valid $\forall\exists$-sentences in $\mathcal{B}$, the boolean algebra of recursive sets (see Corollary 14). An $\forall\exists$-sentence $S = (\forall V_1 \ldots \forall V_n)(\exists U_1 \ldots \exists U_n) F[V_1, \ldots, V_n, U_1, \ldots, U_n]$ with matrix F is called *uniformly* valid in $\mathcal{B}$ if there is an effective procedure to compute from indices $i_1, \ldots, i_n$ of characteristic functions of V_i's indices $j_1, \ldots, j_n$ of characteristic functions of the U_j's such that $F[M_{i_1}, \ldots, M_{i_n}, M_{j_1}, \ldots, M_{j_n}]$ holds. Here M_k denotes the recursive set with characteristic function φ_k.

For games on recursive sets we can allow the entire specification language of Lachlan still preserving effective determinacy:

Theorem 13. *The enumeration games on recursive sets with the predicates* Infinite *and* Card$_k$ *for* $k \in \omega$ *and the set operations* $\cap$, $\cup$ *and* ^{C} *are effectively determined by reductions to graph games.*

Proof. If player I extends a move $b = b_1, \ldots, b_n \in \{0,1\}^n$ of player II with $a = a_1, \ldots, a_n \in \{0,1\}^n$ this means that the corresponding $x \in \omega$ is enumerated into the set

$$S(ba) := \bigcap_{a_i=1} U_i \cap \bigcap_{b_i=1} V_i \cap \bigcap_{a_i=0} U_i^C \cap \bigcap_{b_i=0} V_i^C.$$

For $ab \neq a'b'$ the sets $S(ab)$ and $S(a'b')$ never have an element in common. Each set expression built from the sets $U_1, \ldots, U_n, V_1, \ldots, V_n$ and the operations $\cap$, $\cup$ and ^{C} can be represented as a disjoint union of sets $S(c)$ where $c \in \{0,1\}^{2n}$. Because of (1) and

$$Card_k\Big(\bigcup_{c \in C} S(c)\Big) \iff \sum_{c \in C} |S(c)| = k \iff \bigvee_{\substack{\{k_c \in \omega:\ c \in C\}\\ \sum_{c \in C} k_c = k}} \ \bigwedge_{c \in C} Card_{k_c}(S(c))$$

for $C \subseteq \{0,1\}^{2n}$, we can restrict the specification language by admitting only set expressions $S(c)$ for $c \in \{0,1\}^{2n}$.

With every play of the game an interpretation of the winning formulas is associated:

$$\mathit{Infinite}(S(c)) \text{ is } \mathit{true} \iff c \text{ is produced infinitely often,}$$

$$\mathit{Card}_k(S(c)) \text{ is } \mathit{true} \iff c \text{ is produced exactly } k \text{ times.}$$

Player I wins a play in the game with winning formula F iff the play is complete and F is true under this interpretation.

We now describe how these games can be reduced to a special kind of games, in which the rules are more restrictive. We call the original games the *target games* and the second games *restricted games.* The reductions of restricted games to graph games are straightforward.

Restricted Games: We fix a winning formula F in the target game. Let k_1 be a number such that $k < k_1$ for all atoms $\mathit{Card}_k(S(c))$ occurring in F.

A central idea of the reduction is that if player II plays $m := 2^n k_1$-times the same move $b \in \{0,1\}^n$, then at least one word ba will be produced at least k_1-times. So there is no more chance for atoms $\mathit{Card}_k(S(ba))$ occurring in F to become *true*.

The rules of the restricted games are as follows. At stage $t = 1$ player II plays a single move b_1^1 and m-times a move b_2^1 which we indicate by writing $(b_2^1)^m$. At stage $t = 2$ player I extends b_1^1 to $b_1^1 a_1^2$, and k_1 moves from $(b_2^1)^m$ with the same element a_2^2. At stage $t = 3$ player II again plays a single move b_1^3 and a *block* $(b_2^3)^m$. At stage $t = 4$ player I accordingly extends b_1^3 and k_1 moves from $(b_2^3)^m$ with a_1^4 and a_2^4, respectively. But additionally he extends all $m - k_1$ remaining moves from the block $(b_2^1)^m$. These $m - k_1$ extensions are called the *update* in state t. From now on the following stages proceed like the stages 3 and 4.

Reducing target games to restricted games: We have to show that if a player has an effective winning strategy in the restricted game with formula F, this player also has an effective winning strategy in the target game. For player I this is easy. He only has to reorder the moves of player II in the target game into the form $b_1^1(b_2^1)^m b_1^2(b_2^2)^m \ldots$. This is always possible, because the alphabet $\{0,1\}^n$ is finite and player I can pass in the target game as long as there are not enough moves of player II to build the next block. His strategy in the restricted games then tells him, how to extend all moves to win the game.

Assume now that player II has an effective winning strategy in the restricted game. There occurs the following problem. Consider the moves $b_1^t(b_2^t)^m$ from player II at a stage $t \geq 3$ in the restricted game. Player II can translate these moves by playing correspondingly one time b_1^t and m-times b_2^t in the target game. Now he has to translate the next moves from player I from the target game into the restricted game. For this he needs the extension of b_1^t, k_1 equal extensions of the played b_2^t's, and all extensions of the moves b_2^{t-2}. But by passing, player I can wait with these extensions as long as he wants to, while player II has to perform a proper move in each step. And player II gets the next suggestion, how to move, from his strategy in the restricted game not earlier than he has simulated the next moves of player I.

Player II solves this problem by playing additional moves b_2^t, until player I has done all extensions needed for the next translation step. The intuition is that player I already can produce at least k_1-times the word $b_2^t a$ for each $a \in \{0,1\}^n$, if he wants to. In other words, player I gets no further advantage.

In particular, at each stage $t \geq 3$ player II waits, until all of his b_2^{t-2}-moves from the stage $t-2$ have been extended. These may be more than m extensions. For the update in stage t he has to select exactly $m-k_1$ of those extensions which are not among the k_1 extensions a_2^{t-2} of stage $t-2$. He selects all extensions which occur less than k_1-times. From each of the others (excluding the a_2^{t-2}-extensions) he selects k_1 occurrences. He fills up this selection with arbitrary additional extensions of the b_2^{t-2}-moves such that at all exactly $m-k_1$ extensions are selected. Player II then translates the selected extensions into the restricted game.

At each stage player II plays at most finitely many additional moves in the target game. So he only plays a move infinitely often iff the appropriate move also occurs infinitely often in the restricted game. By the translation an extension occurs infinitely often in the target game iff it occurs infinitely often in the restricted game. For the extensions which occur less than k_1-times there is a one-to-one correspondence between the two games. Hence in both plays exactly the same atomic formulas are valid. Therefore the translated strategy is an effective winning strategy for player II in the target game.

Reducing restricted games to graph games: The nodes of the graph games are composed of three types of information. Of course, we need the letters b_1, b_2 and a_1, a_2 used in the current moves, and for each $a \in \{0,1\}^n$ the number of extensions in the current update step. The nodes in Q_{II}^n contain the b_i, and the nodes in Q_{I}^n the a_i and the update information.

In order to define the edges and the winning sets we also need some book-keeping of the letters used in preceeding moves. To the nodes of player II we add a component b_3 which stores the component b_2 of the preceeding node of player II. The nodes of player I are equipped with components b_1, b_2, b_3 holding the values of the corresponding components of the preceeding node of player II.

At last, we need a counter in each node analogously to the proof of Theorem 7. The counter holds the number of occurences of each word $ba \in \{0,1\}^{2n}$. We only count until the boundary k_1 is reached.

Now it is straightforward to define the edges and the winning sets. For the definition of $\Omega(\mathit{Infinite}(S(c)))$ one has to notice that there are three possibilities of building a word $c \in \{0,1\}^{2n}$: as a single extension $b_1 a_1$, as a block extension $b_2 a_2$ or as an extension of b_3 in an update step. Because there is a one-to-one correspondence between the moves in the two games, it is easy to translate strategies from the graph game into the restricted game. □

An interesting consequence of the given proof is that if player I has a winning strategy, he actually has a winning strategy which extends every move of player

II after a constant amount of time. This is because he only has to await a constant number of player II-moves, until he can build the next input $b_1^t(b_2^t)^m$ for the restricted game.

Corollary 14. *The* $\forall\exists$*-sentences which are uniformly valid in the boolean algebra of recursive sets are decidable.*

Proof sketch. Given an $\forall\exists$-sentence S with matrix F we consider the enumeration game on recursive sets with winning formula F. The sets which are universally quantified in S belong to player II, the sets which are existentially quantified belong to player I. Similarly as in Proposition 2 one can show that S is uniformly valid in the boolean algebra of recursive sets iff player I has an effective winning strategy. The latter is decidable by Theorem 13. □

7 Conclusion

There are many more interesting specification languages which remain to be considered. An open problem of Lachlan [Lac70] is whether the enumeration games with predicates $Card_0$ and the set operations $\cap, \cup$ and ^{C} are effectively determined. An enumeration game on partial functions was studied in [Ott95] motivated by a question from inductive inference. Here the effective determinacy result yields a decision procedure for parallel learning [KS94].

In this paper we have presented the notion of enumeration game and clarified the connection with graph games by giving several nontrivial reductions. Enumeration games may be a suitable framework for modelling reactive systems. From the standpoint of computability they offer a rich source for studying effective strategies. In contrast, if recursive games are approached by effectivizing the definition of Borel games, then already in the basic case of recursive winning conditions there may be only non-arithmetical winning strategies [Bla72].

Acknowledgement: We would like to thank Susanne Kaufmann for helpful discussions.

References

[ALW89] Martin Abadi, Leslie Lamport, Pierre Wolper. Realizable and unrealizable specifications of reactive systems. In *Proc. of 16th Int'l Colloquium on Automata, Languages and Programming*, Lect. Notes in Comput. Sci., Vol. 372, pages 1–17. Springer-Verlag, 1989.

[BL69] J. Richard Büchi, Lawrence H. Landweber. Solving sequential conditions by finite-state strategies. *Trans. Amer. Math. Soc.*, 138:295–311, 1969.

[Bla72] Andreas Blass. Complexity of winning strategies. *Discrete Mathematics*, 3:295–300, 1972.

[Chu63] Alonzo Church. Logic, arithmetic and automata. In *Proceedings of the International Congress of Mathematicians, August 1962*, pages 23–35, Stockholm, 1963.

[Gur89] Yuri Gurevich. The logic in computer science column: Infinite games. *Bulletin of the European Association for Theoretical Computer Science*, 38:93–100, 1989.

[KS94] Martin Kummer, Frank Stephan. Inclusion problems in parallel learning and games. *Proceedings of the Seventh Annual ACM Conference on Computational Learning Theory, COLT 94*, pages 287-298, ACM Press, 1994.

[Lac70] Alistair H. Lachlan. On some games which are relevant to the theory of recursively enumerable sets. *Ann. of Math.*, 91(2):291–310, 1970.

[Les95] Helmut Lescow. On Polynomial-Size Programs Winning Finite-State Games. *CAV: International Conference on Computer Aided Verification*, Lect. Notes in Comput. Sci., Vol. 939, pages 239–252. Springer-Verlag, 1995.

[McN93] Robert McNaughton. Infinite games played on finite graphs. *Annals of Pure and Applied Logic*, 65:149–184, 1993.

[Mos89] Yiannis N. Moschovakis. A game-theoretic modeling of concurrency. In *Proceedings, Fourth Annual Symposium on Logic in Computer Science*, pages 154–163. IEEE Computer Society Press, 1989.

[MPS95] Oded Maler, Amir Pnueli, Joseph Sifakis. On the synthesis of discrete controllers for timed systems. In *STACS 95*, Lect. Notes in Comput. Sci., Vol. 900, pages 229–242. Springer-Verlag, 1995.

[NY92] Anil Nerode, Alexander Yakhnis. Modelling hybrid systems as games. Technical Report 92-36, Mathematical Sciences Institute, Cornell University, October 1992.

[NYY92] Anil Nerode, Alexander Yakhnis, Vladimir Yakhnis. Concurrent programs as strategies in games. In *Logic from Computer Science: Proceedings of a Workshop held November 13-17, 1989.* Springer-Verlag, 1992.

[Odi89] Piergiorgio Odifreddi. *Classical recursion theory.* North-Holland, Amsterdam, 1989.

[Ott95] Matthias Ott. Strategien in Aufzählungsspielen. Diplomarbeit, Institut für Logik, Komplexität und Deduktionssysteme, Universität Karlsruhe, February 1995.

[PR89] Amir Pnueli, Roni Rosner. On the synthesis of a reactive module. In *Conference Record of the Sixteenth Annual ACM Symposium on Principles of Programming Languages*, pages 179–190, Austin, Texas, 1989.

[Rog67] Hartley Rogers. *Theory of recursive functions and effective computability.* McGraw-Hill, New York, 1967.

[Soa87] Robert I. Soare. *Recursively enumerable sets and degrees.* Perspectives in Mathematical Logic. Springer-Verlag, Berlin, 1987.

[Tho90] Wolfgang Thomas. Automata on infinite objects. In Jan van Leeuwen, editor, *Handbook of Theoretical Computer Science*, pages 133–191. Elsevier Science Publishers B. V., 1990.

[Tho95] Wolfgang Thomas. On the synthesis of strategies in infinite games. In *STACS 95*, Lect. Notes in Comput. Sci., Vol. 900, pages 1–13. Springer-Verlag, 1995.

[TW94] J. G. Thistle, W. M. Wonham. Supervision of infinite behaviour of discrete-event systems. *SIAM Journal on Control and Optimization*, 32(4):1098–1113, 1994.

[WD91] Howard Wong-Toi, David L. Dill. Synthesizing processes and schedulers from temporal specifications. In *Computer-Aided Verification '90*, pages 177–186. American Mathematical Society, 1991.

Bounded Fixed-Point Definability and Tabular Recognition of Languages

Hans Leiß

Centrum für Informations-
und Sprachverarbeitung
Universität München
Wagmüllerstr. 23
D-80538 München
leiss@cis.uni-muenchen.de

Abstract. By relating positive inductive definitions to space-bounded computations of alternating Turing machines, Rounds, *Comp. Linguistics 14, 1988*, has given uniform grammatical characterizations of the *EXPTIME* and *PTIME* languages. But his proof gives fairly poor bounds for language recognition with context-free resp. head grammars.
We improve Rounds' analysis in two respects: first, we introduce a modified class of language definitions that allow restricted forms of negative inductions, and second, we show how to build table-driven recognizers from such definitions. For a wide and natural class of language definitions we thereby obtain fairly efficient recognizers; we can recognize the boolean closure of context-free resp. head languages in the well-known $O(n^3)$ resp. $O(n^6)$ steps on a *RAM*. Our 'bounded' fixed-point formulas apparently can not define an arbitrary *PTIME* language.
Our method is based on the existence of fixed-points for a class of operators that need neither be monotone nor increasing, but assume a norm or at least a well-founded quasi-ordering on the underlying set.

1 Introduction

Vardi[14] and Immerman[7] have shown that languages $L \in PTIME$ are those that can be defined by a formula φ in a first-order relational language (with ordering) extended by a least-fixed-point operator:

$$L = L(\varphi) := \{ w \in \Sigma^* \mid \mathcal{A}_w \models \varphi(0, |w|) \}, \tag{1}$$

where a word $w = a_1 \cdots a_{|w|}$ over a finite alphabet Σ is seen as the finite relational structure

$$\mathcal{A}_w := (|w| + 1, +, \cdot, <, R_a)_{a \in \Sigma}, \tag{2}$$

an initial segment of the natural numbers $\mathcal{N} = (I\!N, +, \cdot, <)$ (modulo $|w| + 1$), expanded by relations R_a between positions connected by a in w. Rounds[12] has given a characterization of the *EXPTIME* languages in the same spirit, implicitly using 'initial segments' of the monoid $\mathcal{L} = (\Sigma^*, \cdot, a)_{a \in \Sigma}$, i.e. finite models

$$\mathcal{L}^{\leq |w|} = (\Sigma^{\leq |w|}, \cdot, a)_{a \in \Sigma},$$

where $\Sigma^{\leq n}$ is the set of words over Σ whose length is at most n. Moreover, Rounds shows that both the *PTIME* and his *EXPTIME* characterization have a uniform proof: a least fixed-point formula φ corresponds to a space-bounded alternating Turing machine $\mathcal{M}_\varphi$ (modified to cover fixed-points). For φ in the arithmetical language, a binary representation of numbers (for positions in w) leads to a $log(n)$-space-bounded machine $\mathcal{M}_\varphi$, hence

$$L(\varphi) = L(\mathcal{M}_\varphi) \in ASPACE(\log n) = PTIME,$$

while for φ in the language of concatenation, one gets an n-space-bounded machine $\mathcal{M}_\varphi$, and hence

$$L(\varphi) = L(\mathcal{M}_\varphi) \in ASPACE(n) = EXPTIME.$$

In both cases, the positive inductive definition φ leads to a complexity bound for recognition of $L(\varphi)$ with deterministic Turing machines: in the *PTIME* case, the number of configurations of the corresponding *ATM* $\mathcal{M}_\varphi$ is $O(|w|^{p+3})$ where $p := |free(\varphi)| + |bound(\varphi)|$, and hence, by a result of Chandra e.a.[1], a simulation of $\mathcal{M}_\varphi$ by a *DTM* can be done in $O(|w|^{2(p+3)})$ steps.

Rounds counts $p = 3$ for context-free grammars and hence obtains a *DTM*-recognition algorithm of time complexity $O(|w|^{12})$ for context-free languages. This is far worse than the well-known algorithms by Cocke, Younger, Kasami, and Earley that do it in $O(|w|^3)$ steps on a *RAM* or even a Turing machine (see Harrison[4], p.437 ff). A similar defect of $O(n^{18})$ versus a known bound of $O(n^6)$ (cf. Joshi and Vijay-Shanker[15]) resulted in the case of head grammars, a class of grammars studied in theoretical linguistics (c.f. Section 5.1). [1]

Our aim was to understand why the method yields very poor bounds in these cases and what improvement on an abstract level could be made in reading off the recognition complexity from an inductive language definition. Since the best known recognition algorithms use a well-formed substring table to store intermediate results, our second aim was to find a logical characterization of 'languages that admit a tabular parser'.

First, we observe that the monotonicity of the induction behind least-fixed-point definitions of context-free languages is not essential – neither for the existence of fixed points nor for the efficiency of language recognition. Instead, we use a fixed-point construction for generally non-monotone, 'bounded' operators on sets with a reflexive transitive relation $\leq$ where $<$ is well-founded.

Second, we give a syntactic characterization of first-order formulas $\varphi(x, S)$ that define such operators and are invariant under going from structures $\mathcal{A}$ to 'local' substructures $\mathcal{A}^{\leq a}$ consisting of all elements $b \leq a$ in $\mathcal{A}$, in the sense that

$$\mathcal{A} \models \varphi(a, B) \iff \mathcal{A}^{\leq a} \models \varphi(a, \{\, b \in B \mid b < a \,\}).$$

Interpreting these 'bounded' formulas over $\mathcal{L}$ and exploiting more closely the syntactic form of context-free grammars, the construction of recognition tables

[1] Rounds' $p = 3$ is the *quantifier depth* of φ for a context-free grammar G in Chomsky normal form, but the *number* p of bound individual quantifiers of φ is $3n$, if G has n nonterminals A with a branching rule $A \rightarrow B\,C$. Thus, one only obtains a bound of $O(|w|^{2(3n+3)})$ for context-free and $O(|w|^{2(6n+3)})$ for head-languages.

and the staging of a bounded induction on certain finite substructures $\mathcal{L}^{\leq w}$ of $\mathcal{L}$ turn out to be essentially the same.

The efficiency of the tabular recognizers of Cocke e.a. depends on two parameters: the size of the table and the effort to compute a new table entry from given ones, which reflects a sharing of subcomputations by using stored results.

Restricting a positive induction over $\mathcal{L}$ to $\mathcal{L}^{\leq |w|}$ would in general define a language in *EXPTIME*. To obtain small recognition tables, we interprete bounded inductive definitions in the smaller finite structures

$$\mathcal{L}^{\leq w} = (\Sigma^{\leq w}, \cdot, a)_{a \in \Sigma},$$

where $\Sigma^{\leq w}$ is the set of subwords of w: for intuitively context-free language definitions $\varphi(x)$, we expect the global reading of φ in the infinite structure $\mathcal{L}$ to coincide with its local readings in the finite structures $\mathcal{L}^{\leq w}$, i.e.

$$\{\, w \in \Sigma^* \mid \mathcal{L} \models \varphi(w) \,\} = \{\, w \in \Sigma^* \mid \mathcal{L}^{\leq w} \models \varphi(w) \,\}. \tag{3}$$

This reflects, we think, the proper *logical notion*[2] *of context-independence*: grammatical properties of a string depend only on the grammatical properties of its substrings. All our bounded fixed-point formulas satisfy (3) and define operators Γ which reach their fixed point in $O(|w|^2)$ many stages of constant size, corresponding to a small recognition table with $O(|w|^2)$ fields.

The efficiency of computing a table entry is related to a peculiarity of individual quantification in the language definition that has been overlooked in Rounds' analysis. Not only do context-free or head grammars just quantify over *sub*strings of the input; more restrictively, they *decompose* it into segments of non-overlapping consecutive substrings. Restricting individual quantifiers accordingly, we introduce a class of 'decomposition grammars' that contain the boolean closure of context free ones. For these the tabular recognizers yield $O(n^3)$ recognition algorithms on a *RAM*, since computing a field can be done in $O(|w|)$ steps.

Head grammars, which define languages of splitted strings – i.e. binary relations between strings –, are similar to context-free grammars, except that concatenation is replaced by a number of 'head wrapping' operations. We generalize these to a class of operations on m-tuples of strings. Decomposition grammars using these operations define languages of strings with m segments, and the table-recognizers we obtain yield $O(n^{3m})$ recognition algorithms; a subclass has recently been introduced by Hotz and Pitsch[6]. In particular, a language in the boolean closure of the head languages is recognized in $O(n^6)$ steps.

2 Non-Monotone Operators with Fixed Points

For easier comparison we recall the Tarski/Knaster-fixed-point construction for monotone operators. An operator $\Gamma : 2^A \rightarrow 2^A$ is *monotone*, if $\Gamma(S) \subseteq \Gamma(T)$

[2] The *technical* notion of context-freeness can be expressed in second-order logic, cf. Lautemann and Schwentick[8], or by regular fixed-point expressions, cf. Leiß[9]. We remark that structures $\mathcal{A}_w$ and binary second order quantifieres are used in [8], but with structures $\mathcal{L}^{\leq w}$ one can use fixed-point formulas of monadic second order logic.

whenever $S \subseteq T \subseteq A$, and Γ is *increasing* (or *inflationary*, see Gurevich and Shelah[3]), if $S \subseteq \Gamma(S)$ for each $S \subseteq A$.

Theorem 1 (Tarski/Knaster). *If $\Gamma : 2^A \to 2^A$ is monotone or increasing, then Γ has a distinguished fixed point $\Gamma^\infty \subseteq A$, defined in stages $\Gamma^{<\alpha} \subseteq A$ by*

$$\Gamma^\infty := \bigcup\{\, \Gamma(\Gamma^{<\alpha}) \mid \alpha \textit{ an ordinal}\}, \quad \Gamma^{<\alpha} := \bigcup\{\, \Gamma(\Gamma^{<\beta}) \mid \beta < \alpha \,\}. \tag{4}$$

Recall that Γ^∞ is the least fixed point if Γ is monotone, but not in general.

A *norm* on a set S is a function $|\cdot| : S \to \eta$ onto an ordinal η. Each monotone operator Γ on A gives rise to a norm on its fixed point Γ^∞ by associating to each $a \in \Gamma^\infty$ the least ordinal α such that $a \in \Gamma(\Gamma^{<\alpha})$. Conversely, in situations where a norm or just a well-founded transitive relation $<$ on the universe is given, there are additional (definable) operators that do have fixed points.

Definition 2. Let $(A, \leq)$ be a quasi-ordering, i.e. a set A with a reflexive and transitive relation $\leq$. For $a, b \in A$, define $a < b :\iff a \leq b \wedge b \not\leq a$ and $a \sim b :\iff a \leq b \wedge b \leq a$, and for $S \subseteq A$ use

$$S^{\leq a} := \{\, b \in S \mid b \leq a \,\},\ S^{<a} := \{\, b \in S \mid b < a \,\},\ S^{a} := \{\, b \in S \mid b \sim a \,\}. \tag{5}$$

We call $\leq$ a *well-founded quasi-ordering on A*, if $\leq$ is a quasi-ordering and $<$ is well-founded. An operator $\Gamma := (\Gamma_1, \ldots, \Gamma_n)$ with $\Gamma_i : 2^A \times \cdots \times 2^A \to 2^A$ is called *$<$-bounded*, if for each Γ_i, each $a \in A$ and all sets $S_1, \ldots, S_n \subseteq A$,

$$a \in \Gamma_i(S_1, \ldots, S_n) \iff a \in \Gamma_i(S_1^{<a}, \ldots, S_n^{<a}).$$

Γ is *norm-bounded*, if $(A, \leq)$ is given by a norm $|\cdot| : A \to \eta$, with $a \leq b$ iff $|a| \leq_{On} |b|$.

Example 1. If $A = \{a, b, c\}$ with $a < b \not\leq c$ and $a < c \not\leq b$, the operator $\Gamma(S) :=$ **if** $a \in S$ **then** $\{b\}$ **else** $\{c\}$ is $<$-bounded, but neither monotone nor increasing.

The relations $\leq$ and $<$ are invariant under the equivalence $\sim$, and $S^{<a}$, $S^{\leq a}$ and S^a depend on the equivalence class $[a]$ of a only. We write $S^{<|a|}$ etc. when $\leq$ on A comes from a norm. Well-foundedness of $<$ holds trivially in all finite structures. In the unary case, Γ is $<$-bounded iff $\Gamma(S)^a = \Gamma(S^{<a})^a$ for all $a \in A$ and $S \subseteq A$, whence $\Gamma(S) = \bigcup\{\, \Gamma(S^{<a})^a \mid a \in A \,\}$ for all $S \subseteq A$.

Theorem 3. *Each $<$-bounded operator $\Gamma := (\Gamma_1, \ldots, \Gamma_n) : (2^A)^n \to (2^A)^n$ on a well-founded quasi-ordering $(A, \leq)$ has a unique fixed-point $\Gamma^\infty = (\Gamma_1^\infty, \ldots, \Gamma_n^\infty)$, where the Γ_i^∞ are simultaneously defined by*

$$\begin{aligned} \Gamma_i^\infty &:= \bigcup\{\, \Gamma_i(\Gamma_1^{<a}, \ldots, \Gamma_n^{<a})^a \mid a \in A \,\} \quad \textit{and} \\ \Gamma_i^{<a} &:= \bigcup\{\, \Gamma_i(\Gamma_1^{<b}, \ldots, \Gamma_n^{<b})^b \mid b < a \,\}. \end{aligned}$$

In fact,

$$\begin{aligned} \Gamma_i(\Gamma_1^{<a}, \ldots, \Gamma_n^{<a})^a &= \{\, b \sim a \mid b \in \Gamma_i(\Gamma_1^{<b}, \ldots, \Gamma_n^{<b}) \,\}, \\ \Gamma_i^\infty &= \{\, b \in A \mid b \in \Gamma_i(\Gamma_1^{<b}, \ldots, \Gamma_n^{<b}) \,\}. \end{aligned}$$

The difference between the subset $S^{<a}$ of $S \subseteq A$ and the $\Gamma^{<a} = (\Gamma_1^{<a}, \dots, \Gamma_n^{<a})$ obtained from an operator Γ should be clear from the context.

Proof. Consider the unary case. Since $<$ is well-founded, $\Gamma^{<a}$ is well-defined. Note that $a \sim b$ implies $\Gamma^{<a} = \Gamma^{<b}$ and so $\Gamma(\Gamma^{<a})^a = \Gamma(\Gamma^{<b})^b$. We get

$$\Gamma(\Gamma^{<a})^a = \{ b \sim a \mid b \in \Gamma(\Gamma^{<a}) \} = \{ b \sim a \mid b \in \Gamma(\Gamma^{<b}) \},$$

from which the characterization for Γ^∞ follows. For each $a \in A$ we have

$$(\Gamma^\infty)^a = \Gamma^\infty \cap [a] = \bigcup \{ \Gamma(\Gamma^{<b}) \cap [b] \cap [a] \mid b \in A \}$$
$$= \bigcup \{ \Gamma(\Gamma^{<b})^b \mid b \sim a \} = \Gamma(\Gamma^{<a})^a, \qquad \text{and so}$$
$$(\Gamma^\infty)^{<a} = \bigcup \{ (\Gamma^\infty)^b \mid b < a \} = \bigcup \{ \Gamma(\Gamma^{<b})^b \mid b < a \} = \Gamma^{<a}.$$

Putting these together, we obtain that Γ^∞ is a fixed point of Γ:

$$\Gamma^\infty = \bigcup \{ \Gamma(\Gamma^{<a})^a \mid a \in A \} = \bigcup \{ \Gamma((\Gamma^\infty)^{<a})^a \mid a \in A \}$$
$$= \bigcup \{ \Gamma(\Gamma^\infty)^a \mid a \in A \} = \Gamma(\Gamma^\infty),$$

using the $<$-boundedness of Γ in the third step. If $S = \Gamma(S)$ is another fixed point, then $S^b = \Gamma(S)^b = \Gamma(S^{<b})^b$ for each b, and by well-foundedness of $<$ one gets $\Gamma^{<a} = S^{<a}$ for each $a \in A$. This gives $\Gamma^\infty = \bigcup \{ \Gamma(S^{<a})^a \mid a \in A \} = S$.

We still have $\Gamma^{<a} \subseteq \Gamma^{<b}$ for $a \leq b$. The stages are similar to the stages $\Gamma^{<\alpha} = \bigcup \{ \Gamma(\Gamma^{<\beta}) \mid \beta < \alpha \}$ of Tarski's construction for monotone operators. The basic difference is that from $\Gamma(\Gamma^{<b})$ we only select the $c \sim b$, while for elements $c \not\sim b$, membership in Γ^∞ is fixed at other stages. As with monotone operators, nested recursions can be transformed into simultaneous ones:

Lemma 4. *Let $\Gamma, \Delta : 2^A \times 2^A \to 2^A$ be $<$-bounded on the well-founded quasi-ordering $(A, \leq)$. Then $\Delta_S(T) := \Delta(S,T)$ and $\Theta(S) := \Gamma(S, \Delta_S^\infty)$ are $<$-bounded operators on 2^A, and Θ^∞ is the first component Γ^∞ of the fixed-point of the simultaneous $<$-bounded operator (Γ, Δ).*

The class of $<$-bounded operators can be extended somewhat, without loosing the existence of fixed points. Call $\Gamma : 2^A \to 2^A$ *$\leq$-bounded*, if for each $a \in A$ and $S \subseteq A$, $a \in \Gamma(S)$ iff $a \in \Gamma(S^{\leq a})$. Fixed points can no longer be constructed via

$$\Gamma^{\leq a} := \bigcup \{ \Gamma(\Gamma^{\leq b})^b \mid b \leq a \},$$

as this would not be well-defined. We have to insist that $\Gamma(S)^a$ monotonically depends on S^a. We call Γ *locally monotone*, if $\Gamma(S^{\leq a})^a \subseteq \Gamma(T^{\leq a})^a$ for each $a \in A$ and $S, T \subseteq A$ such that $S^{<a} = T^{<a}$ and $S^a \subseteq T^a$.

Theorem 5. *If Γ is $\leq$-bounded and locally monotone on a well-founded quasi-ordering $(A, \leq)$, then Γ has a fixed point Γ^∞, which is defined using*

$$\Gamma^\infty := \bigcup \{ \Gamma(\Gamma^{\leq a})^a \mid a \in A \}, \qquad \Gamma^{<a} := \bigcup \{ \Gamma(\Gamma^{\leq b})^b \mid b < a \},$$
$$\Gamma^{\leq a} := \bigcup \{ \Gamma_a^{<\beta} \mid \beta \in On \}, \qquad \Gamma_a^{<\beta} := \Gamma^{<a} \cup \bigcup \{ \Gamma(\Gamma_a^{<\gamma})^a \mid \gamma < \beta \},$$

for elements $a \in A$ and ordinals β. In fact, $\Gamma^\infty = \{ a \in A \mid a \in \Gamma(\Gamma^{\leq a}) \}$.

3 Definable Bounded Fixed-Point Operators

To apply the fixed-point constructions of the previous section on first-order structures $\mathcal{A}$ with a norm $|\cdot| : A \rightarrow \eta$, or a well-founded quasi-ordering $\leq$ on A, we will consider formulas $\varphi(x, S)$ with a free set variable S such that

$$\mathcal{A} \models \forall S \forall x\, (\varphi(x,S) \leftrightarrow \varphi(x, S^{<|x|})), \text{ resp. } \mathcal{A} \models \forall S \forall x\, (\varphi(x,S) \leftrightarrow \varphi(x, S^{<x})).$$

Each such formula defines a norm- resp. <-bounded operator

$$\Gamma_\varphi(S) := \{\, a \in A \mid \mathcal{A} \models \varphi(a, S)\,\}$$

on A whose fixed-point Γ_φ^∞ is taken as the meaning of a new predicate $\mu S \lambda x \varphi$. Our intended application is the structure $\mathcal{A} = \mathcal{L}$ of strings over a finite alphabet Σ, with $|\cdot|$ being the length of strings and $\leq$ the substring relation.

Definition 6. *Concatenation bounded fixed-point formulas* over Σ, or *CBFP-formulas*, are given by

$$\begin{aligned} \varphi :\equiv\ & x = a \mid x_1 = x_2 \mid x_1 = x_2 \cdot x_3 \mid S(x) && (a \in \Sigma) \\ & \mid \neg\varphi_1 \mid (\varphi_1 \vee \varphi_2) \mid \exists x_1 < x_2\, \varphi && (x_1 \not\equiv x_2) \\ & \mid \mu(S_1, \ldots, S_n)(\lambda x_1\, \varphi_1, \ldots, \lambda x_n\, \varphi_n)(x), \end{aligned}$$

where in the last clause, the set variables S_i and individual variables x_i are pairwise distinct, $\mathit{freeIndV}(\varphi_i) \subseteq \{\, x_i\,\}$, and no φ_i contains an atomic subformula $S(x_i)$ with a set variable S (not necessarily among $S_1, \ldots, S_n$).

Remark. Officially, we consider $x = a$ and $x = y \cdot z$ as syntactic sugar for atomic formulas $a(x)$ and $Cat(x, y, z)$ in a *relational* language. We use $x = \epsilon$ for the formula saying that x is neither a letter nor composed of strict substrings.

Our 'bounded fixed point' formulas are different from those of 'bounded fixed point logic' as described in Ebbinghaus and Flum[2], Section 7.7.

Definition 7. Let $\mathcal{L} = (\Sigma^*, \cdot, \{a\})_{a \in \Sigma}$ be the set of all finite strings over the alphabet Σ, equipped with the concatenation relation $\cdot$ and predicates for the letters a. Let $<$ be the relation of strict subword (resp. stricly shorter word). Satisfaction in $\mathcal{L}$ of a bounded formula $\varphi(y_1, \ldots, y_n, S_1, \ldots, S_k)$ under an environment $[\mathbf{v}, \mathbf{R}] = [v_1, \ldots, v_n, R_1, \ldots, R_k]$ is defined via

$$\begin{aligned} &\mathcal{L} \models \exists y_{n+1} < y_i\, \varphi\, [\mathbf{v}, \mathbf{R}] < \iff \text{there is } v_{n+1} < v_i \text{ with } \mathcal{L} \models \varphi[\mathbf{v}, v_{n+1}, \mathbf{R}] \\ &\mathcal{L} \models (\mu(S_{k+1}, \ldots, S_{k+m}).(\lambda x_1.\varphi_1, \ldots, \lambda x_m.\varphi_m))(y_i)\ [\mathbf{v}, \mathbf{R}] \iff v_i \in \Gamma_1^\infty, \\ &\qquad \text{where } \Gamma = (\Gamma_1, \ldots, \Gamma_n) \text{ with } \Gamma_i(\mathbf{U}) := \{\, v \mid \mathcal{L} \models \varphi_i[v, \mathbf{R}, \mathbf{U}]\,\}. \end{aligned}$$

An m-ary relation L between words is *definable by a bounded fixed-point formula* $\varphi(y_1, \ldots, y_m)$, if $L = \{\, (u_1, \ldots, u_m) \mid \mathcal{L} \models \varphi(u_1, \ldots, u_m)\,\}$. Depending on which relation $<$ on Σ^* we use, we talk of *length-bounded* and *subword-bounded* formulas.

3.1 Bounded Fixed-Point Formulas Define Bounded Operators

The last clause in the definition of satisfaction makes sense only if we can show that the operator Γ is $|\cdot|$- or $<$-bounded. We use bounded fixed-point formulas over any primitive relations and constants instead of the *CBFP*-formulas above.

Theorem 8. *Let $\mathcal{A}$ be a first-order relational structure with a well-founded quasi-ordering $\leq$ on A. Let $\varphi(x, \mathbf{y}, \mathbf{S}) := \varphi(x, y_1, \ldots, y_m, S_1, \ldots, S_n)$ be a bounded fixed-point formula such that for no set variable T, $T(x)$ is a subformula of φ. Then for all $a \in A$, $b_1 < a, \ldots, b_m < a$ and sets $R_1 \ldots R_m \subseteq A$,*

$$\mathcal{A} \models \varphi(a, b_1, \ldots, b_m, R_1, \ldots, R_n) \leftrightarrow \varphi(a, b_1, \ldots, b_m, R_1^{<a}, \ldots, R_n^{<a}). \tag{6}$$

Proof. We only consider the case $\varphi \equiv \mu(T_1, \ldots, T_k)(\lambda x_1\, \varphi_1, \ldots, \lambda x_k\, \varphi_k)(x)$: By definition, for each i we have $\mathit{freeIndV}(\varphi_i) \subseteq \{ x_i \}$ and there is no subformula $Y(x_i)$ in $\varphi_i(x_i, \mathbf{S}, \mathbf{T})$ with Y among $\mathbf{S}, \mathbf{T}$. By induction, for each $a \in A$ and each sequence $\mathbf{U} = U_1, \ldots, U_k$ of subsets of A we have

$$\mathcal{A} \models \varphi_i(a, \mathbf{R}, \mathbf{U}) \leftrightarrow \varphi_i(a, \mathbf{R}^{<a}, \mathbf{U}^{<a}). \tag{7}$$

By taking $\mathbf{R}^{<a}$ instead of $\mathbf{R}$ and, respectively, $\mathbf{U}^{<a}$ instead of $\mathbf{U}$, this gives

$$\begin{aligned} &\mathcal{A} \models \varphi_i(a, \mathbf{R}^{<a}, \mathbf{U}) \leftrightarrow \varphi_i(a, \mathbf{R}^{<a}, \mathbf{U}^{<a}), \\ &\mathcal{A} \models \varphi_i(a, \mathbf{R}, \mathbf{U}^{<a}) \leftrightarrow \varphi_i(a, \mathbf{R}, \mathbf{U}). \end{aligned} \tag{8}$$

Define k-ary operators $\Gamma_\varphi = (\Gamma_{\varphi_1}, \ldots, \Gamma_{\varphi_k})$ and $\tilde{\Gamma}_\varphi = (\tilde{\Gamma}_{\varphi_1}, \ldots, \tilde{\Gamma}_{\varphi_k})$ using

$$\begin{aligned} \Gamma_{\varphi_i}(\mathbf{U}) &:= \{ a \in A \mid \mathcal{A} \models \varphi_i(a, \mathbf{R}, \mathbf{U}) \}, \\ \tilde{\Gamma}_{\varphi_i}(\mathbf{U}) &:= \{ a \in A \mid \mathcal{A} \models \varphi_i(a, \mathbf{R}^{<a}, \mathbf{U}) \}. \end{aligned}$$

By (8), Γ_φ and $\Gamma_{\tilde{\varphi}}$ are $<$-bounded operators and by Theorem 3 have fixed points $\Gamma_\varphi^\infty = (\Gamma_{\varphi_1}^\infty, \ldots, \Gamma_{\varphi_k}^\infty)$ and $\tilde{\Gamma}_\varphi^\infty = (\tilde{\Gamma}_{\varphi_1}^\infty, \ldots, \tilde{\Gamma}_{\varphi_k}^\infty)$. Thus the formula $\varphi(x, \mathbf{S})$ has a meaning with respect to both environments $[a, \mathbf{R}]$ and $[a, \mathbf{R}^{<a}]$, given by

$$\mathcal{A} \models \varphi(a, \mathbf{R}) \iff a \in \Gamma_{\varphi_1}^\infty \quad \text{and} \quad \mathcal{A} \models \varphi(a, \mathbf{R}^{<a}) \iff a \in \tilde{\Gamma}_{\varphi_1}^\infty. \tag{9}$$

To show $\mathcal{A} \models \varphi(a, \mathbf{R}) \iff \mathcal{A} \models \varphi(a, \mathbf{R}^{<a})$, we first show that

$$\Gamma_\varphi^{<b} = \tilde{\Gamma}_\varphi^{<b} \quad \text{for all } b \leq a. \tag{10}$$

Suppose this is false. Since $<$ is well-founded, there is $b \leq a$ such that for all $c < b$, $\Gamma_\varphi^{<c} = \tilde{\Gamma}_\varphi^{<c}$, but $\Gamma_{\varphi_i}^{<b} \neq \tilde{\Gamma}_{\varphi_i}^{<b}$ for some i. But then, using (7),

$$\begin{aligned} c \in \Gamma_{\varphi_i}(\Gamma_\varphi^{<c}) &\iff c \in \Gamma_{\varphi_i}(\tilde{\Gamma}_\varphi^{<c}) \iff \mathcal{A} \models \varphi_i(c, \mathbf{R}, \tilde{\Gamma}_\varphi^{<c}) \\ &\iff \mathcal{A} \models \varphi_i(c, \mathbf{R}^{<c}, \tilde{\Gamma}_\varphi^{<c}) \iff c \in \tilde{\Gamma}_{\varphi_i}(\tilde{\Gamma}_\varphi^{<c}). \end{aligned}$$

This implies $\Gamma_{\varphi_i}(\Gamma_\varphi^{<c})^c = \tilde{\Gamma}_{\varphi_i}(\tilde{\Gamma}^{<c})^c$ for all $c < b$, which means $\Gamma_{\varphi_i}^{<b} = \tilde{\Gamma}_{\varphi_i}^{<b}$, a contradiction. Using a for c in the above calculation, the claim follows by

$$\begin{aligned} \mathcal{A} \models \varphi(a, \mathbf{R}) &\iff a \in \Gamma_{\varphi_1}^\infty \iff a \in \Gamma_{\varphi_1}(\Gamma_\varphi^{<a}) \\ &\iff a \in \tilde{\Gamma}_{\varphi_1}(\tilde{\Gamma}_\varphi^{<a}) \iff a \in \tilde{\Gamma}_{\varphi_1}^\infty \iff \mathcal{A} \models \varphi(a, \mathbf{R}^{<a}). \end{aligned}$$

Corollary 9. *On each structure $\mathcal{A}$ where $\leq$ is a well-founded quasi-ordering, every bounded fixed-point-formula $\varphi(x) := \mu(S_1, \ldots, S_n)(\lambda x_1\, \varphi_1, \ldots, \lambda x_n\, \varphi_n)(x)$ defines a simultaneous $<$-bounded operator $\Gamma_\varphi := (\Gamma_{\varphi_1}, \ldots, \Gamma_{\varphi_n})$ by*

$$\Gamma_{\varphi_i}(S_1, \ldots, S_n) := \{ a \in A \mid \mathcal{A} \models \varphi_i(a, S_1, \ldots, S_n) \}.$$

In particular, the meaning of φ is well defined:

$$\mathcal{A} \models \mu(S_1, \ldots, S_n)(\lambda x_1\, \varphi_1, \ldots, \lambda x_n\, \varphi_n)(a) \iff a \in \Gamma^{\infty}_{\varphi_1}.$$

Fixed points $\Gamma^{\infty}_{\varphi}$ need not exist if we allow a subformula $S(x)$ in φ.[3] Positive inductive definitions ban *all* negative occurrences of recursively bound relation variables. Our class of formulas shows that this is unnecessarily restrictive in case there is a well-founded $<$ available. While we have to exclude $\mu(S)(\lambda x.\neg S(x))(x)$, we can allow formulas like $\mu(S)(\lambda x.\forall y < x.\neg S(y))(x)$.

Example 2. Let $\mathcal{A}$ be the structure $\mathcal{L}$ of words over Σ and $\leq$ be the subword-relation or the comparison by word-length.

1. Every context-free language over Σ is definable in $\mathcal{L}$ by a bounded fixed-point formula. The converse is false, since we have negation.
2. The non-context-free language $L_0 := \{ www \mid w \in \Sigma^* \}$ is explicitly definable using $\mu(S)(\lambda x\,(x = \epsilon \vee \exists y < x.x = yyy))(x)$.
   The non-context-free $L_1 = \{ a^n b^n c^n \mid n < \omega \}$ is definable by simultaneously defining $L_1 = L_2 L_3 \cap L_4 L_5$, with $L_2 = \{ a^n b^n \mid n < \omega \}$, $L_3 = \{ c^n \mid n < \omega \}$, $L_4 = \{ a^n \mid n < \omega \}$, and $L_5 = \{ b^n c^n \mid n < \omega \}$. This can be done as a positive induction $\mu(S_1, \ldots, S_5)(\lambda x\, \varphi_1, \ldots, \lambda x\, \varphi_5)(x)$ with, for example,

$$\begin{aligned}\varphi_1(x, \mathbf{S}) \equiv x = \epsilon \ \vee\ [&\exists y < x\, \exists z < x\,(x = yz \wedge S_2(y) \wedge S_3(z))\\ &\wedge \exists y < x\, \exists z < x\,(x = yz \wedge S_4(y) \wedge S_5(z))].\end{aligned}$$

3. Universal quantification and boolean operations could be mixed as in the formula $\mu(S)\,(\lambda x\, \varphi)(x)$ with

$$\varphi(x, S) := \ x = a \ \vee\ \forall y < x\, \forall z < x\,(x = y \cdot z \rightarrow (S(y) \leftrightarrow \neg S(z)).$$

Using Theorem 8 and Lemma 4, nested applications of bounded fixed-point operators can be combined to a single application of a simultaneous bounded fixed point operator:

Lemma 10. *('Bekič-Scott principle' for bounded recursion) Let $\varphi(x, S, T)$ and $\tilde{\varphi}(x, S, T)$ be bounded fixed-point formulas, without subformulas $U(x)$ for set variables U. Then*

$$\mathcal{L} \models \ \mu(S, T)(\lambda x.\varphi, \lambda x.\tilde{\varphi})(x) \ \leftrightarrow\ (\mu S \lambda x.\varphi[(\mu T \lambda x.\tilde{\varphi})/T])(x).$$

[3] Positive occurrences of $S(x_i)$ in φ_i could be allowed when working with locally monotone bounded operators (cf. Theorem 5).

3.2 An Invariance Property of Bounded Fixed-Point Formulas

Notions of grammaticality should have both a global and a local reading. Globally, a grammatical property $\varphi(x)$ is used to select a language

$$L(\varphi) = \{ w \in \Sigma^* \mid \mathcal{L} \models \varphi(w) \}$$

from an *infinite* interpretation $\mathcal{L}$. Locally, φ should express a property of w that depends only on a *finite* substructure $\mathcal{L}(w) \subset \mathcal{L}$ and is effectively testable.

For example, note that the construction of the fixed point corresponding to a context free grammar and the construction of a recognition table for input w are related: the recognition table is a kind of 'goal oriented' selection from the stages of the inductive generation of all strings in the language.

More generally, in 'intuitively context-free' languages, grammaticality of a string w should be an 'internal' property of the string, i.e. only depend on properties of its substrings. Here the local reading of φ is its interpretation in the substructure of $\mathcal{L}$ whose universe are the subwords of w. Length-bounded fixed-point formulas $\varphi(x)$, however, can express properties of w by referring to any string v with $|v| < |w|$, and so cover some 'contextual' notions of grammaticality.

The bounded formulas all have a local reading in the sense that they are satisfied by an element w in $\mathcal{A}$ iff they are satisfied in a submodel $\mathcal{A}^{\leq w}$ defined via the quasi-ordering $\leq$ on A.

Definition 11. For a first-order relational structure $\mathcal{A}$ with a binary relation $\leq$, let $\mathcal{A}^{\leq a}$ be the substructure of $\mathcal{A}$ with universe $A^{\leq a}$ (containing the constants). A formula $\varphi(x, y_1, \ldots, y_m, S_1, \ldots, S_n)$ is *$\leq$-local in x*, if for all $\mathcal{A}$, $a \in A$, $b_1, \ldots, b_m < a$ and $S_1, \ldots, S_n \subseteq A$

$$\mathcal{A} \models \varphi(a, b_1, \ldots, b_m, S_1, \ldots, S_n) \iff \mathcal{A}^{\leq a} \models \varphi(a, b_1, \ldots, b_m, S_1^{\leq a}, \ldots, S_m^{\leq a}).$$

If $\mathcal{A}$ is $\mathcal{L}$, we write $\mathcal{L}^{\leq w}$ for the substructure of $\mathcal{L}$ whose universe consists of all subwords of w and $\mathcal{L}^{\leq |w|}$ for the substructure whose universe consists of all words of Σ^* of length at most $|w|$.

Theorem 12 (Local Substructure Invariance). *Let $\varphi(x)$ be the bounded fixed-point formula $= \mu(S_1, \ldots, S_n)(\lambda x_1 \varphi_1, \ldots, \lambda x_n \varphi_n)(x)$. Then for any structure $\mathcal{A}$ with a well-founded quasi-ordering $\leq$ and any $a \in A$,*

$$\mathcal{A} \models \varphi(a) \iff \mathcal{A}^{\leq a} \models \varphi(a).$$

For $\varphi(x)$ as above, by induction on the well-founded relation $<$ the stages $\Gamma_{\varphi_i}^{\leq a}$ of the induction in $\mathcal{A}^{\leq a}$ are the intersection of those in $\mathcal{A}$ with $A^{\leq a}$. Note that *least* fixed-point formulas do not satisfy the 'local substructure invariance', because of their unbounded individual quantifiers.

As one expects, context-free grammars – as fixed-point formulas – are 'invariant under local substructures' in the sense of Theorem 12, with $\leq$ as the subword relation. Theorem 17 below shows that the converse does not hold: there are more 'intuitively context-free' than context-free languages.

3.3 Syntactic Characterization of Invariance and <-Boundedness

As is well known, a first-order formula $\varphi(x, S)$ defines a monotone operator Γ_φ iff it is logically equivalent to one where the variable S does not occur negatively. We give a similar characterization of first-order formulas $\varphi(x, S)$ that both (a) define $<$-bounded operators Γ_φ and (b) express 'intuitively context-free' properties. Identifying these with properties 'invariant under going to the substructure of all subwords', i.e. the 'local' properties in $\mathcal{L}$, (a) and (b) mean

$$\forall w \in \Sigma^* \, \forall S \subseteq \Sigma^* \, [\mathcal{L} \models \varphi(w, S) \iff \mathcal{L}^{\leq w} \models \varphi(w, S^{<w})].$$

In order to replace $\exists y \leq x \, \varphi$ equivalently by $\varphi[x/y] \vee \exists y < x \, \varphi$, our characterization needs $\leq$ to be antisymmetric, and hence does not cover the case of norm-bounded operators.

Definition 13. Let a first-order relational language with a binary relation $\leq$ be given. A formula $\varphi(x, y_1, \ldots, y_m, S_1, \ldots, S_n)$ is *$<$-bounded in x*, if for each structure $\mathcal{A}$, all $w \in A$, $v_1, \ldots, v_m < w$ and $S_1, \ldots, S_n \subseteq A$

$$\mathcal{A} \models \varphi(w, v_1, \ldots, v_m, S_1, \ldots, S_n) \iff \mathcal{A} \models \varphi(w, v_1, \ldots, v_m, S_1^{<w}, \ldots, S_n^{<w}),$$

and $\varphi(x, y_1, \ldots, y_m, S_1, \ldots, S_n)$ is (syntactically) *$<x$-bounded*, if all individual quantifiers are of the form $\exists y < x$ or $\forall y < x$ and each S_i occurs only in the form $S_i(y_j)$ or $S_i(y)$ for a bound variable y.

Theorem 14 (Preservation Theorem). *For a first-order formula $\varphi(x, S)$, the following conditions are equivalent:*

(i) On structures with a partial order $\leq$, $\varphi(x, S)$ is $\leq$-local and $<$-bounded in x.
(ii) There is a $<x$-bounded formula $\chi(x, S)$ such that: "$\leq$ is a partial order" $\models \varphi(x, S) \leftrightarrow \chi(x, S)$.

Our semantic proof of (i) $\Rightarrow$ (ii) is too long to be included here. It derives χ as an interpolant of "$\leq$ is a partial order" $\wedge$ $\varphi^{\leq}(x, S^{<x}) \models \varphi(x, S)$. The assumption $\exists T \, (\varphi^{\leq}(x, T) \wedge T = S^{<})$ is equivalent on countable structures to a first-order theory Φ describing a consistency property for constructing T, and χ is obtained from Φ by compactness.

4 Tabular Recognizers for Bounded Fixed-Point Definitions

To evaluate monotone inductive definitions, Rounds uses an *ATM* modified by adding (i) oracle states to handle free relation variables, and (ii) recursion states that allow arbitrarily many iterations of a recursively defined predicate.

To handle bounded inductions, besides the oracle states our *ATM*'s have two new kinds of states, one for bounded individual quantification and one for bounded fixed-points.

- $\mathcal{M}_{\exists y < x . \varphi}$ has an initial $\exists$-state in which it can write to its work tape y an arbitrary string u such that $u < v$, where v is the content of the input tape x (used as a length bound resp. source for copying); control is then given to the submachine $\mathcal{M}_\varphi$ with u on its input tape y. $\mathcal{M}_{\exists y < x . \varphi}$ returns the maximum of the acceptance values of these calls to $\mathcal{M}_\varphi$.

- $\mathcal{M}_{(\mu(T_1,\ldots,T_n)(\lambda y_1 \cdot \varphi_1,\ldots))(x_1)}$ is built using the machines $\mathcal{M}_{\varphi_i(y_i,\mathbf{S},T_1,\ldots,T_n)}$. We assume oracle states for all free relation variables of the formula. Let w be the input on tape x_1 and oracles $\mathbf{R}$ for $\mathbf{S}$ be given. Let $\Gamma_\varphi^\infty(v)$ be the bit-vector of the boolean values of $v \in \Gamma_{\varphi_1}^\infty, \ldots, v \in \Gamma_{\varphi_n}^\infty$.
First, build a 'table' $\Gamma_\varphi^{<w}$ of all $\Gamma_\varphi^\infty(v)$ for $v < w$: in a loop through all $v < w$, respecting $<$, check whether $\Gamma_\varphi^\infty(v)$ is already stored; if not, compute its bits $\Gamma_{\varphi_i}^\infty(v) = \Gamma_{\varphi_i}(\Gamma_\varphi^{<v})$ using the submachines $\mathcal{M}_{\varphi_i}$ with v on its input tape y_i and oracles $\mathbf{R}$ for $\mathbf{S}$ and $\Gamma_\varphi^{<v}$ for $\mathbf{T}$, and store the results. Second, evaluate φ_1 on input w, using $\mathcal{M}_{\varphi_1}$ with w on its input tape y_1 and oracles $\mathbf{R}$ for $\mathbf{S}$ and the 'table' $\Gamma_\varphi^{<w}$ for $\mathbf{T}$. Finally, return the acceptance value of $\mathcal{M}_{\varphi_1}$.

Thus we first *expand* the finite structure $\mathcal{L}^{\leq w}$ by $\Gamma_\varphi^{<v}$ and then can test $\mathcal{L} \models \varphi(v)$ quickly as $\mathcal{L}^{\leq w} \models \varphi_1(v, \Gamma_\varphi^{<v})$. In contrast to the case of least-fixed points, *before computing* $\Gamma_\varphi^{<v}$ *we know its size*; this could be relevant for 'bounded' queries in databases with flat quasi-ordering $\leq$. Note also that the values $\Gamma_{\varphi_j}^\infty(v)$ are computed only once. Whether this is an advantage over recursive computation (as used by Rounds), depends of course also on the costs of the read/write operations from/to the table.

Lemma 15. *If* $\varphi(x) := \mu(S_1, \ldots, S_n)(\lambda x_1\, \varphi_1, \ldots, \lambda x_n\, \varphi_n)(x)$ *is a bounded fixed-point formula,*

$$\{\, w \in \Sigma^* \mid \mathcal{L}^{\leq |w|} \models \varphi(w) \,\} \in \mathit{EXPTIME}, \;\; \{\, w \in \Sigma^* \mid \mathcal{L}^{\leq w} \models \varphi(w) \,\} \in \mathit{PTIME}.$$

Concerning the converse, note that a bounded recursive definition of the set of configurations that lead to acceptance could recur to accepting configurations of *smaller* size only, but related machine configurations have *the same* length. So it seems impossible to define all *EXPTIME* resp. *PTIME*-languages by length- resp. subword-bounded fixed-point formulas, even if we allow k-ary relation variables rather than just set variables. From a language definability point of view, this might even be expected: ordinary grammars would hardly allow multiple scanning and arbitrary rewriting(!) of an input string to test its grammaticality.

5 Tabular Recognizers for Decomposition Grammars

We now further restrict bounded inductive language definitions to obtain tabular recognition algorithms of time complexity $O(|w|^3)$ on a *RAM*. We generalize a peculiarity of *individual* quantification in the fixed-point formulation of context-free grammars which has been overlooked in Rounds' analysis. It allows to fill a field of the recognition table for input w in $O(|w|)$ steps (cf. Proposition 20 a)).

Definition 16. A bounded fixed-point definition $\mu(S_1, \ldots, S_n)(\lambda x \varphi_1, \ldots, \lambda x \varphi_n)(x)$ is *a decomposition grammar* if each $\varphi_i(x, \mathbf{S})$ is a boolean combination of formulas

$$\exists x_1 < x \ldots \exists x_k < x\, (x = t(x_1, \ldots, x_k) \wedge \psi(x_1, \ldots, x_k, S_1, \ldots, S_n)), \qquad (11)$$

where $x, x_1, \ldots, x_k$ are pairwise distinct individual variables, $t(x_1, \ldots, x_k)$ is a term (here: a word made of x_i's and constants a) in which each variable occurs at most once, and $\psi(\mathbf{x}, \mathbf{S})$ is a conjunction of formulas $S_i(x_j)$ and their negations. The grammar is *in normal form*, if in each subformula (11) either $k = 0$ and $t \equiv a$ for some $a \in \Sigma$, or $k = 2$ and $t \equiv x_1 \cdot x_2$.

We can test property (11) by 'decomposing' its argument string x into strict substrings $x_1, \ldots, x_k$ according to the pattern t and checking which of the predicates $S_1, \ldots, S_k$ hold true of the substrings $x_1, \ldots, x_k$.

Each language $L \subseteq \Sigma^*$ definable by decomposition grammars can also be defined by decompostion grammars in normal form. We could allow ψ in (11) to be a boolean combination of $S_j(x_i)$'s; having disjuncts there amounts to delaying decisions in the parsing process. We could also allow μ-formulas in ψ and have nested recursive definitions. This is possible since the class of definable languages is closed under substitution, for which we need Lemma 10.

Theorem 17. *The class of languages definable by decomposition grammars contains the context-free languages, is closed under the boolean operations* $\cup, \cap, \neg$, *the regular operations of* $\cdot, ^*$, *and under substitution.*

Decomposition grammars seem equally expressive as the *hierarchical complement intersection grammars* of Heilbunner and Schmitz [5], but we have not checked the details.

Before turning to the recognition complexity of decomposition grammars, we generalize these to allow a *relational* interpretation of the syntactic categories.

5.1 Head Grammars and Languages of Segmented Strings

In the syntax of natural languages, concatenation is not the only primitive used to combine expressions. Other operations have been studied (cf. [10, 11]), such as the insertion of one string into another one, or the wrapping of a splitted string around the 'head' (for example: stem) of another one. Technically, one uses *string pairs* over Σ and the following *wrapping operations* $\circ_i : \Sigma^{*2} \times \Sigma^{*2} \to \Sigma^{*2}$

$$(v_1, v_2) \circ_1 (w_1, w_2) := (v_1 w_1, w_2 v_2) \qquad (v_1, v_2) \circ_2 (w_1, w_2) := (v_1, w_1 w_2 v_2)$$

$$(v_1, v_2) \circ_3 (w_1, w_2) := (v_1 w_1 w_2, v_2) \qquad (v_1, v_2) \circ_4 (w_1, w_2) := (v_1, v_2 w_1 w_2)$$

$$(v_1, v_2) \circ_5 (w_1, w_2) := (v_1 v_2 w_1, w_2)$$

More generally, we consider *segmented strings* $(w_1, \ldots, w_m)$, i.e. strings $w = w_1 \cdots w_m$ segmented into several consecutive substrings $w_1, \ldots, w_m$. These are useful at various places in language description: on the word level to decompose a string w into segments such as verb stem, prefixes, infixes and suffixes, or on the phrasal level to handle 'discontinuous constituents', such as a noun phrase whose noun and relative clause are separated by the verb. For simplicity, we fix the number m of segments; but we enlarge the class of operations:

Definition 18. Let *Op* be the set of operations $\circ : (\Sigma^*)^m \times (\Sigma^*)^m \to (\Sigma^*)^m$ that are definable by

$$(x_1, \ldots, x_m) \circ (y_1, \ldots, y_m) := (v_1, \ldots, v_m), \tag{12}$$

where $v_1, \ldots, v_m$ are words over $\{x_1, \ldots, x_m, y_1, \ldots, y_m\}$ and each x_i and y_j occurs exactly once[4] in $v_1 \cdots v_m$. Let *the structure of m-fold segmented strings* be

$$\mathcal{L}_m := ((\Sigma^*)^m, \circ, (a, \epsilon, \ldots, \epsilon), \ldots, (\epsilon, \ldots, \epsilon, a))_{a \in \Sigma, \circ \in Op}.$$

Definition 19. A *normal form decomposition grammar for m-fold segmented strings* is a formula $\varphi(x) = \mu(S_1, \ldots, S_n)(\lambda x \varphi_1, \ldots, \lambda x \varphi_n)(x)$, where each formula $\varphi_i(x, S_1, \ldots, S_n)$ is a boolean combination of formulas

$$\exists x_1 < x \, \exists x_2 < x \, (x = t(x_1, x_2) \wedge \psi(x_1, x_2, S_1, \ldots, S_n)), \tag{13}$$

in which either $t \equiv a$ for some $a \in \Sigma$, or $t \equiv (x_1 \circ x_2)$ for some $\circ \in Op$, and ψ is a conjunction of formulas $S_i(x_j)$ and their negations. *The language of m-fold segmented strings defined by* $\varphi(x)$ is

$$L(\varphi) := \{ (w_1, \ldots, w_m) \mid \mathcal{L}_m \models \varphi((w_1, \ldots, w_m)) \}.$$

To interprete $<$, use comparison by the length $|(w_1, \ldots, w_m)| = |w_1| + \cdots + |w_m|$ of segmented strings. A *head grammar* is a normal form decomposition grammar for 2-fold segmented strings over the set $Op = \{\circ_1, \ldots, \circ_5\}$, where each φ_i is a disjunction of formulas (13) in which ψ has no negations.

C. Pollard[10] introduced head grammars, in a more complicated 'rewriting' format, as context-free grammars where concatenation is replaced by the (non-associative) wrapping operations $\circ_1, \ldots, \circ_5$. Formal properties of head languages have been studied by K. Roach[11].

5.2 Complexity of Recognition with Decomposition Grammars

Let $\mu(S_1, \ldots, S_n)(\lambda x_1 \varphi_1, \ldots, \lambda x_n \varphi_n)(x)$ be a decomposition grammar, and $w \in \Sigma^*$. In order to decide whether $\mathcal{L} \models \mu(S_1, \ldots, S_n)(\lambda x_1 \varphi_1, \ldots, \lambda x_n \varphi_n)(w)$, one proceeds as follows:

1. For each subword v of w and each $i \leq n$, compute the boolean value $\Gamma^\infty_{\varphi_i}(v)$, and store the bitvector $(\Gamma^\infty_{\varphi_1}(v), \ldots, \Gamma^\infty_{\varphi_n}(v))$ as field $M(v)$ of a table with $|subwords(w)|$ many fields.
2. To compute $\Gamma^\infty_{\varphi_i}(v)$, where $\varphi_i(x, \mathbf{S})$ is a boolean combination of subformulas φ as in (iii), determine the corresponding values $\Gamma^\infty_\varphi(v)$ as explained in (iii) and evaluate the boolean combination of the results.
3. To compute $\Gamma^\infty_\varphi(v)$ for $\varphi(x, \mathbf{S}) = \exists x_1 < x \ldots \exists x_k < x \, (x = t(\mathbf{x}) \wedge \psi(\mathbf{x}, \mathbf{S}))$, where $\psi(\mathbf{x}, \mathbf{S})$ is a boolean combination of formulas $S_i(x_j)$ with $1 \leq i \leq n$ and $1 \leq j \leq k$,
   (a) determine all splittings of v into substrings $v_1, \ldots, v_k$ such that $v = t(v_1, \ldots, v_k)$, and
   (b) for each such splitting $\mathbf{v}$, evaluate $\psi(\mathbf{v}, \mathbf{S})$ by looking up the values for $S_i(v_j)$ in $M(v_j)$.

[4] After finishing this work, I found the same restriction used in the 'multiple context-free grammars' of Seki e.a.[13] for a complexity result related to Theorem 21.

The complexity of computing the table M for an input w is proportional to the number of substrings v of w times the cost of computing a field $M(v)$. Since only splittings into strict substrings are allowed in (iii), the table M can be filled by computing $M(v)$ with subwords v of w of increasing length.

Remark. If $\Gamma = \Gamma_\varphi$ for a context-free grammar $\varphi(x)$ in Chomsky normal form and $<$ is the strict subword relation, $\Gamma(\Gamma^{<w})$ is the familiar recognition table for w in the algorithm of Cocke-Younger-Kasami. Different ways of computing $\Gamma(\Gamma^{<w})$ correspond to different versions of the recognizer. In an off-line version, one can compute $\Gamma(\Gamma^{<v})$ for all subwords v of *increasing length*. On-line versions compute $\Gamma(\Gamma^{<v})$ for *increasing prefixes* v of w: if $w = va$ ends in a letter a we first determine the table $\Gamma(\Gamma^{<v})$ of the prefix v, then that of the next input symbol, $\Gamma(\Gamma^{<a})$, and finally compute $\Gamma(\Gamma^{<ua})$ for increasing suffixes u of v.

We now estimate the number of RAM-steps needed to construct a recognition table $M(w_1, \ldots, w_m)$ for a decomposition grammar for m-segmented strings.

Proposition 20. *Let $\circ$ be any such $2m$-ary operation as just defined.*

a) There are $O(\max_i |w_i|^m)$ many decompositions $(u_1, \ldots, u_m) \circ (v_1, \ldots, v_m)$ of $(w_1, \ldots, w_m) \in (\Sigma^*)^m$.
b) The table $M(w_1, \ldots, w_m)$ has $O(\max_i |w_i|^{2m})$ fields.

Proof. a) Each of the v_i that define $\circ$ contains at least one of the variables $x_1, \ldots, y_m$. To consume the remaining m variables one needs m applications of concatenations (giving adjacent variables in the $v_1, \ldots, v_m$). To find substrings of $w_1, \ldots, w_m$ that match the variables, we therefore have to find m splitting positions $i_0, \ldots, i_m$ in $w_1, \ldots, w_m$. There are $O(|w|^k)$ many k-tuples $i_1 \leq i_2 \ldots \leq i_k \leq |w|$ in a string w and so $O(|w_1|^{k_1} \cdots |w_m|^{k_m})$ many splittings with k_i splitting positions in w_i. It follows that there are at most $O(\max |w_i|^m)$ splittings $(u_1, \ldots, u_m) \circ (v_1, \ldots, v_m) = (w_1, \ldots, w_m)$.

b) For a subword $(v_1, \ldots, v_m) \leq (w_1, \ldots, w_m)$ of $(w_1, \ldots, w_m)$, the v_i must be empty or occur as non-overlapping subwords of the $w_1, \ldots, w_m$. The total number of k nonoverlapping subwords of w_i is bounded by the beginning and end positions $i_1 \leq j_1 \leq \ldots \leq i_k \leq j_k \leq |w_i|$ of the subwords, which makes $O(|w_i|^{2k})$ possibilities. There are $O(|w_1|^{2k_1} \cdots |w_m|^{2k_m})$ subwords $(u_1, \ldots, u_m) \leq (w_1, \ldots, w_m)$ such that k_i out of the $u_1, \ldots, u_m$ are nonoverlapping subwords of w_i. Hence the number of all subwords $(u_1, \ldots, u_m) \leq (w_1, \ldots, w_m)$ is bounded by the sum of values $O(|w_1|^{2k_1} \cdots |w_m|^{2k_m})$ over all $k_1, \ldots, k_m$ where $\sum k_i = m$, giving $O(\max_i |w_i|^{2m})$. Multiplying a) and b), we get

Theorem 21. *For any normal form decomposition grammar $\varphi(x)$ for m-segmented strings, a recognition table M for input $(w_1, \ldots, w_m)$ can be constructed in $O(\max_i |w_i|^{3m})$ many RAM-steps.*

For $m = 1$, this gives the familiar $O(|w|^3)$ bound for language recognition with respect to context-free grammars in Chomsky normal form. For $m = 2$, we get an $O(|(w_1, w_2)|^6)$ bound for head grammars in 'Chomsky' normal form.

6 Open Problems

Bounded fixed-point formulas may be applied on other structures, like the finite trees with the subtree relation. They might also be useful to develop relational query languages with low complexities, since the number and size of the inductive stages depend on the quasi-ordering rather than the size of the domain.

An extension of our monadic bounded inductive definability to the n-ary case should present no difficulties. We also expect that the (subword-) boundedly definable languages strictly contain the boolean closure of context-free languages.

We have indicated why the inclusion of subword- resp. length-bounded inductive definability in *PTIME* resp. *EXPTIME* should be strict. A precise characterization of the boundedly definable languages in terms of complexity is open.

Acknowledgement: This work has partially been supported by ESPRIT BRA 7230, GENTZEN.

References

1. A. K. Chandra, D. C. Kozen, and L. J. Stockmeyer. Alternation. *Journal of the Association for Computing Machinery*, 28(1):114–133, 1981.
2. H.-D. Ebbinghaus and J. Flum. *Finite Model Theory*. Springer, Berlin 1995.
3. Y. Gurevich and S. Shelah. Fixed-point extensions of first-order logic. In *Proceedings of the 26th IEEE Symposium on Foundations of Computer Science*, 1985.
4. M. Harrison. *Introduction to Formal Languages*. Addison Wesley, Reading 1978.
5. S. Heilbrunner and L. Schmitz. An efficient recognizer for the boolean closure of context-free languages. *Theoretical Computer Science*, 80:53–75, 1991.
6. G. Hotz and G. Pitsch. Fast uniform analysis of coupled-context-free languages. In S. Abiteboul and E. Shamir, editors, *21st International Colloquium on Automata, Languages and Programming*, pages 412–423. Lecture Notes in Computer Science 820, Springer, Berlin 1994.
7. N. Immerman. Relational queries computable in polynomial time. *Information and Control*, 68:86–104, 1986.
8. C. Lautemann, T. Schwentick, and D. Thérien. Logics for context-free languages. In *Computer Science Logic '94*, pages 205–216. Lecture Notes in Computer Science 933, Springer, Berlin 1995.
9. H. Leiß. Towards Kleene Algebra with Recursion. In E. Börger e.a., editors, *Computer Science Logic '91*, pages 242–256. Lecture Notes in Computer Science 626, Springer, Berlin 1992.
10. C. Pollard. *Generalized Phrase Structure Grammars, Head Grammars, and Natural Language*. PhD thesis, Department of Linguistics, Stanford University, 1984.
11. K. Roach. Formal properties of head grammars. In A. Manaster-Ramer, editor, *Mathematics of Language*, pages 293–348. John Benjamins, Amsterdam 1987.
12. W. Rounds. A logic for linguistic descriptions and an analysis of its complexity. *Computational Linguistics*, 14(4):1–9, 1988.
13. H. Seki, T. Matsumura, M. Fujii and T. Kasami. On multiple context-free grammars. *Theoretical Computer Science*, 88(2):191–229, 1991.
14. M. Vardi. Complexity of relational query languages. In *14th ACM Symposium on the Theory of Computing*, pages 137–146, 1982.
15. K. Vijay-Shanker and A. Joshi. Some computational properties of tree adjoining grammars. In *Proceedigs of the 23rd Meeting of the Association for Computational Linguistics*, pages 82–93, Chicago 1988.

Equivalences among Various Logical Frameworks of Partial Algebras

Till Mossakowski

University of Bremen, Dept. of Computer Science, P.O.Box 33 04 40, D-28334 Bremen
Phone: +49-421-218-2935, E-mail: till@informatik.uni-bremen.de

Abstract. We examine a variety of liberal logical frameworks of partial algebras. Therefore we use simple, conjunctive and weak embeddings of institutions which preserve model categories and may map sentences to sentences, finite sets of sentences, or theory extensions using unique-existential quantifiers, respectively. They faithfully represent theories, model categories, theory morphisms, colimit of theories, reducts etc. Moreover, along simple and conjunctive embeddings, theorem provers can be re-used in a way that soundness and completeness is preserved.
Our main result states the equivalence of all the logical frameworks with respect to weak embeddability. This gives us compilers between all frameworks. Thus it is a chance to unify the different branches of specification using liberal partial logics.
This is important for reaching the goal of formal interoperability of different specification languages for software development. With formal interoperability, a specification can contain parts written in different logical frameworks using a multiparadigm specification language, and one can re-use tools which are available for one framework also for other frameworks.

1 Introduction

Logical frameworks are widely used in computer science, in particular for the specification of correct software systems with the help of specification languages [6, 38]. Each specification language is based on an underlying logical framework, consisting of signatures, models, theories, sentences and so on. Now the large variety of existing specification languages and underlying logical frameworks has lead to incompatibilities and confusion. It is therefore an important task to compare logical frameworks.

Considering the kind of logical frameworks to study, we will start with the logical framework of partial algebras with universal Horn sentences, introduced by Burmeister [4, 5] and others. This seems to be the strongest framework among the "liberal" [16, 37] logical frameworks admitting initial and free constructions which are important for specification languages with module concepts [11]. Now there are various restrictions of this logical framework, namely Reichel's Hep-theories [33], called essentially algebraic theories by Freyd [14], theories formed with ECE-equations [4], Jarzembski's weak varieties of partial algebras [22], and theories formed with strong equations [4, 20, 23, 31]. Further, there are other logical frameworks capturing partiality as well. We only mention left exact sketches [3, 19], Coste's limit theories [9] and Meseguer's and Goguen's order-sorted theories with sort constraints [18]. It is a folklore theorem, that Hep-theories are "the same" as left exact sketches, see [15, 32]. And sort constraints of order sorted algebra are introduced to capture "the same" partiality as partial algebras with universal Horn sentences. But how to make this "the same" precise and how to study the relations between the above mentioned logical frameworks systematically?

We use the notion of institution from [16] as a formalization of "logical framework". Institutions are a version of abstract model theory and come along with at least three notions of representation [25, 30]:

1. Simple maps of institutions allow to map signatures to theories, sentences to sentences and models to models. Theorem-provers can be re-used along such maps.
2. Conjunctive maps of institutions are like simple maps, except that a sentence may be translated to a finite set of sentences. Theorem-provers can still be re-used.
3. Weak maps of institutions map theories to theories and models to models. Under some condition, this can be made modular, such that sentences are mapped to theory extensions, and for mapping a theory, we then have to collect all the theory extensions. Semantic properties are kept along such maps, but since sentences are mapped to whole theory extensions, there is no straightforward re-use of theorem provers.

We restrict each notion to the case of embeddings, which means that signatures and sentences are embedded while model categories are linked via equivalences of categories. Now a systematic study of expressiveness of logical frameworks should order them by their embeddability into each other. Thus equivalent expressiveness means embeddability in both directions.

Our main theorem states the equivalence of all of the above mentioned logical frameworks with respect to weak embeddings of institutions. This extends the following results: The equivalence of Hep-theories and left exact sketches is proved in [1] by showing that both have exactly the locally finitely presentable categories as model categories. Limit-theories are shown to have exactly locally finitely presentable categories as model categories in [9]. In this paper, we strengthen these results by constructing weak embeddings of institutions, which not only follow categorical constructions, but also act at the level of syntax. Furthermore, we give some new, perhaps even unexpected, results concerning other frameworks. Partial algebras with strong equations are equivalent to partial algebras with universal Horn sentences. The exact relation of order-sorted algebra with sort constraints to partial algebras is clarified.

The main result gives us compilers between all logical frameworks under consideration. Thus it is a chance to unify the different branches of specification of partial algebras. Further, it is a step towards the goal of formal interoperability, multiparadigm specification languages and re-use of theorem provers mentioned above.

The organization of the paper is as follows: In Sect. 2, institutions (and logics) and the corresponding notions of map and of embedding are recalled. The notion of weak embedding of institutions from [29] is introduced. Section 3 introduces the logical frameworks mentioned above, while in Sect. 4 the main theorem is proved. Section 5 concludes the paper.

This paper continues the studies begun in [24, 29]. Some of the results were announced in [27].

2 Preliminaries

How can the notion of logical framework be formalized? In this section, we recall some answers to this problem.

2.1 Specification Frames

Specification frames by Ehrig, Pepper and Orejas [12] formalize abstract theories and models of theories, while there are no notions of sentence and satisfaction:

A *specification frame* $F = (\underline{Th}^F, \underline{Mod}^F)$ consists of

1. a category $\underline{Th}^F$ of theories
2. a functor $\underline{Mod}^F: (\underline{Th}^F)^{op} \longrightarrow \underline{CAT}$ giving the category of *models* of a theory

We omit the index F when it is clear from the context and write $M'|_\sigma$ (the *σ-reduct* of M' under σ) for $\underline{Mod}(\sigma)(M')$. M' is called an *expansion* of $M'|_\sigma$.

A map of specification frames $\mu: F \longrightarrow F'$ consists of

1. a functor $\Phi: \underline{Th}^F \longrightarrow \underline{Th}^{F'}$ and
2. a natural transformation $\beta: \underline{Mod}^{F'} \circ \Phi^{op} \longrightarrow \underline{Mod}^F$

Composition of maps $F \xrightarrow{\mu''} F'' = F \xrightarrow{\mu} F' \xrightarrow{\mu'} F''$ is defined by $\Phi'' = \Phi' \circ \Phi$ and $\beta'' = \beta \circ (\beta'_\Phi)$. This gives us a (quasi-)category $\underline{SpecFram}$ of specification frames.

2.2 Institutions

Institutions introduced by Goguen and Burstall [16] split theories into signatures and sentences, thus the area of logic starts here:

An *institution* $I = (\underline{Sign}^I, sen^I, \underline{Mod}^I, \models^I)$ consists of

1. a specification frame $(\underline{Sign}^I, \underline{Mod}^I)$, where $\underline{Sign}^I$ is the category of *signatures*,
2. a functor $sen^I: \underline{Sign}^I \longrightarrow \underline{Set}$ giving the set of *sentences* over a given signature,
3. a satisfaction relation $\models^I_\Sigma \subseteq |\underline{Mod}^I(\Sigma)| \times sen^I(\Sigma)$ for each $\Sigma \in \underline{Sign}^I$

such that for each morphism $\sigma: \Sigma \longrightarrow \Sigma'$ in $\underline{Sign}^I$ the *Satisfaction Condition*

$$M' \models^I_{\Sigma'} sen^I(\sigma)(\varphi) \iff M'|_\sigma \models^I_\Sigma \varphi$$

holds for each model $M' \in |\underline{Mod}^I(\Sigma')|$ and each sentence $\varphi \in sen^I(\Sigma)$.

Given institutions I and J, an *institution representation* or *plain map of institutions* [25] $\mu = (\Phi, \alpha, \beta): I \longrightarrow J$ consists of

- a map of specification frames $(\Phi, \beta): (\underline{Sign}^I, \underline{Mod}^I) \longrightarrow (\underline{Sign}^J, \underline{Mod}^J)$ and
- a natural transformation $\alpha: sen^I \longrightarrow sen^J \circ \Phi$

such that the following property is satisfied for $M' \in |\underline{Mod}^J(\Phi(\Sigma))|$ and $\varphi \in sen^I(\Sigma)$:

$$M' \models^J_{\Phi(\Sigma)} \alpha_\Sigma(\varphi) \iff \beta_\Sigma(M') \models^I_\Sigma \varphi \tag{1}$$

An *embedding of specification frames* is a map of specification frames $\mu = (\Phi, \beta): F \longrightarrow F'$ with Φ an embedding and β a natural equivalence. If there is such a map, F is called *subframe* of F'.

An *embedding of institutions* [24] is a simple map of institutions $\mu = (\Phi, \alpha, \beta): I \longrightarrow J$, with (Φ, β) an embedding of specification frames and α pointwise injective. If there is such a map, I is called *subinstitution* of J.

We call two specification frames resp. institutions *equivalent in expressiveness*, if there are embeddings in both directions.

If we have two institutions which are equivalent in expressiveness, satisfaction is represented faithfully, and each sentence, theory, model category, theory morphism, colimit of theories, reduct etc., taken in one institution, can be faithfully simulated in the other. With this, it is easy to show that institution independent specification language constructs [34, 7] are preserved in both directions.

We now recall three different notions of map of institution from [25, 30].

2.3 Simple Maps of Institutions

An institution $I = (\underline{Sign}, sen, \underline{Mod}, \models)$ induces the category of *theories with axiom-preserving theory morphisms* $Th_0(I)$.
Objects are theories $T = (\Sigma, \Gamma)$, where $\Sigma \in |\underline{Sign}|$ and $\Gamma \subseteq sen(\Sigma)$ (with Γ not necessarily closed under consequence). We set $sign(T) = \Sigma$ and $ax(T) = \Gamma$. Morphisms $\sigma: (\Sigma, \Gamma) \longrightarrow (\Sigma', \Gamma')$ in $Th_0(I)$ are signature morphisms $\sigma: \Sigma \longrightarrow \Sigma'$

such that $\sigma(\Gamma) \subseteq \Gamma'$. *sen*, $\underline{Mod}$ and $\models$ can be easily extended to theories as well. Thus we get a new institution $\underline{Th_0}(I) = (Th_0(I), sen^{\underline{Th_0}}, \underline{Mod}^{\underline{Th_0}}, \models^{\underline{Th_0}})$.

Given a plain map $\mu = (\Phi, \alpha, \beta): I \longrightarrow J$, let Φ^α, the α-extension to theories of Φ, map (Σ, Γ) to $(sign(\Phi(\Sigma)), ax(\Phi(\Sigma)) \cup \alpha_\Sigma(\Gamma))$. Likewise, α and β can easily be extended to $\underline{Th_0}(I)$, so we get a plain map of institution $\underline{Th_0}(\mu) = (\Phi^\alpha, \alpha^{\underline{Th_0}}, \beta^{\underline{Th_0}}): \underline{Th_0}(I) \longrightarrow \underline{Th_0}(J)$, and $\underline{Th_0}: \underline{PlainInst} \longrightarrow \underline{PlainInst}$ becomes a functor. There is an obvious inclusion $\eta_I: I \longrightarrow \underline{Th_0}(I)$, and a projection $\xi_I: \underline{Th_0}(\underline{Th_0}(I)) \longrightarrow \underline{Th_0}(I)$ mapping $((\Sigma, \Gamma), \Gamma')$ to $(\Sigma, \Gamma \cup \Gamma')$ for signatures and keeping sentences and models.

Definition 1. A simple map of institutions $\mu: I \longrightarrow J$ is a plain map of institutions $\mu: I \longrightarrow \underline{Th_0}(J)$. Thus we are allowed to map a signature not just to a signature, but to a theory, which gives us more flexibility when setting up maps of institutions.

Identities are given by η_I, and composition is done using ξ. This gives us a category $\underline{Inst}$. (Technically speaking, $\underline{\boldsymbol{Th_0}} = (\underline{Th_0}, \eta, \xi)$ is a monad over $\underline{PlainInst}$ and $\underline{Inst}$ its Kleisli category.)

A simple embeddings of institutions is a simple map which also is an embedding.

2.4 Conjunctive Maps of Institutions

Now simple maps of institutions cover more, but still not all desirable representations of institutions. A second step is to allow sentences being mapped not to single sentences, but to (finite) sets of sentences.

An institution $I = (\underline{Sign}, sen, \underline{Mod}, \models)$ can be enriched to the institution $\bigwedge(I) = (\underline{Sign}, sen^\wedge, \underline{Mod}, \models^\wedge)$, where $sen^\wedge = \mathcal{P}_{fin} \circ sen$, the composition of *sen* with the functor $\mathcal{P}_{fin}: \underline{Set} \longrightarrow \underline{Set}$ giving the set of finite subsets, and $M \models^\wedge_\Sigma S$ iff for all $\varphi \in S$, $M \models_\Sigma \varphi$.

Definition 2. A conjunctive map of institutions $\mu: I \longrightarrow J$ is a simple map of institutions $\mu: I \longrightarrow \bigwedge(J)$.

Again, this construction can be turned into a monad **Conj** $= (\bigwedge, \eta, \xi)$ (this time acting on $\underline{Inst}$) with Kleisli category $\bigwedge\underline{Inst}$.

A conjunctive embeddings of institutions is a conjunctive map which also is an embedding.

2.5 Weak Maps of Institutions

Still, there is the need for even more complex representations of institutions. In many examples, it is only possible to map theories to theories. Now the theory functor $\underline{Th_0}$ from subsection 2.3 can be viewed as a functor $\underline{Inst} \longrightarrow$

$\underline{SpecFram}$: it takes an institution $I = (\underline{Sign}, sen, \underline{Mod}, \models)$ to the specification frame $(Th_0(I), \underline{Mod})$. By abuse of language, we also denote it by $\underline{Th_0}$.

Definition 3. A weak map of institution $\mu: I \longrightarrow J$ is a map of specification frames $\mu: \underline{Th_0}(I) \longrightarrow \underline{Th_0}(J)$. Composition is that of $\underline{SpecFram}$. This gives us a category $\underline{WeakInst}$ of institutions and weak maps of institutions.

In some cases, a weak map can be shown to be modular. That means, the mapping of theories to theories can be split into two maps: one mapping signatures to theories, and the other mapping sentences to extensions of these theories. Therefore we need to define a functor $\exists!$ which goes from specification frames to institutions and just adds theory extension as axioms.

For a specification frame $F = (\underline{Th}, \underline{Mod})$, we set $\exists!(F) = (\underline{Th}, sen, \underline{Mod}, \models)$, where $sen(T)$ is the set of all theory extensions, i. e. theory morphisms $\sigma: T \longrightarrow T'$ in $\underline{Th}$ such that $M_1' |_\sigma \cong M_2' |_\sigma \Rightarrow M_1' \cong M_2'$. Sentences are translated by pushing out. Now $M \models \sigma: T \longrightarrow T'$ iff "$M \in \underline{Mod}(T')$", i. e. iff there is some $M' \in \underline{Mod}(T')$ with $M' |_\sigma \cong M$. Note that M' has to be unique up to isomorphism. For morphisms, $\exists!(\Phi, \beta) = (\Phi, \Phi, \beta)$.

Unfortunately, this seems not to be a functor between specification frames and institutions in general, so we have to restrict both categories.

Let $\underline{SpecFram}^{amal}$ (resp. $\underline{Inst}^{amal}$) be the restriction of $\underline{SpecFram}$ (resp. $\underline{Inst}$) to those objects having *amalgamation* and those maps preserving amalgamation. A specification frame resp. institution has amalgamation, if $\underline{Th}$ (resp. $\underline{Sign}$) has canonical multiple pushouts and $\underline{Mod}$ maps multiple pushouts to multiple pullbacks in $\underline{\mathcal{CAT}}$. A map of specification frames preserves amalgamation, iff (1) Φ preserves multiple pushouts and (2) β_T is a natural equivalence. A simple map of institutions preserves amalgamation, iff (1) Φ preserves multiple pushouts and (2) β_Σ is a natural equivalence with $M \models_\Sigma \varphi \iff \beta'_\Sigma(M) \models_{\Phi(\Sigma)} \alpha_\Sigma(\varphi)$ where β'_Σ is an inverse-up-to-isomorphism of β_Σ.

Now $\underline{Th_0}$ can be restricted to $\underline{Th_0}: \underline{Inst}^{amal} \longrightarrow \underline{SpecFram}^{amal}$. This theory functor has $\exists!$ as a right adjoint. The unit $\eta_I: I \longrightarrow \exists!(\underline{Th_0}(I))$ of the adjunction is given by mapping a signature Σ to the theory $(\Sigma, \emptyset)$, mapping a Σ-sentence φ to the theory extension $(\Sigma, \emptyset) \hookrightarrow (\Sigma, \{\varphi\})$ and leaving models unchanged. The counit $\epsilon_F: \underline{Th_0}(\exists!(F)) \longrightarrow F$ of the adjunction maps a theory $TT = (T, \{T \xrightarrow{\sigma_i} T_i \mid i \in I\})$ to T', where $(T', (\theta_i: T_i \longrightarrow T')_{i \in I}) = Colim(T, (T \xrightarrow{\sigma_i} T_i)_{i \in I})$. Let $\sigma: T \longrightarrow T'$ denote $\theta_i \circ \sigma_i$ (note that, by $(T', (\theta_i: T_i \longrightarrow T')_{i \in I})$ being a cocone, this is independent of i). Then β_{TT} is $\underline{Mod}(\sigma)$, being a natural equivalence.

Theorem 4. *$(\eta, \epsilon): \underline{Th_0} \dashv \exists!: \underline{SpecFram}^{amal} \longrightarrow \underline{Inst}^{amal}$ is an adjoint situation, inducing a monad* $\boldsymbol{Ext}$ *on $\underline{Inst}^{amal}$ with Kleisli category $\underline{Inst}^{amal}_{\boldsymbol{Ext}}$. Thus $\underline{Inst}^{amal}_{\boldsymbol{Ext}}$ has as objects institutions and as morphisms $\mu: I \longrightarrow J$ simple maps of institutions $\mu: I \longrightarrow \exists!(\underline{Th_0}(J))$.*

Proposition 5. *The functor* $K\colon \underline{Inst}^{amal}_{\mathbf{Ext}} \longrightarrow \underline{WeakInst}^{amal}$ *being the identity on objects and mapping morphisms* $\mu\colon I \longrightarrow \exists!(\underline{Th}_0(J))$ *to weak maps* $K(\mu) = \underline{Th}_0(I) \xrightarrow{\underline{Th}_0(\mu)} \underline{Th}_0(\exists!(\underline{Th}_0(J))) \xrightarrow{\epsilon_{\underline{Th}_0(J)}} \underline{Th}_0(J)$ *is an isomorphism with* $K^{-1}(\underline{Th}_0(I) \xrightarrow{\rho} \underline{Th}_0(J))$ *being* $I \xrightarrow{\eta_I} \exists!(\underline{Th}_0(I)) \xrightarrow{\exists!(\rho)} \exists!(\underline{Th}_0(J))$.

Thus a weak map of institutions $\rho\colon \underline{Th}_0(I) \longrightarrow \underline{Th}_0(J) \in \underline{WeakInst}^{amal}$ can be modularized as a simple map of institutions $K^{-1}(\rho)\colon I \longrightarrow \exists!(\underline{Th}_0(J))$. Vice versa, a modularized map $\mu)\colon I \longrightarrow \exists!(\underline{Th}_0(J))$ can be made into a map $K(\mu)\colon \underline{Th}_0(I) \longrightarrow \underline{Th}_0(J)$ by mapping a theory just is the multiple pushout of all theory extensions resulting from the application of μ to each sentence of the theory.

It is easy to see that each conjunctive map also is a weak map of institutions, this gives us an embedding $weak_\wedge\colon \bigwedge \underline{Inst}^{amal} \longrightarrow \underline{WeakInst}$.

Now a weak embedding is a weak map which also is an embedding of specification frames. Two institutions are called *weakly equivalent expressive*, if there are weak embeddings in both directions.

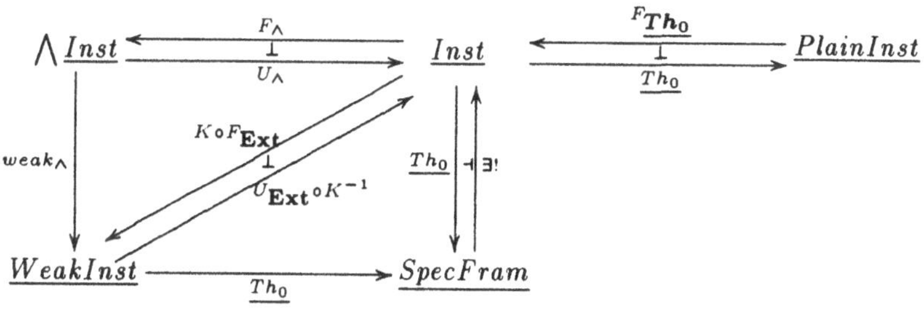

Fig. 1. Functors and adjunctions between different categories of logical frameworks

2.6 Re-Use of Theorem Provers

The following theorem is proved in [8]:

Theorem 6. *Let* $\mu\colon I \longrightarrow J$ *be a simple map of institutions with surjective model components (all simple embeddings have this property). Then semantical entailment is preserved:*

$$\Gamma \models^I_\Sigma \varphi \text{ iff } \alpha_\Sigma[\Gamma] \models^J_{sign\,\Phi\,\Sigma} \alpha_\Sigma \varphi$$

Corollary 7. *Let* $\mu\colon I \longrightarrow J$ *be a conjunctive map of institutions with surjective model components. Then*

$$\Gamma \models^I_\Sigma \varphi \text{ iff } \forall \psi \in \alpha_\Sigma \varphi . \bigcup \alpha_\Sigma[\Gamma] \models^J_{sign\,\Phi\,\Sigma} \psi$$

So we can re-use a theorem-prover which is designed for J also for proofs within I.

2.7 Liberality

Definition 8. An institution I is called *liberal*, if for each theory morphism $\sigma: T \longrightarrow T'$ in $\underline{Th_0}(I)$, $\underline{Mod}^{\underline{Th_0}(I)}(\sigma)$ has a left adjoint.

Liberality means that free constructions which are needed for parameterization and module concepts [11] always exist. Moreover, we can use initiality and freeness constraints which state that some part of a theory has to be interpreted in a fixed canonical way. The restriction to liberal institutions also has the effect that theorem proving becomes more feasible (conditional term rewriting, paramodulation), at least in the well-known liberal institutions.

Proposition 9. *Suppose that there is a weak map of institutions* $(\Phi, \beta): \underline{Th_0}(I) \longrightarrow \underline{Th_0}(J)$ *from* I *to* J. *If* β_T *is a natural equivalence for each theory* T *(in particular, if* (Φ, β) *is a weak embedding), then*

$$J \text{ is liberal} \Rightarrow I \text{ is liberal}$$

Proof:
Let $\sigma: T \longrightarrow T'$ be a theory morphism is $\underline{Th_0}(I)$. Since β_T and $\beta_{T'}$ are natural equivalences, we can choose β'_T left adjoint to β_T and $\beta'_{T'}$ right adjoint to $\beta_{T'}$ such that units and counits are isomorphisms. By naturality of β, $\beta_T \circ \underline{Mod}^{\underline{Th_0}(J)}(\Phi(\sigma)) = \underline{Mod}^{\underline{Th_0}(I)}(\sigma) \circ \beta_{T'}$. Multiplying right with $\beta'_{T'}$ yields $\beta_T \circ \underline{Mod}^{\underline{Th_0}(J)}(\Phi(\sigma)) \circ \beta'_{T'} \cong \underline{Mod}^{\underline{Th_0}(I)}(\sigma)$. By liberality of J, $\underline{Mod}^{\underline{Th_0}(J)}(\Phi(\sigma))$ has a left adjoint $F_{\Phi(\sigma)}$. By compositionality of left adjoints, $\beta_{T'} \circ F_{\Phi(\sigma)} \circ \beta'_T$ is left adjoint to $\underline{Mod}^{\underline{Th_0}(I)}(\sigma)$. □

2.8 Locally finitely presentable categories

Definition 10 [1]. An object K of a category $\mathcal{K}$ is called *finitely presentable* provided that its hom-functor

$$hom(K, \_): \mathcal{K} \longrightarrow \underline{Set}$$

preserves directed colimits.

For example, a set is finitely presentable in $\underline{Set}$ iff it is finite. A many-sorted algebra is finitely presentable in $\underline{Mod}(S, OP)$ iff it can be presented by finitely many generators and finitely many equations in the usual algebraic sense.

Definition 11 [1]. A category $\mathcal{K}$ is called *locally finitely presentable* provided that is cocomplete and has a set $\mathcal{A}$ of finitely presentable objects such that every object is a directed colimit of objects from $\mathcal{A}$.

Proposition 12 [1]. *Each locally finitely presentable category is complete*

Locally finitely presentable categories are categories which satisfy some completeness properties (completeness and cocompleteness) and some smallness properties (roughly speaking, they are categories of structures with operations of finite arities).

3 A Variety of Liberal Institutions

In this section, we formally introduce a variety of liberal institutions. Our list of institutions contains the most expressive liberal institutions studied in the literature.

3.1 Relational Partial Conditional Existence-Equational Logic

We now recall the institution $RP(R \overset{e}{=}\longrightarrow R \overset{e}{=})$ (Relational Partial Conditional Existence-Equational Logic) of partial algebraic systems with universal Horn sentences over existential atomic formulas (see [4, 28]).

This institution has a semantics of atomic formulas and conditional axioms which leads to a two-valued logic of partial algebras, see [4]. Undefinedness of terms and falsehood of relations are not distinguished (as it would be possible within three-valued logics). An overview over different semantics and a justification of the two-valued semantics can be found in [13].

Signatures $\Sigma = (S, OP, POP, REL)$ consist of (finite sets) of sort symbols $s \in S$, total operation symbols $op: s_1, \dots, s_n \longrightarrow s \in OP$, partial operation symbols $pop: s_1, \dots, s_n \longrightarrow s \in POP$, and relation symbols $R : s_1, \dots, s_n \in REL$. $\overline{s} = s_1, \dots, s_n$ is called the *arity*, s the *coarity* of an operation symbol. Signature morphisms map symbols of the appropriate kind to each other, respecting the sorting. A Σ-model (or Σ-algebra) A consists of a family $|A| = (A_s)_{s \in S}$ of carrier sets, a family $(op_A: A_{\overline{s}} \longrightarrow A_s)_{op:\overline{s} \longrightarrow s \in OP}$ of total operations, a family $(pop_A\colon \text{dom } pop_A \longrightarrow A_s)_{pop:\overline{s} \longrightarrow s \in POP}$, where dom $pop_A \subseteq A_{\overline{s}}$ is the domain of pop_A, of partial operations, and a family $(R_A \subseteq A_{\overline{s}})_{R:\overline{s} \in REL}$ of relations[1].
A Σ-homomorphism $h: A \longrightarrow B$ is a family $h = (h_s: A_s \longrightarrow B_s)_{s \in S}$ of total functions, such that for any $op: \overline{s} \longrightarrow s \in OP$ and any $\overline{a} \in A_{\overline{s}}$ we have $h_s(op_A(\overline{a})) = op_B(h_{\overline{s}}(\overline{a}))$, for any $pop: \overline{s} \longrightarrow s \in POP$, $\overline{a} \in A_{\overline{s}}$ and $a \in A_s$ we have

$$\overline{a} \in \text{dom } pop_A \text{ and } pop_A(\overline{a}) = a$$

implies

$$h_{\overline{s}}(\overline{a}) \in \text{dom } pop_B \text{ and } pop_B(h_{\overline{s}}(\overline{a})) = h_s(a)$$

[1] We abbreviate $s_1, \dots, s_n$ by $\overline{s}$, $A_{s_1} \times \dots \times A_{s_n}$ by $A_{\overline{s}}$. $h_{\overline{s}}(\overline{a})$ abbreviates $h_1(a_1), \dots, h_n(a_n)$ and so on.

and for any $R : \bar{s} \in REL$ and $\bar{a} \in A_{\bar{s}}$ we have $\bar{a} \in R_A \Rightarrow h_{\bar{s}}(\bar{a}) \in R_B$.

If $\Sigma = (S, OP, POP, REL)$, $\sigma: \Sigma \longrightarrow \Sigma'$ is a signature morphism and $A' \in |\underline{Mod}^{\mathcal{RPCEL}}\ \Sigma'|$, then $A' |_\sigma$ is the Σ-algebra A with $A_s := A'_{\sigma(s)}$ $(s \in S)$, $op_A := (\sigma(op))_{A'}$ $(op \in OP)$ and so on. Similarly, for homomorphisms we define $(h' |_\sigma)_s := h_{\sigma(s)}$.
A sentence over a signature $\Sigma = (S, OP, POP, REL)$ is a conditional formula

$$\forall X. e_1 \wedge \ldots \wedge e_n \longrightarrow e$$

where X is an S-sorted system of variables and the atomic formulas e and e_i are of two kinds: Either

$$t_1 \stackrel{e}{=} t_2$$

where t_1, t_2 are terms with same sort (from the term algebra with variables $T_\Sigma(X)_s$ using total and partial operation symbols. See, e.g., [10]). Or

$$R(t_1, \ldots, t_n)$$

where $R : \bar{s} \in REL$ and t_i is a term of sort s_i (from $T_\Sigma(X)_{s_i}$). Sentence translation is defined inductively, where X is mapped to $\sigma(X)$ with $\sigma(X)_{s'} = \bigcup_{\sigma(s)=s'} X_s$.
Finally, satisfaction is defined as follows: $A \models_\Sigma (X.e_1 \wedge \ldots \wedge e_n \longrightarrow e)$ if and only if all valuations $\nu: X \longrightarrow A$ which satisfy the premises satisfy the conclusion as well. Satisfaction of atomic formulas is defined as

$$\nu \models t_1 \stackrel{e}{=} t_2 \iff \nu^\#(t_1) \text{ and } \nu^\#(t_2) \text{ are both defined and equal}$$

$$\nu \models R(\bar{t}) \iff \nu^\#(\bar{t}) \text{ is defined and } \in R_A$$

where $\nu^\#$ is the partial homomorphic extension of ν from X to $\operatorname{dom} \nu^\# \subseteq T_\Sigma(X)$ (see [33]).

For sets of variables, we use the following notation: $X = \{ x : s_1; y : s_2 \}$ means that $X_{s_1} = \{ x \}$, $X_{s_2} = \{ y \}$ and $X_s = \emptyset$ otherwise. □

3.2 Restrictions of $RP(R \stackrel{e}{=}\!\!\rightarrow R \stackrel{e}{=})$

Some natural restrictions of $RP(R \stackrel{e}{=}\!\!\rightarrow R \stackrel{e}{=})$ can now be defined immediately:

$P(\stackrel{e}{=}\!\!\rightarrow\!\stackrel{e}{=})$ (Partial Conditional Existence Equational Logic) is the subinstitution of $RP(R \stackrel{e}{=}\!\!\rightarrow R \stackrel{e}{=})$ defined by requiring $REL = \emptyset$ for signatures $\Sigma = (S, OP, POP, REL)$. □

Let $P(D \rightarrow\!\stackrel{e}{=})$ (Partial Existentially-Conditioned Existence-Equational Logic) be the subinstitution of $P(\stackrel{e}{=}\!\!\rightarrow\!\stackrel{e}{=})$ defined by requiring sentences to have the form

$$\forall X. t_1 \stackrel{e}{=} t_1 \wedge \cdots \wedge t_n \stackrel{e}{=} t_n \longrightarrow t \stackrel{e}{=} t'$$

that is, the premises contain only definedness conditions. $P(D \rightarrow \stackrel{e}{=})$ was introduced by Burmeister [4]. But also Jarzembski's weak varieties [21, 22], when restricted to the liberal case, are of this form. □

$P(\stackrel{s}{=})$ is the institution with signatures and models from $P(\stackrel{e}{=} \rightarrow \stackrel{e}{=})$. A Σ-sentence has the form

$$\forall X.t_1 \stackrel{s}{=} t_2 \quad (t_1, t_2 \in T_\Sigma(X)_s)$$

Satisfaction is defined as follows: $A \models_\Sigma \forall X.t_1 \stackrel{s}{=} t_2$ iff for all valuations $\nu: X \longrightarrow A$, $\nu^\#(t_1)$ is defined if and only if $\nu^\#(t_2)$ is defined, and if this is the case, both are equal.

These "strong equations" are cited in the literature quite frequently, see [4, 20, 23, 31]. □

Note that in the literature, total operations are often omitted in presence of partial operations: a total operation can be viewed as a partial operations satisfying $pop(\overline{x}) \stackrel{e}{=} pop(\overline{x})$, if existence equations are available. In $P(\stackrel{s}{=})$, there are no existence equations, and in fact, $P(\stackrel{s}{=})$ without total operations is slightly weaker than with: the algebra with totally undefined partial operations is a model of every sentence containing partial operation symbols on both sides, while this does not happen in presence of a total operation *op* with same arity and coarity as a partial operation *pop*: then the equation

$$\forall \{ x : s \} : op(x) \stackrel{s}{=} pop(x)$$

forces *pop* to be total, so $\forall \{ x : s \} : pop(x) \stackrel{s}{=} pop(x)$ holds as well.

$HEP(\stackrel{e}{=} \rightarrow \stackrel{e}{=})$ (for Hierarchical Equationally Partial Theories) [33] is the institution with signatures $\Sigma = (S, OP, POP, \preceq, Def)$ consisting of $P(\stackrel{e}{=} \rightarrow \stackrel{e}{=})$-signatures (S, OP, POP) together with a well-founded partial order $\preceq$ on POP and a mapping Def, which assigns to each $pop: \overline{s} \longrightarrow s \in POP$ a finite set of existence equations

$$Def(pop) = X.E \text{ with } E \subseteq T_\Sigma(\{ \overline{x} : \overline{s} \}) \times T_\Sigma(\{ \overline{x} : \overline{s} \})$$

such that all partial operation symbols occurring in $Def(pop)$ are strictly less than *pop*.

Signature morphisms are those from $P(\stackrel{e}{=} \rightarrow \stackrel{e}{=})$ with the additional requirement that

$$Def(\sigma(pop)) = \sigma \times \sigma(Def(pop))$$

Σ-models are (S, OP, POP)-models A in $P(\stackrel{e}{=} \rightarrow \stackrel{e}{=})$ such that dom pop_A equals

$$\{ \overline{a} \in A_{\overline{s}} \mid \nu \models t_1 \stackrel{e}{=} t_2 \text{ for all } (t_1, t_2) \in Def(pop), \text{ with } \nu(x_i) = a_i \text{ for } i = 1, \ldots, n \}$$

Reducts, sentences and satisfaction are defined as in $P(\stackrel{e}{=} \rightarrow \stackrel{e}{=})$.

Note that Reichel's theory morphisms defined in [33] are slightly more general than theory morphisms in $HEP(\overset{e}{=}\!\rightarrow\!\overset{e}{=})$. But Reichel only defines a specification frame. If signatures and sentences have to be separated, a slight restriction has to be made.

Freyd's essentially algebraic theories [14] are essentially the same (Freyd does not define signatures, reducts and the like).

We define two restrictions of $HEP(\overset{e}{=}\!\rightarrow\!\overset{e}{=})$: First, let $HEP1(\overset{e}{=}\!\rightarrow\!\overset{w}{=})$ be restricted to those signatures where the hierarchy of operations has only height one, that is, the domain of each partial operation is defined using total operations only. Axioms have to be of form

$$\forall X.e_1 \wedge \cdots \wedge e_n \wedge t \overset{e}{=} t \wedge u \overset{e}{=} u \longrightarrow t \overset{e}{=} u$$

which can equivalently be written as

$$\forall X.e_1 \wedge \cdots \wedge e_n \longrightarrow t \overset{w}{=} u$$

where $t \overset{w}{=} u$ is a weak equation, which is satisfied if in case of definedness of both sides, they are equal.

$HEP1(\overset{w}{=})$ is the restriction of $HEP1(\overset{e}{=}\!\rightarrow\!\overset{w}{=})$ to unconditional axioms. □

3.3 Limit Theories

$R(R =\!\rightarrow \exists!R =)$ is the following institution: Signatures $\Sigma = (S, OP, REL)$ are $RP(R \overset{e}{=}\!\rightarrow R \overset{e}{=})$-signatures with no partial operations. Signature morphisms, models and reducts are inherited from $RP(R \overset{e}{=}\!\rightarrow R \overset{e}{=})$. Σ-sentences have the form

$$\forall X.e_1 \wedge \cdots \wedge e_n \longrightarrow \exists!Y.(e'_1 \wedge \cdots \wedge e'_m)$$

where X and Y are disjoint S-sorted variable sets and the e_i are atomic formulas with terms over X, while the e'_i are atomic formulas with terms over $X \cup Y$. The atomic formulas may be either relation applications or equalities. Coste's limit theories [9] have more general sentences, but can be shown to be equivalent to conjunctions of sentences in the above form.

Signature morphisms and reducts are defined as in $RP(R \overset{e}{=}\!\rightarrow R \overset{e}{=})$. Satisfaction is defined as follows:

$$A \models_\Sigma \forall X.e_1 \wedge \cdots \wedge e_n \longrightarrow \exists!Y.(e'_1 \wedge \cdots \wedge e'_m)$$

if for all valuations $\nu: X \longrightarrow A$ satisfying all the e_i $(i = 1, \ldots, n)$, there exists a unique extension $\xi: X \cup Y \longrightarrow A$ of ν which satisfies all the e'_i $(i = 1, \ldots, m)$. □

3.4 Left Exact Sketches

The institution $\mathcal{LESKETCH}$ (left exact sketches, see [19, 3]) has signatures $\Sigma = (G, U)$, where G is a (finite) directed graph and U is a map assigning to each vertex (or object, to keep close to categorical terminology) a in G an arrow $U(a)$ from a to a. Signature morphisms $\sigma: (G, U) \longrightarrow (G', U')$ are graph homomorphisms $\sigma: G \longrightarrow G'$ such that $\sigma \circ U = U' \circ \sigma$.

Let $|\underline{Set}|$ be the signature which is the underlying graph of the category of sets with U assigning to each set the identity function on that set. Then a Σ-model is a signature morphism $M: \Sigma \longrightarrow |\underline{Set}|$ and a model morphism is a natural transformation $\eta: M \longrightarrow M'$ (note that this is well defined because the target of M and M' is a category). If $\sigma: \Sigma \longrightarrow \Sigma'$ is a signature morphism, then $\underline{Mod}\,\sigma$ is the functor $(\_ \circ \sigma)$ given by composing with σ.

A (G, U)-sentence is either

(1) a finite diagram in G, that is, a graph homomorphism $D: I \longrightarrow G$ (where I is some finite index graph), or
(2) a finite cone over a finite diagram $D: I \longrightarrow G$ in G, that is, an object L in G and arrows $\pi_i: L \longrightarrow D_i$ in G for $i \in |I|$.

Sentences are translated along σ by composing with σ, that is, $sen\,\sigma = (\sigma \circ \_)$.

A model $M: \Sigma \longrightarrow |\underline{Set}|$ satisfies a diagram, if M takes it to a commutative diagram in $\underline{Set}$, and M satisfies a cone, if M takes it to a limit cone in $\underline{Set}$.

$\mathcal{LESKETCH}$-theories are called left exact sketches (see [19]). □

3.5 Order-Sorted Algebra with Sort Constraints

Finally, $COSASC(=\rightarrow=)$ is the institution of coherent order sorted signatures, algebras and theories [17] with conditional sort constraints [18].

Order signatures are triples $\Sigma = (S, \leq, OP)$, where $\leq$ is a partial order on S and OP may contain the same operation with different arities and coarities ("overloading"): for example, we may have $op: \overline{s} \longrightarrow s \in OP$ and $op: \overline{s'} \longrightarrow s' \in OP$.

A signature is called *regular*, if for each $op \in OP$ and $\overline{s} \in S^n$, there is a least arity for op that is greater than or equal to $\overline{s}$.

A signature is called *coherent*, if it is regular and locally filtered. The latter means that each connected component of $(S, \leq)$ must be filtered, i. e. any two elements (of the connected component) have a common upper bound.

$(S, \leq, OP)$-models are $(S, OP, \emptyset)$-models A in $P(\stackrel{e}{=}\rightarrow\stackrel{e}{=})$, such that

1. $s \leq s'$ implies $A_s \subseteq A_{s'}$

2. $op: \overline{s} \longrightarrow s \in OP$, $op: \overline{s}' \longrightarrow s' \in OP$ and $\overline{s} \leq \overline{s}'$ imply $op_A: A_{\overline{s}} \longrightarrow A_s$ equals $op_A: A_{\overline{s}'} \longrightarrow A_{s'}$ on $A_{\overline{s}}$.

For homomorphisms $h: A \longrightarrow B$, $s \leq s'$ and $a \in A_s$ must imply $h_s(a) = h_{s'}(a)$.

Terms are defined inductively as usual, by additionally requiring that $T_\Sigma(X)_s \subseteq T_\Sigma(X)_{s'}$ for $s \leq s'$. Because of that, a term can have many different sorts. But for regular signatures, each term t has a least sort $LS(t)$.

Order-sorted algebra can be translated to many-sorted algebra by introducing, for each order-sorted signature Σ a many-sorted signature $(\Sigma^\#, J)$ where for $\Sigma = (S, \leq, OP)$, $\Sigma^\#$ has sorts S, an operation symbol $op_{\overline{s},s}: \overline{s} \longrightarrow s$ for $op: \overline{s} \longrightarrow s \in OP$ plus additional coercion operation symbols $c_{s,s'}: s \longrightarrow s'$ whenever $s \leq s'$. The axioms in J state identity, injectivity, transitivity and compatibility for the coercions.

A $(\Sigma^\#, J)$-algebra B can be mapped to a Σ-algebra $B^\bullet$, where coercions in B are replaced by set inclusions in $B^\bullet$ using colimits of filtered diagrams built up by the coercions. Vice versa, any Σ-algebra A can be mapped to a $(\Sigma^\#, J)$-algebra $A^\#$ by just adding inclusions as coercions. Goguen and Meseguer show this to be a natural equivalence of categories [17].

A *conditional Σ-sort constraint* with operation symbol *op* is a formula

$$\delta = \forall\{\, x_1 : s_n, \ldots, x_n : s_n \,\}.e_1 \wedge \ldots \wedge e_n \longrightarrow op(x_1, \ldots, x_n) : s$$

where

1. *op* is a Σ-operation symbol $op: s'_1, \ldots, s'_n \longrightarrow s'$ with $s'_i \geq s_i$ and $s' \geq s$,
2. no operation symbol in Σ has arity smaller than $s_1, \ldots, s_n$, and all operation symbols of arity $s_1, \ldots, s_n$ have coarity strictly bigger than s ($s_1, \ldots, s_n$ is called the arity of the constraint)
3. the e_i are Σ-equations in the variables in X.

A signature with sort constraints (Σ, Δ) consists of a coherent order-sorted signature Σ and a set Δ of conditional Σ-sort constraints with different operation symbols. $\underline{Sign}^{COSASC(=\rightarrow=)}$ is the category of coherent order sorted signatures with sort constraints and signature morphisms preserving the sort constraints.

A Σ-algebra A *satisfies* a conditional Σ-sort constraint $\forall X.e_1 \wedge \ldots \wedge e_n \longrightarrow op(x_1, \ldots, x_n) : s$ iff for all assignments $\nu : X \rightarrow A$ that satisfy $e_1, \ldots, e_n$, we have that $\nu^\#(op(x_1, \ldots, x_n))$ belongs to A_s. $\underline{Mod}^{COSASC(=\rightarrow=)}(\Sigma, \Delta)$ is the category of $\Sigma = (S, \leq, OP)$-algebras satisfying all the sort constraints in Δ.

Given a signature (Σ, Δ), we can form the signature $\Sigma(\Delta)$ by adding an operation symbol $\delta: s_1, \ldots, s_n \longrightarrow s$ for each sort constraint $\delta = \forall\{\, x_1 : s_n, \ldots, x_n : s_n \,\}.e_1 \wedge \ldots \wedge e_n \longrightarrow op(x_1, \ldots, x_n) : s$ in Δ. With this, [18] define the intended parse for $\Sigma(\Delta)$-terms t to be some $\Sigma(\Delta)^\#$-term $IP(t)$ plus a set $cond(IP(t))$ of Σ-equations expressing the conditions under which the term can be interpreted.

Any valuation $\nu: X \longrightarrow A$ into a Σ-algebra A can be homomorphically extended to a partial function $\nu^{\natural}: T_{\Sigma(\Delta)\#}(X) \longrightarrow A^{\#}$. A Σ-algebra A satisfy an (Σ, Δ)-axiom

$$\forall X.t_1 = u_1 \wedge \cdots \wedge t_n = u_n \longrightarrow t = u$$

consisting of $\Sigma(\Delta)$-terms iff all valuations $\nu: X \longrightarrow A$ which satisfy $cond(IP(t_1)) \wedge cond(IP(u_1)) \wedge \cdots cond(IP(t)) \wedge cond(IP(u))$ we have:

$$\nu^{\natural}(IP(t_i)) = \nu^{\natural}(IP(u_i)) \ (i = 1, \ldots, n) \text{ implies } \nu^{\natural}(IP(t)) = \nu^{\natural}(IP(u)) \quad \square$$

All frameworks introduced so far are institutions with amalgamation. Thus we can use the modular definition of weak maps of institutions when proving our main theorem.

4 The Main Theorem

Theorem 13. *Between the institutions introduced in Sect. 3, there are the maps of institutions shown in Fig. 2.*

Corollary 14. *All the institutions in Fig. 2 are weakly equivalent expressive. In particular, considered as specification frames, they are equivalent expressive.*

Proof:

By composability of weak embeddings of institutions. $\square$

Corollary 15. *All institutions in Fig. 2 are liberal.*

Proof. $HEP(\stackrel{e}{=}\rightarrow\stackrel{e}{=})$ has shown to be liberal by Reichel [33]. By the Theorem and Proposition 9, this carries over to the other institutions. $\square$

Corollary 16. *We can re-use theorem provers along all except the dashed arrows in Fig. 2.*

Proof. By Theorem 6 and Corollary 7.

Corollary 17. *(1) All model categories specifiable in any of the above institutions are locally finitely presentable.*

(2) In all of the above institutions, the same subclass of locally finitely presentable categories can be specified.

(3) If we extend the above institutions to infinite signatures (consisting of infinite sets of sorts, infinite sets of (finitary) operation and relation symbols, and infinite graphs), then in each such extended institution, exactly the locally finitely presentable categories can be specified as model categories of theories.

Proof. (1) See [9, 1, 15] and use Corollary 14 and the fact that locally finite representability is invariant under equivalences of categories.

(2) Follows from Corollary 14.

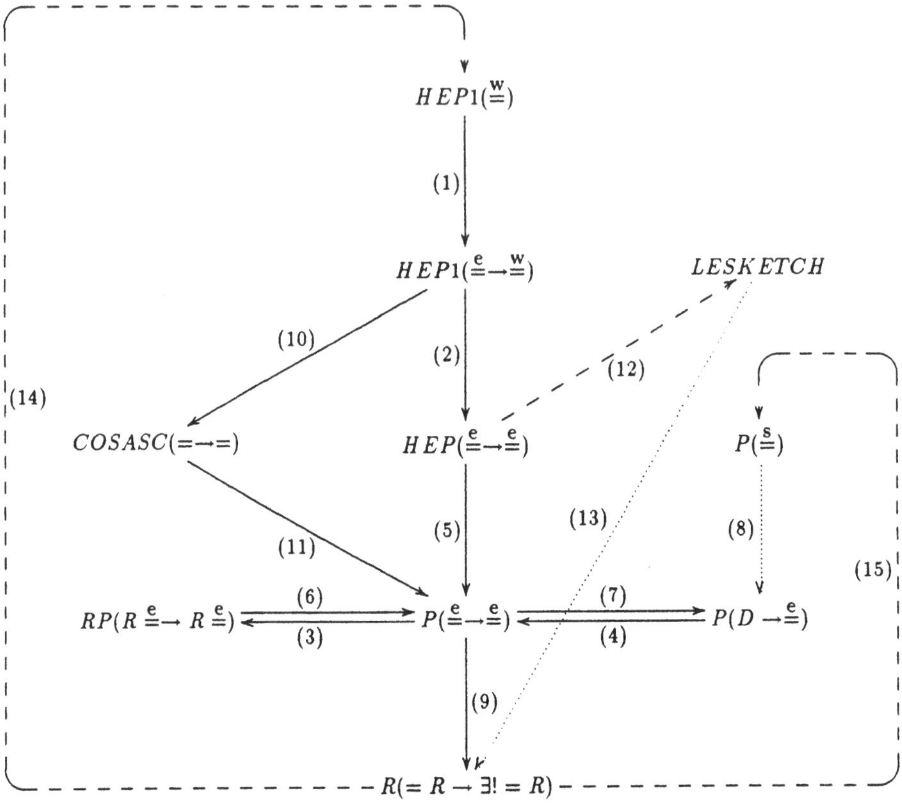

Fig. 2. Embeddings among institutions of partial algebras. A solid arrow denotes an embedding of institutions, a dotted arrow denotes a conjunctive embedding of institutions, and a dashed arrow denotes a weak embedding of institutions.

(3) Coste [9] shows the statement for $R(R =\rightarrow \exists! R =)$, Adamek and Rosický [1] show it for HEP and $\mathcal{LESKETCH}$. This carries over to the other institutions by noticing that the proof of Theorem 13 below can easily be extended to infinite signatures. □

Proof of Theorem 13, (1), (2), (3) and (4)

Obvious subinstitutions.

Proof of Theorem 13, (5)

We define a simple embedding of institutions $\mu^{hep}: HEP(\stackrel{e}{=}\rightarrow\stackrel{e}{=}) \longrightarrow P(\stackrel{e}{=}\rightarrow\stackrel{e}{=})$:

- $\Phi^{hep}(S, OP, POP, \preceq, Def)$ is the theory with signature (S, OP, POP) and the following circumscription of the $Def(pop)$-condition as axioms

$$\forall\{\,\overline{x} : \overline{s}\,\}.pop(\overline{x}) \stackrel{e}{=} pop(\overline{x}) \longrightarrow e \quad (e \in Def(pop))$$

$$\forall\{\,\overline{x} : \overline{s}\,\}. \bigwedge_{e \in Def(pop)} e \longrightarrow pop(\overline{x}) \stackrel{e}{=} pop(\overline{x})$$

  for $pop: \overline{s} \longrightarrow s \in POP$.
- $\Phi^{hep}(\sigma) = \sigma$
- α^{hep}_{Σ} and β^{hep}_{Σ} are the identity □

Proof of Theorem 13, (6)

The embedding $\mu^{chardom}$ from [24], representing relations by domains of partial operations, can easily be extended to a simple embedding of institutions $\mu^{chardom}: RP(R \stackrel{e}{=}\rightarrow R \stackrel{e}{=}) \longrightarrow P(\stackrel{e}{=}\rightarrow\stackrel{e}{=})$.

- $\Phi^{chardom}(S, OP, POP, REL)$ is the theory with signature

$$(S, OP, POP \cup \{\,\chi^{R}: s_1 \,\ldots\, s_n \longrightarrow s_1 \mid R : s_1, \,\ldots\,, s_n \in REL\,\})$$

  and axioms

$$\forall\{\,\overline{s} : \overline{x}; y : s_1\,\}.\chi^{R}(\overline{x}) \stackrel{e}{=} y \longrightarrow \chi^{R}(\overline{x}) \stackrel{e}{=} x_1)$$

  for each $R : \overline{s} \in REL$.
- $\alpha^{chardom}_{\Sigma}$ doesn't change the variable system. On atomic formulas, the action is

$$\alpha^{chardom}_{\Sigma}[\![t_1 \stackrel{e}{=} t_2]\!] = [\![t_1 \stackrel{e}{=} t_2]\!]$$

$$\alpha^{chardom}_{\Sigma}[\![R(\overline{t})]\!] = [\![\chi^{R}(\overline{t}) \stackrel{e}{=} t_1]\!]$$

  This can be easily extended to conditional formulas. □

Proof of Theorem 13, (7)

The simple embedding of institutions $\mu^{pp}: P(\stackrel{e}{=}\rightarrow\stackrel{e}{=}) \longrightarrow P(D \rightarrow\stackrel{e}{=})$ is defined as follows:

A signature $\Sigma = (S, OP, POP)$ is translated by Φ^{pp} to Σ extended by

partial opns $\chi^{s}_{=}: s\ s \longrightarrow s$
axioms $\chi^{s}_{=}(x, x) \stackrel{e}{=} x$
$\chi^{s}_{=}(x, y) \stackrel{e}{=} \chi^{s}_{=}(x, y) \longrightarrow x \stackrel{e}{=} y$

for each sort s in S.

An atomic formula $t_1 \stackrel{e}{=} t_2$ (of sort s) is translated by α^{pp} to

$$\chi^s_=(t_1, t_2) \stackrel{e}{=} \chi^s_=(t_1, t_2)$$

This translation is easily extended to conditional formulas.

β^{pp} translates a model by simply forgetting the $\chi^s_=$-operations. Since the latter are defined uniquely by the axioms, β^{pp} is an isomorphism of categories. □

Proof of Theorem 13, (8)

The conjunctive embedding of institutions $\mu^{se}: P(\stackrel{s}{=}) \longrightarrow P(D \rightarrow \stackrel{e}{=})$ is defined by:

- Φ^{se} and β^{se}_Σ are identities
- $\alpha^{se}_\Sigma(X : t_1 \stackrel{s}{=} t_2) = \{\forall X.t_1 \stackrel{e}{=} t_1 \longrightarrow t_1 \stackrel{e}{=} t_2, \forall X.t_2 \stackrel{e}{=} t_2 \longrightarrow t_1 \stackrel{e}{=} t_2\}$ which state that if either side of $t_1 \stackrel{s}{=} t_2$ is defined, the other side is defined as well and both sides are equal. Thus (1) follows. □

Proof of Theorem 13, (9)

The simple embedding of institutions $\mu^{limgra}: P(\stackrel{e}{=} \rightarrow \stackrel{e}{=}) \longrightarrow R(R = \longrightarrow \exists! R =)$ is defined as follows:

- $\Phi^{limgra}(S, OP, POP)$ is the theory $((S, OP, REL), \Gamma)$, where REL contains a relation

$$G^{pop} : \overline{s}\ s$$

  and Γ contains an axiom

$$\forall\{\overline{x} : \overline{s}; y, z : s\}.G^{pop}(\overline{x}, y) \land G^{pop}(\overline{x}, z) \longrightarrow y = z$$

  for each $pop: \overline{s} \longrightarrow s \in POP$. The relation G^{pop} shall hold the graph of a partial operation pop, and the axiom states that G^{pop} is right-unique, that is, the graph of a partial operation.
- Following Burmeister [4, p. 325], we translate existence equations in a relational form. $(t_1 \stackrel{e}{=} t_2)^*$ is defined inductively as follows:
  - $(pop(t_1, \ldots, t_n) \stackrel{e}{=} t_0)^* = (\exists y_0 : s_0 \ldots y_n : s_n(G^{pop}(y_1, \ldots, y_n, y_0) \land (t_0 \stackrel{e}{=} y_0)^* \land \cdots \land (t_n \stackrel{e}{=} y_n)^*))$ for $pop: s_1 \ldots s_n \longrightarrow s_0 \in POP$
  - $(op(t_1, \ldots, t_n) \stackrel{e}{=} t_0)^* = (\exists y_0 : s_0 \ldots y_n : s_n(op(y_1, \ldots, y_n) \stackrel{e}{=} y_0 \land (t_0 \stackrel{e}{=} y_0)^* \land \cdots \land (t_n \stackrel{e}{=} y_n)^*))$ for $op: s_1 \ldots s_n \longrightarrow s_0 \in POP$
  - $(x \stackrel{e}{=} t)^* = (t \stackrel{e}{=} x)^*$, if t is not a variable
  - $(x \stackrel{e}{=} y)^* = (x \stackrel{e}{=} y)$

Considering a $P(\stackrel{e}{=}\rightarrow\stackrel{e}{=})$-axiom

$$\varphi = \forall X.e_1 \wedge \cdots \wedge e_n \longrightarrow e$$

we can assume that e_i^* has form $\exists Y_i \psi_i$ and e^* has form $\exists Y \psi$, where the ψ_i and ψ consist of conjunctions of atomic formulas. Then

$$\alpha_{\Sigma}^{limgra}(\varphi) = \forall X \cup Y_1 \cup \cdots \cup Y_n.\psi_1 \wedge \cdots \wedge \psi_n \longrightarrow \exists! Y.\psi$$

- β_{Σ}^{limgra} takes a $\Phi\,\Sigma$-model A and replaces each relation G_A^{pop} by the partial operation with graph G_A^{pop}

Now (1) essentially is the proposition on page 326 of [4], using the observation that

$$\forall X.(\exists Y_1.\psi_1 \wedge \cdots \wedge \exists.Y_n\ \psi_n \longrightarrow \exists Y.\psi)$$

is equivalent to

$$\forall X.\forall Y_1 \ldots \forall Y_n.(\psi_1 \wedge \cdots \wedge \psi_n \longrightarrow \exists Y.\psi)$$

by the rules for prenex normal form from [35], which in turn is equivalent to

$$\forall X \forall Y_1 \ldots \forall Y_n.(\psi_1 \wedge \cdots \wedge \psi_n \longrightarrow \exists! Y.\psi)$$

by the uniqueness axioms above. □

Proof of Theorem 13, (10)

The simple embedding of institutions μ^{hc}: $HEP1(\stackrel{e}{=}\rightarrow\stackrel{w}{=}) \longrightarrow COSASC(=\rightarrow=)$ is defined by

- $\Phi^{hc}(S, OP, POP, \preceq, Def) = (S, =, OP)$ plus the following theory added for each pop: $s_1, \ldots, s_n \longrightarrow s \in POP$:
  sorts $dom(pop) \leq s_1 \times \cdots \times s_n$
  opns π_i: $s_1 \times \cdots \times s_n \longrightarrow s_i$ for $i = 1, \ldots, n$
  $<\_, \ldots, \_>$: $s_1 \ldots s_n \longrightarrow s_1 \times \cdots \times s_n$
  pop: $dom(pop) \longrightarrow s$
  axioms $\forall\{x_1 : s_1, \ldots, x_n : s_n\}.\pi_i(< x_1, \ldots, x_n >) = x_i$
  $\forall x : s_1 \times \cdots \times s_n. < \pi_1(x), \ldots, \pi_n(x) >= x$
  $\forall x : dom(pop).Def(pop)[x_i/\pi_i(x)]$
  $\forall\{x_1 : s_1, \ldots, x_n : s_n\}.Def(pop) \longrightarrow < x_1, \ldots, x_n >: dom(pop)$

- $\alpha_{\Sigma}(\forall X.t_1 = u_1 \wedge \cdots \wedge t_n = u_n \longrightarrow t = u)$ is

$$\forall X.\tilde{t_1} = \tilde{u_1} \wedge \cdots \wedge \tilde{t_n} = \tilde{u_n} \longrightarrow \tilde{t} = \tilde{u}$$

where $\tilde{x} = x$

$\widetilde{op(t_1, \ldots, t_n)} = op(\tilde{t_1}, \ldots, \tilde{t_n})$

$\widetilde{pop(t_1, \ldots, t_n)} = pop(< \tilde{t_1}, \ldots, \tilde{t_n} >)$

- $\beta_\Sigma(A)$ forgets the product structure and otherwise keeps carriers and total operations, while an operation $pop_A: A_{dom(pop)} \longrightarrow A_s$ is now understood as a partial operation $A_{s_1} \times \cdots \times A_{s_n} \longrightarrow A_s$ with domain $A_{dom(pop)}$. By the sort constraint and the axiom $\forall x : dom(pop).Def(pop)[x_i/\pi_i(x)]$ above $\beta_\Sigma(A)$ satisfies the domain conditions in Def.
  Vice versa, a Σ-model can be mapped to a $\Phi(\Sigma)$-model by adding a product structure (which is determined up to isomorphism) and considering each partial operation as a total operation on the subsort $dom(pop)$.

Condition 1 can be verified by noting that on both sides, satisfaction is defined by considering those valuations only for which all terms (both in the premises and in the conclusion) are defined. □

Proof of Theorem 13, (11)

Define the simple embedding of institutions $\mu^{ch}: COSASC(=\rightarrow=) \longrightarrow P(\stackrel{e}{=}\rightarrow\stackrel{e}{=})$ by

- $\Phi^{ch}(\Sigma) = (\Sigma(\Delta)^\#, J)$ from subsection 3.5 plus axioms

$$\forall\{\, x_1 : s_n, \ldots, x_n : s_n \,\}.C \longleftrightarrow \delta(x_1, \ldots, x_n) \stackrel{e}{=} \delta(x_1, \ldots, x_n)$$

$$\forall\{\, x_1 : s_n, \ldots, x_n : s_n \,\}.C \longrightarrow \delta(x_1, \ldots, x_n) \stackrel{e}{=} op(x_1, \ldots, x_n)$$

  for all sort constraints $\delta = \forall\{\, x_1 : s_n, \ldots, x_n : s_n \,\}.e_1 \wedge \ldots \wedge e_n \longrightarrow op(x_1, \ldots, x_n) : s$ in Δ.
- $\alpha_\Sigma(\forall X.t_1 = u_1 \wedge \cdots \wedge t_n = u_n \longrightarrow t = u)$ is

$$\forall X.cond(IP(t_1)) \wedge \cdots \wedge cond(IP(u))$$
$$\wedge IP(t_1) \stackrel{e}{=} IP(u_1) \wedge \cdots \wedge IP(t_n) \stackrel{e}{=} IP(u_n) \longrightarrow IP(t) \stackrel{e}{=} IP(u)$$

- $\beta_\Sigma(B) = B^\bullet$. Note that the fact that under condition C op yields values in s is easy shown to be equivalent to the existence of a partial operation $\delta: s_1, \ldots, s_n \longrightarrow s$ that, under condition C, is defined and equal to op.

(1) follows from Theorem 4.4 (2) of [17] and the coincidence of partial homomorphic extensions of valuations in B and $B^\bullet$.

□

Proof of Theorem 13, (12)

The weak embedding of institutions $\mu^{hs}: HEP(\stackrel{e}{=}\rightarrow\stackrel{e}{=}) \longrightarrow \mathcal{LESKETCH}$ has already been sketched in [32].

- $\Phi^{hs}(S, OP, POP, \preceq, Def)$ is a sketch with an object (vertex) s for each $s \in S$ and an object together with projection arrows for each of the limits introduced below. Each operation $op: \overline{s} \longrightarrow s \in OP$ becomes an arrow

$s_1 \times \cdots \times s_n \xrightarrow{op} s$, together with a limit cone for $s_1 \times \cdots \times s_n$ and the projections $\pi_i : s_1 \times \cdots \times s_n \longrightarrow s_i$. Partial operations are translated by a well-founded induction along $\preceq$. For the induction step concerning $pop \in POP$, terms $t \in T_\Sigma(X)$ $(X = \{x_1 : s_1; \ldots ; x_n : s_n\})$, which consist of partial operation symbols less than *pop* and total operation symbols only, are translated to partial arrows, that is, pairs of arrows

$$s_1 \times \cdots \times s_n \xleftarrow{[\![t]\!]^-} D_t \xrightarrow{[\![t]\!]^+} s$$

as described by Poigné [32]. Since only partial operations less than *pop* are used in t, we can assume the existence of partial arrows corresponding to these operations when constructing $[\![t]\!]^+$ and $[\![t]\!]^-$. Now an existence equation $e = X.t_1 \stackrel{e}{=} t_2 \in Def(pop)$ is translated to $D_e \longrightarrow s_1 \times \cdots \times s_n$, which is the equalizer of a pullback (#):

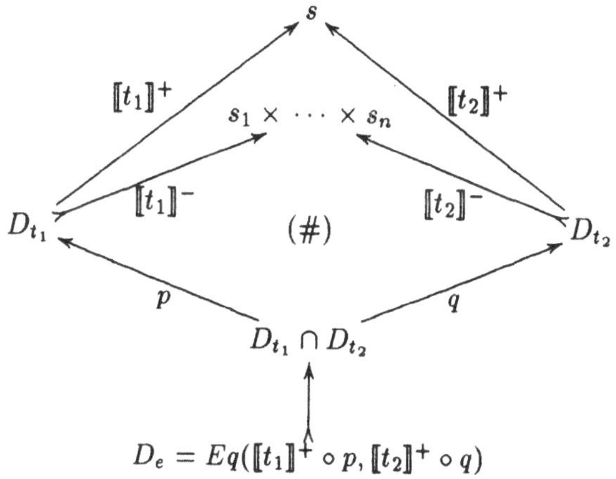

Now $pop : \overline{s} \longrightarrow s$ is translated to the partial arrow

$$s_1 \times \cdots \times s_n \xleftarrow{[\![pop]\!]^-} \mathrm{dom}\ pop = \bigcap\nolimits_{e \in Def(pop)} D_e \xrightarrow{[\![pop]\!]^+} s$$

where the intersection is a categorical intersection, thus a limit.
$\alpha^{hs}_\Sigma(\forall\{x_1 : s_1; \ldots ; x_n : s_n\}..e_1 \wedge \cdots \wedge e_k \longrightarrow e)$ is $\exists ! \Sigma' \hookrightarrow T$, where $\Sigma' = sign\Phi^{hs}\, \Sigma$ and T is $\Phi^{hs}\, \Sigma$ expanded by equalizers of pullbacks for $D_{e_1}, \ldots, D_{e_n}, D_e$, an arrow $m : D_{e_1} \cap \ldots \cap D_{e_k} \longrightarrow D_e$ and a diagram

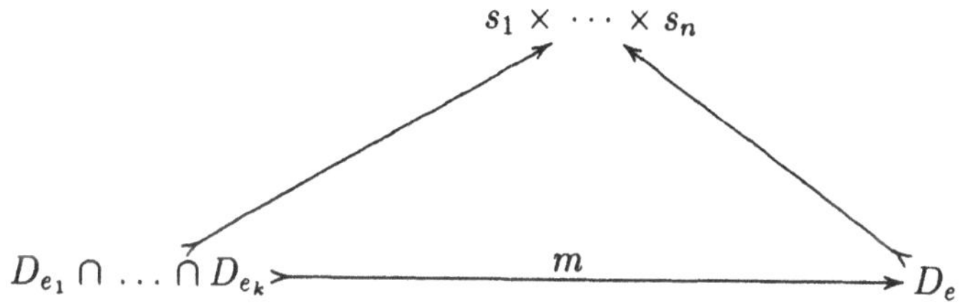

where uniqueness of m follows from the other two arrows being monic.

- β_Σ^{hs} maps a sketch model $M'\colon \Sigma' \longrightarrow |\underline{Set}|$ to the partial algebra with carriers $M'(s)$ $(s \in S)$, total operations $M'(op)$ $(op \in OP)$ and partial operations $M'(pop)\colon M'(\text{dom } pop) \longrightarrow M'(s)$ $(pop\colon \overline{s} \longrightarrow s \in POP)$. A natural transformation $\eta\colon M' \longrightarrow M''$ is translated to the homomorphism of partial algebras $(\eta_s)_{s\in S}$.
  Vice versa, given a partial Σ-algebra M, we construct a sketch model $\beta_\Sigma^{hs'} M$ by interpreting each object (resp. arrow) corresponding to a sort or domain (resp. operation symbol) by the corresponding set (resp. operation). The interpretation of the other parts of the sketch is then determined by the limit cones, if we chose a canonical limit structure on $\underline{Set}$. Similarly for the homomorphisms. Then $\beta_\Sigma^{hs} \circ \beta_\Sigma^{hs'} = Id$, while $\beta_\Sigma^{hs'} \circ \beta_\Sigma^{hs}$ is an isomorphism.

Satisfaction of (1): Poigné's construction satisfies

$M'(D_e \longrightarrow s_1 \times \cdots \times s_n) \cong \{\, \nu\colon X \longrightarrow \beta^{hs} M' \mid \nu \models e \,\} \hookrightarrow \beta^{hs} M'_{s_1} \times \cdots \times \beta^{hs} M'_{s_n}$

Therefore, a model expansion of M' interpreting $m\colon D_{e_1} \cap \ldots \cap D_{e_k} \longrightarrow D_e$ exists if and only if

$$\bigcap_{i=1,\ldots,k} \{\, \nu\colon X \longrightarrow \beta^{hs} M' \mid \nu \models e_i \,\} \subseteq \{\, \nu\colon X \longrightarrow \beta^{hs} M' \mid \nu \models e \,\}$$

if and only if $\beta^{hs} M' \models \forall\{\, x_1 : s_1; \ldots ; x_n : s_n \,\}.e_1 \wedge \cdots \wedge e_k \longrightarrow e$ □

Proof of Theorem 13, (13)

The conjunctive embedding of institutions $\mu^{sc}\colon \mathcal{LESKETCH} \longrightarrow R(= R \rightarrow \exists! = R)$ is defined by expressing the universal property of limits within $R(= R \rightarrow \exists! = R)$.

$\Phi^{sc}(G, U)$ is the theory with a sort s for each object s in G and a total operation $f\colon s \longrightarrow s'$ for each arrow $f\colon s \longrightarrow s'$ in G. $\beta^{sc}_{(G,U)}(M')$ is the model $M\colon \Sigma \longrightarrow |\underline{Set}|$ with $M(s) = M'_s$ for objects s of G and $M(f) = f_{M'}$ for arrows f of G, the converse direction being defined analogously.

Diagrams can be easily translated to equations.

Considering cones over a a diagram $I \xrightarrow{D} G$, $(L, (\pi_i)_{i\in|I|})$ is a cone if in the interpretation, $D_m \circ \pi_i = \pi_j$ for each $m\colon i \longrightarrow j \in I$, and it is a limiting cone if for all other cones $(P, (p_i)_{i\in|I|})$ there exists a unique $p\colon P \longrightarrow L$ with $\pi_i \circ p = p_i$ for all $i \in |I|$.

This property is a second-order property: the existence of a unique $\underline{Set}$-morphism, i. e. function p is required. But we can express this with first-order axioms by replacing cones $(P, (p_i)_{i\in|I|})$ by elements $(y_i = p_i(y) : D_i)_{i\in|I|}$ and maps $p\colon P \longrightarrow L$ by elements $x = p(y) : L$ (for a given $y : P$). Then the limiting property can be expressed with the following axioms:

$$\forall x : L.D_m(D_i(x)) = D_j(x) \text{ for } m\colon i \longrightarrow j \in I$$
$$\forall\{\, y_i : D_i \mid i \in |I| \,\}. \textstyle\bigwedge_{m:i\longrightarrow j\in I} D_m(y_i) = y_j \longrightarrow \exists! x : L.(\bigwedge_{i\in|I|} \pi_i(x) = x_i)$$ □

Proof of Theorem 13, (14)

We first define a weak embedding $\mu^{rs} = (\Phi^{rs}, \alpha^{rs}, \beta^{rs})\colon R(R = \longrightarrow \exists! R =) \longrightarrow HEP1(\overset{e}{=}\!\!\rightarrow\!\overset{w}{=})$. We have to represent relations from $R(R = \longrightarrow \exists! R =)$ within $HEP1(\overset{e}{=}\!\!\rightarrow\!\overset{w}{=})$. The idea is that additional sorts R hold relations $R : s_1 \ldots s_n$. A sort R must be in some sense a "subsort" of $s_1 \times \cdots \times s_n$. Instead of introducing an injection from R to $s_1 \times \cdots \times s_n$ (which is possible only indirectly since we do not have product sorts), we introduce projections $\pi_i^R\colon R \longrightarrow s_i$ for $i = 1, \ldots, n$, which are "together injective", that is, $< \pi_1^R, \ldots, \pi_n^R >\colon R \longrightarrow s_1 \times \cdots \times s_n$ is injective.

Thus let Φ^{rs} extend a signature (S, OP, REL) by the following theory:

sorts R for each $R \in REL \cup \{ =_s \mid s \in S \}$
opns $\pi_i^R\colon R \longrightarrow s_i$ for $R : s_1 \ \ldots \ s_n \in REL \cup \{ =_s\colon s\ s \mid s \in S \},\ i = 1, \ldots, n$
$\Delta_s\colon s \longrightarrow =_s$ for $s \in S$
axioms $\forall \{ x, y : R \}. \bigwedge_{i=1,\ldots,n} \pi_i^R(x) = \pi_i^R(y) \longrightarrow x = y$
for $R : s_1 \ \ldots \ s_n \in REL \cup \{ =_s\colon s\ s \mid s \in S \}$
$\forall \{ x : s \}. \pi_i^{=_s}(\Delta_s(x)) = x$ for $s \in S$, $i = 1, 2$
$\forall \{ y : =_s \}. \pi_1^{=_s}(y) = \pi_2^{=_s}(y)$ for $s \in S$

The first axiom states that the π_i^R are "together injective", that is, $< \pi_1^R, \ldots, \pi_n^R >$ is injective. The other two axioms (together with the diagonal functions Δ_s) ensure that $=_s$ exactly holds the equality relation on s.

To translate a $R(R = \longrightarrow \exists! R =)$-axiom φ, replace all equations $t_1 = t_2$ in φ by relation applications $=_s (t_1, t_2)$ to gain uniformity. Let the thus modified axiom be

$$\forall X. Q_1(t_1^1, \ldots t_{m_1}^1) \wedge \cdots \wedge Q_q(t_1^q, \ldots t_{m_q}^q) \quad \longrightarrow$$
$$\exists! Y. (R_1(u_1^1, \ldots u_{n_1}^1) \wedge \cdots \wedge R_r(u_1^r, \ldots u_{n_r}^r))$$

(with $X = \{ x_1 : s_1, \ldots, x_m : s_m \}$, $Y = \{ y_1 : s_1', \ldots, y_n : s_n' \}$). Thus φ states that for all relation members of $Q_1, \ldots, Q_q$ of a certain form, there are relation members of $R_1, \ldots, R_r$ of a certain form depending on some additional variables Y. We want to simulate the effect of φ by introducing partial operations *proj_R*, *proj_y* and *other_y*. The first two of these have as arguments a valuation of the variables in X and relation members of $Q_1, \ldots, Q_q$. They have as values the corresponding relation members of $R_1, \ldots, R_r$ resp. the values of the variables in Y:

$$proj\_R_k^{\varphi}\colon s_1 \ldots s_m\ Q_1 \ldots Q_q \longrightarrow R_k \quad (k = 1, \ldots, r)$$

$$proj\_y_k^{\varphi}\colon s_1 \ldots s_m\ Q_1 \ldots Q_q \longrightarrow s_k' \quad (k = 1, \ldots, n)$$

The ordering on these partial operations is discrete. Let $Q = \{ v_1 : Q_1, \ldots, v_q : Q_q \}$ and $Def(proj\_R_k^{\varphi}) = Def(proj\_y_k^{\varphi}) =$

$$X \cup Q. \{ \pi_j^{Q_i}(v_i) = t_j^i \mid i = 1, \ldots, q, j = 1, \ldots, m_i \} \tag{2}$$

Thus the $proj\_R_k^{\varphi}$ and the $proj\_y_k^{\varphi}$ are defined if and only if for $i = 1, \ldots, q$, the value of v_i represents a member of Q_i which makes the premise $Q_i(t_1^i, \ldots, t_{m_i}^i)$ true. This is the case if and only if for $x_1, \ldots, x_m$, the premises hold with relation members $v_1, \ldots, v_q$.

Next we have to state that if the premises hold, the conclusion holds as well. That is, $proj\_y_k^{\varphi}(x_1, \ldots, x_m, v_1, \ldots, v_q)$ should yield some value which has the following property: When it is substituted for $y_k : s'_k \in Y$, $R_k(u_1^k, \ldots, u_{m_k}^k)$ becomes true, and $proj\_R_k^{\varphi}(x_1, \ldots, x_m, v_1, \ldots, v_q)$ represents the corresponding member of R_k. This is expressed by the following axioms:

$$\forall X \cup Q.\pi_l^{R_k}(proj\_R_k^{\varphi}(x_1, \ldots, x_m, v_1, \ldots, v_q)) \stackrel{W}{=} \omega_l^k \tag{3}$$

for $k = 1, \ldots, r$ and $l = 1, \ldots, n_k$, where ω_l^k is the term u_l^k with y_i replaced by $proj\_y_i^{\varphi}(x_1, \ldots, x_m, v_1, \ldots, v_q)$ for $i = 1, \ldots, n$.

Now the $proj\_y_k^{\varphi}(x_1, \ldots, x_m, v_1, \ldots, v_q)$ have to be the unique y_k with the above property. This is expressed by introducing partial operations

$$other\_y_k^{\varphi}: s_1 \ldots s_m\ s'_1 \ldots s'_n\ R_1 \ldots R_r \longrightarrow s'_k$$

with $Def(other\_y_k^{\varphi}) =$

$$X \cup Y \cup R.\{\, \pi_l^{R_j}(w_j) = u_l^j \mid j = 1, \ldots, r, l = 1, \ldots, n_j \,\}$$

(where $R = \{\, w_1 : R_1, \ldots, w_r : R_r \,\}$) and axioms:

$$\forall X \cup Y \cup Q \cup R.proj\_y_k^{\varphi}(x_1, \ldots, x_m, v_1, \ldots, v_q) \stackrel{W}{=} other\_y_k^{\varphi}(x_1, \ldots, x_m, y_1, \ldots, y_n, w_1, \ldots, w_r) \tag{4}$$

$$\forall X \cup Y \cup R.other\_y_k^{\varphi}(x_1, \ldots, x_m, y_1, \ldots, y_n, w_1, \ldots, w_r) \stackrel{W}{=} y_k \tag{5}$$

for $k = 1, \ldots, n$.

Note that when passing from $proj\_y_k^{\varphi}(x_1, \ldots, x_m, v_1, \ldots, v_q)$ to arbitrary y_k, we have also to pass from $proj\_R_j^{\varphi}(x_1, \ldots, x_m, v_1, \ldots, v_q)$ to arbitrary w_j, since the w_j have the y_k as components.

Now $\alpha_{\Sigma}^{rs}(\varphi)$ is $\exists!\Sigma' \hookrightarrow T$, where $\Sigma' = sign(\Phi^{rs}\ \Sigma)$ and T is the extension of $\Phi^{rs}\ \Sigma$ outlined above. We have to prove uniqueness of $\Sigma' \hookrightarrow T$-expansions (if existing) for Σ'-models M'. Let N and N' be two $\Sigma' \hookrightarrow T$-expansions of M'. Arguments for $proj\_y_k^{\varphi}$ and $proj\_R_k^{\varphi}$ in N (resp. N') can be identified with valuations $\nu: X \cup Q \longrightarrow M'$. For such a valuation satisfying $Def(proj\_R_k^{\varphi})$, extend ν to $\nu': X \cup Y \cup Q \cup R \longrightarrow N$ with $\nu'(y_k) = proj\_y_{k,N'}^{\varphi}(\nu)$ and $\nu'(w_j) = proj\_R_{j,N'}^{\varphi}(\nu)$. Since (3) holds in N', the definedness condition of (4) holds for ν', so $proj\_y_{k,N}^{\varphi} = proj\_y_{k,N'}^{\varphi}$. By (3) and the injectivity of $< \pi_1^{R_k}, \ldots, \pi_{n_k}^{R_k} >$, we have also $proj\_R_{j,N}^{\varphi} = proj\_R_{j,N'}^{\varphi}$. Thus $N = N'$.

Considering models, $\beta_{((S,OP,REL),\emptyset)}^{rs}$ takes a Σ'-model M' and replaces for each relation symbol $R : s_1 \ldots s_n \in REL$ the components M'_R and $\pi_{i,M'}^R: M'_R \longrightarrow M'_{s_i}$

$(i = 1, \ldots, n)$ by the relation $< \pi^R_{1,M'}, \ldots, \pi^R_{n,M'} > [M'_R]$. Homomorphisms are left unchanged, except that the components for the R fall away. This can easily shown to be a natural equivalence.

To prove (1), assume that $M = \beta^{rs}_{\Sigma} M' \models_{\Sigma} \varphi$ with φ as above. To show that $M' \models_{\Sigma'} \exists!\Sigma' \hookrightarrow T$ (with $\Sigma' \hookrightarrow T$ as above), we have to construct a $\Sigma' \hookrightarrow T$-expansion N of M'. For simplicity, we assume that for $R : s_1, \ldots, s_n \in REL$, the injection $< \pi^R_{1,M'}, \ldots, \pi^R_{n,M'} >: M'_R \longrightarrow M'_{s_1} \times \cdots \times M'_{s_n}$ is an inclusion (without that, we would have to deal with some extra isomorphisms). For valuations $\nu: X \cup Q \longrightarrow M'$ satisfying $Def(proj\_R^{\varphi}_k)$, that is, $\pi^{Q_i}_{j,M'}(\nu(v_i)) = \nu^{\#}(t^i_j)$, we have to define $proj\_R^{\varphi}_{k,N}(\nu)$ and $proj\_y^{\varphi}_{k,N}(\nu)$. Now by the equations satisfied by ν, $(\nu^{\#}(t^i_1), \ldots, (\nu^{\#}(t^i_{m_i})) \in Q_{i,M'}$, that is, $\nu|_X$, the restriction of ν to X, satisfies the premises of φ. By the assumption, there is a unique extension $\nu': X \cup Y \longrightarrow M'$ of ν satisfying the conclusion of φ. Now define

$$proj\_y^{\varphi}_{k,N}(\nu) = \nu'(y_k) \quad (k = 1, \ldots, n)$$

$$proj\_R^{\varphi}_{k,N}(\nu) = (\nu'^{\#}(u^k_1), \ldots, \nu'^{\#}(u^k_{n_k})) \quad (k = 1, \ldots, r)$$

$other\_y^{\varphi}_{k,N}$ is determined directly by the axioms. This guarantees (3) and (4).

The other way round, assume that $M' \models_{\Sigma'} \exists!\Sigma' \hookrightarrow T$ holds. Assume further that a valuation $\nu: X \longrightarrow M = \beta^{rs}_{\Sigma} M'$ satisfies the premises of φ. Let N be the unique $\Sigma' \hookrightarrow T$-expansion of M'. Define $\xi: X \cup Q \longrightarrow N$ by $\xi(x_i) = \nu(x_i)$ and $\xi(v_i) = (\nu^{\#}(t^i_1), \ldots, \nu^{\#}(t^i_{m_i}))$. Then ξ satisfies $Def(proj\_R^{\varphi}_k)$, so $proj\_y^{\varphi}_{k,N}$ and $proj\_R^{\varphi}_{k,N}$ are defined on ξ. Define $\nu': X \cup Y \longrightarrow M$ by $\nu'(x_i) = \nu(x_i)$ and $\nu'(y_k) = proj\_y^{\varphi}_{k,N}(\xi)$. By (3), ν' satisfies the conclusion of φ. By (4), ν' is unique with that property. Thus φ holds in M.

Note that the map we have constructed uses a conditional equation

$$\forall\{ x, y : R \}. \bigwedge_{i=1,\ldots,n} \pi^R_i(x) = \pi^R_i(y) \longrightarrow x = y$$

Thus its codomain is $HEP1(\stackrel{e}{=}\rightarrow\stackrel{w}{=})$. But we can replace this equation by the following

partial opns $member^R: R\ R \longrightarrow R$ for $REL \cup \{ =_s : s\ s \mid s \in S \}$
$\qquad Def(member^R) = \{ x, y : R \}.\{ \pi^R_i(x) = \pi^R_i(y) \mid i = 1, \ldots, n \}$
axioms $\forall\{ x, y : R \}.member^R(x, y) \stackrel{w}{=} x$
$\qquad \forall\{ x, y : R \}.member^R(x, y) \stackrel{w}{=} y$

and thus we end in $HEP1(\stackrel{w}{=})$. □

We illustrate how $\mu^{rs}: R(R = \!\!\rightarrow \exists!R =) \longrightarrow \exists!(HEP1(\stackrel{e}{=}\rightarrow\stackrel{w}{=}))$ works by giving an example. Consider the specifications of simple and transitive graphs in $R(R = \!\!\rightarrow \exists!R =)$:

GRAPH1 =
  sorts *nodes*
  rels *Edge* : *nodes nodes*

TRANSITIVE1 = **GRAPH1** +
  axioms $\forall\{x, y, z : nodes\}.Edge(x, y) \wedge Edge(y, z) \longrightarrow Edge(x, z)$

This is translated via μ^{rs} to $HEP1(\overset{e}{=}\!\rightarrow\overset{w}{=})$ (up to a renaming and omission of $=_s$ and Δ_s which are needed only for equations):

GRAPH2 =
  sorts *nodes*, *edges*
  opns *source*, *target*: *edges* $\longrightarrow$ *nodes*
  axioms $\forall\{e, f : edges\}.source(e) = source(f) \wedge target(e) = target(f) \longrightarrow e = f$

TRANSITIVE2 = **GRAPH2** +
  partial opns $proj\_edge$: $nodes^3\ edges^2 \longrightarrow edges$
  $$Def(proj\_edge) = \{e, f : edges; x, y, z : nodes\}.$$
  $$\{source(e) = x, target(e) = y, source(f) = y, target(f) = z\}$$
  axioms $\forall\{e, f : edges; x, y, z : nodes\}.source(proj\_edge(x, y, z, e, f)) \overset{w}{=} x$
  $\forall\{e, f : edges; x, y, z : nodes\}.target(proj\_edge(x, y, z, e, f)) \overset{w}{=} z$

Since $k = 0$ in this case, there are no axioms of form (4).

Now axiom (2) expresses the first three arguments of *proj_edge* in terms of the last two. Thus the redundant arguments of *proj_edge* can be omitted, and it becomes a concatenation operation:

TRANSITIVE3 = **GRAPH2** +
  partial opns $\_ \circ \_ : edges\ edges \longrightarrow edges$
  $$Def(\circ) = \{e, f : edges\}.\{source(f) = target(e)\}$$
  axioms $\forall\{e, f : edges\}.source(e \circ f) \overset{w}{=} source(e)$
  $\forall\{e, f : edges\}.target(e \circ f) \overset{w}{=} target(f)$

By the way: using this representation of simple graphs, we can easily pass over to multigraphs by omitting the **GRAPH2**-axiom.

Of course, translations of complex theories may become very unreadable. They should better be viewed as the output of a compiler, which can be fed into (semi-)automatic tools.

Proof of Theorem 13, (15)

The construction of $\mu^{ls}: R(R =\!\rightarrow \exists! R =) \longrightarrow P(\overset{S}{=})$ is similar to that of μ^{rs}. The new idea is here to represent relations R as domains of partial operations χ_R (with irrelevant values). Then an atomic relation application

$$R(\bar{t})$$

is translated to

$$\chi_R(\bar{t}) \text{ is defined}$$

Conjunctions can be handled by nested terms with the outer operation symbol chosen to be total, since such a nested term is defined if and only if all subterms are defined. An equivalence

$$\forall X.R(\bar{t}) \longleftrightarrow Q(\bar{t}')$$

can be translated to

$$\forall X.\chi_R(\bar{t}) \stackrel{S}{=} \chi_Q(\bar{t}')$$

Since in propositional logic, implications $p \longrightarrow q$ are equivalent to equivalences $p \longleftrightarrow p \wedge q$, we also can represent conditional axioms.

Now $\mu^{ls}: R(R = \!\!\rightarrow \exists! R =) \longrightarrow P(\stackrel{S}{=})$ is defined as follows:

- $\Phi^{ls}(S, OP, REL)$ is the theory with
  - sort set S plus a sort $bool1$
  - total operations OP plus $true1 : bool1$
  - partial operations
    - $first^s : s\ bool1 \longrightarrow s$ for $s \in S$
    - $\chi_R : s_1 \ldots s_n \longrightarrow bool1$ for $R : \bar{s} \in REL$
    - $\chi_{=_s} : s\ s \longrightarrow bool1$ for $s \in S$
  - and the following axioms
    - $\forall\{\, x, y : bool1 \,\}.x \stackrel{S}{=} y$
    - $\forall\{\, x : s; y : bool1 \,\}.first^s(x, y) \stackrel{S}{=} x$ for $s \in S$
    - $\forall\{\, x : s \,\}.\chi_{=_s}(x, x) \stackrel{S}{=} true1$ for $s \in S$
    - $\forall\{\, x, y : s \,\}.first^s(x, \chi_{=_s}(x, y)) \stackrel{S}{=} first^s(y, \chi_{=_s}(x, y))$

  The first axiom ensures that $bool1$ is one-point, so the values of χ_R are irrelevant. The other axioms ensure that the domain of $\chi_{=_s}$ is the equality relation on s.

  $\Phi^{ls}(\sigma)$ maps $bool1$ to $bool1$, $true1$ to $true1$, χ_R to $\chi_{\sigma(R)}$ and so on.
- Consider a $R(R = \!\!\rightarrow \exists! R =)$-sentence $\varphi =$

$$\forall X.Q_1(t_1^1, \ldots t_{m_1}^1) \wedge \cdots \wedge Q_q(t_1^q, \ldots t_{m_q}^q) \longrightarrow$$
$$\exists! Y(R_1(u_1^1, \ldots u_{n_1}^1) \wedge \cdots \wedge R_r(u_1^r, \ldots u_{n_r}^r))$$

  (with $X = \{\, x_1 : s_1, \ldots, x_m : s_m \,\}$, $Y = \{\, y_1 : s_1', \ldots, y_n : s_n' \,\}$ and equations $t_1 = t_2$ replaced by relation applications $=_s (t_1, t_2)$ to gain uniformity). To translate φ, introduce some auxiliary partial operations

  partial opns $and_n : bool1^n \longrightarrow bool1$
  $and_q : bool1^q \longrightarrow bool1$
  $and_{r+1} : bool1^{r+1} \longrightarrow bool1$
  $forget^s : s \longrightarrow bool1$

  axioms $\forall\{\, x_1, \ldots, x_n : bool1 \,\}.and_n(x_1, \ldots, x_n) \stackrel{S}{=} true1$
  $\forall\{\, x_1, \ldots, x_q : bool1 \,\}.and_q(x_1, \ldots, x_q) \stackrel{S}{=} true1$
  $\forall\{\, x_1, \ldots, x_{r+1} : bool1 \,\}.and_{r+1}(x_1, \ldots, x_{r+1}) \stackrel{S}{=} true1$
  $\forall\{\, x : s \,\}.forget^s(x) \stackrel{S}{=} true1$

Further introduce partial operations

$$proj\_y_k^{\varphi} : s_1 \ldots s_m \longrightarrow s'_k \quad (k = 1, \ldots, n)$$

As in the proof of (14), $proj\_y_k^{\varphi}$ shall be defined if and only if its arguments, considered as valuation, make the premises of φ true. This is expressed by the axioms:

$$\forall X.and_q(\chi_{Q_1}(t_1^1, \ldots t_{m_1}^1), \ldots, \chi_{Q_q}(t_1^q, \ldots t_{m_q}^q)) \stackrel{s}{=} forget_1^{s'_k}(proj\_y_k^{\varphi}(x_1, \ldots, x_m))$$

$(k = 1, \ldots, n)$

Further, the conclusion shall hold in that case and the $proj\_y_k^{\varphi}(x_1, \ldots, x_m)$ shall be unique with that property:

$$\forall X \cup Y.proj\_y_k^{\varphi}(x_1, \ldots, x_m) \text{ defined} \longrightarrow$$
$$(R_1(u_1^1, \ldots, u_{n_1}^1) \wedge \cdots \wedge R_r(u_1^r, \ldots, u_{n_r}^r)$$
$$\longleftrightarrow y_1 = proj\_y_1^{\varphi}(x_1, \ldots, x_m) \wedge \cdots \wedge y_n = proj\_y_n^{\varphi}(x_1, \ldots, x_m))$$

This is translated by the above discussion to $P(\stackrel{s}{=})$-axioms

$$\forall X \cup Y.and_{r+1}(\chi_{R_1}(u_1^1, \ldots, u_{n_1}^1), \ldots, \chi_{R_r}(u_1^r, \ldots, u_{n_r}^r), proj\_y_1^{\varphi}(x_1, \ldots, x_m))$$
$$\stackrel{s}{=} and_n(\chi_{=_{s'_1}}(y_1, proj\_y_1^{\varphi}(x_1, \ldots, x_m)), \ldots, \chi_{=_{s'_n}}(y_n, proj\_y_n^{\varphi}(x_1, \ldots, x_m)))$$

Now $\alpha_{\Sigma}^{ls}(\varphi)$ is $\exists! \Sigma' \hookrightarrow T$, where $\Sigma' = sign(\Phi^{ls}\ \Sigma)$ and T is the extension of $\Phi^{ls}\ \Sigma$ outlined above.

– β_{Σ}^{ls} takes a Σ'-model M' and replaces the operations $\chi_{R,M'}$ by their domains (considered as relations), while the other operations introduced in T are forgotten. Homomorphisms are left unchanged.
Vice versa, $\beta_{\Sigma}^{ls^{-1}}$ replaces all relations R_M by partial operations $\chi_{R,M'}$ with the corresponding relation as domain. By the axiom $\forall\{\, x, y : bool1 \,\}.x \stackrel{s}{=} y$, the value of $\chi_{R,M'}$, if defined, is $true1_M$. The other operations introduced in T are determined by the axioms.

Now (1) can be verified as follows: Suppose $M = \beta_{\Sigma}^{ls} M' \models_{\Sigma} \varphi$ holds with φ as above. To show that $M' \models_{\Sigma'} \exists! \Sigma' \hookrightarrow T$ (with Σ' and T as above), we have to construct a $\Sigma' \hookrightarrow T$-expansion N of M'. Now $and_{n,N}$, $and_{q,N}$, $and_{r+1,N}$ and $forget_N$ are determined by the axioms. By noticing that $\chi_{R,N}(\overline{x})$ is defined if and only if $R_{M'}(\overline{x})$ holds, and $and_{n,N}$, $and_{q,N}$ and $and_{r+1,N}$ act as conjunction of definedness, we can proceed similar to (14). □

Note that in $P(\stackrel{e}{=} \rightarrow \stackrel{e}{=})$, we always can take $OP = \emptyset$ by regarding total operations as partial operations with $op(\overline{x}) \stackrel{e}{=} op(\overline{x})$. μ^{limgra} translates this to a $R(R = \rightarrow \exists! R =)$-theory without total operations, and μ^{ls} further translates it into a $P(\stackrel{s}{=})$-theory with $OP = \{\, true1 : bool1 \,\}$. Thus, we need just one existence equation $true1 \stackrel{e}{=} true1$ to express $P(\stackrel{e}{=} \rightarrow \stackrel{e}{=})$ or $R(R = \rightarrow \exists! R =)$ within $P(\stackrel{s}{=})$ *without* total operations. But this single existence equation is needed, since purely partial theories of strong equations all have the totally undefined algebra as a model, while this is not always the case in $P(\stackrel{e}{=} \rightarrow \stackrel{e}{=})$.

5 Conclusion

With the help of three notion of maps between institutions, namely simple, conjunctive and weak maps, we can draw a detailed picture of the relations between various well-known institutions of partial algebras. Our main result states that the following institutions are weakly equivalent expressive and that there are ten simple embeddings, two conjunctive embeddings and three weak embeddings among them:

1. Relational Partial Conditional Existence-Equational Logic $RP(R \stackrel{e}{=}\rightarrow R \stackrel{e}{=})$ [4]
2. Partial Conditional Existence Equational Logic $P(\stackrel{e}{=}\rightarrow\stackrel{e}{=})$ [4, 5]
3. Partial Existentially-Conditioned Existence-Equational Logic $P(D \rightarrow\stackrel{e}{=})$ [4, 21, 22]
4. Partial Logic With Strong Equations $P(\stackrel{s}{=})$ [4, 20, 23, 31]
5. Hierarchical Equationally Partial Theories $HEP(\stackrel{e}{=}\rightarrow\stackrel{e}{=})$, $HEP1(\stackrel{e}{=}\rightarrow\stackrel{w}{=})$, $HEP1(\stackrel{w}{=})$ [14, 33]
6. Limit Theories $R(R =\rightarrow \exists! R =)$ [9]
7. Left Exact Sketches $\mathcal{LESKETCH}$ [3, 19]
8. Coherent Order Sorted Algebras With Sort Constraints $COSASC(=\rightarrow=)$ [26]

We conjecture that the shown results are optimal in the sense that there is no embedding of institutions where we only weakly embed institutions. For some cases, we already managed to prove this.

The main result helps to unify the different branches of specification of partial algebras from a semantical point of view. Further, one can combine specifications written in different logical frameworks by multiparadigm specification [2] using the embeddings. The ten simple and two conjunctive embeddings of institutions embed also sentences faithfully, so entailment systems and theorem provers can be re-used along them [8].

Future work should examine the properties of weak embeddings of institutions, which translate semantics faithfully, but not theorem provers. We conjecture that semantical consequence in the source institution can be expressed with semantical consequence in the target institution plus some other relation like persistency of parameterizations. This would imply that we can at least partially translate theorem provers also along weak embeddings of institutions.

Another possibility is that there may also be categorical retractive simulations in the sense of [24], which do not translate models by an equivalences of categories, but which still allow borrowing theorem provers.

Another direction of future research is the examination of institutions and logics with weaker or stronger expressiveness (cf. also [29]), such that a partial order or even a hierarchy of equivalence classes of expressiveness emerges.

Acknowledgements

I wish to thank Andrzej Tarlecki, Horst Reichel and many other people for fruitful discussions.

References

[1] J. Adámek, J. Rosický. *Locally Presentable and Accessible Categories*. Cambridge University Press, 1994.

[2] E. Astesiano, M. Cerioli. Multiparadigm specification languages: a first attempt at foundations. In J.F. Groote C.M.D.J. Andrews, ed., *Semantics of Specification Languages (SoSl 93)*, Workshops in Computing, 168–185. Springer Verlag, 1994.

[3] M. Barr, C. Wells. *Toposes, Triples and Theories, Grundlehren der mathematischen Wissenschaften* **278**. Springer Verlag, 1985.

[4] P. Burmeister. Partial algebras — survey of a unifying approach towards a two-valued model theory for partial algebras. *Algebra Universalis* **15**, 306–358, 1982.

[5] P. Burmeister. *A model theoretic approach to partial algebras*. Akademie Verlag, Berlin, 1986.

[6] R. M. Burstall, J. A. Goguen. Putting theories together to make specifications. In *Proceedings of the 5th International Joint Conference on Artificial Intelligence*, 1045–1058. Cambridge, 1977.

[7] M. Cerioli. *Relationships between Logical Formalisms*. PhD thesis, TD-4/93, Università di Pisa-Genova-Udine, 1993.

[8] M. Cerioli, J. Meseguer. May I borrow your logic? In A.M. Borzyszkowski, S.Sokolowski, eds., *Proc. MFCS'93 (Mathematical Foundations of Computer Science), LNCS* **711**, 342–351. Springer Verlag, Berlin, 1993. To appear in Theoretical Computer Science.

[9] M. Coste. Localisation, spectra and sheaf representation. In M.P. Fourman, C.J. Mulvey, D.S. Scott, eds., *Application of Sheaves, Lecture Notes in Mathematics* **753**, 212–238. Springer Verlag, 1979.

[10] H. Ehrig, B. Mahr. *Fundamentals of Algebraic Specification 1*. Springer Verlag, Heidelberg, 1985.

[11] H. Ehrig, B. Mahr. *Fundamentals of Algebraic Specification 2*. Springer Verlag, Heidelberg, 1990.

[12] H. Ehrig, P. Pepper, F. Orejas. On recent trends in algebraic specification. In *Proc. ICALP'89, LNCS* **372**, 263–288. Springer Verlag, 1989.

[13] W. A. Farmer. A partial functions version of Church's simple type theory. *Journal of Symbolic Logic* **55**, 1269–1291, 1991.

[14] P. Freyd. Aspects of topoi. *Bull. Austral. Math. Soc.* **7**, 1–76, 1972.

[15] P. Gabriel, F. Ulmer. *Lokal präsentierbare Kategorien, Lecture Notes in Mathematics* **221**. Springer Verlag, Heidelberg, 1971.

[16] J. A. Goguen, R. M. Burstall. Institutions: Abstract model theory for specification and programming. *Journal of the Association for Computing Machinery* **39**, 95–146, 1992. Predecessor in: LNCS 164(1984):221–256.

[17] J. A. Goguen, J. Meseguer. Order-sorted algebra I: equational deduction for multiple inheritance, overloading, exceptions and partial operations. *Theoretical Computer Science* **105**, 217–273, 1992.

[18] Joseph Goguen, Jean-Pierre Jouannaud, José Meseguer. Operational semantics of order-sorted algebra. In Wilfried Brauer, ed., *Proceedings, 1985 International Conference on Automata, Languages and Programming.* Springer, 1985. Lecture Notes in Computer Science, Volume 194.

[19] J. W. Gray. Categorical aspects of data type constructors. *Theoretical Computer Science* **50**, 103–135, 1987.

[20] H.-J. Hoehnke. On partial algebras. In *Universal Algebra (Proc. Coll. Esztergom 1977), Colloq. Math. Soc. J. Bolyai* **29**, 373–412. North Holland, Amsterdam, 1981.

[21] G. Jarzembski. Weak varieties of partial algebras. *Algebra Universalis* **25**, 247–262, 1988.

[22] G. Jarzembski. Programs in partial algebras. *Theoretical Computer Science* **115**, 131–149, 1993.

[23] S.C. Kleene. *Introduction to Metamathematics.* North Holland, 1952.

[24] H.-J. Kreowski, T. Mossakowski. Equivalence and difference of institutions: Simulating horn clause logic with based algebras. *Mathematical Structures in Computer Science* **5**, 189–215, 1995.

[25] J. Meseguer. General logics. In *Logic Colloquium 87*, 275–329. North Holland, 1989.

[26] J. Meseguer, J. Goguen. Order-sorted algebra solves the constructor, selector, multiple representation and coercion problems. *Information and Computation* **103**(1), 114–158, March 1993.

[27] T. Mossakowski. Simulations between various institutions of partial and total algebras. Talk at the Workshop of the ESPRIT Basic Research Working Group COMPASS, Dresden, September 1993.

[28] T. Mossakowski. Parameterized recursion theory – a tool for the systematic classification of specification methods. In M. Nivat, C. Rattray, T. Rus, G. Scollo, eds., *Proceedings of the Third International Conference on Algebraic Methodology and Software Technology, 1993*, Workshops in Computing, 139–146. Springer-Verlag, London, 1993. Also to appear in Theoretical Computer Science.

[29] T. Mossakowski. A hierarchy of institutions separated by properties of parameterized abstract data types. In *Recent Trends in Data Type Specification. Proceedings, Lecture Notes in Computer Science* **906**, 389–405. Springer Verlag, London, 1995.

[30] T. Mossakowski. Different types of arrow between logical frameworks. In *ICALP 96*, LNCS. To appear. Springer Verlag, 1996.

[31] J. Słominski. *Peano-algebras and quasi-algebras, Dissertationes Mathematicae (Rozprawy Mat.)* **62**. 1968.

[32] A. Poigné. Algebra categorically. In D. Pitt et al., ed., *Category Theory and Computer Programming, Lecture Notes in Computer Science* **240**, 76–102. Springer Verlag, 1986.

[33] H. Reichel. *Initial Computability, Algebraic Specifications and Partial Algebras.* Oxford Science Publications, 1987.

[34] D. Sannella, A. Tarlecki. Specifications in an arbitrary institution. *Information and Computation* **76**, 165–210, 1988.

[35] J.R. Shoenfield. *Mathematical Logic.* Addison-Wesley, Reading, Massachusetts, 1967.

[36] A. Tarlecki. Working with multiple logical systems. Unpublished manuscript.

[37] A. Tarlecki. On the existence of free models in abstract algebraic institutions. *Theoretical Computer Science* **37**, 269–304, 1985.

[38] M. Wirsing. Structured algebraic specifications: A kernel language. *Theoretical Computer Science* **42**, 123–249, 1986.

Some Extensions to Propositional Mean-Value Calculus: Expressiveness and Decidability

Paritosh K. Pandya

Tata Institute of Fundamental Research
Homi Bhabha Road, Colaba,
BOMBAY 400 005 India
email: pandya@tcs.tifr.res.in

Abstract. Two extensions to the propositional mean-value calculus of Zhou and Li [27] are given. The first enriches the logic with outward looking modalities D_1/D_2 and $D_1 \setminus D_2$, and the second allows quantification over state varaibles in formulae. The usefulness of these extensions is demonstrated by some examples. The expressive power and decidability of the resulting logics are analysed. This analysis is achieved by reducing the decidability/expressiveness questions to the corresponding questions in the monadic theory of order [19].

1 Introduction

The Mean-Value Calculus [27, 12] (and its antecedent Duration Calculus [26]) provide a simple and elegant logic for the specification of real-time systems. This logic has been used in a number of applications including requirement capture of real-time systems, giving semantics to real-time and distributed programming languages, capturing circuit behaviour etc. We refer the reader to many papers on this (see [23] for a survey).

The mean-value calculus (or MVC) is an *interval based* logic of time. It uses the notion of *mean-value of a predicate* representing the fraction of the time for which the predicate holds in a bounded closed time interval. The mean-value of a predicate allows real-time behaviour of systems to be described. Foundations of MVC have been studied by Hansen, Zhou, Sestoft and Li [9, 25, 12].

The propositional fragment of Mean-Value Calculus (called $PMVC$), which in fact does not make use of the mean-values, is a significantly weaker logic. Li [12] has shown that under the assumption of finite variability (see Sect. 2), $PMVC$ is decidable for real valued time and has the expressive power of a sub-class of star-free regular languages. In this paper, we shall consider $PMVC$ without any assumption of finite variability.

For many applications of interest, $PMVC$ turns out to have limited expressive power. For example, liveness properties stating that something good will *eventually* happen cannot be formalised. Properties such as fairness also cannot be formalised. This is because the only modality available in MVC is $\frown$ which allows the current interval to be chopped into two parts. This has been termed as an "inward looking" modality as it only allows reference to the *subintervals* of the current interval. In this paper, we will introduce modalities allowing access to *superintervals*.

In this paper, we give two extensions of $PMVC$ which we have found useful in a number of applications. We study the resulting logics especially from the point of view of decidability and expressive power.

Firstly, we enrich $PMVC$ with two operators D_1/D_2 and $D_2 \setminus D_1$ to get the logic $PMVC^{-1}$. These operators provide outward looking modalities and enable properties like liveness and fairness to be stated. Next, we extend the logic with quantification over state variables giving us the logic $QPMVC^{-1}$. Such quantification arises naturally in definitions of "refinement" of systems, and in compositional semantics of concurrent and distributed programs. We also show how assumptions about the structure of time can be axiomatised in these logics.

Many existing logics and models of computation can be encoded in our enriched $QPMVC^{-1}$ (but not in original $PMVC$). For example,

- $PMVC^{-1}$ can express all the formulae of Propositional Linear Temporal Logic (PTL). (See Sect. 4.)
- $QPMVC^{-1}$ can express observable behaviours of Buchi Automata [15].
- $QPMVC^{-1}$ can express observable behaviours of Timed Buchi Automata using formulae *with mean-values* [15]. Logics for real-time systems such as MTL and $TPTL$ [2] can also be encoded.

Thus, in principle, everything modelled by these formalisms can also be formalised in $QPMVC^{-1}$. In practice, $PMVC$ has been used in many interesting applications (see the beginning of this section). Recently, $QPMVC^{-1}$ has been used to provide compositional verification systems for distributed programming languages **ESTEREL** [17] and Timed CSP [24, 8]. All this indicates that $PMVC^{-1}$ and $QPMVC^{-1}$ are interesting logics for specification and verification of reactive systems.

Next, we consider the expressive power and decidability of $QPMVC^{-1}$. These are analysed by relating $QPMVC^{-1}$ to other logics for which expressiveness and decidability results are known. An important technique which we will use is the establishment of a **linear embedding** of a logic A into a logic B (defined in Sect. 4). Such an embedding, denoted by $A \hookrightarrow B$, implies that logic B is at least as expressive as logic A, and it allows us to use the decision procedures of logic B for logic A.

Many of the decidability and expressiveness results in this paper are proved by establishing a linear embedding of $QPMVC^{-1}$ into the *monadic theory of order* [19]. We also establish an embedding of a point-based temporal logic $QPTnL$ into our interval-based $QPMVC^{-1}$, thus showing that all properties expressible in the point based temporal logic can be expressed in the interval based logic.

The rest of the paper is organised as follows. Section 2 briefly defines the logic $PMVC$. This logic is extended to $PMVC^{-1}$ and $QPMVC^{-1}$ in Sect. 3. Section 4 investigates decidability and expressiveness of these logics. Thus, an embedding of the point-based $QPTnL$ into $QPMVC^{-1}$ is established in section 4.1 and an embedding of $QPMVC^{-1}$ into the *monadic theory of order* is established in Sect. 4.2. Section 5 gives conclusions about decidability and expressiveness of $QPMVC^{-1}$ and $PMVC^{-1}$ based on these embeddings. In Appendix A, we define a first-order version of $QPMVC^{-1}$, which is often required in practice [17]. We show that when interpreted over finite domains, this logic has the same expressiveness and decidability properties as $QPMVC^{-1}$.

2 Propositional Mean Value Calculus

The mean value calculus of Zhou and Li [27] is an extension of first-order real arithmetic and interval temporal logic [13]. In this logic, formulae are interpreted over bounded closed intervals of time. The notion of *mean value* of a boolean (i.e. 0, 1 valued) function over bounded closed intervals plays a central role in expressing real-time properties. The reader is referred to the original papers for details [27, 26].

In this paper, we shall consider only the propositional fragment of this logic as investigated by Li [12], and denote it by $PMVC$. This is a significantly weaker logic where the concept of mean value is not required. In this sense, the logic could be called "Interval Temporal Logic of Boolean functions of Time" [13]. But we retain the name $PMVC$ used by Li for historical reasons. This logic is briefly described below.

Let $Pvar$ (with typical elements p, q, r) denote the set of ***propositional variables***. These will be interpreted as boolean functions of time representing some aspect of the dynamical system behaviour. Boolean combinations of propositional variables will be called ***propositions***. We use constants 0, 1 for the propositions which are everywhere $false$ and $true$, respectively. Variables P, Q, R will range over propositions. $PMVC$ formulae are constructed from propositions as follows. Let $D, D_1, D_2, \ldots$ range over formulae.

$$\begin{array}{lll} P & ::= & p \mid 0 \mid 1 \mid P \wedge Q \mid \neg P \\ D & ::= & \lceil P \rceil^0 \mid D_1 \frown D_2 \mid D_1 \wedge D_2 \mid \neg D \end{array}$$

Semantics. Let $TM = (T, \leq)$ denote a *time-frame* with a set of time points T and a *partial order* relation $\leq \subseteq T \times T$. The relation $t_1 \leq t_2$ represents that t_1 is not later than t_2. Define $t_1 < t_2$ as $t_1 \leq t_2 \wedge t_1 \neq t_2$.

Let $Intv$ be the set of bounded closed time intervals $\{[b, e] \mid b, e \in T, \quad b \leq e\}$ (where $[b, e]$ is denoted by the ordered-pair of its end points).

A *valuation* θ over a time-frame $TM = (T, \leq)$ assigns to each variable $p \in Pvar$ a boolean function of time, i.e.

$$\theta : Pvar \rightarrow T \rightarrow \{true, false\}$$

This extends uniquely to a map $\hat{\theta} : Prop \rightarrow T \rightarrow \{true, false\}$ using the standard interpretation for boolean connectives. We shall often simply use θ in place of $\hat{\theta}$. The set of all valuations is denoted by Θ. A pair $\mathcal{S} = (TM, \theta)$ is called a $PMVC$ *structure*.

$PMVC$ formulae are interpreted over a structure and a time interval. The formula $\lceil P \rceil^0$ holds only for point intervals where P is true. The formula $D_1 \frown D_2$ is satisfied by an interval if it can be "chopped" into two subintervals such that the first part satisfies D_1 and the second satisfies D_2. The semantics of $PMVC$ is defined inductively as follows.

$$
\begin{array}{l}
(TM, \theta, [b,e]) \models \lceil P \rceil^0 \quad \textbf{iff} \quad b = e \wedge \theta(P)(b) = true \\
(TM, \theta, [b,e]) \models \neg D \quad \textbf{iff} \quad (TM, \theta, [b,e]) \not\models D \\
(TM, \theta, [b,e]) \models D_1 \wedge D_2 \quad \textbf{iff} \\
\quad (TM, \theta, [b,e]) \models D_1 \text{ and } (TM, \theta, [b,e]) \models D_2 \\
(TM, \theta, [b,e]) \models D_1 \frown D_2 \quad \textbf{iff} \quad \text{for some } m : b \leq m \leq e. \\
\quad (TM, \theta, [b,m]) \models D_1 \text{ and } (TM, \theta, [m,e]) \models D_2
\end{array}
$$

Validity and satisfiability are defined below as usual. Let $(TM, \theta) \models D$ **iff** for all $[b,e] \in Intv$, $(TM, \theta, [b,e]) \models D$. Similarly, $TM \models D$ **iff** for all $\theta \in \Theta$, $(TM, \theta) \models D$. Further, $\models D$ **iff** for all time-frames TM, $TM \models D$. A formula D is satisfiable over (TM, θ) if for some $[b,e]$, $(TM, \theta, [b,e]) \models D$. It is satisfiable over TM if for some $\theta \in \Theta$ it is satisfiable over (TM, θ). Formula D is satisfiable if for some time-frame TM it is satisfiable over TM.

Derived Operators. Several useful formulae and modalities can be defined in terms of the basic formulae given above. These will be used later in the paper.

- $Pt \stackrel{\text{def}}{=} \lceil 1 \rceil^0$ holds for all point intervals.
- $Ext \stackrel{\text{def}}{=} \neg Pt$ holds for all extended (i.e. non-point) intervals.
- The modalities: "for some subinterval D" and "for all subintervals D" can be defined respectively by

$$
\begin{array}{l}
\Diamond D \stackrel{\text{def}}{=} true \frown D \frown true \\
\Box D \stackrel{\text{def}}{=} \neg(\Diamond \neg D)
\end{array}
$$

  Modalities like "for all prefix subintervals" and "for all proper prefix subintervals" can also be defined analogously.
- $\lceil P \rceil \stackrel{\text{def}}{=} Ext \wedge (\neg(Ext \frown \lceil \neg P \rceil^0 \frown Ext))$ holds for all non-point intervals where state P is true *everywhere inside* the interval. $\lceil\lceil P \rceil\rceil \stackrel{\text{def}}{=} \lceil P \rceil^0 \frown \lceil P \rceil \frown \lceil P \rceil^0$ additionally requires P to be true at both the end points of the interval.
- $EP(D) \stackrel{\text{def}}{=} true \frown (Pt \wedge D)$ states that formula D holds at the end-point of the interval. Similarly, $BP(D) \stackrel{\text{def}}{=} (Pt \wedge D) \frown true$ states that D holds at the beginning point.

Finite Variability. The original mean value calculus [27] assumes *finite variance* of propositions. Thus, valuations θ assign only finitely variable boolean functions of time to each propositional variable. Such a function changes value only finitely often in any finite time interval. The following formula characterises such interpretations and was taken as an axiom schema in the original MVC.

$$\begin{array}{ll} & \Box(Pt \vee \lceil p \rceil ^\frown true \vee \lceil \neg p \rceil ^\frown true) \\ \wedge & \Box(Pt \vee true ^\frown \lceil p \rceil \vee true ^\frown \lceil \neg p \rceil) \end{array} \qquad (1)$$

Under the assumption of finite variability, Li [12, 24] has shown that $PMVC$ over the time-frame $(\Re, \leq_{\Re})$ has the expressive power of star-free regular expressions, and that it is decidable.

Finite Divergence. A more general class of valuations has been considered by Hansen, Pandya and Zhou [10] where arbitrary *integrable* boolean functions of time are allowed.
In this paper, we shall allow *arbitrary* boolean functions of time in the valuations. In this setting, the expressiveness and decidability results of Li do not carry over. We shall address these issues in Sect. 4.

3 Extending Propositional Mean Value Calculus

We consider two useful extensions of Propositional Mean-Value Calculus. Actually, the extensions proposed here are also applicable to the full Mean-Value calculus of Zhou and Li (see [15]).

3.1 Weakest Inverses of $^\frown$

We shall now extend the $PMVC$ with operators: D_1/D_2 and $D_1 \backslash D_2$. The resulting logic is called $PMVC$ **with chop inverses**, or $PMVC^{-1}$. The semantics of these operators is as follows.

Definition 1.

$$\begin{array}{l} (TM, \theta, [b,e]) \models D_1/D_2 \;\; \textbf{iff} \;\; \forall m : e \leq m. \\ \qquad ((TM, \theta, [e,m]) \models D_2 \;\; \Rightarrow \;\; (TM, \theta, [b,m]) \models D_1) \end{array}$$

$$\begin{array}{l} (TM, \theta, [b,e]) \models D_1 \backslash D_2 \;\; \textbf{iff} \;\; \forall m : m \leq b. \\ \qquad ((TM, \theta, [m,b]) \models D_1 \;\; \Rightarrow \;\; (TM, \theta, [m,e]) \models D_2) \end{array}$$

These operators can also be called weakest inverses of $^\frown$ as they are the unique operators satisfying following conditions.

$$X \Rightarrow D_1/D_2 \;\; \textbf{iff} \;\; X ^\frown D_2 \Rightarrow D_1 \qquad (2)$$

$$X \Rightarrow D_1 \backslash D_2 \;\; \textbf{iff} \;\; D_1 ^\frown X \Rightarrow D_2 \qquad (3)$$

Formula D_1/D_2 denotes the weakest solution in X of $X ^\frown D_2 \Rightarrow D_1$ and $D_1 \backslash D_2$ denotes the weakest solution (w.r.t. $\Rightarrow$ order) in X of $D_1 ^\frown X \Rightarrow D_2$.

Derived Operators. Several useful modalities can be derived from these chop inverse modalities.

$$\overrightarrow{\Box}\, D \stackrel{\text{def}}{=} D/true \qquad\qquad \overrightarrow{\Diamond}\, D \stackrel{\text{def}}{=} \neg\, \overrightarrow{\Box}\, \neg D$$
$$\overleftarrow{\Box}\, D \stackrel{\text{def}}{=} true \setminus D \qquad\qquad \overleftarrow{\Diamond}\, D \stackrel{\text{def}}{=} \neg\, \overleftarrow{\Box}\, (\neg D)$$

$\overrightarrow{\Box}\, D$ states that every extension of the current interval in the forward direction satisfies D. Its dual $\overrightarrow{\Diamond}\, D$ states that the current interval can be extended in the forward direction to an interval where D holds. Similarly for the backward operators.

$$\overrightarrow{\otimes}\, D \stackrel{\text{def}}{=} false/(\neg D) \qquad\qquad \overleftarrow{\otimes}\, D \stackrel{\text{def}}{=} (\neg D) \setminus false$$
$$\overrightarrow{\bigcirc}\, D \stackrel{\text{def}}{=} \neg\, \overrightarrow{\otimes}\, \neg D \qquad\qquad \overleftarrow{\bigcirc}\, D \stackrel{\text{def}}{=} \neg\, \overleftarrow{\otimes}\, \neg D$$

Operator $\overrightarrow{\otimes}\, D$ states that all the intervals immediately following the current interval satisfy D. Its dual $\overrightarrow{\bigcirc}\, D$ states that the current interval is immediately followed by an interval where D holds. Observe that this is different from $\overrightarrow{\Diamond}\, D$. Similarly for the backward operators $\overleftarrow{\otimes}\, D$ and $\overleftarrow{\bigcirc}\, D$.

Venema [22] has studied interval temporal logic with operators C, D, T. These have been incorporated in MVC by Skakkebaek [20]. These can be derived in $PMVC^{-1}$. Operators C, D, T correspond to the operators $\frown$, $\overset{\frown}{+}$, $\overset{\frown}{-}$ respectively, where

$$D_1 \overset{\frown}{+} D_2 \stackrel{\text{def}}{=} \neg(\neg D_1/D_2)$$
$$D_1 \overset{\frown}{-} D_2 \stackrel{\text{def}}{=} \neg(D_1 \setminus \neg D_2)$$

Applications. Many properties which arise in the specification of program behaviours can be captured in $PMVC^{-1}$. Especially, the liveness properties become expressible. We give some examples below. In section 4.1 we will show that all the formulae of the propositional linear temporal logic, PTL, can be encoded in $PMVC^{-1}$ (but not in $PMVC$).

Fairness. Zhou *et al* [24] have given a semantics of a simple CSP-like programming language in the Mean-Value Calculus. An interesting feature of this semantics is that assumptions about resource sharing and process scheduling can be elegantly specified. In aid of brevity we do not reproduce the semantics here. We describe some of the propositional variables used in this semantics.

$p_j.ready$ – process p_j is ready to run on a processor.
$p_j.run$ – process p_j is running on a processor.
$c!$ – process waits to send on channel c.
$c?$ – process waits to receive on channel c.
c – a communication is taking place on channel c.

The formula $\bigwedge_{j,k:\, k\neq j} (\lceil\lceil p_j.run \Rightarrow \neg p_k.run\rceil\rceil \vee Pt)$ specifies the behaviours where only one process may execute at a time.

The semantics of Zhou *et al* can be extended to specify fairness properties using the weakest inverses of chop.
Weak Process Fairness states that no process can remain perpetually in a ready state without running.

$$\bigwedge_j \neg \overrightarrow{\Diamond}\, \overrightarrow{\otimes}\, (Ext \Rightarrow \lceil p_j.ready \wedge \neg p_j.run \rceil)$$

Strong Process Fairness states that a process which becomes ready infinitely often will run infinitely often.

$$\bigwedge_j \; (\overrightarrow{\Box}\, \overrightarrow{\Diamond}\, \overrightarrow{\bigcirc}\, \lceil p_j.ready \rceil) \;\Rightarrow\; (\overrightarrow{\Box}\, \overrightarrow{\Diamond}\, \overrightarrow{\bigcirc}\, \lceil p_j.run \rceil)$$

Proposition $c? \wedge c!$ denotes that both the sender and the receiver are ready and waiting to communicate over c. Proposition c denotes that a communication over c is taking place.
Weak Channel Fairness. $\neg \overrightarrow{\Diamond}\, \overrightarrow{\otimes}\, (Ext \Rightarrow \lceil c? \wedge c! \rceil)$.
Strong Channel Fairness. $(\overrightarrow{\Box}\, \overrightarrow{\Diamond}\, \overrightarrow{\bigcirc}\, \lceil c? \wedge c! \rceil) \;\Rightarrow\; (\overrightarrow{\Box}\, \overrightarrow{\Diamond}\, \overrightarrow{\bigcirc}\, \lceil c \rceil)$.

Axiomatising Classes of Temporal Frames. We are often interested in interpreting $PMVC^{-1}$ on a class of time-frames satisfying some natural conditions. For example, time is dense and extends infinitely into future. Several such conditions are listed in the survey article on Tense logics by Burgess [4]. Let $\mathcal{F}$ denote a class of time-frames. An axiom AX for $\mathcal{F}$ is a formula D such that $TM \models D$ **iff** $TM \in \mathcal{F}$.

We give axioms in $PMVC^{-1}$ characterising many natural classes of frames. In aid of brevity we only give a verbal description of the classes of frames and omit the proof of correctness of these axioms.

1. *Time has a minimal point.* $\overleftarrow{\Diamond}\, (\neg\, \overleftarrow{\bigcirc}\, Ext)$.
   Similarly one could axiomatize that time has a maximal point.
2. *Time extends infinitely in future.* $\overrightarrow{\Box}\, \overrightarrow{\bigcirc}\, Ext$.
   Similarly one could axiomatise that time extends backwards infinitely.
3. *Discreteness.* Let $Unit \stackrel{\text{def}}{=} Ext \wedge \neg(Ext \frown Ext)$. Thus, $Unit$ holds for non-point time intervals which cannot be further sub-divided.
   Each time-point has a successor. $BP(\overrightarrow{\Diamond}\, Unit)$.
   Each time-point has a predecessor. $EP(\overleftarrow{\Diamond}\, Unit)$.
   Each non-minimal time-point has a predecessor. $Ext \Rightarrow EP(\overleftarrow{\Diamond}\, Unit)$.
4. *Time is everywhere dense.* $Ext \;\Rightarrow\; Ext \frown Ext$.

Similarly, we can give axioms for *Time is totally ordered*, *Time is well-founded*, *Time in complete* (see Burgess [4] for details). These conditions can be combined. For examples, (a) Time has a minimal point, (b) Time is linearly ordered, (c) Time is well-founded, (d) Every time point has a successor and (e) every non-minimal time point has a predecessor together characterise the time-frame $(\omega, \leq_\omega)$ where ω is the set of natural numbers.

3.2 Quantified Propositional MVC

We now extend the mean-value calculus with quantification over propositional variables. Recall that such variables represent boolean functions of time, and hence we have a second-order logic.
Consider $PMVC^{-1}$ extended with formulae of the form:

$$\exists p.D$$

The resulting logic is called **Quantified** $PMVC^{-1}$ (or $QPMVC^{-1}$).

A valuation θ' is called p-variant of θ if for all $q \in Pvar.\ q \neq p \Rightarrow \theta'(q) = \theta(q)$. Thus, θ and θ' agree on the interpretation of all propositional variables except possibly p. Let,

$$(TM, \theta, [b, e]) \models \exists p.D \quad \textbf{iff} \quad (TM, \theta', [b, e]) \models D \text{ for some } p\text{-variant } \theta' \text{ of } \theta$$

Define $\forall p.D \quad \stackrel{\text{def}}{=} \quad \neg\exists p.\neg D$.

Applications. In context of temporal logic, Manna and Pnueli [14] have advocated the usefulness of such quantification construct in the specification of reactive systems. The same motivation holds for our logic too. We give some examples of the use of quantification construct.

Compositional Semantics. The logic $QPMVC^{-1}$ can be used to give compositional semantics of programming languages. We list some examples.

Pandya *et al* [17] have given a compositional semantics of the synchronous programming language **ESTEREL** using $QPMVC^{-1}$. This semantics makes an essential use of the quantification construct. For each construct of **ESTEREL**, the semantics relates the observable variables of the components to the observable variables of the composite statements. The observable variables of the components are then hidden using the existential quantification. We do not reproduce the semantics here and refer the reader to the original paper [17].

The semantics of Timed CSP, given by Zhou *et al* [24], and by Hansen, Olderog *et al* [8], also requires the quantification construct for modelling the hiding operator.

Specifications with Auxiliary Variables and Refinement. Specification of system behaviour can typically be given as a $PMVC^{-1}$ formula D over *observable* variables $p_1, \ldots, p_n$ together with *auxiliary* variables $a_1, \ldots, a_m$. Such auxiliary variables represent some internal unobservable aspects of the system behaviour. Their presence makes the task of specifying the systems considerably simpler (see [1]). The *observable behaviour* of the system is then given by the formula $\exists a_1, \ldots, a_m.\ D$ of logic $QPMVC^{-1}$.

We say that a specification D_1 with auxiliary variables $a_1, \ldots, a_n$ *refines* the specification D_2 with auxiliary variables $b_1, \ldots, b_m$ if

$$\exists a_1, \ldots, a_n.D_1 \quad \Rightarrow \quad \exists b_1, \ldots, b_m.D_2$$

Intuitively, this means that each observable behaviour of D_1 is also an observable behaviour of D_2. Lamport and Abadi have investigated some proof methods for establishing such refinement [1].

Note that it is not always possible to find a formula $D' \in PMVC^{-1}$ such that $D' \Leftrightarrow \exists a_1, \ldots, a_m. D$. Thus, $QPMVC^{-1}$ often provides the necessary expressive power for proving refinement which is not available in $PMVC^{-1}$

4 Expressiveness and Decidability

We relate $QPMVC^{-1}$ to Propositional linear temporal logic, $QPTL$, and to monadic theory of linear order, MLO, for which expressiveness and decidability results are known.

Definition 2 Linear Embedding. Given logics A and B, *linear embedding* $A \hookrightarrow B$ is said to holds if

- There is a bijection s from the structures interpreting A to the structures interpreting B.
- There is an effective map α from (formulae of) A to B such that
  $\mathcal{U} \models_A \phi$ if and only if $s(\mathcal{U}) \models_B \alpha(\phi)$.
- Map α can be implemented by a *linear-time* algorithm (i.e. linear in the size of input formula ϕ). Note that this also implies that the size of $\alpha(\phi)$ is linear in the size of ϕ. □

Then, it is easy to see that $A \hookrightarrow B$ implies that

- map α preserves validity/satisfiability of formulae.
- if logic B is decidable, then so is logic A and with complexity not greater than that of B.
- logic B is at least as expressive as logic A.

This holds for arbitrary classes of structures.

4.1 Expressing Propositional Tense Logic

Temporal logic (or TL) is a well-known logic of programs [14]. It is a *point based* logic as it talks about the truth of a formula at a time point in a structure. In TL, time is taken to be of the form $(\omega, \leq_\omega)$. We can straightforwardly generalise this logic to arbitrary time-frames. We briefly describe one such formulation and call it the **Quantified Propositional Tense Logic** (or $QPTnL$). Let ϕ, ψ range over formulae of $QPTnL$ and P range over propositions as in Sect. 2.

$$\phi \quad ::= \quad P \mid \phi \wedge \psi \mid \neg\psi \mid \phi\, \mathcal{U}\, \psi \mid \phi\, \mathcal{S}\, \psi \mid \exists p.\psi$$

The subset of this logic without the quantification construct $\exists p.\psi$ will be called **Propositional Tense Logic** (or $PTnL$).

Let (TM, θ) be a $PMVC$ structure as in Sect. 2. The propositional tense logic is a point based logic. Its formulae can be interpreted to be true in a structure at a time-point t as follows.

$(TM, \theta, t) \models P$ **iff** $\theta(P)(t) = true$
$(TM, \theta, t) \models \neg\psi$ **iff** $(TM, \theta, t) \not\models \psi$
$(TM, \theta, t) \models \phi \wedge \psi$ **iff** $(TM, \theta, t) \models \phi$ and $(TM, \theta, t) \models \psi$
$(TM, \theta, t) \models \phi\, \mathcal{U}\, \psi$ **iff**
$\exists t'.t < t' \wedge (TM, \theta, t') \models \psi$ and $\forall t''.\ (t < t'' < t') \Rightarrow (TM, \theta, t'') \models \phi$
$(TM, \theta, t) \models \phi\, \mathcal{S}\, \psi$ **iff**
$\exists t'.t' < t \wedge (TM, \theta, t') \models \psi$ and $\forall t''.\ (t' < t'' < t) \Rightarrow (TM, \theta, t'') \models \phi$
$(TM, \theta, t) \models \exists p.\psi$ **iff** for some p-variant θ' of θ $(TM, \theta', t) \models \psi$

For convenience, we have chosen the interpretations of the $\mathcal{U}$ and the $\mathcal{S}$ operators slightly differently than in the literature. It can be easily seen that this does not alter the logic in any significant way.

Note. If the time frame TM is taken to be $(\omega, \leq_\omega)$, the set of natural numbers with usual order, then $PTnL$ gives us the *Linear Propositional Temporal Logic* (or PTL) and $QPTnL$ gives the *Quantified Linear Propositional Temporal Logic* (or $QPTL$). See [6] for an overview of these logics. For example, the formula $false\ \mathcal{U}\ \phi$ represents the "next" operator $\bigcirc\, \phi$ of PTL. □

We shall now set up the embeddings $QPTnL \hookrightarrow QPMVC^{-1}$ and $PTnL \hookrightarrow PMVC^{-1}$.

Definition 3. For each $QPTnL$ formula ϕ let $\alpha(\phi)$ be the $QPMVC^{-1}$ formula defined below. Recall that $BP(D) \stackrel{\text{def}}{=} (Pt \wedge D)^\frown true$ states that the beginning point of the interval satisfies D, and $EP(D)$ means D holds at the end-point.

$\alpha(P) \stackrel{\text{def}}{=} BP(\lceil P \rceil^0)$
$\alpha(\phi \wedge \psi) \stackrel{\text{def}}{=} \alpha(\phi) \wedge \alpha(\psi)$
$\alpha(\neg\psi) \stackrel{\text{def}}{=} \neg\alpha(\psi)$
$\alpha(\phi\, \mathcal{U}\, \psi) \stackrel{\text{def}}{=} BP(\overrightarrow{\Diamond}\ (\ Ext \wedge EP(\alpha(\psi))) \wedge \neg(Ext^\frown \alpha(\neg\phi)^\frown Ext)\ ))$
$\alpha(\phi\, \mathcal{S}\, \psi) \stackrel{\text{def}}{=} BP(\overleftarrow{\Diamond}\ (\ Ext \wedge BP(\alpha(\psi))) \wedge \neg(Ext^\frown \alpha(\neg\phi)^\frown Ext)\ ))$
$\alpha(\exists p.\psi) \stackrel{\text{def}}{=} \exists p.\ \alpha(\psi)$

Remark. $\phi \in PTnL$ implies $\alpha(\phi) \in PMVC^{-1}$. Also note that the encoding $\alpha(\phi)$ can be implemented by a *linear* time algorithm. □

Proposition 4. *For any $\phi \in QPTnL$, we have $(TM, \theta, [b, e]) \models \alpha(\phi)$* **iff** *for all $e' : b \leq e'$. $(TM, \theta, [b, e']) \models \alpha(\phi)$.*

Proof Method. By induction on the structure of ϕ. □

Theorem 5. *For any $\phi \in QPTnL$,*

$$(TM, \theta, b) \models \phi \quad \textbf{iff} \quad \textit{for all } e : b \leq e.\ (TM, \theta, [b, e]) \models \alpha(\phi)$$

Proof Method. By induction on the structure of ϕ. □

Corollary 6. $(TM,\theta) \models \phi$ **iff** $(TM,\theta) \models \alpha(\phi)$.
ϕ is satisfiable over (TM,θ) in $QPTnL$ **iff** *$\alpha(\phi)$ is satisfiable over (TM,θ) in $QPMVC^{-1}$.* □

This implies that

$$PTnL \hookrightarrow PMVC^{-1}$$
$$QPTnL \hookrightarrow QPMVC^{-1}$$

Thus, we can reduce the satisfiability/validity of a $QPTnL$ formula on a class of structures to the satisfiability/validity of a corresponding $QPMVC^{-1}$ formula on the same class of structures.

4.2 Embedding $QPMVC^{-1}$ into the Monadic Second-order Logic of Partial Orders

In this section, we shall reduce the satisfiability/validity questions of $QPMVC^{-1}$ to the corresponding questions in the classical first/second order logic. This allows us to use several important and well-known results from the *first order* and the *monadic second order theories of order* to obtain decidability results for $QPMVC^{-1}$. A similar approach has been used in past to study $QPTL$ and PTL by reducing them to systems $S1S$ and $F1S$ resp. (see [21] for an overview).

Monadic second order logic is obtained by adding *set variables* to first order logic and by allowing quantification over set variables. The monadic logic of order is such a logic over the signature $\{\leq\}$ where $\leq$ is a binary predicate symbol.

Let $Svar$ (with typical elements X, Y) be a countable set of *set variables* and $Ivar$ (with typical elements v_1, v_2) be the countable set of individual variables. The syntax of **monadic logic of order** (or MLO) is given below. Let ϕ, ψ range over formulae of this logic.

$$\phi \quad ::= \quad v_1 = v_2 \mid v_1 \leq v_2 \mid v \in X \mid \phi \wedge \psi \mid \neg\phi \mid \exists v.\phi \mid \exists X.\phi$$

The subset of this logic without the set quantification construct $\exists X.\psi$ will be called the **First-order logic of Order** (or FLO). Note that formulae of FLO may still have atomic sub-formulae of the form $v \in X$. (To be completely formal, we must treat X as unary predicate symbol and write $X(v)$ instead of $v \in X$.)

Let $TM = (T, \leq)$ be a time-frame (a partial order) as in Sect. 2. A *set valuation* $V : Svar \to 2^T$ assigns a subset of T to each set variable and an *individual valuation* $U : Ivar \to T$ assigns members of T to individual variables. (Here notation 2^T denotes the set of all subsets of T). Then, the truth of ϕ in a model (TM, V, U), denoted by $(TM, V, U) \models \phi$, can be defined inductively in the standard manner. For example,

$(TM, V, U) \models v \in X$ **iff** $U(v) \in V(X)$
$(TM, V, U) \models \exists X.\phi$ **iff** $(TM, V', U) \models \phi$ for some X-variant V' of V

A pair (TM, V) will be called an MLO structure.

We shall now establish the embeddings $QPMVC^{-1} \hookrightarrow MLO$ and $PMVC^{-1} \hookrightarrow FLO$.

Convention. Since both $Pvar$, the set of state variables used in $QPMVC^{-1}$, and $Svar$, the set of set variables used in MLO, are countable, we shall assume the following bijection between these sets. For each $p \in Pvar$ let $X_p \in Svar$ denote the set variable corresponding to it.

Given a $PMVC$ structure $((T, \leq), \theta)$, define an MLO structure $((T, \leq), V_\theta)$ such that $t \in V_\theta(X_p)$ **iff** $\theta(p)(t) = true$. It is easy to see that there is a *bijection* between $PMVC$ structures and MLO structures. □

Definition 7. Given a $QPMVC^{-1}$ formula D define the MLO formula $\beta(D)$ as follows. Each such formula $\beta(D)$ has only two free individual variables x, y. Notation $\phi[t_1/x_1, \ldots, t_n/x_n]$ denotes the formula obtained by simultaneously substituting each free occurrence of x_i by term t_i in formula ϕ.

$$\beta(\lceil p \rceil^0) \stackrel{\text{def}}{=} x = y \wedge x \in X_p$$
$$\beta(D_1 \wedge D_2) \stackrel{\text{def}}{=} \beta(D_1) \wedge \beta(D_2)$$
$$\beta(\neg D) \stackrel{\text{def}}{=} x \leq y \wedge \neg\beta(D)$$
$$\beta(D_1 \frown D_2) \stackrel{\text{def}}{=} \exists m.\ \beta(D_1)[m/y] \wedge \beta(D_2)[m/x]$$
$$\beta(D_1 / D_2) \stackrel{\text{def}}{=} \forall m.\ (\beta(D_2)[y/x, m/y] \ \Rightarrow\ \beta(D_2)[m/y])$$
$$\beta(D_2 \setminus D_1) \stackrel{\text{def}}{=} \forall m.\ (\beta(D_2)[m/x, x/y] \ \Rightarrow\ \beta(D_1)[m/x])$$
$$\beta(\exists p.D) \stackrel{\text{def}}{=} \exists X_p.\ \beta(D)$$

Remark. If $D \in PMVC^{-1}$ then $\beta(D) \in FLO$. Also, $\beta(D)$ can be implemented by a linear-time algorithm. □

The following theorem gives the relationship between D and $\beta(D)$.

Theorem 8. *For any* $D \in QPMVC^{-1}$,

$$(TM, \theta, [b, e]) \models D \quad \textbf{iff} \quad (TM, V_\theta, U[b/x, e/y]) \models \beta(D)$$

Proof Method. By induction on the structure of D. □

Corollary 9. $(TM, \theta) \models D$ **iff** $(TM, V_\theta) \models (b \leq e \ \Rightarrow\ \beta(D))$
D is satisfiable over (TM, θ) **iff** *$\beta(D)$ is satisfiable over (TM, V_θ).* □

This implies that

$$PTnL \hookrightarrow PMVC^{-1}$$
$$QPTnL \hookrightarrow QPMVC^{-1}$$

Hence, $QPMVC^{-1}$ is no more expressive than MLO and $PMVC^{-1}$ is no more expressive than FLO.

5 Conclusions and Discussion

We have defined logics $PMVC^{-1}$ and $QPMVC^{-1}$ by extending $PMVC$ of Zhou and Li [27] with outward looking modalities D_1/D_2 and $D_1 \setminus D_2$, and with quanfication over propositional variables. We have discussed some examples of usefulness of these extensions, and referred to other such uses. Outward looking modalities enable properties like *liveness* and *fairness* to be stated. Quantification over propositional variables arises naturally in the formulation of *compositional semantics* of concurrent and distributed programs, and in proofs of *refinement* of systems. These examples indicate that $PMVC^{-1}$ and $QPMVC^{-1}$ are interesting logics for the specification and verification of reactive systems. They provide a novel interval based description of such systems as compared to the conventional point based description given by linear temporal logics. We feel that many systems are more naturally described in such a framework. For example, consider the semantics of sequential composition operator of **ESTEREL** [17] or CSP [24].

We have studied the expressive power and decidabilty of our logics, as summarised below.

In Sect. 4, we have established the following linear embeddings.

$$\begin{array}{ccccc} QPTnL & \hookrightarrow & QPMVC^{-1} & \hookrightarrow & MLO \\ PTnl & \hookrightarrow & PMVC^{-1} & \hookrightarrow & FLO \end{array} \tag{4}$$

Here, $QPTnL$ and $PTnL$ are propositional linear tense logics with and without quantification, respectively. They are a generalisation of the propositional linear temporal logics PTL and $QPTL$ [6] to arbitrary time-frames. FLO and MLO stand for the first order and the monadic second order logics of order [19].

As stated in Sect. 4, an embedding $A \hookrightarrow B$ implies that if logic B is decidable, then so is logic A and with complexity not greater than that of logic B. It also means that logic B is at least as expressive as logic A. This holds for arbitrary classes of structures.

By establishing the embeddings (4), we have shown that our interval based logics $QPMVC^{-1}$ and $PMVC^{-1}$ are at least as expressive as the point based logics $QPTnL$ and $PTnL$ respectively, for any class of time-frames. We do not know whether the converse is true in general.

The embeddings (4) allow us to use many of the well-known decidability results for FLO and MLO to obtain similar results for $QPMVC^{-1}$.

Let $(\omega, \leq_\omega)$ represent the set of natural numbers with usual order, $(Q, \leq_Q)$ the set of rational numbers, $(Q^0, \leq_{Q^0})$ the set of non-negative rational numbers, $(\Re, \leq_\Re)$ the set of real numbers and $(\Re^0, \leq_{\Re^0})$ the set of non-negative real numbers.

Theorem 10. *(1)* **[Buchi [3]]** *Satisfiability/validity of MLO over the time-frame $(\omega, \leq_\omega)$ is decidable. (2)* **[Rabin [18]]** *Satisfiability/validity of MLO over the time-frames $(Q, \leq_Q)$ and $(Q^0, \leq_{Q^0})$ is decidable.* □

Corollary 11. *(1) Satisfiability/validity of $QPMVC^{-1}$ over the time-frame $(\omega, \leq_\omega)$ is decidable. (2) Satisfiability/validity of $QPMVC^{-1}$ over the time-frames $(\mathcal{Q}, \leq_\mathcal{Q})$ and $(\mathcal{Q}^0, \leq_{\mathcal{Q}^0})$ is decidable.*

Proof. Immediate from Theorem 10 and the embedding (4). □

Shelah [19] has also shown that satisfiability/validity of MLO over the time-frame $(\Re, \leq_\Re)$ is undecidable. However, this does not imply that $QPMVC^{-1}$ is undecidable over frame $(\Re, \leq_\Re)$. We do not know the answer to this question. But below we prove a more restricted result.

Theorem 12. *Satisfiability/Validity of FLO over the time-frames $(\Re, \leq_\Re)$ and $(\Re^0, \leq_\Re^0)$ is decidable.*

Proof. We give the proof for $\Re$. The proof for $\Re^0$ is similar. Consider the FLO structure $RS^\Re = ((\Re, \leq_\Re), V)$. By the Löwenheim-Skolem theorem for first-order-logic, there exists a *countable* model $RS^c = ((\Re^c, \leq_\Re^c), V^c)$ which is elementarily equivalent to $RS^\Re$. (This means that any formula of FLO is satisfiable/valid in $RS^\Re$ **iff** it is satisfiable/valid in RS^c.) But, by Cantor's lemma [7](page 150), any two countable dense linear orders without end-points are isomorphic. Hence, we can construct a $V^\mathcal{Q}$ such that RS^c is isomorphic to $RS^\mathcal{Q} = ((\mathcal{Q}, \leq_\mathcal{Q}), V^\mathcal{Q})$. Isomoporphic structures preserve the satisfiability of first-order-logic (and even second order logic) formulae. Hence, any formula of FLO is satisfiable/valid in $RS^\Re$ **iff** it is satisfiable/valid in $RS^\mathcal{Q}$.

Now, the satisfiability/validity of FLO over $(\mathcal{Q}, \leq_\mathcal{Q})$ is decidable by Theorem 10(2). Hence, the satisfiability/validity of FLO over $(\Re, \leq_\Re)$ is also decidable. □

Corollary 13. *Satisfiability/Validity of $PMVC^{-1}$ over the time-frames $(\Re, \leq_\Re)$ and $(\Re^0, \leq_{\Re^0})$ is decidable.* □

A Comparison with PTL. For the time-frame $(\omega, \leq_\omega)$, logics $PTnL$ and $QPTnL$ give precisely the propositional linear temporal logic, PTL, and the quantified propositional linear temporal logic, $QPTL$. Logics FLO and MLO over this time frame are known in the literature as $F1S$ and $S1S$, respectively [21]. These stand for the first order and the monadic second order logics of one successor function.

It is a well-known that logics PTL and $F1S$ have the same expressive power, and logics $QPTL$ and $S1S$ also have the same expressive power (see [6] for an overview of these results). Hence, by the embedding (4), we can conclude that $QPMVC^{-1}$ over the time-frame $(\omega, \leq_\omega)$ has precisely the expressive power of $S1S$ and $QPTL$. Similarly, $PMVC^{-1}$ over the time-frame $(\omega, \leq_\omega)$ has precisely the expressive power of $F1S$ and PTL.

In spite of their same expressive power, there are interesting differences between $PMVC$ and PTL. The complexity of the decision procedure for $PMVC^{-1}$ is non-elementary [5] whereas that for PTL is exponential in the size of the formula (see [6]). This suggests that there are some properties which can be expressed very succinctly in $PMVC^{-1}$ as compared to PTL.

The non-elementary complexity of the decision procedure for $PMVC^{-1}$ is discouraging, if the aim is to build mechanical verification systems for the logic. Actually, the complexity grows by an additional exponent for each alternation of $\neg$ and $\frown$. However, for many applications the number of such alternations in the formulae turn out to be low. For example, in the semantics of **ESTEREL** using $QPMVC^{-1}$ [17], formulae describing statements of **ESTEREL** are free of such alternation. The formula stating that one statement implies (or refines) another statement introduces one level of alteration of $\neg$ and $\frown$ whose validity can be checked in time doubly exponential in the size of the formula. Thus, it may still be feasible to mechanically verify the correctness of some specifications in $PMVC^{-1}$.

Further differences between $PMVC^{-1}$ and PTL become apparant when these logics are extended with fixed point operators. Logic μPTL remains decidable and has the expressive power of $S1S$ [6] whereas the logic $\mu PMVC^{-1}$ becomes undecidable [16].

A Comparison with other Interval Logics. $PMVC$ and its extension $QPMVC^{-1}$ give interval-based description of boolean functions of time. This must be contrasted with the ***propositional interval logics*** studied by studied by Halpern and Shoham [11], and Venema [22]. In these logics, temporal variables are assigned boolean values over *time intervals* (and not over *time points* as in our logic).

We have shown that $PMVC^{-1}$ is decidable over the time frame $(\Re, \leq_\Re)$ whereas the propositional interval logics of Halpern, Shoham and Venema are not decidable [11, 22].

Acknowledgements. The author is indebted to Y.S. Ramakrishna for his expert advise on the Monadic Theory of Order. The author thanks K. Narayan Kumar and Y.S. Ramakrishna for numerous discussions on the ideas in this paper. The author also thanks Prof. Rohit Parikh for his helpful comments.

References

1. M. Abadi, L. Lamport: The existence of refinement mappings, *Theoretical Computer Science*, 82(2), 1991.
2. R. Alur, T.A. Henzinger: Logics and models of real time: a survey. In *Real Time: Theory in Practice*, Mook, The Netherlands, June 1991, *LNCS 600*, pp 74-106, 1992.
3. J.R. Buchi: Weak second order arithmetic and finite automata, *Z. Math. Logik und Grundl. Math.* 6, 1960.
4. J.P. Burgess: Basic tense logic, in *Handbook of Philosophical Logic*, Vol.2, D. Reidel Publ. Co., 1984.
5. A.K.Chandra, J. Halpern, A. Meyer, R. Parikh: Equations between regular terms and an application to process logic, in *Proc. 13 ACM Symp. on Theory of Computing*, 1991.

6. E.A. Emerson: Temporal and modal logics, in *Handbook of Theo. Comp. Science*, Vol. B, The MIT Press, Cambridge, 1990.
7. H.B. Enderton: *A mathematical introduction to logic*, Academic Press, 1972.
8. M.R. Hansen, E.R. Olderog *et al*: A Duration Calculus Semantics for Real-Time Reactive Systems, *ProCoS-II Project Report OLD MRH 1/1*, Universitat Oldenburg, Germany, 1993.
9. M.R. Hansen, Zhou Chaochen: Semantics and Completeness of Duration Calculus, *J.W. de Bakker, C. Huizing, W.-P. de Roever, G. Rozenberg, (Eds) Real-Time: Theory in Practice, REX Workshop, LNCS 600,* pp 209-225, 1992
10. M.R. Hansen, P.K. Pandya, Zhou Chaochen: Finite divergence, *Theoretical Computer Science*, 138 (1995).
11. J. Halpern, Y. Shoham: A propositional modal logic of time intervals, *JACM*, 38(4), 1991.
12. Li Xiaoshan: A Mean-Value Duration Calculus, *Ph.D. Thesis, Institute of Software, Academia Sinica, Beijing*, September 1993.
13. B. Moszkowski: A Temporal Logic for Multi-level Reasoning about Hardware. In *IEEE Computer, Vol. 18(2)*, pp10-19, 1985.
14. Z. Manna and A. Pnueli. *The Temporal Logic of Reactive and Concurrent Systems: Specification.* Springer-Verlag, New York, 1991.
15. P.K. Pandya: Weak chop inverses and liveness in Mean-value Calculus, *Technical Report TR-CS-95/2*, Computer Science Group, TIFR, Bombay (August, 1994).
16. P.K. Pandya: A Recursive Mean Value Calculus, *Technical Report TR-CS-95/3*, Computer Science Group, TIFR, Bombay, (August 1994).
17. P.K. Pandya, Y.S. Ramakrishna, R.K. Shyamasundar: A Compositional Semantics of Esterel in Duration Calculus, *in proc. Second AMAST workshop on Real-time systems: Models and Proofs*, Bordeux, (June, 1995).
18. M.O. Rabin: Decidability of second order theories and automata on infinite trees, *Trans. A.M.S.* 149 (1969).
19. S. Shelah: Monadic Theory of Order, *Annals of of Math.*, 102 (1975).
20. J.U. Skakkebaek: Liveness and Fairness in Duration Calculus, in *Proc CONCUR'94*, LNCS 836, Springer-Verlag, 1994.
21. W. Thomas: Automata on infinite words, in *Handbook of Theo. Comp. Science*, Vol. B, The MIT Press, Cambridge, 1990.
22. Y. Venema: A modal logic for Chopping Intervals, *Jour. Logic Computation*, 1(4), 1991.
23. Zhou Chaochen: Duration Calculi: An Overview, in *Formal methods in programming and their applications*, D. Bjorner, M. Broy and I.V. Pottosin (Eds.), LNCS 735, 1993.
24. Zhou Chaochen, M.R. Hansen, A.P. Ravn, H. Rischel: Duration Specifications for Shared Processors, *Proc. of the Symposium on Formal Techniques in Real-Time and Fault-Tolerant Systems, Nijmegen*, January 1992, LNCS 571, pp 21-32, 1992.
25. Zhou Chaochen, M.R. Hansen, P. Sestoft: Decidability and Undecidability Results for Duration Calculus, *Proc. of STACS '93. 10th Symposium on Theoretical Aspects of Computer Science, Würzburg*, Feb. 1993.
26. Zhou Chaochen, C.A.R. Hoare, A.P. Ravn: A Calculus of Durations. In *Information Processing Letters* 40(5), 1991, pp.269-276.
27. Zhou Chaochen, Li Xiaoshan: A Mean-Value Duration Calculus, in *A classical mind: Essays in honour of C A R Hoare*, Prentice-Hall international series in computer science, Prentice-Hall International, 1994.

A Mean-Value Calculus with First-Order States

In this section, we shall generalise the logic $QPMVC^{-1}$ with first-order-logic formulae in place of propositions. The resulting logic will be called $QPMVCFS^{-1}$. This logic is often required in practice. Moreover, over finite domains, it has the same expressiveness and decidability properties as $QPMVC^{-1}$. For a typical use of this logic see the semantics of synchronous programming language **ESTEREL** [17].

Let $Tvar$ (with typical elements $v_1, v_2, \ldots$) denote the set of *state variables*. These will be interpreted as (not necessarily boolean) functions of time representing some aspect of the dynamical system behaviour. Further $Tvar$ is partitioned into $Rvar$ and $Svar$ where $Rvar$ (called "rigid variables") will represent constant functions of time. We shall use x, y to range over the members of $Rvar$.

Let $SG = (F, G)$ be a signature as in the first-order logic where F is the set of function symbols and G is the set of predicate symbols. A distinguished predicate symbol $=$ denotes equality. Let a **State formula** (or, state in brief,) denote a first-order logic formula over the variables $Tvar$ and the signature SG. (For a precise syntax refer to any book on first-order logic such as [7].) Metavariables P, Q, R will range over states.

The formulae of $QPMVCFS^{-1}$ are constructed from states as follows. Let $D, D_1, D_2, \ldots$ range over formulae.

$$\begin{array}{lll} D & ::= & \lceil P \rceil^0 \mid D_1 \wedge D_2 \mid \neg D \mid D_1 {}^\frown D_2 \mid \\ & & D_1 / D_2 \mid D_1 \setminus D_2 \mid \exists v.D \end{array}$$

Semantics. Let TM be a time-frame and $Intv$ be the set of bounded closed time intervals as in $QPMVC^{-1}$ (see Sect. 2).

An interpretation $\mathcal{I}$ for a signature SG consists of $|\mathcal{I}|$, the domain of values, together with a function $f^{\mathcal{I}}$ for each function symbol $f \in F$ and a predicate $g^{\mathcal{I}}$ for each predicate symbol $g \in G$.

A *valuation* θ over a time-frame $TM = (T, \leq)$ and an interpretation $\mathcal{I}$ assigns to each variable $v \in Tvar$ a function of time, i.e.

$$\theta \; : \; Tvar \rightarrow T \rightarrow |\mathcal{I}|$$

Further, for each rigid variable $x \in Rvar$, the function $\theta(x)$ is required to be a constant function. Call a valuation θ' to be v-variant of θ if for all $w \in Tvar$, $w \neq v \;\Rightarrow\; \theta'(w) = \theta(w)$. Thus, θ and θ' agree on the interpretation of all state variables except possibly v.

Let $\hat{\theta} : T \rightarrow Tvar \rightarrow |\mathcal{I}|$ be such that $\hat{\theta}(t)(v) = \theta(v)(t)$. Then, for every $t \in T$, $\hat{\theta}(t)$ gives a valuation in the sense of first-order logic. Hence, we can define $(\mathcal{I}, \hat{\theta}(t)) \models_{fol} P$ as usual in the first-order logic with equality. (See any book on first-order logic such as [7] for this definition.) It denotes that the f.o.l formula P is true in the interpretation $\mathcal{I}$ and the valuation θ at the time point t. A tuple $\mathcal{S} = (TM, \mathcal{I}, \theta)$ is called a $QPMVCFS^{-1}$ *structure*.

$QPMVCFS^{-1}$ Formulae are interpreted over a structure and a time interval. A tuple $(TM, \mathcal{I}, \theta, [b,e])$ is called a model. The semantics of $QPMVCFS^{-1}$ is defined inductively as follows.

$$
\begin{array}{l}
(TM,\mathcal{I},\theta,[b,e]) \models \lceil P \rceil^0 \ \ \textbf{iff} \ \ b = e \wedge (\mathcal{I}, \hat{\theta}(b)) \models_{fol} P \\
(TM,\mathcal{I},\theta,[b,e]) \models \neg D \ \ \textbf{iff} \ \ (TM,\mathcal{I},\theta,[b,e]) \not\models D \\
(TM,\mathcal{I},\theta,[b,e]) \models D_1 \wedge D_2 \ \ \textbf{iff} \\
\quad (TM,\mathcal{I},\theta,[b,e]) \models D_1 \ \text{and} \ (TM,\mathcal{I},\theta,[b,e]) \models D_2 \\
(TM,\mathcal{I},\theta,[b,e]) \models D_1 {}^\frown D_2 \ \ \textbf{iff} \ \ \text{for some } m : b \leq m \leq e. \\
\quad (TM,\mathcal{I},\theta,[b,m]) \models D_1 \ \ \text{and} \ \ (TM,\mathcal{I},\theta,[m,e]) \models D_2 \\
(TM,\mathcal{I},\theta,[b,e]) \models D_1 / D_2 \ \ \textbf{iff} \ \ \forall m : e \leq m. \\
\quad ((TM,\mathcal{I},\theta,[e,m]) \models D_2 \ \ \Rightarrow \ \ (TM,\mathcal{I},\theta,[b,m]) \models D_1) \\
(TM,\mathcal{I},\theta,[b,e]) \models D_1 \setminus D_2 \ \ \textbf{iff} \ \ \forall m : m \leq b. \\
\quad ((TM,\mathcal{I},\theta,[m,b]) \models D_1 \ \ \Rightarrow \ \ (TM,\mathcal{I},\theta,[m,e]) \models D_2) \\
(TM,\mathcal{I},\theta,[b,e]) \models \exists v.D \ \ \textbf{iff} \\
\quad (TM,\mathcal{I},\theta',[b,e]) \models D \ \ \text{for some } v\text{-variant } \theta' \text{ of } \theta
\end{array}
$$

It is easy to see that if $|\mathcal{I}|$ is taken to be the set of boolean values $0, 1$ and F is taken to be the boolean connectives $\wedge, \neg$ with usual interpretation, then logic $QPMVCFS^{-1}$ reduces to logic $QPMVC^{-1}$. Below, we consider a more general case.

Proposition 14. *if $|\mathcal{I}|$ is finite then $QPMVCFS^{-1}$ over $(TM, \mathcal{I})$ is decidable if and only if $QPMVC^{-1}$ is decidable over TM.*

Proof Outline. Let $\mathcal{I}$ be a f.o.l. structure with a finite domain $|\mathcal{I}| = \{c_1, \ldots, c_n\}$. We can define an effective translation $\phi(X)$ such that a f.o.l. formula P with variables $v_1, \ldots, v_n$ maps to the formula $\phi(P)$ of propositional logic with propositional variables $\{p_{(v_i,c_j)}\}$ such that P is satisfiable over $\mathcal{I}$ if and only if $\phi(P)$ is propositionally satisfiable. The main idea is that $p_{(v_i,c_j)} = true$ denotes $v_i = c_j$. We omit the details.

Given such a ϕ, we can translate a $QPMVCFS^{-1}$ formula D to $QPMVC^{-1}$ formula $\psi(D)$ by replacing each $\lceil P \rceil^0$ by $\lceil \phi(P) \rceil^0$. The formula $\exists v.D$ can be translated to $\exists\ p_{(v,c_1)}, \ldots, p_{(v,c_n)}.\ \psi(D) \wedge Excl$. Here, $Excl$ states that exactly one of $p_{(v,c_1)}, \ldots, p_{(v,c_n)}$ can be true at a time. We omit the details of the simple proof that $\psi(D)$ is satisfiable over TM if and only if D is satisfiable over $(TM, \mathcal{I})$. □

Thus, decidability of $QPMVCFS^{-1}$ over a given finite domain reduces to the decidability of $QPMVC^{-1}$. However, the complexity of the decision procedure depends on the size of $|\mathcal{I}|$.

Theorem Proving modulo Associativity*

Albert Rubio

Universtitat Politècnica de Catalunya,
Pau Gargallo 5, 08028 Barcelona, Spain
E-mail: `rubio@lsi.upc.es`. Tel. 34-3-4017330

Abstract. We present an inference system for first-order constrained clauses with equality modulo associativity (A). Our procedure is refutationally complete and reduces to Knuth-Bendix completion modulo A in the equational case. As an essential ingredient we present the first —as far as we know— A-compatible reduction ordering total on the ground A-congruence classes.

1 Introduction

In some cases, in automated theorem proving special treatments for some equational subset of the axioms are useful. Historically, these special treatments were motivated by the fact that equations like the commutativity axiom $f(x,y) \simeq f(y,x)$ cannot be oriented into a (terminating) rewrite rule. Although this problem was overcome by the ordered rewriting approach, there are two other good reasons for applying specific methods for some particular equations. On one hand, some axioms generate many slightly different permuted versions of clauses, and for efficiency reasons it is many times better to treat all these clauses together as a single one representing the whole class. In the case modulo associativity (A), like it also happens in the case modulo associativity and commutativity (AC), there is a second advantage: sets like $f(a,b) \rightarrow b$ and $f(a,f(x,b)) \rightarrow f(x,b)$ are complete modulo A, but cannot be completed without building-in associativity of f [14].

Also, as observed by Bachmair in [1], some equations like the commutativity axiom are more naturally viewed as "structural" axioms (defining a congruence relation on terms) rather than as "simplifiers" (defining a reduction relation). This leads to extending completion procedures to deal with congruence classes of terms instead of single terms, i.e. working with a *built-in* equational theory E, and performing rewriting and inferences with special E-matching and E-unification algorithms [8, 5, 14, 6, 7, 2], some of them for specific sets E and for wider classes of sets others, but all of them requiring that a complete E-unification algorithm is given.

In general there is no unique most general E-unifier for a given E-unification problem. In the case of A-unification, unlike in AC-unification, the *minimal complete* set of unifiers needs not even to be finite: $f(a,x)$ and $f(x,a)$ have an infinite

* This work has been partially supported by the Esprit Working Group CCL, ref. 6028

set of independent A-unifiers: $a, f(a,a), f(a,a,a), \ldots$ Due to this, equality constraints [11, 12, 13] are extremely useful in this context: instead of E-unifying the terms, the unification problem is kept in an (E-)equality constraint. Dealing with a constrained clause $C\ [\![\ s = t\ ]\!]$ can be much more efficient than having n clauses $C_1, \ldots, C_n$, one for each E-unifier that is a solution of $s = t$, since e.g. many inferences can be computed at once, and each inference generates *one single conclusion* with an additional equality $s = t$ in its constraint. Furthermore, computing A-unifiers is not needed at all, which is of course crucial, due its well-known computational and algorithmic complexity [9]. A clause C with an A-equality constraint T can be proved redundant by means of efficient incomplete methods detecting cases of unsatisfiability of T. Only if C is the empty clause one has to decide the A-unifiability of T to know whether an inconsistency has been derived or not. By means of the model generation method [3], we proved the completeness of such a basic strategy for the AC-case in [12] (see also [17]), combined with ordering constraints. Here we develop a similar inference system for the case modulo A, together with an essential ingredient for these methods, namely the first —as far as we know— A-compatible reduction ordering total on the ground A-congruence classes.

This paper is structured as follows. After the introduction some basic notions and definitions are given. In section 3 the A-compatible ordering is defined. Section 4 is devoted to the inference system and section 5 to prove its refutationally completeness. In section 6 the usefulness of saturated sets is studied. All proofs and detailed explanations of the following can be found in [15].

2 Preliminaries

Below let s and t (possibly indexed) be terms in $\mathcal{T}(\mathcal{F})$ and f a function symbol in $\mathcal{F}$ and let E be an equational theory. A (strict partial) ordering on $\mathcal{T}(\mathcal{F})$ (a transitive irreflexive relation) $\succ$ fulfills the *subterm property* if $f(\ldots t \ldots) \succ t$ for all f and t. It is *monotonic* if $s \succ t$ implies $f(\ldots s \ldots) \succ f(\ldots t \ldots)$. A monotonic ordering fulfilling the subterm property is a *simplification ordering* and for finite signatures it is *well-founded*: there is no infinite sequence $t_1 \succ t_2 \succ \ldots$ An ordering $\succ$ is *E-compatible* if $s' =_E s \succ t =_E t'$ implies $s' \succ t'$. Finally we say that an ordering is E-total on $\mathcal{T}(\mathcal{F})$ if $s \neq_E t$ implies $s \succ t$ or $t \succ s$ for all terms $s, t \in \mathcal{T}(\mathcal{F})$. Any well-founded monotonic ordering $\succ$ total on $\mathcal{T}(\mathcal{F})$ is a simplification ordering.

An ordering on $\mathcal{T}(\mathcal{F}, \mathcal{X})$ is *stable* under substitutions if $s \succ t$ implies $s\sigma \succ t\sigma$ for all terms s and t and substitutions σ. A well-founded monotonic ordering stable under substitutions is called a *reduction ordering*.

Here an *equation* is a multiset of terms $\{s, t\}$, which will be written in the form $s \simeq t$. A first-order clause is a pair of (finite) multisets of equations Γ (the *antecedent*) and Δ (the *succedent*), denoted by $\Gamma \rightarrow \Delta$. By *(ordering and equality) constraints* we mean quantifier-free first-order formulae built over the binary predicate symbols $\succ$ and $=$ relating terms in $\mathcal{T}(\mathcal{F}, \mathcal{X})$, where, in what follows, $=$ will be interpreted as A-equality $=_A$, and $\succ$ as an A-compatible simplification ordering A-total on ground terms. We say that a ground substitution σ *satisfies* a constraint T if $T\sigma$ is (or evaluates to) true in this sense.

We extend $\succ$ to an ordering on ground equations (in fact, to their *occurrences* in clauses) and to clauses, s.t. terms in the antecedent get a slightly higher complexity than in the succedent. An occurrence of an equation $t \simeq t'$ in an antecedent is (the two-fold multiset) $\{\{t, t'\}\}$, and in a succedent it is $\{\{t\}, \{t'\}\}$. Now the two-fold multiset extension of $\succ$ is A-total on ground equations, and the three-fold multiset extension of $\succ$ is an A-total ordering on ground clauses. We will ambiguously use $\succ$ to denote all these orderings on terms, equations and clauses. An equation e is called *maximal* in a ground clause C if there is no equation e' in C such that $e' \succ e$ and *strictly maximal* if there is no e' with $e' \succeq e$ (i.e. $e' \succ e$ or $e' =_A e$).

If C is a ground clause and S is a set of clauses, then we denote by $S^{\prec C}$ (resp. $S^{\preceq C}$) the set of ground instances of clauses in S that are smaller wrt. $\succ$ than C (resp. smaller than or equal to C).

An interpretation I is a congruence on ground terms, which satisfies a ground clause $\Gamma \rightarrow \Delta$, denoted $I \models \Gamma \rightarrow \Delta$, if $I \not\supseteq \Gamma$ or else $I \cap \Delta \neq \emptyset$. It is said to be an A-interpretation when it satisfies the A-axiom for all A-operators. An interpretation I satisfies (is a model of) a constrained clause $C \llbracket T \rrbracket$, denoted $I \models C \llbracket T \rrbracket$, if it satisfies every ground instance of $C \llbracket T \rrbracket$, i.e. every $C\sigma$ such that σ is ground and $T\sigma$ is true. Therefore, clauses with unsatisfiable constraints are tautologies, and $C \llbracket T \rrbracket$ is the *empty clause* only if C is empty and T is satisfiable. I satisfies a set of clauses S, denoted by $I \models S$, if it satisfies every clause in S. A clause C follows from a set of clauses S (denoted by $S \models C$), if C is satisfied by every model of S. For dealing with non-equality predicates, atoms A can be expressed by equations $A \simeq true$ where $true$ is a special symbol (minimal in $\succ$).

We use the definitions of [4] for rewriting-related notions. However, to avoid confusion with the arrow $\rightarrow$ of clauses, we denote ground rewrite rules (ground equations $s \simeq t$ with $s \succ t$) by $s \Rightarrow t$. The congruence generated by a set of equations (or rewrite rules) E (which is an interpretation) will be denoted by E^*.

It is well-known that a term s can be *flattened* by removing all A-operators f that are immediately below another f. For example, if f and g are A-operators, then $h(f(f(a,a), f(b, g(c, g(d,e)))))$ is flattened into $h(f(a,a,b,g(c,d,e)))$. We do not use flattening in this paper, except for illustrating the following. The symbols that are not removed under flattening are in a *maximal position*: if p is a position in a ground term s, we define $maxpos(s,p)$ to be p if $top(s|_p)$ is not an A-operator and else $maxpos(s,p)$ is the maximal prefix p' of p such that $p' = \lambda$ or $p' = p'' \cdot n$ with $top(s|_{p''}) \neq top(s|_p)$. Let s and t be two A-equal terms, i.e. $s =_A t$. Then their flattened forms are equal: a one-to-one correspondance can be established in this way between maximal positions in s and in t. We will sometimes speak about the *corresponding* position in t of some maximal position in s. Note that if u and v are subterms at corresponding maximal positions of resp. s and t, then $u =_A v$. Moreover, if $f(t_1, \ldots t_n)$ is the term resulting of applying flattening only at top-most position then *top-flattening* of a term t, denoted $tf(t)$ is $\{t_1,\ldots,t_n\}$. For example, if f is an A-operator, $tf(f(a,f(g(f(f(a,b),c)),f(a,b))))$ is $\{a,g(f(f(a,b),c)),a,b\}$.

3 A total A-compatible reduction ordering

As for the C-case, it is clear that AC-compatible orderings are also A-compatible orderings (when the associative symbols are also considered commutative), but what is not so clear is how to get an A-compatible reduction ordering A-total on $\mathcal{T}(\mathcal{F})$. Suppose we are trying to extend a path ordering. Then the first attempt could be to flatten terms to ensure A-compatibility and then apply a *lexicographic path ordering* (LPO; see e.g. [4]) to ensure totality. But due to flattening, we have variable arity function symbols (the A-symbols), and this leads to loose well-foundedness, since LPO is a simplification ordering only when all symbols have fixed arity (as it does not fulfil the deletion property): if $a \succ b$ then $f(b,a) \succ f(b,b,a) \succ f(b,b,b,a) \succ \ldots$. Another attempt could be to normalize terms wrt. associativity rules (moving A-symbols to the right or to the left) and then apply LPO (on terms with fixed-arity function symbols), but again monotonicity is lost: suppose f associative and $f \succ g$, and that we normalize wrt. the rule $f(f(x,y),z) \rightarrow f(x,f(y,z))$ (i.e. we move A-symbols to the right); then $f(a,a) \succ_A g(a)$ but $f(g(a),a) \succ_A f(f(a,a),a)$.

In the following we will define an A-compatible reduction (simplification) ordering $\succ_A$ extending an AC-compatible reduction (simplification) ordering $\succ_{AC}$ s.t. $\succ_A$ is A-total on $\mathcal{T}(\mathcal{F})$ whenever $\succ_{AC}$ is AC-total on $\mathcal{T}(\mathcal{F})$, provided that $\mathcal{F}$ is a set of fixed-arity function symbols and $\mathcal{F}_A$ the subset of associative function symbols (cosidered associative-commutative when using $\succ_{AC}$).

Definition 1. Let $\mathcal{F}$ be a set of fixed-arity function symbols, $\succ_{AC}$ an ordering on $\mathcal{T}(\mathcal{F},\mathcal{X})$ and s and t terms in $\mathcal{T}(\mathcal{F},\mathcal{X})$, with $tf(s) = \langle s_1,\ldots,s_m\rangle$ and $tf(t) = \langle t_1,\ldots,t_n\rangle$ (here we have flattening rules for all symbols in $\mathcal{F}_A$, but since they are only applied at top-most position all terms in the top-flattening are in $\mathcal{T}(\mathcal{F},\mathcal{X})$, i.e. there is no problem with the requirement of having fixed-arity function symbols). Then $s \succ_A t$ iff

$$s \succ_{AC} t \quad \text{or} \quad s =_{AC} t \quad \text{and} \quad \langle s_1,\ldots,s_m\rangle \succ_A^{lex} \langle t_1,\ldots,t_n\rangle$$

where $\succ_A^{lex}$ is the lexicographic extension of $\succ_A$ wrt. $=_A$ (note that if $s =_{AC} t$ then $top(s) = top(t)$ and $m = n$), and $tf(u)$ for some term u headed by f denotes the list of subterms of u at maximal position not headed by f if f is in $\mathcal{F}_A$, and the list of the arguments of u otherwise.

Theorem 2. *Let $\succ_{AC}$ be an AC-compatible reduction (simplification) ordering on terms in $\mathcal{T}(\mathcal{F},\mathcal{X})$. Then $\succ_A$ is an A-compatible reduction (simplification) ordering on $\mathcal{T}(\mathcal{F},\mathcal{X})$. Moreover, if $\succ_{AC}$ is AC-total on $\mathcal{T}(\mathcal{F})$ then $\succ_A$ is A-total on $\mathcal{T}(\mathcal{F})$.*

Proof. All properties are proved separately by induction on the size of the involved terms. Assume $tf(s) = \langle s_1, \ldots, s_m \rangle$ and $tf(t) = \langle t_1, \ldots, t_n \rangle$.

1. Irreflexivity and transitivity follow from the irreflexivity and transitivity of $\succ_{AC}$ and $\succ_A^{lex}$ (by induction hypothesis).
2. Monotonicity. Suppose $s \succ_A t$: If $s \succ_{AC} t$ then $f(\ldots s \ldots) \succ_{AC} f(\ldots t \ldots)$ (by monotonicity of $\succ_{AC}$) and hence $f(\ldots s \ldots) \succ_A f(\ldots t \ldots)$. If $s =_{AC} t$ then $top(s) = top(t)$, $m = n$, $tf(s) \succ_A^{lex} tf(t)$ and $f(\ldots s \ldots) =_{AC} f(\ldots t \ldots)$. There are two cases to be considered: if $top(s) = f$ is an A-symbol then $tf(f(\ldots s \ldots)) = \langle \ldots s_1, \ldots, s_m \ldots \rangle \succ_A^{lex} \langle \ldots t_1, \ldots, t_n \ldots \rangle = tf(f(\ldots t \ldots))$. Otherwise, $tf(f(\ldots s \ldots)) = \langle \ldots, s \ldots \rangle \succ_A^{lex} \langle \ldots, t \ldots \rangle = tf(f(\ldots t \ldots))$.
3. Well-foundedness. Suppose there exists an infinite decreasing sequence $u_1 \succ_A u_2 \succ_A u_3 \succ_A \ldots$. Since $\succ_{AC}$ is well-founded and by transitivity of $\succ_A$, there exists k s.t. $u_k =_{AC} u_j$ for all $j \geq k$. But there is only a finite number of (syntactically different) terms AC-equivalent to u_k, which implies that there must be two terms u_q and u_p with $p > q \geq k$ s.t. u_q and u_p are the same term (i.e. they are syntactically equal). Therefore by transitivity we have $u_q \succ_A u_p$ which contradicts the irreflexivity.
4. Stability under substitutions (when dealing with terms with variables). Suppose $s \succ_A t$. If $s \succ_{AC} t$ then by stability of $\succ_{AC}$ we have $s\sigma \succ_{AC} t\sigma$, and hence $s\sigma \succ_A t\sigma$, for all ground substitutions σ. If $s =_{AC} t$ then $s\sigma =_{AC} t\sigma$ for all ground substitutions σ and $\langle s_1, \ldots, s_m \rangle \succ_A{}^{lex} \langle t_1, \ldots, t_n \rangle$, i.e. $s_1 =_A t_1 \wedge \ldots \wedge s_{i-1} =_A t_{i-1} \wedge s_i \succ_A t_i$, which implies by induction hypothesis $s_1\sigma =_A t_1\sigma \wedge \ldots \wedge s_{i-1}\sigma =_A t_{i-1}\sigma$ and $s_i\sigma \succ_A t_i\sigma$. Now suppose $tf(s\sigma) = \langle s'_1, \ldots, s'_p \rangle$ and $tf(t\sigma) = \langle t'_1, \ldots, t'_p \rangle$ (note that due to the existence of variables $tf(s\sigma)$ could be different from $tf(s)\sigma$ as well as for t). Since s_i can not be a variable (otherwise it would not be greater than any term), there must be some $j = 1 \ldots p$ s.t. s'_j is $s_i\sigma$ and therefore $s'_1 =_A t'_1 \wedge \ldots \wedge s'_{j-1} =_A t'_{j-1} \wedge s'_j \succ_A t'_j$ (since s'_j is $s_i\sigma$ and t'_j is $t_i\sigma$ or one of its subterms), which implies $s\sigma \succ_A t\sigma$.
5. Subterm property (note that the deletion property trivially holds since all symbols are supposed to have fixed arity). Since $\succ_{AC}$ satisfies this property we have $f(\ldots s \ldots) \succ_{AC} s$ and hence $f(\ldots s \ldots) \succ_A s$.
6. A-compatibility. Suppose we have $s' =_A s \succ_A t =_A t'$. If $s \succ_{AC} t$, since $s' =_A s$ and $t' =_A t$ implies $s' =_{AC} s$ and $t' =_{AC} t$, by AC-compatibility of $\succ_{AC}$ we have $s' \succ_{AC} t'$ and hence $s' \succ_A t'$. If $s =_{AC} t$ then $s' =_{AC} t'$ and $tf(s) \succ_A{}^{lex} tf(t)$. Suppose $tf(s') = \langle s'_1, \ldots, s'_m \rangle$ and $tf(t') = \langle t'_1, \ldots, t'_n \rangle$. Therefore $s_i =_A s'_i$ and $t_i =_A t'_i$ for all $i = 1 \ldots m$ (note that $m = n$) and by induction hypothesis $tf(s') \succ_A{}^{lex} tf(t')$, which implies $s' \succ_A t'$.
7. A-totality. By AC-totality of $\succ_{AC}$ we know that either $s \succ_{AC} t$ or $t \succ_{AC} s$ or $s =_{AC} t$ for all ground terms s and t. Therefore, either $s \succ_A t$ or $t \succ_A s$ or we have to compare $\langle s_1, \ldots, s_m \rangle$ and $\langle t_1, \ldots, t_n \rangle$. But, by induction hypothesis for all $i = 1 \ldots m$, either $s_i \succ_A t_i$ or $t_i \succ_A s_i$ or $s_i =_A t_i$, and hence either $s =_A t$ or $tf(s) \succ_A{}^{lex} tf(t)$ implying $s \succ_A t$ or $tf(t) \succ_A{}^{lex} tf(s)$ implying $t \succ_A s$. □

As seen in the proof, the only restriction needed is the fact that all function symbols have fixed arity. Terms compared must be built fulfilling this condition, but we do not mind about how these terms are compared under $\succ_{AC}$, i.e. if terms are flattened or not, or if $\succ_{AC}$ is based on polynomial interpretation or on a path ordering, etc. Therefore, there are no other restrictions on the ordering $\succ_{AC}$ but to be an AC-compatible reduction (simplification) ordering (possibly AC-total on $\mathcal{T}(\mathcal{F})$). Since such an AC-total ordering for the AC-case indeed exists (e.g. [10, 16]), from the previous theorem the existence of an A-total A-compatible reduction ordering follows.

4 The inference system I_A

The following inference system called I_A extends the classical strict superposition inference system I given in e.g. [13].

Definition 3. In the inference rules the ordering constraints (OC) always encode that the equations $s \simeq t$ and $s' \simeq t'$ are maximal wrt. $\succ$ (which is an A-compatible reduction ordering total on the A-congruence classes) in the premise to which they belong (strictly maximal if they belong to the succedent), with $s \succ t$ and $s' \succ t'$, and that $s \simeq t$ is bigger than $s' \simeq t'$ except in A-top superposition.

In the A-superposition rules the variables x and x' (which are new variables) can be empty. Furthermore if x or x' are not empty then the term s' can be restricted to be headed by the A-symbol f. This can be expressed in the constraint language and added to the constraint. Similarly to the AC-case, A-top superposition is only needed if s and s' are headed by f and the top-flattening (i.e. applying flattening only at top-most position) of x is a proper prefix of the top-flattening of s' and the top-flattening of x' is a proper suffix of the top-flattening of s. Note that here we cannot restrict the inference to consider only the longest shared prefix and suffix respectively of s and s' (see example 1).

Of course, the superposition inferences are needed only if $s|_p$ is non-variable, and A-superposition is needed only if moreover $s|_p$ (which has an f as top symbol) is not immediately below another f.

1. *A-strict superposition right*:

$$\frac{\Gamma' \rightarrow \Delta', s' \simeq t' \, [\![T']\!] \qquad \Gamma \rightarrow \Delta, s \simeq t \, [\![T]\!]}{\Gamma', \Gamma \rightarrow \Delta', \Delta, s[f(x, f(t', x'))]_p \simeq t \, [\![T' \wedge T \wedge s|_p = f(x, (s', x')) \wedge OC]\!]}$$

2. *A-strict superposition left*:

$$\frac{\Gamma' \rightarrow \Delta', s' \simeq t' \, [\![T']\!] \qquad \Gamma, s \simeq t \rightarrow \Delta \, [\![T]\!]}{\Gamma', \Gamma, s[f(x, f(t', x'))]_p \simeq t \rightarrow \Delta', \Delta \, [\![T' \wedge T \wedge s|_p = f(x, f(s', x')) \wedge OC]\!]}$$

3. *A-top-superposition*:

$$\frac{\Gamma' \rightarrow \Delta', s' \simeq t' \, [\![T']\!] \qquad \Gamma \rightarrow \Delta, s \simeq t \, [\![T]\!]}{\Gamma', \Gamma \rightarrow \Delta', \Delta, f(x, t) \simeq f(t', x') \, [\![T' \wedge T \wedge f(x, s) = f(s', x') \wedge OC]\!]}$$

4. *equality resolution:*

$$\frac{\Gamma, s \simeq t \to \Delta\, [\![\, T \,]\!]}{\Gamma \to \Delta\, [\![\, T \wedge OC \wedge\ s = t \,]\!]}$$

5. *factoring:*

$$\frac{\Gamma \to \Delta, s' \simeq t', s \simeq t\, [\![\, T \,]\!]}{\Gamma, t \simeq t' \to \Delta, s \simeq t\, [\![\, T \wedge OC \wedge\ s = s' \,]\!]}$$

In the rules of A-strict superposition right and left the fact that x or x' can be empty means that apart from $f(x, f(s', x'))$ we have to consider in addition $f(x, s')$, $f(s', x')$ and s' to superpose with.

Example 1. For simplicity in this example we use string notation (but there is no λ) for the terms. Suppose a simplification ordering on strings extending $a \succ b \succ c \succ d \succ e$. Then the following set:

1. $\to baa \simeq d$
2. $\to aac \simeq e$
3. $\to be \simeq dc$
4. $bae \simeq dac \to$

is inconsistent, but due to the ordering restrictions (note that $baa \succ d$ and $aac \succ e$ by the transitivity and the subterm property), the only one possible inference is by A-top superposition between 1. and 2. but, instead of taking the longest shared part (getting 3.), considering just one a symbol to be shared, which produces 5. $\to bae \simeq dac$. Finally 5. and 4. lead to the empty clause.

5 Refutational completeness

Definition 4. Let $C\, [\![\, T \,]\!]$ be a constrained clause and let σ be a ground substitution such that $T\sigma$ is true. Then $C\sigma$ is called a ground *instance* with σ of $C\, [\![\, T \,]\!]$.

If moreover $C\sigma$ is of the form $\Gamma \to \Delta, s \simeq t$ where $top(s)$ is an A symbol f, and $s \simeq t$ is the strictly maximal equation in $C\sigma$ with $s \succ t$, then for every ground terms v and v', the clauses (i) $\Gamma \to \Delta, f(s, v) \simeq f(t, v)$ (ii) $\Gamma \to \Delta, f(v, s) \simeq f(v, t)$ and (iii) $\Gamma \to \Delta, f(v, f(s, v')) \simeq f(v, f(t, v'))$ are called *extended* (ground) instances of $C\, [\![\, T \,]\!]$ wrt. $C\sigma$ (with the *context* v and v');

Sometimes, to distinguish between extended instances and the usual instances, we will call the latter *non-extended instances*.

Similarly, if π is an inference (by I_A) with premises $C_1\, [\![\, T_1 \,]\!], \ldots C_n\, [\![\, T_n \,]\!]$ and conclusion $C\, [\![\, T \,]\!]$ and σ is a ground substitution satisfying T, then the inference $\pi\sigma$ with premises $C_1\sigma, \ldots, C_n\sigma$ and conclusion $D\sigma$ is a *ground instance with* σ of π.

Definition 5. If, for a given ground instance $C\sigma$ of a clause C, a variable x only appears in equations $x \simeq t$ of the succedent of C with $x\sigma \succ t\sigma$ then x is called a *succedent-top* variable of $C\sigma$, denoted $x \in stvars(C, \sigma)$.

Definition 6. A variable x is called an *extension variable* for the A-symbol f if it is the new variable x introduced in an inference by A-strict superposition (right or left). The set of all extension variables for the function symbol f is denoted by $\mathcal{X}_f$.

Definition 7. Let R be a set of ground rewrite rules, let $C\sigma$ be a ground instance of a clause C and let x be a variable in $\mathcal{V}ars(C)$. Then x is said to be *variable irreducible* in $C\sigma$ (wrt. R) if,

1. $x\sigma$ is irreducible wrt. R, or
2. $x \in stvars(C, \sigma)$ and $x\sigma$ is irreducible wrt. all rules $l \to r \in R$ s.t. $x\sigma \simeq t\sigma \succ l \simeq r$ for all $x \simeq t$ in C, or
3. $x \in \mathcal{X}_f$ for some A-symbol f and all subterms t of $x\sigma$ with $top(t) \neq f$ are irreducible wrt. R.

If the property holds for all $x \in \mathcal{V}ars(C)$ then $C\sigma$ is variable irreducible wrt. R.

Definition 8. Let R be a set of ground rewrite rules, C $[\![T]\!]$ a constrained clause, S a set of constrained clauses and π an inference.

1. The set of variable irreducible (wrt. R) ground instances of C $[\![T]\!]$ is $Ir_R(C\,[\![T]\!]) = \{C\sigma \,|\, T\sigma \equiv true \wedge \sigma \text{ ground} \wedge C\sigma \text{ variable irreducible wrt.} R\}$.
2. Similarly, $Ir_R(S) = \{C\sigma \mid C\,[\![T]\!] \in S \wedge C\sigma \in Ir_R(C\,[\![T]\!])\}$.
3. $Ir_R(\pi)$ is the set of ground instances $\pi\sigma$ of π such that $C\sigma \in Ir_R(C\,[\![T]\!])$ for each $C\,[\![T]\!]$ that is premise or conclusion of π.

Definition 9. Let $D\,[\![T]\!]$ be a constrained clause and let π be an inference.

1. $D\,[\![T]\!]$ is *redundant* in a set of constrained clauses S if $Ir_R(S)^{\preceq C} \cup A^{\preceq C} \cup R \models C$
2. π is *redundant* in a set S if $Ir_R(S)^{\prec C} \cup A^{\prec C} \cup R \models D$

for every set of rules R s.t. $\to_R \subseteq \succ$ and C in $Ir_R(D\,[\![T]\!])$, and for every inference in $Ir_R(\pi)$ with maximal premise C and conclusion D.

At the end of this section we will provide some sufficient conditions for proving redundancy which include well-known *practical* methods like subsumption or rewriting.

Now we define the set of rewrite rules R_S for a set S by induction. Each instance C may *generate* a rule depending on the set R_C of rules generated by smaller instances:

Definition 10. Let S be a set of constrained clauses. Now for each ground extended and non-extended instance C of a constrained clause in S, we inductively define the cases in which C *generates* certain ground rewrite rules, in terms of the set R_C of rules generated by instances smaller (wrt. $\succ$) than C.

Let A_C denote the set of ground instances $s \simeq s'$ of equations in A with $C \succ s \simeq s'$ and s and s' irreducible wrt. R_C, and let I_C denote the interpretation $(R_C \cup A_C)^*$.

Let C be a ground clause of the form $\Gamma \to \Delta, s \simeq t$ where $s \simeq t$ is strictly maximal (wrt. $\succ$) in C and $s \succ t$.

1. If C is a (non-extended) instance of a clause in S that is variable irreducible wrt. R_C then it generates all rules $u \Rightarrow t$ with $u =_A s$ if:
   (a) $I_C \not\models C$,
   (b) $I_C \not\models t \simeq t'$, for every $s' \simeq t'$ in Δ with $s' =_A s$, and
   (c) u is irreducible by R_C for all u with $u =_A s$.
2. If C is an extended instance of a clause in S wrt. some D that has generated some rule, then for each u with $u =_A s$ and u irreducible by R_C, C generates a rule $u \Rightarrow t$.

Finally[2], we define $R_S = \bigcup R_C$, $A_S = \bigcup A_C$, and $I_S = (R_S \cup A_S)^*$.

Note that since $\succ$ is A-compatible $s \succ t$ implies $u \succ t$ for all u with $u =_A s$.

Lemma 11. *Let S be a set of constrained clauses, and C and D instances of clauses in S with $C \succ D$. Then $R_C \supseteq R_D$, $A_C \supseteq A_D$, and $I_C \supseteq I_D$.*

Lemma 12. *Let S be a set of constrained clauses.*

1. *If instances C and D with $C \succ D$ generate resp. $l \Rightarrow r$ and $l' \Rightarrow r'$ then $l \succ l'$.*
2. *For all $s_1 \simeq s_2$ in A_S, the terms s_1 and s_2 are irreducible wrt. R_S.*
3. *For all $l \Rightarrow r$ and $l' \Rightarrow r'$ in R_S, if $l =_A l'$ then r and r' are the same term.*
4. *There are no overlaps between left hand sides of rules of R_S.*
5. *If $u =_A v$ for ground terms u and v, then u is reducible by R_S iff v is.*

Lemma 13. *Let S be a set of constrained clauses, and let s and t be ground terms. Then $I_S \models s \simeq t$ implies $s \rightarrow^*_{R_S} s' =_{A_S} t' \leftarrow^*_{R_S} t$ for some s' and t'.*

Lemma 14. *If $\Gamma\sigma \rightarrow \Delta\sigma, s\sigma \simeq t\sigma$ is an instance C of S that generates rules $u \Rightarrow t\sigma$ for all $u =_A s\sigma$ then $I_S \supseteq \Gamma\sigma$ and $I_S \cap \Delta\sigma = \emptyset$.*

Lemma 15. *Let S be a set of constrained clauses. If a ground instance $C\sigma$ of a clause C [[T]] in S, with C of the form $\Gamma \rightarrow \Delta, s \simeq t$ generates rules $u \Rightarrow t\sigma$ with $u =_A s\sigma$ then $C\sigma$ is variable irreducible wrt. R_S.*

Definition 16. A set of constrained clauses S is *saturated* if all inferences by I_A with premises in S are redundant in S.

Lemma 17. *Let S be a saturated set of constrained clauses not containing the empty clause. Then $I_S \models Ir_{R_S}(S) \cup A$.*

[2] to ensure that in this inductive definition all instances of A are generated, even if there is some greatest instance C of S (e.g. when all clauses in S are ground), only for this definition it is supposed that the clause $\rightarrow x \simeq x$ [[*true*]] is in S (note that this clause cannot generate any rule).

Proof. We will derive a contradiction from the existence of a minimal (wrt. $\succ$) instance C in $Ir_{R_S}(S) \cup A$ such that $I_S \not\models C$.

If C is an instance $f(f(u_1,u_2),u_3) \simeq f(u_1,f(u_2,u_3))$ of the associativity axiom, then since $C \notin A_S$, one of $f(f(u_1,u_2),u_3)$ and $f(u_1,f(u_2,u_3))$ must be reducible by R_S and by lemma 12 point 5 both of them, since they are A-equal. Consider u_1, u_2 and u_3 irreducible (otherwise a contradiction is directly obtained).

Let the rule reducing $f(f(u_1,u_2),u_3)$ be $l \Rightarrow r$ with (i) $l =_A s\sigma$ and $r = t\sigma$, (ii) $l =_A f(s\sigma, v)$, and $r = f(t\sigma, v)$ (iii) $l =_A f(v, s\sigma)$ and $r = f(v, t\sigma)$ or (iv) $l =_A f(v, f(s\sigma, w))$ and $r = f(v, f(t\sigma, w))$, generated by an instance with σ (possibly extended with the context v (and w)) of a clause D of the form $\Gamma \rightarrow \Delta, s \simeq t$, where $top(s\sigma) = f$. Then $f(f(u_1,u_2),u_3) =_A f(s\sigma, v_1)$ or $f(f(u_1,u_2),u_3) =_A f(v_2, s\sigma)$ or $f(f(u_1,u_2),u_3) =_A f(v_3, f(s\sigma, v_4))$ for some v_1, v_2, v_3 and v_4; and $f(f(u_1,u_2),u_3)$ is rewritten into some s_1 with $s_1 =_{A^{\prec C}} f(t\sigma, v_1)$ or $s_1 =_{A^{\prec C}} f(v_2, t\sigma)$ or $s_1 =_{A^{\prec C}} f(v_3, f(t\sigma, v_4))$ (we use $A^{\prec C}$ to denote the instances of A that are smaller wrt. $\succ$ than C; note that $I_S \models A^{\prec C}$ by minimality of C).

Similarly, let the rule reducing $f(u_1,f(u_2,u_3))$ be $l' \Rightarrow r'$ with (i) $l' =_A s'\sigma$ and $r' = t'\sigma$, (ii) $l' =_A f(s'\sigma, v')$, and $r' = f(t'\sigma, v')$ (iii) $l' =_A f(v', s'\sigma)$ and $r' = f(v', t'\sigma)$ or (iv) $l' =_A f(v', f(s'\sigma, w'))$ and $r' = f(v', f(t'\sigma, w'))$, generated by an instance with σ (possibly extended with the context v' (and w')) of a clause D' of the form $\Gamma' \rightarrow \Delta', s' \simeq t'$, where $top(s'\sigma) = f$. Then $f(f(u_1,u_2),u_3) =_A f(s'\sigma, v_1')$ or $f(f(u_1,u_2),u_3) =_A f(v_2', s'\sigma)$ or $f(f(u_1,u_2),u_3) =_A f(v_3', f(s'\sigma, v_4'))$ for some v_1', v_2', v_3' and v_4'; and $f(f(u_1,u_2),u_3)$ is rewritten into some s_2 with $s_2 =_{A^{\prec C}} f(t'\sigma, v_1')$ or $s_2 =_{A^{\prec C}} f(v_2', t'\sigma)$ or $s_2 =_{A^{\prec C}} f(v_3', f(t'\sigma, v_4'))$.

It can be assumed wlog. that $s\sigma \succ s'\sigma$ or $s\sigma =_A s'\sigma$. Let $tf(f(f(u_1,u_2),u_3))$ (and hence $tf(f(u_1,f(u_2,u_3))))$ be $\langle w_1,\ldots,w_n \rangle$ with $n \geq 3$. Therefore, as u_1, u_2 and u_3 are irreducible, $tf(s\sigma) = \langle w_i,\ldots,w_j \rangle$ for some p and q with $1 \leq i < j \leq n$ and $tf(s'\sigma) = \langle w_k,\ldots,w_r \rangle$ for some k and r with $1 \leq k < r \leq n$.

Now there are several cases to be considered, depending on the order relation between i, j, k and r.

If $i = k \leq r < j$ then $s\sigma =_A f(s'\sigma, v_5)$ with $tf(f(s'\sigma, v_5)) = \langle w_i,\ldots,w_j \rangle$, and therefore the following inference by A-strict superposition right 1

$$\frac{\Gamma' \rightarrow \Delta', s' \simeq t' \; [\![T']\!] \qquad \Gamma \rightarrow \Delta, s \simeq t \; [\![T]\!]}{\Gamma', \Gamma \rightarrow \Delta', \Delta, s[f(t',x)]_p \simeq t \; [\![T' \wedge T \wedge OC \wedge \; s|_p =_A f(s',x)]\!]}$$

can be made (with $p = \lambda$), and, since all the conditions for its application hold, its conclusion D_1 has an instance with a ground substitution θ defined by $\theta = \sigma \cup \{x \mapsto v_5\}$.

$D_1\theta$ is variable irreducible wrt. R_S since $D'\theta$ and $D\theta$ are variable irreducible wrt. R_S (by lemma 15) and for every variable $y \in Vars(D_1)$, either $y\theta$ is irreducible wrt. R_S or we have:

1. $y \in stvars(D,\theta)$ or $y \in stvars(D',\theta)$ in some $y \simeq t_y$. Then also $y \in stvars(D_1,\theta)$ in the same $y \simeq t_y$, and therefore y is variable irreducible in $D_1\theta$ wrt. R_S.

2. $y \in \mathcal{X}_g$ for some A-symbol g in D or D'. Then also $y \in \mathcal{X}_g$ in D_1 and therefore it is variable irreducible in $D_1\theta$ wrt. R_S.
3. y is x, then, since v_5 must be a proper subterm of u for some $u =_A s\sigma$, v_5 is irreducible wrt. R_S (as the rule $s\sigma \Rightarrow t\sigma$ has been generated). Therefore y is variable irreducible in $D_1\theta$ wrt. R_S.

$D_1\theta$ is an existing instance smaller than C, and moreover variable irreducible. Since S is saturated, $R_S \cup A^{\prec D\theta} \cup Ir_{R_S}(S)^{\prec D\theta} \models D_1\theta$ (as $\rightarrow_{R_S} \subseteq \succ$ by construction), so from the minimality of C (note that $C \succ D\theta$) we have $I_S \models D_1\theta$. We know $I_S \not\models \Gamma'\sigma, \Gamma\sigma \rightarrow \Delta'\sigma, \Delta\sigma$, so it must be the case that $I_S \models f(t', x)\theta \simeq t\theta$, i.e. $I_S \models f(t'\sigma, v_5) \simeq t\sigma$, but since
$s_1 =_{A^{\prec C}} f(w_1, f(\ldots, f(w_{j-1}, f(\quad t\sigma \quad, f(w_{r+1}, f(\ldots, f(w_{n-1}, w_n))))) \ldots))$ and
$s_2 =_{A^{\prec C}} f(w_1, f(\ldots, f(w_{j-1}, f(f(t'\sigma, v_5), f(w_{r+1}, f(\ldots, f(w_{n-1}, w_n))))) \ldots))$,
it contradicts $I_S \not\models C$.

Similarly if $i < k \leq j = r$ another A-strict superposition inference is needed (in this case with $f(x, s')$instead of $f(s', x)$) and when $i < k \leq j < r$ we apply an A-top superposition rule. In all other cases a contradiction is directly obtained.

If C is an instance with σ of a clause $D \llbracket T \rrbracket$ in S, then there are several cases to be analyzed, depending on the maximal equation in C:

1. C has a maximal equation in its succedent.
2. C has a maximal equation $s\sigma \simeq t\sigma$ in its antecedent, with $s\sigma =_A t\sigma$.
3. C has a maximal equation $s\sigma \simeq t\sigma$ in its antecedent, with $s\sigma \succ t\sigma$.

1. C has a maximal equation $s\sigma \simeq t\sigma$ in its succedent, with $s\sigma \succ t\sigma$: note that $s\sigma \neq_A t\sigma$, since if C consists only of the equation $s\sigma \simeq t\sigma$ then $s\sigma =_A t\sigma$ would follow from $A^{\prec C}$ plus instances of A that are A-equal to C, which are shown true in I_S by the first part of this proof; otherwise in fact $s\sigma =_{A^{\prec C}} t\sigma$, which, since $I_S \models A^{\prec C}$, would contradict $I_S \not\models C$.

Since $I_S \not\models C$, the instance C has not generated the rule $s\sigma \Rightarrow t\sigma$. This must be because conditions 1.b) or 1.c) of definition 10 do not hold:

If condition 1.b) does not hold then an inference by factoring can be made and its conclusion contradicts the assumption.

If condition 1.c) does not hold then let $s\sigma \simeq t\sigma$ be a strictly maximal equation in $D\sigma$ (note that if $s\sigma \simeq t\sigma$ is only maximal then we are in the previous case) s.t. some u with $s\sigma =_A u$ is reducible by R_C with a rule generated by an instance C' smaller than C.

Let this rule be the one that reduces u at a position p with $top(u|_p) = f$ (for some A or non-A symbol f) where p is innermost in the following sense: no other rule reduces u in a position p' below $maxpos(u, p)$ with $top(u|_{p'}) \neq f$. Note that such a rule always exists. Now there are two main subcases **1.2.1** and **1.2.2**, depending on whether the rule has been generated by an extended instance or by a non-extended instance.

Let C' be a non-extended instance $D'\sigma$ of some clause $D' \llbracket T' \rrbracket$ (the case where C' is an extended instance is proved similarly) with D' of the form $\Gamma' \rightarrow \Delta', s' \simeq$

t', where the rule is $u' \Rightarrow t'\sigma$ for some u' with $s'\sigma =_A u' = u|_p$ (we can use the same σ since D and D' do not share variables). Two cases have to be considered:

(a) If $maxpos(u,p) = p$ then $u' =_A s\sigma|_{p'}$ for the corresponding maximal position p' in $s\sigma$ and therefore $s'\sigma =_A s\sigma|_{p'}$. Then $s\sigma|_{p'}$ cannot be below a variable, as $D\sigma$ is variable irreducible wrt. R_S: if s were in $stvars(D,\sigma)$, then it would be irreducible wrt. rules smaller than $s\sigma \simeq t\sigma$, which is not the case; case 3. of definition 7 does not apply either, since $maxpos(s\sigma, p') = p'$. Then the inference by A-strict superposition right

$$\frac{\Gamma' \rightarrow \Delta', s' \simeq t' \, [\![T']\!] \qquad \Gamma \rightarrow \Delta, s \simeq t \, [\![T]\!]}{\Gamma', \Gamma \rightarrow \Delta', \Delta, s[t']_{p'} \simeq t \, [\![T' \wedge T \wedge OC \wedge \; s|_{p'} =_A s']\!]}$$

can be made, and, since all the conditions for its application hold, its conclusion D_1 has a ground instance $D_1\sigma$ of the form $\Gamma'\sigma, \Gamma\sigma \rightarrow \Delta'\sigma, \Delta\sigma, s\sigma[t'\sigma]_{p'} \simeq t\sigma$ that is not satisfied by I_S, is smaller than C, and (as above) variable irreducible wrt. R_S. Since S is saturated, as before, a contradiction is obtained.

(b) If $p_1 = maxpos(u,p) \neq p$ then $u|_{p_1} =_A s\sigma|_{p'}$ for the corresponding maximal position p' in $s\sigma$ and either (i) $u|_{p_1} =_A f(u',v) =_A f(s'\sigma, v)$ or (ii) $u|_{p_1} =_A f(v,u') =_A f(v, s'\sigma)$ or (iii) $u|_{p_1} =_A f(v, f(u',v')) =_A f(v, f(s'\sigma, v'))$, for some v and v', and therefore either (i) $s\sigma|_{p'} =_A f(s'\sigma, v)$ or (ii) $s\sigma|_{p'} =_A f(v, s'\sigma)$ or (iii) $s\sigma|_{p'} =_A f(v, f(s'\sigma, v'))$. Then $s\sigma|_{p'}$ cannot be below a variable, as before, since again $maxpos(s\sigma, p') = p'$. These three cases correspond to three different A-strict superposition right inferences that can be made, respectively with the extension $f(s',x)$, $f(x,s')$ and $f(x, f(s',x))$, which conclusions contradict the assumption.

2. When C has a maximal equation in its antecedent whose members are A-equal, then an following inference by equality resolution can be made and its conclusion contradicts the assumption.

3. If $D\sigma$ is $\Gamma\sigma, s\sigma \simeq t\sigma \rightarrow \Delta\sigma$, with a maximal equation $s\sigma \simeq t\sigma$, and $s\sigma \succ t\sigma$. Since $I_S \not\models C$, we have $I_S \models s\sigma \simeq t\sigma$, and by lemma 13 $s\sigma$ must be reducible by R_C (with a rule generated by an instance C' smaller than C).

Let this rule be the one that reduces $s\sigma$ in an innermost position p with $top(s\sigma|_p) = f$ as in case 1: no other rule reduces $s\sigma$ in a position p' below $maxpos(s\sigma, p)$ with $top(u|_{p'}) \neq f$. Now a contradiction is obtained exactly as it is done in case 1.2, but always inferences by A-superposition left are considered instead of superposition right. □

Now our aim will be to compute saturated sets, by means of *theorem proving derivations*. The following definition of such derivations is still parameterized by R, so from the definition it is not clear how to compute derivations if R is not known, because e.g. the redundancy of clauses depends on R. Later on this becomes clear, and sufficient conditions for redundancy will be given.

Definition 18. Let R be a ground rewrite system.

1. A *theorem proving derivation* is a sequence of sets of constrained clauses $S_0, S_1, \ldots$, such that each S_{i+1} is obtained from S_i by adding a logical consequence of S_i or by removing a clause $C \llbracket T \rrbracket$ that is redundant in $S_i \backslash C \llbracket T \rrbracket$.
2. The set S_∞ of *persistent* clauses in $S_0, S_1, \ldots$ is defined as $\cup_j (\cap_{k \geq j} S_k)$.
3. A theorem proving derivation is *fair* if every inference by I_A with persisting premises is redundant in some S_j.

Lemma 19. *Let $S_0, S_1, \ldots$ be a theorem proving derivation, let π be an inferences and let $C \llbracket T \rrbracket$ a constrained clause. (i) If π is redundant in some S_j then π is redundant in S_∞, and (ii) if $C \llbracket T \rrbracket$ is redundant in some S_j then $C \llbracket T \rrbracket$ is redundant in S_∞, for $j \geq 0$.*

If we instantiate R by the set R_{S_∞} for some derivation $S_0, S_1, \ldots$, then we get the following theorem. Again, note that R_{S_∞} is not known in advance, and that therefore in practice sufficient conditions for purity and redundancy have to be used.

Theorem 20. *If $S_0, S_1, \ldots$ is a fair theorem proving derivation and S_0 is a set containing only clauses with empty contraints, then (i) S_∞ is saturated, and (ii) either the empty clause is in some S_j (hence S_0 is inconsistent) or else $I_{S_\infty} \models S_j \cup A$ for $j \geq 0$ (hence S_0 is consistent) and $I_{S_\infty} \models S_\infty \cup A$.*

Proof. (i) By fairness of the derivation, we have that for every inference π with premises in S_∞ there is some S_j s.t. π is redundant wrt. R_{S_∞} in S_j. But, by lemma 19, π is also redundant wrt. R_{S_∞} in S_∞.

(ii) by lemma 17 (applied to S_∞ and R_{S_∞}) and (i), we have that either the empty clause is in S_∞ or else $I_{S_\infty} \models Ir_{R_{S_\infty}}(S_\infty) \cup A$. Obviously if the empty clause is in S_∞ then it is also in some S_j (and by soundness of the derivation the empty clause is consequence of S_0). Otherwise, by lemma 19, we have $R_{S_\infty} \cup Ir_{R_{S_\infty}}(S_\infty) \cup A \models Ir_{R_{S_\infty}}(S_0)$, and, since all clauses in S_0 have empty contraints, $R_{S_\infty} \cup Ir_{R_{S_\infty}}(S_0) \models S_0$. Therefore, as $I_{S_\infty} \models R_{S_\infty}$, it follows that $I_{S_\infty} \models S_0 \cup A$ (which proves the consistency of S_0). Furthermore, as by soundness of the derivation $S_0 \cup A \models S_j$ for $j \geq 0$ and $S_0 \cup A \models S_\infty$, we have $I_{S_\infty} \models S_j \cup A$ for $j \geq 0$ and $I_{S_\infty} \models S_\infty \cup A$. □

Recall that $C \llbracket T \rrbracket$ is the empty constrained clause if C is empty and T is satisfiable, and that our inference rules are sound also if no ordering constraints are added, but that the A-equality constraints are essential for soundness. Therefore we only have to decide the satisfiability of the A-equality part of T to know whether $C \llbracket T \rrbracket$ implies the inconsistency of S_0 or not. It is an open problem whether the satisfiability of our kind of ordering constraints is decidable or not, but this is not needed here. We only need sufficiently powerful methods for detecting as many unsatisfiable ordering constraints as possible. For instance, we can simply check whether there is some $s \succ t$ in the ordering constraint s.t. $t \succ_A s$, which by stability under subtitutions of $\succ_A$ implies the unsatisfiability of the constraint. On the other hand we can look for loops or contradictions with the monotonicity or subterm properties.

Note that, since the word problem modulo associativity is undecidable even in ground equational theories, there may be ground sets of clauses for which there is no finite saturated system, and for which derivations indeed do not terminate.

Finally, let us remark that this result also holds when certain initial constraints are allowed. This problem is studied in [15].

5.1 Redundancy tests

First of all note that in this framework a simplification step, replacing a clause C by its simplified clause C', can be performed with two steps in the derivation: the first one adding C' (which is a consequence) and the second one deleting C (which becomes redundant).

Therefore, we will concentrate in giving sufficient conditions to ensure the redundancy of clauses and inferences.

Lemma 21. *Let S be a set of constrained clauses. A clause C $[\![T]\!]$ is redundant in S if for every ground instance $C\sigma$ of it, there are ground instances $e_1 \dots e_r$ of $A^{\preceq C\sigma}$ and ground instances $D_i\sigma_i$ in $S^{\preceq C\sigma}$ of clauses D_i $[\![T_i]\!]$ with $\{e_1 \dots e_r, D_1\sigma_1, \dots, D_m\sigma_m\} \models C\sigma$ and T_i is true for all $i = 1 \dots m$.*

This result can be slightly strengthened (see [15] or [12] for the AC-case), but for simplicity reasons we present it here like this. Also note that it is straightforward to adapt this lemma for redundancy of inferences.

With respect to practice, first of all, note that for the "classical" saturation methods without constraint inheritance, the previous lemma shows that the usual redundancy notions are correct, since the condition on the constraints is always true, i.e. a clause C is redundant in S if $S^{\preceq C\sigma} \cup A^{\preceq C\sigma} \models C\sigma$ for every ground σ. This means that our framework can deal uniformly with constrained and unconstrained clauses, obtaining exactly the known results for the unconstrained case. On the other hand, our concept of redundant clause allows to include subsumption without the need of combining the underlying orderings with special subsumption orderings.

In the constraint case, if the condition on the constraints of the previous lemma fails for some constraint T_i of a clause D_i, and we still want to carry out the redundancy proof, then sometimes we can make T_i to be true (ensuring soundness) by propagating the information of the literals in the equality constraint part. Note that if we have started with an initial set of clauses without ordering constraints we can always delete the ordering constraint part without loosing soundness. On the other hand, weakening constraints may increase the number of inferences. Therefore there is sometimes a trade-off between the possibility of carrying out redundancy proofs and restrictedness of the constraints.

6 Saturated sets and Knuth-Bendix completion

Suppose S is a finite saturated set without the empty clause, obtained from an initial set without constraints (in the following, such a set will be simply called saturated). Since $I_S \models S \cup A$, obtaining such an S proves the consistency of the theory (one can normally only prove inconsistencies), and on the other hand it is an efficient tool for theorem proving in this theory, since no inferences have to be computed between clauses of S. In fact, in some cases, depending on the syntactic properties of S, decision procedures for the theory are obtained. This is the case e.g. for saturated sets of equations E, which are convergent for both *rewriting modulo A*, denoted $\rightarrow_{E/A}$, and for *extended A-rewriting* denoted $\rightarrow_{E\backslash A}$. Let $l\sigma \simeq r\sigma$ be an instance of an equation of E with $l\sigma \succ r\sigma$. Then $s \rightarrow_{E/A} u[r\sigma]$ if $s =_A u[l\sigma]$. Furthermore, extended A-rewriting is defined as $s[u] \rightarrow_{E\backslash A} s[f(x, f(r, x'))\sigma]$ if $u =_A f(x, f(l, x'))\sigma$ (where $f = top(l)$, and x and x' are empty when f is not an A-symbol and they both or one can be non-empty when f is an A-symbol).

Theorem 22. *Let E be a saturated set of constrained equations. For all terms s and t*

$$E \cup A \models s \simeq t \quad \textit{iff} \quad s \rightarrow^*_{E/A} \circ \leftrightarrow^*_A \circ \leftarrow^*_{E/A} t \quad \textit{iff} \quad s \rightarrow^*_{E\backslash A} \circ \leftrightarrow^*_A \circ \leftarrow^*_{E\backslash A} t.$$

Let us remark that if r has no "extra variables" (variables that are not in l), then A-matching provides such a ground σ and we can check whether σ fulfils the equality constraint part T' of T (the ordering part can be ignored). Otherwise, it suffices to instantiate the extra variables with the adequate mgu of T', and the remaining variables with the smallest constant (this provides a smaller *ground* term of the same $(E \cup A)$-congruence class iff such a term exists). The mgu's can also be computed once and for all for E before rewriting. For this particular purpose, computing A-unifiers may even be unnecessary, but this has to be studied in detail. Note that this is crucial here since if the A-unification problem has an infinite minimal complete set of A-unifiers then we may not be able to find the needed substitution.

A similar decision result (by refutation or by conditional rewriting) holds for conditional equations or Horn clauses.

Due to this relation with Knuth-Bendix completion modulo A, the application of these techniques to completion of string rewriting systems or, in particular, to Thue systems should be studied. Note that the presence of equality constraints could be important to obtain finite complete systems, since they can capture some divergences.

References

1. Leo Bachmair. *Canonical equational proofs.* Birkhäuser, Boston, Mass., 1991.
2. Leo Bachmair and Nachum Dershowitz. Completion for rewriting modulo a congruence. In Pierre Lescanne, editor, *Rewriting Techniques and Applications, [2nd International Conference]*, LNCS 256, pages 192–203, Bordeaux, France, May 25–27, 1987. Springer-Verlag.

3. Leo Bachmair and Harald Ganzinger. Rewrite-based equational theorem proving with selection and simplification. *Journal of Logic and Computation*, 4(3):1–31, 1994.
4. Nachum Dershowitz and Jean-Pierre Jouannaud. Rewrite systems. In Jan van Leeuwen, editor, *Handbook of Theoretical Computer Science*, volume B: Formal Models and Semantics, chapter 6, pages 244–320. Elsevier Science Publishers B.V., Amsterdam, New York, Oxford, Tokyo, 1990.
5. G. Huet. Confluent reductions: abstract properties and applications to term rewriting systems. *Journal of the ACM*, 27(4):797–821, October 1980.
6. Jean-Pierre Jouannaud. Confluent and coherent equational term rewriting systems: Applications to proofs in abstract data types. In *Proc. 8th Colloquium on Trees in Algebra and Programming*, LNCS 59, pages 269–283. Springer-Verlag, 1983.
7. Jean-Pierre Jouannaud and Hélène Kirchner. Completion of a set of rules modulo a set of equations. *SIAM Journal of Computing*, 15:1155–1194, 1986.
8. D. S. Lankford and A. M. Ballantyne. Decision procedures for simple equational theories with commutative-associative axioms: Complete sets of commutative-associative reductions. Technical Report Memo ATP-39, Dept. of Mathematics and Computer Science, Univ. of Texas, Austin, TX, August 1977.
9. G.S. Makanin. The problem of solvability of equations in a free semigroup. *Math. USSR Sbornik*, 32(2):129–198, 1977.
10. Paliath Narendran and Michael Rusinowitch. Any ground associative commutative theory has a finite canonical system. In *Fourth int. conf. on Rewriting Techniques and Applications*, LNCS 488, pages 423–434, Como, Italy, April 1991. Springer-Verlag.
11. Robert Nieuwenhuis and Albert Rubio. Basic superposition is complete. In B. Krieg-Brückner, editor, *European Symposium on Programming*, LNCS 582, pages 371–390, Rennes, France, February 26–28, 1992. Springer-Verlag.
12. Robert Nieuwenhuis and Albert Rubio. AC-Superposition with constraints: No AC-unifiers needed. In Allan Bundy, editor, *12th International Conference on Automated Deduction*, LNAI, Nancy, France, June 1994. Springer-Verlag.
13. Robert Nieuwenhuis and Albert Rubio. Theorem Proving with Ordering and Equality Constrained Clauses. *J. of Symbolic Computation*, 19(4):321–351, April 1995.
14. G.E. Peterson and M.E. Stickel. Complete sets of reductions for some equational theories. *Journal Assoc. Comput. Mach.*, 28(2):233–264, 1981.
15. Albert Rubio. Automated deduction with ordering and equality constrained clauses. PhD. Thesis, Technical University of Catalonia, Barcelona, Spain, 1994.
16. Albert Rubio and Robert Nieuwenhuis. A total AC-compatible ordering based on RPO. *Theoretical Computer Science*, 142(2):209–227, May 15, 1995.
17. Laurent Vigneron. Associative Commutative Deduction with constraints. In Allan Bundy, editor, *12th International Conference on Automated Deduction*, LNAI, Nancy, France, June 1994. Springer-Verlag.

Positive Deduction modulo Regular Theories *

Laurent Vigneron

CRIN-CNRS & INRIA Lorraine
B.P.239, 54506 Vandœuvre-lès-Nancy Cedex, France
E-mail: Vigneron@Loria.Fr

Abstract. We propose a *new technique* for dealing with an equational theory $\mathcal{E}$ in the clausal framework. This consists of the definition of two inference rules called *contextual superposition* and *extended superposition*, and of an *algorithm* for computing the only needed applications of these last inference rules only by examining the axioms of $\mathcal{E}$. We prove the refutational completeness of this technique for a class of theories $\mathcal{E}$ that include *all the regular theories*, i.e. any theory whose axioms preserve variables. This generalizes the results of Wertz [31] and Paul [17] who could not prove the refutational completeness of their superposition-based systems for any regular theory.
We also combine a *collection of strategies* that decrease the number of possible deductions, without loss of completeness: the superposition strategy, the positive ordering strategy, and a simplification strategy.
These results have been implemented in a theorem prover called DATAC, for the case of commutative, and associative and commutative theories. It is an interesting tool for comparing the efficiency of strategies, and practical results will follow.

1 Introduction

The paramodulation rule permits one to deal with the equality predicate without explicitly describing its properties of reflexivity, symmetry, transitivity and functional reflexivity. It is also based on a notion of replacement. Over time, several refinements have been added to this rule. Brand [6] has shown that only the reflexivity axiom $x \simeq x$ is needed. Peterson [18] has shown that paramodulations into variables are useless. Hsiang and Rusinowitch [10] have introduced ordering restrictions to the application of these rules, and have proved the completeness of the following *ordering strategy*: *each inference step has to be applied between maximal (w.r.t. an ordering) literals in clauses, and in each paramodulation step, a term cannot be replaced by a bigger one.*
Other refinements, such as the superposition strategy which applies replacements only in biggest sides of equations, and clausal simplifications which delete redundant clauses, have followed [4].

* This work was done during a fellowship at the University of Stony Brook (NY, USA), funded by the *Institut National de Recherche en Informatique et en Automatique* (France).

The complete Hsiang-Rusinowitch strategy and others are unfortunately often inefficient in the presence of clauses such as the associativity property of an operator f, $f(f(x,y),z) \simeq f(x,f(y,z))$, which produces the divergence of derivations by successive superpositions into the subterm $f(x,y)$. Other properties, such as the commutativity of an operator, induce problems with the superposition rule because they cannot be oriented.

The most established solution was proposed by Plotkin [20]. He proposed to define an equational theory $\mathcal{E}$, by extracting the above properties from the set of clauses, and to define a *unification algorithm modulo* $\mathcal{E}$. This result has been the basis of much work: Lankford and Ballantyne [14] for the particular case of associative and commutative theories, and Peterson and Stickel [19] for completion. When applying ordering strategies to theorem proving in equational theories, we need to add various additional techniques. The techniques usually proposed in equational deduction are:

1. either to add an inference rule applying replacements into axioms of $\mathcal{E}$, and therefore generating *extensions* of these axioms,
2. or to associate to each equation the set of its possible extensions, which may be used later by the superposition rule.

These extensions have been studied by Jouannaud and Kirchner [13], and Bachmair and Dershowitz [1]. Both techniques have been used by Wertz [31]; the second has been used by Paul [17] too.

We propose in this paper a *new technique* for dealing with these extensions in the clausal framework, by defining two inference rules called *contextual superposition* and *extended superposition*. We also define an *algorithm* for computing the only needed applications of these last inference rules, only by examining the axioms of $\mathcal{E}$ and generalizing the $\mathcal{E}$-redundant context notions of Jouannaud and Kirchner [13] defined for equational completion. Our inference system is defined by combining the superposition strategy and the positive ordering strategy; it is also compatible with the simplification strategy.

The positive strategy was initially proposed by Robinson [21] and has been transformed many times later. Our definition of this strategy, whose first version was presented in [25], is a much more attractive one. The usual condition is to apply superposition steps from a positive clause. Here, we mention that whenever we want to use a positive literal, it has to belong to a positive clause. A similar strategy has also been independently defined by Paul in [17].

Our positive strategy uses a particular case of the superposition calculus with selection, defined by Bachmair and Ganzinger in [3], for selecting negative literals. But in addition we define a new kind of selection on positive literals: a positive literal can be used in a deduction if it belongs to a positive clause and if it is maximal in this clause (for a given ordering).

We prove the refutational completeness of our inference system for all the equational theories $\mathcal{E}$ allowed by Wertz [31] and Paul [17], but in addition we prove it *for any regular theory* $\mathcal{E}$, i.e. any theory whose axioms preserve variables.

Moreover, our algorithm for detecting $\mathcal{E}$-redundant contexts permits a significant decreasing of the number of possible deductions.

These results have been implemented in a theorem prover called **DATAC**, for commutative, and associative and commutative theories. It is an interesting tool for comparing the efficiency of strategies, and practical results will follow.

The layout of this paper is the following: after introducing the basic notions in Sect. 2, we describe our inference rules in Sect. 3. Section 4 presents a procedure to compute useful contexts for extended equations. The proof of refutational completeness of the inference system is sketched in Sect. 5, but it is detailed in [30] (see also [26, 29]). Section 6 presents an example of trace with our system **DATAC**.

2 Notations and Definitions

Let us define some basic notions, based on the standard notations and definitions for term rewriting and unification given in [8, 12].

Let $\mathcal{E}$ be an equational theory, i.e. a set of equations. The congruence generated by this set $\mathcal{E}$ is called *$\mathcal{E}$-equality* and written $=_{\mathcal{E}}$. A *substitution* is a function replacing some variables by terms. A substitution σ is said to *$\mathcal{E}$-unify* two terms s and t if $s\sigma$ and $t\sigma$ are $\mathcal{E}$-equal, and if σ is a most general $\mathcal{E}$-unifier of s and t (see [12]). In this case, σ is a solution of the $\mathcal{E}$-unification problem $s =^?_{\mathcal{E}} t$.

An *atom* is an equality $l \simeq r$. A *clause* is denoted $A_1, \ldots, A_n \rightarrow B_1, \ldots, B_m$, where $A_1, \ldots, A_n, B_1, \ldots, B_m$ are atoms; this means A_1 *and... and* A_n *implies* B_1 *or... or* B_m. A *literal* is an atom appearing in a clause. A *literal is positive* (resp. *negative*) if it appears on the right-hand side (resp. left-hand side) of $\rightarrow$. A *clause is positive* if it contains only positive literals, i.e. if the left-hand side of $\rightarrow$ is empty.

To express subterms and substitutions, we use *positions*. Envision a term represented as a tree; a position in a term is a node of this tree. The subterm at position p of a term t is written $t|_p$. A position is a sequence of integers: $f(t_1, \ldots, t_n)|_{i \cdot p} = t_i|_p$; the empty sequence (*empty position*) is denoted ϵ ($t|_\epsilon = t$). A position p in a term t is a *non-variable position* if $t|_p$ is not a variable. The set of all non-variable positions of a term t is denoted $\mathcal{FP}os(t)$. The term $s[t]_p$ represents the term s whose subterm at position p is t.

To decrease the number of possible deductions, we use an ordering strategy. So, we assume we are given a *simplification ordering* $>$, defined on terms and atoms. For the sake of completeness, it has to be *total* on ground $\mathcal{E}$-congruence classes and *$\mathcal{E}$-compatible*, i.e.

$$\forall s, t \text{ ground terms, if } s > t \text{ and } s \neq_{\mathcal{E}} t, \text{ then } \forall s' =_{\mathcal{E}} s,\ \forall t' =_{\mathcal{E}} t,\ s' > t'$$

So, in our inference rules, we will use this ordering to orient equations and to check the maximality of an equation w.r.t. other equations. However terms may be incomparable; we will write that a term is maximal w.r.t. another term, if it

is not smaller than or equal to this second term.
Given an equality $l \simeq r$, we will assume l is maximal w.r.t. r.

3 Inference Rules

We describe in this section a set of inference rules for applying deductions modulo an equational theory $\mathcal{E}$. These rules are based on the *superposition strategy*, a variant of the paramodulation strategy; it applies replacements only in maximal sides of equations. This superposition strategy is combined with a positive ordering strategy to prune the search space. This strategy is described in the next definition, and needs a total simplification ordering for comparing terms.

Definition 1 (Positive Ordering Strategy).

- If an inference rule uses a positive literal in a clause, this clause has to be positive. In addition, the positive literal used has to be maximal in the clause.
- If an inference rule uses a negative literal in a clause, this literal has to be maximal w.r.t. the other negative literals of the clause.

The first inference rule is the Equational Factoring. Its purpose is to derive clauses in which two positive equations do not have $\mathcal{E}$-equal left-hand sides. This inference rule is essential for the completeness of the superposition strategy. Note that it is applied only on positive clauses.

Definition 2 (Equational Factoring). $\dfrac{\to l_1 \simeq r_1, l_2 \simeq r_2, R}{r_1\sigma \simeq r_2\sigma \to l_2\sigma \simeq r_2\sigma, R\sigma}$

where σ $\mathcal{E}$-unifies l_1 and l_2, $l_1\sigma \simeq r_1\sigma$ is maximal w.r.t. $l_2\sigma \simeq r_2\sigma$ and each equation of $R\sigma$. Moreover, $l_1\sigma$ has to be maximal w.r.t. $r_1\sigma$.

The next rule stands for avoiding the addition of the reflexivity axiom $x \simeq x$ of the equality predicate. It is the only rule which can derive the empty clause, symbolizing an incoherence in the initial set of clauses, since it is the only rule which deletes a literal.

Definition 3 (Reflexion). $\dfrac{l \simeq r, L \to R}{L\sigma \to R\sigma}$

where σ $\mathcal{E}$-unifies l and r, and $l\sigma \simeq r\sigma$ is maximal w.r.t. each equation of $L\sigma$.

The superposition rule applies the replacement of a term by an equal one, from a positive clause. It is decomposed into a *Left* and a *Right Superposition* rule, respectively defined by

$$\frac{\to l_1 \simeq r_1, R_1 \qquad l_2 \simeq r_2, L_2 \to R_2}{l_2[r_1]_{p_2}\sigma \simeq r_2\sigma, L_2\sigma \to R_1\sigma, R_2\sigma} \quad \text{and} \quad \frac{\to l_1 \simeq r_1, R_1 \qquad \to l_2 \simeq r_2, R_2}{\to l_2[r_1]_{p_2}\sigma \simeq r_2\sigma, R_1\sigma, R_2\sigma}$$

where σ is a $\mathcal{E}$-unifier of l_1 and the subterm at position p_2 of l_2. But, even with these two inference rules, the procedure of deduction is not complete, as shown in the next example.

Example 1. Let $\mathcal{E} = \{ f(f(x_1, x_2), x_3) \simeq f(x_1, f(x_2, x_3)) \}$. The following clauses

$$(1) \ \rightarrow f(a,b) \simeq c \qquad (2) \ \rightarrow f(a, f(b,d)) \simeq e \qquad (3) \ f(c,d) \simeq e \rightarrow$$

form an incoherent set with $\mathcal{E}$, since: $\mathcal{E}$ permits a modification of the parentheses in the left-hand side of the second clause, to obtain $\rightarrow f(f(a,b),d) \simeq e$, and replacing $f(a,b)$ by c in this term (thanks to (1)), we deduce $\rightarrow f(c,d) \simeq e$ which contradicts (3).
However, there is no possible inference step between the three initial clauses. $\diamond$

We solve this problem by applying superpositions from *extended equations*, i.e. from equations $e[l_1]_p \simeq e[r_1]_p$, where e is a term and p a non-variable position in e. Such a pair (e,p) is called a *context*. In the previous example, a contradiction can be derived using the context $(f(f(x_1, x_2), x_3), 1)$, producing the extended equation $f(f(a,b), x_3) \simeq f(c, x_3)$ from $f(a,b) \simeq c$.

By the Critical Pairs Lemma of Jouannaud and Kirchner [13], we know that contexts can be computed. We define in Sect. 4 a procedure to compute all the possible contexts for a given equational theory $\mathcal{E}$. Given a term l, $\mathit{Cont}(l)$ is the set of all contexts (e,p) for $\mathcal{E}$ such that $e|_p$ and l are $\mathcal{E}$-unifiable. These contexts are used in three new inference rules.

The first two rules simulate replacements from an equation or an extended equation. Indeed, we assume that the context (l, ϵ) belongs to $\mathit{Cont}(l)$. Left and right superposition rules are therefore particular cases of the next inference rules.

Definition 4 (Left Contextual Superposition).

$$\frac{\rightarrow l_1 \simeq r_1, R_1 \qquad l_2 \simeq r_2, L_2 \rightarrow R_2}{l_2[e_1[r_1]_{p_1}]_{p_2}\sigma \simeq r_2\sigma, L_2\sigma \rightarrow R_1\sigma, R_2\sigma}$$

where p_2 is a non-variable position in l_2, (e_1, p_1) is a context[2] in $\mathit{Cont}(l_1)$, σ $\mathcal{E}$-unifies $l_2|_{p_2}$ and $e_1[l_1]_{p_1}$, $l_1\sigma \simeq r_1\sigma$ is maximal for $>$ in its clause, and $l_2\sigma \simeq r_2\sigma$ is maximal w.r.t. each atom of $L_2\sigma$. Moreover, $l_1\sigma$ has to be maximal w.r.t. $r_1\sigma$, and $l_2\sigma$ has to be maximal w.r.t. $r_2\sigma$. The replacing term in the deduced clause is the extension of the right-hand side, $e_1[r_1]_{p_1}$.

Definition 5 (Right Contextual Superposition).

$$\frac{\rightarrow l_1 \simeq r_1, R_1 \qquad \rightarrow l_2 \simeq r_2, R_2}{\rightarrow l_2[e_1[r_1]_{p_1}]_{p_2}\sigma \simeq r_2\sigma, R_1\sigma, R_2\sigma}$$

where the only difference with Left Contextual Superposition is that $l_2\sigma \simeq r_2\sigma$ is maximal in its clause and maximal w.r.t. $l_1\sigma \simeq r_1\sigma$.

The next inference rule simulates a superposition between two extended equations, at the top of their maximum side.

Definition 6 (Extended Superposition).

$$\frac{\rightarrow l_1 \simeq r_1, R_1 \qquad \rightarrow l_2 \simeq r_2, R_2}{\rightarrow e_1[r_1]_{p_1}\sigma \simeq e_2[r_2]_{p_2}\sigma, R_1\sigma, R_2\sigma}$$

[2] (e_1, p_1) may be an empty context, i.e. $p_1 = \epsilon$.

where, given a non-empty context (e_1, p_1) in $Cont(l_1)$ and a non-empty context (e_2, p_2) in $Cont(l_2)$, σ $\mathcal{E}$-unifies $e_1[l_1]_{p_1}$ and $e_2[l_2]_{p_2}$. Each equation has to be maximal in its clause, and their left-hand side has to be maximal w.r.t. their right-hand side.

3.1 About the Superposition Strategy

The principle of the superposition strategy is *to apply replacements only into maximal sides of equations*, and has been extensively used for term rewriting and completion. But, the completeness of inference systems representing this strategy has been a longstanding open problem. For completeness, either some deductions using non-maximal literals [24], or some replacements into minimal sides of equations [3], were needed. Bachmair and Ganzinger [2] have proved the completeness in the empty theory of the entire superposition strategy by adding two *Equational Factoring* rules (one for negative and one for positive literals). Defining a particular ordering for comparing negative and positive literals, Nieuwenhuis and Rubio [16] have proved that the rule on negative literals is useless.

In our inference rules, we never need to compare such literals: we always compare literals of the same sign. So for us, *specifying a special ordering on literals is useless.*

3.2 Other Predicate Symbols

Our five inference rules have been defined for deduction in first-order logic with a unique predicate, the equality predicate. This restriction has been decided only for simplifying notations, but it is easy to adapt the inference rules to the presence of other predicate symbols. And we have to add a Factoring rule (applied only on positive clauses) and a Resolution rule (applied with a positive clause) for dealing with the non-equational literals (see [26]). The new system of deduction remains complete if the equality symbol is minimal in precedence.

Now that we have defined all the inference rules, let us show how to compute extended equations with contexts.

4 Extended Equations

An extension of an equation $l \simeq r$ is an equation $e[l]_p \simeq e[r]_p$, also called an *extended equation* of $l \simeq r$, where e is a term, p a non variable position in this term. The subterm at position p in e is $\mathcal{E}$-unifiable with l, the maximum side of the equation. The couple (e, p) is called the *context* of this extension.

The set of all possible contexts for a theory $\mathcal{E}$, written $\mathcal{C}_\mathcal{E}$, is defined by $\bigcup_{k \geq 0} Cont_k$, where the sets $Cont_k$ are inductively defined by:

$$\begin{array}{rcl} Cont_0 & = & \{\ (e,p)\ \mid\ \exists e \simeq e' \text{ or } e' \simeq e \in \mathcal{E},\ p \in \mathcal{FP}os(e) \text{ and } p \neq \epsilon\ \} \\ Cont_{k+1} & = & \{\ (e_1[e_2]_{p_1}, p_1 \cdot p_2)\ \mid\ (e_1,p_1) \in Cont_0,\ (e_2,p_2) \in Cont_k, \\ & & \qquad \text{and } e_1|_{p_1} \text{ and } e_2 \text{ are } \mathcal{E}\text{-unifiable}\ \} \end{array}$$

Then, given an equation $l \simeq r$ where l is maximal w.r.t. r, the set of all possible contexts which can extend $l \simeq r$ is defined by:

$$Cont(l) = \{ (e,p) \in \mathcal{C}_{\mathcal{E}} \mid e|_p \text{ and } l \text{ are } \mathcal{E}\text{-unifiable} \} \cup \{ (l,\epsilon) \}$$

We have added (l,ϵ) for avoiding the definition of special inference rules, applying superpositions without context.

Let $l \rightarrow r$ be a ground rewrite rule. Let C_l be the set of all ground instances of contexts of $Cont(l)$. We define the relation $\longrightarrow_{C_l,\mathcal{E}}$ by:

$$t_1 \longrightarrow_{C_l,\mathcal{E}} t_2 \text{ if } \exists (e_l,p_l) \in C_l,\ \exists q \in \mathcal{FP}os(t_1),\ t_1|_q =_{\mathcal{E}} e_l,\ t_2 = t_1[e_l[r]_{p_l}]_q$$

This relation $\longrightarrow_{C_l,\mathcal{E}}$ satisfies a property called *$\mathcal{E}$-closure* if: whenever a term t is reducible into a term t_1 by the relation $\longrightarrow_{C_l,\mathcal{E}}$, then for each term t_2, $\mathcal{E}$-equal to t, t_2 and t_1 are reducible by $\longrightarrow_{C_l,\mathcal{E}}$ into two $\mathcal{E}$-equal terms.
A set of contexts C is said to be *$\mathcal{E}$-covering* if, for any ground term l, the relation $\longrightarrow_{C_l,\mathcal{E}}$ satisfies the property of $\mathcal{E}$-closure, where $C_l = C \cap Cont(l)$.

Proposition 7. *Let $\mathcal{E}$ be an equational theory. The set of contexts $\mathcal{C}_{\mathcal{E}}$ is $\mathcal{E}$-covering.*

This Proposition means that the role of the equations of $\mathcal{E}$ is entirely simulated by superpositions with contexts of $\mathcal{C}_{\mathcal{E}}$. Its proof is similar to the proof of the Critical Pairs Lemma of Jouannaud and Kirchner [13] (see [29]), and consists of simple case analyses.

However, the definition of $\mathcal{C}_{\mathcal{E}}$ is very general, and for efficiency we combine it with a procedure deleting redundant contexts. Before describing this procedure, let us introduce some definitions.

Definition 8. A context (e_1,p_1) is **redundant at a position p** w.r.t. a set of contexts C, if p is a non-variable position in e_1 and $p_1 = p{\cdot}q$ (where $q \neq \epsilon$), and if there is a context (e_2,p_2) in C and a substitution σ such that:

1. $e_2[\cdot]_{p_2}\sigma =_{\mathcal{E}} (e_1|_p)[\cdot]_q$ for guaranteeing the equivalence of terms $e_2\sigma$ and $e_1|_p$,
2. $(e_2|_{p_2})\sigma =_{\mathcal{E}} e_1|_{p_1}$ for guaranteeing the equivalence of subterms where replacements will apply.

where the symbol $\cdot$ is a new constant. (e_1,p_1) is said to be redundant at p w.r.t. C, by $(e_2\sigma,p_2)$. If p is ϵ, the context (e_1,p_1) is said to be top-redundant.

Definition 9. Let (e_1,p_1) be a context. Let e'_1 be a ground term and σ a ground substitution such that e'_1 is $\mathcal{E}$-equal to $e_1\sigma$. The representation e'_1 of the context (e_1,p_1) is said to be **$\mathcal{E}$-redundant at a position p** w.r.t. a set of contexts C, if there is a term e_2 $\mathcal{E}$-equal to $e'_1|_p$ and a non-variable position p_2 in e_2, s.t. :

1. (e_2,p_2) is top-redundant w.r.t. C, by a context (e_3,p_3),
2. $(e_1\sigma,p_1)$ is top-redundant by $(e'_1[e_3]_p, p{\cdot}p_3)$.

Note that the position p may be the empty position.

A context (e_1, p_1) is **$\mathcal{E}$-redundant** w.r.t. a set of contexts $\mathcal{C}$ if,

1. either (e_1, p_1) is top-redundant w.r.t. $\mathcal{C}$,
2. or, for each term e'_1, $\mathcal{E}$-equal to a ground instance $e_1\sigma$ of e_1,
   (a) either there is a non-variable position p'_1 in e'_1 such that (e'_1, p'_1) is top-redundant by (e_1, p_1),
   (b) or the representation e'_1 of the context (e_1, p_1) is $\mathcal{E}$-redundant at a position p' w.r.t. $\mathcal{C}$.

Fig. 1. Redundancy criteria of a context in $\mathcal{E}$.

Proposition 10. *Let $\mathcal{E}$ be an equational theory. The set of contexts $\mathcal{C}_\mathcal{E}$, constructed with the $\mathcal{E}$-redundancy criteria described in Fig. 1, is $\mathcal{E}$-covering.*

Proof. Uselessness of redundant contexts is easily derived from the algorithm described in Fig. 1 as follows:

1. *If there is a context (e_2, p_2) in $\mathcal{C}$ such that any replacement with the context (e_1, p_1) is an instance of a replacement with this context (e_2, p_2), then to use (e_2, p_2) instead of (e_1, p_1) generates the same result, or a more general one.*
2. *Let us study the terms in which the context (e_1, p_1) could be applied. A first remark is there is no need to use this context with terms that are instances of e_1; the replacement can be applied directly at the position p_1. We can generalize this remark: (e_1, p_1) is useless if all terms in which it could be applied can be treated without context or with another context of $\mathcal{C}$. But to test this for each term $\mathcal{E}$-equal to e_1 is not sufficient, because a term $\mathcal{E}$-equal to an instance of e_1 may not be an instance of a term $\mathcal{E}$-equal to e_1. So, the context (e_1, p_1) is $\mathcal{E}$-redundant if, for each term e'_1 $\mathcal{E}$-equal to a ground instance $e_1\sigma$ of e_1,*
   (a) either a term $\mathcal{E}$-equal to $e_1|_{p_1}$ appears at a position p'_1 of e'_1, i.e. the replacement can be directly done at this position; in addition, we have to check that the result is identical to the one obtained with the context (e_1, p_1),
   (b) or a context of $\mathcal{C}$ can be applied at a position p' of e'_1, producing the same result as applying the context (e_1, p_1) to the top of e'_1.

In practice, to check the second point does not consist of studying all the ground instances of e_1, but of enumerating the different forms that can have these instances. And we can note that if the context (e_1, p_1) is redundant at a non-empty position p by a context (e_2, p_2), then all its representations $e'_1 =_\mathcal{E} e_1\sigma$ such that

$$\exists p' \in \mathcal{FP}os(e'_1),\ e'_1|_{p'} =_\mathcal{E} (e_1|_p)\sigma \text{ and } e'_1[\cdot]_{p'} =_\mathcal{E} e_1[\cdot]_p\sigma$$

are $\mathcal{E}$-redundant at the position p' by the context (e_2, p_2). □

A simple algorithm for constructing the contexts with the redundancy criteria of Fig. 1 is, for each context newly created, to verify it is not $\mathcal{E}$-redundant w.r.t. the set C of the contexts already constructed; then, we delete from C the contexts $\mathcal{E}$-redundant by the addition of this new context. Moreover, it would be interesting, when applying an inference rule involving a context, to check the non-redundancy of the instance of this context used, and even to check the non-redundancy of the representation of its term in the clause where the replacement is going to apply.

Let us give two examples of the construction of contexts.

Example 2 (Associativity and Commutativity). If $\mathcal{E}$ represents properties of associativity and commutativity of an operator f,

$$\mathcal{E} = \{ f(f(x_1, x_2), x_3) \simeq f(x_1, f(x_2, x_3)),\ f(x_1, x_2) \simeq f(x_2, x_1) \}$$

$Cont_0$ contains two contexts, $(f(f(x_1, x_2), x_3), 1)$ and $(f(x_1, f(x_2, x_3)), 2)$, but the second one is top-redundant by the first one. $(f(f(f(x_1, x_2), x_3), x_4), 1{\cdot}1)$, the unique context of $Cont_1$, is top-redundant by $(f(f(x_1, x_2), x_3), 1)$ too. Hence, $C_{AC} = \{ (f(f(x_1, x_2), x_3), 1) \}$, which means that the only possible extension of an equation $l \simeq r$ is $f(l, x_3) \simeq f(r, x_3)$. ◇

Example 3 (Associativity). If $\mathcal{E}$ contains the property of associativity of f,

$$\mathcal{E} = \{ f(f(x_1, x_2), x_3) \simeq f(x_1, f(x_2, x_3)) \}$$

the non-redundant contexts are

$$Cont_0 = \{ (f(f(x_1, x_2), x_3), 1),\ (f(x_1, f(x_2, x_3)), 2) \}$$
$$Cont_1 = \{ (f(f(x_1, f(x_2, x_3)), x_4), 1{\cdot}2) \}$$

So, there are three useful extensions of an equation $l \simeq r$ where f is the top-symbol of l: to add a new variable, either on the right, $f(l, x_3) \simeq f(r, x_3)$, or on the left, $f(x_1, l) \simeq f(x_1, r)$, or on both sides, $f(f(x_1, l), x_4) \simeq f(f(x_1, r), x_4)$. ◇

4.1 Refining the Construction of Contexts

In the construction of the sets of contexts $Cont_k$, we have used the notion of $\mathcal{E}$-unifiability. For instance, for building a context $(e_1[e_2[e_3]_{p_2}]_{p_1}, p_1{\cdot}p_2{\cdot}p_3)$, we have assumed that $e_2|_{p_2}$ and e_3 are $\mathcal{E}$-unifiable, and that $e_1|_{p_1}$ and $e_2[e_3]_{p_2}$ are $\mathcal{E}$-unifiable. But, in this last test, we have lost the information that $e_2|_{p_2}$ and e_3 have to be $\mathcal{E}$-unifiable. There may be no substitution satisfying both conditions, and therefore the context may be useless.

A simple way for avoiding such cases, is to add a third element to each context: *the conjunction of the $\mathcal{E}$-unification constraints* encountered to construct it. In the previous example, the context would be:

$$(e_1[e_2[e_3]_{p_2}]_{p_1},\ p_1{\cdot}p_2{\cdot}p_3,\ \{e_2|_{p_2} \stackrel{?}{=}_{\mathcal{E}} e_3 \ \wedge\ e_1|_{p_1} \stackrel{?}{=}_{\mathcal{E}} e_2[e_3]_{p_2}\})$$

Hence, a context is created only if its unification problems admit at least one solution. As a second consequence, for applying an inference rule using a context, we solve the specific unification problem of this rule, but in conjunction with the unification problems of the context.

With this additional parameter, less contexts are constructed, less inference rules are applicable and their unification problems have less solutions.

However, even with this optimization, there is an infinite number of contexts for a lot of theories, as shown in the next example. This can be dealt with using the algorithm building contexts with incrementality.

Example 4 (Distributivity). Let $\mathcal{E} = \{ f(x_1, g(x_2, x_3)) \simeq g(f(x_1, x_2), f(x_1, x_3)) \}$. $Cont_0$ contains the three contexts

$$(f(x_1, g(x_2, x_3)), 2), \ (g(f(x_1, x_2), f(x_1, x_3)), 1), \ (g(f(x_1, x_2), f(x_1, x_3)), 2)$$

The context $(f(x_1, f(x_2, g(x_3, x_4))), 2{\cdot}2)$ belongs to $Cont_1$, and so on... We can build an infinite sequence of contexts of the form:

$$(f(x_1, f(x_2, \ldots f(x_n, g(x_{n+1}, x_{n+2})))), 2^n)$$

These contexts are all useful: they permit to recover the subterm $g(x_{n+1}, x_{n+2})$, where the replacement occurs, from the representation:

$$g(f(x_1, f(x_2, \ldots f(x_n, x_{n+1}))), f(x_1, f(x_2, \ldots f(x_n, x_{n+2})))) \qquad \diamond$$

5 Refutational Completeness

A set of clauses S is said to be *$\mathcal{E}$-incoherent* if there is no model such that $S \cup \mathcal{E}$ is valid in this model. Let us define two properties of a theory $\mathcal{E}$:

- **(P1)** *Regularity.* For any equation $e_1 \simeq e_2$ in $\mathcal{E}$, each variable of e_1 is a variable of e_2, and vice-versa.
- **(P2)** For any ground term s that is $\mathcal{E}$-equal to one of its strict subterms $s|_p$ ($p \neq \epsilon$), for any ground term t, $s[t]_p$ has to be $\mathcal{E}$-equal to t.

Let *INF* be the set of the five inference rules described in Sect. 3. Let us state the theorem of refutational completeness of *INF*.

Theorem 11 (Completeness). *Let $\mathcal{E}$ be an equational theory satisfying at least one of the properties (P1) and (P2), and let S be a set of clauses. If S is $\mathcal{E}$-incoherent, INF will always derive a contradiction from S.*

This theorem states that our inference system is refutationally complete if $\mathcal{E}$ satisfies (P1) or (P2). This result is an important improvement of previous works of Wertz [31] and Paul [17], since they proved the completeness of their systems only if $\mathcal{E}$ satisfies (P2). Moreover, our inference system limits the number of possible deductions much more than Wertz' and Paul's systems, thanks to the positive ordering strategy and the notion of $\mathcal{E}$-redundant contexts.

Note that many theories satisfy (P1) but not (P2). For instance, if $\mathcal{E}$ is $\{f(x, 0) \simeq x\}$, $\mathcal{E}$ is regular but: given the ground term $f(0, 0)$, it is $\mathcal{E}$-equal to 0; however, for a constant a, $f(0, a)$ is not $\mathcal{E}$-equal to a. (P2) is not satisfied.

There are also some particular theories $\mathcal{E}$ that satisfy (P2) but not (P1). For instance[3], if $\mathcal{E}$ is $\{f(x,y) \simeq x\}$, f is the only functional symbol and a is the only constant, the term $f(a,a)$ is $\mathcal{E}$-equal to a, and for any ground term t, $f(a,t) =_{\mathcal{E}} t$. Indeed, since f and a are the only symbols, any ground term (a, $f(a,a)$, $f(f(a,a),a)$,...) is $\mathcal{E}$-equal to a.

We prove the Theorem of Completeness by the transfinite semantic tree method of Hsiang and Rusinowitch [10], extended to deduction modulo an equational theory in [26, 29]. Let us give a sketch of this proof, as it is rather similar to the proof for the particular case of associative and commutative theories [26] (see [29, 30] for the detailed proofs).

Proof. Let $\mathcal{E}$ be a theory satisfying (P1) or (P2). Let S be an $\mathcal{E}$-incoherent set of clauses. Let us describe the main steps of the proof of refutational completeness. It is realized in the ground case, because each deduction step with ground instances clauses can be lifted to the general case.

Given a total $\mathcal{E}$-compatible ordering on ground atoms, we sort them by increasing order, and we construct the transfinite semantic tree $\mathcal{T}$ (in the empty theory). An interpretation *is a node of this tree.*
As S is $\mathcal{E}$-incoherent, each branch of the semantic tree $\mathcal{T}$ has a node that falsifies either a ground instance of a clause of S, or a trivial equation $t \simeq t'$ where $t =_{\mathcal{E}} t'$. Such nodes are called failure nodes. *The maximal subtree of $\mathcal{T}$ which does not contain a failure node is called the* maximal consistent tree, *and written $MCT(S)$.*
Our inference system INF is refutationally complete if it is always able to derive a contradiction (the empty clause) from S. Let $INF^*(S)$ be the set of all clauses deduced by INF from S, in any number of steps. For proving that $INF^*(S)$ contains the empty clause, we show that the maximal consistent tree for $INF^*(S)$, $MCT(INF^*(S))$, is reduced to an empty tree.

The first step is to choose a branch in $MCT(INF^*(S))$ that is consistent with the theory $\mathcal{E}$. This is done by adding new special failure nodes: distant failure nodes *and* quasi-failure nodes.

- *Let K be a failure node at the level of an atom $u \simeq w$ s.t. $u > w$, w is reducible and $u \simeq w$ is falsified by K. If there is an irreducible atom $u \simeq v$, smaller than $u \simeq w$ and s.t. K satisfies $w \simeq v$ (therefore K falsifies $u \simeq v$), the restriction of K to the level of $u \simeq v$ is a* distant failure node.
  This distant failure node permits to avoid a branch where there is a failure node falsifying an equation in which only the smallest side is reducible (condition of the superposition strategy).
- *Let K be an interpretation defined on atoms $A_1, \ldots, A_n$. Let A_{n+1} be an irreducible equation $u_1 \simeq v$ s.t. $u_1 > v$. K has two extensions: L, satisfying $u_1 \simeq v$, and R, falsifying $u_1 \simeq v$. R is a* quasi-failure node *if there is a term u_2, $\mathcal{E}$-equal to u_1, s.t. $u_2 \simeq v$ is reducible by an equation $l \simeq r$ into $u_2[r] \simeq v$,*

[3] This example has been suggested to me by Wayne Snyder.

and K satisfies $u_2[r] \simeq v$.
This quasi-failure node avoids to have $u_1 \simeq v$ *satisfied and* $u_2 \simeq v$ *falsified in the same branch; this would be inconsistent with* $\mathcal{E}$.

In the proof of consistency with $\mathcal{E}$ *of this branch, we encounter a major problem; we have to prove that the following case cannot happen in the chosen branch: two* $\mathcal{E}$*-equal atoms* $u_1 \simeq v$ *and* $u_2 \simeq v$ *are interpreted differently,* $u_1 \simeq v$ *is reducible in* u_1 *by* $l_1 \simeq r_1$*, and* $u_2 \simeq v$ *is reducible in* u_2 *by* $l_2 \simeq r_2$*. For the case of associative and commutative theories [26], we show that the branch falsifies a ground instance of a clause of* $INF^*(S)$*, produced by an extended superposition between* $l_1 \simeq r_1$ *and* $l_2 \simeq r_2$*. But, for a general theory* $\mathcal{E}$*, it is not so easy. The terms* $u_1[l_1]$ *and* l_1 *may be* $\mathcal{E}$*-equal, and in such a situation, we have to prove that* $u_1[r_1] \simeq r_1$ *is valid in the chosen branch.*
Wertz [31] and Paul [17] have decided to only consider theories $\mathcal{E}$ *such that, whenever* $u_1[l_1]$ *and* l_1 *are* $\mathcal{E}$*-equal,* $u_1[r_1]$ *and* r_1 *are* $\mathcal{E}$*-equal too (Property (P2)).*
In addition, studying the transformation of $u_1[l_1]$ *into* l_1 *by* $\mathcal{E}$*-equality steps, we prove that* $u_1[r_1] \simeq r_1$ *is always valid if the theory* $\mathcal{E}$ *is regular (Property (P1)).*

The last step of the proof is to show that the branch is empty. This implies that $MCT(INF^*(S))$ *is empty, and also that the empty clause belongs to* $INF^*(S)$*. A study of the leaves of this branch, i.e. of failure nodes, distant failure nodes and/or quasi-failure nodes cutting it, shows that this branch falsifies a clause of* $INF^*(S)$*, deduced from clauses falsified by the leaves.*
The final solution is that the branch is empty, and therefore the empty clause belongs to $INF^*(S)$*.*

The compatibility with the positive strategy is a consequence of the following property: if a (distant) failure node along the chosen branch, occuring at the level of an atom A_i*, falsifies* A_i*, then it falsifies a positive clause of* $INF^*(S)$*. The proof of this property is done by induction on the failure and distant failure nodes, as in [23] for the deduction in the empty theory.* □

Our inference system *INF* is compatible with the *simplification strategy*, if the derivations are fair, i.e. do not infinitely forget a possible deduction. This strategy has for purpose the deletion of redundant clauses. Let us give some examples of simplification rules:

- *Simplification* (also called *Demodulation*): it consists of applying a term rewriting step, using a procedure of matching modulo $\mathcal{E}$.
- *Clausal Simplification*: if there is a clause $\rightarrow A$ (resp. $A \rightarrow$), then each clause of the form $A', L \rightarrow R$ (resp. $L \rightarrow A', R$), where A' is $\mathcal{E}$-equal to an instance of A, is replaced by $L \rightarrow R$.
- *Trivial Reflexion*: a clause of the form $l \simeq r, L \rightarrow R$, where l is $\mathcal{E}$-equal to r, is replaced by $L \rightarrow R$.
- *Tautology Deletion*: each clause of the form $L \rightarrow l \simeq r, R$ where $l =_{\mathcal{E}} r$, or $A, L \rightarrow A', R$ where $A =_{\mathcal{E}} A'$, is deleted.

INF is also compatible with the subsumption: if a clause C_1 subsumes a clause C_2 thanks to a substitution σ, i.e. each literal of $C_1\sigma$ is $\mathcal{E}$-equal to a literal of C_2, the clause C_2 is deleted.

6 Implementation

The inference system described in this paper is implemented in the system **DATAC** for the case where $\mathcal{E}$ represents properties of commutativity, or associativity and commutativity (AC), of operators.

DATAC is a theorem prover written in CAML Light (18000 lines), a functional language of the ML family; it has a graphical interface written in Tcl/Tk, X11 Toolkit based on the language Tcl. It runs on SUN, HP and IBM PC workstations.
It uses an AC-unification algorithm based on the algorithm of Stickel [27] and the technique for solving Diophantine equations of Fortenbacher [9]. The algorithm for AC-matching is inspired by the algorithm of Hullot [11]. The ordering for comparing terms is the APO of Bachmair and Plaisted [5] with the improvements of Delor and Puel [7].

Let us detail an example of execution in modular lattices, where $\cdot$ denotes the function *meet*, $+$ the function *join*, 1 the greatest element and 0 the least element. The predicate symbol *Comp* denotes the complementarity of two elements (*Comp* is commutative). The equational theory $\mathcal{E}$ is the following:

$$\mathcal{E} = \left\{ \begin{array}{rcl} (x_1 + x_2) + x_3 & \simeq & x_1 + (x_2 + x_3) \\ x_1 + x_2 & \simeq & x_2 + x_1 \\ (x_1 \cdot x_2) \cdot x_3 & \simeq & x_1 \cdot (x_2 \cdot x_3) \\ x_1 \cdot x_2 & \simeq & x_2 \cdot x_1 \end{array} \right\}$$

There are only two useful contexts for this theory $\mathcal{E}$ (cf. Example 2):

$$C_{\mathcal{E}} = \{ ((x_1 + x_2) + x_3, 1),\ ((x_1 \cdot x_2) \cdot x_3, 1) \}$$

The initial set of clauses is:

(1) $\rightarrow x_1 \cdot x_1 \simeq x_1$ *(2)* $\rightarrow x_1 + x_1 \simeq x_1$
(3) $\rightarrow x_1 \cdot (x_1 + x_2) \simeq x_1$ *(4)* $\rightarrow x_1 + (x_1 \cdot x_2) \simeq x_1$
(5) $\rightarrow x_1 \cdot 0 \simeq 0$ *(6)* $\rightarrow x_1 + 0 \simeq x_1$
(7) $\rightarrow x_1 \cdot 1 \simeq x_1$ *(8)* $\rightarrow x_1 + 1 \simeq 1$
(9) $x_1 \cdot x_2 \simeq x_1 \rightarrow x_2 \cdot (x_1 + x_3) \simeq x_1 + (x_3 \cdot x_2)$
(10) $Comp(x_1, x_2) \rightarrow x_1 \cdot x_2 \simeq 0$ *(11)* $Comp(x_1, x_2) \rightarrow x_1 + x_2 \simeq 1$
(12) $x_1 + x_2 \simeq 1,\ x_1 \cdot x_2 \simeq 0 \rightarrow Comp(x_1, x_2)$

The property we want to prove is:

> *For all elements a and b, let c_1 be the complement of $a \cdot b$ and let c_2 be the complement of $a + b$; then $c_2 + (c_1 \cdot b)$ is the complement of a.*

For this purpose, we add three new clauses that represent the negation of this property (A, B, C_1 and C_2 are new constants):

(13) $\rightarrow Comp(C_1, A \cdot B)$ *(14)* $\rightarrow Comp(C_2, A + B)$

(15) $Comp(A, C_2 + (C_1 \cdot B)) \rightarrow$

The theorem prover **DATAC** is run with these 15 initial clauses, and with the precedence ordering $\cdot > + > B > A > C_1 > C_2 > 1 > 0$ on functional operators, and $Comp > \simeq$ on predicate operators. Deductions are applied thanks to the inference rules defined in Sect. 3, combined with a resolution rule (for dealing with the predicate *Comp*). These deduction rules combine the positive ordering strategy with the superposition strategy. When a contextual superposition uses an empty context, we simply call it a superposition.
Note that we are going to use a flattened representation under AC operators, i.e. a term $C_1 \cdot (A \cdot B)$ will be written $C_1 \cdot A \cdot B$.
DATAC automatically derives a contradiction, the empty clause written □, in the following way:

Resolution between 10 and 13
(16) $\rightarrow A \cdot B \cdot C_1 \simeq 0$

Resolution between 11 and 13
(17) $\rightarrow (A \cdot B) + C_1 \simeq 1$

Resolution between 10 and 14
(18) $\rightarrow (A + B) \cdot C_2 \simeq 0$

Resolution between 11 and 14
(19) $\rightarrow A + B + C_2 \simeq 1$

Left Contextual Superposition from 1 into 9
(32) $x_1 \cdot x_2 \simeq x_1 \cdot x_2 \rightarrow x_1 \cdot ((x_1 \cdot x_2) + x_3) \simeq (x_1 \cdot x_2) + (x_3 \cdot x_1)$

Trivial Reflexion in 32
(32) $\rightarrow x_1 \cdot ((x_1 \cdot x_2) + x_3) \simeq (x_1 \cdot x_2) + (x_3 \cdot x_1)$

Left Contextual Superposition from 3 into 9
(63) $x_1 \cdot x_3 \simeq x_1 \cdot x_3 \rightarrow (x_1 + x_2) \cdot ((x_1 \cdot x_3) + x_4) \simeq (x_1 \cdot x_3) + (x_4 \cdot (x_1 + x_2))$

Trivial Reflexion in 63
(63) $\rightarrow (x_1 + x_2) \cdot ((x_1 \cdot x_3) + x_4) \simeq (x_1 \cdot x_3) + (x_4 \cdot (x_1 + x_2))$

Right Superposition from 17 into 32
(131) $\rightarrow (B \cdot A) + (C_1 \cdot B) \simeq B \cdot 1$

Simplification from 7 into 131
(131) $\rightarrow (B \cdot A) + (C_1 \cdot B) \simeq B$

Extended Superposition between 3 and 63
(197) $\rightarrow ((x_2 \cdot x_3) + (x_4 \cdot (x_2 + x_1))) \cdot x_1 \simeq x_1 \cdot ((x_2 \cdot x_3) + x_4)$

Extended Superposition between 4 and 131
(267) $\rightarrow A + (C_1 \cdot B) \simeq B + A$

Right Superposition from 18 into 197
(397) $\rightarrow A \cdot ((B \cdot x_1) + C_2) \simeq ((B \cdot x_1) + 0) \cdot A$

Simplification from 6 into 397
(397) $\rightarrow A \cdot ((B \cdot x_1) + C_2) \simeq B \cdot x_1 \cdot A$

`Left Superposition from 397 into 12`

(1214) $(B \cdot x_1) + C_2 + A \simeq 1,\ B \cdot x_1 \cdot A \simeq 0 \rightarrow Comp((B \cdot x_1) + C_2, A)$

`Left Superposition from 16 into 1214`

(2541) $(B \cdot C_1) + C_2 + A \simeq 1,\ 0 \simeq 0 \rightarrow Comp((B \cdot C_1) + C_2, A)$

`Trivial Reflexion in 2541`

(2541) $(B \cdot C_1) + C_2 + A \simeq 1 \rightarrow Comp((B \cdot C_1) + C_2, A)$

`Clausal Simplification in 2541 thanks to 15`

(2541) $(B \cdot C_1) + C_2 + A \simeq 1 \rightarrow$

`Simplification from 267 into 2541`

(2541) $B + A + C_2 \simeq 1 \rightarrow$

`Clausal Simplification in 2541 thanks to 19`

(2541) $\square$

The following table compares our positive ordering strategy with the classical ordering strategy [10], which requires only that deductions have to apply between maximal literals of clauses. For this comparison, we applied two linear completion steps on the 12 initial clauses of the previous example. A step of linear completion consists of applying all possible deductions between the initial clauses, but none with one of the deduced clauses. The second step for the ordering strategy was stopped because of a lack of memory while solving a tricky AC-unification problem.
The last column of this table presents statistics for the example traced above. For this example, we have used a simplified version of the AC-unification algorithm that permits not to compute all the minimal solutions and not to solve tricky problems. A consequence is the loss of the completeness of the strategy, but the main advantage is that we avoid problems of memory size.

Linear Completion	First step		Second step		Example
	Ordering	Positive	Ordering	Positive	
Initial Clauses	12	12	53	19	15
Generated Clauses	111	63	>3336	240	2526
Final Clauses	53	19	>1508	46	258
Resolutions	0	0	0	0	4
Superpositions	14	12	>554	59	783
Cont. Superpositions	20	14	>74	24	125
Ext. Superpositions	9	6	>67	12	748
Deductions	43	32	>695	95	1660
Simplifications	132	109	>4410	413	5086
Deletions	151	133	≫1881	324	3407

These statistics give an idea of the advantage of the positive strategy, but the proportions cannot be generalized. Indeed, the positive strategy may be less powerful if some initial clauses have several negative literals. In addition, if the positive strategy reduces the width of the search space, it increases the depth of the proofs (depth 5 for previous example, while depth 4 with the ordering strategy).

7 Conclusion

In this paper, we have defined an inference system for automated deduction modulo equational theories. This system combines the superposition strategy with a positive ordering strategy to prune the search space. Moreover, we have described a procedure for computing contexts, from the theory $\mathcal{E}$ only, i.e. without the use of the initial set of clauses.

Our system has been proved refutationally complete for a large class of equational theories, including all the regular theories. This and our algorithm for constructing non-redundant contexts are important improvements of previous results of Wertz [31] and Paul [17]. One of our further works is to implement this algorithm and to study theories where there is an infinity of non-redundant contexts.

Our technique of deduction modulo some equations has shown its interest in our theorem prover **DATAC**, for the case of associative and commutative theories. However, for testing it on other theories, we need to study orderings for comparing terms and unification algorithms, since there are very few in the literature. This lack of orderings may be solved by term rewriting techniques as in [7, 22]. Unification algorithms may be solved by term rewriting techniques too, for dealing with parts of these theories such as in [15].

However, it seems that one of the most interesting ways for dealing with these problems of $\mathcal{E}$-unification is to use symbolic constraints, as in [28].

Acknowlegments: I would like to thank Prof. Anita Wasilewska of Stony Brook for the numerous discussions we had on the history of the bases of this paper.

I would like to dedicate this paper to the memory of my colleague Valentin Antimirov of INRIA Lorraine (France), with whom I had very interesting discussions while preparing a first version of this paper.

References

1. L. Bachmair and N. Dershowitz. Completion for Rewriting Modulo a Congruence. *Theoretical Computer Science*, 67(2-3):173–202, October 1989.
2. L. Bachmair and H. Ganzinger. On Restrictions of Ordered Paramodulation with Simplification. In M. E. Stickel, editor, *Proceedings 10th International Conference on Automated Deduction, Kaiserslautern (Germany)*, volume 449 of *Lecture Notes in Computer Science*, pages 427–441. Springer-Verlag, July 1990.
3. L. Bachmair and H. Ganzinger. Rewrite-based Equational Theorem Proving with Selection and Simplification. *Journal of Logic and Computation*, 4(3):1–31, 1994.
4. L. Bachmair, H. Ganzinger, C. Lynch, and W. Snyder. Basic Paramodulation. *Information and Computation*, 121(2):172–192, 1995.

5. L. Bachmair and D. Plaisted. Associative Path Orderings. In *Proceedings 1st Conference on Rewriting Techniques and Applications, Dijon (France)*, volume 202 of *Lecture Notes in Computer Science*. Springer-Verlag, 1985.
6. D. Brand. Proving Theorems with the Modification Method. *SIAM Journal of Computing*, 4:412–430, 1975.
7. C. Delor and L. Puel. Extension of the Associative Path Ordering to a Chain of Associative Symbols. In C. Kirchner, editor, *Proceedings 5th Conference on Rewriting Techniques and Applications, Montreal (Canada)*, volume 690 of *Lecture Notes in Computer Science*, pages 389–404. Springer-Verlag, 1993.
8. N. Dershowitz and J.-P. Jouannaud. Rewrite Systems. In J. van Leeuwen, editor, *Handbook of Theoretical Computer Science*. Elsevier Science Publishers B. V. (North-Holland), 1990.
9. A. Fortenbacher. *Effizientes Rechnen in AC-Gleichungstheorien*. PhD thesis, Universität Karlsruhe (Germany), February 1989.
10. J. Hsiang and M. Rusinowitch. Proving Refutational Completeness of Theorem Proving Strategies: The Transfinite Semantic Tree Method. *Journal of the ACM*, 38(3):559–587, July 1991.
11. J.-M. Hullot. *Compilation de Formes Canoniques dans les Théories équationelles.* Thèse de Doctorat de Troisième Cycle, Université de Paris Sud, Orsay (France), 1980.
12. J.-P. Jouannaud and C. Kirchner. Solving Equations in Abstract Algebras: a Rule-based Survey of Unification. In Jean-Louis Lassez and G. Plotkin, editors, *Computational Logic. Essays in honor of Alan Robinson*, chapter 8, pages 257–321. MIT Press, Cambridge (MA, USA), 1991.
13. J.-P. Jouannaud and H. Kirchner. Completion of a Set of Rules Modulo a Set of Equations. *SIAM Journal of Computing*, 15(4):1155–1194, 1986. Preliminary version in Proceedings 11th ACM Symposium on Principles of Programming Languages, Salt Lake City (USA), 1984.
14. D. S. Lankford and A. Ballantyne. Decision Procedures for Simple Equational Theories with Associative Commutative Axioms: Complete Sets of Associative Commutative Reductions. Technical report, Univ. of Texas at Austin, Dept. of Mathematics and Computer Science, 1977.
15. C. Marché. *Réécriture modulo une théorie présentée par un système convergent et décidabilité du problème du mot dans certaines classes de théories équationnelles.* Thèse de Doctorat d'Université, Université de Paris-Sud, Orsay (France), October 1993.
16. R. Nieuwenhuis and A. Rubio. Basic Superposition is Complete. In B. Krieg-Brückner, editor, *Proceedings of ESOP'92*, volume 582 of *Lecture Notes in Computer Science*, pages 371–389. Springer-Verlag, 1992.
17. E. Paul (E-mail: etienne.paul@issy.cnet.fr). E-Semantic Tree. Unpublished paper, 70 pages, 1994.
18. G. E. Peterson. A Technique for Establishing Completeness Results in Theorem Proving with Equality. *SIAM Journal of Computing*, 12(1):82–100, 1983.
19. G. E. Peterson and M. E. Stickel. Complete Sets of Reductions for Some Equational Theories. *Journal of the ACM*, 28:233–264, 1981.
20. G. Plotkin. Building-in Equational Theories. *Machine Intelligence*, 7:73–90, 1972.
21. J. A. Robinson. A Machine-oriented Logic Based on the Resolution Principle. *Journal of the ACM*, 12:23–41, 1965.
22. A. Rubio and R. Nieuwenhuis. A Precedence-Based Total AC-Compatible Ordering. In C. Kirchner, editor, *Proceedings 5th Conference on Rewriting Techniques*

and Applications, Montreal (Canada), volume 690 of *Lecture Notes in Computer Science*, pages 374–388. Springer-Verlag, 1993.

23. M. Rusinowitch. *Démonstration automatique — Techniques de réécriture*. InterEditions, 1989.
24. M. Rusinowitch. Theorem-proving with Resolution and Superposition. *Journal of Symbolic Computation*, 11:21–49, 1991.
25. M. Rusinowitch and L. Vigneron. Associative Commutative Deduction. In E. Domenjoud and Claude Kirchner, editors, *Proceedings of the 1st CCL Workshop, Le Val d'Ajol (France)*, October 1992.
26. M. Rusinowitch and L. Vigneron. Automated Deduction with Associative-Commutative Operators. *Applicable Algebra in Engineering, Communication and Computing*, 6(1):23–56, January 1995.
27. M. E. Stickel. A Unification Algorithm for Associative-Commutative Functions. *Journal of the ACM*, 28:423–434, 1981.
28. L. Vigneron. Associative-Commutative Deduction with Constraints. In A. Bundy, editor, *Proceedings 12th International Conference on Automated Deduction, Nancy (France)*, volume 814 of *Lecture Notes in Artificial Intelligence*, pages 530–544. Springer-Verlag, June 1994.
29. L. Vigneron. *Automated Deduction with Symbolic Constraints in Equational Theories*. PhD Thesis, Université Henri Poincaré - Nancy 1, November 1994. Available as Research Report *CRIN 94-T-266* (in French).
30. L. Vigneron. Theorem Proving modulo Regular Theories. Technical report 95-1, Department of Computer Science, SUNY at Stony Brook, Stony Brook, January 1995.
31. U. Wertz. First-Order Theorem Proving Modulo Equations. Technical Report MPI-I-92-216, Max Planck Institut für Informatik, April 1992.

Author Index

Springer-Verlag and the Environment

We at Springer-Verlag firmly believe that an international science publisher has a special obligation to the environment, and our corporate policies consistently reflect this conviction.

We also expect our business partners – paper mills, printers, packaging manufacturers, etc. – to commit themselves to using environmentally friendly materials and production processes.

The paper in this book is made from low- or no-chlorine pulp and is acid free, in conformance with international standards for paper permanency.

Lecture Notes in Computer Science

For information about Vols. 1–1019

please contact your bookseller or Springer-Verlag

Vol. 1020: I.D. Watson (Ed.), Progress in Case-Based Reasoning. Proceedings, 1995. VIII, 209 pages. 1995. (Subseries LNAI).

Vol. 1021: M.P. Papazoglou (Ed.), OOER '95: Object-Oriented and Entity-Relationship Modeling. Proceedings, 1995. XVII, 451 pages. 1995.

Vol. 1022: P.H. Hartel, R. Plasmeijer (Eds.), Functional Programming Languages in Education. Proceedings, 1995. X, 309 pages. 1995.

Vol. 1023: K. Kanchanasut, J.-J. Lévy (Eds.), Algorithms, Concurrency and Knowlwdge. Proceedings, 1995. X, 410 pages. 1995.

Vol. 1024: R.T. Chin, H.H.S. Ip, A.C. Naiman, T.-C. Pong (Eds.), Image Analysis Applications and Computer Graphics. Proceedings, 1995. XVI, 533 pages. 1995.

Vol. 1025: C. Boyd (Ed.), Cryptography and Coding. Proceedings, 1995. IX, 291 pages. 1995.

Vol. 1026: P.S. Thiagarajan (Ed.), Foundations of Software Technology and Theoretical Computer Science. Proceedings, 1995. XII, 515 pages. 1995.

Vol. 1027: F.J. Brandenburg (Ed.), Graph Drawing. Proceedings, 1995. XII, 526 pages. 1996.

Vol. 1028: N.R. Adam, Y. Yesha (Eds.), Electronic Commerce. X, 155 pages. 1996.

Vol. 1029: E. Dawson, J. Golić (Eds.), Cryptography: Policy and Algorithms. Proceedings, 1995. XI, 327 pages. 1996.

Vol. 1030: F. Pichler, R. Moreno-Díaz, R. Albrecht (Eds.), Computer Aided Systems Theory - EUROCAST '95. Proceedings, 1995. XII, 539 pages. 1996.

Vol.1031: M. Toussaint (Ed.), Ada in Europe. Proceedings, 1995. XI, 455 pages. 1996.

Vol. 1032: P. Godefroid, Partial-Order Methods for the Verification of Concurrent Systems. IV, 143 pages. 1996.

Vol. 1033: C.-H. Huang, P. Sadayappan, U. Banerjee, D. Gelernter, A. Nicolau, D. Padua (Eds.), Languages and Compilers for Parallel Computing. Proceedings, 1995. XIII, 597 pages. 1996.

Vol. 1034: G. Kuper, M. Wallace (Eds.), Constraint Databases and Applications. Proceedings, 1995. VII, 185 pages. 1996.

Vol. 1035: S.Z. Li, D.P. Mital, E.K. Teoh, H. Wang (Eds.), Recent Developments in Computer Vision. Proceedings, 1995. XI, 604 pages. 1996.

Vol. 1036: G. Adorni, M. Zock (Eds.), Trends in Natural Language Generation - An Artificial Intelligence Perspective. Proceedings, 1993. IX, 382 pages. 1996. (Subseries LNAI).

Vol. 1037: M. Wooldridge, J.P. Müller, M. Tambe (Eds.), Intelligent Agents II. Proceedings, 1995. XVI, 437 pages. 1996. (Subseries LNAI).

Vol. 1038: W: Van de Velde, J.W. Perram (Eds.), Agents Breaking Away. Proceedings, 1996. XIV, 232 pages. 1996. (Subseries LNAI).

Vol. 1039: D. Gollmann (Ed.), Fast Software Encryption. Proceedings, 1996. X, 219 pages. 1996.

Vol. 1040: S. Wermter, E. Riloff, G. Scheler (Eds.), Connectionist, Statistical, and Symbolic Approaches to Learning for Natural Language Processing. IX, 468 pages. 1996. (Subseries LNAI).

Vol. 1041: J. Dongarra, K. Madsen, J. Waśniewski (Eds.), Applied Parallel Computing. Proceedings, 1995. XII, 562 pages. 1996.

Vol. 1042: G. Weiß, S. Sen (Eds.), Adaption and Learning in Multi-Agent Systems. Proceedings, 1995. X, 238 pages. 1996. (Subseries LNAI).

Vol. 1043: F. Moller, G. Birtwistle (Eds.), Logics for Concurrency. XI, 266 pages. 1996.

Vol. 1044: B. Plattner (Ed.), Broadband Communications. Proceedings, 1996. XIV, 359 pages. 1996.

Vol. 1045: B. Butscher, E. Moeller, H. Pusch (Eds.), Interactive Distributed Multimedia Systems and Services. Proceedings, 1996. XI, 333 pages. 1996.

Vol. 1046: C. Puech, R. Reischuk (Eds.), STACS 96. Proceedings, 1996. XII, 690 pages. 1996.

Vol. 1047: E. Hajnicz, Time Structures. IX, 244 pages. 1996. (Subseries LNAI).

Vol. 1048: M. Proietti (Ed.), Logic Program Syynthesis and Transformation. Proceedings, 1995. X, 267 pages. 1996.

Vol. 1049: K. Futatsugi, S. Matsuoka (Eds.), Object Technologies for Advanced Software. Proceedings, 1996. X, 309 pages. 1996.

Vol. 1050: R. Dyckhoff, H. Herre, P. Schroeder-Heister (Eds.), Extensions of Logic Programming. Proceedings, 1996. VII, 318 pages. 1996. (Subseries LNAI).

Vol. 1051: M.-C. Gaudel, J. Woodcock (Eds.), FME'96: Industrial Benefit and Advances in Formal Methods. Proceedings, 1996. XII, 704 pages. 1996.

Vol. 1052: D. Hutchison, H. Christiansen, G. Coulson, A. Danthine (Eds.), Teleservices and Multimedia Communications. Proceedings, 1995. XII, 277 pages. 1996.

Vol. 1053: P. Graf, Term Indexing. XVI, 284 pages. 1996. (Subseries LNAI).

Vol. 1054: A. Ferreira, P. Pardalos (Eds.), Solving Combinatorial Optimization Problems in Parallel. VII, 274 pages. 1996.

Vol. 1055: T. Margaria, B. Steffen (Eds.), Tools and Algorithms for the Construction and Analysis of Systems. Proceedings, 1996. XI, 435 pages. 1996.

Vol. 1056: A. Haddadi, Communication and Cooperation in Agent Systems. XIII, 148 pages. 1996. (Subseries LNAI).

Vol. 1057: P. Apers, M. Bouzeghoub, G. Gardarin (Eds.), Advances in Database Technology — EDBT '96. Proceedings, 1996. XII, 636 pages. 1996.

Vol. 1058: H. R. Nielson (Ed.), Programming Languages and Systems - ESOP '96. Proceedings, 1996. X, 405 pages. 1996.

Vol. 1059: H. Kirchner (Ed.), Trees in Algebra and Programming - CAAP '96. Proceedings, 1996. VIII, 331 pages. 1996.

Vol. 1060: T. Gyimóthy (Ed.), Compiler Construction. Proceedings, 1996. X, 355 pages. 1996.

Vol. 1061: P. Ciancarini, C. Hankin (Eds.), Coordination Languages and Models. Proceedings, 1996. XI, 443 pages. 1996.

Vol. 1062: E. Sanchez, M. Tomassini (Eds.), Towards Evolvable Hardware. IX, 265 pages. 1996.

Vol. 1063: J.-M. Alliot, E. Lutton, E. Ronald, M. Schoenauer, D. Snyers (Eds.), Artificial Evolution. Proceedings, 1995. XIII, 396 pages. 1996.

Vol. 1064: B. Buxton, R. Cipolla (Eds.), Computer Vision - ECCV '96. Volume I. Proceedings, 1996. XXI, 725 pages. 1996.

Vol. 1065: B. Buxton, R. Cipolla (Eds.), Computer Vision - ECCV '96. Volume II. Proceedings, 1996. XXI, 723 pages. 1996.

Vol. 1066: R. Alur, T.A. Henzinger, E.D. Sontag (Eds.), Hybrid Systems III. IX, 618 pages. 1996.

Vol. 1067: H. Liddell, A. Colbrook, B. Hertzberger, P. Sloot (Eds.), High-Performance Computing and Networking. Proceedings, 1996. XXV, 1040 pages. 1996.

Vol. 1068: T. Ito, R.H. Halstead, Jr., C. Queinnec (Eds.), Parallel Symbolic Languages and Systems. Proceedings, 1995. X, 363 pages. 1996.

Vol. 1069: J.W. Perram, J.-P. Müller (Eds.), Distributed Software Agents and Applications. Proceedings, 1994. VIII, 219 pages. 1996. (Subseries LNAI).

Vol. 1070: U. Maurer (Ed.), Advances in Cryptology - EUROCRYPT '96. Proceedings, 1996. XII, 417 pages. 1996.

Vol. 1071: P. Miglioli, U. Moscato, D. Mundici, M. Ornaghi (Eds.), Theorem Proving with Analytic Tableaux and Related Methods. Proceedings, 1996. X, 330 pages. 1996. (Subseries LNAI).

Vol. 1072: R. Kasturi, K. Tombre (Eds.), Graphics Recognition. Proceedings, 1995. X, 308 pages. 1996.

Vol. 1073: J. Cuny, H. Ehrig, G. Engels, G. Rozenberg (Eds.), Graph Grammars and Their Application to Computer Science. Proceedings, 1994. X, 565 pages. 1996.

Vol. 1074: G. Dowek, J. Heering, K. Meinke, B. Möller (Eds.), Higher-Order Algebra, Logic, and Term Rewriting. Proceedings, 1995. VII, 287 pages. 1996.

Vol. 1075: D. Hirschberg, G. Myers (Eds.), Combinatorial Pattern Matching. Proceedings, 1996. VIII, 392 pages. 1996.

Vol. 1076: N. Shadbolt, K. O'Hara, G. Schreiber (Eds.), Advances in Knowledge Acquisition. Proceedings, 1996. XII, 371 pages. 1996. (Subseries LNAI).

Vol. 1077: P. Brusilovsky, P. Kommers, N. Streitz (Eds.), Mulimedia, Hypermedia, and Virtual Reality. Proceedings, 1994. IX, 311 pages. 1996.

Vol. 1078: D.A. Lamb (Ed.), Studies of Software Design. Proceedings, 1993. VI, 188 pages. 1996.

Vol. 1079: Z.W. Raś, M. Michalewicz (Eds.), Foundations of Intelligent Systems. Proceedings, 1996. XI, 664 pages. 1996. (Subseries LNAI).

Vol. 1080: P. Constantopoulos, J. Mylopoulos, Y. Vassiliou (Eds.), Advanced Information Systems Engineering. Proceedings, 1996. XI, 582 pages. 1996.

Vol. 1081: G. McCalla (Ed.), Advances in Artificial Intelligence. Proceedings, 1996. XII, 459 pages. 1996. (Subseries LNAI).

Vol. 1082: N.R. Adam, B.K. Bhargava, M. Halem, Y. Yesha (Eds.), Digital Libraries. Proceedings, 1995. Approx. 310 pages. 1996.

Vol. 1083: K. Sparck Jones, J.R. Galliers, Evaluating Natural Language Processing Systems. XV, 228 pages. 1996. (Subseries LNAI).

Vol. 1084: W.H. Cunningham, S.T. McCormick, M. Queyranne (Eds.), Integer Programming and Combinatorial Optimization. Proceedings, 1996. X, 505 pages. 1996.

Vol. 1085: D.M. Gabbay, H.J. Ohlbach (Eds.), Practical Reasoning. Proceedings, 1996. XV, 721 pages. 1996. (Subseries LNAI).

Vol. 1086: C. Frasson, G. Gauthier, A. Lesgold (Eds.), Intelligent Tutoring Systems. Proceedings, 1996. XVII, 688 pages. 1996.

Vol. 1087: C. Zhang, D. Lukose (Eds.), Distributed Artificial Intelliegence. Proceedings, 1995. VIII, 232 pages. 1996. (Subseries LNAI).

Vol. 1088: A. Strohmeier (Ed.), Reliable Software Technologies - Ada-Europe '96. Proceedings, 1996. XI, 513 pages. 1996.

Vol. 1089: G. Ramalingam, Bounded Incremental Computation. XI, 190 pages. 1996.

Vol. 1090: J.-Y. Cai, C.K. Wong (Eds.), Computing and Combinatorics. Proceedings, 1996. X, 421 pages. 1996.

Vol. 1091: J. Billington, W. Reisig (Eds.), Application and Theory of Petri Nets 1996. Proceedings, 1996. VIII, 549 pages. 1996.

Vol. 1092: H. Kleine Büning (Ed.), Computer Science Logic. Proceedings, 1995. VIII, 487 pages. 1996.